NEW TESTAM

JOHN 11-21

EDITED BY

JOEL C. ELOWSKY

GENERAL EDITOR

THOMAS C. ODEN

An imprint of InterVarsity Press
Downers Grove, Illinois

InterVarsity Press
P.O. Box 1400, Downers Grove, IL 60515-1426
ivpress.com
email@ivpress.com

InterVarsity Press® is the book-publishing division of InterVarsity Christian Fellowship/USA®, a movement of students and faculty active on campus at hundreds of universities, colleges, and schools of nursing in the United States of America, and a member movement of the International Fellowship of Evangelical Students. For information about local and regional activities, visit intervarsity.org.

Cover design: David Fassett
Images: gold texture background: © Katsumi Murouchi / Getty Images
stained glass cathedral window: © elzauer / Getty Images
gold texture: © Katsumi Murouchi / Getty Images
abstract marble pattern: © NK08gerd / iStock / Getty Images Plus

ISBN 978-0-8308-4356-5 (paperback)
ISBN 978-0-8308-1099-4 (hardcover)
ISBN 978-0-8308-9746-9 (digital)

Printed in the United States of America ♾

InterVarsity Press is committed to ecological stewardship and to the conservation of natural resources in all our operations. This book was printed using sustainably sourced paper.

Library of Congress Cataloging-in-Publication Data
A catalog record for this book is available from the Library of Congress.

P 32 31 30 29 28 27 26 25 24 23 22 21 20 19 18 17 16 15 14 13 12 11 10 9 8 7 6 5 4 3 2 1
Y 47 46 45 44 43 42 41 40 39 38 37 36 35 34 33 32 31 30 29 28 27 26 25 24 23 22 21 20 19

Contents

THE GOSPEL ACCORDING TO JOHN

11:1-5 JESUS IS INFORMED THAT LAZARUS IS SICK

[1]Now a certain man was ill, Lazarus of Bethany, the village of Mary and her sister Martha. [2]It was Mary who anointed the Lord with ointment and wiped his feet with her hair, whose brother Lazarus was ill. [3]So the sisters sent to him, saying, "Lord, he whom you love is ill." [4]But when Jesus heard it he said, "This illness is not unto death; it is for the glory of God, so that the Son of God may be glorified by means of it."

[5]Now Jesus loved Martha and her sister and Lazarus.

Overview: In the raising of Lazarus, whose name means "helped" (Isidore), the Lord accomplishes one of his greatest miracles as he, the Creator, raises his own creation (Augustine). John mentions not only Lazarus by name, but also his sisters Mary and Martha, whose tears for Lazarus become the focus of the Orthodox liturgy for Lazarus Saturday, which precedes Palm Sunday (Romanus). John focuses at the beginning on Mary's anointing of Jesus as a testament to her piety and her attachment to him (Cyril). This makes it all the more important to note that the Mary mentioned here is not Mary the harlot mentioned in Matthew's and Luke's accounts (Chrysostom), although John does seem to confirm Luke's account in other details (Augustine). Since Jesus, the Life, was absent from Lazarus and his sisters, death had room to do its work through the agency of disease (Gregory of Nyssa). Mary and Martha's report to Jesus of their brother and his friend's illness reminds us that even friends of Christ suffer (Chrysostom).

The raising of Lazarus is unique among the resurrections Jesus performed in the Gospels because rather than leaving immediately at the request of Lazarus's sisters, Jesus had allowed death to have full reign so that in Lazarus, the sign of the resurrection would be shone in all its fullness (Peter Chrysologus). Lazarus's sisters, nevertheless, demonstrate great faith in approaching Jesus to heal Lazarus since they were convinced that Jesus is not one who loves and then abandons those he loves (Augustine). Although Lazarus's death is for the glory of God, God does not cause Lazarus's illness (Cyril). The resurrection of Lazarus is for the glory of the Father and the Son since the glory of the Father and the Son is one. We should also note that Jesus' glory is the consequence, not the cause, of Lazarus's death (Chrysostom). Mary, Martha and Lazarus are loved by the one who can bring them true comfort and healing (Augustine).

11:1 *Lazarus, Mary and Martha*

LAZARUS SIGNIFIES "HELPED." ISIDORE OF SEVILLE: Lazarus means "helped,"[1] referring to him who was [helped] when raised from the dead. ETYMOLOGIES 7.10.5.[2]

THE MAKER RAISES HIS CREATION. AUGUSTINE: Among all the miracles done by our Lord Jesus Christ, the resurrection of Lazarus holds a prime place in preaching. But if we consider attentively who did it, our duty is to rejoice rather than to wonder. A man was raised up by him who made humankind. He is the only one of the Father by whom, as you know, all things were made. And if all things were made by him, why is anyone amazed that one was raised by him when so many are daily brought into the world by his power? It is a greater deed to create men and women than to raise them again from the dead. Yet he decided both to create and to raise again; to create all, to resuscitate some. TRACTATES ON THE GOSPEL OF JOHN 49.1.[3]

THE TEARS OF MARY AND MARTHA. ROMANUS MELODUS:

Let us all, with love, hurry to Bethany to see
Christ there, weeping for His friend.
For wishing all things to be ordained by law,
He controls all things in His dual nature.
He suffers as son of David; as Son of God,
He redeems the whole world from all the evil
of the serpent,
And on the fourth day, He raised up Lazarus,
taking pity on
The tears of Mary and Martha.

Together sustained by faith, the two
announced to Christ and God the death
Of their brother, saying, "Hasten, come, Thou
who art always present in all places,
For Lazarus whom Thou dost love is ill: if
Thou come near,
Death will vanish, and Thy friend will be
saved from corruption,
And the Jews will see that Thou, the Merciful
One, hast taken pity on
The tears of Mary and Martha."

KONTAKION ON THE RAISING OF LAZARUS 15.2-3.[4]

11:2 *Mary, Who Anointed the Lord*

EDIFYING DESCRIPTION OF THE SISTERS. CYRIL OF ALEXANDRIA: The Evangelist has a purpose in mentioning the names of the women, showing that they were distinguished for their piety, which is why the Lord loved them. And of the many things that probably had been done for the Lord by Mary, he mentions the ointment, not in a haphazard way but in order to show that Mary had such a thirst for Christ that she wiped his feet with her own hair, seeking to fasten to herself in a more real way the spiritual blessing that comes from his holy flesh. Indeed, she often appears with much warmth of attachment, sitting close to Christ without being distracted by any interruption and to have been drawn into a close relationship of friendship with him. COMMENTARY ON THE GOSPEL OF JOHN 7.[5]

MARY IS NOT THE HARLOT MENTIONED IN LUKE. CHRYSOSTOM: First we are to observe that this was not the harlot mentioned in Matthew[6] or Luke,[7] but a different person. Those mentioned in Matthew and Luke were harlots full of many vices, but she was an honest woman, who treated our Lord with marked reverence. HOMILIES ON THE GOSPEL OF JOHN 62.1.[8]

JOHN CONFIRMS LUKE'S ACCOUNT. AUGUSTINE: John here confirms the passage in Luke, where this is said to have taken place in the house of one Simon a Pharisee: Mary had done this act

[1] "Lazarus" is a shortened form of "Eleazar," meaning "God has helped." Origen *Fragments on the Gospel of John* 77 explores the possibility that the Lazarus mentioned in Luke 16 is the same as here but ultimately dismisses the idea. [2] Cetedoc 1186, 7.10.5. [3] NPNF 1 7:270**; CCL 36:419. [4] *KRBM* 1:151-52. More of the sermon follows below. [5] LF 48:110*. [6] Mt 26:7. [7] Lk 7:37. [8] NPNF 1 14:227**. However, Augustine (see below), Origen (Fragment 78) and a number of others identify Lazarus's sister Mary as the "notorious sinner" of Lk 7.

therefore on a former occasion. That she did it again at Bethany is not mentioned in the narrative of Luke, but it is in the other three Gospels. Harmony of the Gospels 2.79.154.[9]

11:3 *The One You Love Is Ill*

Death Has Room to Work. Gregory of Nyssa: One of the Lord's companions and friends is ill (Lazarus is the sick man's name). The Lord refuses any visiting of his friend, though far away from the sick man, that in the absence of the Life, death might find room and power to do his own work by the agency of disease. On the Making of Man 25.11.[10]

Friends of Christ Do Suffer. Chrysostom: Many are offended when they see any of those who are pleasing to God suffering anything terrible. There are those, for instance, who have fallen ill or have become impoverished or have endured some other tragedy. Those who are offended by this do not know that those who are especially dear to God have it as their lot to endure such things, as we see in the case of Lazarus, who was also one of the friends of Christ but was also sick. Homilies on the Gospel of John 62.1.[11]

Conquering Death More Important. Peter Chrysologus: Our Lord had raised up the daughter of Jairus, the ruler of the synagogue.[12] Although he restored life to the dead girl, he left the law of death still in force. He also raised the widow's only son.[13] He halted the bier, forestalled the young man's burial, arrested the onset of physical decay. But the life he restored had not completely fallen in to the power of death. The case of Lazarus was unique. His death and resurrection to life had nothing in common with the other two. Death had already exerted its full power over him, so that in him the sign of the resurrection shone out in all its fullness. I think it is possible to say that if Lazarus had remained only three days in the tomb it would have deprived our Lord's resurrection of its full significance, since Christ proved himself Lord by returning to life after three days, whereas Lazarus, as his servant, had to lie in the grave for four days before he was recalled. However, let us see if we can verify this suggestion by reading the Gospel text further.

"His sisters sent a message to Jesus saying, Lord, the friend whom you love is sick." By these words they appeal to his affection, they lay claim to his friendship, they call on his love, urging their familiar relationship with him to persuade him to relieve their distress. But for Christ it was more important to conquer death than to cure disease. He showed his love for his friend not by healing him but by calling him back from the grave. Instead of a remedy for his illness, he offered him the glory of rising from the dead. Sermon 63.1-2.[14]

Love Does Not Abandon. Augustine: But what was the message sent by his sisters? "Lord, behold, he whom you love is ill." They did not say, "Come," for the intimation was all that was needed for one who loved. They did not venture to say, "Come and heal him," nor did they venture to say, "Command there, and it shall be done here." And why would it be any different with them if, on these very grounds, the centurion's faith was commended? For he said, "I am not worthy that you should enter under my roof. But only say the word, and my servant shall be healed."[15] These women said nothing like this, but only, "Lord, behold, he whom you love is ill"—as if to say: It is enough that you know. For you are not one that loves and then abandons. Tractates on the Gospel of John 49.5.[16]

11:4 *For the Glory of the Son of God*

[9]CSEL 43:261; NPNF 1 6:174**. [10]NPNF 2 5:416*. [11]NPNF 1 14:227**. [12]See Mk 5:37-43; Lk 8:49-56. [13]See Lk 7:11-15. [14]*JFA* 44-45; PL 52:376. [15]Mt 8:8. [16] NPNF 1 7:272**; CCL 36:422.

God Is Not the Cause of Lazarus's Illness. Cyril of Alexandria: Jesus saw that in the end, Lazarus's illness and death would be for the glory of God. This is not to say that the sickness came on Lazarus so that God should be glorified, for it would be silly to say this, but rather, since the sickness had come upon Lazarus, Jesus foresaw the wonderful conclusion to Lazarus's illness. Commentary on the Gospel of John 7.[17]

The Glory of Father and Son Is One. Chrysostom: Observe how he again asserts that his glory and the Father's is one. For, after saying "of God," he has added, "that the Son of God might be glorified." Homilies on the Gospel of John 62.1.[18]

Jesus' Glory Is the Consequence of Lazarus's Death. Chrysostom: The word "that" [which is in the phrase "*that* the Son of God may be glorified,"] here signifies not the cause but the consequence. The sickness sprang from other [natural] causes, but he turned it to the glory of God. Homilies on the Gospel of John 62.1.[19]

11:5 *Jesus' Love for Mary, Martha and Lazarus*

Loved by the Comforter and Healer. Augustine: Lazarus is sick, his sisters are sorrowful, all of them are loved. But [they had hope because the] one who loved them was the healer of the sick—even more, he was the raiser of the dead and the comforter of the sorrowful. Tractates on the Gospel of John 49.7.[20]

[17]LF 48:111**. [18]NPNF 1 14:227*. [19]NPNF 1 14:227**. [20]NPNF 1 7:272**; CCL 36:422-23.

11:6-10 Jesus Delays Seeing Lazarus

[6]So when he heard that he was ill, he stayed two days longer in the place where he was. [7]Then after this he said to the disciples, "Let us go into Judea again." [8]The disciples said to him, "Rabbi, the Jews were but now seeking to stone you, and are you going there again?" [9]Jesus answered, "Are there not twelve hours in the day? If any one walks in the day, he does not stumble, because he sees the light of this world. [10]But if any one walks in the night, he stumbles, because the light is not in him."

Overview: Why wait two days longer instead of coming immediately—unless Jesus wanted to give free reign to death before he conquered it so that no one could doubt Lazarus had truly died (Peter Chrysologus)? Then Jesus tells his disciples to return with him to Judea, where the Jews had previously sought to stone him (Augustine). His disciples' reaction to this is one of fear for themselves and for him because they lack faith (Chrysostom). They presume to give advice to God, and so he rebukes them by asking a question concerning the twelve hours of daylight, in which there is great symbolism, pointing for instance to Christ as the day and his twelve disciples as the hours (Augustine). It may also refer to the twelve patriarchs or apostles who look to the Sun, Christ, who is the spiritual day (Origen). Christ is telling his disciples that now is not the time for the Sun/Son to withdraw from the Jews since while there is daylight, there is still time for them to be illumined (Cyril). Apart from the light of Christ there is only stumbling in the darkness of the devil (Athanasius). But those who walk uprightly, as though during the day, need have no fear of evil (Chrysostom).

11:6 *Jesus Stayed Two Days Longer*

Jesus Grants Free Reign to the Grave. Peter Chrysologus: You see how he gives full scope to death. He grants free reign to the grave. He allows corruption to set in. He prohibits neither putrefaction nor stench from taking their normal course. He allows the realm of darkness to seize his friend, drag him down to the underworld, and take possession of him. He acts like this so that human hope may perish entirely and human despair reach its lowest depths. The deed he is about to accomplish may then clearly be seen to be the work of God, not of man.

[Jesus] waited for Lazarus to die, staying in the same place until he could tell his disciples that he was dead. Then he announced his intention of going to him. "Lazarus is dead," he said, "and I am glad." Was this a sign of his love for his friend? Not so. Christ was glad because their sorrow over the death of Lazarus was soon to be changed into joy at his restoration to life. "I am glad for your sake," he said. Why for their sake? Because the death and raising of Lazarus were a perfect prefiguration of the death and resurrection of the Lord himself. What the Lord was soon to achieve in himself had already been achieved in his servant. . . . This explains why he said to them, "I am glad for your sake not to have been there, because now you will believe." It was necessary that Lazarus should die, so that the faith of the disciples might also rise with him from the dead. Sermon 63.2.[1]

11:7-8 *Going Again to Judea*

The Attempted Stoning Was in Judea. Augustine: [Judea is] where he had just escaped being stoned. For this was the cause of his leaving. He left indeed as man: he left in weakness, but he returns in power. Tractates on the Gospel of John 49.7.[2]

Jesus Tries to Prepare the Disciples. Chrysostom: He had not as yet told his disciples where he was going. But now he tells them, in order to prepare them beforehand because they are so worried when they hear about it. . . . They feared both for him and for themselves. For they were not yet established in faith. Homilies on the Gospel of John 62.1.[3]

11:9-10 *Daylight versus Stumbling in the Dark*

Christ Is the Day, the Disciples Are Twelve Hours. Augustine: What did the Lord mean? As far as I can judge . . . he wanted to dissuade them from their doubting and unbelief. For their words were meant to keep the Lord from death, who had come to die, in order to save themselves from death too.[4] . . . And so, when [these] men presumed to give advice to God, disciples to their Master, servants to their Lord, patients to their physician, our Lord reproved them, saying, "Are there not twelve hours in the day? If anyone walks during the day, he does not stumble." Follow me if you do not want to stumble. Do not give counsel to me when you should be receiving it from me instead. . . . He showed himself to be the day by appointing twelve disciples. If I am the day, he says, and you are the hours, is it for the hours to give counsel to the day? The day is followed by the hours, not the hours by the day. . . . Even when Judas fell, he was still succeeded by Matthias, and the number twelve was preserved. Our Lord did not make the choice of twelve disciples arbitrarily, then, but to indicate that he himself is the spiritual Day. Let the hours be lightened by the day so that by the

[1]JFA 45; PL 52:376-77. [2]NPNF 1 7:272**; CCL 36:423. [3]NPNF 1 14:228**. [4]Peter had done something similar in Mt 16:22-23.

preaching of the hours, the world may believe on the day. Follow me, then, says our Lord, if you wish not to stumble. Tractates on the Gospel of John 49.8.[5]

Twelve Patriarchs, Twelve Apostles, Twelve Days. Origen: As the day is divided into twelve hours, accordingly the twelve patriarchs and the choir of the apostles are equal in number with the hours of the day, having as their Sun Christ our God, who is also the spiritual Day, from whom there is learning and the enlightenment of its knowledge. Fragment 137 on the Gospel of John.[6]

It Is Not the Time for the Sun/Son to Withdraw. Cyril of Alexandria: Perhaps he compares to the ever-moving course of the day, the easily-swayed and novelty-loving mind of people, which is not established in one opinion but vacillates from one way of thinking to another, just as the day changes from one hour to another. This is also how the words "are there twelve hours in the day" can be understood. In other words, "I," he says, "am the Day and the Light. Therefore, just as it is not possible for the light of the day to fail without having completed its appointed time, so it is not among possibilities that the illumination that proceeds from me should be shrouded from the Jews without having fully reached its fitting measure of love for humankind." And he speaks of the time of his presence as "day," and of that before it as "night," as the Lord also does when he says, "We must work the works of him that sent us while it is day."[7] This therefore is what he says here: "This is not the time for me to separate myself from the Jews, even though they are unholy. Instead, I must do everything that I can for their healing. For they must not now be punished by having the divine grace (like the light of the sun) withdrawn from them. But just as the light of the day does not fail until the twelve hours have been completed, so the illumination that proceeds from me is not shrouded before the proper time. However, until I am crucified I remain among the Jews, sending forth unto them like light the understanding of the knowledge of God. For since the Jews are in the darkness of unbelief, and so stumble on me as on a stone, I must go back to them and enlighten them so that they may desist from their madness in fighting against God." Commentary on the Gospel of John 7.[8]

Stumbling Without the Light of Christ. Athanasius: Consider what I have said, that the Light is Christ. Everyone who will walk in his commandments will not be laid hold of by evil. These twelve hours that are in the day are the twelve apostles. The devil . . . is compared with the night. He who walks in the will of the devil will stumble because he does not have the light of Christ. Homily on the Resurrection of Lazarus.[9]

The Upright Need Fear No Evil. Chrysostom: It is as if Jesus is saying that the upright need fear no evil. It is only the wicked who have cause to fear. We have done nothing worthy of death, and therefore we are in no danger. Or, he is saying, If any one sees this world's light, he is safe. The one who is with me is even safer. Homilies on the Gospel of John 62.1.[10]

---

[5] NPNF 1 7:272-73**; CCL 36:424. [6] *AEG* 4:165-66*; GCS 10(4):573. [7] See Jn 9:4. [8] LF 48:112-13**. [9] *AJSL* 57:264*. [10] NPNF 1 14:228**.

11:11-16 LAZARUS IS ONLY SLEEPING

[11]Thus he spoke, and then he said to them, "Our friend Lazarus has fallen asleep, but I go to awake him out of sleep." [12]The disciples said to him, "Lord, if he has fallen asleep, he will recover." [13]Now Jesus had spoken of his death, but they thought that he meant taking rest in sleep. [14]Then Jesus told them plainly, "Lazarus is dead; [15]and for your sake I am glad that I was not there, so that you may believe. But let us go to him." [16]Thomas, called the Twin, said to his fellow disciples, "Let us also go, that we may die with him."

Overview: The fact that Jesus says Lazarus is only sleeping is a promise of things to come since, from Jesus' perspective, Lazarus was sleeping and not dead (Augustine). Jesus did not need to go to Lazarus to raise him, but he chose to go so that no one could doubt that he had performed the miracle (Hippolytus). Thinking this was another one of Jesus' enigmatic statements (Chrysostom), the disciples misunderstand what Jesus means about Lazarus sleeping, unaware of what kind of sleep it was (Romanus). They are soon informed that Lazarus has died, returning to the clay from which he was taken (Potamius). But Jesus does not yet tell them that he is going to raise Lazarus (Chrysostom), knowing that he had been sent to heal sickness, but it was death that could not remain in hiding from him (Augustine). Unlike normal physicians, who wear themselves out to save life, Lazarus's physician waited for his death in order to establish the victory of life over death (Ephrem). Jesus uses Lazarus's death, in other words, to establish his disciples' faith (Hippolytus). His delay not only ensures Lazarus's death will occur but was also necessary, since his love might otherwise have moved him to heal Lazarus, leaving no opportunity for the greater miracle of resurrection. Knowing that Lazarus has died, he then decides to go to him and Thomas volunteers to go with him, asserting that he will join Jesus in death. This is either an expression of audacity from one who has a false sense of bravery, although he may indeed have understood Jesus' true power over death (Cyril), or it is the expression of a coward who later, however, is the most zealous of the disciples (Chrysostom). Or, perhaps Thomas unwittingly knows that one must die with Jesus in order to live with him (Origen).

11:11 *Lazarus Sleeps*

From Jesus' Perspective, Lazarus Was Sleeping. Augustine: It was really true that he was sleeping. To his sisters he was dead; to our Lord, he was sleeping. To those who could not raise him again, he was dead. Our Lord awoke him with as much ease from his grave as you might awake a sleeper from his bed. He calls him then "asleep," with reference to his own power, . . . as the apostle says, "But I would not have you to be ignorant, concerning those who are asleep."[1] . . . Asleep, he says, because he is foretelling their resurrection. And so, all the dead are sleeping, both good and bad. But just as it matters to those who sleep and wake again daily, what they see in their sleep—some having pleasant dreams, others nightmares so scary that they are afraid to fall asleep again in case they reoccur—so it is [in death]. Everyone sleeps and wakes up again in circumstances peculiar to his own situation. Tractates on the Gospel of John 49.9.[2]

[1]1 Thess 4:13. [2]NPNF 1 7:273**; CCL 36:424.

JESUS' PRESENCE CONFIRMS HE PERFORMED A MIRACLE. HIPPOLYTUS: For truly the death of human beings is counted with the Lord as sleep. Why does he say "I go"? Are you unable to enliven the dead while remaining here? But, [Jesus says], the Jews in my absence do not receive the grace. For perhaps on his arising they will think Lazarus has come to life by some chance. I therefore am coming so that, if I am there, they will be eyewitnesses of the miracles done by me. And when they receive this grace from me, they can then be brought to a sure and certain faith. ON THE GOSPEL OF JOHN AND THE RESURRECTION OF LAZARUS.[3]

ANOTHER ENIGMATIC STATEMENT OF JESUS? CHRYSOSTOM: If anyone asks, "How did the disciples imagine Lazarus was only sleeping? Why didn't they understand that death was meant when Jesus said, 'I go to awake him?' for it was foolishness of them to expect that he would go fifteen stadia[4] to awake him"—we would reply, that they thought this was another one of Jesus' dark sayings, such as he often spoke to them. HOMILIES ON THE GOSPEL OF JOHN 62.2.[5]

THE DISCIPLES ARE IGNORANT, BUT PAUL WOULD HAVE KNOWN. ROMANUS MELODUS:

Again the Lord spoke to the disciples;
"See now, Lazarus, our friend, has fallen asleep,
And I wish to go and awaken him."
But they did not understand that the Redeemer referred to death as sleep,
Indeed if Paul had been there,[6] he would have known the word of the Word,
For, instructed by Him, he sent to his churches epistles
Calling the dead those who have fallen asleep.
For who can die if he loves Christ? How can he fall if he eats the living bread?[7]
He has in his heart the miracle
As a phylactery,[8] so even if he perish,
He will be resurrected and he will rise up
Saying, "Thou art the Life and the Resurrection."

KONTAKION ON THE RAISING OF LAZARUS 14.6.[9]

11:12-13 *If Asleep, He Will Recover*

SLEEP EXISTS FOR ONE'S SAFETY. ROMANUS MELODUS:

The Creator of all spoke on behalf of the disciples, saying: "Friends and companions, our friend has fallen asleep."
He was secretly teaching them in advance, because he knows and cares for all things—
"Let us go, then, let us advance and see the unusual tomb,[10]
And let us cause the mourning of Mary and Martha to cease
As I raise up Lazarus from the tomb, and as the Merciful One take pity on
The tears of Mary and Martha."

When they heard these words, the apostles as with one voice cried out to the Lord,
"Sleep exists for man for his safety and not at all for his destruction."[11]
And so He spoke to them openly: "He is dead.
As mortal I am away from him; but as God, I know all things.
If we truly arrive in time,
I shall resurrect the dead, and cause to cease
The tears of Mary and Martha."

KONTAKION ON THE RAISING OF LAZARUS 15.4-5.[12]

11:14 *Lazarus Is Dead*

[3]*AEG* 4:166*; GCS 1 2:217. [4]About two miles. [5]NPNF 1 14:228**. [6]Paul makes the connection: 1 Cor 15:20; 1 Thess 4:13. [7]Jn 6:51. [8]The editor notes phylacteries were used to ward off illness and accidents. They were also used as reminders of the law among the Pharisees. [9]*KRBM* 1:142-43. [10]Unusual because neither the son of the widow of Nain or Jairus's daughter, whom Jesus had also raised, had been buried as Lazarus had. [11]Sleep, as Chrysostom notes, was a good sign when someone was sick (*Homilies on the Gospel of John* 62.1). [12]*KRBM* 1:152.

Lazarus Begins to Be What He Had Been. Potamius of Lisbon: Lazarus, this intimate friend of God, died, as is known through the testimony of the Gospel. According to John, for forty years he had compensated for the losses of the flesh by the actions of his will. And so after a quick death which was due to his earthly frame, that is, to earth itself more than humanity—according to the book of Genesis[13] the rich fluidity of clay is responsible for us as well—while Christ the judge was far away, imparting the gifts of salvation on the borders of Judea, Lazarus was buried and placed in the tomb in order that he might begin to be what he had been—clay. On Lazarus.[14]

No Hint Yet of the Miracle to Come. Chrysostom: When he said, "He sleeps," he added, "I go to awake him." But when he said, "He is dead," he did not add, "I go to raise him." For he would not foretell in words what he was about to confirm by his deeds. He is always teaching us not to look for glory and not to make promises without a reason for doing so. Homilies on the Gospel of John 62.2.[15]

Physicians Normally Do Everything to Save Life. Ephrem the Syrian: All physicians wear themselves out for their patient lest he die. But Lazarus's physician was waiting for his death in order to show his victory over death. Commentary on Tatian's Diatessaron 17.3.[16]

Jesus Heals Death. Augustine: He had been sent for in order to restore Lazarus from sickness, not from death. But how could the death be hidden from him into whose hands the soul of the dead had flown? Tractates on the Gospel of John 49.11.[17]

11:15 *For Your Sake I Am Glad I Was Not There*

Establishing the Disciples' Faith. Hippolytus: Is he who does not desire the death of a sinner,[18] now glad of the death of a friend? I rejoice, [Jesus says], not for my own sake, nor for the sake of the dead, but for your sake. For I need this death as the foundation for your faith. On the Gospel of John and the Resurrection of Lazarus.[19]

Christ's Love Would Have Overcome Him. Cyril of Alexandria: Here it is as though Jesus says, If I had been there, he would not have died, because I would have had pity on him when he was suffering only a little. But now in my absence his death has taken place, so that, by raising him to life I shall bestow upon you a great advantage through your faith in me. And Christ says this, not to indicate that he is only able to do his divine work when present, but rather to show that if he had been present he would not have been able to neglect helping his friend who was dying. Commentary on the Gospel of John 7.[20]

11:16 *That We May Die with Him*

Thomas Later Becomes the Most Zealous of All the Disciples. Chrysostom: Some say that Thomas himself wanted to die. But this is not the case. The expression is rather one of cowardice. And yet Christ does not rebuke him but instead supports his weakness. The result is that in the end he became stronger than them all—in fact, invincible. For the wonderful thing is this: We see one who was so weak before the crucifixion become more tenacious than any of them after the crucifixion and after he comes to believe in the resurrection. This is how great the power of Christ was. The very man who dared not go in company with Christ to Bethany, the same person, while not seeing Christ, ran practically through the entire inhabited world, living in the midst of nations that

[13]See Gen 2:7. [14]CCL 69A:166. [15]NPNF 1 14:228**. [16]*ECTD* 262*. [17]NPNF 1 7:274**; CCL 36:425. [18]Ezek 18:23, 32; 33:11. [19]*AEG* 4:167*; GCS 1 2:218. [20]LF 48:114-15**.

were full of murder and wanting to kill him.[21] HOMILIES ON THE GOSPEL OF JOHN 62.2.[22]

THOMAS EXPECTS DEATH WHEN HE SHOULD EXPECT LIFE. CYRIL OF ALEXANDRIA: There is audacity in Thomas's words, but also timidity. It was the outflow of a devout heart, but it was mixed with a small faith. For he does not endure being left behind and even tries to persuade the others to adopt a similar resolution. Nevertheless, he thinks that they are destined to suffer [death] at the hands of the Jews, even against the will of Christ. . . . He neglects to look at the power of the Deliverer as he should have. And Christ made them timid, by enduring with patience beyond measure the sufferings he did experience at the hands of the Jews. Thomas therefore says that they should not separate themselves from their teacher, although undoubted danger lay before them. So, perhaps with a knowing smile, he said, "Let us go," that is, "Let us die." Or, maybe he meant, If we go, we certainly will die. Nevertheless, let us not refuse to suffer, for that would be too cowardly. Because if he raises from the dead, fear is superfluous seeing that we have someone who is able to raise us again after we have fallen. COMMENTARY ON THE GOSPEL OF JOHN 7.[23]

THOMAS MUST DIE WITH JESUS IN ORDER TO LIVE WITH HIM. ORIGEN: Perhaps Thomas also knew that it would not be possible to live with Jesus except by having died with him, as Paul taught.[24] But those who disagree say that he said this because he suspected the envy of the Jews that would arise from the resurrection of Lazarus, and the ensuing danger. FRAGMENT 79 ON THE GOSPEL OF JOHN.[25]

---

[21]Eugene LaVerdiere, in his article on Thomas in EEC 900, notes that Thomas was particularly influential in early church history as an apostle to Syria and its environs. Eusebius says he brought the Gospel to Parthia (*Ecclesiastical History* 3.1). Jerome and Rufinus of Aquileia (*Ecclesiastical History* 2.4) mention his influence in Persia. Gregory of Nazianzus in his *Oration* 25, as well as the *Acts of Thomas* 1, note that he preached the gospel in India where he also ultimately received martyrdom. [22]NPNF 1 14:228**. [23]LF 48:115**. Theodore expresses many of the same points. [24]Rom 6:8. [25]*AEG* 4:167*; GCS 10(4):546.

11:17-27 JESUS ARRIVES AT BETHANY

[17]Now when Jesus came, he found that Lazarus[x] had already been in the tomb four days. [18]Bethany was near Jerusalem, about two miles[y] off, [19]and many of the Jews had come to Martha and Mary to console them concerning their brother. [20]When Martha heard that Jesus was coming, she went and met him, while Mary sat in the house. [21]Martha said to Jesus, "Lord, if you had been here, my brother would not have died. [22]And even now I know that whatever you ask from God, God will give you." [23]Jesus said to her, "Your brother will rise again." [24]Martha said to him, "I know that he will rise again in the resurrection at the last day." [25]Jesus said to her, "I am the resurrection and the life;[z] he who believes in me, though he die, yet shall he live, [26]and whoever lives and believes in me shall never die. Do you believe this?" [27]She said to him, "Yes, Lord; I believe that you are the Christ, the Son of God, he who is coming into the world."

x Greek *he* **y** Greek *fifteen stadia* **z** Other ancient authorities omit *and the life*

Overview: The elapsed four days can be accounted for according to the letter (Chrysostom). Under such an understanding, after four days, Lazarus's body would be subjected to miserable corruption in the grave, testifying against anyone who doubted he had died (Potamius). Because Bethany was only two miles from Jerusalem means that Christ could have arrived earlier had he wanted to. Many—even the enemies of Christ—come to console his friends Mary and Martha because he did not (Chrysostom). Mary is not there to greet him, which may perhaps lie in the fact that Mary is here and elsewhere more a type of the contemplative life, while Martha personifies the active life (Origen). It may also be true, however, that Martha simply wants to speak to Christ alone, and when comforted, then she retrieves her sister (Chrysostom). She expresses her disappointment at his absence, although he was indeed there (Andrew) despite her lack of recognition of his divinity (Chrysostom). Such ignorance, however, does not imply a lack of faith (Andrew). Martha trusts that Jesus knows what is best (Augustine) as Jesus leads Martha to higher truths (Chrysostom) while she herself struggles to believe (Peter Chrysologus). He tests her faith in his promises (Theodore), knowing that her brother could have been raised right then and there if Jesus had chosen to do so (Peter Chrysologus).

Jesus is the voice of life and joy that awakens the dead (Athanasius). He has always been and continues to be the God not of the dead but of the living (Irenaeus). He is the pledge of our resurrection, which was already prophesied in the Old Testament (Apostolic Constitutions). There is therefore no need for those who are at the tomb to weep who believe Jesus' words (Romanus). Believers never die, although their bodies may (Methodius, Augustine). He gives us a joyful hope and security in him where we would otherwise be overcome by grief, as the world is (Cyprian). In Jesus' resurrection of Lazarus we see then a foretaste of the general resurrection (Cyril). Even though we may die, we are still alive if we believe (Augustine). Such a confession of faith is the confession Jesus seeks to elicit from Martha (Origen) and from us (Cyril). While Martha, perhaps in her grief, does not answer Jesus' question about the resurrection (Chrysostom), she does confess that he is the Christ, as also Peter and Nathanael had done (Tertullian), and expresses her belief in the Son, which is ultimately belief in the resurrection (Augustine).

11:17 *Dead for Four Days*

An Accounting of the Four Days. Chrysostom: Our Lord had stayed two days, and the messenger had come the day before—the very day on which Lazarus died. This brings us to the fourth day. Homilies on the Gospel of John 62.2.[1]

The Corruption of Lazarus's Body in the Tomb. Potamius of Lisbon: Here indeed, throughout the gloomy spheres of darkness and the shades of black horror, that is, throughout the course of four days that are renewed in accordance with the alternate interchange of increase and diminution—throughout eight days, we may say, by including also the dark nights—he lay with his jaws gaping and hanging down, the teeth in his mouth dropping, his mouth obstructed since he was really putrefying like a crumbly clod, consumed by earthly destruction, and his unhappy burial condemned his nerve bundles with the essence of his body to a miserable corruption. Thus, with the contraction of his limbs, his blackened skin is stretched over the dry and easy-to-count ribs, and a stream of bodily fluid, which is released from the cavity of the entrails, an already foul-smelling sewer, flowed filthy and dark to the feet of the corpse. On Lazarus.[2]

[1]NPNF 1 14:228**. Augustine provides an allegorical understanding of the four days of death that the law brings; *Tractates on the Gospel of John* 49.12. [2]CCL 69A:166. While this detail is rather gruesome, it was a staple description in many patristic homilies emphasizing the power and finality of death that was overcome by Jesus.

11:18-19 *Bethany Was Near Jerusalem*

WHY DO ENEMIES OF CHRIST CONSOLE HIS FRIENDS? CHRYSOSTOM: "Two miles." This is mentioned to account for so many coming from Jerusalem. . . . But how could the Jews console the loved ones of Christ, when they had resolved that whoever confessed Christ should be put out of the synagogue? Perhaps the extreme affliction of the sisters excited their sympathy, or they wished to show respect for their rank. Or perhaps those who came were of the better sort, as we find that many of them believed. Their presence is mentioned to do away with all doubt that Lazarus was really dead. HOMILIES ON THE GOSPEL OF JOHN 62.2.[3]

11:20 *Martha Goes While Mary Stays*

MARY AS ALLEGORY OF THE SOUL'S QUIET RECEPTIVITY. ORIGEN: Since Mary is a type of the contemplative life, Martha of the active, Lazarus of him who has fallen into sins after believing, naturally Mary and Martha mourn for Lazarus, and in mourning they need the comfort concerning their brother which the Jews wish to bring them. But before the fullness of time, words despair of being able to make the sister of the dead cease from weeping over him.

Martha seems more eager than Mary, since Martha first ran to Jesus, while Mary remained sitting in the house. . . . Therefore Martha, who was somewhat inferior in this regard, ran to Jesus while Mary remains in the house to receive him as one who was able to bear his presence. And she would not have gone out from her house if she had not heard her sister say, "The teacher has arrived and is calling you." And she did not simply get up but did so quickly, and falling at Jesus' feet said what she said. The other sister had not fallen at his feet. FRAGMENT 80 ON THE GOSPEL OF JOHN.[4]

MARTHA WANTS TO SPEAK TO CHRIST ALONE. CHRYSOSTOM: Martha does not take her sister with her because she wants to speak with Christ alone and tell him what has happened. When her hopes had been raised by him, then she went her way and called Mary. HOMILIES ON THE GOSPEL OF JOHN 62.3.[5]

11:21 *Lord, If You Had Been Here*

CHRIST WAS THERE. ANDREW OF CRETE: Do you see her faith? Do you see her undoubting mind? She affirmed in two ways that he was God and the Giver of life, even though she was led astray on account of her simple nature: "If you had been here," she said. What are you saying, Martha? Your reasoning is false. For he was there and he has been and still is present everywhere. . . . "If you had been here, my brother would not have died." Do you see how she believed him to be God and able with his power to restrain death and to raise the dead? For she was saying, I know that if you had been here, death would not have prevailed. HOMILY 8 ON LAZARUS.[6]

IGNORANCE CONCERNING JESUS' DIVINITY. CHRYSOSTOM: See how great the heavenly wisdom of the women is, although their understanding is weak. For when they saw Christ, they did not break out into mourning and wailing and loud crying, as we do when we see any of those we know coming in on our grief. Rather, immediately they reverence their Teacher. So then both these sisters believed in Christ, but not in a right way. For they did not yet certainly know either that he was God or that he did these things by his own power and authority, although on both points he had taught them. For they showed their ignorance of the former by saying, "If you had been here, our brother would not have died" and of the latter by saying, "Whatever you will ask of God, he will give it to you." HOMILIES ON THE GOSPEL OF JOHN 62.3.[7]

11:22 *Ask, and God Will Give*

[3]NPNF 1 14:229**. [4]*AEG* 4:168-69*; GCS 10(4):547-48. [5]NPNF 1 14:229**. [6]StPatr 31:35; PG 97:969-72. [7]NPNF 1 14:229*.

Martha Trusts That Jesus Knows What Is Best. Augustine: She does not say to him, "Bring my brother to life again." For how could she know that it would be good for him to come to life again? She says, I know that you can do so, if you want to, but what you will do is for your judgment, not for my presumption, to determine. Tractates on the Gospel of John 49.13.[8]

Jesus Leads Martha to Higher Truths. Chrysostom: He leads her to the knowledge of higher truths. Even though she had been inquiring only about the resurrection of Lazarus, he tells her of a resurrection in which both she and those with her would share. Homilies on the Gospel of John 62.3.[9]

Martha Is Trying to Believe. Peter Chrysologus: This woman does not believe, but she is trying to believe, while her unbelief is disturbing her belief. "Whatever you ask of God. . . ." God gives of his own accord; he does not ask of himself. Why, woman, do you delay in making your request when the one to grant it stands before you? Woman, he is the Judge himself whom you desire merely as an advocate. In him there is the power to give, not the need to make any request. "I know," she says, "that whatever you ask of God, he will give you." Woman, to believe this means that you do not believe. To know this means that you do not know. The apostle has indicated this, that the moment when a person thinks that he knows something, he does not know it.[10] Sermon 63.3.[11]

11:23-24 *The Resurrection on the Last Day*

The Future Resurrection. Theodore of Mopsuestia: From this it appears that they, even though they believed somehow in the power of the Lord, were still in doubt because of the greatness of the task. . . . On the one hand, she has no doubts about his promise. On the other hand, however, she considers the task superior to human power. Indeed, we said above that they still thought they were speaking to a man who does everything through his own strength. This is why she said to him, "I know that he will rise again in the resurrection of the last day." Commentary on John 5.11.23-24.[12]

Her Brother Could Be Raised Here and Now. Peter Chrysologus: Martha, again you know but you do not know. Martha, again do you really know, when you do not know that your brother can rise here and now? Or is it perhaps that God who at that future time is able to raise up all is now unable to raise up even one from the dead? He is able, yes, God is able to raise up one from the dead as a sign for this time, God who will later raise up all the dead to eternal life. . . . Martha, right in front of you is the Resurrection that you are putting so far into the future. Sermon 63.4.[13]

11:25 *I Am the Resurrection and the Life*

The Voice of Life and Joy That Wakens the Dead. Athanasius: I am the voice of life that wakens the dead. I am the good odor that takes away the foul odor. I am the voice of joy that takes away sorrow and grief. . . . I am the comfort of those who are in grief. Those who belong to me are given joy by me. I am the joy of the whole world. I gladden all my friends and rejoice with them. I am the bread of life.[14] Homily on the Resurrection of Lazarus.[15]

The Old Testament Fathers Are Christ's Children. Irenaeus: If he is not the God of the dead but of the living, yet was called the God of the fathers[16] who were sleeping, they do undoubtedly live to God and have not passed out of existence, since they are children of the resurrection. But our Lord is himself the resurrection, as he himself declares, "I am the resurrection and the

[8]NPNF 1 7:275**; CCL 36:427. [9]NPNF 1 14:229**. [10]See 1 Cor 8:2. [11]FC 109:253*. [12]CSCO 4 3:224-25. [13]FC 109:253. [14]Jn 6:35. [15]*AJSL* 57:265-66*. [16]The Old Testament patriarchs.

life." But the fathers are his children, for it is said by the prophet: "In the place of ancestors you, O king, shall have sons."[17] Christ himself, therefore, together with the Father, is the God of the living who spoke to Moses and who was also made known to the fathers. Against Heresies 4.5.2.[18]

Christ As Pledge of Our Resurrection Foreshadowed in Old Testament. Apostolic Constitutions: For the almighty God himself will raise us up through our Lord Jesus Christ, according to his infallible promise, and grant us a resurrection with all those that have slept from the beginning of the world. And we shall then be such as we now are in our present form, without any defect or corruption. For we shall rise incorruptible: whether we die at sea, or are scattered on the earth or are torn to pieces by wild beasts and birds, he will raise us by his own power. For the whole world is held together by the hand of God. . . .

This resurrection was not believed by the Jews, when of old they said, "Our bones are withered, and we are gone."[19] To whom God answered and said, "Behold, I open your graves and will bring you out of them. And I will put my Spirit into you, and you shall live: and you shall know that I the Lord have spoken it and will do it."[20] And he says by Isaiah: "The dead shall rise, and those that are in the graves shall be raised up. And those that rest in the earth shall rejoice, for the dew which is from you shall be healing to them."[21] There are indeed many and various things said concerning the resurrection, and concerning the continuance of the righteous in glory and concerning the punishment of the ungodly, their fall, rejection, condemnation, shame, "eternal fire and endless worm."[22] Now in order to show that it was in his power, if it had pleased him, that all men and women should be immortal, he provided the examples of Enoch and Elijah, who he did not allow to have any experience of death. Or if it had pleased him in every generation to raise those that died, that this also he was able to do he has made evident by himself and by others as when he raised the widow's son by Elijah[23] and the Shunammite's son by Elisha.[24] But we are persuaded that death is not a retribution of punishment, because even the saints have undergone it. In fact, even the Lord of the saints, Jesus Christ, the life of those who believe and the resurrection of the dead, [experienced it]. . . . For it is he who raised Lazarus when he had been in the grave four days, and Jairus's daughter[25] and the widow's son.[26] It is he who raised himself by the command of the Father in the space of three days who is the pledge of our resurrection. For he says, "I am the resurrection and the life." Constitutions of the Holy Apostles 5.1.7.[27]

11:26a *Believers Die, Yet Live*

Why Do We Not Trust Christ's Words? Romanus Melodus:

Taking pity on the tears of Mary and Martha,
  Thou hast said to them:
    "He will be resurrected and he will rise up
    Saying, 'Thou art the Life and
      Resurrection.' "

In considering the tomb and those in the
      tomb, we weep,
  But we should not; for we do not know
      whence they have come,
  And where they are now, and who has them.
They have come from temporal life, released
      from its sorrows;
  They are at peace, waiting for the receiving
      of divine light.[28]
  The Lover of man has them in His charge,
      and He has divested them of their
        temporal clothing
  In order that He may clothe them with an
      eternal body.
Why, then, do we weep in vain? Why do we
      not trust Christ, as He cries:

[17]Ps 45:16 (44:17 LXX). [18]SC 100:430; ANF 1:467. [19]Ezek 37:11. [20]Ezek 37:13-14. [21]Is 26:19. [22]Is 66:24. [23]1 Kings 17. [24]2 Kings 4. [25]Mk 5. [26]Lk 7. [27]ANF 7:439-40*. [28]See Wis 4:7.

"He who believes on me shall not perish,
For even if he knows corruption, after that corruption,
He will be resurrected and he will rise up
Saying, 'Thou art the Life and the Resurrection' "?

The man of faith always has power for whatever he wishes,
Since he possesses a faith which lends strength to all things;
From it, he gains power from Christ for whatever he asks.
This faith is a great possession; if a man have it, he has control of everything.
Mary and Martha had it and were renowned for it.
Kontakion on the Raising of Lazarus 14.1-2.[29]

Believers Are Always Alive. Methodius: Here he says believers live; they never die. Their bodies die but are brought back to life again. On the Resurrection 3.21.6.[30]

Faith Is the Life of the Soul. Augustine: What does this mean? "He who believes in me, though he were dead." Just as Lazarus is dead, "yet shall he live," for he is not the God of the dead but of the living. Such was the answer he gave the Jews concerning their fathers, long ago dead, that is, concerning Abraham and Isaac and Jacob: "I am the God of Abraham, and the God of Isaac and the God of Jacob: He is not the God of the dead but of the living. For all live unto him."[31] Believe then, and though you were dead, yet shall you live; but if you do not believe, even while you are alive you are dead. Let us prove this also by the fact that if you do not believe, though you live you are dead. To one who was delaying to follow him and saying, "Let me first go and bury my father," the Lord said, "Let the dead bury their dead. But come and follow me."[32] There was there a dead man needing to be buried, there were there also dead people to bury the dead: the one was dead in the flesh, the others in soul. And how does death come to the soul? When faith is wanting. How does death come to the body? When the soul is wanting. For faith is the life of the soul. Tractates on the Gospel of John 49.15.[33]

Living in the Hope of the Resurrection. Cyprian: The apostle Paul reproaches and rebukes those who show sorrow for those who have left this world. "I would not," he says, "like you to be ignorant, my dear brothers and sisters, about those who are sleeping, so that you feel sorrow like those who have no hope. If we believe that Jesus died and rose again, then God will bring those who are asleep in Jesus with him."[34] Those who show sorrow at the departure of their friends reveal their own lack of hope. But we who live by hope and believe in God and are convinced that Christ suffered for us and that he rose again, who remain with Christ and find our resurrection by him and in him, why should we either show reluctance when we ourselves have to depart or lament and grieve for others who depart as though they were dying forever? Christ himself, our Lord and God, tells us, "I am the resurrection and the life, he that believes in me, though he should die, shall live, and whoever lives and believes in me shall never die." If we believe in Christ, let us put faith in his words and promises. Since we shall not die once and for all, let us pass into Christ in joy and confidence since we shall live and reign with him forever. On Mortality, 21.[35]

The Grace of the General Resurrection. Cyril of Alexandria: If anyone notices that even the saints who have received promises of life die, this is no reason for concern, since it is what naturally happens. The display of the grace [of resurrection] has been reserved until the appointed time. This grace is powerful, not partially but effectually, in the case of all, even of those saints who have died in time past and are

[29]*KRBM* 1:140-41. [30]*AEG* 4:170**; *MOS* 279. [31]Mt 22:32; Lk 20:37-38. [32]Mt 8:21-22. [33]NPNF 1 7:275*; CCL 36:427. See also *Sermon* 173 (*WSA* 3 5:254). [34]1 Thess 4:13-14. [35]*BTNL* 122-23; CCL 3A:28.

tasting death for a short time until the general resurrection. For then, together, all will enjoy the good things. Commentary on the Gospel of John 7.[36]

11:26b *Do You Believe This?*

Whether a Question or a Statement. Origen: The Savior does not inquire "Do you believe this?" in ignorance as to whether Martha did or did not believe what was said. Rather, he did so in order that we, or indeed those who were then present, might learn from her answer what her disposition was. But another will say that it is not a question but a statement: "You believe this." In this case, Martha then completes the Savior's statement saying, Yes, Lord, and not only do I believe what you now say, but I believe now that you are the Christ, something I also believed before. And I believe that you are the Son of God who comes into the world and lives with all who believe in you. Fragment 81 on the Gospel of John.[37]

Martha's "Amen" on Behalf of Lazarus. Cyril of Alexandria: Having previously explained the force of the mystery in himself and shown plainly that he is by nature life and true God, he demands assent to the faith, furnishing in this matter a model to the churches. For we should not vainly cast our words into the air when we confess the venerable mystery but rather fix the roots of the faith in heart and mind and then allow it to bear fruit in our confession. And we ought to believe without any hesitation or double-mindedness. . . . Nevertheless, it is necessary to know that we make the confession of our faith to God, although we are questioned by others, I mean those whose responsibility it is to minister in sacred things, when we say the "I believe" at the reception of holy baptism. Certainly therefore to speak falsely and to slip aside toward unbelief is a most awful thing. . . . In a certain way, as Lazarus was lying dead, the assent to the faith is demanded of the woman on his behalf. The same can be seen in the churches when a newborn child is brought either to receive the anointing of the catechumenate or to be fully initiated into the Christian faith at holy baptism. In these instances, the person who brings the child repeats aloud the "Amen" on the child's behalf[38]. . . something we also see in the case of Lazarus and his sister. Martha wisely and prudently sows the confession of faith first so that afterward she may reap the fruit of it. Commentary on the Gospel of John 7.[39]

11:27 *The Christ, the Son of God*

Asked One Thing, Answers Another. Chrysostom: Martha seems not to have understood his words, that is, she saw that he meant something great but did not see what that was. She is asked one thing and answers another. Yet for a while at least she had this in her favor, that she moderated her grief. Such was the power of the words of Christ. This is why Martha went out first and Mary followed. For their affection for their teacher did not allow them to feel their present sorrow so strongly, so that the minds of these women were truly wise as well as loving. Homilies on the Gospel of John 62.3.[40]

Martha Confesses Christ. Tertullian: Martha confesses him to be the Son of God, being no more astray than Peter and Nathanael, though even if she had been astray she should at once have learned [the truth]. For the Lord, for the raising up of her brother from the dead, looked up to heaven and to the Father and said, "Father"—evidently a son [speaks]—"I thank you that you hear me always: for the sake of these multitudes that stand by, I said it that they may believe that you have sent me."[41] Against Praxeas 23.[42]

---

[36]LF 48:118**. [37]*AEG* 4:170-71*; GCS 10(4):548. [38]In an intriguing analogy, Martha's "Amen" on behalf of Lazarus is here compared by Cyril with the "Amen" of the parents on behalf of a newborn child in baptism. This more corporate understanding of faith and the Christian life in early Christianity ensured mutual consolation and support within the Christian family. [39]LF 48:119-20**. [40]NPNF 1 14:230**. [41]Jn 11:41-42. [42]*TTAP* 165.

Belief in the Son Is Belief in the Resurrection. Augustine: When I believed [that you were the Son of God], I believed that you were the resurrection, that you were life and that he that believes in you, though he were dead, shall live. Tractates on the Gospel of John 49.15.[43]

[43]NPNF 1 7:275**; CCL 36:428.

11:28-37 Mary and Martha Come to Meet Jesus

[28]When she had said this, she went and called her sister Mary, saying quietly, "The Teacher is here and is calling for you." [29]And when she heard it, she rose quickly and went to him. [30]Now Jesus had not yet come to the village, but was still in the place where Martha had met him. [31]When the Jews who were with her in the house, consoling her, saw Mary rise quickly and go out, they followed her, supposing that she was going to the tomb to weep there. [32]Then Mary, when she came where Jesus was and saw him, fell at his feet, saying to him, "Lord, if you had been here, my brother would not have died." [33]When Jesus saw her weeping, and the Jews who came with her also weeping, he was deeply moved in spirit and troubled; [34]and he said, "Where have you laid him?" They said to him, "Lord, come and see." [35]Jesus wept. [36]So the Jews said, "See how he loved him!" [37]But some of them said, "Could not he who opened the eyes of the blind man have kept this man from dying?"

Overview: Jesus calls for Mary, although the text does not say where, when or how (Augustine). When Mary, who bears the same name as his mother, comes to Jesus (Peter Chrysologus), her ardent love for him is evident (Theodore). As if by providential design, the Jews follow her so that they too will become witnesses to the miracle that is going to take place (Cyril). They, along with Mary and Jesus, all wept together, but Mary even more so, having her brother separated from her (Peter Chrysologus). Her initial reaction to Jesus is the same as Martha's, but also more intense as she falls at Jesus' feet (Theodore). But Jesus too is disturbed over Lazarus's death as one who is human just as we are (Hippolytus). John chooses to show Jesus' grief here—or perhaps his anger at death (Diadochus)—as he groans on coming to the tomb, rather than later, at the passion, where Jesus' divinity is much more evident than his humanity in John's account (Chrysostom).

In coming to Lazarus's grave, Jesus asks where they have laid him, not out of ignorance but in order to get them to follow him to the tomb as witnesses (Chromatius). He has come out of pity for the tears of Mary and Martha, although the crowd thinks he has come to mourn (Chrysostom) as he also does with our sin (Augustine). Jesus wept, but he did not mourn (Hippolytus). Could it be possible that they may have been tears of joy knowing that Lazarus would be returned (Peter Chrysologus)? Or, is it more likely that God wept, moved by the mortality of those created to be immortal (Potamius)? He wept to teach us to weep (Augustine) and how to weep because there are limits to grief for Christians who know of the resurrection (Basil of Seleucia). It was Jesus' mother who gave him the gift of weeping (Irenaeus). His tears were like the watering rain that would cause the seed of Lazarus's body to sprout back to life (Ephrem). He wept out of compassion, not only for Lazarus but for all humanity, which is subject to death (Cyril). But there were still those who saw not compassion or power but only weakness in Jesus because of the delay in raising Lazarus (Chrysostom).

11:28 *The Teacher Calls for You*

No Mention of Where, When or How Jesus Called Mary. Augustine: We may observe that the Evangelist has not said where, when or how the Lord called Mary, but for brevity's sake he has left it to be gathered from Martha's words. Tractates on the Gospel of John 49.16.[1]

11:29-30 *Mary Quickly Comes to Jesus*

The One Who Bears the Name of His Mother. Peter Chrysologus: When Martha professed her faith in Christ and wiped out by her reverent confession whatever blame there was in womanhood, a message is sent to Mary, because without Mary death could not be banished or life be restored.[2] Let Mary come; let the one who bears the name of his mother come so that humanity might see that as Christ dwelt enclosed in the Virgin's womb, so too to that extent the dead will come forth from the underworld, the dead will come forth from the tombs. Sermon 64.2.[3]

11:31 *Jews Suppose Mary Goes to Weep at the Tomb*

Mary's Ardent Love for Jesus. Theodore of Mopsuestia: The Jews who were there to console her in her grief, as they saw that Mary had suddenly gotten up and gone out, thinking that she went to the sepulcher to weep, followed her as if she, being overwhelmed by her sorrow, might be about to do something[4] that was their duty to prevent. This was ordered by the providence of God, that they came there against their will and became the witnesses of the miracle to be performed. Commentary on John 5.11.29.[5]

The Providence of God. Cyril of Alexandria: The Jews who follow Mary are doing the will of God in order that they might go to see the marvelous deed, even without wishing to do so. Had this not taken place by the providence of God, the Evangelist would not have mentioned it, neither would he have written down the reason they followed Mary to Lazarus's tomb if he had not been continuously zealous for the truth. Thus, he states the reason why many ran to the tomb, and were found there, and became witnesses of the marvelous deed and reported it to others. Commentary on the Gospel of John 7.[6]

Mary, the Jews, Christ and We All Weep. Peter Chrysologus: Mary weeps, the Jews weep, and Christ also weeps: do you think [all wept] with a similar emotion? So be it that Mary the sister wept since she was unable to hold on to her brother and was unable to prevent his death. Although she was certain about the resurrection, nevertheless, because she was without comfort at the moment, because its delay meant that his absence would be lengthy and because she was sad about his being separated from God, she could not but weep. At the same time since when death appears it is so grim, so morbid, so very cruel, it could not but unsettle and disturb any mind, no matter how full of faith....

The Jews were in tears, being both mindful of

[1]NPNF 1 7:275**; CCL 36:428. [2]Chrysologus, here and elsewhere, interprets Martha and Mary as symbols of Eve and the Virgin Mary. [3]FC 109:256-57. [4]Perhaps suicide? [5]CSCO 4 3:226-27. [6]LF 48:120-21**.

their condition and overcome by despair concerning the future life. . . . As often as one sees a dead person, that often does he lament that he is destined to die. So a mortal cannot but grieve concerning death.

For which of these reasons was Christ weeping? And if for none of them, then why was he in tears? Certainly he is the same one who had said, "Lazarus is dead, and I rejoice."[7] . . . When he loses him he sheds no tears, but when he lifts him up it is then that he weeps. He pours out mortal tears just at the time when he is pouring back in the spirit of life. Brothers, the nature of our human body has this tendency, that the force of joy and the force of sorrow both produce tears. . . . This is why Christ wept, not from grief in the face of death but from calling to mind that happiness when by his own voice, and solely by his voice, he would raise up all the dead to eternal life. Sermon 64.3.[8]

11:32 *Lord, If You Had Been Here*

Mary's Love and Devotion More Intense. Theodore of Mopsuestia: As Mary came to Jesus, she immediately fell at his feet saying the same things as Martha, "Lord, if you had been here, my brother would not have died." Martha is not actually said to have fallen at his feet but only to have come to him, so that it seems to many that Mary had a greater love for the Lord. This also appears from the fact that, while the Lord was at their house, Martha was intent on her service, whereas Mary, because of her great love, sat at his feet, as she did not want to be separated from her teacher even for a short time. Therefore the Lord exalted her in his praise more than Martha. Commentary on John 5.11.32.[9]

11:33 *Jesus Deeply Moved in Spirit*

Jesus Showed Himself Human. Hippolytus: "He troubled himself" not as we are troubled by fear or pain, but "he troubled himself." "Where have you laid him?" Did he who had known when he had died not know where he was buried? But he mingles human words with divine miracles in order to show that he was also human, as also the prophet says, "And he is a human, and who will know him?"[10] And he wanted it to be clear that he who is God is also something else. . . . But he showed himself actually as man also by the fact that he wept. On the Gospel of John and the Resurrection of Lazarus.[11]

The Benefits of a Troubled Spirit. Diadochus of Photice: Becoming incensed usually spells trouble and confusion for the soul more than any other passion, yet there are times when it greatly benefits the soul. For when with inward calm we direct it against blasphemers or other sinners in order to induce them to mend their ways or at least feel some shame, we make our soul more gentle. In this way we put ourselves completely in harmony with the purposes of God's justice and goodness. In addition, through becoming deeply angered by sin we often overcome weaknesses in our soul. Thus there is no doubt that if, when deeply depressed, we become indignant in spirit against the demon of corruption, this gives us the strength to despise even the presumptuousness of death. In order to make this clear, the Lord twice became indignant against death and troubled in spirit.[12] And despite the fact that, untroubled, he could by a simple act of will do all that he wished, nonetheless when he restored Lazarus's soul to his body he was indignant and troubled in spirit—which seems to me to show that becoming incensed in a controlled manner can be viewed as a weapon implanted in our nature by God when he creates us. If Eve had used this weapon against the serpent, she would not have been impelled by sensual desire. In my view, then, the person who in a spirit of devotion makes controlled use of the power of his anger will without doubt be judged more favorably than

[7]Jn 11:14-15. [8]FC 109:257-58. [9]CSCO 4 3:227. [10]Jer 17:9 (LXX). [11]AEG 4:171-72*; GCS 1 2:219-20, 224. [12]See Jn 12:27; 13:21.

the one who . . . has never become incensed. The latter seems to have an inexperienced driver in charge of his emotions, while the former, always ready for action, drives the horses of virtue through the midst of the demonic host, guiding the four-horsed chariot of self-control in the fear of God. On Spiritual Perfection 62.[13]

Jesus' Grief. Chrysostom: He comes then to the tomb and again curbed his emotions. Why does the Evangelist carefully mention in several places that "he wept" and that "he groaned"? He mentions these so that you may learn that he had truly put on our nature. For while this Evangelist is remarkable for the great things he says about Christ more than the others in matters relating to the body, [at the passion] he also speaks much more humbly than they. For instance, he says nothing about Jesus' sorrow concerning his death, while the other Evangelists declare that he was exceedingly sorrowful, that he was in fact in an agony. But John, on the contrary, says that he even threw the officers backwards. The result is that [John] here has made up for what is omitted there by mentioning his grief. Homilies on the Gospel of John 63.2.[14]

11:34 *Where Have You Laid Him?*

Jesus Asks Not Out of Ignorance. Chromatius of Aquileia: When therefore the Lord comes to Mary and Martha the sisters of Lazarus, seeing the crowd of the Jews, he says, "Where have they laid him?" But could the Lord truly be ignorant of where the body of Lazarus was placed, who while being absent at the death of Lazarus had already announced his death and who in his divine majesty was everywhere? But this the Lord did out of ancient custom. For to Adam he had similarly said, "Where are you, Adam?"[15] This was not because he was ignorant of where Adam was but that he might therefore question him so that Adam would openly confess his sin. . . It is the same here. He does not ask because he is ignorant of Lazarus's whereabouts[16] but so that the crowd of the Jews would follow him to Lazarus's tomb so that, seeing the divine power of Christ exhibited in the resurrection of Lazarus, they might be exposed as his enemies if they did not believe this display of his power. For the superior Lord said to them, "If you do not believe me, believe the works and know that the Father is in me and I in him."[17] Sermon 27.3.[18]

They Thought Jesus Came to Mourn. Chrysostom: Jesus had not yet raised anyone from the dead and seemed as if he came to mourn, not to resurrect him. For the Jews seem to indicate that he was coming to mourn, not to raise him. Homilies on the Gospel of John 63.1.[19]

Seeing, He Pities. Augustine: When the Lord sees, he pities, as we read, "Look upon my adversity and misery, and forgive me all my sin."[20] Tractates on the Gospel of John 49.20.[21]

11:35 *Jesus Wept*

He Wept but Did Not Mourn. Hippolytus: What need was there to weep for him whom he was soon about to raise? But Jesus wept to give us an example of sympathy and kindliness toward our fellow human beings. Jesus wept that he might by deed rather than word teach us to "weep with those that weep."[22] He wept but did not mourn—avoiding absolute tearlessness as harsh and inhuman but rejecting love of mourning as ignoble and cowardly. He wept, assigning due measure to his sympathy. On the Gospel of John and the Resurrection of Lazarus.[23]

Tears at Welcoming Lazarus Back? Peter Chrysologus: Christ was deeply agitated with his inner organs all in turmoil, because at this

[13]*TP* 1:272*. [14]NPNF 1 14:233*. [15]Gen 3:9. [16]This is a common emphasis in patristic commentary that seeks to emphasize that Christ was all-knowing as God. [17]Jn 10:38. [18]CCL 9A:125-26. [19]NPNF 1 14:232**. [20]See Ps 51:1 (50:3 LXX, Vg). [21]CCL 36:430; NPNF 1 7:277**. [22]Rom 12:15. [23]*AEG* 4:173*; GCS 1 2:224.

point he was going to raise up only Lazarus and not yet all the dead. Who then could think that Christ shed tears on this occasion out of human weakness when the heavenly Father weeps over the prodigal son, not when he goes away but at the moment when he welcomes him back?[24] And so, Christ shed tears over Lazarus because he was welcoming him back, not because he lost him. And to be sure, it is not when he sees the crowd weeping that Jesus weeps, but when he asks them questions and sees in their responses no trace of faith.[25] Sermon 64.3.[26]

God Wept, Moved by Mortals' Tears. Potamius of Lisbon: God wept, moved by the tears of mortals, and although he was about to release Lazarus from the bond of death by the exercise of his power, he fulfilled the component of human affection with the comfort of his sympathetic tears. God wept, not because he learned that the young man had died before him but in order to moderate the sisters' outpourings of grief. God wept, in order that God might do, with tears and compassion, what human beings do on behalf of their fellow human beings. God wept, because human nature had fallen to such an extent that, after being expelled from eternity, it had come to love the lower world. God wept, because those who could be immortal, the devil made mortal. God wept, because those whom he had rewarded with every benefit and had placed under his power, those whom he had set in paradise, among flowers and lilies without any hardship, the devil, by teaching them to sin, exiled from almost every delight. God wept, because those whom he had created innocent, the devil through his wickedness, caused to be found guilty. On Lazarus.[27]

He Wept to Teach Us to Weep. Augustine: Why did Christ weep except to teach us to weep? Tractates on the Gospel of John 49.19.[28]

Jesus Showed There Are Limits to Grief for Christians. Basil of Seleucia: Jesus wept by the tomb in order to give a limit for grief to lovers of Christ. By weeping, he ordained a law with his tears. He wept, he did not lament, or wail, or moan, or rend his garments or tear his hair. He defined the bounds of grief [as extending] only as far as the first tears. For why do you weep for a corpse that will be raised? Why do you weep for one who is awaiting the trumpet? Why do you lament as a corpse one who is [merely] sleeping? Why do you trouble one who is in repose with your cries? "Christ is arisen and became the first-fruits of those that slept."[29] On hearing of one who is asleep, do not lament him as a corpse. Moderate your love by means of your tears. Do not offend the one who has experienced the resurrection by weeping immoderately.[30] For it is on this account that he is weeping by the tomb and allowing himself to suffer now, in order that he may expel your grief. Homily on Lazarus 6.[31]

Jesus' Mother Gave Him the Gift of Weeping. Irenaeus: Why did he come down into [Mary his mother] if he were to take nothing of her? If he had taken nothing of Mary, he . . . would never have wept over Lazarus. Against Heresies 3.22.2.[32]

Jesus' Tears Are Like the Rain That Waters the Earth. Ephrem the Syrian: His tears were like the rain, and Lazarus like a grain of wheat, and the tomb like the earth. He gave forth a cry like that of thunder, and death trembled at his voice. Lazarus burst forth like a grain of wheat. He came forth and adored his Lord who had raised him. Commentary on Tatian's Diatessaron 17.7.[33]

[24]See Lk 15:20. [25]See also Chromatius of Aquileia *Sermon* 27.2 for a similar opinion regarding the tears of agitation. [26]FC 109:258*. [27]CCL 69A:172. [28]NPNF 1 7:276*; CCL 36:430. [29]1 Cor 15:20. [30]The disapproval of the Greek fathers toward the expression of violent grief and ritual lamentation of the dead is discussed at length by Margaret Alexiou, *The Ritual Lament in Greek Tradition* (Cambridge: Cambridge University Press, 1974), 28ff. [31]*AnBoll* 104:180*. [32]SC 34:376; ANF 1:454. For further reflection on the human nature of Christ and this passage, see Tertullian *Against Praxeas* 16; Gregory of Nazianzus *Oration* 38.15; Theodore *Dialogues* (FC 106:150). [33]*ECTD* 264.

11:36 *See How He Loved Him!*

Jesus Weeps for All Humanity. Cyril of Alexandria: The Jews thought that Jesus wept on account of the death of Lazarus, but in fact he wept out of compassion for all humanity, not mourning Lazarus alone but all of humanity, which is subject to death, having justly fallen under so great a penalty. Commentary on the Gospel of John 7.[34]

11:37 *Power over Blindness and Death*

Wickedness Even in the Face of Calamity. Chrysostom: They do not relax their wickedness even in the face of calamity. And yet, what he was about to do was something far more wonderful. For it is a much greater thing to dispel death that has come and conquered than to ward off death that is imminent. They therefore slander him by those very points through which they ought to have marveled at his power. They allow for the time that he opened the eyes of the blind. And, when they ought to have admired him because of that miracle, they use this latter case as a way to cast a slur upon it, as though it had not even taken place. And not only this . . . but even before he has arrived or done anything, they try to prevent him with their accusations without even waiting to see how things will turn out. Homilies on the Gospel of John 63.1.[35]

[34]LF 48:123-24**. [35]NPNF 1 14:233**.

11:38-44 THE RAISING OF LAZARUS: THE SEVENTH SIGN

[38]*Then Jesus, deeply moved again, came to the tomb; it was a cave, and a stone lay upon it.* [39]*Jesus said, "Take away the stone." Martha, the sister of the dead man, said to him, "Lord, by this time there will be an odor, for he has been dead four days."* [40]*Jesus said to her, "Did I not tell you that if you would believe you would see the glory of God?"* [41]*So they took away the stone. And Jesus lifted up his eyes and said, "Father, I thank thee that thou hast heard me.* [42]*I knew that thou hearest me always, but I have said this on account of the people standing by, that they may believe that thou didst send me."* [43]*When he had said this, he cried with a loud voice, "Lazarus, come out."* [44]*The dead man came out, his hands and feet bound with bandages, and his face wrapped with a cloth. Jesus said to them, "Unbind him, and let him go."*

Overview: Tragedies such as sickness and death cause even our Lord to groan (Peter Chrysologus). When Jesus was far from the tomb, he groaned in spirit, but when he neared the tomb, the groan was compressed inward (Origen) as an indication of the turmoil he was going through inside (Cyril). He groans because that is what faith does when it sees something that has gone wrong and is not right (Augustine). Jesus then arrives at the tomb—the prison from which Lazarus will be freed (Peter Chrysologus).

The stone in front of the cave, the stench of

the body, all indicate there was no opportunity for deception (Hippolytus). The stench of Lazarus's body highlights how miraculous the resurrection was (Theodore). In allegorizing concerning the stench of Lazarus—and allegorizing need not deny its historicity (Augustine)—parallels are drawn between sin and death, repentance and resurrection (Augustine). Jesus commands the stone to be removed, but Martha's words temporarily intervene (Origen), only to give way to faith—her faith as one living that trusts Jesus on behalf of Lazarus, who is dead (Cyril). As they roll away the stone, the Storehouse of life approaches the tomb of death (Athanasius).

Jesus' eyes focus upward, taking our attention away from daily concerns to what is above (Origen). Jesus knows that the Father has already anticipated his prayer, which is why he offers a prayer of thanks rather than petition (Origen). Our Lord's prayer also makes clear to the crowd that he never acts against the will of his Father (Chrysostom) and lets us know that those who truly pray are always heard (Origen). Christ did not need to pray (Hilary), but because they had leveled a charge of blasphemy against him, the tomb becomes a court of justice where Jesus is vindicated (Hippolytus). His prayer knocks on the doors of hell, demanding the release of Lazarus from the grip of Tartarus, who in futility appeals to heaven as the Trinity commands Lazarus to be returned (Peter Chrysologus).

Lazarus's friend and Lord commands him to come out (Andrew). The voice longing for Lazarus frees him from his prison (Hesychius). It is a loud, singular voice that calls to his friend by name (Apollinaris). Had he not called him by name, the great power of Jesus would have summoned all those in their graves (Maximinus). The voice that speaks also spoke at creation (Athanasius), and will speak again when it calls us out of our graves at the general resurrection (Gregory of Nyssa). When Jesus raises Lazarus through prayer, he demonstrates his own power while also showing his oneness with the Father (Chrysostom).

As Lazarus is bid to come forth, so also are those with a guilty conscience (Gregory the Great, Augustine). The unbinding of the linens that bound Lazarus parallels our being unbound from the deadness of sin (Irenaeus, Origen), as the church and its ministers are charged with the task of unloosing sinners from their sins (Augustine). There are many like Lazarus trapped in their own tombs until released by the words of Jesus (Origen). The resurrection of Lazarus teaches us that death has lost its kingdom forever (Basil of Seleucia). We can now look forward to Lazarus offering the toast at the resurrection feast he has already sampled when we together with him celebrate Christ's return (Peter Chrysologus).

11:38 *Jesus Comes to the Tomb*

Groaning in the Face of Death. Peter Chrysologus: Spirit groans, so that flesh would come back to life. Life groans, so that death would be put to flight. God groans, so that humanity would rise. Pardon groans, lest the verdict be unfavorable. Christ groans as he subdues death, because one who snatches an unparalleled victory over an enemy cannot but groan. But with regard to the fact that he said that he "groaned again," he does groan again in order to provide evidence of a twofold resurrection, since at Christ's voice just as those dead in body are raised to life from their graves, so too those dead in faithfulness rise to a life of faith. Sermon 65.1.[1]

Two Different Groanings of Christ. Origen: When he was far from the tomb, he groaned in spirit. But when he comes near to the tomb, he no longer groans in spirit but compresses his groaning in himself. . . . Again he rebukes the feeling that we may learn that he has become unchangeably human like ourselves. Fragment 84 on the Gospel of John.[2]

[1]FC 109:260*. [2]AEG 4:173*; GCS 10(4):549.

The Struggle Within. Cyril of Alexandria: Here we understand the groaning as if it were the will struggling with a sort of movement according to its power, both because he rather sternly reproved his grief and [because of] the tears that were about to be shed from his grief. For, as God he, in the way of a master, reproves his humanity, looking for it to be strong in sorrowful circumstances. . . . "He groaned," which means that through the outward action of his body he indicated his inner distress. Commentary on the Gospel of John 7.[3]

Christ Groans Because Faith Groans. Augustine: Why did Christ trouble himself except to intimate to you how you should be troubled when you are weighed down and crushed by so great a mass of iniquity? For here you have been looking to yourself, seeing your own guilt, doing an accounting of yourself. I have done this, and God has spared me. I have committed this, and he has still stayed with me. I have heard the gospel and despised it. I have been baptized and returned again to my old habits. What am I doing? Where am I going? How shall I escape? When you speak in this way, Christ is already groaning, for your faith is groaning. In the voice of one who groans like this, the hope of that person's rising again comes to light. If this kind of a faith is within, Christ is there too, groaning. For if there is faith in us, Christ is in us. . . . Why did he groan and trouble himself, but to intimate that the faith of one who has just cause to be displeased with himself should be, in a sense, groaning over the accusation of wicked deeds so that the habit of sinning may give way to the vehemence of penitential sorrow? Tractates on the Gospel of John 49.19.[4]

The Cave As Prison. Peter Chrysologus: It would have sufficed for him to have said that he had come to the tomb. Why is it that the Evangelist makes special mention of the cave? Certainly it is a cave, where the devil's thievery has lodged human beings. It is a cave where a woman's wiles buried the man, a cave where the greediness of death imprisoned God's handiwork. "And a stone had been placed in front of it." The door of hard death was bolted harder still by a very hard stone. What good does weeping at a grave do since the voice of the one weeping does not penetrate such hard and thick barriers? Christians, let us weep before God for our sins, and let us not weep with the pagans before the dead who do not hear us. Sermon 65.2.[5]

11:39 *Odor of Death After Stone's Removal*

No Chance for Deception. Hippolytus: Are you—as someone who has bestowed the kind of power on your apostles that can remove mountains[6]—are you not able to roll away a small stone from the entrance of the cave? But he chose not to roll the stone away because the spectators did not believe. Otherwise, they might have been able to say that what he did relied on trickery and deceiving the eyes. They would say there had been an apparently dead man laid in the grave, and that [Jesus] wanted to make it look like he called and the other heard. And so now he leads them to the grave, so that after they have rolled away the stone, the foul smell might reach them and furnish them with testimony that the man was actually dead. And then, once they believe Lazarus has died, they will no longer doubt his resurrection. The Lord had already planned for this when he came. Notice what immediately follows. Martha approaches the stone and says, "Lord, by this time there will be an odor, for he has been dead for four days." But the ever-living one, who is fully conscious of his power, says, "I chose to learn this from you, [Martha]. In fact, repeat what you said about him, 'By this time he stinks.' Repeat it, proclaiming that his resurrection is real." His death was established several times in order that the fact of his resurrection

[3]LF 48:124*. [4]NPNF 1 7:276**. [5]FC 109:260-61. Origen also compares Lazarus coming out of the cave to Joseph's release from the well as a prefiguring of the Resurrection. See *Fragment 84 on the Gospel of John*. [6]Mt 17:20.

might be established. . . . He commanded the Jews to roll away the stone with their own hands, reserving for himself the greatest sign so that they might be witnesses of the sign done by him. On the Gospel of John and the Resurrection of Lazarus.[7]

Flesh and Soul of Lazarus Are Resurrected. Tertullian: In the case of Lazarus, which we may take as the most outstanding instance of a resurrection, the flesh lay prostrate in weakness, almost putrid in the dishonor of its decay. The flesh smelled of corruption, and yet it was as flesh that Lazarus rose again—with his soul, no doubt. But that soul was incorrupt. Nobody had wrapped it in its linen swathes. Nobody had deposited it in a grave. Nobody had yet perceived its "smell," nobody for four days had seen it "sown." Well, now, this entire condition, this whole end of Lazarus, is indeed what the flesh of all humanity is still experiencing, but no one's soul is experiencing it. That substance, therefore, to which the apostle's whole description clearly refers,[8] of which he clearly speaks, must be both the natural (or animate) body when it is sown and the spiritual body when it is raised again. On the Resurrection of the Flesh 53.3-4.[9]

The Stench Highlights the Extent of the Miracle. Theodore of Mopsuestia: "Lord, already there is a stench because he has been dead four days." These words were spoken by the woman who doubted, but they also referred to the greatness of the miracle to be performed. Indeed, the more they knew that his body was putrefying and was in a state of mutation according to nature, the more the miracle to be performed for Lazarus appeared to be extraordinary. So the Lord by reproving her said, "Did I not tell you that if you believed, you would see the glory of God?" From this it is evident that she was not free from doubts even when she had said the words mentioned above and seemed to assent to and believe them. Commentary on John 5.11.39-40.[10]

Allegorizing Does Not Have to Deny Historicity. Augustine: Although according to the gospel history, we hold that Lazarus was really raised to life, yet I do not doubt that his resurrection is an allegory as well. We do not, because we allegorize facts, however, lose our belief in them as facts. On Eighty-three Varied Questions 65.[11]

Three Deaths, Three Resurrections. Augustine: If, then, the Lord in the greatness of his grace and mercy raises our souls to life so that we may not die forever, we may well understand that those three dead persons whom he raised in the body have some figurative significance of that resurrection of the soul that is effected by faith. He raised up the ruler of the synagogue's daughter, while still lying in the house.[12] He raised up the widow's young son, while being carried outside the gates of the city.[13] And he raised up Lazarus when four days in the grave. Let each one pay attention to his own soul: in sinning he dies; sin is the death of the soul. But sometimes sin is committed only in thought. You have felt delight in what is evil, you have assented to its commission, and you have sinned. That assent has killed you, but the death is internal because the evil thought had not yet ripened into action. The Lord intimated that he would raise such a soul to life in raising that girl who had not yet been carried out for burial but was still lying dead in the house as if sin still lay concealed. But if you have not only harbored a feeling of delight in evil but have also done the evil thing, you have, so to speak, carried the dead outside the gate: you are already outside and being carried to the tomb. Yet the Lord also raised such a person to life and restored him to his widowed mother. If you have sinned, repent, and the Lord will raise you up and restore you to your mother church. The

[7]AEG 4:173-74*; GCS 1 2:222-23, 225. [8]See 1 Cor 15. [9]ANF 3:586*; CCL 2:998. [10]CSCO 4 3:228. [11]FC 70:136**; PL 35:1746. [12]See Mk 5:41ff. [13]See Lk 7:14ff.

third example of death is Lazarus. It is a horrible kind of death and is distinguished as a habit of wickedness. For it is one thing to fall into sin, another to form the habit of sinning. The one who falls into sin and immediately submits to correction will be quickly restored to life, for he is not yet entangled in the habit, he is not yet laid in the tomb. But whoever has become habituated to sin is buried and has it properly said of him, "he stinks." For his character, like some horrible smell, begins to be of the worst repute. Such are all who are habituated to crime or abandoned in morals. You say to such a person, "Don't act like that." But when will you be listened to by one on whom the earth is thus heaped who is breeding corruption and pressed down with the weight of habit? And yet the power of Christ was not unequal to the task of restoring such a person to life. Tractates on the Gospel of John 49.3.[14]

11:40 *Faith Sees the Glory of God*

Martha Hindered the Removal of the Stone. Origen: But now, between the words "Take away the stone" and "therefore, they took away the stone," the words of the dead man's sister hindered the removal of the stone. And it would not have been taken away at all even later had not Jesus answered and said to her unbelief, "Did I not say to you that if you believe, you will see the glory of God?" It is good, then, that nothing intervenes between Jesus' command and the action enjoined by his bidding. Commentary on the Gospel of John 28.17.[15]

The Faith of One Serving to Assist Another. Cyril of Alexandria: Faith is a truly excellent thing when it is produced from an ardent mind. It has such great power that not only is the believer healed but in fact others also can be healed besides those who believe. For instance . . . Lazarus is saved by the faith of his sister to whom the Lord said, "If you believe you shall see the glory of God," which is like saying, "Since Lazarus, being dead, is not able to believe, you then are to fill up the faith that is lacking in him that is dead."[16] Commentary on the Gospel of John 7.[17]

11:41 *The Stone Removed, Jesus Lifts His Eyes in Prayer*

The Storehouse of Life Approaches the Tomb of Death. Athanasius: They took, then, the stone there from the mouth of the tomb. The whole crowd marveled, witnessing the smell of pus of Lazarus, who was decayed. He had rotted so that they were not able to approach within the tomb because of the smell of his body and its decay. But into the midst came Jesus, the storehouse that is full of life, the mouth that is full of sweet odor, the tongue that frightens death, the Mighty One in his commands, the joy of those who are sorrowful, the rising of those who have fallen, the resurrection of the dead, the assembly of the strong, the hope of the hopeless.

He came and stood openly by the mouth of the tomb, with the preparations of salvation in his divine mouth. Now all of the crowd were standing and beholding and wondering what he would do in starting to raise him from the dead. Now the body was lying dead, but God himself was standing over it, looking down on him and grieving for him. Homily on the Resurrection of Lazarus.[18]

Pay Attention to the Eyes. Origen: We must carefully observe and examine what has been written concerning the position of Jesus' eyes. . . . He had changed his thought from his conversation with those below and lifted it up and exalted it, bringing it in prayer to the Father who is over all. . . . The one who imitates Christ's prayer, lifting up the eyes of his soul and bringing

[14]NPNF 1 7:271*; CCL 36:420-21. See also Augustine *On Eighty-three Varied Questions* 65, *Sermon* 128.14, and Gregory the Great *Morals on the Book of Job* 4.27. [15]FC 89:295; SC 385:66. [16]See Cyril's comment on Jn 11:26 concerning Martha's "Amen" on behalf of Lazarus. [17]LF 48:125**. [18]*AJSL* 57:267*.

them up in this way from everyday concerns, memories, thoughts and intention must in this way address to God the great and heavenly words of prayer concerning great and heavenly matters. ... If indeed God makes such a promise for those who pray in a worthy manner ... that "while you are still speaking, I will say, 'Here I am,'"[19] what answer do we think our Savior and Lord would receive? Commentary on the Gospel of John 28.23-25, 39.[20]

11:42 *A Prayer of Thanks to the Father*

Christ Offers Thanks. Origen: He was about to pray for the resurrection of Lazarus when the only good God and Father anticipated his prayer and heard the words about to be spoken in his prayer. So the Savior begins by giving thanks in place of prayer in the hearing of the crowd. Commentary on the Gospel of John 28.42.[21]

A Prayer to Demonstrate Unity of Will. Chrysostom: Who ever prayed like Jesus did? Even before uttering any petition, he says, "I thank you that you have heard me," demonstrating that he did not need prayer. He goes on to say, "And I knew that you always hear me," not as though he himself were powerless but to show that his will and the Father's are one. But then why did he pray? He says he did so "for the sake of the people standing by so that they may believe that you have sent me."... All but saying, If I had been an enemy of God, what is done would not have succeeded. Homilies on the Gospel of John 64.2.[22]

Those Who Pray Are Always Heard. Origen: "I knew that you hear me always," which is reported by John as said by the Lord, makes clear that those who pray are *always* heard. On Prayer 13.1.[23]

Christ Did Not Need to Pray. Hilary of Poitiers: When he was about to restore Lazarus, he prayed to the Father. But he did not need to pray.... "But for the benefit of the people standing nearby I said it, that they may believe that you have sent me." He prayed then for us so that we might know that he is the Son. His prayer did not benefit himself but benefited our faith. He did not need any help, but we needed instruction. On the Trinity 10.71.[24]

The Tomb As a Court of Justice. Hippolytus: Because they considered it a blasphemy that he called God his Father, he used the tomb as a court of justice and set the truth as judge, while the surrounding unthankful multitude formed the witnesses, so that those who had said "You blaspheme by naming yourself in your own sense Son of God and him as your Father" were to see with their own eyes and hear with their own ears, while he as good as said to them, "I appeal to him here before you. If he is displeased because I call him Father, and it is a blasphemy as you think, he will not hear me. But if he hears me, it is certainly clear that he is actually my Father.... If I call the dead and he obeys my command and arises, it is not the work of a blasphemer but the command of God and of the Son of God." That this is the meaning of the prayer and that it did not spring from any deficiency on his part is shown by his words. On the Gospel of John and the Resurrection of Lazarus.[25]

Knocking on the Doors of Hell. Peter Chrysologus: When Christ began to strike the doors of the underworld, to break through the gates of Tartarus, to open the entrance of death, to dissolve the old law of Gehenna, to do away with the age-old right to punish and to demand the return of Lazarus's soul, the power of Tartarus with all its fury confronted him, brandish-

[19]Is 58:9. [20]FC 89:296-97, 300**; SC 385:68-70, 78. [21]FC 89:300-301; SC 385:80. [22]NPNF 1 14:238**. See also Theodore's comments (CSCO 4 3:229). [23]ACW 19:48*; GCS 3(2):326. [24]NPNF 2 9:202**; CCL 62A:526-27. [25]AEG 4:176*; GCS 1 2:223-24.

ing the edict of the Ruler of heaven, bearing the decree of the King most high, presenting the sentence rendered by the mouth of God and in effect for so many years.[26] And on seeing the man, [Tartarus] asked who [Christ] was, what his intentions were, what his purpose was and why all by himself he was fearlessly challenging and attacking the fearsome entrance to death.

As he asked who he was, the angels serving as ministers of the resurrection answered him in the words of the prophet: "He is the King of glory," he is "the One who is strong and mighty in battle."[27] But Tartarus responded, "I know that the King of glory is in charge in heaven of all the celestial powers, and the whole of creation is unable to bear his will. However, this one that I see is one of the earthlings, made out of mud, enclosed in a mortal body, and in his human condition viler than human beings, and, in short, soon to be handed over to the grave and very shortly destined to come under my jurisdiction."

But the angels persisted and kept repeating, "He is 'the Lord of hosts, he is the king of glory,' he is the Ruler of heaven, the Creator of the earth, the Savior of the world, the Redeemer of all, he is the one who rendered the death sentence that has you in a fury, he is about to tread on your head,[28] crush your authority and issue his own judgment of condemnation on you, who, although ordered to seize the guilty, drag away the innocent, abduct the saints and now threaten the Son of God himself. So give back one before you are forced to release all." Sermon 65.6.[29]

A Futile Appeal to Heaven. Peter Chrysologus: But Tartarus, still not believing the report he received from the customary messengers, and deploring the situation, with a complaint full of envy makes this appeal to heaven: "O Lord, even though I am the lowest of your creatures, even though I am subjected to grim servitude, I am unfailing in keeping your precepts. I am ever vigilant so that no rash innovator alter the age-old authority of your sentence. But a man has appeared, who is called Christ, bragging that he is your Son, and he reprimands your priests, he rebukes your scribes, he violates your sabbath, he abolishes your law, and he compels souls, released from the flesh and assigned now to my custody for punishment, to return to the bodies in which they had lived wickedly.

"And his audacity, which is growing stronger day by day, has reached the point that he has broken the barriers of the underworld and is attempting to rescue Lazarus, already locked in our prison, already bound by our law and already subject to our authority. Either quickly come to the aid, or, once he opens the doors, you are now going to lose all those whom we have kept in custody for so long a time."

To this the Son from the bosom of his Father responds, "Father, it is just that a prison holds not the innocent but the guilty. That punishment torments the unrighteous, not the righteous. For how long for the offense of one man, on account of Adam's guilt alone, will this executioner continue to drag down to himself with his cruel violence patriarchs, prophets, martyrs, confessors, virgins, widows, those abiding in the chastity of marriage, people of all ages and of both sexes, even little children who do not know good or evil? Father, I shall die so that all may not die. Father, I shall pay Adam's debt so that through me those who die through Adam for the underworld may live for you. Father, because of your sentence I shall shed my blood. That is how important it is to me that your creation should return to you. May the price of my blood so dear to you be the redemption of all the dead."

To this the whole Trinity agreed and ordered

[26]The personification of Tartarus, who is the keeper of the underworld, the vivid description of Lazarus's liberation from the underworld and the dialogue among Tartarus, the angels, God the Father, and the Son are thought by one scholar to come from a lost apocryphon (see C. Jenkins, "Aspects of the Theology of St. Peter Chrysologus," *Church Quarterly Review* 103 [1927]:259). There are many similarities with this text and that of the *Gospel of Nicodemus* 4.20.3-11.27. In Greek mythology, Tartarus was a place even lower than Hades. In Roman mythology, it was the place where sinners were sent. [27]Ps 24:8, 10 (23:8, 10 LXX). [28]See Gen 3:15. [29]FC 109:263-65.

Lazarus to leave, and Tartarus was commanded to obey Christ in giving back all the dead. This is why the Son proclaims, "Father, I thank you for having heard me." The apostle bears witness that Christ is our advocate in the presence of the Father.[30] And so, when he is seated he judges together with the Father. When he stands, he functions in the capacity of advocate. Sermon 65.6-8.[31]

11:43 *Lazarus, Come Out!*

Come Out! Andrew of Crete:

Lazarus, Come out!
It is the voice of the Lord, the proclamation of the king—an authoritative command.
Come out!
Leave corruption behind and receive the flesh of incorruption.
Lazarus, Come out!
Let them know that the time has come when those in the tombs will hear the voice of the Son of man. Once they have heard they will come alive.
Come out!
The stumbling block is taken away.
Come to me—I am calling you.
Come out!
As a friend, I am calling you; as Lord I am commanding you. . . .
Come out
Covered with the burial cloth so that they won't think you were only pretending to be dead. Let them see your hands and feet bound and your face covered. Let them see if they still do not believe the miracle.
Come out!
Let the stench of your body prove the resurrection. Let the burial linen be undone so that they can recognize the one who was put in the tomb.
Come out!
Come alive and enliven! Come out of the tomb. Teach them how all creation will be enlivened in a moment when the trumpet's voice proclaims the resurrection of the dead.
Come out!
Let breath appear in your nostrils, let blood pulse through your veins, let the voice sound in your larynx, let words fill your ears, let vision enlighten your eyes, let the sense of smell fill your senses, walk as nature intended as your earthly tent is enlivened by your soul.
Come out!
Leave behind the burial cloth and glorify the miracle. Leave the revolting stench of death and proclaim the strength of my power.
I'm calling you out!
Come out.
I, who said, "Let there be light, let there be firmament."[32]

Homily 8 on Lazarus.[33]

The Voice Longing for Lazarus. Hesychius of Jerusalem: The voice longed for Lazarus, its call freeing up the wings of the prisoner so that he rises up from the earth. Homily 11 on St. Lazarus.[34]

Jesus Will Call His Friends by Name at the Resurrection. Apollinaris of Laodicea: The one whom he loved and who was his friend he calls by name so that [Lazarus] serves as a sign of the resurrection of all those who are called friends by the Lord whom the apostle says have died in the Lord. Fragments on John 75.[35]

A Particular Example of General Resurrection Yet to Come. Maximinus: For all the dead, most beloved, would have arisen out of their graves [on hearing] that one voice if he had not called out that single name. Therefore he spoke in particular, "Lazarus, come forth." . . . It is also in this singular name that he called, I say,

[30]The designation "apostle" refers not to Paul but uncustomarily to John. See 1 Jn 2:1. [31]FC 109:265-66*. [32]Gen 1:3, 6—a reference to Christ, the Word, present at creation. [33]PG 97:980-81. [34]*SubHag* 59:412. [35]*JKGK* 31.

that we see in a single instance what is to be understood more generally of all in the future. Sermon 14.3.[36]

The Same Voice Spoke at Creation. Hippolytus: O power of the voice, arousing the four days' dead as from sleep and bringing forth from the grave as well loosed and swiftly running the one who was bound with grave bands. Give your attention, beloved, to the voice, and you will find him to be the Word that spoke at the creation.... "Lazarus, come forth," and the dead arose, and he who had reached the fourth day was equal to one who had not died at all. "Lazarus, come forth," and the soul was drawn up from the realms below ... and joyfully recognized its own dwelling. On the Gospel of John and the Resurrection of Lazarus.[37]

The Sweet Odor of Paradise Invades the Stench of Death. Athanasius: "Come forth." See, I am standing by you. I am your Lord. You are the work of my hands. Why have you not known me, because in the beginning I myself formed Adam from the earth and gave him breath? Open your mouth yourself so that I may give you breath. Stand on your feet and receive strength for yourself. For I am the strength of the whole creation. Stretch out your hands, and I shall give them strength. For I am the straight staff. I command the foul odor to depart from you. For I am the sweet odor of the trees of paradise. Behold, the prophecy of Isaiah the prophet will be fulfilled in you, namely, "I shall open your tombs, and I shall bring you forth."[38] Homily on the Resurrection of Lazarus.[39]

The Same Voice That Called Lazarus Will Call Us at the Resurrection. Gregory of Nyssa: Here we have a man past the prime of life, a corpse, decaying, swollen, in fact, already in a state of dissolution, so that even his own relatives did not want the Lord to draw near the tomb because the decayed body enclosed there was so offensive. And yet, he is brought into life by a single call, confirming the proclamation of the resurrection, that is to say, that expectation of it as universal that we learn by a particular experience to entertain. For as in the regeneration of the universe the apostle tells us that "the Lord himself will descend with a shout, with the voice of the archangel,"[40] and by a trumpet sound raise up the dead to incorruption—so now too he who is in the tomb, at the voice of command, shakes off death as if it were only sleep. He rids himself of the corruption that had come on his condition of a corpse, leaps forth from the tomb whole and sound, not even hindered as he leaves by the bonds of the grave cloths round his feet and hands. On the Making of Man 25.11.[41]

Divine Power of the Father and Son. Chrysostom: Why did he not say, "In the name of my Father come out"? Or why not, "Father, raise him up"? Why did he omit all these expressions and, after assuming the attitude of one praying, show by his actions his independent authority? Because this was also a mark of his wisdom: to show condescension by his words but power by his deeds. For since [the Jewish leaders] had nothing else to charge him with except that he was not of God, and since in this way they deceived many, for this reason he more than sufficiently proves this very point by what he says in a way their weakness required. For it was in his power to show in another way his agreement with the Father as well as his own dignity, but the multitude could not ascend so far. And so he simply says, "Lazarus, come forth." Homilies on the Gospel of John 64.2.[42]

11:44 *Lazarus Comes Out and Is Unbound*

The Coming Out of a Guilty Conscience. Gregory the Great: Lazarus is bid to come forth, that is, to come forth and condemn himself with his own mouth, without excuse or reserva-

[36]CCL 87:28. [37]*AEG* 4:180*; GCS 1 2:226-27. [38]See Is 25:8. [39]*AJSL* 57:268**. [40]1 Thess 4:16. [41]NPNF 2 5:416-17*. [42]NPNF 1 14:238**.

tion. In the same way, the one who lies buried in a guilty conscience may come forth out of himself by confession. Morals on the Book of Job 22.15.31.[43]

Come Out of the Hiding of Your Sin. Augustine: Do you wonder how it is that he came forth with his feet bound, but forget about the fact that after four days he rose from the dead? In both events it was the power of the Lord that operated and not the strength of the dead. He came forth and yet was still bound. Still in his burial shroud, he has already come outside the tomb. What does it mean? When you despise [Christ], you lie dead. . . . When you confess, you come forth. For what is to come forth, but to come out, as it were, from your hiding place and show yourself? But you cannot make this confession unless God moves you to do it, by crying with a loud voice, that is, calling you with abundant grace. But even after the dead man has come forth, he remains bound for some time, that is, he is as yet only a penitent. Then our Lord says to his ministers, "Loose him, and let him go," that is, forgive his sins: "Whatever you shall bind on earth shall be bound in heaven, and whatever you shall loose on earth shall be loosed in heaven."[44] Tractates on the Gospel of John 49.24.[45]

Unbound from Sin. Irenaeus: Concerning Lazarus, who had lain four days in the tomb: In what [body did he] rise again? In the same, no doubt, in which he had also died. For if it were not in the very same [body], then certainly he who had died did not rise again. . . . "The dead man came out, his hands and feet bound with strips of cloth." This was symbolic of that man who had been bound in sins. And therefore the Lord said, "Unbind him, and let him go." Therefore, since those who were healed were made whole in those members that had in times past been afflicted, and the dead rose in the identical bodies, their limbs and bodies receiving health, so also that life that was granted by the Lord who prefigures eternal things by temporal ones shows that it is he who is himself able to extend both healing and life to his handiwork so that his words concerning its [future] resurrection may also be believed. Against Heresies 5.13.1.[46]

The Church Unbinds. Augustine: So someone says, "What's the use of the church, if you can confess, and be brought back to life by the voice of the Lord and come out immediately?" "What use is the church to you as you confess—the church to which the Lord said, 'What you loose on earth shall be loosed in heaven?' "[47] Look at Lazarus's case. He came out, all tied up. He was already alive, by confessing, but he was not yet walking around freely, being still entangled with the bandages. So what does the church do, told as it has been, "Whatever you loose shall be loosed"? The church does what the Lord went on at once to tell the disciples, of course: "Unbind him and let him go." Sermon 67.3.[48]

The Land of Dead Prayer. Origen: Now, we ought to be aware that there are some Lazaruses even now who, after they have become Jesus' friends, have become sick and died, and as dead persons they have remained in the tomb and the land of the dead with the dead who were later made alive by Jesus' prayer. They were summoned from the tomb to the things outside it by Jesus with his loud voice. He who trusts in Jesus comes forth wearing bonds worthy of death from his former sins and still bound around his face, so that he can neither see nor walk nor do anything because of the bonds of death until Jesus commands those who are able to loose him and let him go. Commentary on the Gospel of John 28.54.[49]

Death Itself Cast into Affliction. Basil of Seleucia: Lazarus appeared, resembling an

[43]LF 21:573**. [44]Mt 16:19. [45]NPNF 1 7:277-78**; CCL 36:431. See also his *On Eighty-three Varied Questions* 65 (FC 70:137). [46]ANF 1:539*; SC 153:162-66. [47]Mt 18:18. [48]*WSA* 3 3:216*; PL 38:434. [49]FC 89:303; SC 385:86-88.

impromptu trophy over death. He appeared without having left to Hades any of the burial wrappings. For, bound [in these], he came forth. His feet did not bear him, rather, grace provided him with wings.[50] Lazarus appeared, having left Hades behind mourning. As he put an end to the grief of [his] brothers, he cast death into affliction.

Seeing his kingdom destroyed and unable to prevent this, [death] lamented, crying, "What is this change in my affairs, what is this miraculous alliance of nature? The dead are returning to life, and the tombs have become wombs of the living. Alas, for these misfortunes! Even the tombs are faithless to me with regard to the dead, and the dead, although putrefying, are leaping out. They are all dancing in their swathing bands, mocking my laugh. Still mourned, they are going up toward those that mourn them. By showing themselves, they undo the tragedy, leaving me an heir to grief. Who is it who teaches the dead to challenge death? Who is it who is enlisting the deceased against death? Who is the One whose voice the prisons underground cannot support? Who is the One before whom the tombs tremble? He merely speaks, and I am not able to hold on to those whom I have in my power. Oh, in vain was I entrusted with a kingdom! Oh, in vain was I confident in an angry God! Homily on Lazarus 11-12.[51]

Lazarus's Sip of the Resurrection. Peter Chrysologus: Pray, brothers, that we who have taken a sip of the resurrection with Lazarus offering the toast at Christ's return may merit drinking the whole draft of the universal resurrection. Sermon 65.9.[52]

[50]See also earlier the imagery of Hesychius. [51]*AnBoll* 104:183*. [52]FC 109:266.

11:45-53 THE PLOT TO KILL JESUS

[45]*Many of the Jews therefore, who had come with Mary and had seen what he did, believed in him;* [46]*but some of them went to the Pharisees and told them what Jesus had done.* [47]*So the chief priests and the Pharisees gathered the council, and said, "What are we to do? For this man performs many signs.* [48]*If we let him go on thus, every one will believe in him, and the Romans will come and destroy both our holy place*[a] *and our nation."* [49]*But one of them, Caiaphas, who was high priest that year, said to them, "You know nothing at all;* [50]*you do not understand that it is expedient for you that one man should die for the people, and that the whole nation should not perish."* [51]*He did not say this of his own accord, but being high priest that year he prophesied that Jesus should die for the nation,* [52]*and not for the nation only, but to gather into one the children of God who are scattered abroad.* [53]*So from that day on they took counsel how to put him to death.*

a Greek *our place*

Overview: There are some who believe Jesus after Lazarus is raised to life, but others doubt (Theodore). Those who react negatively to the miracle, either out of jealousy or unbelief (Origen, Augustine), fear that such "apostasy" of the Jews from their Jewish faith might provoke the Romans (Origen). In this they demonstrated audacity and blindness to the signs Jesus had given them, thinking they could resist someone who had the power Jesus had demonstrated, and blind to what his power proved (Origen). They sought to hold on to the temple and their nation's temporal power in the Roman system (Augustine), falsely accusing Jesus of sedition (Chrysostom). Their fear that the Romans would destroy their place and nation was ultimately realized, however, despite their planning (Origen). They were afraid of losing temporal power without any thought of the eternal consequences (Augustine). And so, the Gentiles, represented by the Romans, displaced those who had forsaken their calling as his people (Origen).

A number of questions emerge regarding Caiaphas's prophecy: How is it that Caiaphas was high priest that year when, according to the law, there was to be one hereditary high priest appointed by God (Chrysostom)? The Romans, however, were in charge of the high priest's office at this time, and much corruption had entered into the process (Augustine). In the official position of a prophet, much as Balaam had done in the Old Testament, Caiaphas proclaims the good that would come from Christ's death, even if he himself did not understand what he was saying and intended something quite different and malevolent (Cyril). This leads to the larger question of how inspiration might indeed occur in someone who did not know what he was saying (Origen). But it was not by virtue of the person that he prophesied (Chrysostom) but the office of high priest that he was able to do so (Augustine). The Evangelist then extends Caiaphas's prophecy to include not only the Jewish nation, as Caiaphas intended, but also the lost sheep of the Gentiles Jesus had spoken of (in Jn 10) who would be brought into the fold as one flock under one shepherd (Augustine). This prophecy was accomplished in Jesus' death (Gregory the Great), although not in the way the Jewish leaders envisioned (Origen).

11:45-46 *Many Believed in Jesus*

Reactions of the Jews After the Miracle. Theodore of Mopsuestia: The Jews, who were present, had different opinions about what had happened. Some believed in him because of the miracle, which he had performed. Others, on the contrary, were so far away from believing that they went to denounce him to the Pharisees, as if he had dared do something unlawful. But even what they did out of hatred and evil desire still contributed to making the accomplished miracle well known to everyone. Commentary on John 5.11.44.[1]

The Announcement Produces Jealousy in Pharisees. Origen: The text has a certain ambiguity. Were those who went to the Pharisees and told them the things Jesus had done—were they from those many Jews who saw the things that he had done and believed in him and wished to win over those who were hostile to him by the announcement about Lazarus? Or were they the others not among the many who believed who, since what had happened did not bring about faith in Jesus, intended as much as possible to stir up the wicked jealousy in the Pharisees against him by the announcement about Lazarus? The Evangelist seems to me to be leaning toward this latter meaning. Commentary on the Gospel of John 28.77-78.[2]

11:47 *Jesus' Signs and the Chief Priests and Pharisees*

They Gather Out of Envy, Not Out of Faith. Augustine: None of them said, "Let us believe." For these abandoned men were more preoccupied in considering what evil they could do to bring down Jesus than in consulting about how they might be preserved from death. Tractates on the Gospel of John 49.26.[3]

[1]CSCO 4 3:229-30. [2]FC 89:309*; SC 385:100-102. [3]NPNF 1 7:278**.

Audacious and Blind. Origen: I think the phrase "this man" was used to diminish [Jesus'] glory because they did not believe what was said above about him being God. . . . Notice both the audacity and the blindness of their evil. It was audacious because they had already witnessed the fact that he had performed many signs, and yet they thought they could plot against him—as if he could do nothing when they plotted against him. On the other hand, they were no less blind either because it makes more sense to be on the side of someone who performs such miracles than [to be a part of] the plot of those who do not want to allow him to live. Or perhaps they thought that he performed signs that were not the result of divine power and that this was why he could not do all things or deliver himself from their plot. They resolved, therefore, not to let him live, thinking that they would place an impediment in the way of those who believed in him and also prevent the Romans from taking away their place and nation. Commentary on the Gospel of John 28.88-90.[4]

11:48 *The Romans Will Destroy the Temple and the Nation*

The Pharisees' Insincerity. Augustine: Insincerity speaks in the Pharisees: "If we let him go, the Romans will come and take away our nation and place." It was not the reality of justice that they wished to have but its name, and they desired to hold on dishonestly to the honor owed to just men and women. Sermon 10.8.[5]

The Failure of the Plan. Chrysostom: But what is it that these leaders are planning to do? They want to stir up the people, as though they themselves would be in danger on suspicion of establishing a kingdom. "For if," says one of them, "the Romans learn that this man is leading the multitudes, they will suspect us and will come and destroy our city." Tell me, where did he teach revolt? Did he not permit you to give tribute to Caesar? Didn't you want to make him a king and instead he fled from you? Didn't he lead a normal and unpretentious life, homeless and having no possessions of his own? Therefore they said this, not from any such expectation but out of malice. And yet things happened contrary to their expectations, so much so that the Romans took their nation and city when they had killed Christ. For everything he did was beyond all suspicion. Homilies on the Gospel of John 64.3.[6]

The Romans Did Destroy Their Holy Place. Origen: The Romans did come and take away their place. For where is that which they call a sanctuary? And they also took away the nation, casting them out of the place and scarcely permitting them to be where they wish even in the Diaspora. Commentary on the Gospel of John 28.91-92.[7]

Afraid of Temporal Loss. Augustine: They were afraid of losing temporal things with no thought for that which is eternal and so lost both. For the Romans, after our Lord had suffered and was glorified, did come and take away their place and nation, reducing the one by siege and dispersing the other. . . . Or they were afraid that if all believed in Christ, none would remain to defend the city of God and the temple against the Romans, since they thought that Christ's teaching was directed against the temple and their laws. Tractates on the Gospel of John 49.26.[8]

The Romans Represent the Gentiles. Origen: The mystical meaning of these words is that the Gentiles occupied the place of those of the circumcision, "For by their transgression salvation has come to the Gentiles to stir them to envy."[9] The Romans represent the Gentiles because they are the rulers of the Gentile world. But the nation also was taken away by the Gen-

[4]FC 89:312**; SC 385:106-8. [5]*WSA* 3 1:288*; CCL 41:159. [6]NPNF 1 14:239**. [7]FC 89:313. [8]NPNF 1 7:278**; CCL 36:432. [9]See Rom 11:11.

tiles because those who had been the people of God were made not a people,[10] and those of Israel are no longer Israel, and their seed did not attain the status of becoming children.[11] Commentary on the Gospel of John 28.93-94.[12]

11:49 *Caiaphas Was High Priest*

The Authority of the Involuntary Prophecy. Chrysostom: But what does it mean when it says "being high priest that year"? This matter as well as the rest had been corrupted. For from the time that offices became matters of purchase, they were no longer priests for the whole period of their lives but for a year. Notwithstanding, even in this state of things the Spirit was still present. But when they lifted up their hands against Christ, then it left them and went to the apostles. Homilies on the Gospel of John 65.1.[13]

How Was Caiaphas High Priest That Year? Augustine: How is it that he is called the high priest of that year, when God appointed one hereditary high priest? This was owing to the ambition and contention of parties among the Jews themselves, which had ended in the appointment of several high priests, who took the office in turn, year by year. . . . And sometimes there even seems to have been more than one in office. Tractates on the Gospel of John 49.27.[14]

11:50 *Expedient That One Man Should Die*

Christ Does Die for One People. Cyril of Alexandria: Caiaphas makes a true statement, his words being verified not by the perversity of the people but by the power and wisdom of God. . . . Nevertheless, his language was made to indicate something true, spoken by one in the official position of a prophet. For he proclaims beforehand of what good things the death of the Christ would become the source. He speaks of what he does not understand, glorifying God (as Balaam did[15]) under constraint, since he was holding the prerogative of the priestly order. The prophecy was given, as it were, not to him personally but to the outward representative of the priesthood. Or, indeed, it may have been the case that the words spoken by Caiaphas were accomplished and happened afterward without his having received any prophetic gift whatever. For it is probable that what some people say will really happen, although they may say it without really knowing whether or not it will happen. Caiaphas then said that the death of Christ would be for the Jews only. But the Evangelist says that it would be for all humankind. For we are all called the offspring and children of God inasmuch as he is the Father of all, having by way of creation begotten as it were and brought into existence the things that were not. And also [we are called his children] because we had from the first the honor of being made in his image, and were allotted the supremacy over earthly things, and were accounted worthy of the divine covenant and enjoyed the life and bliss of paradise. But Satan, unwilling to let us remain in that condition, scattered us and in diverse ways led humanity astray from its nearness to God. And the Christ collected us all together again and brought us through faith into one fold, the church. He united us under one yoke, all being made one, Jews, Greeks, Barbarians, Scythians. We are fashioned again into one new person[16] and worship one God. Commentary on the Gospel of John 7.[17]

11:51 *Caiaphas Did Not Prophesy on His Own*

Whether Caiaphas Understood What He Said. Origen: I think we learn from this that we say some things on our own, by ourselves, where there is no power that inspires us to speak. But there are other things that we say when some power prompts us (as it were), dictating what we

[10]See Hos 1:9; 1 Pet 2:10. [11]See Rom 9:6-8; Jn 8:39. [12]SC 385:110; FC 89:313**. [13]NPNF 1 14:241*. [14]NPNF 1 7:278**. [15]Num 22:38. [16]Eph 2:15. [17]LF 48:133-34*.

say, even if we do not fall completely into a trance and lose full possession of our own faculties, but seem to understand what we say. Now, it is possible for us, while we understand what we say on our own, not to understand the meaning of the words that are spoken. This is what happened in the case of Caiaphas the high priest. He did not speak on his own, by himself, nor did he understand the meaning of what he said, since it was a prophecy that was spoken. Commentary on the Gospel of John 28.171-72.[18]

Caiaphas Was Unworthy of the Office He Occupied. Chrysostom: Do you see the great power in the high priest's authority? . . . Even though he was unworthy of the office of the high priest, he prophesied, although he did not know what he was saying. Divine grace merely made use of his mouth, without touching his corrupt heart. . . . See how great the power of the Spirit is. It was able to bring forth a marvelous prophecy even from an evil imagination. Homilies on the Gospel of John 65.1.[19]

The Office, Not the Person, Prophesied. Augustine: We are here taught that the Spirit of prophecy used the agency even of wicked people to foretell the future. The Evangelist, however, attributes this power to the divine sacramental fact that he was pontifex, that is, the high priest. Tractates on the Gospel of John 49.27.[20]

11:52 *Bring Them Together As One*

John Extends Caiaphas's Prophecy to the Gentiles. Augustine: "That Jesus should die for the nation. And not for the nation only but that also he should gather together in one the children of God that were scattered abroad" were words added by the Evangelist. Caiaphas had prophesied only about the Jewish nation in which there were sheep of whom our Lord himself had said, "I am not sent but unto the lost sheep of the house of Israel."[21] But the Evangelist knew that there were other sheep who were not of this fold but who also had to be brought so that there would be one fold and one shepherd.[22] But he says this in the way of predestination since those who were still unbelieving were neither yet sheep nor children of God. Tractates on the Gospel of John 49.27.[23]

Jesus' Death Did Bring Children of God Together. Gregory the Great: His persecutors accomplished this wicked purpose and put him to death, thinking to extinguish the devotion of his followers. But faith grew from the very thing that these cruel and unbelieving men thought would destroy it. . . . Even that which human cruelty had executed against him he reduced to the purposes of his mercy. Morals on the Book of Job 6.18.32.[24]

11:53 *Plotting to Put Jesus to Death*

They Misunderstood Their Own Prophecy. Origen: Spurred on by Caiaphas's words, they took counsel together to kill the Lord. From what sort of spirit then did Caiaphas prophesy that Jesus was to die for the nation, and was the Holy Spirit at work in such a man, and thus became the cause of the plot against Jesus? Or was it not then the Holy Spirit but another spirit which was able both to speak in the impious man and to move those like him against Jesus? . . . Just as those who deliberately put the worst construction on things misrepresent the holy meaning of the Scriptures . . . so did the Pharisees and the chief priests. For they did not understand correctly the prophecy about our Savior that Caiaphas spoke. It is a prophecy that is true in that it is better for us that one man die for the people and the whole nation not perish. But they thought the meaning and intention of his counsel was something else, and so they took counsel together from that day to kill Jesus. Now, I say

[18]FC 89:327-28**; SC 385:144-46. [19]NPNF 1 14:241**. [20]NPNF 1 7:278*. [21]Mt 15:24. [22]See Jn 10:16. [23]NPNF 1 7:278*. [24]LF 18:336-37**; ODGM 1 1:504.

these things to answer the argument that it was the Holy Spirit who prophesied through Caiaphas. I personally do not in the least maintain that this was the case but leave it to the readers to decide what one must recognize as correct concerning Caiaphas and whether he was moved by the Spirit. Commentary on the Gospel of John 28.186-87, 190-91.[25]

Plans Move into Action. Chrysostom: Before they only looked for ways to kill him. Now they ratify their determination and get down to business in determining how to carry it out. Homilies on the Gospel of John 65.1.[26]

[25]FC 89:330-32**; SC 385:152-54. [26]NPNF 1 14:241**.

11:54-57 JESUS WITHDRAWS TO THE WILDERNESS

[54]Jesus therefore no longer went about openly among the Jews, but went from there to the country near the wilderness, to a town called Ephraim; and there he stayed with the disciples.

[55]Now the Passover of the Jews was at hand, and many went up from the country to Jerusalem before the Passover, to purify themselves. [56]They were looking for Jesus and saying to one another as they stood in the temple, "What do you think? That he will not come to the feast?" [57]Now the chief priests and the Pharisees had given orders that if any one knew where he was, he should let them know, so that they might arrest him.

Overview: John mentions that Jesus no longer went about openly because of opposition, which teaches Christians that it can be expedient to avoid opposition and unnecessary conflict, at times, in the face of martyrdom or unnecessary conflict (Origen, Cyril). And so Jesus retreats to the city of Ephrem, which means "fruitfulness," indicative of the fruit Jesus will bring about in the church through his impending death (Origen). While the Passover of the Jews is at hand, it is only a shadow of the reality of Christ (Augustine), the true Passover Lamb who purified us by taking away the sin of the world (Origen) and giving us his flesh to eat (Cyril). As the crowd awaited Jesus' attendance at the festival (Theodore), those who plot against him cannot find him then—or now (Origen). If only the descendants of those who were looking for Jesus would still seek him. Let us at least for our part show the Jews where Christ can be found (Augustine).

11:54 *Restricting His Movements, Jesus Goes to Ephrem*

Avoid Martyrdom. Origen: I think that these words and those like them have been recorded because the Word wishes to turn us back from rushing too hastily and irrationally to struggle unto death on behalf of the truth and to suffer martyrdom. For, on the one hand, it is right not to shun the confession or to hesitate to die for the truth if one has been caught in the struggle about confessing Jesus. But, on the other hand, it is no less right also not to provide an opportunity for such a great trial but to avoid it by every means, not only because the outcome of such an act is unclear to us but also so that we may not be responsible for causing those who would not, in actual fact, have become guilty of pouring out our blood, to have become more sinful and impious [by doing so], if we act in our own interest and take no thought for those who plot against us unto death. These people will experience greater and more serious punishment because of us if we are self-centered and do not consider the things of others and deliver ourselves to be killed when this necessity has not overtaken us. COMMENTARY ON THE GOSPEL OF JOHN 28.192-94.[1]

AVOIDING UNNECESSARY CONFLICT. CYRIL OF ALEXANDRIA: As God, Jesus knows the secret plans of the Jews even though no one reported them to him, and he withdraws, not because he is afraid but so that his presence might not irritate those who were already seeking to kill him. Here, he also teaches us to avoid stirring up the passions of those who are angry and not to thrust ourselves into dangers, not even when it may be for the sake of truth. When we are overtaken by dangers, he teaches us to stand firm, but when we see them coming, since it is unclear what the actual terms of the conflict will be, it is best for us to get out of their way. COMMENTARY ON THE GOSPEL OF JOHN 7.[2]

EPHREM MEANS FRUITFULNESS. ORIGEN: Mystically, these words mean that long ago Jesus walked boldly among the Jews when the Word of God dwelled among them through prophets. . . . But now Jesus no longer walks boldly among the Jews but has departed from there. . . . He then entered the country near the desert of which it is said, "Many are the children of the desolate, more than of her who has a husband."[3] . . . Now Ephrem means "fruitfulness." He was the brother of Manasseh, who stands for the elder people who were forgotten. For after the forgotten people were left behind, an abundant harvest from the Gentiles occurred. . . .

"Jesus," therefore, "no longer walks openly among the Jews but has departed from there into the country" of the whole world, "near the desert" of the church, "into the city that is called Ephrem," that is, "fruitful," "and there he has remained with his disciples." And up to this moment, Jesus is with his disciples near the desert in the city called Ephrem, for he is present in "fruitfulness." And at the birth, indeed, of this Ephrem, our Lord, magistrate of the grain,[4] who begot him, who humbled himself and became obedient unto death, even death of the cross,[5] might say, "God increased me in the land of my humility."[6] COMMENTARY ON THE GOSPEL OF JOHN 28.211-14, 221-23.[7]

11:55 *Passover and Purification*

THE TRUE PASSOVER AT HAND. AUGUSTINE: "And the Jews' Passover was near at hand." They had resolved to celebrate that Passover by shedding our Lord's blood, the blood that consecrated the Passover, the blood of the Lamb. There was a plot among the Jews to slay Jesus, and he who came from heaven to suffer wanted to draw near the place of his suffering because the hour of his passion was now at hand. Therefore "many went out of the country up to Jerusalem before the Passover to sanctify themselves." The Jews did so, following the command of the Lord delivered by holy Moses in the Law, which commanded that on the feast day of the Passover everyone should come together from every part of the land and be sanctified in celebrating the services of the day. But that celebration was a shadow of the future. It was a prophetic intimation of the Christ to come, a prophecy of him who on that day was to suffer for us. The shadow would vanish, and the light would come. The sign would pass away, and the truth would remain. The Jews held their Passover in the shadows, we in the light. Otherwise, why was it necessary for the Lord to command them to slay a sheep on the very day of the feast unless it was only because of him that it was

[1]FC 89:332-33; SC 385:156. [2]LF 48:135**. [3]Is 54:1; Gal 4:27. [4]See Gen 47:12. [5]See Phil 2:8. [6]See Gen 41:52. [7]FC 89:335-37**; SC 385:162-68.

prophesied, "He is led as a sheep to the slaughter"?[8] Their posts were stained with the blood of a slain animal; our foreheads are signed with the blood of Christ. Tractate on the Gospel of John 50.2.[9]

Christians and Their Passover Lamb. Cyril of Alexandria: He calls it "the Passover of the Jews" as a type, for [he refers to] the true Passover, not of the Jews but of Christians who eat the flesh of Christ the true Lamb. And, according to the ancient custom those who sin, whether willfully or inadvertently, purify themselves before the feast. Commentary on the Gospel of John 7.[10]

True Purification. Origen: But the true purification was not before the Pasch but during the Pasch, when Jesus died as the Lamb of God for those who were purifying themselves and took away the sin of the world.[11] Commentary on the Gospel of John 28.237.[12]

11:56 *Will Jesus Attend the Festival?*

The Crowd Is Waiting. Theodore of Mopsuestia: Many who had come up from the country to Jerusalem in order to purify themselves according to the precepts of the Law before the Passover . . . gathered together in the temple and discussed among themselves whether the Lord would come out of respect for the festival or would avoid coming in order to protect himself from the ambushes of his enemies. These were the words of those who desired to see him. With good reason the crowd was close to him because of the miracles he had performed. Commentary on John 5.11.55-56.[13]

11:57 *The Leaders Seek to Arrest Jesus*

Plotters Never Know Where Jesus Is. Origen: Observe how it has been testified that he has withdrawn, that we too might know to do such at the proper time. And notice indeed that neither the chief priests nor the Pharisees knew where he was, and because they did not know, they gave commands that if anyone should know where he was, he should reveal it to them and they would seize him. But you will say in addition that anyone who plots against Jesus does not know where he is. This is why they give commands that are other than those of God, "teaching as doctrines the commandments of men."[14] Commentary on the Gospel of John 28.244-46.[15]

Let Us Show the Jews Where Christ Is. Augustine: Let us at least for our part show the Jews where Christ is. If only the descendants of those who demanded to be shown where Christ was would listen! Let them come to the church and hear where Christ is and take hold of him for themselves. Let them hear it from us. Let them hear it from the gospel. Tractates on the Gospel of John 50.4.[16]

---

[8]Is 53:7. [9]NPNF 1 7:279**; CCL 36:433-34. [10]LF 48:135*. [11]See Jn 1:29. [12]FC 89:340; SC 385:172. [13]CSCO 4 3:232-33. [14]Mt 15:9. [15]FC 89:341*; SC 385:174-76. [16]NPNF 1 7:279**.

12:1-3 The Preparation: The Anointing at Bethany

[1]Six days before the Passover, Jesus came to Bethany, where Lazarus was, whom Jesus had raised from the dead. [2]There they made him a supper; Martha served, and Lazarus was one of those at table with him. [3]Mary took a pound of costly ointment of pure nard and anointed the feet of Jesus and wiped his feet with her hair; and the house was filled with the fragrance of the ointment.

Overview: John mentions the time, "six days before the Passover," because Christ was the spotless lamb who would take away the sins of the world, just as Israel purchased and kept its lamb until the fourteenth day (Bede, Cyril). Jesus goes to the house of Mary and Martha, where both serve him (Athanasius). Martha serves the meal, while Mary serves in a more spiritual way (Chrysostom). The Evangelist then provides further proof of Lazarus's resurrection in telling us of Lazarus's dining with Jesus (Chrysostom), as Lazarus has been privileged to eat wih both Christ and his Father (Athanasius).

The Mary who anointed Jesus' head in Matthew and Mark is not the same Mary who anointed his feet in Luke and John (Origen). Taking the Evangelists together, it appears that the ointment was poured on the head and the feet (Augustine). In this case, Mary's anointing of Jesus' feet demonstrates her humility in not presuming to anoint the head first, but only doing so after she had shown her humility in service, as the church also is called to do (Chromatius). Her care for his body, the church, should move us to provide the healing oil of forgiveness not only to those enmeshed in sin but also to those who are not at peace (Ambrose). The ointment and Mary's hair are also a sacramental symbol of righteousness for those who give their excess to the poor and thus wipe Jesus' feet (Augustine). Just as the house was filled with the fragrance of the ointment, so also the world is to be filled with the fragrance of the Christian's good deeds (Origen). An abundance of oil covers an abundance of sin as the Anointed forgives the anointer (Ephrem).

12:1 *At Lazarus's Home in Bethany*

The Stainless Lamb. Bede: "The Mediator between God and man, the man Christ Jesus,"[1] who had come down to earth from heaven in order to suffer for the salvation of the human race, as the hour of his passion was drawing near, willed to draw near the place of his passion. Even by this it was to become apparent that he would not be suffering unwillingly but of his own volition. . . . He willed to come five days before the Passover[2] . . . that by this again he might show that he was the stainless lamb who would take away the sins of the world. It was commanded that the paschal lamb, by whose immolation the people of Israel were freed from slavery in Egypt, should be selected five days before the Passover, that is, on the tenth day of the month,[3] and immolated on the fourteenth day of the month.[4] Homilies on the Gospels 2.3.[5]

Proof of Lazarus's Resurrection. Cyril of Alexandria: [Jesus went] to Bethany. He

[1]1 Tim 2:5. [2]John mentions that it was six days before the Passover, and Christ would be leaving for Jerusalem the next day after dining with Lazarus. [3]Ex 12:3. [4]Ex 12:18. [5]CS 111:23; CCL 122:200.

did not actually go into Jerusalem, since if he suddenly appeared to the Jews, he might kindle their anger. Instead the rumor of his being so near gradually softens the rage of their wrath. He eats with Lazarus, reminding those who saw them of his divine power. And by telling us this, the Evangelist shows that Christ did not despise the Law. This is also why the text mentions that it was "six days before the Passover," when it was necessary that the lamb should be purchased and kept until the fourteenth day. This is when he ate with Lazarus and his friends, doing so perhaps because it was a custom not of law but from long usage, for the Jews to have some little merrymaking on the day before the lamb was taken, in order that after the lamb was obtained they might devote themselves, from that time until the feast, to fasting or a lesser amount of food and to purifications. The Lord therefore is shown to have given honor even to these customs of the feast. And in amazement the Evangelist says that he who had been four days dead was eating with the Christ, to remind us of his divine power. And he adds that Martha, out of her love toward Christ, served and ministered at the labors of the table. COMMENTARY ON THE GOSPEL OF JOHN 7.[6]

IMPRINTING THE MEMORY OF LAZARUS'S RESURRECTION. BEDE: Being sure of the glory of his resurrection, Jesus first came to Bethany, a town near Jerusalem, where Lazarus was, whom he had raised from the dead. Then he went to Jerusalem, where he himself was to suffer and rise from the dead. He went to Jerusalem so that he might die there, but to Bethany so that the raising up of Lazarus might be imprinted more deeply on the memory of all. HOMILIES ON THE GOSPELS 2.4.[7]

12:2 *Martha Serves in Presence of Lazarus*

THE DEVOTED SERVICE OF MARY AND MARTHA. ATHANASIUS: Martha herself was taking great care with the service and was ministering to Christ with all her heart. Mary herself was seated at the feet of Jesus and kissing them. . . . Christ beholds them both with his divine eyes and is cheered and rejoices over the purity of their mode of life and the offering to him of their undefiled service. HOMILY ON THE RESURRECTION OF LAZARUS.[8]

MARY DIRECTS HER SERVICE TO GOD. CHRYSOSTOM: "And Martha served" makes it clear that the meal was in her house, for they received Jesus as loving and beloved. Some, however, say that it took place in the house of another. Mary did not serve because she was a disciple.[9] Here again she acted in the more spiritual manner. For she did not serve as though invited, nor did she offer her service to all alike. Rather she directed the honor to him alone and approached him not as a man but as God. HOMILIES ON THE GOSPEL OF JOHN 65.2.[10]

LAZARUS ALIVE AND EATING. CHRYSOSTOM: This was a proof of the genuineness of Lazarus's resurrection, that after many days he both lived and ate. HOMILIES ON THE GOSPEL OF JOHN 65.2.[11]

LAZARUS PRIVILEGED TO EAT WITH CHRIST AND THE FATHER. ATHANASIUS: You have seen this great public favor, that Lazarus was one of those who were reclining with Jesus. You saw not only that he gave him life again and took him from the hand of death but also that he granted him this great honor of eating with him at his supper. O these great favors that God grants to those who love him and keep his commandments! Moreover, you have seen the favor well fulfilled. Lazarus was reclining, eating with Jesus. For Jesus relied on his holy apostles to [eat and drink] with humankind. . . . Lazarus,

[6]LF 48:137. [7]CS 111:35*. [8]*AJSL* 57:272-73. [9]Chrysostom speaks of Mary's discipleship, focusing on her spiritual attitude toward Jesus in contrast to Martha's preoccupation with more earthly concerns. Both served Jesus as his disciples, but in different ways. [10]NPNF 1 14:242*. See also Theodoret *Dialogues* (FC 106:127). [11]NPNF 1 14:242**

on the other hand, [Jesus says], ate and drank with my Father. Come to me, Lazarus, and I shall take away the evil odor that is in your flesh over which death ruled, and I shall give you the sweet odor. See, I shall go to Jerusalem, and everyone will see you going with me in this body in which you have slept in the grave for four days. Afterward I gave you life, for truly again you yourself have served others. For in accordance with the measure that someone measures, it will be measured to himself. HOMILY ON THE RESURRECTION OF LAZARUS.[12]

12:3a *Which Mary Anoints Jesus?*

WHO IS THIS MARY? ORIGEN: There seems then much likeness and some connection about the woman in the four Evangelists. Yet I would say to those who think that all wrote of the same woman, "Do you think that the very same woman who poured precious ointment on Jesus' head, as Matthew and Mark have related, also anointed his feet with ointment (or "myrrh," "myrrha") as Luke and John have related?

But it is not possible that the Evangelists should have contradicted one another in relating about the same woman, since they were perfected in the same understanding and the same spirit and the same mind, and they had been seeking to minister to the welfare of the church. But if anyone thinks it is the same woman in Luke and John, let him tell us if Mary was the woman who is said in Luke to have been a sinner in a city who, learning that Jesus had sat down to meet in a Pharisee's house, brought an alabaster box of ointment and stood behind his feet weeping, washing his feet with her tears.

It is incredible that Mary, whom Jesus loved, the sister of Martha, who had chosen the better portion, should be said to have been a sinner in the city. And the woman who, according to Matthew and Mark, poured precious ointment on Jesus' head is not actually written to have been a sinner. But she who according to Luke is described as a sinner did not dare to reach to Christ's head but washed his feet with her tears—as if scarcely worthy of his very feet—from sorrow that brought about sincere repentance with salvation.

The woman in Luke wails and weeps much so that she may wash Jesus' feet. But she, who according to John is Mary, is introduced neither as a sinner nor as weeping. Perhaps then one will say that four different women are recorded by the Evangelists. But I rather agree that there were three. There was the one of whom Matthew and Mark wrote in complete agreement. There was also the woman of whom Luke wrote, while John wrote of yet another, differing from the other woman not only in what is written about the ointment but also because Jesus loved Mary and Martha—although she also is related to have been at Bethany like the woman in Matthew and Mark. COMMENTARY ON MATTHEW 77.[13]

HARMONY MAINTAINED. AUGUSTINE: Harmony is maintained here between the three Evangelists: Matthew, Mark and John. There is no doubt that they record the same occurrence at Bethany. This is the occasion when the disciples also, as all three mention, murmured against the woman, ostensibly on the ground of her having wasted this very precious ointment. There is the further fact that Matthew and Mark tell us that it was the Lord's head on which the ointment was poured, while John says it was his feet. This can be shown to involve no contradiction if we apply the principle . . . that even where the several Evangelists introduce only the one fact each, we should take the case to have been really that both things were elements in the actual occurrence. In the same way, our conclusion with regard to the passage now before us should be that the woman poured the ointment not only on the Lord's head but also on his feet. HARMONY OF THE GOSPELS 2.79.155.[14]

[12]*AJSL* 57:271-72. [13]*AEG* 4:302-4*; GCS 38 2 (11):178-80. For the identity of Mary, see also the discussion in Jn 11:2. [14]NPNF 1 6:174**; CSEL 43:262.

She Does Not Presume to First Anoint His Head. Chromatius of Aquileia: See the humility of this holy woman. She does not anoint his head but his feet. It is only afterward that she anoints the Lord's head. Therefore, first she washes his feet and then his head. But she began at his feet so that she might be found worthy to proceed [to anoint] his head. For "those who are humble," as it is written, "will be exalted, and those who are exalted will be humbled."[15] . . . And she wipes his feet not with a towel but with her hair so that she might exhibit even greater service to the Lord. . . . Allegorically, the woman was anticipating the figure of the church who truly in the fullness of faith brings its devotion to Christ. And this he freely receives as a very precious perfume. Sermon 11.2-3.[16]

Pouring Ointment on Jesus' Feet. Ambrose: In loving this body, that is, the church, bring water for his feet and kiss his feet, not only pardoning those who have become enmeshed in sin but by your peace giving them harmony and putting them at peace. Pour ointment on his feet, that the whole house wherein Christ reclines at table may be filled with the odor of your ointment, that all at table with him may be pleased with your perfume. In other words, pay honor to the least. Letter 62 (to his sister).[17]

Give Your Excess to the Poor. Augustine: Let us look into the mystery this incident imported. Whatever soul among you wishes to be truly faithful, anoint the feet of the Lord with precious ointment like Mary did. That ointment was righteousness, and therefore it was [exactly] a pound weight: but it was ointment of pure nard, very precious. From his calling it "pistici"[18] we ought to infer that there was some locality from which it derived its preciousness; but this does not exhaust its meaning, and it harmonizes well with a sacramental symbol. The root of the word in the Greek [*pistis*] is by us called "faith." You were seeking to work righteousness: "The just shall live by faith."[19] Anoint the feet of Jesus: follow the Lord's footsteps by living a good life. Wipe them with your hair: what you have in excess, give to the poor, and then you have wiped the feet of the Lord. For the hair seems to be the superfluous part of the body. You have something to spare of your abundance: it is superfluous to you but necessary for the feet of the Lord. Perhaps on this earth the Lord's feet are still in need. For of whom but of his members is he yet to say in the end, "Inasmuch as you did it to one of the least of mine, you did it unto me"?[20] You spent what was superfluous for yourselves, but you have done what was grateful to my feet. Tractates on the Gospel of John 50.6.[21]

12:3b *House Filled With Fragrance*

The Ointment of Good Deeds to God's Glory. Origen: Everything by which anyone is anointed is called oil. Ointment is one form of oil. So one form of ointment is costly; another is not. And so, every righteous action is called a good work. But one kind of good work is what we do for our fellow human beings or according to their [expectations]. Another kind of good work is something we do because of God and according to [his expectations]. Of the latter, one form is profitable to humanity; another serves only to the glory of God. For example, a person does something well under the influence of natural justice, not because of God, as sometimes even heathen or a lot of other people do. This kind of work is common oil, not of great fragrance, and yet it is duly accepted by God. . . .

Peter says [in the Clementines] that good works done by unbelievers profit them in this world but not also in the other to the attainment of eternal life. This is only right, since they are

[15]Lk 18:14. [16]CCL 9A: 48-49. [17]FC 26:395-96*; CSEL 82 3:160. [18]The term for "pure nard," which Augustine provides in the transliterated Greek, is "*nardi pistici.*" Because *pistici*, which means trustworthy or authentic, derives from the Greek term for "faith," which is *pistis*, Augustine will draw further inferences. [19]See Rom 1:17. [20]Mt 25:40. [21] NPNF 1 7:280*; CCL 36:435.

not done because of God but because of human nature itself. But those who do them because of God, that is, believers, profit not only in this world but more especially in the one to come. What believers do because of God is a kind of ointment that has a pleasing fragrance. But part of this very work that believers do because of God . . . is done for the welfare of humanity, such as the giving of alms, visitations of the sick, entertainments of strangers, humility, kindness. . . . Those who do these things to Christians anoint the Lord's feet with ointment because they are the Lord's feet with which he always walks—something that penitents are especially accustomed to do in the remission of their sins. This is a work called a fragrant ointment, but it is not the best. Rather, those who pursue charity, continue in fasting and prayer, have patience in adversities like Job, in temptations, those who are not afraid to confess the truth of God—all of which are things that are of no benefit to other people but only promote the glory of God—this is the ointment that anoints the head of the Lord Christ and from there runs down through his whole body, that is, the whole church. And this is very costly ointment whose fragrance fills the whole house, that is, the church of Christ. COMMENTARY ON MATTHEW 77.[22]

ABUNDANCE OF OIL COVERS ABUNDANCE OF SIN. EPHREM THE SYRIAN:

An abundance is oil with which sinners do business: the forgiveness of sins.
By oil the Anointed[23] forgave the sins of the sinner who anointed [his] feet.[24]
With [oil] Mary poured out her sin upon the head of the Lord of her sins.
It wafted its scent; it tested the reclining as in a furnace:
It exposed the theft clothed in the care of the poor.[25]
It became the bridge to the remembrance of Mary to pass on her glory from generation to generation.[26]
In its flowings is hidden joy, for oil does indeed gladden the face.
It brings its shoulder to all burdens in rejoicing and grieving with everyone:
For it serves joy yet is obeyed by gloom,
For faces joyful of life by it are resplendent,
And with it, the gloomy face of death is prepared for burial and dies.

HYMNS ON VIRGINITY 4.11-12.[27]

[22]GCS 38 2 (11):185-86; *AEG* 4:307-8**. [23]Athanasius too speaks of Jesus anointing Mary with the oil of the unbreakable seal of the Trinity in a reference to baptism (*Homily on the Resurrection of Lazarus* [*AJSL* 57:264]). [24]Ephrem identifies the sinful woman as Mary, presumably Mary Magdalene. [25]A reference to Jude's later objections. [26]Mk 14:9. [27]ESH 278-79.

12:4-8 CARING FOR THE POOR AND HONORING JESUS

[4]But Judas Iscariot, one of his disciples (he who was to betray him), said, [5]"Why was this ointment not sold for three hundred denarii[b] and given to the poor?" [6]This he said, not that he cared for the poor but because he was a thief, and as he had the money box he used to take what was put into it.

[7]Jesus said, "Let her alone, let her keep it for the day of my burial. [8]The poor you always have with you, but you do not always have me."

b The denarius was a day's wage for a laborer

Overview: Even though Jesus foreknows Judas's treachery, he tolerates him among his company of disciples (Augustine). Under the guise of religion (Gaudentius), Judas places a higher value on the perfume than he would later place on Jesus' life when he betrayed him (Ambrose). Judas may have been speaking for the whole company of the disciples if one compares the other Gospel accounts, but John focuses on Judas's propensity for greed (Augustine). Jesus hoped to restrain Judas's greedy impulses by placing him in the position of treasurer (Ephrem), which would have been one of the loftier positions among the disciples (Ambrose). But a greedy person is always in need, and Judas's heart was already polluted by the stain of avarice (Bede). He seems callous to Jesus' allusion to his impending death (Chrysostom) as Mary, in anointing his body for burial, was allowed to do at that time what she would not be able to do later (Bede). In this anointing, the powerlessness of death and greed are exposed (Ephrem).

Mary's act of love should be seen for what it was, an honor given to our Lord, who would not be long among them, rather than pitted against the idea of caring for the poor, which was not really Judas's primary concern (Theodore). Jesus wants the poor taken care of, but not at the expense of serving him (Cyril). Ideally, both occur together since caring for the poor is a kind of anointing of Jesus' head (Origen). In speaking of his own presence with them, which was drawing to a close, Jesus is telling Judas, and all those present, that his incarnate presence would soon be withdrawn, but his divine presence would still remain with them always by faith (Augustine). Even now his presence is with us in the sacraments, but those who are wicked, whom Judas represents, will not always have him present with them (Augustine). And yet none of this, or the many acts of love Jesus did and spoke about that night, dissuaded Judas (Chrysostom).

12:4 *Judas Iscariot*

Jesus' Toleration of Judas. Augustine: Judas did not become perverted only at the time when he yielded to the bribery of the Jews and betrayed his Lord. For not a few, not paying attention to the Gospel itself, suppose that Judas perished only when he accepted money from the Jews to betray the Lord. It was not at that point that he perished. But he was already a thief, already lost, and he followed our Lord in body but not with his heart. He made up the apostolic number of twelve but had no part in the apostolic blessedness—he had been made the twelfth in semblance. On his departure and the succession of another, the apostolic reality was completed, and the completeness of the number was preserved. What lesson was our Lord Jesus Christ trying to impress on the church when he decided to have one castaway among the twelve? We are taught the duty of tolerating the wicked and to refrain from dividing the body of Christ. Here you have Judas among the saints—that Judas, mind you, who was a thief!—and do not overlook this fact, since he was no ordinary thief, but a thief who also committed sacrilege. He was a robber of money bags—not just any money bags, but those of the Lord. . . . The one who robs the church stands side by side with the castaway Judas. This was the kind of man Judas was, and yet he went in and out with eleven holy disciples. . . . Tolerate the wicked, you that are good, that you may receive the reward of the good and not fall into the punishment of the wicked. Follow our Lord's example while he lived with humanity on earth. Why did he have bags to whom the angels ministered, except because his church should afterward have bags?[1] Why did he admit thieves but to show that his church should tolerate thieves even while it suffered from them? It is not surprising that Judas, who was accustomed to steal money from the bags, should betray our Lord for money. Tractates on the Gospel of John 50.10-11.[2]

12:5 *Judas's Concern About the Price of the Perfume*

Under the Guise of Religion. Gaudentius of Brescia: Judas valued cheating above everything else—except his hatred of the Savior. Nevertheless, under the pretext of piety, he brings out these deceitful words. . . . Impious beyond measure and filled with a savage disposition, influenced by his fraudulent greed, it is evident that he expresses this particular charge, attempting to hide it under the guise of religion. Sermon 13.[3]

Judas Devalues Forgiveness and Christ's Passion. Ambrose: O traitor Judas, you value the ointment of his passion at three hundred pence, and you sell his passion at thirty pence. Rich in valuing, cheap in wickedness! On the Holy Spirit 3.17.128.[4]

12:6 *Judas the Thief Did Not Care About the Poor*

Who Murmured Against the Waste of Perfume? Augustine: In the other Gospels it is the disciples who murmured at the waste of the ointment. . . . I think myself that Judas is put for the whole body of disciples; the plural used for the singular.[5] . . . But at any rate we may supply for ourselves that the other disciples said it, or thought it or were persuaded by this very speech of Judas. The only difference is that Matthew and Mark expressly mention the concurrence of the others, whereas John only mentions Judas, whose habit of thieving he takes occasion to notice. Harmony of the Gospels 2.79.156.[6]

Not Forced into Betrayal. Ambrose: [Judas] was chosen among the twelve apostles and had charge of the money bag, to distribute it among the poor, so that it might not seem as though he had betrayed the Lord because he was not honored or in want. And so, the Lord granted him this office so that he might also be shown to be just in his dealings with him. Judas would be guilty of a greater fault, not as one driven to it by a wrong done to him but as one misusing grace. Duties of the Clergy 1.16.64.[7]

Jesus Tried to Restrain Judas's Greed. Ephrem the Syrian: Our Lord, because he saw that Judas was greedy for money, had placed him in charge of the money to satisfy him and to prevent him becoming a traitor for the sake of money. It would have been better for him, however, to have stolen the money rather than to have betrayed the Creator of money. . . . Should not the thief of money fear the Creator of money? Perhaps that is what he remembered when he hanged himself.[8] Commentary on Tatian's Diatessaron 17.13.[9]

A Greedy Person Is Always in Need. Bede: Because "a greedy person always is in need,"[10] [Judas], being faithless and wicked, never remembered the trust [placed in him] but went on from the theft of the money that he had been asked to carry to betraying our Lord who showed confidence [in him]. Homilies on the Gospels 2.4.[11]

12:7 *The Day of Jesus' Burial*

[1]See note on Augustine at 13:29. [2]NPNF 1 7:281-82**; CCL 36:437. [3]PL 20:935-36. [4]FC 44:200*; CSEL 79:205. [5]Gaudentius makes a similar point, inferring that Jesus was trying to spare Judas from a direct accusation; see his *Tractate* 13 (PL 20:935), where he compares *sine* with *sinite*. [6]CSEL 43:263; NPNF 1 6:174**. [7]NPNF 2 10:12*; CCL 15:23-24. [8]See Mt 27:5. [9]*ECTD* 267-68. [10]Horace *Epistle* 1.2.56. [11]CS 111:39*. Ephrem makes a similar comment; see his *Commentary on Tatian's Diatessaron* 17.13.

A Reminder to Judas Elicits No Pity. Chrysostom: Again, as if to remind his betrayer, Jesus alludes to his burial. But the reproof does not reach him, nor does the expression soften him, although it should have been sufficient to inspire him with pity—almost as if Jesus had said, "I am a burden, and I know I cause a lot of trouble for you, but wait a little while, and I will leave." Homilies on the Gospel of John 65.2.[12]

Mary Allowed to Anoint Him. Bede: It is as though Judas were asking an innocent question, and so our Lord simply and gently explained the mystery of what Mary's action meant, namely, that he himself was about to die and that he was to be anointed for his burial with the spices. It was being granted to Mary (to whom it would not be permitted to anoint his dead body, although she greatly desired this) to render a service [to him while he was] still alive, since she would be unable [to perform it] after his death, for she would be prevented by his swift resurrection. Homilies on the Gospels 2.4.[13]

The Ointment of His Burial. Ephrem the Syrian: He restored Lazarus to life and died in his stead. For after he had drawn [Lazarus] from the tomb and had seated himself at table with him, he was himself buried by the symbol of the ointment that Mary "poured over his head."... Thus, [the Lord] came to Bethany, raised his friend and buried himself through the symbol of the ointment. He made Mary and Martha joyful and exposed both Sheol and greed, Sheol because it would not always be holding onto him and greed because it would not always be selling him. Commentary on Tatian's Diatessaron 17.7-8.[14]

12:8a *The Poor*

Care, Reproof and Vindication. Theodore of Mopsuestia: If, he says, you are really sincere in your mercy for the poor, there is much time left for you to benefit them. There will never be a shortage of them in this world. But it will not always be easy for you to perform a service for me: I am staying with you for a short time, and then I will leave. First he purified the woman from the blame with these words by modestly saying that a greater honor had to be attributed to him than to the poor because he was staying with them for a short time. Then he reproved the intention of Judas because Judas did not care about the poor at all, nor should the woman be reproached because of the perfume she had poured. Commentary on John 5.12.8.[15]

Care for the Poor. Cyril of Alexandria: And the Savior also brings forward an argument that convinces us that nothing is better than devotion toward him. For, he says, love for the poor is very praiseworthy, only let it be put after veneration of God. And what he says amounts to this: The time, he says, that has been appointed for my being honored, that is to say, the time of my sojourn on earth, does not require that the poor should be honored before me. And this he said with reference to the incarnation. He does not, however, in any way forbid the sympathetic person to exercise love toward the poor. Therefore, when there is need of service or of singing, these must be honored before love toward the poor. For it is possible to do good after the spiritual services are over. He says therefore that it is not necessary always without intermission to devote our time to honoring himself or to spend everything on the priestly service but to lay out the greatest part on the poor. Or think of it this way: As he asks his disciples to fast after he had ascended to the Father,[16] so also he says that then they may more freely give attention to the care of the poor and exercise their love for the poor with less disturbance and more time, which indeed was the case. For after the ascension of the Savior, when they were no longer following their Master on his journeys but had leisure, then they eagerly spent all the offerings that were brought to them

[12]NPNF 1 14:243**. [13]CS 111:39*. [14]*ECTD* 264-65. [15]CSCO 4 3:235-36. [16]See Mt 9:15.

on the poor. Commentary on the Gospel of John 8.[17]

Anoint the Lord's Head by Caring for the Poor. Origen: So powerful is the praise of a good work of this kind that it exhorts all of us to fill the Lord's head with fragrant and rich works so that it may be said also of us that we have done a good work on his head. Because as long as we are in this life we will always have the poor with us, and those who have advanced in word and have become rich in the wisdom of God need to care for them, but [this] cannot be equal to having always with them, by night and day, the Son of God, the Word and Wisdom of God, and whatever also the Lord our Savior is. Commentary on Matthew 77.[18]

12:8b *Jesus' Presence Soon Gone*

Jesus' Incarnate Presence Withdrew. Augustine: It may be also understood in this way: . . . The good may take it also as addressed to themselves, but not so as to be any source of anxiety. For he was speaking of his bodily presence. For in respect of his majesty, his providence, his ineffable and invisible grace, his own words are fulfilled, "Lo, I am with you always, even to the end of the world."[19] But in respect of the flesh he assumed as the Word . . . "you will not have him always." And why is this? Because in respect of his bodily presence he associated for forty days with his disciples, and then, having brought them forth for the purpose of beholding and not of following him, he ascended into heaven and is no longer here. He is there, indeed, sitting at the right hand of the Father. And he is here also, having never withdrawn the presence of his glory. In other words, in respect of his divine presence we always have Christ. In respect of his presence in the flesh it was rightly said to the disciples, "You will not always have me." In this respect the church enjoyed his presence only for a few days; now it possesses him by faith without seeing him with the eyes. In whichever way, then, it was said, "But me you will not have always," it can no longer, I suppose, after this twofold solution, remain as a subject of doubt. Tractates on the Gospel of John 50.13.[20]

The Wicked Will Not Have Christ Always. Augustine: We can certainly understand "the poor you have always." What he has said here is true. When were the poor ever lacking in the church? "But you will not always have me." What does he mean by this? How are we to understand "you will not always have me"? Do not be alarmed: it was addressed to Judas. Why, then, didn't he say, "You (sg.) will have" instead of "You (pl.) will have"? [He used the plural form] because Judas is not here just an individual. One wicked man represents the whole body of the wicked. . . . And so it was said [to Judas], "But you will not always have me." But what does the "not always" and "always" mean? If you are good, if you belong to the body represented by Peter, you have Christ both now and hereafter: now by faith, by sign, by the sacrament of baptism, by the bread and wine of the altar. You have Christ now, but you will have him always. For, when you have gone from here, you will come to him who said to the robber, "Today you shall be with me in paradise."[21] But if you live wickedly, you may seem to have Christ now, because you enter the church, sign yourself with the sign of Christ, are baptized with the baptism of Christ, mingle with the members of Christ and approach his altar: now you have Christ, but by living wickedly you will not have him always. Tractates on the Gospel of John 50.12.[22]

The Madness of Sin. Chrysostom: But none of these things [that he said] turned back that savage madman [i.e., Judas]. And yet, really Jesus said and did far more than this: he washed his feet that night, made him a sharer in the table and

[17]LF 48:139-40**. [18]AEG 4:306*; GCS 38 2 (11):184. [19]Mt 28:20. [20]NPNF 1 7:282*; CCL 36:438-39. [21]Lk 23:43. [22]NPNF 1 7:282-83*; CCL 36:438.

the salt, which is a thing that should restrain even the souls of robbers. He also spoke other words, enough to melt a stone, and he did this, not a long time before but on the very day in order that not even time might cause it to be forgotten. But none of this affected Judas. Homilies on the Gospel of John 65.2.[23]

[23]NPNF 1 14:243**.

12:9-11 Lazarus and the Plot Against Him

[9]When the great crowd of the Jews learned that he was there, they came, not only on account of Jesus but also to see Lazarus, whom he had raised from the dead. [10]So the chief priests planned to put Lazarus also to death, [11]because on account of him many of the Jews were going away and believing in Jesus.

Overview: Many Jews came not only to see Jesus but also to see Lazarus, from whom perhaps they expected to hear something extraordinary. He was considered to be dangerous by the Jewish leaders since the people might then be led to Christ (Theodore). Lazarus's popularity spurs the Jewish leaders to plot his murder too, which is indeed foolish since there was no reason to believe he could not be raised from the dead again (Bede). But the leaders are envious (Ambrose) and exasperated (Chrysostom), frantically believing they can erase not only Lazarus but also any memory of the miracle of his coming back to life (Cyril).

12:9 *The Crowd Came to See Jesus and Lazarus*

Jewish Leaders Seek Containment. Theodore of Mopsuestia: The Jews discovered that Jesus was again in Bethany, staying with Lazarus and his sisters, and was in fact with them at that moment. Many came . . . perhaps expecting to hear something extraordinary from him, like somebody who comes back to civilization from a strange and remote land. For this reason the chief priests, when they saw that the crowd was also greatly attracted by the desire to see Lazarus, thought to kill Lazarus together with Christ. They obviously had the idea that the crowds would have not confined themselves to see Lazarus but by seeing him would have been led to faith in Christ—as if he who had raised [Lazarus] from the dead once could not bring him back to life again. Commentary on John 5.12.9.[1]

12:10 *Plotting of the Murder of Lazarus*

The Foolishness of Killing One Already Raised. Bede: Blind cunning of the blind, to wish to kill one who had been restored to life! As if [Jesus] could not restore to life one who had been killed when he had been able to restore to life one who had died! And, indeed, he taught that he was about do both, since he restored to life both Lazarus, who had died, and himself, who had been killed. Homilies on the Gospels 2.4.[2]

[1]CSCO 4 3:237. [2]CS 111:40.

Envy Seeks to Kill Those Raised to Life. Ambrose: In the presence of such grace given by the Lord, of such a miracle of divine bounty, when all ought to have rejoiced, the wicked were stirred up and gathered a council against Christ[3] and wished moreover to kill Lazarus also. Do you not recognize that you are the successors of those whose hardness you inherit? For you too are angry and gather a council against the church, because you see the dead come to life again in the church and raised again by receiving forgiveness of their sins. And thus, so far as you are concerned, you desire to slay again through envy those who are raised to life. Concerning Repentance 2.7.59.[4]

12:11 *How Can Defections to Jesus Be Prevented?*

Lazarus Exasperates Jewish Leaders. Chrysostom: No other miracle of Christ exasperated the Jewish leaders as much as this one. . . . It was so public, and so wonderful, to see a man walking and talking after he had been dead four days. And the fact was so undeniable. . . . In the case of some other miracles, they had charged him with breaking the sabbath[5] and so diverted people's minds; but here there was nothing to find fault with, and therefore they vent their anger upon Lazarus. . . . They would have done the same to the blind man, had they not had the charge to make of breaking the sabbath. Then again the latter was a poor man, and they cast him out of the temple, but Lazarus was a man of rank, as is plain from the number who came to comfort his sisters. . . . It exasperated them to see all leaving the feast, which was now beginning, and going to Bethany. Homilies on the Gospel of John 66.1.[6]

Frantic to Stop Christ. Cyril of Alexandria: See now how frantic the rulers seem to become, wildly rushing here and there under the influence of their envy and saying nothing coherently. They seriously meditate murder on murder, thinking they can remove the force of the miraculous deed at the same time as their victim in order to stop the people from running to believe Christ. Commentary on the Gospel of John 8.[7]

[3]Jn 11:47. [4]NPNF 2 10:353*. [5]E.g., Jn 5:16. [6]NPNF 1 14:244-45**. [7]LF 48:140.

12:12-19 The Triumphal Entry into Jerusalem

[12]The next day a great crowd who had come to the feast heard that Jesus was coming to Jerusalem. [13]So they took branches of palm trees and went out to meet him, crying, "Hosanna! Blessed is he who comes in the name of the Lord, even the King of Israel!" [14]And Jesus found a young ass and sat upon it; as it is written,

[15]"Fear not, daughter of Zion;
behold, your king is coming,
sitting on an ass's colt!"

[16]His disciples did not understand this at first; but when Jesus was glorified, then they remembered

that this had been written of him and had been done to him. [17]*The crowd that had been with him when he called Lazarus out of the tomb and raised him from the dead bore witness.* [18]*The reason why the crowd went to meet him was that they heard he had done this sign.* [19]*The Pharisees then said to one another, "You see that you can do nothing; look, the world has gone after him."*

Overview: The large crowd that greets Jesus on his entry into Jerusalem demonstrates that the people knew better than their leaders the truth of who Jesus was (Chrysostom). The crowd, many of whom had witnessed Lazarus's coming out of the tomb, is there to greet Jesus because of this great sign he had done (Athanasius). They wave their palms of victory over the tomb of Lazarus as they (and we) sing psalms of victory over the tomb of sin and death (Romanus, Augustine).

They praise him with Scripture (Cyril), with shouts of Hosanna, which means "Lord save us" (Eusebius). They call for the blessing of the one who comes in the name of the Lord, that is, of the Father (Bede). This was a claim that previously had been divisive when it came from the mouth of Jesus (Chrysostom), a further point that the same psalm had also prophesied (Bede). He is recognized as the Son of David, the king returning to Jerusalem (Irenaeus)—although human kingship for the Lord of the universe is more of a demotion than a promotion (Augustine). To stress this point, Jesus borrows a donkey for his ride into Jerusalem, in contrast with the Roman trust in princes and horses rather than in the Lord (Tertullian).

In explaining both the donkey and colt as present in the narrative, it is most likely that while the disciples were bringing the donkey, Jesus found the colt and sat on it (Chrysostom). By sitting on the colt, which represents the Gentiles, Jesus indicates their future subjection to himself as a new people (Cyril). Zechariah prophesied the return of the king, but there is no record of any Jewish king fulfilling this role except Jesus the Christ (Eusebius), who, as a king of peace, contrasts with Israel's wicked kings (Chrysostom). The daughter of Zion need not fear if it acknowledges the one it praises as he whose blood will cleanse their sins (Augustine).

Jesus' disciples did not understand the significance of the events since our Lord did not reveal everything to them (Chrysostom). John includes this so we can see the power of the Spirit in the change we see in the disciples after the resurrection when Jesus was glorified (Cyril). Those at Lazarus's tomb for his resurrection readily persuaded the crowd who welcomed Jesus to Jerusalem (Cyril) that Jesus was the one who defeated death (Theodore). Some of them were Pharisees favorable to Jesus (Chrysostom). In fact, Jesus' popularity is so far advanced that the leaders wish they had taken action sooner (Cyril). The shouts of the crowd were evidence enough (Proclus) that "all the world," that is, the Gentiles, were going after him (Cyril).

12:12 *Crowd Hears of Jesus Entering Jerusalem*

The Crowd Knows Better Than Their Leaders. Chrysostom: Wealth is just as liable as power to destroy those who are not careful. The first leads into covetousness; the second, into pride. See, for instance, how the multitude of the Jews is sound while their rulers are corrupt. For the first of these believed Christ, as the Evangelists continually assert, saying that "many of the multitude believed on him,"[1] but those who were of the ruling party did not believe. . . . But how is it that he now enters openly into Jerusalem whereas before he had not walked openly among the Jews and had withdrawn into the wilderness? Having quenched their anger by withdrawing, he comes to them now when they are calmer. Moreover, the multitude that went before him and

[1]See Jn 7:31, 48.

then followed after him was enough to throw them into an agony of fear. For no miracle so attracted the people as that of Lazarus. And another Evangelist says that they threw their garments under his feet[2] and that "the whole city was moved."[3] This is the kind of honor he had when he entered the city. Homilies on the Gospel of John 66.1.[4]

12:13a *Branches of Palm Trees and Hosannas*

The Crowd Hails Jesus. Athanasius: When the crowd took the palm branches from the date palms and went before Christ as he was about to go up to the feast, all of them bore witness that he had called Lazarus forth from the grave and had raised him from the dead. Because of this, this great throng believed on him when they heard that he had done this sign. For all the people had come out of the tomb before they buried him and closed the mouth of the tomb. A great wonder seized them all when they heard that he was alive again. Homily on the Resurrection of Lazarus.[5]

Palms of Victory over Death. Romanus Melodus:

O Savior, all came with palms on the occasion of Thy arrival, crying out, "Hosanna" to Thee,
Now all of us bring hymns to Thee out of piteous mouths,
As we wave the branches of our spirit and cry out:
"O Thou, truly among those on high, save the world which Thou hast created, Lord,
And blot out our sins, just as formerly Thou hast dried
The tears of Mary and Martha."

O Lover of man, the holy church holds a high festival, faithfully calling together her children;
It meets Thee with palms and spreads out garments of joy
So that with Thy disciples and with Thy friend,
Thou mayst advance and legislate a deep peace for Thy servants,
And release them from oppression, as formerly Thou hast checked
The tears of Mary and Martha.

Incline Thy ear, O God of the universe, and hear our prayers, and snatch us from the bonds of death. . . .
Let us who are dead because of our sins and who dwell in the tomb because of our knowledge of evil imitate
The sisters of faithful Lazarus as we cry to Christ with tears, in faith and in love:
"Save us, Thou who didst will to become man.
And resurrect us from the tomb of our sins, Thou, alone immortal."

Kantakion on the Raising of Lazarus 15.14-17.[6]

Palms Are Psalms of Praise for Victory. Augustine: See how great the fruit of his preaching was and how large a flock of the lost sheep of the house of Israel heard the voice of their Shepherd. . . . "On the next day many people that came to the feast, when they heard that Jesus was coming to Jerusalem, took branches of palm trees." . . . The branches of palms are psalms of praise for the victory that our Lord was about to obtain by his death over death and his triumph over the devil, the prince of death, by the trophy of the cross. Tractates on the Gospel of John 51.1-2.[7]

Multitudes Praise Using Scripture. Cyril of Alexandria: The multitudes do not praise Jesus with ordinary language but quote from the inspired Scripture[8] that which was

[2]Mt 21:8. [3]Mt 21:10. [4]NPNF 1 14:244-45**. [5]*AJSL* 57:271. [6]*KRBM* 1:155-56. [7]NPNF 1 7:283**; CCL 36:440. [8]Ps 118:26 (117:26 LXX).

beautifully spoken regarding him. Confessing that he was indeed the King of Israel, they call him their own king and accept the lordship of the Christ. Commentary on the Gospel of John 8.[9]

Old and New Testaments Praise the Christ. Bede: Those who went ahead and those who followed exalted our Lord with one and the same voice of praise, for undoubtedly the faith of those who were approved before our Lord's incarnation and of those after it is one [faith], although they had sacraments that differed according to the customs of the times. Peter bears witness [to this] when he says, "But we believe that we are being saved in the same way as they also were, through the grace of the Lord Jesus."[10] As for their saying, "Hosanna," that is, "salvation to the Son of David," this is the same thing we read in the psalm, "The Lord is [our] salvation, [let] your blessing [be] on your people."[11] It is the same as the chorus that the saints echo with a chant of great praise in the Apocalypse, "Salvation to our God, who sits on the throne, and to the Lamb."[12] Homilies on the Gospels 2.3.[13]

Hosanna Means Saved. Eusebius of Caesarea: As, therefore, hosanna is said in the psalm we are considering, which is translated "Save us now," and the Hebrew has "Lord, save us," and the words "blessed is he that comes in the name of the Lord" are taken from the same psalm, and these words can only refer to the Christ of God, we naturally apply the rest of the prediction to him as well. Proof of the Gospel 9.18.[14]

Same Psalm Spoke of the Rejected Cornerstone. Bede: The crowd took this verse of praise from the one hundredth and seventeenth psalm,[15] and there is no one who doubts that it is sung about the Lord. Hence it is appropriate that there is previously sung of him in the same psalm, "The stone which the builders rejected has become the cornerstone,"[16] for Christ, whom the Jews rejected as they were building the decrees of their own traditions, became a memorial[17] for believers from among both peoples, namely, the Jews and the Gentiles. For as to the fact that Christ is called the cornerstone in this psalm, this is what was being chanted in high praise in the Gospel by the voice of those who followed and those who went ahead. Homilies on the Gospels 2.3.[18]

12:13b *The King Who Comes in the Lord's Name*

In the Name of the Father. Bede: "In the name of the Lord" signifies "In the name of God the Father,"[19] just as [our Lord] himself said elsewhere to the unbelieving Jews, "I have come in the name of my Father, and you do not receive me; another will come in his own name, him you will receive."[20] Christ came in the name of God the Father because in everything that he did and said he was concerned with glorifying his Father and with proclaiming to human beings that he is to be glorified. The antichrist will come in his own name, and although he may be the wickedest person of all and a great help to the devil, he will see fit to call[21] himself the Son of God while "being opposed to and raised above everything that is said to be God and is worshiped."[22] Homilies on the Gospels 2.3.[23]

The Divisive Claim. Chrysostom: Do you see how this [praise] choked them the most, that is, the belief everyone had that he was not an enemy of God? And this is what had most divided the people, when he said that he came from the Father. Homilies on the Gospel of John 66.1.[24]

[9]LF 48:141**. [10]Acts 15:11. [11]Ps 3:8 (3:9 LXX). [12]Rev 7:10. [13]CS 111:28; CCL 122:204. [14]*POG* 2:188-89*. [15]Ps 118:26 (117:26 LXX). [16]Ps 118:22 (117:22 LXX). [17]Lat *monimentum*. [18] CS 111:29; CCL 122:204-5. [19]Although Augustine notes it might also be understood that he came "'in his own name' inasmuch as he is also himself the Lord," quoting, interestingly enough, Jn 5:43 (*Tractate on the Gospel of John* 51.3 [NPNF 1 7:284]). [20]Jn 5:43. [21]Lat *dignatur . . . cognominare.* [22]2 Thess 2:4. [23]CS 111:28-29; CCL 122:204. [24]NPNF 1 14:245**.

The Return of the King. Irenaeus: The Lord granted, by means of his advent, a greater gift of grace to those of a later period than what he had granted to those under the Old Testament dispensation. For they indeed used to hear, from his servants, about the King who would come, and they rejoiced to a certain extent, inasmuch as they hoped for his coming. But those who have actually been in his presence and have been freed and made partakers of his gifts—they possess a greater amount of grace and a higher degree of exultation in their rejoicing because the King has arrived. This is also what David says, "My soul shall rejoice in the Lord; it shall be glad in his salvation."[25] And for this reason, on his entrance into Jerusalem, all those who were in the way recognized David their king in the sorrow of his soul, and spread their garments for him and ornamented the way with green boughs, crying out with great joy and gladness, "Hosanna to the Son of David; blessed is he who comes in the name of the Lord: hosanna in the highest."[26] . . . What had been declared by David concerning the Son of God was accomplished in his own person. . . . It was he himself who was announced by the prophets as Christ, whose name is praised in all the earth. Against Heresies 4.11.3.[27]

Becoming a King Is Not a Promotion for the Lord. Augustine: What a cross of mental suffering the Jewish rulers must have endured when they heard such a great multitude proclaiming Christ as the King! But what honor was it to the Lord to be King of Israel? How great was it for the King of eternity to become the King of humanity? Christ was not the King of Israel so that he could exact tribute, put swords in his soldiers' hands and subdue his enemies by open warfare. He was King of Israel in exercising kingly authority over their souls, in consulting for their eternal interests, in bringing into his heavenly kingdom those whose faith, hope and love were centered in himself. For the Son of God, the Father's equal, the Word by whom all things were made, in his good pleasure to be King of Israel was a demotion not a promotion, a sign of his pity not an increase of his power. For he who was called on earth the King of the Jews is in heaven the King of angels. Tractates on the Gospel of John 51.4.[28]

12:14 *Jesus Sits on a Young Donkey*

Jesus' Borrowed Donkey. Tertullian: For state reasons, the various orders of the [Roman] citizens . . . are crowned with laurel crowns. . . . There are also provincial crowns of gold, needing now the larger heads of images instead of those of men. But your orders,[29] and your magistracies and your very place of meeting, that is, the church, are Christ's. You belong to him, for you have been enrolled in the books of life.[30] There the blood of the Lord serves for your purple robe, and your broad stripe is his own cross. There the axe is already laid to the trunk of the tree.[31] There the branch is from the root of Jesse.[32] Never mind the state horses with their crown. Your Lord, when, according to the Scripture, he would enter Jerusalem in triumph, had not even a donkey of his own. These [put their trust] in chariots, and these in horses. But we will seek our help in the name of the Lord our God.[33] The Chaplet 13.1-2.[34]

The Donkey and the Colt. Chrysostom: But how does it happen that the other evangelists say that he sent disciples and said, "Loose the donkey and the colt,"[35] while John says nothing of the kind but that, "having found a young donkey, he sat on it"? Because it is likely that both circumstances took place, and that after the donkey was loosed, while the disciples were bringing it, he found [the colt] and sat on it. Homilies on the Gospel of John 66.1.[36]

---

[25]Ps 35:9 (34:9 LXX). [26]Mt 21:9. [27]ANF 1:474-75; SC 100:502-6. [28]NPNF 1 7:284**; CCL 36:440-41. [29]The various clerical offices of those to whom he is writing. [30]Phil 4:3. [31]Mt 3:10. [32]Is 11:1. [33]Ps 20:7 (19:8 LXX, Vg). [34]ANF 3:101; CCL 2:1060-61. [35]Mt 21:2. [36]NPNF 1 14:245*.

Subjection of Gentiles. Cyril of Alexandria: And since, contrary to his usual habits, on this occasion only, Christ appears seated on a donkey, we do not say that he sat on it because it was a long distance to the city. For it was not more than two miles away.[37] Nor do we say that it was because there was a multitude. For it is certain that on other occasions when he was found with a multitude he did not do this; but he does this to indicate that he is about to make subject to himself as a new people the unclean among the Gentiles, and to lead them up to the prerogative of righteousness and to the Jerusalem above of which the earthly is a type. It is into this Jerusalem that this people, being made clean, shall enter with Christ, who will be hymned by the guileless angels of whom the babes are a type. And he calls the donkey a colt, because the people of the Gentiles had been untrained in the piety that faith produces. Commentary on the Gospel of John 8.[38]

12:15 *Zion's King Arrives on a Donkey's Colt*[39]

No Record of Jewish King Except Christ. Eusebius of Caesarea: Zechariah gave this prophecy after the return from Babylon toward the conclusion of prophecy. But there is no record of a Jewish king since that time, such as the prophecy predicts, except our Lord and Savior Jesus Christ, in whom this prediction was fulfilled. . . . But what was his riding on a donkey meant to show but the lowly and humble manner that marked his first coming? Proof of the Gospel 9.17.[40]

Wicked Kings Contrasted with the King of Peace. Chrysostom: Because all their kings had mostly been unjust and covetous and subjected them to wars . . . he said to them, "Trust me, I am not like them. I am gentle and mild." He demonstrated this by the manner of his entrance, not entering at the head of an army but simply riding on a donkey. Homilies on the Gospel of John 66.1.[41]

Acknowledge Him Whom You Praise. Augustine: This act of our Lord's is pointed to in the prophets, though the malignant rulers of the Jews did not see in it any fulfillment of prophecy. . . . Yes, in that nation though reprobate, though blind, there remained still the daughter of Zion, which is Jerusalem. . . . It is said to her, "Fear not." . . . Acknowledge him whom you praise, and do not tremble when he suffers. That is the blood that shall wipe away your sins and redeem your life. Tractates on the Gospel of John 51.5.[42]

12:16 *Jesus' Disciples Do Not Understand*

The Former Ignorance of the Apostles. Chrysostom: But observe the wisdom of the Evangelist, how he is not ashamed to parade the disciples' former ignorance. He writes how they were ignorant of what was happening. For it would have offended them if, as a king, they found out that he was about to suffer such things and be betrayed like he was. Besides, they could not have immediately absorbed the knowledge of the kingdom of which he spoke. For another Evangelist says that they thought the words were spoken of a kingdom of this world.[43] Homilies on the Gospel of John 66.2.[44]

The Disciples' Understanding. Cyril of Alexandria: The Evangelist does not hesitate to mention the ignorance of the disciples, nor their subsequent understanding, since he did not care about the respect of people but pleads for the glory of the Spirit and shows what kind of men the disciples were before the resurrection and what sort of men they had become after the resurrection. Commentary on the Gospel of John 8.[45]

12:17-18 *The Crowd at Lazarus's Tomb Bore Witness*

[37]See Jn 11:18. [38]LF 48:142. [39]Origen notes how neither Matthew nor John quotes the prophecy exactly. See his *Commentary on Matthew* 16.14. [40]POG 2:185-86*. [41]NPNF 1 14:245**. [42]NPNF 1 7:284**; CCL 36:441. [43]Cf. Mt 20:21. [44]NPNF 1 14:245**. [45]LF 48:142*.

The Crowd Readily Persuaded by Witnesses. Cyril of Alexandria: The gathering of the common people, having heard what had happened, were readily persuaded by those who had witnessed that the Christ had raised Lazarus to life and annulled the power of death, as the prophets said. This is why they too went and met him. Commentary on the Gospel of John 8.[46]

The One Who Has Defeated Death. Theodore of Mopsuestia: Since through Adam death came, which subjected everyone, they had heard through their prophets and believed that death would be defeated. When they saw that this had been done by our Lord, who raised a man dead for four days, they took branches of palm trees and went out to meet him as the victor over death, which oppresses humankind, and praised him with appropriate hymns. Since the Pharisees did not like this, they reproached them by saying that they followed him in vain, but it was their reproach that was in vain, since all the people went after him anyway. Commentary on John 5.12.17-18.[47]

12:19 *The Pharisees Perceive Jesus' Popularity*

Some Pharisees Favorable to Jesus. Chrysostom: Now this seems to me to be said by those who thought correctly about Jesus but did not have the courage to speak up. [It would seem] that they were trying to restrain the others by pointing to the result, as though they would be attempting the impossible if they went ahead with it. Homilies on the Gospel of John 66.2.[48]

Leaders Wish They Had Taken Action Sooner. Cyril of Alexandria: They say this, finding fault with themselves because they had not put both Jesus and Lazarus to death a long time ago, wishing they had murdered them then. They were angry concerning the "believing multitude," as though they [as the people's leaders] were being deprived of their special possessions comprised of those who really belonged to God. Commentary on the Gospel of John 8.[49]

Praises of the Crowd Irritate Pharisees. Proclus of Constantinople:

It irritated the high priests and Pharisees to hear from the crowds:
"The King of Israel."
They were hearing what they did not wish to hear.
They were used to addressing him as one possessed by demons,[50]
But these were proclaiming him "King":
"Blessed is he who comes in the name of the Lord, even the King of Israel."
Who is the one who suggested this utterance to the crowds?
Who is the one who put this praise into their minds?
Who is the one who entrusted them with branches from the palm trees?
Who is the one who suddenly at a fixed signal acted as military commander of them all?
Who is the one who taught them this harmony of voice?
The grace from above, the revelation of the Holy Spirit.
And therefore they called out with boldness:
"Blessed is he who comes in the name of the Lord, even the King of Israel."

Homily 9.3, On the Palm Branches.[51]

Salvation for the Gentiles. Cyril of Alexandria: Even though they did not know it, the Pharisees were telling the truth when they said, "Look, the world has gone after him," for not only Jews but Gentiles as well were destined to accept the faith. Commentary on the Gospel of John 8.[52]

---

[46]LF 48:143. [47]CSCO 4 3:238-39. [48]NPNF 1 14:245**. [49]LF 48:143*. [50]See Mt 12:22. [51]ECS 1:151. [52]LF 48:145*.

12:20-26 The Greeks' Request to See Jesus

[20]Now among those who went up to worship at the feast were some Greeks. [21]So these came to Philip, who was from Bethsaida in Galilee, and said to him, "Sir, we wish to see Jesus." [22]Philip went and told Andrew; Andrew went with Philip and they told Jesus. [23]And Jesus answered them, "The hour has come for the Son of man to be glorified. [24]Truly, truly, I say to you, unless a grain of wheat falls into the earth and dies, it remains alone; but if it dies, it bears much fruit. [25]He who loves his life loses it, and he who hates his life in this world will keep it for eternal life. [26]If any one serves me, he must follow me; and where I am, there shall my servant be also; if any one serves me, the Father will honor him."

Overview: The Greeks, having been impressed by the Jewish customs and temple, were present for the feast in order to honor the one, all-supreme God (Cyril). John provides us with an instance of Jews and Greeks joined together in praise of their king (Augustine). In fact, the proclamation of the crowds that Jesus was king is more than likely what drew the Greeks to Jesus (Proclus). With the arrival of the firstfruits of the Gentiles to see Jesus (Cyril), the time of Jesus' glorification before Jews and Gentiles, which would occur at the passion, must be near (Augustine) as he here speaks of the glory of the cross, which the Gentiles too would now take up (Proclus).

Jesus provides the Greeks who come to see him with a parable. He tells them about a seed that is planted and dies, which sprouts again as new life from the ground and reveals the nature of the plant from which it came (Ambrose). When Christ was planted in Calvary, the church sprouted into a multitude of grains (Theodore) baked into the bread of life of the Eucharist, which is multiplied in us who receive it (Irenaeus). Christ is the one sheaf of wheat made up of many individual stalks, since he contains in himself all believers (Cyril).

Jesus goes on to speak of losing and gaining one's life, which in the Greek refers to the soul. There is a wrong way and a right way to love your soul (Augustine). If we love our soul in sin, that is wrong, but if we love that which is in the image of God, then we love rightly (Caesarius). It is a painful thing to lose the one you love, especially if that person is yourself (Augustine). If you want to keep your soul safe forever, you have to hate it for a time (Augustine), since it is important not only to protect your life but also to submit it to testing; otherwise it may be lost in the future (Theodore). He is not talking here about taking your life into your own hands either (Augustine). Rather, Jesus is calling us to turn away from evil as if we hated it (Chrysostom) so that, like the martyrs, we may gain a crown in exchange for the life that is sown here (Augustine). Imitating Christ in service to our fellow human beings is another way that we serve him (Augustine), becoming partners with him in service here and in eternity (John Cassian). The path of service leads ultimately to the path of glory, as long as we follow Christ and not ourselves (Cyril). Jesus says the honor conferred on one who serves is given by the Father, since his hearers at that time had more respect for the Father than for him (Chrysostom).

12:20 *Some Greeks Went to the Feast*

What Were Greeks Doing at the Feast? Cyril of Alexandria: Anyone might be perplexed at these words and wonder with what motive certain Greeks should be going up to Jerusalem to worship. Note that they were doing this at the time when the feast was being celebrated according to the Law. For surely no one will say that they went up merely to look at the people there. Certainly it was with the intention of participating in the feast that was suitable for Jews and Jews only that they were journeying up in the company of the Jews. What was the point as regards the motive of worship that was common to both Greeks and Jews? . . .

Since the territory of the Jews was situated near that of the Galileans, and since both they and the Greeks had cities and villages in close vicinity to each other, they were continually intermingling together and interchanging visits, being invited for a variety of occasions. And since it somehow happens that the disposition of idol worshipers is very easily brought to welcome a change for the better, and since nothing is easier than to convict their false worship of being utterly unprofitable, some among them were easily persuaded to change. This does not mean that they fully and perfectly worshiped him who alone is truly God, since they were somewhat divided with regard to the arguments in favor of abandoning idolatry and following the precepts of their own teachers. . . .

It was then a custom for certain of the inhabitants of Palestine, especially the Greeks, who had the territory of the Jews closely adjoining and bordering on their own, to be impressed in some way by the Jewish habits of thought and to honor the name of one sovereign [deity]. And this was the view current among those Greeks whom we just now mentioned, albeit they did not express it in the same way that we do. And they, not having the tendency to Judaism in full force, nor even having separated themselves from the habits dear to the Greeks but holding an intermediate opinion that inclined both ways, are called "worshipers of God." People of this kind, therefore, seeing that their own habits of thought were not very sharply distinguished from those of the Jews . . . were in the habit of going up with the Jews to worship, especially at the national gatherings, not meaning to slight their own religion but as an act of honor to the one all-supreme God. Commentary on the Gospel of John 8.[1]

12:21-22 *The Request to Philip to See Jesus*

Jews and Gentiles Joined in Praise. Augustine: Look how the Jews want to kill him, the Gentiles to see him.[2] But they also were there with the Jews who cried, "Blessed is he who comes in the name of the Lord, the king of Israel." Here then are both those of the circumcision and those of the uncircumcision, once so wide apart, coming together like two walls and meeting in the one faith of Christ by the kiss of peace. Tractates on the Gospel of John 51.8.[3]

The Crowds Draw the Greeks to Jesus. Proclus of Constantinople:

[The crowds] caused the Pharisees to turn away.
They loathed the high priests.
They lifted up in song their voices befitting to God.
They caused creation to rejoice.
They sanctified the air.
They shook the dead beforehand.
They opened heaven.
They planted paradise.
They stirred up the dead to the same zeal.
For that reason some of the Greeks at that time were urged on toward that zeal for God, because of this utterance befitting to God;
And having reached a turning about, they approached . . . one of the apostles by the name of Philip, saying to him:

[1]LF 48:143-45*. Cyril here provides a sociological-historical observation that helps account for the interest in Christ among the Gentiles prior to his resurrection. Theodore notes that they were also attracted to Jerusalem because of the miracles God had performed among the Jews. See *Commentary on the Gospel of John* 5.12.20-23 (CSCO 4 3:239). [2]See also Bede, *loc. cit.*, PL 92:788. [3]NPNF 1 7:285**; CCL 36:442.

"Sir, we wish to see Jesus."
Behold the preaching of the crowd,
And how they moved the Greeks to
conversion.
Homily 9.3, On the Palm Branches.[4]

Firstfruits of the Gentiles Arrive to See Jesus. Cyril of Alexandria: This approach of the Greeks [to Philip] happened at that time as a sort of firstfruits. And the Galileans came to Philip as being himself a Galilean, asking him to show them Jesus whom they wanted to see because they were continually hearing good things about Jesus. They wanted to worship him and attain the object of their desires. But Philip remembered what the Lord had said to them, "Do not go into any area of the Gentiles or enter any city of the Samaritans."[5] And so Philip was afraid that he might give offense by bringing to Christ those who had not believed, not realizing that it was for a set purpose that the Lord had forbidden the disciples to approach the Gentiles until the Jews should first have rejected the grace given to them. And so Philip tells Andrew, who was more disposed for and accustomed to such things, and then, with his approval they both carry the message to the Lord. Commentary on the Gospel of John 8.[6]

12:23 *The Hour for Glorification Has Arrived*

The Hour Looks Toward the Fullness of the Gentiles. Augustine: We listen to the voice of the cornerstone. . . . Did he think of himself as glorified because the Gentiles wished to see? No. But he saw that after his passion and resurrection, the Gentiles in all lands would believe in him . . . and took occasion from this request of some Gentiles to see him to announce the approaching fullness of the Gentiles. For the Gentiles would believe that the hour of his being glorified was now at hand and that after he was glorified in the heavens the Gentiles would believe, as it is written in the psalm, "Set yourself up, O God, above the heavens, . . . and your glory above all the earth."[7] . . . But it was necessary that his exaltation and glory should be preceded by the humiliation of his passion. Tractates on the Gospel of John 51.8-9.[8]

The Glory Is the Cross. Proclus of Constantinople:
[The Greeks say,] "We wish to see Jesus"—
not so much in order to look him in his face,
as to carry the cross.
And therefore Jesus, having seen their
intention,
Openly said to those present:
"The hour has come
for the Son of man to be glorified."
Glorified—referring to the conversion of the
Greeks;
A glory that the Jews donned
But that the nations put on.
Therefore Jesus said concerning the Gentiles:
"The hour has come
For the Son of man to be glorified."
Glorified—referring to the cross.
For from it the power of the Lord was made
known,
Because it changed the shame into glory—
the insult into honor,
the curse into blessing,
the gall into sweetness,
the vinegar into milk,
the slap in his face into freedom,
death into life.
The hour has come,
For the Son of man to be glorified.
Glorified—referring to the cross,
For from it the cross is even now glorified.
For the cross itself even now still glorifies
kings,
and gives radiance to priesthood,
and preserves virginity,

[4]ECS 1:152. [5]Mt 10:5. [6]LF 48:145*. [7]Ps 57:5 (56:6 LXX, Vg) and Ps 108:5 (107:6 LXX, Vg). [8]NPNF 1 7:285**; CCL 36:442. See also Hilary *On the Trinity* 3.10 (NPNF 2 9:64).

and establishes asceticism,
and strengthens union,
and guards widowhood,
and protects orphans,
and increases the blessing of children,
and multiples the church,
and enlightens the people,
and preserves a spiritual lifestyle,[9]
and opens paradise,
and guides the robber,
and roots out enmity,
and extinguishes hatred,
and puts demons to flight,
and drives the devil away.

Homily 9.3, On the Palm Branches.[10]

12:24 *Unless a Grain of Wheat Falls to the Earth and Dies*

The Seed Must Die Before Being Resurrected. Ambrose: How many more wonders appear, if you examine each plant, noticing how the seed when laid in the earth decays and, if it did not die, would bear no fruit. But when it decays, by that very act of death, it rises up to bear fruit in greater abundance. The pliable sod receives, then, a grain of wheat. The scattered seed is controlled by the use of the hoe, and mother earth cherishes it in firm embraces to her breast. When that grain decays, there comes the pleasing aspect of the green burgeoning shoot, which immediately reveals its kind from its similarity to its own seed, so that you may discover the nature of the plant even in the very beginning of its growth, and its fruit, too, is made evident to you. Six Days of Creation 3.8.34.[11]

Jesus As the Grain of Wheat. Theodore of Mopsuestia: However, he says, my death must not upset you. As indeed a grain of wheat is just a single grain before falling into the earth, after it has fallen and decomposed, it sprouts forth in great glory and produces double fruit by showing before everyone its riches in its ears and displaying the spectacle of its beauty to those looking on. This is the same way you should think about me. Now I am alone, and just one more man among obscure people without any glory. But when I undergo the passion of the cross, I will be raised in great honor. And when I produce much fruit then everyone will know me—not only the Jews but also the people of the entire world will call me their Lord. Then, not even the spiritual powers will refuse to worship me. Commentary on John 5.12.24.[12]

Dying Grain Becomes the Eucharist. Irenaeus: A cutting from the vine planted in the ground bears fruit in its season, or a kernel of wheat falling into the earth and becoming decomposed rises and is multiplied by the Spirit of God, who contains all things. And then, through the wisdom of God, it serves for our use when, after receiving the Word of God, it becomes the Eucharist, which is the body and blood of Christ. In the same way our bodies, being nourished by it, and deposited in the earth and suffering decomposition there, shall rise at their appointed time. The Word of God grants them resurrection to the glory of God, even the Father who freely gives to this mortal immortality, and to this corruptible incorruption.[13] This is so because the strength of God is made perfect in weakness[14] in order that we may never become puffed up, as if we had life from ourselves, or become exalted against God with ungrateful minds. Against Heresies 5.2.3.[15]

Christ the One Sheaf Made Up of Many Stalks. Cyril of Alexandria: Christ is also symbolized by a sheaf of grain, as a brief explanation will show.

The human race may be compared with stalks of wheat in a field rising, as it were, from the earth, awaiting their full growth and development, and then in time being cut down by the

[9]Gk *erēmos* is often used in patristic texts as metaphor for a spiritual lifestyle, as Barkhuizen the editor notes. [10]ECS 1:152-53*. [11]FC 42:92-93*; CSEL 32 1:81. [12]CSCO 4 3:240. [13]1 Cor 15:53. [14]See 1 Cor 15:43; 2 Cor 13:4. [15]ANF 1:528; SC 153:36-38. See also *Against Heresies* 5.7.2.

reaper, which is death. The comparison is apt, since Christ himself spoke of our race in this way when he said to his holy disciples, "Do you not say, 'Four months and it will be harvest time?' Look at the fields; I tell you, they are already white and ready for harvesting. The reaper is already receiving his wages and bringing in a crop for eternal life."[16] . . .

Now Christ became like one of us. He sprang from the holy Virgin like a stalk of wheat from the ground. Indeed, he spoke of himself as a grain of wheat when he said, "I tell you truly, unless a grain of wheat falls into the ground and dies, it remains as it was, a single grain, but if it dies its yield is very great." And so, like a sheaf of grain, the firstfruits, as it were, of the earth, he offered himself to the Father for our sake.

For we do not think of a stalk of wheat in isolation any more than we do of ourselves. We think of it rather as part of a sheaf, which is a single bundle made up of many stalks. The stalks have to be gathered into a bundle before they can be used, and this is the key to the mystery they represent, the mystery of Christ, who, though one, appears in the image of a sheaf to be made up of many, as in fact he is. Spiritually, he contains in himself all believers. "As we have been raised up with him," writes Paul, "so we have also been enthroned with him in heaven."[17] He is a human being like ourselves, and this had made us one body with him, the body being the bond that unites us. We can say, therefore, that in him we are all one, and indeed he himself says to God, his heavenly Father, "It is my desire that as you and I are one, so they also may be one in us."[18] Glaphyra on Numbers 2.[19]

12:25 *Losing One's Soul*[20] *and Keeping It for Eternity*

When You Love Yourself. Augustine: Only a human being would ask, "How can someone who loves himself deny himself?" God . . . says to such a person, "Let him deny himself, if he loves himself." By loving himself, you see, he loses himself; by denying himself, he finds himself. "Whoever loves his soul," he says, "let him lose it." . . . It is a painful thing to lose what you love. . . .

There is not anyone, after all, who does not love himself. But we have to look for the right sort of love and avoid the wrong sort. You see, anyone who loves himself by leaving God out of his life (and leaves God out of his life by loving himself), does not even remain *in* himself. He actually leaves his self. He goes away into exile from his own heart by taking no notice of what is inside and instead only loving what is outside. . . . For instance, let me ask you this: Are you money? . . . And yet, by loving money, you end up abandoning yourself. First you abandon and then later end up destroying yourself. Love of money, you see, has caused you to destroy yourself. You tell lies on account of money.[21] . . . While looking for money, you have destroyed your soul.

Bring out the scales of truth . . . and put on one side money, on the other the soul. . . . But do not weigh it yourself. You want to cheat yourself. . . . Let God do the weighing—the one who does not know how to deceive or be deceived. . . . Watch him weighing them and then listen to him announce the result: "What does it profit someone if he gains the whole world but suffers the loss of his own soul?"[22] . . . . You were willing to lose your soul in order to acquire the earth. This soul, however, outweighs heaven and earth combined. But you do this because by leaving God out of your life and loving yourself, you have also gone away from yourself. You end up valuing other things, which are outside you, more than yourself. Come back to yourself. But then turn upward when you have come back to yourself; do not stay in yourself. First come back to yourself from the things outside you, and then give yourself back to the one who made you, who looked for you when you were lost and found you when you were a runaway. Sermon 330.2-3.[23]

[16]Jn 4:35-36. [17]Eph 2:6. [18]See Jn 17:11. [19]*JFB* 38-39*; PG 69:621-24. [20]Gk *psychēn*. [21]See Wis 1:11. [22]Mt 16:26. [23]*WSA* 3 9:186-87**; PL 38:1456-57.

Love What Is in the Image of God. Caesarius of Arles: Whatever you love is either the same as yourself, below you or above you. If what you love is beneath you, love it to comfort it, care for it and to use it but not to cling to it. For example, you love gold. Do not become attached to the gold, for how much better are you than gold? Gold, indeed, is a shining piece of earth, while you have been made in the image of God in order that you may be illumined by the Lord. Although gold is a creature of God, still God did not make it according to his own image, but you he did. Therefore, he put the gold beneath you. This kind of love should be despised. Those things are to be acquired for their usefulness, but we should not cling to them with the bond of love as if with glue. Do not make for yourself members over which, when they have begun to be cut away, you will grieve and be afflicted. What then? Rise from that love with which you love things that are lower than you, and begin to love your equals, that is, things that are what you are. . . . The Lord himself has told us in the Gospel and clearly showed us in what order we may have true love and charity. For he spoke in this way, "You shall love the Lord your God with your whole heart, and with your whole soul and with your whole strength. And your neighbor as yourself."[24] Therefore, first love God and then yourself. After these, love your neighbor as yourself. Sermon 173.4-5.[25]

How to Lose Eternal Life. Theodore of Mopsuestia: Therefore, he says, not only must you not be upset by my suffering or have doubts about my words that will be confirmed by the facts later on, but you must also be drawn to that suffering so that you might enjoy the same things I do by suffering the same things I do. The one who appears to be so concerned with his life here that he does not want to submit it to testing will lose it in the future world. The one who hates his life, and in this world exposes it to afflictions, gathers much more fruit for himself. Jesus does not express this idea as if he wants to reveal here something about life. Rather, he simply identifies love for life as something that is prevalent among us as we seek to defend, preserve and protect our body and life from any possible danger. Commentary on the Gospel of John 5.12.25.[26]

Suicide Is Not Meant Here. Augustine: But do not think for an instant that by hating your soul, it means that you may kill yourself. For wicked and perverse people have sometimes so mistaken it and have burned and strangled themselves, thrown themselves from precipices, and in other ways put an end to themselves. This is not what Christ taught. In fact, when the devil tempted him to cast himself down, he said, "Get behind me, Satan."[27] . . . But when no other choice is given you, when the persecutor threatens death and you must either disobey God's law or leave this life . . . then hate your life in this world so that you may keep it to life eternal. Tractates on the Gospel of John 51.10.[28]

Turn Away from Evil. Chrysostom: The present life is sweet and full of much pleasure—not for everyone, although it is for those riveted to it. The moment anyone looks to heaven, however, and sees the beauty that is there, he will soon despise this life as if it counted for nothing. The beauty of an object is admired, in other words, as long as there is nothing more beautiful to be seen. But when something better comes along, the earlier object loses its luster. . . . The one who loves his life in this world loses it by indulging its inordinate desires. . . . The one who hates it resists them. Notice, it does not say "who does not yield to" but "who hates." For as we cannot bear to hear the voice or see the face of those whom we hate, so when the soul invites us to things contrary to God, we should turn it away from them with all our might. Homilies on the Gospel of John 67.1.[29]

[24]Lk 10:27. [25]FC 47:431-32*. [26]CSCO 4 3:241. [27]Augustine conflates Mt 4:7-10 with Mt 16:23. [28]NPNF 1 7:285**. [29]NPNF 1 14:248**.

Losing Straw, Gaining a Crown. Augustine: If you love [your soul], lose it. Sow it here, and you will reap it in heaven. If the farmer does not lose wheat in the seed, he does not love it in the harvest. . . . Do not love your soul so much that you lose it. People who are afraid to die seem to love their souls. If the martyrs had loved their souls like that, they would undoubtedly have lost them. . . . What good, after all, would it be to hold on to the soul on earth and lose it in heaven? And what does holding on to it amount to? Keeping it for how long? What you keep eventually vanishes from you. If you lose it, you find it in yourself. . . . The martyrs lost their souls at a great profit—losing straw, earning a crown. Earning a crown, I repeat, and keeping hold of life without end. Sermon 331.1.[30]

12:26 *Serving and Following*

Imitation of Christ Is Service to Christ. Augustine: Christ's servants are those who look out for his things rather than their own.[31] "Let him follow me" means "Let him walk in my ways and not in his own," as it is written elsewhere.[32] . . . For if he supplies food for the hungry, he should do so in the way of mercy, not to brag about it. He should be looking for nothing else there but to do good and not letting his left hand know what his right hand does.[33] In other words, any work of charity should be utterly devoid of any thought of "what's in it for me." The one who serves in this way serves Christ and will have it rightly said to him, "Inasmuch as you did it unto one of the least of those who are mine, you did it unto me."[34] . . . And the one who serves Christ in this way will be honored by his Father with the peculiar honor of being with his Son and having nothing lacking in his happiness ever again. And so, when you hear the Lord saying, "Where I am, there shall also my servant be," do not think merely of good bishops and clergy. But you yourselves should also serve Christ in your own way by good lives, by giving to the poor, by preaching his name and doctrine as best as you can too. Every father [or mother] . . . too will be filling an ecclesiastical and episcopal kind of office by serving Christ in their own homes when they serve their families so that they too may be with him forever. Tractates on the Gospel of John 51.12-13.[35]

Partners with Christ in Ministry. John Cassian: Everyone who lives in this body knows that he must be committed to that special task or ministry to which he has given himself in this life as a participant and a laborer, and he ought not to doubt that in that everlasting age he will also be the partner of him whose servant and companion he now wishes to be, according to what the Lord says, "If anyone serves me, let him follow me, and where I am, there also will my servant be." For just as the kingdom of the devil is gained by deceiving people with vices, so the kingdom of God is possessed in purity of heart and spiritual knowledge by practicing the virtues. And where the kingdom of God is, there without a doubt is eternal life, and where the kingdom of the devil is, there—it is not to be doubted—are death and hell. Whoever is there cannot praise the Lord. Conference 1.14.1-2.[36]

The Path to Divine Glory Leads to God. Cyril of Alexandria: Since the author of our salvation did not travel by the path of glory and luxury but by that of dishonor and hardships, we must do the same thing without complaining if we are to reach the same destination and share in the divine glory. But what honor shall we receive if we refuse to endure sufferings like those of our Master? . . . The one who does things pleasing to God serves Christ, but the one who follows his own wishes is a follower of himself and not of God. Commentary on the Gospel of John 8.[37]

[30]*WSA* 3 9:190*. [31]See Phil 2:21. [32]1 Jn 2:6. [33]See Mt 6:3. [34]Mt 25:40. [35]NPNF 1 7:286-87**; CCL 36:444-45. [36]ACW 57:52*. [37]LF 48:149-50*.

Valuing the Father More Than Christ. Chrysostom: Why didn't he say that the Father will honor "me"? Because at that time they did not have the proper opinion of him but held a higher opinion of the Father. Homilies on the Gospel of John 67.1.[38]

[38]NPNF 1 14:248**.

12:27-36 The Prediction of Jesus' Death

[27]"Now is my soul troubled. And what shall I say? 'Father, save me from this hour'? No, for this purpose I have come to this hour. [28]Father, glorify thy name." Then a voice came from heaven, "I have glorified it, and I will glorify it again." [29]The crowd standing by heard it and said that it had thundered. Others said, "An angel has spoken to him." [30]Jesus answered, "This voice has come for your sake, not for mine. [31]Now is the judgment of this world, now shall the ruler of this world be cast out; [32]and I, when I am lifted up from the earth, will draw all men to myself." [33]He said this to show by what death he was to die. [34]The crowd answered him, "We have heard from the law that the Christ remains for ever. How can you say that the Son of man must be lifted up? Who is this Son of man?" [35]Jesus said to them, "The light is with you for a little longer. Walk while you have the light, lest the darkness overtake you; he who walks in the darkness does not know where he goes. [36]While you have the light, believe in the light, that you may become sons of light."

When Jesus had said this, he departed and hid himself from them.

Overview: Jesus' troubled soul is indicative of a humanity that has feelings in no way different from ours (Chrysostom). And so, when I see him troubled, I am consoled, knowing that if he ultimately triumphed over his fears, I can too (Augustine). He went through all of our fears and troubles so that he might transform them in such a way that they no longer overtake him or us (Cyril). We see Jesus struggling with the fear of death (Chrysostom), but we also view an example of how, even in the face of death, he chose his Father's will over his own (Augustine). The glory that would come to the Father's name through Jesus' crucifixion and resurrection (Cyril) was something he chose over his own comfort and safety (Chrysostom). The Father's name, in and of itself, received no further glory except in the sense of humanity being made aware of his glory through the action of his Son. As a result, the voice from heaven confirms Jesus' divinity—not to Jesus (Apollinaris) but to those who were capable of hearing the voice (Ambrose). His name was glorified before the creation of the world, it was glorified throughout the life of Jesus, from his birth and the visit of the magi, through his transfiguration and miracles, and it would be glorified at the cross and the resurrection (Augustine). The voice that had spoken at the moment must have been the voice of an angel (Gregory the Great). When the Jews said "it thundered on him," they unwittingly confirmed Jesus' sonship with the Father (Ambrose). Although God chose to reveal himself by this voice from heaven for the crowd, we should not continue to seek this kind of revelation for the senses but rather worship him in awe and reverence (Hilary).

The present judgment that Jesus speaks of is the judgment of the devil (Augustine), who will be deposed from his throne (Theodore). His lifting up is his exaltation (Cyril) as Christ the head of the church will draw all things to himself at the proper time (Irenaeus) when he is lifted up from the earth on the tree of martyrdom (Irenaeus). As he spread out his hands on the cross, he drew the ancient people of the old covenant with one hand and the Gentiles of the new covenant with the other, uniting them in himself (Athanasius). Jesus' previous discussions about his impending death enable the crowd to understand what he meant by being "lifted up" (Chrysostom). Or perhaps their consciences convicted them of what they were about to do (Augustine). Those who live enslaved to bodily desires are living in darkness (Gregory of Nyssa) and not in the light of Christ (Ambrose), who will go away but will return (Chrysostom). But while he is with them, they should believe that he is the light that shines as the radiance of the Father (Origen), and as they are enlightened, they become children of the light of Christ and his Father (Chrysostom).

After speaking these things, Christ withdraws to escape the crowd's wrath, knowing what human nature is capable of (Chrysostom)—only to later yield himself up to suffering (Cyril).

12:27 *Jesus' Troubled Soul and Plea to His Father*

The Infirmity of Human Nature. Chrysostom: Surely this is not the expression of one urging them to go even to death. No, but it is that of one who is greatly urging them on. For they might try to say that he was exempt from mortal pain and so it was easy for him to ruminate about death, and this is how he can exhort us because he himself is in no danger. This is why he shows here that, although he dreaded death, he does not refuse it, because it is efficacious for our salvation. But this is a manifestation of his humanity not of his divinity, which is why he says, "Now my soul is troubled," since if this is not the case, what connection does what was spoken here have with his saying, "Father, save me from this hour"? And he is so troubled that he even looked for deliverance from death if it were possible to escape. These were the infirmities of his human nature. Homilies on the Gospel of John 67.1.[1]

His Suffering Strengthens Us. Augustine: I heard him saying previously . . . "If anyone wants to serve me, let him follow me. And where I am, there my servant shall also be."[2] And so, I was all on fire to despise the world, and the whole of this life, however long it might be, had become only a vapor before my eyes. In comparison with my love for eternal things, everything temporal had lost its value for me. But now, this same Lord, whose words had transported me from the weakness that was mine to the strength that was his—I now hear him saying, "How is my soul troubled." What does this mean? How can you ask my soul to follow you when I see your own in so much turmoil? How can I endure when even a strength as great as yours feels it is a heavy burden? What kind of foundation am I left with when the Rock is giving way? But the Lord is already forming the answer inside my own head, saying: You shall follow me that much better, because it is to strengthen your own endurance that I included this. You have heard, as if addressed to yourself, the voice of my strength. Now hear in me the voice of your infirmity. I supply strength when you need to run without slowing you down, but I take on myself whatever makes you afraid, paving the way for you to continue your march. Lord, I acknowledge your mercy! You, who are so great, allowed yourself to be troubled in order to console all of those in your body who are troubled by the continual experience of their own weakness—keeping them from perishing utterly in despair. Tractates on the Gospel of John 52.2.[3]

[1]NPNF 1 14:249**. [2]Jn 12:26. [3]NPNF 1 7:287**.

Christ's Human Nature Had to Feel What We Feel. Cyril of Alexandria: Only the death of the Savior could bring an end to death, and it is the same for each of the other sufferings of the flesh too. Unless he had felt dread, human nature could not have become free from dread. Unless he had experienced grief, there could have never been any deliverance from grief. Unless he had been troubled and alarmed, there would have been no escape from these feelings. Every one of the emotions to which human nature is liable can be found in Christ. The emotions of his flesh were aroused, not that they might gain the upper hand, as indeed they do in us, but in order that when aroused they might be thoroughly subdued by the power of the Word dwelling in the flesh, human nature as a whole thus undergoing a change for the better. Commentary on the Gospel of John 8.[4]

Jesus Struggles with His Fear. Chrysostom: Although my trouble urges me to say, "Save me," yet I say the opposite, "Glorify your name," that is, "From now on, lead me to your cross." Here he definitely shows his humanity and a nature unwilling to die that is clinging to this present life. It proves that he was not exempt from human feelings. To have a desire for this present life is not necessarily wrong, though, any more than it is to be hungry or to want to sleep. Christ indeed had a body free from sin, and yet it was not free from the natural wants of the body; otherwise it would not have been a body. Homilies on the Gospel of John 67.1.[5]

Jesus Teaches by Example Whose Will We Should Prefer. Augustine: He also teaches you here on whom to call, in whom to hope, and whose sure and divine will you should prefer over your own will which is human and weak. Do not imagine that he has lost any of his exalted position in wanting you to rise out of the depths of your own ruin. . . . He assumed human infirmity in order to teach us, when saddened and troubled, to say, "Nevertheless, Father, not as I will but as you will."[6] For when the will of God is preferred to our own, this is how humanity is turned from the human to the divine. Tractates on the Gospel of John 52.3.[7]

12:28 *Father, Glorify Your Name*

The Name Glorified in the Crucifixion and Resurrection. Cyril of Alexandria: Whether the Gospel has "glorify your Son" or "glorify your name" makes no difference to the interpretation of its precise meaning.[8] Christ, however, despising death and the shame that comes from suffering, focused only on the achievements resulting from the suffering. And immediately seeing the death of all of us departing from our midst as a result of the death of his own flesh, and the power of decay about to be completely destroyed and human nature already formed anew in anticipation of newness of life,[9] he all but says to God the Father something along the following lines: "The body, O Father, shrinks from suffering and is afraid of a death that violates nature. Indeed, it seems scarcely endurable that he who is enthroned with you and has power over all things should be subjected to such outrageous treatment. But since I have come for this purpose, glorify your Son, that is, do not stop him from going to his death, but give your consent to your offspring for the good of all." The Evangelist even calls the cross glory elsewhere.[10] . . . It is clear that in this passage, "glorified" means "crucified." "Glory" is equivalent to "the cross." In fact, his acceptance of suffering for the good of others is a sign of extraordinary compas-

[4]LF 48:154**. See also Athanasius *Against the Arians* 3.26, where he includes this passage in a list of passages the Arians cite as showing Jesus' inferiority to the Father. He refutes the charge by showing how these pertain to his humanity, not his divinity. [5]NPNF 1 14:249**. [6]Mt 26:39. [7]NPNF 1 7:288**. [8]Cyril is aware that there are two different readings of Jn 12:28. The more authentic reading is "glorify your name." A number of manuscripts, including the one used by Cyril, read "glorify your Son," probably through the influence of Jn 17:1. Most modern commentators tend to agree with Cyril that the two readings amount to the same thing, since the Father and Son are one. [9]Rom 6:4. [10]See Jn 7:39.

sion and the highest kind of glory. The glorification of the Son also took place in another way. Through his victory over death we recognize him to be life and the Son of the living God. The Father is glorified then when he is shown to have such a Son begotten from himself and with the same attributes as himself. COMMENTARY ON THE GOSPEL OF JOHN 8.[11]

JESUS CHOOSES THE FATHER'S GLORY. CHRYSOSTOM: He teaches us here that if we ever are in agony and dread, we should not shrink back from what is set before us. . . . He shows us that he is dying for the truth, calling the action "glory to God." And this is indeed how things happened after the crucifixion. The world was about to be converted and to acknowledge the name of God. HOMILIES ON THE GOSPEL OF JOHN 67.2.[12]

THE VOICE CONFIRMS CHRIST'S DIVINITY. APOLLINARIS OF LAODICEA: It was not the utterance in the voice of the Father to the Son, since divinity is beyond all voice, but it was sent from heaven from the face of the Father to the Son as a sound for human beings to hear, in order that those who heard it might contemplate Christ all the more and come to know his divinity beyond his humanity. Glory is not added to the Father, since he has always had it, but it is added in so far as it radiates and is made known so that human beings are aware of it. Likewise, one must not conclude that the Son would be glorified from a state of disgrace, but rather he is glorified in so far as he who had formerly been hidden was made manifest in the flesh to the eyes of people. Moreover, it was not so much the voice that captivated the ears of those present, but rather how it took place that another glorified him. There was an established teaching among them from the fathers that utterances that were heard could not be borne directly from the mouth of God, since also Moses and all the rest who had spoken of the words they had heard from God, wrote down for humanity, while also saying that the manner of the discourse was that of an angel.[13] If then we also posit that it was an angel who emitted the voice, it would be good that the Father's voice, which was spoken from above to people, be heard through an angel. Jesus answered and said, "This voice did not take place for my sake." He who knew the Father and the Father's matters did not need anything. Thus he does not allow us to think little of him at all or to regard him as one would only be regarded as a prophet. Rather, this helps us to know who he was in relation to God. See whether or not "glorify your name" is the same as imposing on the Savior the name of God, since he is the Word of God. So also the "name" is that of the Father, but "name" does not refer to that which is composed of syllables or uttered with human voices, but rather whatever reveals the nature of the Father. One can understand the "name of God" also in the same way as well as the phrase in the psalms: "I will proclaim your name to my brothers."[14] How else can one understand that the name of God can be told? FRAGMENTS ON JOHN 84.[15]

THE MANY INSTANCES OF GLORIFICATION. AUGUSTINE: "I have both glorified it," before I created the world, "and I will glorify it again," when he shall rise from the dead and ascend into heaven. It may also be otherwise understood. "I have both glorified it" could be understood to refer to when he was born of the Virgin; when he exercised miraculous powers; when the magi, guided by a star in the heavens, bowed in adoration before him; when he was recognized by saints filled with the Holy Spirit. It could further refer to when he was openly proclaimed by the descent of the Spirit in the form of a dove and pointed out by the voice that sounded from heaven; when he was transfigured on the mount; when he performed many miracles, cured and cleansed multitudes, fed so vast a number with a very few loaves, commanded the winds and the waves, and to when he raised the dead. "And I

[11]*COA* 120-21*. [12]NPNF 1 14:249**. [13]See Acts 7:53; Gal 3:19. [14]Ps 22:23 (21:23 LXX). [15]*JKGK* 34-35.

will glorify it again" could refer to when he would rise from the dead, when death would no longer have dominion over him. It can also refer to when he would be exalted over the heavens as God and to when his glory would extend over all the earth. Tractates on the Gospel of John 52.4.[16]

12:29 *Thunder or Angels*

God Does Not Speak with the Voice of the Body. Ambrose: How does God speak? Is it with the voice of the body? Not at all. He utters oracular words with a voice that is far more significant than is the voice of the body. The prophets heard this voice. It is heard by the faithful, but the wicked do not comprehend it. And so, we find the Evangelist in the Gospel listening to the voice of the Father speaking: "I have glorified it and will glorify it again." But the Jews did not listen, which is why they said, "It has thundered." . . . Here is an occasion when he was heard speaking, whereas to some people he did not speak. On Paradise 14.69.[17]

When Angels Speak. Gregory the Great: When God speaks audibly, as he does here, but no visible appearance is seen, he speaks through the medium of a rational creature, that is, by the voice of an angel. Morals on the Book of Job 28.1.4.[18]

12:30 *The Voice for the Crowd*

God Is to Be Worshiped. Hilary of Poitiers: We remember, indeed, that a voice was sometimes uttered from heaven for us so that the power of the Father's words might confirm for us the mystery of the Son. . . . But the divine nature can dispense with the various combinations necessary for human functions, the motion of the tongue, the adjustment of the mouth, the forcing of the breath and the vibration of the air. God is a simple being: we must understand him by devotion and confess him by reverence. He is to be worshiped, not pursued by our senses, for a conditioned and weak nature cannot grasp with the guesses of its imagination the mystery of an infinite and omnipotent nature. On the Trinity 9.72.[19]

12:31 *The Judgment of the Ruler of This World*

The World Is Judged in and Through Christ. Theodore of Mopsuestia: What happens, [Jesus says,] now takes place on behalf of the world. For the whole world is judged in me now. You see, the first man, having been condemned to death on account of disobedience, became subject to the devil. Likewise all after him, becoming evil, brought on themselves the devil to be an exceedingly heavy tyrant over them, and because of this they were even more impious, making the kingdom of death worse for themselves. Therefore, because no one was able to wage war against it, Christ, being God, able to do everything, gave himself up on behalf of all people, the ones of old and those who are living now.

The world, therefore, is judged in me and through me. For, having committed no sin but having accomplished every kind of virtue and in no way found worthy of death, I accept death unjustly, so that in this way I may make my case against the devil, the one who himself killed me and was condemned. Having been freed from the bonds of death, I will rise, but I will also raise with me the common race of humanity by the case I make, and all will be acquitted of the verdict. He, on the other hand, who wickedly controlled the people in this life will be deposed from power. And the bonds of death, with which he surrounded people and was easily controlling them, will be taken away. These are the same bonds that caused them to sin all the more, as the devil attained a greater mastery over them. Commentary on the Gospel of John, Fragment 109.12.31.[20]

[16]NPNF 1 7:288*; CCL 36:447. [17]FC 42:347. [18]LF 23:264**; CCL 143B:1397. [19]NPNF 2 9:180*; CCL 62A:452-53. [20]ECS 7:102*.

Removing the Arrogance of the Devil. Ammonius: As if in a court of law, it is said to the devil, "Granted, you have killed everyone else in the human race because they were sinners. But why did you kill the Lord?" The time of sojourning on earth is the "judgment of the world," since Christ is about to justify humanity and to remove the arrogance of the devil. The judgment he speaks of here then is not the condemnation of the human race. Rather, Christ's death justifies all humanity against the devil, who is the one who is under judgment because he had wronged the world. Fragments on John 419.[21]

Not Reigning from Within, Laying Siege Without. Augustine: The judgment that is looked for in the end will be the judging of the living and the dead, the awarding of eternal rewards and punishment. But what kind of judgment, then, [takes place] now? . . . There is a judgment spoken of [now] that is not condemnation but discernment. . . . This is what he calls judgment here, that is, this righteous separation, this expulsion of the devil from Christ's own redeemed. . . . The Lord, therefore, was foretelling what he already knew, that after his own passion and glorification, many nations throughout the whole world, in whose hearts the devil lived as an inmate, would become believers, and the devil when thus renounced by faith would be cast out.

But someone might ask: Wasn't the devil cast out of the hearts of the patriarchs and prophets and the righteous people of old? Certainly he was. How then can it be said that now he shall be cast out? Then it was done in the case of a few individuals, but now it is foretold that it will take place rapidly and among many people and mighty nations. . . . But someone might further ask: Since the devil is cast out of the hearts of believers, does he now stop tempting the faithful? No, he has not stopped tempting. But it is one thing to reign within and another to lay siege from without. Tractates on the Gospel of John 52.6-9.[22]

12:32 *Lifted Up and Drawing All*

The Lifting Up Is His Glorification. Cyril of Alexandria: He keeps the mystery invisible to those intent on killing him, for they were not worthy to learn it. Nevertheless, he allowed those who were wiser to understand that he would suffer because of all and on behalf of all. And it is probably even more the case that anyone might take it in this way, and very appropriately, that is, that the death on the cross was an exaltation that is always associated in our thoughts with honor and glory. For on this account too Christ is glorified, because the benefits he procured for humanity thereby are many. Commentary on the Gospel of John 8.[23]

Christ Sums Up All Things in Himself. Irenaeus: He took up humanity into himself, the invisible becoming visible, the incomprehensible being made comprehensible, the impassible becoming capable of suffering and the Word being made human, thus summing up all things in himself: so that as in supercelestial, spiritual and invisible things, the Word of God is supreme, so also in things visible and corporeal he might possess the supremacy, and, taking to himself the preeminence, as well as constituting himself head of the church, he might draw all things to himself at the proper time.[24] Against Heresies 3.16.6.[25]

Only on a Cross Does One Die with Hands Spread Out. Athanasius: For it is only on the cross that a man dies with his hands spread out. And so it was fitting for the Lord to bear this also and to spread out his hands, that with the one he might draw the ancient people and with the other those from the Gentiles and unite both in himself. For this is what he himself has said, signifying by what manner of death he

[21]*JKGK* 301. [22]NPNF 1 7:288-89**; CCL 36:448-49. [23]LF 48:156-57**. [24]Christ as the "summing up" of all things was an important contribution by Irenaeus to subsequent theology on the meaning of the incarnation. [25]SC 34:292; ANF 1:443*. See also *Against Heresies* 4.2.7.

was to ransom all: "I, when I am lifted up," he says, "shall draw all unto me." On the Incarnation 25.3-4.[26]

12:34 *The Son of Man Lifted Up?*

They Understand "Lifted Up." Chrysostom: And so we see that they understood many of the things that he spoke in parables. . . . As he had talked about death earlier, they saw now what was meant by his being lifted up. Homilies on the Gospel of John 68.1.[27]

A Disturbed Conscience Asks. Augustine: Or they interpreted the word by their own intended act. It was not wisdom imparted but conscience disturbed that disclosed its meaning to them. Tractates on the Gospel of John 52.12.[28]

12:35 *While You Have the Light*

Living Enslaved to the Body. Gregory of Nyssa: The one who is stupid looks downward and hands his soul over to pleasures of the body, as cattle to pasture, living only for the stomach and the organs nearby, being alienated from the life of God. He is a stranger to the promise of the covenants, considering nothing else to be good than pleasing the body. This one, and everyone like him, is the one making his way "in darkness," as the Scripture says. On Virginity 4.[29]

Christ Is the Light the Darkness Cannot Overcome. Ambrose: [In the] form of a servant the fullness of true light was there. And when the form emptied itself, there was the light. Then he said, "Walk while you have the light." Even when he was in death, he was not in the shadow. . . . The true light of wisdom shone there as well. It illumined hell but was not shut up in hell. On the Sacrament of the Incarnation of Our Lord 5.41.[30]

We Will See the Light Again. Chrysostom: He signifies that his death is a transition,[31] for the light of the sun is not destroyed, but having withdrawn for a while appears again. Then he says, "While you have the light," but he does not say of what time he is talking about here. Is he speaking of the whole present life or of the time before the cross? I think both, for because of his ineffable love of humankind many even after the cross believed. He speaks these things to press them on to the faith. Homilies on the Gospel of John 68.1.[32]

12:36a *Believe in the Light and Become Sons of Light*

The Son's Radiance Illumines Us. Origen: Let us see what idea we are to form from the language of Paul regarding Christ where he says that he is the "brightness of the glory of God and the representation of his being."[33] According to John, "God is light." The only-begotten Son, therefore, is the glory of this light, proceeding inseparably from God himself, just as brightness proceeds from light and illuminates the whole creation. . . . Through this brightness, human beings understand and experience what light itself is. And this splendor presents itself gently and softly to the frail and weak eyes of mortals and gradually trains and accustoms them, as it were, to bear the brightness of the light. It removes from them every hindrance and obstruction to their vision, according to the Lord's own command to cast out the beam from your own eye.[34] In this way, it renders them capable of enduring the splendor of the light and becomes, in this respect, also a kind of mediator between human beings and the light. On First Principles 1.2.7.[35]

Jesus Begets Children Too. Chrysostom: He tells them to become sons of light, that is, become my children. Yet in the beginning the

---

[26]NPNF 2 4:49-50*. [27]NPNF 1 14:251**. [28]NPNF 1 7:290**; CCL 36:451. [29]FC 58:24-25. [30]CSEL 79:244; FC 44:234*. [31]Gk *metastasis*. [32]NPNF 1 14:251**. [33]Heb 1:3. [34]Lk 6:42. [35]ANF 4:248*.

Evangelist says these "were born, not of blood, nor of the will of the flesh, but of God,"[36] that is, of the Father, while here Christ himself is said to beget them so that you may understand that the operation of the Father and the Son is One. Homilies on the Gospel of John 68.1.[37]

12:36b *Jesus Withdraws and Hides*

Steer Clear of Rage. Chrysostom: Why does he now "hide himself"? They did not take up stones against him, nor did they blaspheme him in any way as before. Why then did he hide himself? Walking in people's hearts, he knew that their wrath was fierce, although they said nothing. He knew their wrath was boiling and murderous and did not wait until it broke into action, but rather he hid himself to mitigate their ill will. Homilies on the Gospel of John 68.1.[38]

Christ Withdraws. Cyril of Alexandria: Jesus withdraws with a set purpose, his passion being close at hand, showing that it was not his will to be put to death by the Jews. Nevertheless, he willingly yielded himself up to suffer, giving himself as a ransom for our life and accepting death, which is cause for sadness. But he ends up changing sorrow into gladness. Commentary on the Gospel of John 8.[39]

[36]Jn 1:13. [37]NPNF 1 14:251*. [38]NPNF 1 14:251*. [39]LF 48:159**.

12:37-43 THE CULMINATION OF THE JEWISH LEADERS' UNBELIEF

[37]Though he had done so many signs before them, yet they did not believe in him; [38]it was that the word spoken by the prophet Isaiah might be fulfilled:
"Lord, who has believed our report,
and to whom has the arm of the Lord been revealed?"
[39]Therefore they could not believe. For Isaiah again said,
[40]"He has blinded their eyes and hardened their heart,
lest they should see with their eyes and perceive with their heart,
and turn for me to heal them."
[41]Isaiah said this because he saw his glory and spoke of him. [42]Nevertheless many even of the authorities believed in him, but for fear of the Pharisees they did not confess it, lest they should be put out of the synagogue: [43]for they loved the praise of men more than the praise of God.

Overview: Isaiah had foretold the glory of Christ and the opposition of the Jews (Eusebius, Theodore), who he said were incurable in their unbelief (Chrysostom). More specifically, the arm of the Lord, of which Isaiah spoke, is the Son of God by whom all things were made (Augustine). But is God, then, the cause of their unbelief since he has blinded them (Augustine)? Or is it rather that because they willed not to believe, they could not believe (Chrysostom)? It is true that when God blinds and hardens, he does so in righteousness by withdrawing his help through a judgment that is hidden (AUGUSTINE). It is also true that Israel had blinded itself in its pride (AUGUSTINE), and that God also allows an evil people to be blinded by the devil (TERTULLIAN, CYRIL). When the prophet Isaiah saw the Lord sitting on his Father's throne in divine glory, he first foretold his coming and then how his knowledge and praise would be over all the earth (EUSEBIUS). Those who came to believe in Jesus did indeed grow in faith, which Jesus seeks to confirm in his words of deference to the Father that follow (THEODORE). But the love of human praise in these leaders made them slaves to human opinion (CHRYSOSTOM).

12:37 *The Leaders Did Not Believe in Jesus*

THE OPPOSITION OF THE JEWS. EUSEBIUS OF CAESAREA: Here he expressly foretells the opposition of the Jews to him and how they will see him and not understand who he is. He foretells how they will hear him speaking and teaching them but will be quite unable to grasp who it is that speaks with them or the new teaching he offers them. And John the Evangelist witnesses to the fulfillment of these words referring to our Savior where he says, "Though he had done so many signs before them, yet they believed not on him, that Isaiah the prophet's words might be fulfilled which he spoke, 'Lord, who has believed our report, and to whom has the arm of the Lord been revealed?' Therefore they were not able to believe, because again Isaiah said, 'He has blinded their eyes and hardened their heart, so that they should not see with their eyes, and understand with their heart and be converted, and I should heal them.'[1] Isaiah said these things when he saw his glory and bore witness of him." Thus the Evangelist most certainly referred the theophany in Isaiah to Christ and to the Jews who did not receive the Lord that was seen by the prophet, according to the prediction about him. PROOF OF THE GOSPEL 7.1.[2]

12:38 *The Prophecy of Isaiah Fulfilled*

ISAIAH SAW THE GLORY. THEODORE OF MOPSUESTIA: What did he see? In the spiritual vision, in the revelation of divine nature, which is incomprehensible, Isaiah saw the glory that, since it is common to the Father, the Son and the Holy Spirit, Scripture cannot establish precisely whether it is the glory of the Son or the Holy Spirit, and therefore neither the Evangelist nor the apostle[3] are in contradiction by saying that it is the glory of the Son or of the Holy Spirit. COMMENTARY ON JOHN 12.38-41.[4]

ISAIAH PROPHESIED THEY WERE INCURABLE. CHRYSOSTOM: Here again observe that the words "because" and "spoke" refer not to the cause of their unbelief but to the event. For it was not "because" Isaiah spoke that they did not believe. Rather, it was because they were not about to believe, which is why [Isaiah] spoke. Why then doesn't the Evangelist express it this way instead of making the unbelief proceed from the prophecy, not the prophecy from the unbelief? And further on he puts this very thing more emphatically, saying, "Therefore they could not believe, because Isaiah had said." He wants to establish by many proofs the unerring truth of Scripture, and that what Isaiah foretold happened in no other way than what he said would happen. For in case anyone should say, "Why did Christ come? Didn't he know that they would not listen to him?" he introduces the prophets, who knew this also. But he came that they might have no excuse for their sin. For what the prophet foretold, he foretold that it would certainly happen. If they were not most certainly going to happen, he could not have foretold them. And they were certainly going to happen because these people were incurable. HOMILIES ON THE GOSPEL OF JOHN 68.2.[5]

[1]See Is 6:10. [2]POG 2:51-52*. [3]Acts 28:25-26. [4]CSCO 4 3:248. [5]NPNF 1 14:252**.

The Arm of the Lord Is the Son of God. Augustine: It is evident here that the arm of the Lord is the Son of God himself. Not that the Father has a human fleshly form. He is called the arm of the Lord because all things were made by him. . . . If someone had power like this so that, without any motion of his body, what he said was then done, the word of that person would be his arm. . . . There is no ground here to justify, however, the error of those who say that the Godhead is one person only, because the Son is the arm of the Father, and a person and his arm are not two persons, but one. These people do not understand that the most common things are required to be explained often by applying language to them taken from other things in which there happens to be a likeness. . . . But some mutter and ask, What fault was it of the Jews if it was necessary that the sayings of Isaiah should be fulfilled when he said, "Lord, who has believed our report and to whom has the arm of the Lord been revealed?"[6] We answer that God, foreseeing the future, predicted by the prophet the unbelief of the Jews, but did not cause it. God does not compel people to sin, because he knows they will sin. He foreknows their sins, not his own. . . . The Jews committed the sin that he who knows all things foretold they would commit. Tractates on the Gospel of John 53.2-4.[7]

12:39 *Therefore They Could Not Believe*

Because They Would Not, They Cannot Believe. Chrysostom: And if, "on account of this, they could not [believe]"[8] is put instead of "they were not willing [to believe]," do not be surprised. . . . He does not say that it is the doing of virtue that is impossible for them, but that because they *would* not practice virtue therefore they *cannot* practice it. And by what he says, the Evangelist means that it was impossible for the prophet to lie. And yet, this was not the reason why it was impossible for them to believe. Homilies on the Gospel of John 68.2.[9]

Is God the Cause of Unbelief? Augustine: But the words of the Gospel also that follow are still more pressing and start a question of more profound import. For he goes on to say, "Therefore they could not believe, because Isaiah said again, 'He has blinded their eyes and hardened their heart so that they should not see with their eyes or understand with their heart and be converted, and I should heal them.'" For it is almost as if he said, If they could not believe, what sin is it in a person not to do what he cannot do? And if they sinned in not believing, then they had the power to believe and did not use it. If, then, they had the power, how does the Gospel say, "Therefore they could not believe, because Isaiah said again, 'he has blinded their eyes and hardened their heart,'" so that (and this is very important) to God himself is referred the cause of their not believing, inasmuch as it is he who "has blinded their eyes and hardened their heart"? Tractates on the Gospel of John 53.5.[10]

Mercy and Righteousness. Augustine: But the prophet, you say, assigns another cause than that of their will. What cause does the prophet assign? That "God has given them the spirit of remorse, eyes that they should not see, and ears that they should not hear. And has blinded their eyes and hardened their heart." This also, I reply, their will deserved. For God thus blinds and hardens, simply by letting alone and withdrawing his aid. And God can do this by a judgment that is hidden, although not by one that is unrighteous. This is a doctrine that the piety of the God-fearing ought to preserve unshaken and inviolable in all its integrity: even as the apostle, when treating of the same intricate question, says, "What shall we say then? Is there unrighteousness with God? God forbid."[11] If, then, we must be far from thinking that there is unrighteousness with God, this only can it be,

[6]Is 53:1. [7]NPNF 1 7:291-92**; CCL 36:452-53. [8]Gk *dia touto ouk ēdynanto pisteuein.* [9]NPNF 1 14:252**. [10]NPNF 1 7:292*; CCL 36:454. [11]Rom 9:14.

that, when he gives his aid, he acts mercifully. And when he withholds it, he acts righteously. For in all he does, he does not act rashly but in accordance with judgment. Tractates on the Gospel of John 53.6.[12]

Blinded by Pride. Augustine: It is no wonder, then, that they could not believe when such was their pride of will, that, being ignorant of the righteousness of God, they wished to establish their own [righteousness]. As the apostle says of them, "They have not submitted themselves to the righteousness of God."[13] For it was not by faith, but as it were by works, that they were puffed up. And blinded by this very self-elation, they stumbled against the stone of stumbling. And so it is said, "They could not," by which we are to understand that they would not. This is the same as when it was said of the Lord our God, "If we do not believe, yet he remains faithful, he cannot deny himself."[14] It is said of the Omnipotent, "He cannot." And so, just as it is a commendation of the divine will that the Lord "cannot deny himself," that they "could not believe" is a fault chargeable against the will of humankind.

See, I also say, that those who have such lofty ideas of themselves as to suppose that so much must be attributed to the powers of their own will, that they deny their need of the divine assistance in order to attain to a righteous life, cannot believe on Christ. For the mere syllables of Christ's name and the Christian sacraments are of no profit where faith in Christ is itself resisted. For faith in Christ is to believe in him that justifies the ungodly.[15] It means to believe in the Mediator, without whose intervention we cannot be reconciled to God. It means to believe in the Savior who came to seek and to save that which was lost,[16] to believe in him who said, "Without me you can do nothing."[17] Because, then—being ignorant of that righteousness of God that justifies the ungodly—he wishes to set up his own [righteousness] to satisfy the minds of the proud, such a person cannot believe on Christ. And so, those Jews "could not believe" [so to speak,] not that people cannot be changed for the better. But so long as their ideas run in such a direction, they cannot believe. And so they are blinded and hardened. For, denying the need of divine assistance, they are not assisted. God foreknew this regarding these Jews who were blinded and hardened, and the prophet by his Spirit foretold it. Tractates on the Gospel of John 53.9-10.[18]

12:40 *Blinded Eyes and Hardened Hearts*

We Desert God and Cause Our Own Destruction. Chrysostom: Just as the sun blinds the eyes of the weak . . . this is also what happens to those who do not listen to the words of God. As so, in the case of Pharaoh, he is said to have hardened his heart,[19] and so it is with those who are at all contentious against the words of God. This is a peculiar mode of speech of Scripture, as in, "He gave them over to a reprobate mind,"[20] . . . that is, he allowed or permitted them to go. For the writer does not here introduce God as himself doing these things but shows that they took place through the wickedness of others. For when we are abandoned by God, we are given up to the devil. . . . It is to terrify the hearer that the writer says "he hardens" and "he gave over." For to show that he does not give us over or even leave us unless we want him to, listen to what he says, "Isn't it your iniquities that separate me and you."[21] . . . Isaiah also says, "I came, and there was no one; I called, and there was none who listened."[22] He says these things, showing that we begin the desertion and become the causes of our destruction. For God not only desires *not* to leave or to punish us, but even when he punishes, he does it unwillingly. "I desire not," he says, "the death of the sinner but that he should turn and live."[23] . . . Knowing this, let us do everything we can so as not to remove ourselves from God. Let

[12]NPNF 1 7:293*; CCL 36:454-55. [13]Rom 10:3. [14]2 Tim 2:13. [15]See Rom 4:5. [16]See Lk 19:10. [17]Jn 15:5. [18]NPNF 1 7:294*; CCL 36:456. [19]See Ex 10:1. [20]Rom 1:28. [21]Is 59:2 LXX. He also cites Ps 73:27 (72:27 LXX); Hos 4:6 LXX; Lk 13:34. [22]Is 50:2 LXX. [23]Ezek 18:32 LXX.

us instead be concerned about the care of our souls and about our love toward one another. Homilies on the Gospel of John 68.2-3.[24]

Blinded by the Devil. Cyril of Alexandria: In this instance the prophet Isaiah is not quoted as saying that "God" blinded the people."[25] However, it is likely that someone else did the blinding in order that the Jews should not convert and find healing. But, even though we should accept the supposition that God blinded them, it must be understood that God allowed them to suffer blinding at the hands of the devil as a result of their evil character. Commentary on the Gospel of John 8.[26]

12:41 *Isaiah Saw God's Glory*

The Prophet's Witness of God's Glory. Eusebius of Caesarea: In approaching the account of his coming to humanity, the prophecy before us tells first of his divine kingdom, in which it says that the prophet saw him sitting on a throne high and exalted. This is that throne that is mentioned in the psalm of the Beloved.[27] . . . John the Evangelist supports my interpretation of this passage, when he quotes the words of Isaiah, where it is said, "For this people's heart has become fat, and their ears are dull of hearing, and they have closed their eyes,"[28] referring them to Christ, saying, "This is what Isaiah said when he saw his glory and bore witness of him." The prophet then seeing our Savior sitting on his Father's throne in the divine and glorious kingdom, and moved by the Holy Spirit and being about to describe next his coming among humanity and his birth of a Virgin, foretells that his knowledge and praise would be over all the earth. Proof of the Gospel 7.1.[29]

12:42 *Many Believed*

Jesus Seeks to Confirm Their Faith. Theodore of Mopsuestia: Then the Evangelist said that many among the authorities who believed in him hid their opinion about him because of the Pharisees, because they feared they might lose their privileges and because they valued the glory of people more than the glory of God. What did our Lord say? While some believed, others did not even accept the accomplished miracles, others only came to know the truth through the miracles but hid their opinion because of their fear of the Pharisees as they pursued human glory. Commentary on John 5.12.44.[30]

12:43 *Praise of People*

Not Rulers but Slaves to Praise. Chrysostom: See how these men were broken off from the faith through their love of honor. It says that many of the chief rulers believed on him, "but because of the Pharisees they did not confess him lest they should be put out of the synagogue." . . . So then, they were not really rulers at all but slaves subject to the utmost slavery [of human opinion]. Homilies on the Gospel of John 69.1.[31]

---

[24]NPNF 1 14:253**. [25]See Is 6:9. [26]LF 48:161**. [27]Ps 110:1 (109:1 LXX). [28]Is 6:10 (LXX). [29]POG 2:49-50*. [30]CSCO 4 3:248-49. [31]NPNF 1 14:254**.

12:44-50 Belief in the Son Is Belief in the Father

[44]And Jesus cried out and said, "He who believes in me, believes not in me but in him who sent me. [45]And he who sees me sees him who sent me. [46]I have come as light into the world, that whoever believes in me may not remain in darkness. [47]If any one hears my sayings and does not keep them, I do not judge him; for I did not come to judge the world but to save the world. [48]He who rejects me and does not receive my sayings has a judge; the word that I have spoken will be his judge on the last day. [49]For I have not spoken on my own authority; the Father who sent me has himself given me commandment what to say and what to speak. [50]And I know that his commandment is eternal life. What I say, therefore, I say as the Father has bidden me."

Overview: It is through the Son that one believes in the Father (Tertullian), since ignorance of the Son is ignorance of the Father (Ambrose). Christ, who is begotten of the Father, calls for faith in himself but refers the honor to the one who begat him (Augustine). He is seeking to move them slowly from contemplating him, who they can see, to the Father with whom he shares his essence in the Godhead (Cyril), but who they cannot see, at least not in a physical sense (Chrysostom). He distinguishes himself from the Father as being the one sent even as he in the next sentence identifies himself with the Father (Theodore). Contrast such an identification with that of Jesus and the apostles who also were sent—but the apostles neither could nor would identify themselves with Jesus in this way because the difference is so great (Augustine). But perhaps Jesus is also putting forth in a mystical sense a distinction between believing and beholding Christ (Origen).

Christ casts the brilliant beams of his divinity into our hearts to bring us light (Origen). And so, to withdraw from Christ is to enter into darkness (Augustine). He says here that he did not come into the world to judge, so why do we (Ambrose)? Those who refuse to hear Jesus and accept saving faith condemn themselves and cannot blame God for such judgment (Cyril, Chrysostom). The Word ultimately will serve as judge (Augustine) revealing the word and will of his Father to us (Cyril, Basil). The Father's goal is in concert with the Son's, that is, the salvation of everyone (Theodore). But the Son is not awaiting orders, so to speak, from the Father as if he was in need of instruction, since his own will is connected in indissoluble union with the Father (Basil). He does demonstrate his humility and his oneness with the Father in doing what his Father commands (Chrysostom) since he is, in effect, the Father's commandment (Augustine).

12:44 *Belief in the Sender*

Son and Father Affirm Each Other Mutually. Tertullian: It is through the Son that one believes in the Father, while the Father also is the authority from which springs belief in the Son. Against Praxeas 23.8.[1]

Ignorance of the Son Is Ignorance of the Father. Ambrose: The one who confesses the Father believes on the Son. For the one who does not know the Son does not know the Father. For everyone that denies the Son does not have the Father, but the one who confesses the Son has

[1]CCL 2:1193; ANF 3:619*

both the Father and the Son.[2] What, then, is the meaning of "believes not in me"? It speaks not about what you can perceive in bodily form, nor merely on the man whom you see. For he has stated that we are to believe not merely on a man, but that you may believe that Jesus Christ himself is both God and man. This is why, for both reasons, he says, "I came not from myself."[3] And again: "I am the beginning, of which also I speak to you."[4] On the Christian Faith 5.10.119-20.[5]

Deferring Honor to the Begetter. Augustine: What is this we have just heard, brothers and sisters: the Lord saying, "Whoever believes in me does not believe in me, but in the one who sent me"? It is good for us to believe in Christ, especially since he himself also said quite plainly what you heard just now, that is, that he had come as light into the world, and that whoever believes in him will not walk in darkness but will have the light of life.

So it is good to believe in Christ. It is a great good to believe in Christ and a great evil not to believe in Christ. But because Christ the Son is whatever he is from the Father, while the Father is not from the Son but is the Father of the Son, that is why the Son does indeed call for faith in himself but refers the honor of it to his only-begetter. Sermon 140.1.[6]

12:45 *Whoever Sees Jesus Sees the Father*

From the Human to the Divine. Cyril of Alexandria: [Our Lord] gradually accustoms their minds to penetrate the depth of the mysteries concerning himself, [leading them] not to the human person but to that which was of the divine essence. He does this inasmuch as the Godhead is apprehended completely in the person of God the Father, for he has in himself the Son and the Spirit. With exceeding wisdom he carries them onward, . . . for he does not exclude himself from being believed on by us because he is God by nature and has shone forth from God the Father. But skillfully (as has been said) he handles the mind of the weak to mold them to godliness in order that you might understand him to say something like this: "When you believe on me—I who, for your sakes, am a man like yourselves, but who also am God by reason of my own nature and because of the Father from whom I exist—do not suppose that it is on a man you are setting your faith. For I am by nature God, notwithstanding that I appear like one of yourselves, and I have within myself him who begat me. Forasmuch therefore as I am consubstantial with him that has begotten me, your faith will assuredly pass on also to the Father himself." As we said therefore, the Lord, gradually trains them to something better and profitably interweaves the human with what is God-befitting. Commentary on the Gospel of John 8.[7]

Seeing God. Chrysostom: What then! Is God a body?[8] By no means. The "seeing" of which he here speaks is that of the mind. This demonstrates the consubstantiality. And what does it mean when he says "he that believes on me"? It is as though one should say, "He that takes water from the river does not take it from the river but from the spring that supplies the river." Homilies on the Gospel of John 69.1.[9]

A Great Difference and a Perfect Similarity. Theodore of Mopsuestia: [In verse 44], he said, "Whoever believes in me believes not in me but in him who sent me." He said this because they allege they were prosecuting him in order to avenge God. And so he says in effect, "I refer you to [the Father] because, you see, the one who believes in me is the one who comes to know the Father fully through me." That is why he said what he did there. On the other hand, "whoever sees me sees him who sent me" seems to contradict what had just been said. The statement in

[2] 1 Jn 2:23. [3] Jn 7:28. [4] Jn 8:25. [5] NPNF 2 10:299*; CSEL 78:261-62 (*On the Christian Faith* 5.10.120-21). [6] *WSA* 3 4:403; PL 38:773. [7] LF 48:162**. [8] Avoiding anthropomorphisms concerning God is a common theme in patristic commentary. [9] NPNF 1 14:254*.

[verse 44] shows the difference between Father and Son, while [verse 45] shows their perfect similarity. Because the first statement showed such great humility, however, he logically concluded the second in order to declare his similarity with the Father. Both statements, however, show that he never stood far apart from the Father. The first he said for the unbelievers. The second was to indicate how precise his likeness was to the Father's. COMMENTARY ON JOHN 5.12.45.[10]

APOSTLES ARE SEEN, BUT WE DO NOT BELIEVE IN THEM. AUGUSTINE: There is so little difference between me [i.e., the Son] and him who sent me [i.e., the Father] that he that sees me sees him. Certainly, Christ the Lord sent his apostles . . . yet none of them dared to say, "He who believes in me." . . . We believe an apostle, but we do not believe in an apostle, for it is not an apostle who justifies the ungodly. . . . An apostle might say, "He who receives me receives him who sent me," or "He who hears me hears him who sent me," for the Lord tells them so himself.[11] . . . For the master is honored in the servant and the father in the son. But then the father is as it were in the son, and the master as it were in the servant. But the Only Begotten could rightly say, "Believe on God, and believe on me,"[12] as what he also says here, "He who believes in me does not believe in me but on him that sent me." Here he does not deflect the believer's faith from himself but gives him a higher object than the form of a servant for that faith. TRACTATES ON THE GOSPEL OF JOHN 54.3.[13]

BELIEVING AND BEHOLDING. ORIGEN: Notice in the passage before us that there are two aspects about the Savior: first, believing in him, and second, what is above believing, that is, to behold (contemplate)[14] the Word and in beholding the Word to behold the Father. Believing occurs even among the multitude of those who come to religion.[15] But to behold the Word, and in him to regard the Father, does not pertain to all who believe but only to the pure in heart. This is how I understand "He who has seen me has seen the Father." For it is not the one who applies the power of vision lying in the eyes of the body to Jesus and his body who has seen his Father and God. And I think that time and training were needed in order to see Jesus, and seeing the Son to behold also the Father.[16] . . .

For one believing on the Son believes not on the Son but on God the Father of all. But one beholding the Word and Wisdom and Truth beholds not this alone but also the Father. And I think that it is in order to show the greatness of the mystery involved first in believing on the Son and secondly in beholding him that it is prefixed, "Jesus cried and said." For the mystical pronouncement about these things was indeed great. And the Evangelist makes clear elsewhere that it is possible to believe without beholding.[17] FRAGMENT 93 ON THE GOSPEL OF JOHN.[18]

12:46 *Faith Brings Us Out of Darkness*

THE TRUE LIGHT SHINES IN THE DARKNESS. ORIGEN: When the Savior of the world came, he made the true light shine. But they did not want to gaze on it, nor were they willing to walk by the radiance of his teaching. Consequently, darkness overtook them and demanded a penalty for the wickedness that had preoccupied them. And this [darkness] might be said to have reasonably blinded and hardened them. And, just as it follows that the one who has chosen to walk in the light also knows where he is going, so it follows that the one who has not chosen to walk in the light walks in darkness and travels wretchedly along the road of the blind. . . .

For just as the visible sun shoots out its bright beams in order to enlighten those who have ailing eyes, so also does the spiritual Sun, the Light that has no setting or evening, come to the world and

[10]CSCO 4 3:249. [11]Mt 10:40. [12]Jn 14:1. [13]CCL 36:460; NPNF 1 7:296-97**. [14]Gk *theorein*. [15]Gk *theosebeia*. [16]See Jn 14:9. [17]See Jn 8:31-32. [18]AEG 5:109-10*; GCS 10(4):556-57.

through his divine and ineffable miracles cast the brilliant gleam of his deity far and wide. Fragment 94 on the Gospel of John.[19]

To Withdraw from Christ Is Darkness. Augustine: He says in one place to his disciples, "You are the light of the world"[20] . . . but he did not say to them, "You have come as a light into the world, that whosoever believes on you should not abide in darkness." . . . All saints are lights, but they are illuminated by Christ through faith, and everyone that becomes separated from him will be enveloped in darkness. But that light that enlightens them cannot become separated from itself. For it is altogether beyond the reach of change. We believe, then, the light that has thus been lit is the prophet or apostle. But we believe him for this end, that we may not believe on that which is itself enlightened, but, with him, on that light that has given him light. Then we too may be enlightened, not by him, but along with him by the same light as he. And when he says, "That whoever believes on me may not abide in darkness," he makes it sufficiently clear that all have been found by him in a state of darkness. But so that they do not remain in the darkness in which they have been found, they ought to believe on that light that has come into the world, for that is how the world was created. Tractates on the Gospel of John 54.4.[21]

12:47 *Not Judging, but Saving*

He Does Not Judge, Do You? Ambrose: He judges not, and do you judge? He says that "whoever believes in me may not remain in darkness," that is, that if he is in darkness he may not remain that way but may amend his error, correct his fault and keep my commandments. For I have said, "I do not desire the death of the wicked, but their conversion."[22] I said above that he who believes on me is not judged, and I keep to this: "For I have not come to judge the world, but that the world may be saved through me."[23] I pardon willingly, I quickly forgive. "I will have mercy rather than sacrifice,"[24] because by sacrifice the just is rendered more acceptable, by mercy the sinner is redeemed. Concerning Repentance 1.12.54.[25]

Condemnation Is Self-Inflicted. Cyril of Alexandria: Those who refuse to hear Jesus and accept saving faith will condemn themselves, for he who came to illumine came not to judge but to save. Therefore, he who disobeys and subjects himself to the greatest miseries can only blame himself as justly punished. Commentary on the Gospel of John 8.[26]

12:48 *The Word as Judge*

The Word That Will Judge. Chrysostom: The word that I have just said shall be their accusers and deprive them of all excuses. The same word that I have spoken will be the word that will judge them. And what word is this? "That I have not spoken of myself, but the Father who sent me told me what I should say and what I should speak." All these things were said on their account so that they might have no pretense or excuse. Homilies on the Gospel of John 69.2.[27]

Jesus Is the Word Who Will Judge. Augustine: In the meantime, while they were waiting to know who this [judge] was, he went on to add, "The word that I have spoken, the same shall judge him at the last day." He makes it sufficiently clear that he himself will judge at the last day. For the word that he speaks is himself. He speaks himself, announces himself and sets himself as the gate where he enters as the Shepherd to his sheep.[28] We gather too from these words that those who have not heard will be judged differently from those who have heard and despised it. Tractates on the Gospel of John 54.6.[29]

[19]AEG 5:110-11*; GCS 10(4):557-58. [20]Mt 5:14. [21]NPNF 1 7:297**; CCL 36:460-61. [22]Ezek 33:11. [23]Jn 3:17. [24]Hos 6:6. [25]NPNF 2 10:338; SC 179:98-100. [26]LF 48:163-64**. [27]NPNF 1 14:255**. [28]See Jn 10:2. [29]NPNF 1 7:297**; CCL 36:461.

12:49 *Jesus Speaks by the Father's Authority*

Jesus Reveals the Will of God the Father. Cyril of Alexandria: Since Jesus was the living and personal[30] Word of God the Father, he is necessarily the medium of interpreting what is in the Father. Thus, by saying that he has received a commandment, Jesus means that he brings to light that which is, as it were, the set will and purpose of his own Father. Commentary on the Gospel of John 9.[31]

The Word Gives Knowledge of the Father. Basil the Great: Through all these words [Jesus] is guiding us to the knowledge of the Father and referring our wonder at all that is brought into existence to him, to the end that "through him" we may know the Father. On the Holy Spirit 8.19.[32]

Salvation of All Is the Goal of Father and Son. Theodore of Mopsuestia: We need to consider the purpose of the words. Indeed he means This is the purpose of my advent—salvation for all. You who do not believe will be condemned—but not by me because this is contrary to my passion, and it is not your condemnation I am after. Because of your [evil] mind you will be condemned by my own words which leave no excuse to the unbelievers on judgment day. These are the words that I spoke many times. In other words, I want nothing that is against the will of the Father, nor do I intend to establish a congregation for myself alone. I always led you all to the Father with my words by telling you that I was sent by him and that it was from him that I received the command to tell you the right words. Therefore I spoke to you words that were in agreement with his will. And this same thing I testify now to you: By those same words you will be condemned. Indeed you will not be able to come up with any excuses, as if you were defending the honor of God, because I always led you to him. Commentary on John 5.12.47-50.[33]

The Son Is Not Given Orders by the Father. Basil the Great: It is not because Jesus lacks deliberate purpose or initiative, nor is it because he has to wait for some prearranged signal, that he employs language of this kind. His purpose is to make plain that his own will is connected in indissoluble union with the Father. Let us not then understand that what he calls a "commandment" is a peremptory mandate delivered by organs of speech, and giving orders to the Son, as to a subordinate concerning what he ought to do. Let us rather, in a sense befitting the Godhead, perceive a transmission of will, like the reflection of an object in a mirror, passing without note of time from Father to Son. . . . Everything the Father has also belongs to the Son. The Son does not acquire it piecemeal. Rather, he has it all at once. Among people, the workman who has been thoroughly taught his craft through long training and experience is able to work for his own future, utilizing that training he has received. And are we to suppose that the wisdom of God, the Maker of all creation, he who is eternally perfect, who is wise without a teacher, the Power of God, "in whom are hidden all the treasures of wisdom and knowledge,"[34] needs piecemeal instruction to mark out the manner and measure of his operations? . . . If you consistently follow this line of reasoning, you will turn the Son into an eternal student who is never able to graduate since the Father's wisdom is infinite. On the Holy Spirit 8.20.[35]

12:50 *Just as the Father Has Told Me*

The Humility of Jesus. Chrysostom: Do you see the humility of the words? For he who has received a commandment is not his own master. Yet he says, "As the Father raises up the dead and enlivens them, even so the Son enlivens whom he will."[36] Does he have power then to enliven whomever he wants, and does he not have

[30]Or, hypostatic. [31]LF 48:170*. [32]NPNF 2 8:13*. [33]CSCO 4 3:251-52. [34]Col 2:3. [35]NPNF 2 8:14. [36]See Jn 5:21.

the power to say what he wants? What he intends then by the words is this: It is not possible that he [the Father] should speak one set of words and I should utter another. "And I know that his commandment is life everlasting." He said this to those who called him a deceiver and who asserted that he had come to do harm. However, when he says "I judge not," he shows that he is not the cause of their destruction. By this he all but plainly testifies (when he is about to remove himself from them and leave) that "I converse with you, speaking nothing on my own but everything as from the Father." Homilies on the Gospel of John 69.2.[37]

The Son Is the Commandment of the Father. Augustine: If life everlasting is the Son himself and the commandment is life everlasting, what is this but saying, "I am the commandment of the Father"? And in the same way in the following, "Whatever I speak therefore, even as the Father said to me, so I speak," we must not understand "said to me" as if words were spoken to the only Word or that the Word of God needed words from God. The Father spoke to the Son in the same way as he gave life to the Son. It was not that the Son was ignorant or did not [already] have life. Rather, it was simply because the Son was what he was. What, then, is meant by "as he said to me, so I speak" but that I am the Word who speaks. The Father is true, the Son is truth: the True begat the Truth. What then could he say to the Truth if the Truth was perfect from the beginning and no new truth could be added to him? That he spoke to the Truth then means that he begat the Truth. Tractates on the Gospel of John 54.8.[38]

[37]NPNF 1 14:255*. [38]NPNF 1 7:298**; CCL 36:462-63.

13:1-5 Jesus Begins to Wash the Disciples' Feet

[1]Now before the feast of the Passover, when Jesus knew that his hour had come to depart out of this world to the Father, having loved his own who were in the world, he loved them to the end. [2]And during supper, when the devil had already put it into the heart of Judas Iscariot, Simon's son, to betray him, [3]Jesus, knowing that the Father had given all things into his hands, and that he had come from God and was going to God, [4]rose from supper, laid aside his garments, and girded himself with a towel. [5]Then he poured water into a basin, and began to wash the disciples' feet, and to wipe them with the towel with which he was girded.

Overview: The passion narrative begins before the Passover feast (Theodore). The Passover was a type of Christ the Passover lamb sacrificed for us who delivers us from the bondage of sin (Augustine). Here our Lord prepares a blessed "passing over" for his disciples and the whole church when he intercedes for them in prayer (Leo). As he is about to depart from the world, he will leave his emptiness to which he subjected himself at his incarnation in order to return to the fullness of his Godhead (Origen). He leaves nothing left undone for those he loves (Chrysostom) who are left in the very world he is about to leave (Cyril). He loves them to the end in giving his own life (Bede), even as he himself is the end (Augustine).

The order of the washing, which normally would have been conducted before they sat down to eat, serves to signal a higher more spiritual washing that will occur (Origen). Judas is present since not even the prospect of table fellowship will stop him (Chrysostom). But it is questionable as to whether Jesus washed Judas's feet or not, since his betrayal shows he was not clothed with the full armor of God (Origen) as he slept the sleep of avarice (Ambrose). Nonetheless, Jesus was in control of the whole situation since everything had been given into his hands (Origen), including Judas (Augustine) and the salvation of the faithful (Chrysostom). Again, one should notice the washing which occurs after the meal, demonstrating a secondary washing was needed (Origen).

He who feeds everything under the heaven received sustenance himself as he reclined with the apostles as a master among servants (Severian). All of his actions are those of a servant, offering an example for us (Chrysostom). Jesus began to wash his disciples' feet as a servant would do, first laying aside the glory of his status as the Word, symbolized by the garment he laid aside (Origen). The Lord of the universe (Theophilus of Alexandria) then took up the servant's towel (Augustine), a towel of suffering (Bede), and began to wash his disciples' feet as only he could (Origen), cleansing their heels so they would not feel the serpent's bite (Ambrose).

The text tells us Jesus began to wash the disciples' feet, but that washing was not complete until he had cleansed them so that they might no longer be defiled (Origen). The Potter of the universe washes his disciples' feet of clay (Romanus), washing not only their feet but their entire body, which was sanctified, and death itself was washed away (Irenaeus). He humbled himself to teach us a humility that removes any contrast, division or dissension from human beings (Theodore). Feet that are consecrated in this way are not swift to shed blood or run to evil but instead run to the gospel (Gregory of Nazianzus).

13:1a *Before the Passover and Jesus' Departure from This World*

Beginning of the Passion Narrative. Theodore of Mopsuestia: From here the Evangelist passes to the story of the passion. Here also, insofar as is possible, he is careful in saying nothing that has already been related by the other [Evangelists], unless the course of the narrative obliges him [to do so], and it is impossible to construct an accurate order of events without reporting part of the facts already related by his colleagues. When he reports those things done and said by our Lord to his disciples, which we do not find to be mentioned by the others in their books, he wants to show that our Savior did not undergo his passion outside his knowledge and expectation but by his free will. Only when he wanted to did he taste death. . . . In the same way here, by writing, "Jesus knew that his hour had come to depart from this world and go to the Father," he means that he knew exactly the time of his passion and everything that would happen to him. Commentary on John 6.13.1.[1]

The True Passover Comes. Augustine: Pascha (Passover) is not, as some think, a Greek noun, but it is Hebrew, although there is a remarkable amount of agreement between the two languages over this noun. For inasmuch as the Greek word *paschein* means "to suffer," *Pascha* has been supposed to mean suffering, as if the noun derived its name from Christ's passion. But in its own language, that is, in Hebrew, *Pascha* means "Passover,"[2] because the Pascha was then celebrated for the first time by God's people when, in their flight from Egypt, they passed over the Red Sea.[3] And

[1]CSCO 4 3:252-53. [2]Lat *transitus*. [3]From what follows, Augustine surely meant to emphasize the angel of the Lord passing over the houses of the Israelites when killing the firstborn for Egypt. Perhaps we get a glimpse here of a preacher preaching without his notes.

now, that prophetic emblem is fulfilled in truth when Christ is led as a sheep to the slaughter,[4] that by his blood sprinkled on our doorposts, that is, by the sign of his cross marked on our foreheads, we may be delivered from the perdition awaiting this world, just as Israel was delivered from the bondage and destruction of the Egyptians. We perform a most salutary journey when we pass over from the devil to Christ and from this unstable world to his well-established kingdom.... This name, then, of pascha, which, as I have said, is in Latin called *transitus* ("pass over"), is interpreted, as it were, for us by the blessed Evangelist when he says, "Before the feast of pascha, when Jesus knew that his hour was come that he should *pass out of* this world to the Father." Here you see we have both *pascha* and passover. TRACTATES ON THE GOSPEL OF JOHN 55.1.[5]

A MYSTICAL PASSOVER. LEO THE GREAT: The very feast that by us is named Pascha among the Hebrews is called *Phase*,[6] that is, Passover, as the Evangelist attests, saying, "Before the feast of Pascha, Jesus, knowing that his hour was come when he should pass[7] out of this world unto the Father." But what kind of nature was it that he passed out of unless it was ours, since the Father was in the Son and the Son in the Father inseparably? But because the Word and the Flesh is one person, the assumed is not separated from the assuming nature, and the honor of being promoted is spoken of as accruing to him that promotes. This is what the apostle says in a passage we have already quoted, "Wherefore also God exalted him and gave him a name that is above every name."[8] Here, the exaltation of his assumed manhood is no doubt spoken of so that he (in whose sufferings the Godhead remains indivisible) is similarly coeternal in the glory of the Godhead. And to share in this unspeakable gift, the Lord himself was preparing a blessed "passing over" for his faithful ones, when on the very threshold of his passion he interceded not only for his apostles and disciples but also for the whole church, saying, "But not for these only I pray, but for those also who shall believe on me through their word, that they all may be one, as you also, Father, are in me, and I in you, that they also may be one in us."[9] SERMON 72.6.[10]

LEAVING HIS EMPTINESS BEHIND. ORIGEN: Surely this statement does not refer to the idea of a change of place with respect to the Father and the Son toward the one who loves Jesus' word, nor can it be understood in a spatial sense. Rather, the Word of God, by condescending to us and by being humbled, as it were, in regard to his own worth, when he is present with human beings, is said to change places from this world to the Father. The result is that we also see him in his perfection, returning from the emptying with which he emptied himself[11] alongside us, to his own fullness.[12] ON PRAYER 23.2.[13]

13:1b *He Loved His Own to the End*

JESUS LEAVES NOTHING LEFT UNDONE. CHRYSOSTOM: This was not his first inkling that his hour had come. He had known long before that he was going to depart. The Evangelist is most eloquent in calling his death a departure.... Being so near to leaving his disciples, he shows greater love for them. "Having loved his own which were in the world, he loved them to the end," means that he left nothing undone that one who greatly loved should do. Why then didn't he do this from the beginning? He reserved this for the end so that their love might be increased by it and to prepare them by this consolation for the terrible things that were coming. John calls them "his own" in the sense of personal attachment.... The word was used in another sense in the begin-

[4]Is 53:7. [5]NPNF 1 7:299**. See also *Sermon* 155.5 (*WSA* 3 5:87). [6]Lat *Phase id transitus dicitur*. See the Vulgate, Ex 12:11, *est enim Phase* (*id est transitus*) *Domini*. The form of the word is due to defective transliteration, the correct Hebrew form being *Pesach*, which is derived from a root that means to pass over or to overleap, and thus points back to the historical origin of the festival. [7]Gk *metabē*; Lat *transeat*. [8]Phil 2:9. [9]Jn 17:20-21. [10]NPNF 2 12:186**; CCL 138A: 447-48. [11]Phil 2:7. [12]Col 1:19, 2:9; Eph 1:23. [13]*OSW* 126*; GCS 3(2):350.

ning of the Gospel, "His own received him not."[14] Homilies on the Gospel of John 70.1.[15]

He Came for Those in the World. Cyril of Alexandria: The Evangelist says that the Savior, before enduring his suffering for our salvation, was aware that the time of his translation to heaven was now close, "even at the doors,"[16] and he gave a proof of the absolute perfection of his love for his own that were in this world. . . . All things made by Christ our Savior, all intellectual and reasonable creatures, the powers above, and thrones, and principalities and all things related to these, inasmuch as they have all been made [by him], belong to Christ our Savior as his own possessions. Furthermore, all the rational beings on earth particularly belong to him, inasmuch as he is Lord of all, even though some refuse to adore him as Creator. Therefore he loved his own that were in the world. "It is not with angels that he is concerned"[17] according to the voice of Paul . . . but rather for the sake of us who are in the world, he the Lord of all has emptied himself and assumed the form of a servant, called to this by his love for us. Commentary on the Gospel of John 9.[18]

The Passover Cross, Old and New. Bede: He loved them so much that by that very love he would end his bodily life for a time and soon pass from death to life, from this world to the Father. "Greater love has no one than this, that he should lay down his life for his friends."[19] And so, each passing over—the one under the Law and the other under the gospel—was consecrated with blood, the former with the paschal lamb, the latter with "Christ, our Passover, who was sacrificed for us."[20] The latter had his blood poured out on the cross, the former had its blood sprinkled in the manner of a cross in the middle of the lintel and the middle of the door posts. Homilies on the Gospels 2.5.[21]

Christ Is the End. Augustine: For what do these words "to the end" mean but "to Christ"? "For Christ is the end of the law," says the apostle, "for righteousness to everyone that believes."[22] He is the end that consummates, not that consumes. He is the end that we are aiming for, not our end where we perish. It is exactly in this way that we are to understand the passage, "Christ our Passover is sacrificed."[23] He is our end. We pass into him. For I see that these Gospel words may also be taken in a kind of human sense, that Christ loved his own even unto death, so that this may be the meaning of "he loved them to the end." This meaning is human, not divine, for it was not merely up to this point that we were loved by him who loves us always and endlessly. God forbid that he whose death could not end should have ended his love at death. Even after death that proud and ungodly rich man loved his five brothers.[24] And is Christ to be thought of as loving us only till death? God forbid, beloved. He would have come in vain with a love for us that lasted till death, if that love had ended there. But perhaps the words "he loved them unto the end" may have to be understood in this way, that he so loved them as to die for them. For this he testified when he said, "Greater love has no one than this, that he lay down his life for his friends."[25] Tractates on the Gospel of John 55.2.[26]

13:2 *Judas Is Ready to Betray*

Washing Before Supper. Origen: It seems to me that the Evangelist has not preserved the literal sequence concerning the washing in these words that he might raise our understanding to the spiritual sense of the things in the passage, since those who need to wash their feet wash them before supper and before they recline to eat. The Evangelist, however, passed over that proper time for washing in his account, and now, after he has reclined to eat, Jesus arises from supper, that the teacher and Lord might begin to wash the dis-

[14]Jn 1:11. [15]NPNF 1 14:257**. [16]Mt 24:33. [17]Heb 2:16. [18]LF 48:172**. [19]Jn 15:13. [20]1 Cor 5:7. [21]CS 111:44**. [22]Rom 10:4. [23]1 Cor 5:7. [24]See Lk 16:27-28. [25]Jn 15:13. [26]NPNF 1 7:299-300*; CCL 36:464.

ciples' feet after they have eaten. Commentary on the Gospel of John 32.11.[27]

Even Table Fellowship Does Not Stop Judas. Chrysostom: The Evangelist inserts this as if in astonishment, showing that our Lord was about to wash the feet of the very person who had resolved to betray him. This also proves the great wickedness of Judas that even partaking of the same table, which checks the behavior of even the worst people, did not stop him. Homilies on the Gospel of John 70.1.[28]

Judas Not Clothed with the Armor of God. Origen: I would also venture to say, as consistent with the statement, "If I do not wash you, you have no part with me," that he did not wash Judas's feet, [because] the devil had already put into his heart to betray the teacher and Lord, since the devil found him not clothed in the full armor of God and not having the shield of faith with which one can quench all the fiery darts of the wicked one.[29] [The devil] is an archer [who] prepares fiery darts for those who do not keep their heart with all watchfulness.[30] ... In the case of Judas, therefore, it has been written, "The devil had already put it into the heart of Judas Iscariot, Simon's son, to betray him." Consistently with this you might say of each of those wounded in the heart by the devil, the devil having already put it in the heart of so-and-so that he should commit fornication, and of so-and-so that he should commit fraud, and of so-and-so that, mad for fame, he should submit to the idolatry of those who seem to have rank, and so in the case of the other sins that the devil puts into that heart that is not armed with the shield of faith, by which shield of faith one can quench not one, or two, but all the fiery darts of the wicked one.[31] Commentary on the Gospel of John 32.19-20, 24.[32]

Judas Sleeping the Sleep of Avarice. Ambrose: Judas was sleeping; therefore he did not hear the words of Christ. Judas was sleeping, yes, sleeping the sleep of wealth since he sought a reward from his betrayal. The devil saw that he was sleeping, yes, buried in the deep sleep of avarice. He let himself into his heart, wounded the horse and threw the rider whom he had separated from Christ. On the Patriarchs 7.33.[33]

13:3 *All Things in Jesus' Hands*

The Meaning. Origen: The things, therefore, that were not formerly in Jesus' hands are given into his hands by the Father. And it is not some things and not others that are given into his hands, but all things. David, too, seeing in the Spirit, says in relation to this, "The Lord said to my Lord, 'Sit at my right hand until I make your enemies your footstool.' "[34] For Jesus' enemies were also a part of the "all things" that Jesus knew, so far as it was in the power of foreknowledge, to be given to him by the Father. ... The Father has given all things into his hands, that is, into his power. For his hands hold all things. Or, the Father [has given all things] "to him," for his work. "My Father works still, and I work also."[35] Commentary on the Gospel of John 32.26-27, 34.[36]

Even Judas Is in His Hands. Augustine: Since the Evangelist was about to relate such a magnificent instance of our Lord's humility, he first wanted to remind us of his majesty. This is why he says, "Jesus, knowing that the Father had given all things into his hands" ... including his betrayer. Tractates on the Gospel of John 55.6.[37]

"Giving Over" Refers to Salvation. Chrysostom: The Evangelist wonders aloud how one who was so very great, who came from God and went to him and ruled over everything, did not disdain to undertake such an action [of

[27]FC 89:344*; SC 385:190. [28]NPNF 1 14:257**. [29]See Eph 6:13-16. [30]See Prov 4:23. [31]See Eph 6:16. [32]FC 89:345-47; SC 385:194-98. [33]FC 65:261*; CSEL 32 2:144. [34]Ps 110:1 (109:1 LXX). [35]Jn 5:17. [36]FC 89:347, 349**; SC 385:198, 202. [37]NPNF 1 7:300-301**; CCL 36:466.

humility]. And by "giving over" I think John means the salvation of the faithful,[38]... not that Christ would in any way be lessened by this action, since he came from God and went to God and possessed all things. But when you hear of "giving over," you should not think of this action in human terms, because it shows how he honors the Father and demonstrates his unanimity with him. For just as the Father gives over to him, so he also gives over to the Father, as Paul declares saying, "When he shall have given over the kingdom to God, even the Father."[39] But John here means this in a more human sense, showing his great care for them and declaring his unutterable love in now caring for them as for his own. Homilies on the Gospel of John 70.1.[40]

13:4 *Jesus Rose from Supper*

Not the Usual Order of Washing. Origen: In bringing to mind the spiritual meaning of the passage, the Evangelist here seems to me not to have observed the literal sequence of the washing. Normally, it is before supper and before sitting down to supper that those who need to wash their feet wash them. But passing over that time in his account, he says that Jesus, having already sat down for supper, arose from supper so that the Teacher and Lord may begin to wash the feet of the disciples after they had supper. For before the supper, they had been washed and were altogether clean.[41] But after that washing they needed a second water for just their feet, that is, the lowest parts of the body. Commentary on the Gospel of John 32.11-12.[42]

The Company at Supper. Severian of Gabala: The whole visible world proclaims the goodness of God, but nothing proclaims it so clearly as his coming among us, by which he whose state was divine assumed the condition of a slave. This was not a lowering of his dignity, but rather a manifestation of his love for us. The awesome mystery that takes place today brings us to the consequence of his action. For what is it that takes place today? The Savior washes the feet of his disciples.... Although he took upon himself everything pertaining to our condition as slaves, he took a slave's position in a way specially suited to our own arrangements when he rose from the table.

He who feeds everything beneath the heavens was reclining among the apostles, the master among slaves, the fountain of wisdom among the ignorant, the Word among those untrained in the use of words, the source of wisdom among the unlettered. He who nourishes all was reclining and eating with his disciples. He who sustains the whole world was himself receiving sustenance.

Moreover, he was not satisfied with the great favor he showed his servants by sharing a meal with them. Peter, Matthew and Philip, men of the earth, reclined with him, while Michael, Gabriel and the whole army of angels stood by. Oh, the wonder of it! The angels stood by in dread, while the disciples reclined with him with the utmost familiarity!

And even this marvel did not content him. "He rose from the table," as Scripture says. He who is "clothed in light as in a robe" was clad in a cloak. He who wraps the heavens in clouds wrapped round himself a towel. He who pours the water into the rivers and pools tipped some water into a basin. And he before whom every knee bends in heaven and on earth and under the earth knelt to wash the feet of his disciples. Homily on the Washing of the Feet.[43]

The Signs of Humility. Chrysostom: Observe how not only by the washing but also in another way he exhibits humility. For it was not before reclining, but after they had all sat down, then he arose. In the next place, he does not merely wash them, but he does so taking off his garments. And he did not even stop here, but he

[38]He then cites as proof of this understanding Mt 11:27; Jn 3:27; 6:44; 17:6. [39]1 Cor 15:24. [40]NPNF 1 14:257**. [41]See Is 1:16. [42]FC 89:344**; SC 385:190. [43]*JFA* 50-51; *REBy* 25:227-28.

girded himself with a towel. Nor was he satisfied with this, but himself filled [the basin] and did not ask another to fill it. He did all these things himself, showing by all of them that we must do such things when we are engaged in well doing, not merely for the sake of appearance but with every effort. Homilies on the Gospel of John 70.2.[44]

Why Lay Aside Clothing? Origen: What prevented him from washing the disciples' feet clothed? This is not a problem at all if we consider (in a manner worthy of Jesus) the garments that he wore while eating and rejoicing with the disciples and what adornment the Word that became flesh wears. But he lays aside that [kind of a garment] that consists in some weaving of words with words and voices with voices, and he becomes more naked in the fashion of a slave,[45] which is signified by "having taken a towel, he girded himself," both that he might not be completely naked, and that, after washing the disciples' feet, he might dry them with a more appropriate cloth. Commentary on the Gospel of John 32.43-45.[46]

The Lord of the Universe Humbles Himself. Theophilus of Alexandria: What is more contrary to expectation than this, what more awe-inspiring? He who is clothed with light as with a garment[47] is girded with a towel. He who held the waters in the clouds[48] and sealed the abyss with his fearsome name is bound about by a belt. He who gathers the waters of the sea like a wineskin[49] pours water in a bowl. He who covers his upper chambers with waters,[50] with water washed the feet of the disciples. He who measured heaven with his hand's span and holds the earth in his grasp,[51] with his undefiled palms wiped off the feet of servants. He for whom "every knee bends, of those in heaven, and on earth and under the earth"[52] bowed his neck to attendant servants. The angels saw and recoiled; heaven beheld and shuddered; creation observed and trembled. Sermon on the Mystical Supper.[53]

Divine Humility in Taking the Towel of a Servant. Augustine: But why should we wonder that he rose from supper and laid aside his garments who, being in the form of God, emptied himself? And why should we wonder if he girded himself with a towel who took on him the form of a servant and was found in the likeness of a man?[54] Why wonder if he poured water into a basin that he used to wash his disciples' feet who poured his blood upon the earth to wash away the filth of their sins? Why wonder if with the towel in which he was girded he wiped the feet he had washed who with the very flesh that clothed him laid a firm pathway for the footsteps of his Evangelists? In order, indeed, to gird himself with the towel, he laid aside the garments he wore. But when he emptied himself in order to assume the form of a servant, he did not lay down what he had, but he assumed that which he did not have before. When about to be crucified, he was indeed stripped of his garments, and when he was dead, he was wrapped in linen clothes: and all that suffering of his is for our purification. When, therefore, about to suffer the last extremities of humiliation, he here illustrated beforehand its friendly compliances—not only to those for whom he was about to endure death but to him also who had resolved to betray him to death. Because so great is the beneficence of human humility that even the divine Majesty was pleased to commend it by his own example. For proud humans would have perished eternally had they not been found by the lowly God. For the Son of man came to seek and to save that which was lost.[55] And as he was lost by imitating the pride of the deceiver, let him now, when found, imitate the Redeemer's humility. Tractates on the Gospel of John 55.7.[56]

[44]NPNF 1 14:258**. [45]See Phil 2:7. [46]FC 89:350-51**; SC 385:206. [47]Ps 104:2 (103:2 LXX). [48]Job 26:8. [49]Ps 33:7 (32:7 LXX). [50]Ps 104:3 (103:3 LXX). [51]Is 40:12. [52]Phil 2:10. [53]MFC 7:154. [54]See Phil 2:6-7. [55]See Lk 19:10. [56]CCL 36:466; NPNF 1 7:301*.

The Towel of Suffering. Bede: He rose from the table and put aside his [outer] garments when, ceasing the fuller sharing of his life in time with human beings, he put aside on the cross the bodily members that he had assumed. He took up a linen towel with which he girded himself, when, after having taken up for us the mandate of suffering that he had received from his Father, he covered his body with the torment of his passion. A linen towel, which is woven by the endless labor of twisting [flax], is usually taken to signify the pain of suffering. When our Lord had laid aside his [outer] garments, he girded himself with a linen towel to signify that he was putting aside the clothing of the body that he had put on, [and that he was doing this] not without the distress of sorrow but with the prolonged anguish of the cross. Homilies on the Gospels 2.5.[57]

13:5 *Water in a Basin*

Mighty Wisdom Pours Water into a Basin. Anonymous: The Wisdom of God that restrains the untamed fury of the waters that are above the firmament, that sets a bridle on the deep and keeps back the seas, now pours water into a basin; and the Master washed the feet of his servants. The Master shows to his disciples an example of humility . . . as he in whose hand is the life of all things kneels down to wash the feet of his servants. Matins for Holy Thursday, Canticle 5.[58]

The Heavenly Dew Washes the Heel That Was Cursed. Ambrose: I find the Lord divesting himself of his garments and girding himself with a towel, pouring water into a basin, washing the feet of his disciples. This water was that heavenly dew with which, it was prophesied, the Lord Jesus would wash the feet of his disciples.[59] And now let the feet of our souls be extended. The Lord Jesus wishes to wash our feet also. . . .There is a kind of water that we pour into the basin of our soul, water from the fleece and from the book of Judges, water from the book of Psalms.[60] The water is the dew of the heavenly message. Therefore, Lord Jesus, let this water come into my soul, into my flesh, that by the moisture of this rain the valleys of our minds and the fields of our inmost heart may grow green.[61] Let your drops come on me, sprinkling grace and immortality. Wash the steps of my mind that I may not sin again. Wash off the heel of my spirit[62] that I may be able to abolish the curse so that I may not feel the bite of the serpent on my inner foot,[63] but, as you yourself have ordered your followers, that I may have the power with uninjured foot to tread on the serpents and scorpions. You have redeemed the world. Redeem the soul of one sinner. On the Holy Spirit 1, Prologue 12, 16.[64]

Jesus Not Finished Washing the Disciples' Feet. Origen: Why do you suppose it was not written, "He washed the disciples' feet" instead of "And he *began* to wash the disciples' feet"? For is it the custom of the Scriptures to prefix "he began" without a reason, as in the usage of the majority? Or did Jesus then "begin to wash the disciples' feet" and not stop when he had washed their feet at that time? For later he washed them and completed the washing, since they were defiled, according to the saying, "You will all be made to stumble because of me this night,"[65] and what was said to Peter, "The rooster will not crow until you deny me three times."[66] For when these sins occurred, the defiled feet of the disciples were again in need of washing, which he had begun to wash when he rose from supper, [but] he completed the washing when he cleansed them that they might no longer be defiled. Commentary on the Gospel of John 32.51-54.[67]

[57]CS 111:45-46. [58]LT 551. [59]Ps 23:2 (22:2 LXX, Vg). [60]See Ps 23:2 (22:2 LXX, Vg). [61]See Ps 72:6 (71:6 LXX, Vg). [62]See Gen 3:15. [63]See Lk 10:19. [64]FC 44:40-42**; CSEL 79:20, 22. See also *On the Holy Spirit* 1.13, where he speaks of washing the footprints of the mind. [65]Mt 26:31. [66]See Jn 13:38. [67]FC 89:351-52; SC 385:208.

The Potter Washes the Feet of Clay. Romanus Melodus:

The sea washes the brick, the Abyss washes the clay
And it does not destroy its structure,
But binds its substance and wipes clean its purpose.[68]
Behold the disposition of the One who made us.
See of what sort is the attitude of the Creator for His creatures;
They have reclined and He has stood, they are fed and He serves, they are washed
and He wipes them clean;
And the feet of clay are not cast into a mold in the hands of fire.
Have mercy, have mercy, have mercy on us,
Thou who dost bear with all men and receive all men. . . .

May sleep take me to death, if I allow Thee, the Immortal,
To bend down before me, a mortal.
The enemy would laugh at me, if Thou dealest in this way with me.
Is it not enough that Thou dost consider me as Thine?
Is it not much that I am considered and called the first of Thy friends?
But art Thou to wash my feet and limbs of clay, Thou, the Potter of the universe?
O Redeemer, dost Thou wish to wash my mortal limbs and feet?
Have mercy, have mercy, have mercy on us,
Thou who dost bear with all men and receive all men.

Kontakion on Judas 17.8,10.[69]

Death Washed Away. Irenaeus: Now in the last days, when the fullness of the time of liberty had arrived, the Word himself did by himself "wash away the filth of the daughters of Zion"[70] when he washed the disciples' feet with his own hands. For this is the end [result] of the human race inheriting God. In the beginning, by means of our first [parents], we were all brought into bondage by being made subject to death. And so now, at last, by means of the new man, all who from the beginning were his disciples—having been cleansed and washed from whatever pertains to death—come to life with God. For he who washed the feet of the disciples sanctified the entire body and rendered it clean. For this reason, too, he administered food to them while reclining, indicating that those who were lying in the earth were those to whom he came to impart life. Against Heresies 4.22.1.[71]

A Metaphor for Spiritual Zeal. Gregory of Nazianzus: It is good for the [feet and hands] to be consecrated . . . so that they are not swift to shed blood or to run to evil,[72] but that they are prompt to run to the gospel and the prize of the high calling[73] and to receive Christ who washes and cleanses them. On Holy Baptism, Oration 40.39.[74]

A Lesson in Humility. Theodore of Mopsuestia: Humility is the principle of all virtues: it removes any contrast, division or dissension from human beings and plants into them peace and charity. And through charity it grows and increases. Commentary on John 6.13.3-5.[75]

[68]The metaphor here refers to Christ as the abyss, in the sense of the depths of his wisdom and goodness. Adam was formed of clay, and the image presents us with Christ strengthening the clay and purifying it. [69]*KRBM* 1:172-73. [70]Is 4:4. [71]ANF 1:493*; SC 100:684-86. [72]Prov 1:16. [73]Phil 3:14. [74]NPNF 2 7:374. For further explorations of Jn 13 and the theme of humility in Gregory, see also *Oration* 38.14; 43.64; 45.26. [75]CSCO 4 3:254.

13:6-11 Washing Simon Peter's Feet

[6]He came to Simon Peter; and Peter said to him, "Lord, do you wash my feet?" [7]Jesus answered him, "What I am doing you do not know now, but afterward you will understand." [8]Peter said to him, "You shall never wash my feet." Jesus answered him, "If I do not wash you, you have no part in me." [9]Simon Peter said to him, "Lord, not my feet only but also my hands and my head!" [10]Jesus said to him, "He who has bathed does not need to wash, except for his feet,[c] but he is clean all over; and you[x] are clean, but not every one of you." [11]For he knew who was to betray him; that was why he said, "You are not all clean."

c Other ancient authorities omit *except for his feet* **x** The Greek word for *you* here is plural

Overview: Peter cannot understand this expression of humility since he lacks full understanding of the significance of the incarnation at that point (Severian, Ambrose). The washing of the feet, however, is a mystery of sanctification that continues in the life of the church (Ambrose). In washing the feet of his disciples, Jesus had made those feet beautiful, enabling them to preach the good news of salvation (Origen).

Peter's rashness at refusing to be washed inadvertently accuses the other disciples who had submitted to Jesus' washing (Origen). In washing Peter, Jesus protects Peter from himself (Origen) since refusal of the Lord's gifts is ultimately harmful (Theophilus of Alexandria). The slave is appalled at the service of his master, not realizing the mystery of finding honor in lowly things (Flavian) or that purification must occur for there to be fellowship with Jesus (Bede). However, as vehement as Peter was in his self-deprecation, he is even more so once he acquiesces to be washed (Chrysostom). And yet, one only needs one baptism to be clean, and Peter had already received the baptism of remission from John, so only his feet needed to be washed (Theodore) in order to teach humility and that cleansing comes through the Word (Chrysostom).

This continual cleansing is important because of the daily defilements we undergo as our feet touch the filth and dirt of this world (Bede). Our Lord washes away the poisons of the serpent prophesied in Genesis who attacks the feet (Ambrose). Jesus tells his disciples that not all of them are clean. In fact, the filthy such as Judas only become filthier (Origen). Nonetheless, Jesus also washes the feet of his betrayer, bearing with Judas's guilt for a long time until Judas brings his own punishment on himself (Cyril), expressing his gratitude for his cleansing with the nails of the cross (Ephrem).

13:6 *Lord, Are You Going to Wash My Feet?*

Peter Lacks Full Understanding of the Incarnation. Severian of Gabala: The Lord of all creation washed his disciples' feet! This was not an affront to his dignity but a demonstration of his boundless love for us. Yet however great his love was, Peter was well aware of his majesty. Always impetuous and quick to profess his faith, he was quick also to recognize the truth. The other disciples had let the Lord wash their feet, not with indifference but with fear and trembling. They dared not oppose the Master. Out of reverence, however, Peter would not permit it. He said, "Lord, are you going to wash my feet? You shall never wash my feet!"

Peter was adamant. He had the right feelings, but not understanding the full meaning of the incarnation, he first refused in a spirit of faith and afterward gratefully obeyed. This is how religious people ought to behave. They should not be obdurate in their decisions but should surrender to the will of God. For although Peter reasoned in human fashion, he changed his mind out of love for God. Homily on the Washing of the Feet.[1]

Permitting the Servanthood of Jesus. Ambrose: [Peter] did not notice the mystery, and so he refused the ministry because he believed that the humility of the servant was being overtaxed if he patiently permitted the ministry of the Lord. On the Mysteries 6.31.[2]

The Ecclesiastical Practice of Washing Feet. Ambrose: You came up from the font. What followed? You heard the reading. The girded priest—for, although the presbyters also do this, the highest priest, girded, I say, washed your feet.[3] . . . We are not unaware of the fact that the church in Rome does not have this custom whose character and form we[4] follow in all things, except for the fact that it[5] does not have this custom of washing the feet. So note: perhaps on account of the multitude this practice declined. Yet there are some who say and try to allege in excuse that this is not to be done in the mystery, or in baptism or in regeneration, but the feet are to be washed as for a guest. But one belongs to humility, the other to sanctification. Finally, be aware that the mystery is also sanctification: "Unless I wash you, you have no share with me." So I say this, not that I may rebuke others but that I may commend my own ceremonies. In all things I desire to follow the church in Rome, yet we, too, have human feeling. What is preserved more rightly elsewhere we, too, preserve more rightly.[6] The Sacraments 3.1.4-5.[7]

13:7 *You Will Understand Later*

Beautiful Feet to Preach the Gospel. Origen: [Our Lord teaches] that this act was a mystery. But what was it that Jesus was doing when he washed the disciples' feet? Was he, by washing their feet and drying them with the towel with which he had girded himself, making them beautiful,[8] since they were about to preach the good news? . . .

Now the feet of those proclaiming good news became beautiful, so that, when they were washed and cleansed and dried by Jesus' hands, they might be able to walk on the holy way and travel over him who said, "I am the way."[9] For he alone, and everyone who has had his feet washed by Jesus, travels over this way, which is living and which brings one to the Father. This way admits no feet that are defiled and not yet clean. Moses therefore had to loose the sandals from his feet since the place to which he had come, on which he stood, was holy ground.[10] And the same was true of Joshua the son of Nun.[11] . . .

For me to wash your feet [Jesus says] is symbolic of the bases of your souls being purified, that they may be beautiful, since you are to preach the good news and to approach the souls of people with your feet clean. But you do not now know this mystery, inasmuch as you do not yet have knowledge of it. Such knowledge will more appropriately be present in you when I have washed your feet, and after this you will know, when you understand this mystery and are enlightened. Commentary on the Gospel of John 32.76-77, 80-82, 87-88.[12]

13:8 *Peter's Refusal to Be Washed*

Peter Inadvertently Accuses Other Disciples. Origen: When the other disciples entrusted themselves to Jesus and offered no

[1]*JFA* 51; *REBy* 25:228. [2]FC 44:16; CSEL 73:102. [3]In the fourth century, foot washing (*pedilavium*) formed part of the rite of baptism in Milan, which practice Ambrose is here defending. In the East it is still performed on Holy Thursday in the Armenian church, but in the Byzantine rite it is confined to some cathedrals and monasteries. [4]In Milan. [5]The church in Rome. [6]Ambrose provides a glimpse into some of the tension over church authority that existed between Rome, Milan and other churches. [7]CSEL 73:39-40; FC 44:291-92*. [8]See Rom 10:15; Is 52:7. [9]Jn 14:6. [10]See Ex 3:5. [11]See Josh 5:15. [12]FC 89:357-58*; SC 385:220-24.

resistance, [Peter], by what he says (although he seemed well intentioned) not only accuses Jesus of beginning to wash the disciples' feet without a reason but also accuses his companions. For if he acted properly (which he thought he did) when he wanted to hinder Jesus, but the other disciples did not see the propriety in his actions, then he accused those who presented their feet to Jesus, contrary to what was proper at least in his mind. And if he thought that one must not resist what is reasonable and supposed that what happened when the disciples' feet were washed by Jesus was reasonable, he would not have resisted what happened. He appears, therefore, to have assumed rashly that Jesus' desire to wash the disciples' feet was not reasonable. Commentary on the Gospel of John 32.66-68.[13]

Jesus Protects Peter from Himself. Origen: Since Peter's answer was disadvantageous for him, Jesus, who in a manner appropriate to his own goodness prevents those things from becoming true that would prove harmful to the one who speaks them, does not permit Peter's answer to become true. Commentary on the Gospel of John 32.90.[14]

Refusal Is Harmful. Theophilus of Alexandria: When he heard these words, Peter the leader [of the Twelve] was at a loss as to his answer, saying, "Alas, O Lord, I am thwarted in every direction. Presumption is a burden, but refusal is harmful. To say no deserves punishment, but assent is most difficult for me. Nonetheless, let the command of God and not the opposition of the servant prevail, the Wisdom of God and not the excuse of the servant." Sermon on the Mystical Supper.[15]

The Slave Appalled at the Master's Service. Flavian of Chalon-sur-Saône:

Rising from this noble feast
He gives us an example,
For lowliness' sake
Approaching Peter's feet.

The slave is appalled at the service,
When he beholds the angels' Master
Carry water, and a towel,
And kneel upon the ground.

"O Simon, let yourself be washed!
My acts are mysteries, and disclose
—As I, the Highest, fetch lowly things—
The honor due from dust to dust."

A Hymn for Holy Thursday: "Heaven and Earth Rejoice."[16]

No Fellowship with Christ Apart from Purification. Bede: Here it is clearly pointed out that this washing of the feet implies the spiritual purification of body and soul without which we cannot arrive at fellowship with Christ. Homilies on the Gospels 2.5.[17]

13:9 *Wash My Hands and Head*

Peter Always Has a Vehement Response. Chrysostom: As vehement as Peter was in self-deprecation, he was even more vehement in acquiescing. But he did both from love. For why didn't Jesus say why he was doing what he did, instead of adding a threat? He did so because Peter would not have been persuaded. For had he said, "Let this be done to you because I am trying to persuade you to be humble minded," Peter would have promised it ten thousand times so that his Master might not do this thing. But now what does Jesus say? He speaks of that which Peter most feared and dreaded—being separated from him. For it is Peter who continually asks, "Where are you going?" Therefore he also said, "I will give even my life for you." And if, after hearing, "What I do you do not understand now, but you will know later," he still persisted, much more would he have done so had he learned [the meaning of the action]. Therefore Jesus says, "but you shall know later," being aware that should he

[13]FC 89:355; SC 385:216**. [14]FC 89:359; SC 385:226. [15]MFC 7:154-55*. [16]MFC 7:384. [17]CS 111:46.

learn it immediately he would still resist. Homilies on the Gospel of John 70.2.[18]

13:10 *No Need to Wash—Except Feet*

Washing in Place of Baptism? Theodore of Mopsuestia: Simon did not want his teacher to wash his feet. The purpose of our Lord's action was . . . to teach you that you should deeply love and eagerly help one another. Peter did not know that that was the purpose of his action. So again our Lord said to him who was still resisting, "Unless I wash you, you have no share with me." Since from these words Peter believed that this washing of the feet was in place of baptism,[19] and that from it he would have obtained his share with the Lord and therefore might say that he was entirely washed—if this was the present situation, the Lord corrected his ignorance by saying, "One who has bathed does not need to wash, except for the feet, but is entirely clean. And you are clean, but not all of you." Then the Evangelist by explaining the words of our Lord added, "For he knew who was to betray him. For this reason he said, 'Not all of you are clean.' " By speaking to Simon our Lord means to say: "This is not the baptism for the remission of sins. You have already received it once and do not need it twice, because you were made clean by the first you received. Now it is necessary that only your feet are washed, and soon you will know the purpose of this act." Certainly the disciples received the baptism of remission from John, in which the teaching of our Lord confirmed them even more by exhorting them to virtue. And then the descended Spirit perfected them when it later came on them. Commentary on John 6.13.6-13.[20]

Purified Through the Word. Chrysostom: And if they are clean, why does he wash their feet? He does so, so that we may learn to be modest. This is why he came not to any other part of the body, but to that which is considered more dishonorable than the rest. But what is meant by "he that is washed," which is said instead of "he that is clean"? Were they then clean who had not yet been delivered from their sins or deemed worthy of the Spirit, since sin still had the mastery, the handwriting of the curse still remaining, the victim not having yet been offered? Why then does he call them "clean"? That you may not consider them clean as delivered from their sins, he adds, "You are clean through the word that I have spoken unto you." That is, "You are clean insofar as you have received the light and have been freed from error." Homilies on the Gospel of John 70.2.[21]

Feet Symbolize the Daily Defilements to Be Cleansed. Bede: Jesus is giving clear notice that this washing of the feet indicates pardoning of sins, and not only that which is given once in baptism but in addition that by which the daily guilty actions of the faithful that everyone lives with in this life are cleansed by his daily grace. Our feet, by which we move about [and] touch the ground—and for this reason we cannot keep them free from contact with dirt, as we can the rest of our bodies—signify the necessity of our living on earth, by which we who are idle and negligent are daily affected to a great extent. Even outstanding people who live the highest kind of life are distracted from the heavenly contemplation that they love so much, so that "if we say we have no sin, we deceive ourselves and the truth is not in us."[22] . . .

The person who has been cleansed in the baptismal font and has received pardon for all his sins has no need to be cleansed again. Moreover, he cannot be cleansed again in the same way. He finds it necessary only to have the daily defilements of his worldly life wiped away by the daily forgiveness of his Redeemer. His whole body, together with its actions, is clean, with the exception merely of those things that cling to the mind because of the necessities of temporal cares. For their daily polluting and cleansing we say daily in

[18]NPNF 1 14:258**. [19]See also Tertullian *On Baptism* 12. [20]CSCO 4 3:256-57. [21]NPNF 1 14:259**. [22]1 Jn 1:8.

prayer, "And forgive us our debts as we also forgive our debtors."[23] Homilies on the Gospels 2.5.[24]

The Serpent Attacks the Feet. Ambrose: In baptism all fault is washed away. So fault withdraws. But since Adam was overthrown by the devil[25] and venom was poured out on his feet, this is why you wash the feet, so that in this part in which the serpent lay in wait, the greater aid of sanctification can be added so that he cannot conquer you later. Therefore, you wash the feet so that you can wash away the poisons of the serpent. It also benefits humility because then we are not ashamed of what we disdain in obedience in the Mystery. The Sacraments 3.1.7.[26]

13:11 *Not All Were Clean*

The Filthy Become Filthier. Origen: The eleven who had bathed and were clean became even cleaner when they had their feet washed by Jesus. But Judas who was already unclean, for it says, "He who is filthy, let him be filthy still,"[27] became filthier and unclean when Satan entered him after the morsel.[28] Commentary on the Gospel of John 32.110.[29]

Jesus Washes the Feet of His Betrayer. Cyril of Alexandria: Jesus clearly knew that Judas felt no kindness or wise consideration for his master. He also knew that Judas was full of devilishly bitter poison, and even while [his feet were being washed by Jesus] he was devising the means to betray him. Nevertheless, Jesus honored him just as much as the rest of the disciples and washed his feet as well, continually exhibiting his own unique love. Jesus did not express his anger, in fact, until he had tried every kind of objection. Note how this special quality is distinctive of the divine nature. Although God knows what is about to happen, he brings his punishment prematurely on no one. Rather, after bearing with the guilty for as long as is possible or necessary, when he sees them in no way profiting from the delay but instead remaining in their self-chosen evil ways, then he finally punishes them, showing it to be actually the result of their perverse folly and not really an effect of his own counsel or will. Commentary on the Gospel of John 9.[30]

The Nails of Judas's Gratitude. Ephrem the Syrian: In his gentleness our Lord humbled his wise hands by washing the feet of his betrayer, who expressed his gratitude for the cleansing with the nails of the cross. Commentary on Tatian's Diatessaron 18.22.[31]

[23]Mt 6:12, see also Augustine *Tractates on the Gospel of John* 56.4; 57.1. [24]CS 111:47*. [25]See Gen 3:1-6, 15. [26]FC 44:292**; CSEL 73:41. [27]Rev 22:11. [28]See Jn 13:27. [29]FC 89:363*; SC 385:234. [30]LF 48:181**. [31]*ECTD* 282.

13:12-17 THE SIGNIFICANCE OF THE WASHING

[12]When he had washed their feet, and taken his garments, and resumed his place, he said to them, "Do you know what I have done to you? [13]You call me Teacher and Lord; and you are right, for so I am. [14]If I then, your Lord and Teacher, have washed your feet, you also ought to wash one another's feet. [15]For I have given you an example, that you also should do as I have done to you.

[16]Truly, truly, I say to you, a servant[d] is not greater than his master; nor is he who is sent greater than he who sent him. [17]If you know these things, blessed are you if you do them."

d Or slave

Overview: Jesus tells his disciples that he washed their feet as their teacher and the feet of servants as their Lord (Origen). His goal as teacher is to make his disciples like himself (Origen). His title as Lord is his by nature, possessing authority over the universe (Cyril). Our Lord first washed and then taught (Bede). But the kind of washing Jesus commands rarely occurs among his followers (Origen). And yet, when I do wash away the filth of others, I end up washing away my own filth as well (Ambrose). The act of washing feet itself elicits humility by its very nature (Augustine) and helps us avoid the trap of pride (Cyril). Jesus' profound humility is an example for everyone to emulate as he arms the heels of the disciples and all Christians in humility to defeat Satan's pride that strikes at our heels (Theophilus of Alexandria). Jesus is like a schoolmaster who writes the letters beautifully for the children, who then seek to imitate his handwriting, albeit imperfectly (Chrysostom). Such humility has great potential for growth (Cyprian), and Jesus wants his servants to reach the potential of their master, which is the opposite of what most masters want for their servants (Origen). Neither servants nor apostles should overreach their station in life, although Jesus is the kind of loving master who wants his servants to succeed in becoming just like him in reaching their potential of humility (Cyril). It is not sufficient, however, to know about humility unless you also practice it (Cyril).

13:12-13 *You Call Me Teacher and Lord*

Teacher and Lord. Origen: Jesus washed the feet of the disciples insofar as he was their teacher, and the feet of the servants insofar as he was their Lord. For the dust from the earth and from worldly things is cleared away by teaching, since it reaches nothing else than the extremities and lower parts of the disciples. But those things that defile the feet are also removed by the lordship of the ruler, since he has authority over those who still receive common defilement because they still have the spirit of bondage.[1] Commentary on the Gospel of John 32.115-16.[2]

The Goal of the Teacher. Origen: And this is the goal of the teacher, *as teacher,* for the disciple. He wants to make the disciple like himself, so that he may no longer need the teacher, *as teacher,* although he will need him in other respects. Commentary on the Gospel of John 32.118.[3]

The Title of Lord by Nature. Cyril of Alexandria: Christ does not hold the title Lord as an empty name of honor like we do when we are decorated by the favor of others with titles that surpass our nature and merit, even though we remain mere servants by nature. Rather, Jesus is Lord by nature, possessing authority over the universe as God, as it is said somewhere by the psalmist, "all things are your servants."[4] Also, he is Master [or Teacher] by nature, for "all wisdom comes from the Lord,"[5] and all understanding comes by him. For inasmuch as he is wisdom he makes all intelligent beings wise, and in every rational creature, both in heaven and on earth, he implants the intelligence that is appropriate for it. Commentary on the Gospel of John 9.[6]

13:14 *Wash One Another's Feet*

Act, Then Teach. Bede: Our Lord first did something then taught it, because Jesus, estab-

[1]See Rom 8:15. [2]FC 89:364*; SC 385:238. [3]FC 89:364-65*; SC 385:238. [4]Ps 119:91 (118:91 LXX). [5]Sir 1:1. [6]LF 48:183**.

lishing the pattern of a good teacher, taught nothing except those things that he did.[7] COMMENTARY ON THE ACTS OF THE APOSTLES 1.1.[8]

FEET WASHING AS JESUS COMMANDS OCCURS RARELY. ORIGEN: But consider if it is not also difficult for anyone who is a disciple of Christ who wishes to fulfill the command that says, "You also ought to wash one another's feet," since he is obliged to desire to perform the work of washing his brothers' feet, which are physical and perceptible to the senses. Consequently, the faithful [are obliged] to do this in whatever station of life they happen to be, whether bishops and presbyters who seem to be in ecclesiastical prominence, or even those in other positions of honor in the world. This means that the master comes to wash the feet of the believing servant, and parents wash the feet of their son. This custom either does not occur, or it occurs exceedingly rarely and among those who are very simple and rustic. COMMENTARY ON THE GOSPEL OF JOHN 32.133.[9]

WASHING THE FILTH OF OTHERS, I WASH MY OWN. AMBROSE: I also, then, wish to wash the feet of my brothers and sisters. I wish to fulfill the mandate of the Lord. I do not wish to be ashamed of myself or to disdain what he himself did first. The mystery of humility is good because, while I wash the filth of others, I wash away my own. But not all were able to drink in this mystery. Indeed, Abraham also wished to wash feet, but out of a feeling of hospitality.[10] Gideon, too, wished to wash the feet of the angel of the Lord who appeared to him. But he wished to do this as one who was offering obedience, not as one who was offering fellowship. This is a great mystery that no one understands. ON THE HOLY SPIRIT 1, PROLOGUE 15.[11]

THE ACT ITSELF ELICITS HUMILITY. AUGUSTINE: This act is done literally by many when they receive one another in hospitality. . . . For it is unquestionably better that it should be done with the hands and that the Christian does not disdain to do what Christ did. For when the body is bent at the feet of a brother, the feeling of humility is made to rise in the heart, or, if it is already there, it is confirmed. But besides this moral meaning . . . is not a brother able to change a brother from the pollution of sin? . . . Let us confess our faults one to another, forgive one another's faults and pray for one another's faults.[12] . . . In this way we shall wash one another's feet. TRACTATES ON THE GOSPEL OF JOHN 58.4-5.[13]

AVOID THE TRAP OF PRIDE. CYRIL OF ALEXANDRIA: Somehow we are always grasping after what is greater, and the empty honors of life are always persuading our weak minds to vault up toward a more glorious position. In order, therefore, to save ourselves from this disease and obtain final relief from such a loathsome passion—for the passion of vainglory is a mere fraud and nothing less—let us engrave on our inmost hearts the memory of Christ, the King of all, washing his disciples' feet, to teach us also to wash one another's feet. For in this way, every tendency to arrogance will be restrained and every form of worldly pride will depart from among us. COMMENTARY ON THE GOSPEL OF JOHN 9.[14]

13:15 *An Example of Humility*

CHRIST ARMS THE HEEL TO DEFEAT SATAN'S PRIDE. THEOPHILUS OF ALEXANDRIA: Therefore, imitate me, your Lord, that through this sacred work of mine you may become sharers of the divine nature.[15] I decided to portray in advance for you this most excellent path of exaltation. I bent down once to the earth when I gave you existence and my good will as I took the clay of the earth and fashioned humanity, establishing

[7] Acts 1:1. [8] CS 117:9; CCL 121:6. [9] FC 89:367; SC 385:246. [10] See Gen 18:4. [11] FC 44:41**; CSEL 79:21-22. [12] Jas 5:16. [13] NPNF 1 7:306-7**; CCL 36:474-75. [14] LF 48:183-84*. [15] 2 Pet 1:4.

a living being on the earth.[16] And now I have seen fit to bend down that I may strengthen the foundation and pedestal of my collapsing creation. I have placed enmity and cursing between the deceiver and the deceived, a wariness of head and heel.[17] And now I arm the wounded heel against the serpent, that it may no more limp away from the straight path. I have strengthened your feet to walk on serpents and scorpions and every power of the enemy, and they will not harm you at all.[18] Through arrogance the one whispering of exaltation tore down the loftiness of the earth-born, first-created one. Smash his insolence by cheerful humility toward one another. Sermon on the Mystical Supper.[19]

Imitate Christ's Servant Handwriting. Chrysostom: And yet it is not the same thing, for he is Lord and Master, but you are fellow servants one of another. What does "as" mean then [when he says, "If I *as* your Lord and Master do this]? It means we should do it "with the same zeal." For on this account he takes instances from greater actions that we may, if so be it, perform the lesser actions. Thus schoolmasters write the letters for children very beautifully, that they may come to imitate them, though in an inferior manner. Where now are they who spit on their fellow servants? Where now they who demand honors? Christ washed the feet of the traitor, the sacrilegious, the thief—and he did this close to the time of the betrayal—and incurable as [Judas] was, made him a partaker of his table. And are you high minded, and do you raise your eyebrows? "Let us then wash one another's feet." But then someone says, "Then we must wash those of our domestics." And what a great thing it is if we do wash even those of our domestics! In our case "slave" and" free" is a difference of words. But there it is an actual reality. For by nature he was Lord and we were the servants, yet even this he did not refuse to do at that time. But now it is considered praiseworthy if we do not treat free people as bondmen, as slaves bought with money. And what shall we say in that day, if after receiving proofs of such forbearance, we ourselves do not imitate them at all but do the exact opposite and, acting in diametrical opposition to Jesus' words, remain prideful and do not discharge the debt? For God has made us debtors one to another, having first done so himself, and has made us debtors of a lesser amount. For he was our Lord, and he did this. But we do it, if we do it at all, to our fellow servants, a thing that he himself implied by saying, "If I then your Lord and Master do this, so should you." Indeed it would have naturally followed to say, "How much more should you servants," but he left this to the conscience of the hearers. Homilies on the Gospel of John 71.1.[20]

13:16 *No Servant Is Greater Than His Master*

Humility Has Great Potential. Cyprian: [I]f "the servant is not greater than his Lord," let those who follow the Lord humbly and peacefully and silently tread in his steps, since the lower one is, the more exalted one may become, as the Lord says, "He that is least among you shall be the greatest."[21] Letter 6.4.[22]

This Master Wants His Servants to Reach Their Potential. Origen: The Savior, who is Lord, does something that surpasses all other lords, who have no desire to see their servants rise up to their level. He is such a Son of the Father's goodness and love that, although he was Lord, he produced servants who could become like him, their Lord, not having the spirit of bondage, which comes from fear, but the spirit of adoption in which they too cry, "Abba, Father." So then, before becoming like their teacher and lord, they need to have their feet washed because they are still deficient disciples who possess the spirit of bondage to fear. But when they attain the stature of master and lord . . . then they will be

[16]Gen 2:7. [17]Gen 3:15. [18]Lk 10:19. [19]MFC 7:155-56. [20]NPNF 1 14:260**. [21]Lk 9:48. [22]ANF 5:284-85*; *Letter* 13.4 in CCL 3B:76.

able to imitate their master and wash the disciple's feet as the teacher. COMMENTARY ON THE GOSPEL OF JOHN 32.120-22.[23]

OF THE SAME MIND AS THEIR MASTER. CYRIL OF ALEXANDRIA: He points out here what an inadmissible offense it would be for servants to refuse to be of the same mind as their own masters. Such a passionate longing for greater and higher things than our merits deserve is really covetousness and nothing else. And he would be perfectly just in bringing the same charge against the apostles, namely, of seeking to be on a higher level than he who commissioned them, if they acted like this. The mind of the One who sent them should be a sufficient yardstick of the glory they seek. It is as if he were saying You will be laughed right out of the divine tribunal if your pride gets in the way of doing for each other what I have done for you. You are servants. I, on the other hand, have always been from the very beginning, by nature, your God and Lord. It would be preposterous and the height of madness for servants who, by definition, are inferior to their master, to be ashamed at the idea of being servants to one another. COMMENTARY ON THE GOSPEL OF JOHN 9.[24]

13:17 *Knowing and Doing*

PRACTICE VIRTUE. CYRIL OF ALEXANDRIA: It is not the knowledge of virtue but rather the practice of it that may be appropriately called worthy of both love and enthusiasm. . . . Whenever actions go hand in hand with knowledge, then assuredly there is no small gain. But when either is lacking, the other will be seriously crippled. And it is written, even faith apart from works is dead.[25] Although the knowledge of God who is one even in nature, and the confession of God in guilelessness and truth is all included in faith, even this is dead if it is not accompanied by the bright light that proceeds from works. Surely, therefore, it is utterly profitless merely to know what is good and yet have no desire to practice it at once. COMMENTARY ON THE GOSPEL OF JOHN 9.[26]

[23]FC 89:365**; SC 385:240. [24]LF 48:184-85**. [25]See Jas 2:26. [26]LF 48:185-86*.

13:18-22 A BETRAYER AMONG THE DISCIPLES

[18]"I am not speaking of you all; I know whom I have chosen; it is that the scripture may be fulfilled, "He who ate my bread has lifted his heel against me. [19]I tell you this now, before it takes place, that when it does take place you may believe that I am he. [20]Truly, truly, I say to you, he who receives any one whom I send receives me; and he who receives me receives him who sent me."

[21]When Jesus had thus spoken, he was troubled in spirit, and testified, "Truly, truly, I say to you, one of you will betray me." [22]The disciples looked at one another, uncertain of whom he spoke.

OVERVIEW: Jesus is surely aware of what Judas is up to when he says, "I know whom I have chosen" (ORIGEN). That Judas betrays Christ is not, however, the fault of Christ but of Judas (CYRIL). Judas, as the one who lifted up his heel against Christ, was incapable of praise toward the one who made him (Cosmas). Jesus foretold what would happen so that when these things did happen, his disciples would know who he was and believe (Theodore), that is, that they would increase in faith as they continued to believe. Those who are sent by Jesus are his apostles, but they are apostles only to those to whom they are sent. Those who receive these apostles receive Jesus and in turn also receive the Father who sent Jesus (Origen). He is not speaking here about the unity of nature between the sender and the one sent, so much as the authority of the sender (Augustine).

Christ was troubled in spirit about Judas (Chrysostom) and about us, as well as about all the other impending trials he was facing at the moment, which shows that Christians too can be troubled by what they see going on around them (Augustine). His troubled spirit may also be understood as his anger at Judas's betrayal, which he foreknew (Theodore). The disciples too were troubled (Origen), and Jesus does nothing to allay that anxiety when he chooses not to name the betrayer (Chrysostom, Augustine).

13:18 *The Chosen and the Rebellious Heel*

Jesus Is Aware of Judas. Origen: Literally, this means, I know who each person is whom I have chosen. Therefore, I also know who Judas is, and he does not escape my notice, although the devil has already put the things against me into his heart. Commentary on the Gospel of John 32.152.[1]

Was Judas Predestined to Betray Christ? Cyril of Alexandria: Some may raise the following objection, "If we believe that Christ was all-knowing, why did he choose Judas, and why did he include him as one of the disciples if he knew that he would be convicted of treachery and fall prey to the snares of coveting?" Furthermore, another will say, "And if, as Christ himself says, Judas lifted up his heel against his master so that the Scripture may be fulfilled, surely Judas could not be deemed guilty of being responsible for what happened. Rather, the blame must rest with the power that caused the Scripture to be fulfilled."... However, God knew that the first man, Adam, would sin, and yet he was created in the beginning.... And likewise, God anointed Saul to be king, knowing that he too would sin. ... Therefore, in a similar manner, Christ chose Judas and associated him with the holy disciples, since at first he certainly possessed the capacity for discipleship. But when, after the temptations of Satan succeeded in making him captive to base greediness for gain, when he was conquered by passion and had become by this means a traitor, then he was rejected by God. This, therefore, was in no way the fault of him who called this man to be an apostle. For it lay in the power of Judas to have saved himself from falling, namely, by making the more excellent choice and transforming his whole heart and soul in such a way as to become a sincere follower of Christ.... Let no one suppose, as do some ignorant people, that the oracles delivered by the holy prophets are carried onward to final accomplishment simply in order that the Scriptures may be fulfilled.... Who could ever be so utterly void of proper reason as to suppose that the Word of the Holy Spirit should become, to any, a patron of sin? Therefore, we do not believe that the deeds of any were done simply so that the Scriptures might be fulfilled. But the Holy Spirit has spoken in perfect foreknowledge as to what will happen, so that when the event comes to pass we may find in the prediction a pledge to establish our faith that we may from that point on hold our faith without hesitation. Commentary on the Gospel of John 9.[2]

Judas Incapable of Praise. Cosmas of Maiuma:

The hateful Iscariot, heedless,
By intent, of the law of friendship,
Readied for betrayal the feet
Which Christ had washed. And though he ate

[1]FC 89:371; SC 385:254. [2]LF 48:187-90**.

Your bread, the divine Body,
He raised his heel against you, O Christ,
And knew not how to cry out:
"Praise the Lord, O his works,
and exalt him unto all ages."

The man without conscience received
The Body which redeems from sin
And the divine blood poured out
For the sake of the world;
But he was not ashamed to drink
What he sold for a price;
He took no offense at his wickedness,
And knew not how to cry out:
"Praise the Lord, O his works,
and exalt him unto all ages."
Kanon for the Fifth Day of Great Week, Eighth Ode.[3]

13:19 *That You May Believe*

Jesus' Foreknowledge Testifies to His Identity. Theodore of Mopsuestia: I could not reveal what was about to happen, he says. However, in order that you might not think that I did not know the thoughts of those who follow me—or that I was unaware of what was happening to me and therefore striving in vain because of the shameful things that were happening to me—I foretell the facts before the event so that when they happen you will know who I am. Commentary on John 6.18-19.[4]

"Believe" Here Can Also Mean "Increase in Faith." Origen: And understand the words "that you may believe" as capable of being equivalent to the words "that you may be increased in faith," while you continue to believe. Commentary on the Gospel of John 32.176.[5]

13:20 *Receiving the Sender*

Particularity of Apostles of Jesus Christ. Origen: Whomever the Savior sends to minister to the salvation of anyone, that person who is sent is an apostle of Jesus Christ. But just as the apostle is an apostle of the one who sent him, so is he an apostle only to those to whom he is sent. Commentary on the Gospel of John 32.204-5.[6]

Receives the Father. Origen: He who receives whom[ever] Jesus may send, receives Jesus in the one sent, and he who receives Jesus receives the Father. Therefore, he who receives whomever Jesus may send receives the Father who sent Jesus. Commentary on the Gospel of John 32.212.[7]

Receiving the Sender Through the Sent One. Augustine: Did he mean us to understand that there is as little distance between one sent by him and himself as there is between himself and God the Father? If we take it this way, we would have to adopt the Arian system of gradations because, when they hear or read these words of the Gospel, they have immediate recourse to their dogmatic measurements and say, The Son's messenger then stands at the same relative distance from the Son . . . as that in which the Son himself stands from the Father. . . . Listen rather to the Son himself when he says, "I and the Father are one."[8] There is no shadow of distance there between the Begetter and the Only Begotten. There Christ himself has erased your measurements. . . .

But in what sense then are we to take these words of the Lord? "He who receives me receives him who sent me" expresses the oneness in nature of the Father and the Son. The other phrase, then, "He who receives whomever I send, receives me," refers to the unity in nature of the Son and his messenger. And there is no impropriety in understanding it this way, . . . seeing that the Word became flesh, that is, God became man. And so he would have been speaking here with regard to the union with his human nature when

[3]MFC 7:390-91. [4]CSCO 4 3:258-59. [5]FC 89:375; SC 385:262. [6]FC 89:380-81; SC 385:274. [7]FC 89:382*; SC 385:276. [8]Jn 10:30.

he said, "He who receives whomever I send receives me," but speaking of his [divine nature] when he says, "He who receives me [as God] receives him who sent me." But in this passage he was not so much commending the unity of nature as the authority of the Sender in him who is sent. Let everyone, therefore, receive him who is sent [i.e., Christ], that in the person [of Christ] he may listen to the One who sent him [i.e., the Father]. If then, you look for Christ in Peter, you will find Peter's instructor. And if you look for the Father in the Son, you will find the Begetter of the Only Begotten. Therefore, when you receive him who is sent, you are not mistaken when you believe that you are also receiving the Sender. TRACTATES ON THE GOSPEL OF JOHN 59.2-3.[9]

13:21 *Jesus Was Troubled in Spirit*

JESUS IS TROUBLED FOR JUDAS. CHRYSOSTOM: When Jesus reflected on the fact that the traitor would be deprived of [the twofold comfort] he had given . . . Jesus again was troubled. HOMILIES ON THE GOSPEL OF JOHN 72.1.[10]

JESUS TROUBLED FOR US. AUGUSTINE: Was Jesus troubled, not in flesh but in spirit, because he was now about to say, "One of you shall betray me"? Did this occur then for the first time to his mind, or was it at that moment suddenly revealed to him for the first time, and so troubled him by the startling novelty of so great a calamity? . . . Was it because now he had to single out the betrayer so that he should no longer remain concealed among the rest but be separated from the others, that therefore "he was troubled in spirit"? Or was it because now the traitor himself was on the eve of departing to bring those Jews to whom he was to betray the Lord, that he was troubled by his imminent passion, the closeness of the danger and the swooping hand of the traitor, whose resolution was foreknown?

It was for some reason like these that Jesus was "troubled in spirit." . . .

He was troubled, then, who had power to lay down his life and power to take it up again.[11] That mighty power is troubled, that immovable rock is disturbed? Or is it rather our infirmity that is troubling him? Most certainly this is the case. Let servants believe nothing unworthy of their Lord but recognize their own membership in their Head. He who died for us was also himself troubled in our place. He therefore who died in power was troubled in the midst of his power. He who shall transform the body of our humility into similarity of form with the body of his glory has also transferred into himself the feeling of our infirmity. He sympathizes with us in the feelings of his own soul. And so, when it is the great, the brave, the sure, the invincible One that is troubled, let us have no fear for him as if he were capable of failing. He is not perishing but is in search of us [who are]. . . . Away with the reasons of philosophers who assert that a wise person is not affected by mental troubles. . . . It is plain that the mind of the Christian may be troubled, not by misery but by pity. TRACTATES ON THE GOSPEL OF JOHN 60.1-3.[12]

JESUS ANGERED AT JUDAS'S BETRAYAL. THEODORE OF MOPSUESTIA: As in the episode of Lazarus he said that he was troubled in spirit, because he foretold what would happen, and that he was angered in order to show that he had knowledge of the things that still had to happen as if they had already happened, so here too he says he was angered because of Judas's betrayal and was confused by how vicious he was. He also said here the words "Jesus was troubled in spirit" because through the operation of the Spirit that was in him he foreknew the future [and the trouble that awaited him]. COMMENTARY ON JOHN 6.13.21-26.[13]

13:22 *Doubting Themselves and One Another*

[9]NPNF 1 7:308**. [10]NPNF 1 14:263**. [11]See Jn 10:18. [12]NPNF 1 7:309**; CCL 36:478-79. [13]CSCO 4 3:259-60.

The Disciples Were Confused. Origen: The phrase about the disciples, "doubting of whom he spoke," is vivid. For they were unable to conceive of whom this had been said and were in doubt about it, and they found nothing clear either to think or say. Commentary on the Gospel of John 32.259.[14]

Jesus Perpetuates Their Anxiety. Chrysostom: They were in doubt, although they were conscious of nothing evil in themselves. But they considered that the declaration of Christ should be believed more than their own thoughts. And so, "they looked at one another." By singling out one, Jesus would have allayed their fear, but by adding "one of you," he troubled them all. Homilies on the Gospel of John 72.1.[15]

They Knew Themselves, but Not Each Other. Augustine: While the disciples had a reverential love for their master, they were nonetheless affected by human frailty in their feelings toward each other. Each one's own conscience was known to himself. But as he was ignorant of his neighbor's, each one's self-assurance was such that each was uncertain of all the others, and all the others were uncertain of that one. Tractates on the Gospel of John 61.3.[16]

[14]FC 89:390; SC 385:294. [15]NPNF 1 14:263**. [16]NPNF 1 7:311**; CCL 36:481.

13:23-30 Judas Identified as the Betrayer

[23]One of his disciples, whom Jesus loved, was lying close to the breast of Jesus; [24]so Simon Peter beckoned to him and said, "Tell us who it is of whom he speaks." [25]So lying thus, close to the breast of Jesus, he said to him, "Lord, who is it?" [26]Jesus answered, "It is he to whom I shall give this morsel when I have dipped it." So when he had dipped the morsel, he gave it to Judas, the son of Simon Iscariot. [27]Then after the morsel, Satan entered into him. Jesus said to him, "What you are going to do, do quickly." [28]Now no one at the table knew why he said this to him. [29]Some thought that, because Judas had the money box, Jesus was telling him, "Buy what we need for the feast"; or, that he should give something to the poor. [30]So, after receiving the morsel, he immediately went out; and it was night.

Overview: At this point, John inserts himself into the narrative, albeit not by name, which he omits out of modesty (Augustine). He does, however, refer to himself, seemingly immodestly, as the one "whom Jesus loved" (Chrysostom). Peter beckons to John, who was closer to Jesus, in order to get further information (Origen). John was closer to Jesus because perfect love drives out fear (Chrysostom). His presence next to Jesus, reclining on his breast, indicates the love and honor our Lord had for him and for all who are pure in heart who are allowed to see God (Cyril), and it is analogous to the Word that resides in the bosom of the Father (Origen). Judas was present and did partake of the bread but not of its blessing (Ephrem), although it is questionable as to whether this was the bread of the sacrament since Judas and the other disciples, according to Luke, had received this earlier (AUGUSTINE).

The rebuke Jesus issued to Judas was calculated to win Judas over but did not succeed (CHRYSOSTOM). And so, instead of tempting one who belonged to another, Satan took possession of what was his (AUGUSTINE, AMMONIUS) after Judas had partaken of Christ's body to his condemnation (CHRYSOSTOM). Satan attacked Judas's weak points, as he does with us. But Judas also chose the evil as opposed to being forced into it (CYRIL). Satan confirmed that choice (THEODORE). Judas even later repented of that choice, but he lost hope and did not ask for pardon (AUGUSTINE).

Jesus tells Judas (or Satan), "What you are going to do, do quickly," as though summoning his opponent to battle (CYRIL). When Jesus dismisses Judas, he keeps the reason for the dismissal secret in case someone like Peter would kill Judas on the spot (CHRYSOSTOM). John notes, in passing, that Judas was the treasurer, which demonstrates to the church that our Lord approved of church treasuries but also that the service of God should not be neglected in service to that treasury (AUGUSTINE). It is most likely that the money in the treasury came from female disciples, and the existence of a treasury among the disciples also demonstrates our Lord's concern that the poor be cared for by those crucified to this world (CHRYSOSTOM).

When Judas leaves, it is one of the few instances where he obeys his master (ORIGEN). He leaves the stable of the lambs to go out among the beasts (ROMANUS). He hurries out into the darkness, which in itself was an image of his soul (ORIGEN).

13:23 *One of the Disciples Whom Jesus Loved*

THE MODESTY OF JOHN. AUGUSTINE: It was that very John whose Gospel is before us, as he afterward expressly declares.[1] For it was a custom of the sacred writer, when he came to anything relating to himself, to speak of himself as if he were speaking of another. He would give himself a place in the flow of the narrative so that he became one who was the recorder of public events rather than making himself the subject of his preaching. Matthew also acted this way.[2] . . . For what does truth lose by the omission of boasting on the writer's part, as long as the facts themselves are told? TRACTATES ON THE GOSPEL OF JOHN 61.4.[3]

IS JOHN BEING VAIN? CHRYSOSTOM: But it is a question worth asking, why when all were distressed and trembling, when their leader was afraid, John leans on Jesus' bosom like one at ease, and not only leans but even [lies] on his breast? Nor is this the only thing worthy of inquiry, but also what follows, when John refers to himself as the one "whom Jesus loved." Why did no one else say "whom Jesus loved" about himself? The others were surely loved too. But he, more than any. . . . But why did no one else say this concerning him? [They said nothing] because John would not even have said it himself unless he had come to this passage [where Peter beckons]. For if, after telling us that Peter beckoned to John to ask, he had added nothing more, he would have caused considerable doubt and have compelled us to inquire into the reason Peter asked him in particular. HOMILIES ON THE GOSPEL OF JOHN 72.1.[4]

13:24 *Simon Peter Asks John*

PETER BECKONS OUT OF EAGERNESS TO KNOW. ORIGEN: Now, beckoning is taken as slander in proverbs, for the wicked person "beckons with his eyes"[5] . . . Peter's act, however, was to beckon out of his eagerness for knowledge, and subsequent to such beckoning, to say to his fel-

[1]Jn 21:20-24. Augustine affirms John the disciple as the author of the Gospel, which was the consensus of the early church. [2]Mt 9:9. [3]NPNF 1 7:311**; CCL 36:481-82. [4]NPNF 1 14:263-64**. [5]See Prov 6:13.

low disciple, since he was more intimate with the teacher, "Tell us who it is of whom he speaks." Commentary on the Gospel of John 32.275.[6]

Love Drives Out Fear. Chrysostom: In order, therefore, to solve this difficulty [of Peter's beckoning] himself, John says, "He lay on the bosom of Jesus." Do you think that you have learned a little thing when you have heard that "he lay" and that their Master allowed such boldness to them? If you want to know the cause of this, the action was because of love. Therefore he says, "whom Jesus loved." I suppose also that John did this for another reason, wanting to show that he was exempt from the charge and so he speaks openly and out of confidence. Again, why did he use these words, not at any other point of time but only when the chief of the apostles beckoned? That you might not deem that Peter beckoned to him as being greater, he says that the thing took place because of the great love [that Jesus had toward him]. But why does he still lie on his bosom? They had not as yet formed any high assessment concerning him. Besides, in this way he calmed their despondency. For it is probable that at this time their faces were clouded over. If they were troubled in their souls, much more would they be so in their countenances. Soothing them therefore by word and by the question, he makes a way beforehand and allows him to lean on his breast. Observe also his modesty, for he mentions not his own name but the one "whom he loved." Homilies on the Gospel of John 72.1.[7]

13:25 *While Reclining on Jesus' Breast*

A Place of Honor for Those Who See God. Cyril of Alexandria: The Evangelist tells us that he was himself the object of special honor and love on the part of Christ our Savior. He reclines next to Jesus, actually in the very bosom of the Lord, considering this a token of Christ's surpassing affection toward him. Those who are pure in heart are most especially near to God and in the highest place of honor. For the Savior himself assigns them this conspicuous honor when he says that the pure in heart shall be blessed for they shall see God.[8] . . . To those who keep their mind unstained by the world and from an empty preoccupation with the things of this life, it does seem that Christ reveals his own peculiar glory by a subtle and perhaps incomprehensible process, thereby showing also the glory of the Father, which must be what Jesus meant when he said, "Whoever has seen me has seen the Father."[9] Commentary on the Gospel of John 9.[10]

Reclining in the Bosom of the Word. Origen: John, by reclining on the Word and resting on more mystical things, was reclining in the bosom of the Word, analogous also to the Word being in the bosom of the Father, according to the statement, "The only-begotten God who is in the bosom of the Father, he has declared him."[11] Commentary on the Gospel of John 32.264.[12]

13:26 *Judas Gave the Morsel to Judas*

Judas Partakes of the Bread, but Not of the Blessings. Ephrem the Syrian: All approached and drank from the cup, that is, only eleven of them. For when Jesus had given his bread indiscriminately to the eleven, Judas also approached to receive, just as his comrades who had approached and received. But Jesus dipped the bread in water and thus gave it to Judas. He washed the blessing from it and thereby marked off the offender. This is how the apostles recognized that it was he who would betray him. Jesus had dipped the bread and thus gave it to him so that its blessing might be removed from the bread. Thus Judas did not eat the blessed bread, nor did he drink from the cup of life. He grew

[6]FC 89:393-94; SC 385:304-6. [7]NPNF 1 14:264**. [8]Mt 5:8. [9]Jn 14:9. [10]LF 48:197-98**. [11]Origen, again paying careful attention to the text, goes on to make much of the distinction between the different Greek words for "bosom" in verse 23 and "breast" in verse 25 (a distinction ignored in the RSV), asserting that John had moved to a higher level of revelation by moving from Christ's bosom to his breast. See *Commentary on John* 32.276-79. [12]FC 89:391; SC 385:298-300.

angry that his bread had been dipped, for he knew that he was, then, not worthy of life. And the rage about this removed him from drinking from the cup of the blood of Jesus. He went out to the crucifiers and no longer saw the hallowed cup. Satan rushed to drive the Iscariot away from his comrades, so that he would not be a sharer with them of the living and life-giving sacrament. Memra for the Fifth Day of Great Week (Holy Thursday), Sermon 4.[13]

Judas Had Already Received the Sacrament Earlier. Augustine: But it was not then, as some thoughtless readers suppose, that Judas received the body of Christ. For our Lord had already distributed the sacraments of his body and blood to all of them, while Judas was there, as Luke relates.[14] And it was after this that he dipped the bread, as John relates, and gave it to the traitor—the dipping of the bread perhaps intimating the false pretensions of the other. For the dipping of a thing does not always imply its washing. Some things are dipped in order to be dyed. If, however, this dipping meant anything good, he was as ungrateful for it and deserved the damnation that followed him. Tractates on the Gospel of John 62.3.[15]

A Rebuke Calculated to Restore. Chrysostom: Even the way he rebuked Judas was calculated to put him to shame. Judas did not respect the table, though he shared the bread. Be that as it may, who would not have been won over, however, by receiving the bread from Christ's own hand? Yet it did not win Judas over. Homilies on the Gospel of John 72.2.[16]

13:27 *Satan Enters into Judas*

Tempting Gives Way to Possession. Augustine: But now, after the bread, Satan entered into Judas, no longer to tempt one who belonged to another but to take possession of him as his own. Tractates on the Gospel of John 62.2.[17]

The Difference Between Satanic Attack and Possession. Ammonius: Since Satan saw Judas wishing to betray the Lord and hastening to do this, then "he entered him." It is one thing for the devil to assail someone and quite another for the devil to enter him, just as it is one thing to strike someone outwardly and quite a different matter to hit someone's vital organ or thrust a sword into him. Fragments on John 457.[18]

The Devil Enters Judas After Judas Partakes of Supper. Chrysostom: Let no one . . . be a deceiver, no one full of evil, no one holding venom in his mind, lest his partaking lead to condemnation.[19] After Judas took what was offered, the devil hastened into him, not because the devil despised the Lord's body but because he despised Judas for his shamelessness. Thus you may learn concerning those who partake unworthily of the divine mysteries, that these especially are the ones the devil invades and enters at once, just like he did to Judas of old. Honors, indeed, are of benefit to those who are worthy, but those who enjoy them without deserving them are propelled into greater retribution. I say these things not to frighten but to protect you. Sermon on the Betrayal by Judas 1.6.[20]

Satan Attacks Weak Points. Cyril of Alexandria: When a skilled general lays siege to a city, he spares no effort to quickly attack the weakest parts of the wall with his battering rams, knowing that in such areas the capture will be easy. I believe that Satan employs an identical strategy when laying siege to the human heart, attacking at its weakest point, thinking that he will easily bring it into subjection especially when he sees it unfortified by those reinforcements that

[13]MFC 7:140-41. [14]Lk 22:19-21. [15]NPNF 1 7:313**. [16]NPNF 1 14:264**. [17]NPNF 1 7:313**. [18]*JKGK* 310. [19]1 Cor 11:29. [20]MFC 7:145*; PG 49:380. Some Fathers, like Chrysostom, believed Judas partook of the sacrament at its institution but did so unworthily, which led to his destruction. Others, like Ephrem, however, believed that Judas was not allowed to participate, or at least not allowed to fully participate, in the sacrament.

would likely repel the attack of the passions such as emotions that are under control, bold courage, a devotional heart, and most importantly, the mystical Eucharist, for this is the most effective antidote to the murderous poison of the devil. Commentary on the Gospel of John 9.[21]

Satan Confirms the Will of Judas. Theodore of Mopsuestia: What Judas believed to be hidden and turning around in his mind was disclosed through the handing of the bread and made known to all the disciples. He was so far away from the admirable virtue of the one who knows the inner thoughts that, even though he had to feel ashamed and blush because of that public rebuke, he on the contrary confirmed even more inside himself the will of his iniquity. And since he was offended by the blame [he received], he prepared to execute his crime at once. The Evangelist rightly called this thought the entry of Satan by attributing to Satan the confirmation of Judas's will. Commentary on John 6.13.27-30.[22]

Judas Repented but Despaired. Augustine: The one who persuaded Judas to betray Christ is the one who persuaded him to hang himself with a noose. He repented, you remember, of "having betrayed righteous blood,"[23] but his repentance was without hope. He repented, but he also despaired. He did not believe he would receive mercy. He did not come to the one he had betrayed and ask him his pardon. He did not ask for pardon from him; he did not implore him to set him free; he did not entrust himself to his blood for redemption.[24] Sermon 313E.4.[25]

Confidence Motivates Jesus. Cyril of Alexandria: Our Lord Jesus the Christ may now appear to be addressing Satan himself rather than the disciple who by careless infatuation had fallen into Satan's power. . . . It is as though Jesus is saying, "That work of yours, O Satan, which you alone know and which is ever dear to you, see that you do it quickly. You killed the prophets, and you were always leading the Jews to impiety. In time past you obtained the death by stoning of those who were sent as ambassadors to Israel bearing the word of salvation. You did not spare one of those who were sent from God. Toward them you showed your incredible brutality and the excess of your madness. And now I have come following in their steps. . . . I have come to overthrow the sovereignty of sin that you have brought to power and to make clear to everyone the one who is truly God by nature. But I know full well your implacable temper. The harm you desire to inflict on all who wish to accomplish works like I have come to do is what you inflict on me now. But you will cause me no more grief by being swift to attack and quick in your assault, even though you will inflict great pain on me at first.". . . Jesus' words are not so much an exhortation as a threat to his enemy. It is as though some handsome youth in early manhood, his heart swelling with fresh vigor at the sight of an opponent running at full speed to attack him, were to pick up a sharp battle axe in his right hand, and in full knowledge that his enemy will no sooner reach him than die, were to call out, "What you are going to do, do it quickly, for you will feel the force of my right arm." And surely this would not be the cry of one who is eager to die but rather the cry of one who knows certainly that he will be victorious and will prevail over the one who wishes to hurt him. Commentary on the Gospel of John 9.[26]

13:28 *No One Knew Why Jesus Said This*

How and Why Christ Kept Judas's Identity Secret. Chrysostom: It is not easy to see how the disciples did not understand him when they had asked, "Who is he," and he had replied, "He it is to whom I shall give the bread." [How is

[21]LF 48:200**. [22]CSCO 4 3:260. [23]Mt 27:4. [24]In contrast to Peter, who denied his Lord, but in his subsequent repentance trusted also in Christ's mercy. [25]*WSA* 3 9:112; MiAg 1:538. [26]LF 48:202-4**. See also Cyprian *Testimonies Against the Jews* 3.80; Tertullian *Against Marcion* 5.6.

it that they did not understand him], unless it was that he spoke too low to be heard and that John lay on his breast when he asked the question. In other words, he did it for the very reason that the traitor might not be made known.... For had Christ made him known ... perhaps Peter would have killed him. And so it was, then, that none at the table knew what our Lord meant. But why didn't John know? Because he could not conceive how a disciple could fall into such wickedness: he was far from such wickedness himself and therefore did not suspect it of others.... What they thought he meant we are told in what follows. Homilies on the Gospel of John 72.3.[27]

13:29 *Judas Was the Treasurer*

The First Instance of a Church Treasury. Augustine: Our Lord then had a money box in which he kept the offerings of the faithful to supply either the wants of his own followers or the poor. This is where the custom of the church having money was first introduced. Our Lord shows that his commandment not to think about tomorrow does not mean that the saints should never save money but that they should not neglect the service of God for it or let the fear of want tempt them to injustice. Tractates on the Gospel of John 62.5.[28]

Money Provided by Female Disciples. Chrysostom: None of the disciples contributed this money, but it is hinted that it was certain female disciples who, it is said, ministered to him of their means.... But how was it that he, who forbade purses, and staff and money, carried bags for the relief of the poor? It was to show you that even the very poor, those who are crucified to this world, ought to attend to this duty. He did many things in order to instruct us in our duty. Homilies on the Gospel of John 72.3.[29]

13:30 *Judas Leaves*

Judas Obeys the Savior. Origen: The Savior said to Judas, "What you are going to do, do quickly," and for once the betrayer obeys the teacher. For when he had received the morsel, he neither hesitated nor procrastinated, but as it is written, "he went out immediately" to do quickly the work of betrayal in accordance with Jesus' command. And "he went out" truly, for he not only went out of the house in which the supper was held, according to the simpler meaning, but he also went out from Jesus in a final sense, analogous to the statement "they went out from us."[30] Commentary on the Gospel of John 32.300-301.[31]

Judas Hurries to Do Evil. Cyril of Alexandria: In haste Judas hurries away in obedience to the will of Satan. Like one stung and goaded on to madness, he rushes from the house. He sees nothing that can overcome his love of gain, and, marvelous though it is, we shall find him in no way benefited by the gift from Christ due to his irrepressible greed for money. Commentary on the Gospel of John 9.[32]

Judas Leaves the Stable. Romanus Melodus:

And leaving the stable he [Judas] hurried to
the beasts, leaving behind the lambs.

Kontakion on Judas 17.12.[33]

Darkness an Image of Judas's Soul. Origen: "And it was night," has not been interjected in vain by the Evangelist. The perceptible night at that time was symbolic, being an image of the night that was in Judas's soul when Satan, the darkness that lies over the abyss,[34] entered him. Commentary on the Gospel of John 32.313.[35]

[27]NPNF 1 14:264**. [28]NPNF 1 7:314**; CCL 36:485. See further comment on Judas as treasurer in Jn 12:4-6. This passage was also featured in the medieval debate between the Franciscans and the pope over the monastic poverty that William of Ockham championed in *Opus Nonaginta Dierum*. [29]NPNF 1 14:265**. [30]See 1 Jn 2:19. [31]FC 89:398*; SC 385:316. [32]LF 48:206**. [33]*KRBM* 1:173. [34]See Gen 1:2. [35]FC 89:400; SC 385:320-22.

13:31-32 The Glory of the Son of Man

[31]When he had gone out, Jesus said, "Now is the Son of man glorified, and in him God is glorified; [32]if God is glorified in him, God will also glorify him in himself, and glorify him at once."

Overview: The glorification of the Son of man of which Jesus speaks here is that of his humanity, which is glorified in his passion and death for the world and which also brings glory to God (Origen). God is the one who glorifies him, not anyone else (Chrysostom). This glory is not an indifferent entity, as the Greeks use the term, but rather indicates a participation in the divine. This glory may also be perceived in the knowledge and spreading of his name among believers throughout the world after his death and resurrection; those believers then will bring glory to his name (Origen). Or we may also understand Judas's departure here as a foreshadowing of what will take place at Christ's glorification when the tares are separated from the wheat and all that remains are the righteous saints. Jesus goes further in saying that in himself God is glorified, meaning that the human nature is endowed with eternity (Augustine). The Son's glorification ultimately is the Father's glorification (Tertullian).

Not only does this passage speak of the glorification of the Son of man on the cross, which was the immediate reference to glory that Jesus makes, It also speaks of that future glory that shall happen to the human nature when it will be eternally transformed into divinity after the resurrection (Hilary). At that time, the Son will receive in his entire person once again the glory he had with his Father before he became incarnate and laid aside his glory, as the Father glorifies the Son with himself and in himself (Hilary). The glorification that will take place "at once," then, refers first of all to his imminent passion, which is his highest glorification (Theodore), although Augustine believes the glorification refers to Christ's resurrection (Augustine).

13:31a *The Son of Man Is Glorified*

The Glory Belongs to Jesus' Humanity. Origen: After the glory of his miracles and his transfiguration, the next glorifying of the Son of man began when Judas went out with Satan, who had entered into him. . . . Because it is not possible that the Christ is glorified if the Father is not glorified in him, the statement "and God is glorified in him" is added to the words "now is the Son of man glorified." But the glory that resulted from Jesus' death for the human race did not belong to the only-begotten Word, which by nature does not die, nor to wisdom and truth, nor to any of the other titles that are said to belong to the divine aspects in Jesus. They belonged to the man who was also the Son of man born of the seed of David according to the flesh.[1]. . . Now I think God highly exalted this [Son of] man when he became obedient "unto death, even the death of a cross."[2] For the Word in the beginning with God, God the Word, was not capable of being highly exalted. But the high exaltation of the Son of man that occurred when he glorified God in his own death consisted in the fact that he was no longer different from the Word but was the same with him . . . so that the humanity of Jesus became one with the Word when he who "did not consider equality with God as something to be grasped"[3] was highly exalted. The Word, however, remained in his own grandeur or was even restored to it when he was again with God, God the Word being man. But Jesus glorified God in death, and "when he had despoiled the principalities and powers, he exposed them confidently,

[1]See Rom 1:3. [2]Phil 2:8. [3]Phil 2:6.

having triumphed in the cross."[4] "He also "made peace through the blood of his cross, whether they are things in earth or things in heaven."[5] ... For in all these the Son of man was glorified, and God was glorified in him. Now since he who is glorified is glorified by someone, you will ask who this is.[6] Commentary on the Gospel of John 32.318, 321-22, 324-28.[7]

God Glorifies the Son of Man by Himself. Chrysostom: [God] will glorify him "by means of"[8] himself, not by means of another. And he "will immediately glorify him," that is, ... not at some distant time after the resurrection. His glory will appear immediately while he is still on the cross. And indeed, the sun was darkened, the rocks split open, the veil of the temple was parted in two, many bodies of saints that slept arose, the tomb had its seals, the guards sat by, and while a stone lay over the body the body rose. ... This happened not through the agency of angels or archangels, not by any other power, but by himself. Homilies on the Gospel of John 72.3-4.[9]

Glory As Participation in the Divine. Origen: The noun *glory* is not used with reference to an indifferent entity in the way some of the Greeks take it,[10] where they define glory to be approval by the multitude. It is clear that the noun is used of something over and above this from the following words in Exodus. "And the tabernacle was filled with the glory of the Lord."[11] ... "And when [Moses] descended from the mountain [he] also did not know that the appearance of his facial skin had been glorified while he spoke with him."[12] ...

So far as the literal sense is concerned, there was a divine epiphany in the tabernacle and in the temple,[13] which were destroyed, and in the face of Moses when he had conversed with the divine nature. But in a higher and more spiritual sense we are glorified, when with the eye of the understanding we penetrate into the things of God. For the mind, when it ascends above material things and spiritually sees God, is deified. The visible glory on the face of Moses is a figure of this spiritual glory. For it was his mind that was deified by its contemplation of God. Commentary on the Gospel of John 32.330-31, 334, 338-39.[14]

The Son of Man Glorified in Those Who Came to Know Him. Origen: But there is no comparison between the excellent glory of Christ and the knowledge of Moses whereby the face of his soul was glorified. ... For the whole of the Father's glory shines on the Son, who is the brightness of his glory and the express image of his person.[15] Yes, and from the light of this whole glory there go forth particular glories throughout the whole rational creation, though none can take in the whole of the divine glory except the Son. ...

But only insofar as the Son was known to the world, so far was he glorified. And as yet he was not fully known. But afterward the Father spread the knowledge of him over the whole world, and then the Son of man was glorified in those who knew him. And of this glory he has made all who know him partakers, as the apostle said, "We all, with open face beholding as in a glass the glory of the Lord, are changed into the same image, from glory to glory,"[16] that is, from his glory we receive glory. When he was approaching then that dispensation by which he was to become known to the world and to be glorified in the glory of those who glorified him, he says, "Now is the Son of man glorified."[17] And because "no one knows the Father but the Son, and he to whomever the Son will reveal him," and the Son by the dispensation was about to reveal the Father, this is why he said, "And God is glorified in him." Commentary on the Gospel of John 32.342, 353, 356-59.[18]

[4]Col 2:14-15. [5]Col 1:20. [6]Chrysostom answers this query in the next quote. [7]FC 89:402-3**; SC 385:324-28. [8]Gk *dia*. [9]NPNF 1 14:265**. [10]The Stoics classed *doxa* ("glory," "reputation") among indifferent things. [11]Ex 40:34. [12]Ex 34:29. [13]Origen had quoted 1 Kings 8:10-11. Origen also quotes Lk 9:29-31, 2 Cor 3:7-11, 18; 4:3-4, 6. [14]FC 89:404-6**; SC 385:328-34. [15]Heb 1:13. [16]2 Cor 3:18. [17]Mt 11:27. [18]FC 89:407-9**; SC 385:334, 338-42.

The Father's Glory Seen in the Son's Perfection. Origen: But the matters in this passage might be understood even more clearly as follows. Just as the name of God is blasphemed among the Gentiles because of some,[19] so, because of the saints whose good works are seen very distinctly before people, the name of the Father who is in heaven is glorified. In whom, then, was it glorified more than in Jesus, since he committed no sin, nor was deceit found in his mouth, nor did he know sin?[20] And since he is such as this, therefore, the Son is glorified, and God is glorified in him. But if God is glorified in him, the Father presents something to him in return that is greater than what the Son of man has done. For the glory of the Son of man, when the Father glorifies him, far exceeds the Father's glory when he [the Father] is glorified in the Son, since it is only fitting that the greater should return the greater glory. Commentary on the Gospel of John 32.360-63.[21]

His Glory Is in the Remaining Apostles. Augustine: Or think of it in this way: The unclean [i.e., Judas] went out; the clean remained with the one who cleanses them. This is how it will be when the tares are separated from the wheat. "The righteous shall shine forth as the sun in the kingdom of their Father."[22] Our Lord, foreseeing this, said this when Judas went out, as if the tares were now separated and he was left alone with the wheat, the holy apostles. "Now is the Son of man glorified," as if to say, Behold what will take place at my glorifying, at which none of the wicked shall be present; none of the righteous shall perish. He does not say, Now is the glorifying of the Son of man signified. Rather [he says], "Now is the Son of man glorified," just as it is not said, "That rock signified Christ," but "That Rock was Christ."[23] . . . Scripture often speaks of the things signifying as if they were the things signified. And so, the Lord makes use of the words "Now is the Son of man glorified" in order to indicate that, in the completed separation of that arch sinner from their company and in the remaining around him of his saints, we have the foreshadowing of his glorification when the wicked shall finally be separated and he shall dwell with his saints throughout eternity. Tractates on the Gospel of John 63.2.[24]

13:31b *God Is Glorified in the Son of Man*

Human Nature Also Endowed with Eternity. Augustine: But the glorifying of the Son of man is the glorifying of God in him, because he then adds, "And God is glorified in him," which he proceeds to explain. If God is glorified in him—for he came not to do his own will but the will of him that sent him—God shall also glorify him in himself so that the human nature that was assumed by the eternal Word shall also be endowed with eternity. Tractates on the Gospel of John 63.3.[25]

The Son's Glorification Is the Father's Glorification. Tertullian: It was the Son of God who was in the Son of man that was betrayed, as the Scripture says afterward, "Now the Son of man has been glorified, and God has been glorified in him." Who is here meant by *God?* Certainly not the Father,[26] but the Word of the Father who was in the Son of man—that is, in the flesh in which Jesus had been already glorified by the divine power and word. "And God," he says, "will also glorify him in himself." In other words, the Father shall glorify the Son because [the Father] has [the Son] within himself. And even though the Son is prostrated to the earth and put to death, [the Father] would soon glorify [the Son] by his resurrection and make him conqueror over death. Against Praxeas 23.11-12.[27]

The Glorification of Christ's Humanity in the Future. Hilary of Poitiers: In the

[19]See Rom 2:24. [20]See 1 Pet 2:22; 2 Cor 5:21. [21]FC 89:410**; SC 385:342-44. [22]Mt 13:43. [23]1 Cor 10:4. [24]NPNF 1 7:315**; CCL 36:486-87. [25]NPNF 1 7:315**; CCL 36:487. [26]As if separable from the Son. [27]ANF 3:619-20; CCL 2:1193.

words "Now is the Son of man honored, and God is honored in him," we have first the glory of the Son of man, then the glory of God in the Son of man. So there is first signified the glory of the body, which it borrows from its association with the divine nature. And then follows the promotion to a fuller glory derived from an addition to the glory of the body. . . . Already before this [the Son] was reigning in the glory that springs from the divine glory. From this time forward, however, [the Son] is himself to pass into the divine glory . . . leaving behind the dispensation by which he is man so that his whole being may be eternally transformed into divinity. The time when this will happen is not hidden from us either. . . . At the moment when Judas arose to betray him, he signified as present the glory that he would obtain after his passion through the resurrection, but he assigned to the future the glory with which God would glorify him with himself. The glory of God is seen in him in the power of the resurrection. But he himself, after his state of humiliation,[28] will be taken eternally into the glory of God, that is, into God, the all in all. ON THE TRINITY 11.42.[29]

13:32 *God Glorifies Him in Himself*

THE SON RECEIVES AGAIN THE GLORY HE HAD WITH THE FATHER. HILARY OF POITIERS: The meaning of his opening words can hardly be disputed when he says, "Now is the Son of man glorified." He was saying that all the glory that [the Son of man] obtains is not for the Word but for his flesh. . . . What, then, is the meaning of what follows . . . when he says that "God is glorified in him," that is, in the Son of man? Tell me, then, is the Son of man the same as the Son of God?[30] And since the Son of man is not one entity and the Son of God another—but he who is the Son of God is himself also the Son of man—who, pray tell, is the God who is glorified in this Son of man who is also the Son of God? . . . The third clause helps us with this when he adds, "If God is glorified in him, God has also glorified him in himself." . . . Now, a man is not glorified in himself, nor, on the other hand, does God, who is glorified in the man, cease being God just because he receives glory. . . . "God is glorified in him" must certainly be referring either to Christ, who is glorified in the flesh, or to the Father, who is glorified in Christ. If it is Christ, Christ is clearly God who is glorified in the flesh. If it is the Father, we are face to face with the mystery of the unity, since the Father is glorified in the Son. . . . But when we consider that God glorifies in himself God who is glorified in the Son of man, by what loophole, pray tell, can your profane doctrine escape from the confession that Christ is very God according to the truth of his nature? . . . The Father glorifies him, not with a glory from without but in himself. By taking him back into that glory that belongs to himself and that [the Son] had with him before, the Father glorifies [the Son] with himself and in himself. ON THE TRINITY 9.40-42.[31]

THE PASSION IS THE HIGHEST GLORIFICATION. THEODORE OF MOPSUESTIA: The time is near when the Son of man who was assumed will be glorified in a laudable way and in which, above all, God will be revealed before everybody through the things that happen to him. The events that happened at the time of the crucifixion, when the earth shook, the light of the sun was obscured, the darkness covered the earth, the sepulchers opened and the rocks were broken, showed how great was already—and how great would have been—the magnificence of the one who had been crucified. And, at the same time, they were the reason why people admired God who made the Son of man worthy of such an honor. "If God has been glorified in him, God will also glorify him in himself and will glorify him at once." Evidently, he says, God is glorified by those things that are happening in him as

[28]Lit. "out of the dispensation of subjection." [29]NPNF 2 9:215*; CCL 62A:569-70. [30]He expects an answer in the affirmative. [31]NPNF 2 9:168-69*; CCL 62A:414-18.

much as he also glorifies him. It cannot happen that he appears to be admirable because of him if the things that happened to him were not great. And they, he says, had already been given to him. Commentary on John 6.13.31-32.[32]

Jesus Speaks As If the Resurrection Had Taken Place. Augustine: He predicts his own resurrection, which was to follow immediately, not at the end of the world like ours. . . . And so he says, "Now is the Son of man glorified." The now refers not to his approaching passion but to the resurrection that was immediately to follow it, as if that which was so very soon to be had already taken place. Tractates on the Gospel of John 63.3.[33]

[32]CSCO 4 3:261-62. [33]NPNF 1 7:315-16**; CCL 36:488.

13:33-35 The Command to Love One Another

[33]Little children, yet a little while I am with you. You will seek me; and as I said to the Jews so now I say to you, "Where I am going you cannot come." [34]A new commandment I give to you, that you love one another; even as I have loved you, that you also love one another. [35]By this all men will know that you are my disciples, if you have love for one another.

Overview: Jesus alludes to his impending death (Origen). This elicits in his disciples even greater awareness of how they love him (Chrysostom). They attempt to seek him out in the sense that they seek the Word, wisdom, justice, truth and power of God that Christ is (Origen). They did indeed seek him out and found him after the resurrection, although at the time they still could not face death as he would (Theodore).

In this context Jesus gives them a new commandment, which is really a fulfilling of the old based on the song of love. He calls on us to love one another as those who are God's sons and daughters. As brothers and sisters of his Son, we will seek to make each other the dwelling place of God (Augustine). This kind of love that Christ calls for goes further than anything previously commanded (Cyril) because it is a love that is not owed (Chrysostom). In order to show we are his, we are called to love others more than ourselves (Theodore). That kind of love is a greater sign to the world of what God is all about than any miracle would be (Chrysostom). As we express this love toward one another, the artistry of God who paints his portrait in us shines through (Gregory of Nyssa).

13:33 *Jesus' Presence, Departure and Disciples' Seeking*

Jesus' Impending Death. Origen: The statement "Yet a little while I am with you" is clear in the simple sense, so far as the literal sense is concerned, since he would soon no longer be with the disciples. First, he was arrested by the cohort and the tribune and the servants of the Jews who bound him and led him off to Annas first, and after this he was delivered to Pilate. Next, he was condemned to the cross, and then he spent three days and three nights in the heart of the earth.[1] Commentary on the Gospel of John 32.376.[2]

[1]See Mt 12:40. [2]FC 89:412; SC 385:348

Jesus Incites the Disciples' Love for Him. Chrysostom: "Where I go, you cannot come." He shows that his death is a removal and a change for the better to a place that does not admit corruptible bodies. This he says both to excite their love toward him and to make it more fervent. You know that when we see any of our dearest friends departing from us, our affection is warmest, and the more so when we see them going to a place to which it is not even possible for us to go. He said these things then, terrifying the Jews but kindling longing in the disciples. This is such a place that not only they, but not even you, my most beloved, can come there. In this statement he also makes clear his own dignity [since he can go there]. Homilies on the Gospel of John 72.4.[3]

Seeking Jesus As the Word. Origen: For in that "little while" in which they would not see him, they would seek Jesus, and for this reason they would weep and lament, although their grief would change to joy when the saying was fulfilled, "And again a little while and you will see me."[4] But to seek Jesus is to seek the Word, and wisdom, and justice, and truth and the power of God, all of which Christ is. Commentary on the Gospel of John 32.385, 387.[5]

The Apostles Seek and Find Jesus After the Resurrection. Theodore of Mopsuestia: He references the time up until his passion when he says "only a little longer." He says to the Jews, "You will look for me," and adds, "and you will not find me," because they would no longer see him anymore after his passion. But to his disciples he only says, "You will look for me." Indeed, they looked for him and, since they were led by devotion in their search for him and saw themselves deprived of the care of their teacher, they found him. They saw him after his resurrection, and they lived and ate with him until he ascended into heaven. Commentary on John 6.13.33.[6]

The Apostles Cannot Face Death Now, but Will Later. Theodore of Mopsuestia: But, he says, as I said to the Jews that they could not come where I go, "so now I say to you." Notice that he added "now." By saying that they could not come where he goes, he means that they still cannot face death like him. In fact, they all run away. And even Simon denied him. But he added "now" to declare that afterward they would disregard sufferings and trials. Indeed, after the descent of the Holy Spirit they even enjoyed suffering for Christ since they were fully confirmed in faith in him and in the promise of future things. Therefore, he says, even though you are led by love to look for me—I know that you do this because of your love for me—nevertheless you cannot prove now your love with your works since your natural weakness inspires you with fear. Therefore things are going to happen [now] that cannot happen in a different way. If you want, you can do what I am teaching you to do even now while you are still a little apprehensive since it is useful now, and it will be [even more] useful later. Commentary on John 6.13.33.[7]

13:34 *A New Commandment to Love One Another*

Love Fulfills the Law. Apostolic Constitutions: He who then had forbidden murder now forbids anger without cause.[8] He who had forbidden adultery now forbids all unlawful lust. He who had forbidden stealing now pronounces him most happy who supplies those that are in want out of his own labors.[9] He who had forbidden hatred now pronounces him blessed who loves his enemies.[10] Constitutions of the Holy Apostles 6.23.[11]

Love One Another As Those Who Are God's. Augustine: The Lord Jesus declares that

[3]NPNF 1 14:266**. [4]Jn 16:19. [5]FC 89:414; SC 385:352-54. [6]CSCO 4 3:262. [7]CSCO 4 3:262-63. [8]The writer had just quoted Jn 13:34; see also Mt 5:22. [9]Act 20:35. [10]Mt 5:7. [11]ANF 7:460*.

he is giving his disciples a new commandment, that they should love one another. . . . But was not this already commanded in the ancient law of God, where it is written, "You shall love your neighbor as yourself"?[12] Why, then, is it called a new one by the Lord, when it is proven to be so old? Is it a new commandment because he has divested us of the old and clothed us with the new person? For it is not indeed every kind of love that renews him that listens to it, or rather yields it obedience, but that love regarding which the Lord, in order to distinguish it from all carnal affection, added, "as I have loved you.". . . For this they hear and observe, "A new commandment I give unto you, that you love one another," not as those who are corrupt love one another or as human beings who love one another only in a human way. Instead, they are to love one another as those who are God's. All of them are to love as children of the Highest, who are siblings, therefore, of his only Son. They are to love with that mutual love by which he loved them when about to lead them on to the goal where all sufficiency should be theirs and where their every desire should be satisfied with good things.[13] Tractates on the Gospel of John 65.1.[14]

Love God in the Other. Augustine: But do not think that that greater commandment that requires us to love the Lord our God with all our heart, and with all our soul and with all our mind is overlooked. . . . For, if we understand the two commandments correctly, each is implied in the other. One who loves God cannot despise his commandment that he should love his neighbor. And he who loves his neighbor in a heavenly spiritual way, what does he love in that neighbor but God? That is the love that our Lord distinguishes from all human love when he adds, "As I have loved you." For what was it but God that he loved in us? Not because we had him, but in order that we might have him and that he may lead us on . . . to where God is all in all. . . . And so, let each of us so love the other in such a way that by this working of love we make each other the dwelling place of God. Tractates on the Gospel of John 65.2.[15]

Christ's Love Goes Further Than Anything Previous. Cyril of Alexandria: He plainly indicates the novelty involved in his command here—and the extent to which the love he enjoins here surpasses the old idea of mutual love[16]—by adding the words "Even as I have loved you, you also should love one another.". . . The law of Moses mandated the necessity of loving our brothers as ourselves, yet our Lord Jesus the Christ loved us far more than he loved himself. Otherwise, he would have never descended to our humiliation from his original exaltation in the form of God and on an equality with God the Father, nor would he have undergone for our sakes the exceptional bitterness of his death in the flesh, nor have submitted to beatings from the Jews, to shame, to derision, and all his other sufferings too numerous to mention. Being rich, he would never have become poor if he had not loved us far more than he loved himself. It was indeed something new for love to go as far as that! Christ commands us to love as he did, putting neither reputation, wealth or anything else before love of our brothers and sisters. If need be, we even need to be prepared to face death for our neighbor's salvation as our Savior's blessed disciples did, as well as those who followed in their footsteps. To them the salvation of others mattered more than their own lives, and they were ready to do anything or to suffer anything to save souls that were perishing. Commentary on the Gospel of John 9.[17]

A Love That Is Not Owed. Chrysostom: Or think of "as I have loved you" this way: For my love has not been the payment of something owing to you but had its beginning on my side.

[12]Lev 19:18. [13]See Ps 103:5 (102:5 LXX, Vg). [14]NPNF 1 7:317-18*; CCL 36:490-91. See also *Sermon* 33.2 (CCL 41:413-14; *WSA* 3 2:154-55) and *Sermon* 140A (*WSA* 3 4:409). [15]NPNF 1 7:318**; CCL 36:491-92. [16]Deut 6:5. [17]LF 48:217-19*.

And in a similar way you ought to do one another good, though you may not owe it. Homilies on the Gospel of John 72.5.[18]

13:35 *Jesus' Disciples Are Recognized by Their Love for One Another*

Love Others More Than Ourselves. Theodore of Mopsuestia: How is it new? "Just as I have loved you, you also should love one another." The way to love is what is new. In the Law it had been ordered that anyone should love his neighbor like himself.[19] But the voice of the Lord wants our companions in faith to be loved even more than ourselves, because he orders us to imitate his love for us. In the words that follow he shows that accurately. Indeed, in order to amplify the greatness of this precept he says, "By this everyone will know that you are my disciples, if you have love for one another." So excellent is the observation of that command that it is a sign clear enough of my discipleship. Commentary on John 6.13.34-35.[20]

Love Is a Greater Sign Than Miracles. Chrysostom: Passing over the miracles that they were to perform, he makes love the distinguishing mark of his followers. . . . Miracles do not attract unbelievers as much as the way you live your life. And nothing brings about a proper life as much as love. Homilies on the Gospel of John 72.5.[21]

God the Artist Paints Himself As Love in Us. Gregory of Nyssa: It is true, indeed, that the divine beauty is not adorned with any shape or endowment of form, by any beauty of color, but it is contemplated as excellence in unspeakable bliss. As then painters transfer human forms to their pictures by means of certain colors, laying on their copy the proper and corresponding tints so that the beauty of the original may be accurately transferred to the likeness, so I would have you understand that our Maker also, painting the portrait to resemble his own beauty, by the addition of virtues, as it were with colors, shows in us his own sovereignty. There are also many and varied tints, so to say, by which his true form is portrayed: not red or white or the blending of these, whatever it may be called, nor a touch of black that paints the eyebrow and the eye and shades, by some combination, the depressions in the figure, and all such arts that the hands of painters contrive. But instead of these, purity, freedom from passion, blessedness, alienation from all evil and all those attributes of a similar kind that help to form in men and women the likeness of God. With such hues as these did the Maker of his own image mark our nature.

And if you were to examine the other points also by which the divine beauty is expressed, you will find that to them too the likeness in the image that we present is perfectly preserved. . . . God is love and the fount of love: for this the great John declares that "love is of God" and "God is love,"[22] the Fashioner of our nature has made this to be our feature too. For "in this," he says, "shall all know that you are my disciples, if you love one another." And so, if love is absent, the whole stamp of the likeness is transformed. On the Making of Man 5.[23]

[18]NPNF 1 14:266**. [19]Lev 19:18. [20]CSCO 4 3:263. [21]NPNF 1 14:266**. [22]1 Jn 4:8. [23]NPNF 2 5:391*.

13:36-38 The Prediction of Peter's Denials

[36]*Simon Peter said to him, "Lord, where are you going?" Jesus answered, "Where I am going you cannot follow me now; but you shall follow afterward."* [37]*Peter said to him, "Lord, why cannot I follow you now? I will lay down my life for you."* [38]*Jesus answered, "Will you lay down your life for me? Truly, truly, I say to you, the cock will not crow, till you have denied me three times.*

Overview: Jesus speaks of his departure, and Peter, to whom Jesus had entrusted the keys to the kingdom, does not presume to follow but rather only asks as one not yet up to following (Ambrose). Only those who are prepared to walk in Christ's steps persistently can follow (Origen). And so we must rely on the power of the Spirit, who alone enables us to follow as we enter into our greatest trials (Cyril). The brave assertion of Peter that he would lay down his life for Jesus belied his later denial but also confirmed that it is fear of death that kills you (Augustine). Jesus allows Peter to learn his own weaknesses (Chrysostom), but at this point, Peter promises more than he can fulfill, seeking to lead when he should be following (Augustine). At the time, Peter knew his great desire to defend Jesus; what he did not know was his own strength (Augustine). But even though he later failed, the fact that he received pardon is comfort for us when we fall (Bede). Peter dies by denial but lives by tears (Augustine) as he comes to learn who he truly is (Chrysostom). The speech regarding Peter's denial occurs at different points in different Gospels, but they are not in contradiction (Augustine, Theodore).

13:36 *Going And Following*

Peter Was Not Presuming. Ambrose: The soul too wishes to arrive at the prize that it longs to obtain. And so it wisely asks that it be drawn, because not all are able to follow. Indeed, when Peter said, "Where are you going?" the Word of God replied, "Where I am going, you cannot follow me now. But you will follow afterward." The Lord had entrusted to him the keys of the kingdom of heaven,[1] and yet Peter judged himself unequal to following. The Lord did not put off this soul, however, for Peter was not presuming but asking. Isaac, or the Soul 3.10.[2]

Following Christ. Origen: The Word, however, departs on his own courses, and he who follows the Word follows him. But one who is not prepared to walk in his steps persistently cannot follow, since the Word leads those to his Father who do all things that they might be able to follow him and that they may follow him until they may say to the Christ, "My soul has clung to you."[3] Commentary on the Gospel of John 32.400.[4]

The Spirit Empowers Us. Cyril of Alexandria: The disciples had not yet been clothed with the power from on high, neither had they received the strength that was to invigorate them and impart courage to their character—I mean the gift of the Holy Spirit. Thus, they were not able to wrestle with death and engage in a conflict with terrors so hard to face. Commentary on the Gospel of John 9.[5]

13:37 *I Will Lay Down My Life for You*

Being Afraid of Death Is What Kills You. Augustine: Peter had earlier answered the

[1]See Mt 16:19. [2]FC 65:18; CSEL 32 1:650. [3]See Ps 63:8 (62:9 LXX). [4]FC 89:417; SC 385:358-60. [5]LF 48:225*.

Lord out of a kind of proud self-assurance when he had told him, "I will lay down my life for you." He had not yet received the strength to carry out that promise. Now, in order to be able to do so, he is already filled with charity. That is why he is asked, "Do you love me?" And he answers "I do," because it is only charity that can carry it out. So how do things stand, Peter? Dying is what you were afraid of. He is alive and talking to you, the one you saw dead. Do not be afraid of death anymore. It has been conquered in him whose death you dreaded. He hung on the cross, he was fixed there with nails, he gave up the spirit, he was struck with a lance, laid in the tomb. That is what you were afraid of when you denied him, afraid you would suffer this. And by fearing death you denied life. Understand the truth now: when you were afraid of dying, that is when you died. SERMON 253.3.[6]

JESUS LETS PETER LEARN HIS OWN WEAKNESSES. CHRYSOSTOM: [Jesus says to Peter], You shall know from this temptation that your love is nothing without the presence of the impulse from above. From this it is clear that in caring for him, Jesus allowed Peter to fall. Jesus wanted to teach him by what he had said earlier, but in the face of Peter's vehemence,[7] Jesus did not throw or force him into his denial but rather left him alone in order that he might learn his own weakness. . . . Since Peter is in the habit of contradicting Jesus, Jesus next teaches him not to oppose him. . . . In every way, Jesus teaches Peter humility and proves that human nature by itself is nothing. HOMILIES ON THE GOSPEL OF JOHN 73.1.[8]

PETER PROMISES MORE THAN HE CAN FULFILL. AUGUSTINE: Peter promised he would die for him, and he was not even able to die with him. He had staked more, you see, than his credit could stand. He had promised more than he could fulfill, because it was in fact unfitting that he should do what he had promised. "I will lay down my life," he said, "for you." But that is what the Lord was going to do for the servant, not the servant for the Lord. So as he had staked more than he was worth, he was then loving in an inverted sort of way; that is why he was afraid and denied Christ. Later on, though, the Lord, after he has risen, teaches Peter how to love. While he was loving in the wrong way, he collapsed under the weight of Christ's passion. But when he was loving in the right way, Christ promises him a passion of his own. SERMON 296.1.[9]

PETER WANTS TO LEAD. AUGUSTINE: The blessed Peter, as we have just heard, is ordered to follow. And yet he had originally been thinking of going ahead when he said to the Lord, "I will lay down my life for you." He was so sure of himself that he was unaware of his fear. He wanted to go ahead of the one he should be following. It was a good thing he was eager to do, but he did not keep to the right order. SERMON 297.1.[10]

13:38 *Prophecy of Peter's Threefold Denial*

PETER DID NOT KNOW HIS OWN STRENGTH. AUGUSTINE: Peter knew his great desire. What he did not know was his own strength. He boasted of his will while he was still weak. But the Physician had an eye on the state of his health. . . . Will you do for me what I have not done yet for you? "Will you lay down your life for my sake?" Can you go before even though you cannot come after? Why are you so presumptuous? What do you think of yourself and what do you imagine yourself to be? Listen to what you are: "Truly, truly, I say to you, the rooster shall not crow till you have denied me three times." See, that is how you will very quickly get to know who you are—someone who talks big but has no idea that he is only a child. You promise me your death and yet will deny me your life. You, who think you are able to die for me, learn to live first

[6]*WSA* 3 7:149**; SC 116:330. [7]See Mt 16:22; Jn 13:8. [8]NPNF 1 14:267-68**. [9]*WSA* 3 8:203*; MiAg 1:401. [10]*WSA* 3 8:216; PL 38:1359.

for yourself. When you fear the death of your flesh, you occasion the death of your soul. Just as much as it is life to confess Christ, it is death to deny him. . . . The frailty of Peter himself acknowledged its sin when he witnessed by his tears the evil he had done in denying Christ. . . . Nor do we say this because we have pleasure in blaming the first of the apostles. But in looking at him, we learn that no one should place his confidence in human strength. Tractates on the Gospel of John 66.1-2.[11]

Peter Dies by Denial but Lives by Tears. Augustine: That took place in the soul of Peter which he offered in the body, although it happened differently from what he intended. For before the death and resurrection of our Lord, he did both die by his denial and live again by his tears. He died because he was so sure of himself, but he lived again because Jesus looked on him with kindness. Tractates on the Gospel of John 66.2.[12]

Peter Will Learn to Know Himself. Chrysostom: [Jesus] let him go without assistance so that he might learn his own weakness . . . and not fall into such sin again when he received the stewardship of the world, but that remembering what had happened to him, he might know himself. Homilies on the Gospel of John 73.1.[13]

Different Accounts Compared. Augustine: John is not the only Evangelist who details this prophetic announcement of Jesus' own denial to Peter. The other three also record the same thing[14] but not at the same time in all cases. Matthew and Mark introduce it after they have left the house in which they were eating the Passover. Luke and John bring it in before he left that scene. We may suppose either that the two former are referring to what had passed or the two latter are anticipating what is coming. Or the great difference not only of the words but of the subjects that precede the speech and that excite Peter to the presumption of offering to die for or with our Lord may lead us to conclude that he made this offer three times and that our Lord three times replied, "Before the rooster crows, you shall deny me three times." Harmony of the Gospels 3.2.5.[15]

John and Mark Are Not in Contradiction. Theodore of Mopsuestia: This is not contrary to what is said in Mark. For he said, "The rooster will not crow twice before you will deny me three times."[16] You see, as soon as he denied him, the rooster crowed. And as he denied for a third time, the rooster crowed for a second time, in some way bearing witness to the truthfulness of the Lord, as well as reminding Peter both what he said to the Lord and what he heard from him. Therefore, when he denied at first, by the will of the Lord the bird uttered a sound out of its proper time.[17] But when he denied for the third time, then it crowed at the appointed time. However Mark, dictating the Gospel according to Peter's view, also said how many times the bird crowed during the denial, as if he wanted to establish more clearly the reproach of Peter by his own sin. Commentary on the Gospel of John, Fragment 119.13.38.[18]

---

[11]NPNF 1 7:319-20**; CCL 36:493-94. [12]NPNF 1 7:320*; CCL 36:495. [13]NPNF 1 14:267-68**. [14]Mt 26:30-35; Mk 14:26-31; Lk 22:31-34. [15]NPNF 1 6:178-79** ; CSEL 43:272-73. [16]Mk 14:30. [17]The Syriac text of Theodore says, "according to the will and command of the Lord." [18]ECS 7:112*

14:1-6 THE WAY, THE TRUTH AND THE LIFE

[1]"Let not your hearts be troubled; believe[e] in God, believe also in me. [2]In my Father's house are many rooms; if it were not so, would I have told you that I go to prepare a place for you? [3]And when I go and prepare a place for you, I will come again and will take you to myself, that where I am you may be also. [4]And you know the way where I am going."[f] [5]Thomas said to him, "Lord, we do not know where you are going; how can we know the way?" [6]Jesus said to him, "I am the way, and the truth, and the life; no one comes to the Father, but by me."

e Or *you believe* **f** Other ancient authorities read *where I am going you know, and the way you know*

Overview: Jesus sees that his disciples are needlessly afraid for their Lord (Augustine), caught between the hope of his mercy and fear of their own stumbling (Cyril) and the trials that awaited them (Augustine). He calls for faith in them, which is more powerful than anything (Chrysostom), making soldiers out of recent cowards (Cyril). This statement, "Believe in God and believe in me also," demonstrates his unity with the divine nature while also distinguishing his person as Christ the Son in the Trinity (Hilary).

Jesus then speaks of the many mansions in his Father's house for the many members of his body, each allotted according to their readiness to trust (Irenaeus, Tertullian). He will rehabilitate our present fleshly houses into mansions, providing us better living through resurrection (Tertullian). And so, as he prepares the mansions, he is also preparing the dwellers (Augustine). There will be abundance and rest in these plentiful mansions (Gregory of Nazianzus), and Christ has already taken care of the reservations (Theodore). The mansions are already fully prepared, and so Christ goes ahead of us not so much to prepare them but to prepare the way by making our human nature capable of living in those divine dwellings (Cyril). He is going to leave his disciples here in order to elicit faith, which, by definition, would not be possible had he remained (Augustine). But he is coming for them and us to bring all of us into himself where there is life, since he himself is life (Augustine) and the way to the place where we will all go (Cyril).

Thomas's question evidences that they did indeed know the way—they just did not know that they knew (Augustine). To follow Christ as the way is to follow the cross (Leo) toward perfection (Basil) as we come to God through God (Peter Chrysologus). The disciples understand and are comforted by the fact that Christ is the way, but they are not as comprehending of what follows (Chrysostom). Since Jesus is also the truth, he will not mislead us along the way (Hilary). In fact, not only is his name "Truth" (Ambrose), but he is the truth, being equal to the Father (Ambrose). We should then walk by faith in the truth that is Christ so that we may one day see that truth (Augustine).

Our Lord is also "the life" because he is the only one who can restore us to the life of incorruptibility that we hope for and for which we were made (Cyril). What the soul is to the body, Christ is to the soul (Peter Chrysologus), as he himself is immortality, which he gives to us (Gregory of Nyssa). Christ is the only way to the Father (Augustine), and no one can understand the Father apart from the Son (Hilary), nor can anyone partake of the divine nature apart from Christ's mediation (Cyril). May Christ be the way that receives us, the truth that strengthens us and the life that invigorates us (Ambrose).

14:1a *Calm for Troubled Hearts*

The Disciples Needlessly Afraid for Their Lord. Augustine: Our Lord consoles his disciples who, as men, would be naturally alarmed and troubled at the idea of his death, by assuring them of his divinity, . . . "Let not your heart be troubled: you believe in God, believe also in me," as if they must believe in him if they believed in God. This would not follow unless Christ were God. . . . You are in fear for this form of a servant. Let not your heart be troubled. The form of God shall raise it up. Tractates on the Gospel of John 67.1.[1]

Between Hope and Fear. Cyril of Alexandria: In commanding them not to be troubled, Jesus placed them, as it were, on the threshold between hope and fear. This way, if they fell into weakness and suffering in their human frailty, the hope of his mercy might help them to recover. On the other hand, the fear of stumbling might urge them to fall less often inasmuch as they had not yet been endowed with the power from above, from on high—I mean the grace that comes through the Spirit that always keeps them from failure. Commentary on the Gospel of John 9.[2]

Jesus Calms the Disciples' Fear of Death. Augustine: And as the disciples were afraid for themselves when Peter, the boldest and most zealous of them, had been told, "The rooster will not crow until you have denied me thrice, . . ." Jesus adds, "In my Father's house are many mansions," . . . by way of an assurance to them in their trouble that they might with confidence and certainty look forward, after all their trials, to dwelling together with Christ in the presence of God. Tractates on the Gospel of John 67.2.[3]

Faith More Powerful Than Anything. Chrysostom: He shows the power of the Godhead within him, discerning their inward feelings when he says, "Let not your heart be troubled." "Believe in God, believe also in me." . . . Faith, too, in me, and in the Father who begat me, is more powerful than anything that shall come on you. And it will permit no evil thing to prevail against you. Homilies on the Gospel of John 73.1.[4]

Faith As a Weapon. Cyril of Alexandria: Here, Jesus makes an able soldier out of one who recently was a coward. And while the disciples were suffering with the anxieties of fear, he commands them to cling to the intense power of faith. . . . Faith is a weapon whose blade is stout and broad; it drives away all cowardice that may spring from the expectation of coming suffering and renders the darts of evildoers utterly void of effect and makes their temptations utterly profitless. Commentary on the Gospel of John 9.[5]

Unity of Nature, Distinction of Persons. Hilary of Poitiers: Our Lord speaks in words deliberately chosen, so that whatever he claims for the Father, he signifies in modest language to be appropriate to himself. Take for example the command, "Believe in God, and believe in me." He is identified with God in honor. How, I ask you, can he be separated from his nature? He says, "Believe in me also," just as he said "Believe in God." Do not the words "in me" signify his nature? Separate the two natures, but then you must also separate the two beliefs. If it is life that we should believe in God without Christ, strip Christ of the name and qualities of God. But if perfect life is given to those who believe in God only when they believe in Christ also, let the careful reader ponder the meaning of the saying, "Believe in God, and believe in me also," for these words, uniting faith in him with faith in God, unite his nature to God's. He enjoins first of all the duty of belief in God but

[1]NPNF 1 7:321**; CCL 36:495. [2]LF 48:232**. [3]NPNF 1 7:321**; CCL 36:495. [4]NPNF 1 14:268**. [5]LF 48:232-33**.

adds to it the command that we should believe in himself also, which implies that he is God, since those who believe in God must also believe in him. Yet he excludes the suggestion of a unity contrary to religion, for the exhortation "Believe in God, believe in me also" forbids us to think of him as alone in solitude. On the Trinity 9.19.[6]

14:2 *Many Rooms in the Father's House*

Shares Allotted According to Worthiness. Irenaeus: All things belong to God, who supplies all with a suitable dwelling place, even as his Word says that a share is allotted to all by the Father, according as each person is or shall be worthy.[7] And this is the couch on which the guests shall recline, having been invited to the wedding.[8] Against Heresies 5.36.2.[9]

Mansions in the Realm of Rewards. Tertullian: How will there be many mansions in our Father's house, if not to match the diversity of what each deserves? How will one star also differ from another star in glory, unless in virtue of disparity in their rays?[10] Scorpiace 6.[11]

Better Living Through Resurrection. Tertullian: Owing to the fact that our flesh is undergoing dissolution through its sufferings, we shall be provided with a home in heaven. . . . Because he had called the flesh a house, he wanted to use the same term elegantly in his comparison of the ultimate reward, promising to the very house that undergoes dissolution through suffering a better house through the resurrection, just as the Lord also promises us many mansions like that of a house in his Father's home. On the Resurrection of the Flesh 41.1, 3.[12]

Preparing the Dwellers. Augustine: But he is in a certain sense preparing the dwellings by preparing for them the dwellers. As, for instance, when he said, "In my Father's house are many dwellings." What else can we suppose the house of God to mean but the temple of God? And what that is, ask the apostle, and he will reply, "For the temple of God is holy, which temple you are."[13] This is also the kingdom of God that the Son is yet to deliver up to the Father. . . . For it is to this kingdom, standing then at the right hand, that it shall be said in the end, "Come, you blessed of my Father, receive the kingdom."[14] In other words, you who were the kingdom but without the power to rule, come and reign so that what you formerly were only in hope, you may now have the power to be in reality. This house of God, therefore, this temple of God, this kingdom of God and kingdom of heaven, is as yet in the process of building, of construction, of preparation, of assembling. There will be dwellings in it even as the Lord is now preparing them. There are in fact such dwellings already even as the Lord has already ordained them. Tractates on the Gospel of John 68.2.[15]

Plentiful Mansions. Gregory of Nazianzus: Are there many mansions in God's house, as you have heard, or only one? Of course you will admit that there are many, and not just one. Now, are they all to be filled, or only some, and others not, so that some will be left empty and will have been prepared to no purpose? Of course all will be filled, for nothing can be in vain that has been done by God. Against the Eunomians, Theological Oration 1(27).8.[16]

Reservations Are Already Made. Theodore of Mopsuestia: With my Father there is such an abundance that he can give everyone the delights of eternal happiness. . . . He tells us that

[6]NPNF 2 9:161*; CCL 62A:389-90. [7]Irenaeus alludes to the different degrees of glory and rewards believers will experience in heaven. [8]Mt 22:10. [9]ANF 1:567*; SC 153:458. See also *Against Heresies* 3.19.3. [10]1 Cor 15:41. [11]ANF 3:639**; CSEL 20:157. [12]ANF 3:575**; CCL 2:975. See also Tertullian *On Monogamy* 10 (ANF 4:67). [13]1 Cor 3:17. [14]Mt 25:34. [15]NPNF 1 7:323*; CCL 36:498. Augustine also uses this passage to "reject those who infer from there being many mansions that there is a place outside the kingdom of heaven, where innocent souls that have departed this life without baptism . . . remain in bliss," referring to this as akin to secondary housing. *Tractates on the Gospel of John* 67.3 (NPNF 1 7:321). [16]NPNF 2 7:287.

here since the custom among us, when space is scarce, is to reserve a place to stay in advance due to lack of available rooms. Commentary on John 6.14.2.[17]

14:3 *Jesus Prepares a Place for Us with Him*

The Mansions Are Already Prepared. Cyril of Alexandria: If there were not many mansions in God the Father's home, he would have said that he was going on before them to prepare beforehand the homes of the saints. But since he already knew that there were many homes already fully prepared and awaiting the arrival of those who love God, he says that he will depart, but not for this purpose. Rather, he leaves in order to secure the way to the mansions above, to prepare a passage of safety for you and to smooth the paths that were formerly impassible. For in times of old, heaven was utterly inaccessible to mortals, and no flesh as yet had ever traveled that pure and all-holy realm of the angels. But Christ was the first who consecrated for us the means of access to himself and granted to flesh a way of entrance into heaven. He did this by presenting himself as an offering to God the Father, the "firstfruits of those who are asleep"[18] and are lying in the tomb, and by presenting himself as the first human being that ever appeared in heaven. . . . For Christ did not ascend on high in order to present himself before the presence of God the Father. He always was and is and will be continually in the Father, in the sight of him who begat him. For he is the one in whom the Father takes delight. Rather, he who of old was the Word with no part or lot in human nature has now ascended in human form so that he may appear in heaven in a strange and unusual manner. And this he has done on our account and for our sakes in order that he, though "found as a man,"[19] may still in his absolute power as Son—while yet in human form—obey the command, "Sit at my right hand,"[20] and in this way transfer the glory of adoption through himself to the entire human race. For because he has appeared in human form, he is still one of us as he sits at the right hand of God the Father, even though he is far above all creation. He is also consubstantial with his Father due to the fact that he has come forth from him as truly God of God and Light of Light. He has presented himself therefore as man to the Father on our behalf so that he may restore us again, as it were, to behold the Father's face—we who were removed from the Father's presence by the ancient transgression. . . .

"I shall not then," he says, "depart to prepare mansions for you. There are already enough there. There is no need to make new homes for my creation. But I go to prepare a place for you because of the sin that has mastery over you in order that those of you who are on the earth will be able to be mingled with the holy angels. Otherwise, the holy multitude of those above would never mingle with those [below] who were so defiled. But now, when I shall have accomplished the work of uniting the world below with that above—giving you a way of access to the city on high as well—I will return again at the time of regeneration and 'receive you with myself, so that where I am, there you may be also.' " Commentary on the Gospel of John 9.[21]

He Leaves to Elicit Faith. Augustine: But why has he gone away to prepare it, if it is ourselves that he prepares? If he leaves us, how can he prepare us? The meaning is that in order that those mansions may be prepared, the just must live by faith . . . and if you *see*, there is no faith. . . . Let Christ go away then so that he is not seen. Let him remain concealed that faith may be exercised. Then a place is prepared if you live by faith. Let faith desire so that the place desired may itself be possessed. The longing of love is the preparation of the mansion. In this way, Lord, prepare what you are preparing. For you are preparing us for yourself and yourself for us, inas-

[17]CSCO 4 3:265-66. [18]1 Cor 15:20. [19]Phil 2:8. [20]Ps 110:1. [21]LF 48:236-38**. He goes on to cite 1 Thess 4:15-17 as to how this will take place.

much as you are preparing a place both for yourself in us and for us in you. For you have said, "Abide in me, and I in you." [22] As far as each one has been a partaker of you, some less, some more, such will be the diversity of rewards in proportion to the diversity of merits. The multitude of mansions will suit the multitude of inequalities among their occupants. But all of them, nonetheless, will live eternally and will be endlessly blessed. Tractates on the Gospel of John 68.3.[23]

Life Himself. Augustine: When he says, therefore, "That where I am, there you may be also," where else were they to be but in himself? In this way he is also in himself, and they, therefore, are just where he is, that is, in himself. Accordingly, he himself is that eternal life that is yet to be ours, when he has received us unto himself. As he is that life eternal, so is it in him, that where he is there shall we be also, that is to say, in himself. "For as the Father has life in himself"—and certainly that life that he has is in no way different from what he is himself as its possessor—"so has he given to the Son to have life in himself."[24] This is so because he is the very life that he has in himself. But will we then actually be what he is, [namely], the life when we begin our existence in that life, that is, in himself? Certainly not, for he, by his very existence as the life, has life. He is himself what he has. And just as the life is in him, so he is in himself. But we are not that life. We are partakers of his life. And we shall be there in such a way as to be wholly incapable of being in ourselves what he is. But even while we ourselves are not the life, we will be able to have him as our life. And he himself has life because of the very fact that he himself is the life. Tractates on the Gospel of John 70.1.[25]

14:4 *You Know the Way to the Place Where I Am Going*

"The Way" Is Jesus. Cyril of Alexandria: "I myself," he seems to say, "am going ahead to prepare the path of entry into the heavens." But if you wish, and if it is the delight of your heart to rest within those mansions, and if you have devoted everything to reaching that city above and dwelling in the company of the holy spirits—then "you know the way," which is myself. For assuredly it is through me and no one else that you will ever gain that marvelous blessing. No other will ever open the heavens to you or smooth over the ground that one on earth could ever walk—except myself alone. Commentary on the Gospel of John 9.[26]

14:5 *Thomas's Question*

The Disciples Do Not Know They Know. Augustine: The Lord said they knew the place to which and the way whereby he was going. Thomas declares he does not know either the place or the way. But Thomas does not know he is speaking falsely. They knew, but they did not know that they knew. Jesus, however, will convince them of what they already know even though they themselves imagine that they are ignorant about it. Tractates on the Gospel of John 69.1.[27]

14:6 *The Way, the Truth and the Life*

The Way of the Cross. Leo the Great: The cross of Christ, which was set up for the salvation of mortals, is both a sacrament and an example: a sacrament whereby the divine power takes effect, an example whereby one's devotion is excited. For to those who are rescued from the prisoner's yoke, redemption further procures the power of following the way of the cross by imitation. For if the world's wisdom so prides itself in its error that everyone follows the opinions and habits and whole manner of life of him whom he has chosen as his leader, how shall we share in the name of

[22]Jn 15:4. [23]NPNF 1 7:323-24**; CCL 36:498-99. [24]Jn 5:26. [25]NPNF 1 7:326*; CCL 36:502-3. [26]LF 48:238-39**. [27]NPNF 1 7:324**; CCL 36:500.

Christ except by being inseparably united to him who is, as he himself asserted, "the way, the truth and the life"—the way, that is, of holy living, the truth of divine doctrine and the life of eternal happiness. SERMON 72.1.[28]

THE PERFECT WAY. BASIL THE GREAT: We understand the "way" to be the road to perfection, advancing in order step by step through the words of righteousness and the illumination of knowledge, always yearning for that which lies ahead and straining toward the last mile, until we reach that blessed end, the knowledge of God, with which the Lord blesses those who believe in him. For truly our Lord is a good way, a straight road with no confusing forks or turns, leading us directly to the Father. For "no one comes to the Father," he says, "except through me." Such is our way up to God through his Son. ON THE HOLY SPIRIT 8.18.[29]

TO GOD THROUGH GOD. PETER CHRYSOLOGUS: "I am the way," he says, so that the power of demons may not prevail in impeding those coming to the way through the Way, to God through God. It is not possible to attain to God except through God. SERMON 16.4.[30]

DISCIPLES UNDERSTAND THE WAY BUT NOT THE REST. CHRYSOSTOM: "I am the way." This is the proof that "No one comes to the Father but by me." "The truth and the life" prove that these statements will be carried out. "There is, then, no falsehood with me if I am 'the truth.' It is also the same if I am 'life,' since not even death shall be able to stop you from coming to me. Besides, if I am 'the way,' you will need no one to lead you by the hand. And, if I am also 'the truth,' my words are not false. If I am also 'life,' although you die you shall obtain what I have told you." His being "the way" they both understood and allowed, but the rest they did not understand. Indeed they did not venture to say what they did not know. Still they gained great consolation from his being "the way." "If," he says, "I have sole authority to bring you to the Father, you shall surely come this way. For neither is it possible to come by any other way." HOMILIES ON THE GOSPEL OF JOHN 73.2.[31]

JESUS DOES NOT MISLEAD US. HILARY OF POITIERS: He who is the way does not lead us into by-paths or trackless wastes. He who is the truth does not mock us with lies. He who is the life does not betray us into delusions, which are death. He himself has chosen these winning names to indicate the methods that he has appointed for our salvation. As the way, he will guide us to the truth. As the truth, he will establish us in the life. And therefore it is all-important for us to know what the mysterious mode is that he reveals for attaining this life. "No one comes to the Father except through me." The way to the Father is through the Son. ON THE TRINITY 7.33.[32]

JESUS' NAME IS TRUTH. AMBROSE: Christ is not only God but true God indeed—true God of true God[33]—and I approach the true one inasmuch as he himself is the truth. If, then, we inquire his name, it is "the truth." If we seek to know his natural rank and dignity, he is so truly the very Son of God, that he is indeed God's own Son. ON THE CHRISTIAN FAITH 1.17.108.[34]

BEING THE TRUTH, THE SON IS EQUAL TO THE FATHER. AMBROSE: If they say that the Father alone is true God, they cannot deny that God the Son alone is the truth. For Christ is the truth. Is the truth then something inferior to him that is true, seeing that according to the use of terms a person is called true from the word *truth*, as also wise from wisdom, just from justice? We do not consider it so between the Father and the Son. For there is nothing lacking in the Father, because

[28]NPNF 2 12:184*; CCL 138A:441-42. [29]*OHS* 37. [30]FC 109:77; CCL 24:100. [31]NPNF 1 14:269*. [32]NPNF 2 9:132*; CCL 62:300-301. [33]See the Nicene Creed, second article. [34]NPNF 2 10:219*; CSEL 78:46.

the Father is full of truth. And the Son, because he is the truth, is equal to him who is true. On the Christian Faith 5.2.28.[35]

Walk by Faith in the Truth. Augustine: Persevere now in walking by faith in the truth, that you may succeed in coming at a definite and due time to the sight of the same truth. For as the apostle says, "While staying here in the body, we are away from the Lord. For we are walking by faith, not by sight."[36] We are led to the direct sight and vision of the Father by Christian faith. That is why the Lord says, "No one comes to the Father except through me." Sermon 12.5.[37]

He Will Raise Us Again to What We Were Intended. Cyril of Alexandria: There are three means by which we shall reach the divine courts that are above and enter the church of the firstborn:[38] by practicing every kind of virtue; by faith in right doctrine; by hope of the life to come. Is there anyone other than our Lord Jesus the Christ who could ever be a leader, a helper or a means for granting us success in these kinds of things? Surely not! Do not even entertain such an idea! For he himself has taught us things beyond the Law. He has pointed out to us the way that anyone might safely take that would lead to a life of incredible virtue and to a highly motivated and unhindered performance of those actions that follow the pattern of Christ. And so he himself is the truth, he is the way, that is, the true boundary of faith and the exact rule and standard of an unerring conception concerning God. For by a true belief in the Son, namely, as begotten of the very essence of God the Father and as bearing the title of Son in its fullest and truest meaning—and not even in any sense a made or created being—we shall then clothe ourselves in the confidence of a true faith. For one who has received the Son as a Son has fully confessed a belief also in him of whose essence the Son is, and that person knows and will immediately accept God as the Father. Therefore he is the truth, he is the life, for no one else will restore to us the life that is within our hopes, namely, that life that is in incorruption, blessedness and sanctification. For it is he that raises us up and who will bring us back again from the death we died under the ancient curse to the state in which we were at the beginning. Commentary on the Gospel of John 9.[39]

Jesus Enlivens the Soul with Life. Peter Chrysologus: He himself has said, "I am the life." What the soul is to the body is what Christ is to the soul. Without the soul, the body does not live. The soul does not live without Christ. As soon as the soul leaves the body, stench, corruption, rottenness, the worm, ashes, horror and everything that is loathsome to the sight take its place. When God leaves, immediately the stench of faithlessness, the corruption of sin, the rottenness of the vices, the worm of guilt, the ashes of vanities and the horror of infidelity enter the soul, and there comes to pass in the living tomb of the body the death of the soul now buried. Sermon 19.5.[40]

The Son Is Immortality. Gregory of Nyssa: [Eunomius] speaks of God as "without beginning, eternally without end, alone." Once more "understand, you simple ones," as Solomon says, "his subtlety,"[41] in case you might be deceived and fall headlong into the denial of the Godhead of the only-begotten Son. Whatever is devoid of death or decay is that which is without end. That, likewise, is called everlasting that does not exist only for a time. That, therefore, which is neither everlasting nor without end is surely seen in the nature that is perishable and mortal. And so, the one who predicates "unendingness" of the one and only God and does not include the Son in the assertion of "unendingness" and "eternity" maintains by such a proposition that he whom he

[35]NPNF 2 10:288*; CSEL 78:226-27 (Latin designates this quote 5.2.29). See also Athanasius *Against the Arians* 1.20 (NPNF 2 4:318). [36]2 Cor 5:6-7. [37]*WSA* 3 1:300; CCL 41:169. [38]Heb 12:23. [39]LF 48:242*. [40]FC 109:90*; CCL 24:113-14. [41]Prov 8:5 LXX

thus contrasts with the eternal and unending is perishable and temporary. But we, even when we are told that God "alone has immortality,"[42] understand by "immortality" the Son. For life is immortality, and the Lord is that life who said, "I am the Life." Against Eunomius 2.4[43]

Christ Is the Way to the Father. Augustine: The one who is himself the Truth and the Word, by whom all things were made, was made flesh so that he might dwell among us. And yet, the apostle still says, "Even though we have known Christ after the flesh, yet from now on we know him no more."[44] For Christ, desiring not only to give the possession to those who had completed the journey but also to be himself the way to those who were just setting out, determined to take a fleshly body. This is the source of that expression, "The Lord created me in the beginning of his way."[45] Those who desire to come [to the Father] begin their journey in [the Son]. The apostle, therefore, although still on the way . . . had already passed over the beginning of the way and had now no further need of it. And yet, everyone who wants to attain to the truth and to rest in eternal life has to start the journey by this way. For Jesus says, "I am the way, and the truth and the life"; that is, by me men and women come. To me they come, in me they rest. For when we come to him, we come to the Father also, because through an equal an equal is known. Christian Instruction 1.34.38.[46]

God the Father Shows Us Himself in Christ. Hilary of Poitiers: Except through him there is no approach to the Father. But there is also no approach to him unless the Father draws us. Understanding him to be the Son of God, we recognize in him the true nature of the Father. And so, when we learn to know the Son, God the Father calls us. When we believe the Son, God the Father receives us. For our recognition and knowledge of the Father is in the Son who shows us in himself God the Father. The Father draws us by his fatherly love, if we are devout, into a mutual bond with his Son. On the Trinity 11.33.[47]

We Cannot Partake of Divine Nature Apart from Christ. Cyril of Alexandria: We approach the Father in two ways: either by becoming holy,[48] as far as is possible for humanity . . . or else we arrive, through faith and contemplation, at that knowledge of the Father which is as it were "in a mirror darkly."[49] But no one would ever be holy and make progress in a life according to the rule of virtue unless Christ were the guide of his footsteps in everything. And no one would ever be united to God the Father except through the mediation of Christ, for he is the mediator between God and humanity, through himself and in himself uniting humanity to God. . . . No one, therefore, will come to the Father, that is, will appear as a partaker of the divine nature, except through Christ alone. For if he had not become a mediator by taking human form, our condition could never have advanced to such a height of blessedness. But now, if anyone approaches the Father in a spirit of faith and reverent knowledge, he will do so by the help of our Savior Christ himself. Commentary on the Gospel of John 9.[50]

Our Strength, Confidence and Reward. Ambrose: Lord Jesus, we do follow you, but we can come only at your bidding. No one can make the ascent without you, for you are our way, our truth, our life, our strength, our confidence, our reward. Be the way that receives us, the truth that strengthens us, the life that invigorates us. Death as a Good 12.55.[51]

[42]1 Tim 6:16. [43]NPNF 2 5:105*. [44]2 Cor 5:16. [45]Prov 8:22. [46]NPNF 1 2:532**; CCL 32:27-28. See also Cyprian *Epistle* 72.17 (ANF 5:383). [47]NPNF 2 9:212-13*; CCL 62A:561-62. [48]Lev 19:2. [49]1 Cor 13:12. [50]LF 48:243*. [51]*JFA* 65; CSEL 32 1:750.

14:7-14 Knowing the Father

[7]*"If you had known me, you would have known my Father also; henceforth you know him and have seen him."*

[8]*Philip said to him, "Lord, show us the Father, and we shall be satisfied."* [9]*Jesus said to him, "Have I been with you so long, and yet you do not know me, Philip? He who has seen me has seen the Father; how can you say, 'Show us the Father'?* [10]*Do you not believe that I am in the Father and the Father in me? The words that I say to you I do not speak on my own authority; but the Father who dwells in me does his works.* [11]*Believe me that I am in the Father and the Father in me; or else believe me for the sake of the works themselves.*

[12]*"Truly, truly, I say to you, he who believes in me will also do the works that I do; and greater works than these will he do, because I go to the Father.* [13]*Whatever you ask in my name, I will do it, that the Father may be glorified in the Son;* [14]*if you ask*[g] *anything in my name, I will do it."*

g Other ancient authorities add *me*

Overview: Christ reveals knowledge of the Father, who is invisible, through his own manifestations in the flesh (Irenaeus, Hilary). But it is not Christ's human nature that makes the Father known; rather, the Father is known through the evidence of the divine powers and authority Christ has (Hilary). And while it is true that the disciples did know something of God, they did not yet know him as Father (Chrysostom). Philip then asks to be shown the Father, not quite yet understanding how the Father is to be seen in the Son (Hilary) because he did not yet have the eyes of faith (Augustine).

The Son is like a portrait of his Father (Ambrose). The Old Testament says no one can see God's face and live, but Christ is the perfect divine vision, showing in himself the image of the one who begot him (Chrysostom), an image spoken of in Genesis (Ambrose). Such an image has nothing to do with bodily likeness (Hilary) but rather of the will that is the same in both (Basil). In this, there is a perfect likeness between Father and Son (Theodore). If the disciples had known this about Jesus, especially with all the time they had spent with him, they surely would have recognized the Godhead in him that belongs to his Father's nature (Hilary).

The mutual indwelling of the Father and the Son remains incomprehensible (Hilary) as they are, in the entirety of their persons, in one another without any variation in glory or essence of either (Gregory of Nyssa). The Father is in the Son because their substance is one (Ambrosiaster).There is no subterfuge going on here so that one might think he at one time poses as the Son and then at another time poses as the Father; nor can Father and Son be separate and divided when one speaks through the voice of the other (Hilary). It is self-evident that the Father would not have used any different words than the Son has, had he chosen to speak himself (Cyril).

The Father works together with the Son (Augustine), and all three persons of the Trinity are inseparable so that the actions of any one person in the Trinity do not occur without the other two (Augustine). The Son as the image of the Father shares the attributes of the Father (Athanasius). Here again Christ reveals the perfect likeness of his nature, ideas, virtue and even of his very words with that of the Father (Theodore). Christ's actions also show that there is a unity of nature (Hilary) since he could never have performed the miracles unique to the divine nature that he did unless he himself was essentially of the same divine nature (Cyril).

We can do similar works when empowered by Christ, but we do not have the same unity of nature with Christ as Christ has with the Father (Ambrose, Augustine). Christ has equal dignity and consubstantiality with the Father as his words and works demonstrate his unity with the Father—works that he shall also do through us (Theodore). Even our very believing, which is one of the great works to which Christ refers, is the work of Christ (Augustine). But he is also referring to the miracles the apostles would accomplish by his power (Theodore of Heraclea). Because Father and Son share in the divine nature, we can also go to the Son with our requests (Ambrose). But believers do not always receive what they ask for, not because the Son is not able to grant their request, but because, like a physician, God knows when what we ask for is beneficial and when it is not (Augustine).

14:7 *Knowing Christ, You Know the Father*

Christ's Appearance Provides Knowledge of the Father. Irenaeus: The Son reveals the knowledge of the Father through his own manifestation. For the manifestation of the Son is the knowledge of the Father, since all things are manifested through the Word. Against Heresies 4.6.3.[1]

The Time of Seeing and the Time of Knowing. Hilary of Poitiers: How can knowledge of him be knowledge of the Father? For the apostles see him wearing the aspect of that human nature that belongs to him. But God is not encumbered with body and flesh and is unrecognizable by those who dwell in our weak and fleshly body. The answer is given by the Lord, who asserts that under the flesh that, in a mystery, he had taken, his Father's nature dwells within him.... He makes a distinction between the time of seeing and the time of knowing. He says that from this time onward they shall know him whom they had already seen and so shall possess, from the time of this revelation onward, the knowledge of that nature on which, in him, they had gazed for so long. On the Trinity 7.34.[2]

Divine Sonship Produces Recognition of Divine Father. Hilary of Poitiers: It was not the carnal body that he had received by birth from the Virgin that could manifest to them the image and likeness of God. The human aspect that he wore could be no aid toward the mental vision of the incorporeal God. But God was recognized in Christ by those who recognized Christ as the Son on the evidence of the powers of his divine nature. And a recognition of God the Son produces a recognition of God the Father. For the Son is in such a sense the image as to be one in kind with the Father and yet in a way that indicates that the Father is his origin. On the Trinity 7.37.[3]

Seeing the Father in the Son. Chrysostom: He does not contradict himself. They knew him indeed, but not as they should have. God they knew, but they did not yet know the Father. For afterward, when the Spirit came upon them, he formed in them all knowledge. It is as if he had said, "If you had known my essence and my dignity, you would have known that of the Father also. And from this time onward you shall know him, and you have seen him." The [knowing] belongs to the future; the [seeing] belongs to the present. Both are brought about "by me." By "sight," he means knowledge by intellectual perception. For those who are seen we may see but not know. Those, however, who are known we cannot both know and not know.... These words are used so that you may learn that the one who

[1]ANF 1:468*; SC 100:442. [2]NPNF 2 9:132-33*; CCL 62:301. [3]NPNF 2 9:133-34*; CCL 62:304.

has seen him knows him who begat him.[4] But they beheld him not in his unveiled essence but clothed with flesh. Homilies on the Gospel of John 73.2.[5]

14:8 *Lord, Show Us the Father*

Philip Was Not Tampering with the Faith. Hilary of Poitiers: The novel sound of these words of Jesus disturbed the apostle Philip. A man is before their eyes. This man asserts that he is the Son of God and declares that when they have known him they will know the Father. He tells them that they have seen the Father and that, because they have seen him, they shall know him hereafter. . . . And so Philip spoke out with the loyalty and confidence of an apostle, requesting, "Lord, show us the Father, and that will suffice." He was not tampering with the faith. It was only a mistake made in ignorance. . . . Philip did not deny that the Father could be seen but only asked that he might see him. He did not ask that the Father should be unveiled so that he could see him with his bodily eyes, but that he might have some further indication that would enlighten him concerning how the Father could be seen. For he had seen the Son under the aspect of humanity but cannot understand how he could thereby have seen the Father. On the Trinity 7.35.[6]

Show Us the Father? Augustine: When Philip said to him, "Lord, show us the Father, and that is enough for us," he understood well enough that being shown the Father could satisfy him. But if the one who is equal to the Father was not enough for him, how would the Father be enough? And why wasn't he enough for him? Because he was not seen. Why wasn't he seen? Because the eye he could be seen with was not yet whole. As for the Lord's body, which could be seen with these eyes, it was not only the ones who revered him who saw him but also the Jews who crucified him. So if he wanted to be seen in another way, it means he was requiring other eyes. And that is why he gave this reply to the one who said, "Show us the Father, and that is enough for us: Have I been with you all this time, and you do not know me? Philip, whoever sees me also sees the Father." And to heal the eyes of faith in the meantime, he is first admonished in terms of faith, so that he may be enabled to attain to sight. And in case Philip should assume that God is to be thought of in the same way as he saw the Lord Jesus Christ in the flesh, he immediately added, "Do you not believe that I am in the Father, and the Father is in me?" Sermon 88.4.[7]

14:9 *Seeing the Father in and Through the Son*

The Father's Portrait in the Son. Ambrose: By means of this image the Lord showed Philip the Father. Yes, he who looks on the Son sees, in portrait, the Father. Notice what kind of portrait is spoken of. It is truth, righteousness, the power of God. It is not silent, for it is the Word. It is not insensible, for it is Wisdom. It is not vain and foolish, for it is power. It is not soulless, for it is the life. It is not dead, for it is the resurrection. On the Christian Faith 1.7.50.[8]

Seeing the Father in the Son. Chrysostom: In the Old Testament it says, "No one shall see my face and live."[9] What does Christ say? Very reprovingly he says, "Have I been with you for so long, and have you not known me, Philip?" He did not say "have you not seen" but "have you not known me." "Why," Philip might say, "would I want to learn anything concerning you? At present I want to see your Father, and you say to me, 'Have you not known me?'" What connection then does this have with the question? Surely a very close one. For if he is that which the Father is, yet continues to be a Son, there is a definite reason for showing in himself the one who begat

[4]The Son. [5]NPNF 1 14:269**. [6]NPNF 2 9:133**; CCL 62:301-3. [7]*WSA* 3 3:421; *RB* 94:77. See also Augustine *On the Trinity* 1.8.16-17. [8]NPNF 2 10:208*. See also Basil *On the Holy Spirit* 8.21, 45. [9]Ex 33:20.

him. Then to distinguish the persons he says, "He who has seen me has seen the Father," in case anyone should assert that the same person is Father and Son. For had he been the Father, he would not have said, "He who has seen me has seen him." Homilies on the Gospel of John 74.1.[10]

Only One Image of God Spoken of in Scripture. Ambrose: In the church, I know of only one image, that is, the image of the unseen God. God has said about this image, "Let us make man [humankind] in our image."[11] Of this image it is written that Christ is the "effulgence of the glory and impress of his hypostasis."[12] In that image, I perceive the Father as the Lord Jesus himself has said, "The one who has seen me has seen the Father." For this image is not separated from the Father, which indeed has taught me the unity of the Trinity, saying, "I and the Father are one,"[13] and again, "All things whatever the Father has are mine."[14] [In this image, also perceive] the Holy Spirit, seeing that the Spirit is Christ's and has received of Christ, as it is written, "He shall receive of mine and shall announce it to you."[15] Sermon Against Auxentius 32.[16]

Not Speaking of a Bodily Likeness Here. Hilary of Poitiers: I ask whether he is the visible likeness of the invisible God and whether the infinite God can also be presented to view under the likeness of a finite form. For a likeness must necessarily repeat the form of that of which it is the likeness. Let those, however, who want there to be a nature of a different sort in the Son determine what sort of likeness of the invisible God they wish the Son to be. Is it a bodily likeness exposed to the gaze and moving from place to place with human gait and motion? No, rather let them remember that according to the Gospels and the prophets both Christ is a Spirit and God is a Spirit. If they confine this Christ the spirit within the bounds of shape and body, such a corporeal Christ will not be the likeness of the invisible God, nor will a finite limitation represent that which is infinite. On the Trinity 8.48.[17]

The Identification of the Divine Will. Basil the Great: "He who has seen me has seen the Father"; this does not mean that he has seen the image and the form of the divine nature, since the divine nature is simple, not composed of various parts. Goodness of will is a current in the stream of the divine essence, and thus is perceived to be the same in the Father and the Son.[18] On the Holy Spirit 8.21.[19]

A Perfect Likeness Between Father and Son. Theodore of Mopsuestia: So, he says, was not such a long time sufficient to teach you about my Father and me? And yet you still are looking to see him. If you had known me, you would have known the Father through me and would have not thought that he can be seen with bodily eyes. Since the expression "you still do not know me" seemed not to fit in with the words "show us the Father," he clearly explains this by saying, "Whoever has seen me has seen the Father. How can you say, 'Show us the Father?' " There is no difference, he says, so that whoever sees me sees the Father himself. There is a perfect similarity between us two that shows the Father himself in me. Very aptly he adds, "How can you say?" as he confirms through his open amazement the words said above. How can you ask me, he says, to show you the Father, if not for the fact that you ignore me completely? Therefore what I said is true, "You neither know my Father nor me. If you had known me, you would have known him too," because the perfect likeness would have shown him. Commentary on John 6.14.8-9.[20]

Not Recognizing the Father's Nature. Hilary of Poitiers: He rebukes the apostle for

---

[10]NPNF 1 14:271*. [11]Gen 1:26. [12]Heb 1:3. [13]Jn 10:30. [14]Jn 16:15. [15]Jn 16:14. [16]NPNF 2 10:435**. See also *The Sacrament of the Incarnation of the Lord* 10.112. [17]NPNF 2 9:151*; CCL 62A:360-61. [18]Christ is the "express image," or imprint, or form, of the Father (Heb 1:3; Phil 2:6), but not in the sense that his physical appearance is what the Father looks like. [19]*OHS* 41. [20]CSCO 4 3:268.

defective knowledge of himself. For previously he had said that when he was known the Father was known also. But what did they mean when he complained that for so long they had not known him? It means this: that if they had known him, they must have recognized in him the Godhead that belongs to his Father's nature. For his works were the peculiar works of God. ON THE TRINITY 7.36.[21]

14:10a *Mutual Indwelling*

THE MUTUAL INDWELLING IS INCOMPREHENSIBLE. HILARY OF POITIERS: The words of the Lord, "I am in the Father and the Father is in me," confuse many minds, and this is only natural since the powers of human reason cannot provide them with any intelligible meaning. It seems impossible that one object should be both within and without another, or that—since it is laid down that the beings of whom we are treating, although they do not dwell apart, retain their separate existence and condition—these beings can reciprocally contain one another so that one should permanently envelope and be permanently enveloped by the other whom yet he envelopes. This is a problem that human wisdom will never solve, nor will human research ever find an analogy for this condition of divine existence. But God can be what human beings cannot understand. ON THE TRINITY 3.1.[22]

FATHER AND SON ARE IN EACH OTHER. GREGORY OF NYSSA: The Lord speaks the truth who says, "I am in the Father and the Father in me"—plainly, the one in his entirety is in the other in his entirety. The Father does not have an overwhelming presence in the Son. The Son is not deficient in the Father. And the Lord also says that the Son should be honored.[23] And, "The one who has seen me has seen the Father," and, "No one fully knows the Father except the Son."[24] In all of this, there is no hint . . . of any variation in glory or of essence or anything else between the Father and the Son. AGAINST EUNOMIUS 2.4.[25]

THE SON IS GOD'S ENVOY ACCORDING TO NATURE. AMBROSIASTER: For the Son is the envoy of God the Father in accordance with nature. And so he says . . . "I am in the Father and the Father is in me." For the Father is understood through this to be in the Son, because their substance is one. For where there is unity, there is no differentiation. And they are interchangeable, because both their appearance and likeness are the same, with the consequence that he who sees the Son is said to have seen the Father too. As the Lord himself says, "He who has seen me has seen the Father too." Therefore it is correct to say, God was in Christ. COMMENTARY ON 2 CORINTHIANS 5.19-21.2.[26]

THE SON IS NOT FALSELY CONCEALING THAT HE IS THE FATHER. HILARY OF POITIERS: In no other words than these that the Son has used can the fact be stated that Father and Son, being alike in nature, are inseparable. The Son, who is the way and the truth and the life,[27] is not deceiving us by some theatrical transformation of names and aspects when he, while wearing manhood, styles himself the Son of God. He is not falsely concealing the fact that he is God the Father.[28] He is not a single person who hides his features under a mask so that we might imagine that two are present. He is not a solitary being, now posing as his own Son, and then again calling himself the Father, adorning the one unchanging nature with varying names. . . . It is the height of impiety to believe that Father and Son are two gods. It is sacrilege to assert that Father and Son are singularly God.[29] It is blasphemy to deny the unity, consisting in sameness of kind, of God from God. ON THE TRINITY 7.39.[30]

[21]NPNF 2 9:133*; CCL 62:303. [22]NPNF 2 9:62**. [23]Jn 5:23. [24]Mt 11:27. [25]NPNF 2 5:105*. [26]CSEL 81 2:237. [27]Jn 14:6. [28]Sabellianism. [29]Lat *singularem Deum*. Hilary is still asserting the oneness of God. Here, however, he is also guarding against those who denigrate the distinction of person within the monarchy of God. For example, the Sabellians spoke of Father, Son and Spirit as different modes or manifestations of the one God. [30]NPNF 2 9:134-35*; CCL 62:306-7.

No Separation or Division. Hilary of Poitiers: That the Father dwells in the Son proves that the Father is not isolated and alone. That the Father works through the Son proves that the Son is not an alien or a stranger. There cannot be one person only, for he speaks not of himself. And, conversely, they cannot be separate and divided when the one speaks through the voice of the other. These words are the revelation of the mystery of their unity. On the Trinity 7.40.[31]

14:10b *Mutual Words and Works*

The Father Would Not Have Used Different Words. Cyril of Alexandria: If, he would say, my Father had spoken anything to you, he would not have used any other words than these that I am now speaking. For so great is the equality in essence between myself and him that my words are his words, and whatever I do may be believed to be his actions. For, because he "abides in me," by reason of the exact equivalence in essence, he himself does the works. For since the Godhead is one in the Father, in the Son and in the Spirit, every word that comes from the Father comes always through the Son by the Spirit. Every work or miracle is through the Son by the Spirit, and yet it is considered as coming from the Father. For the Son is not apart from the essence of the Father, nor indeed is the Holy Spirit. But the Son, being in the Father and having the Father again in himself, claims that the Father is the doer of the works. For the nature of the Father is mighty in operation and shines out clearly in the Son.

And one might add to this another meaning that is involved, suggested clearly by the principles that underlie the incarnation. He says, "I speak not of myself," meaning, not in separation from or in lack of agreement with God the Father. For since he appeared to those who saw him in human form, he refers his words to the divine nature, as speaking in the person of the Father. It is the same with his actions. He almost seems to say, Do not let this human form deprive me of that reverent estimation that is due and befitting to me, and do not suppose that my words are those of a mere human or of one like yourselves. Rather, believe them to be in very truth divine words that would be just as fitting for the Father as they are for me. And he is the one who works, "abiding in me." For I am in him, and he is in me. Do not think therefore that a mighty and extraordinary privilege was granted to the people of former days because they saw God in a vision of fire and heard his voice speaking to them. For you have in reality seen the Father through me and in me, since I have appeared among you, being in my nature God, and "have come visibly," according to the words of the psalmist.[32] And be well assured that in hearing my words, you heard the words of the Father. And you have been spectators of his works and of the might that is in him. For by me he speaks as by his own Word. And in me he carries out and achieves his wondrous works, as though by his own power. Commentary on the Gospel of John 9.[33]

The Father Works Together with the Son. Augustine: The Father was not born of the Virgin, and yet this birth of the Son from the Virgin was the work of both Father and Son. The Father did not suffer on the cross, and yet the passion of the Son was the work of both Father and Son. The Father did not rise again from the dead, and yet the resurrection of the Son was the work of both Father and Son. You have the persons quite distinct, and their working inseparable. So let us never say that the Father worked anything without the Son, the Son anything without the Father. Or perhaps you are worried about the miracles Jesus did, in case perhaps he did some that the Father did not do? Then what about "But the Father abiding in me does his works"? Sermon 52.14.[34]

[31]NPNF 2 9:135*; CCL 62:308-9. [32]Ps 50:3 (49:3 LXX). [33]LF 48:262-63. [34]*WSA* 3 3:56; *RB* 74:25.

The Divine Three Are Inseparable. Augustine: So then, with all these ways of speaking we still have to understand that the activities of the divine three are inseparable, so that when an activity is attributed to the Father he is not taken to engage in it without the Son and the Holy Spirit. And when it is an activity of the Son, it is not without the Son and the Holy Spirit. And when it is an activity of the Son, it is not without the Father and the Son. That being the case, those who have the right faith, or better still the right understanding as far as they can, know well enough that the reason it is said about the Father, "He does the works," is that the works have their origin in the one from whom the co-working persons have their very existence. The Son, you see, is born of him, and the Holy Spirit proceeds primarily from him of whom the Son is born, being the Spirit common to them both. Sermon 71.26.[35]

The Image Shares Attributes of the Father. Athanasius: Let us proceed then to consider the attributes of the Father, and we shall come to know whether this Image is really his. The Father is eternal, immortal, powerful, light, King, Sovereign, God, Lord, Creator and Maker. These attributes must be in the Image to make it true that whoever "has seen" the Son "has seen the Father." If the Son is not all this, but, as the Arians consider, he is originate and not eternal, this is not a true image of the Father, unless indeed they give up shame and go on to say that the title of image, given to the Son, is not a token of a similar essence, but his name only. Discourses Against the Arians 1.21.[36]

Perfect Likeness. Theodore of Mopsuestia: Among all the words said so far, especially here, he clearly shows that he talks about their likeness. Indeed, in the same way, by turning the speech to the Father and him, he reveals the perfect likeness of their nature, so that, as the Father lives in him, and he in the Father, a perfect likeness can be shown in each of them. Then he proves and confirms his words by saying, "The words that I say to you I do not speak on my own." If you do not believe, he says, in these words, know that so perfect is the conformity of nature, ideas, and virtue that there is no difference in the words either. Whatever I say is in common, and do not only speak on my own. The Father who dwells in me does his works. It would have been opportune to add, "My Father speaks through the words: I do not speak." But he had said above, "The words that I say," and here, "The Father does his works," in order to show that the nature is common, the words are common and the works are common as well. From this it is evident that through the words, "I do not speak on my own," he does not signify an inferior state, but a perfect communion and an inseparable union. And this appears especially from the context. Commentary on John 6.14.10.[37]

14:11 *Believe There Is Mutual Indwelling and Works*

Unity with the Father Is Recognized. Hilary of Poitiers: His power belonged to his nature, and his working was the exercise of that power. In the exercise of that power, then, they might recognize in him the unity with the Father's nature. To the extent that anyone recognized him to be God in the power of his nature, that person would come to know God the Father who was present in that mighty nature. The Son, who is equal with the Father, showed by his works that the Father could be seen in him so that when we perceived in the Son a nature like the Father's in its power, we might know that in Father and Son there is no distinction of nature. On the Trinity 9.52.[38]

Against Those Who Deny the Divinity of Christ. Cyril of Alexandria: In these

[35]*WSA* 3 3:262; *RB* 75:93-94. [36]NPNF 2 4:318*. [37]CSCO 4 3:269. [38]NPNF 2 9:173*; CCL 62A:430.

words Christ distinctly says that he could never have worked and accomplished those miracles that are unique to the divine nature if he, himself, had not been essentially of the same divine nature.... [Only heretics] whose hearts are devoid of the Holy Spirit make separations between the Father and the Son and assert that the Son is essentially and completely severed from the Father in the way that created things and divine works are separate from God the Father. Commentary on the Gospel of John 9.[39]

14:12 *Believers Also Do Even Greater Works*

We Can Do Similar Works. Ambrose: Skillfully inserting here the word *also,* he has allowed us similarity and yet has not ascribed natural unity. The work of the Father and the work of the Son, therefore, are one. On the Christian Faith 3.11.91.[40]

Working in Christ. Augustine: And so he promised that he himself would also do those greater works. Do not let the servant exalt himself above his Lord or the disciple above his Master.[41] He says that they will do greater works than he does himself, but it is all by his doing such works in or by them, and not as if they did them of themselves. And so we have the song that is addressed to him, "I will love you, O Lord, my strength."[42] But what, then, are those greater works? Was it that their very shadow, as they themselves passed by, that healed the sick?[43] For it is a mightier thing for a shadow, than for the hem of a garment, to possess the power of healing.[44] The one work was done by Christ himself, the other by them. And yet it was he that did both. Tractates on the Gospel of John 71.3.[45]

Our Believing Is the Work of Christ. Augustine: But there is still something to excite thought in his doing such greater works by the apostles. For he did not say, as if merely with reference to them, "the works that I do shall you do also. And greater works than these shall you do," but wishing to be understood as speaking of all that belonged to his family, he said, "He who believes in me, the works that I do shall he do also. And greater works than these shall he do." If, then, he who believes shall do such works, he who shall not do them is certainly no believer, just as "He who loves me, keeps my commandments"[46] implies, of course, that whoever does not keep them does not love.... In a similar way, also, it is said here, "He who believes in me shall do such works." The one who does not do good works, therefore, is no believer. What have we here, then, brothers? Is it that one is not to be counted among believers in Christ who will not do greater works than Christ? It would be hard, unreasonable, intolerable to suppose so, that is, unless it is rightly understood. Let us listen, then, to the apostle when he says, "To him who believes in him who justifies the ungodly, his faith is counted for righteousness."[47] This is the work in which we may be doing the works of Christ, for even our very believing in Christ is the work of Christ. Tractates on the Gospel of John 72.2.[48]

Exceeding the Power of Their Teacher. Theodore of Heraclea: This refers to the other miracles that the apostles did, such as healing a man through their shadow falling on him. But this incident did not reveal the fullness of this saying, but rather it was fulfilled in the fact that, when he used the power of the Godhead for an act of kindness, the disciples on the one hand worked through the power given to them for the service of those who believe and the punishment of the extremely wicked, and on the other hand they exceeded the power of their teacher, even though he was mightier in his ability to punish the godless, since he chose to restrain and control his power to punish in the meantime until the

[39]LF 48:265, 286**. [40]NPNF 2 10:255; CSEL 78:141. [41]See Jn 13:16. [42]Ps 18:1 (17:1 LXX, 17:2 Vg). [43]See Acts 5:15. [44]See Mt 14:36. [45]NPNF 1 7:329*; CCL 36:506. [46]Jn 14:21. [47]Rom 4:5. [48]NPNF 1 7:330*; CCL 36:508.

right moment of judgment. Fragments on John 259.[49]

Jesus' Reunion with the Father. Theodore of Mopsuestia: We said above that the words "I am going to the Father" refer to [his union with the Father after his passion]. After ... this union, he will have the power to give everything to those who ask him, because by asking they ask for the greatness dwelling in him.[50] He can give because of his [union with the Father], and the Father then is completely recognized in the Son to be excellent and admirable. Commentary on John 6.14.13-14.[51]

14:13-14 *Asking in Jesus' Name*

Requests Need to Be Made Not Only to the Father. Ambrose: But if we think it impious to believe that the Father has handed over all judgment to the Son in such a way that he does not have it himself—for he has it and cannot lose what the divine majesty has by its very nature—we ought to consider it equally impious to suppose that the Son cannot give what either men and women can merit or any creature can receive, especially as he himself has said, "I go to my Father, and whatever you shall ask of him in my name, that will I do." For if the Son cannot give what the Father can give, the Truth has lied and cannot do what the Father has been asked for in his name. He therefore did not say, "For whom it has been prepared by my Father," in order that requests should be made only of the Father. For all things that are asked of the Father, [the Son] has declared that he [himself] will give. And finally, he did not say, "Whatever you shall ask of me, that will I do" but "Whatever you shall ask of him in my name, that will I do." On the Christian Faith 5.5.66.[52]

Why Don't Believers Always Receive? Augustine: "Whatever you shall ask." Then why do we often see believers asking and not receiving? Perhaps it is that they do not ask correctly. ... When a person would make a bad use of what he asks for, God in his mercy does not grant him it. It is even more the case that if someone asks what would, if answered, only tend to his injury, there is surely greater cause to fear, in case what God could not withhold with kindness, he should give in his anger.... Still if God even in kindness often refuses the requests of believers, how are we to understand "Whatever you shall ask in my name, I will do"? Was this said to the apostles only? No. He says above, "He who believes in me, the works that I do he shall do also." ... And if we go to the lives of the apostles themselves, we shall find that he who labored more than them all prayed that the messenger of Satan might depart from him[53] but was not granted his request.... Wake up then, believer, and note what is stated here: "In my name." That [name] is Christ Jesus. Christ signifies King, Jesus signifies Savior.... Therefore whatever we ask for that would hinder our salvation, we do not ask in our Savior's name, and yet he is our Savior not only when he does what we ask but also when he does not. When he sees us ask anything to the disadvantage of our salvation, he shows himself our Savior by not doing it. The physician knows whether what the sick person asks for is to the advantage or disadvantage of his health. And [the physician] does not allow what would be harmful to him, though the sick person himself desires it. But the physician looks to his final cure.... And some things we may even ask in his name, and he will not grant them to us at the time, though he will some time. What we ask for is deferred, not denied.... He adds, "that the Father may be glorified in the Son." The Son does not do anything without the Father, inasmuch as he does it in order that the Father may be glorified in the Son, ... for the Father and Son are one. Tractates on the Gospel of John 73.1-4.[54]

---

[49]*JKGK* 133. [50]Here again we see Theodore's emphasis on the distinction between Christ's two natures. [51]CSCO 4 3:270-71. [52]NPNF 2 10:293*; CSEL 78:242 (*On the Christian Faith* 5.5.67). [53]See 2 Cor 12:8. [54]CCL 36:509-12; NPNF 1 7:331-33**.

14:15-17 Love and the Spirit of Truth

[15]If you love me, you will keep my commandments. [16]And I will pray the Father, and he will give you another Counselor, to be with you for ever, [17]even the Spirit of truth, whom the world cannot receive, because it neither sees him nor knows him; you know him, for he dwells with you, and will be in you.

Overview: When we love Jesus, we submit to his will and obey his commandments (Chrysostom). This obedience, which is an expression of love, paints a portrait of love in our lives that displays the beauty of what God has created (Cyril). There is no love without the Spirit, however, but the disciples evidenced their love for Jesus and so they must have had the Spirit, although not yet in the fuller way he promised here (Augustine). Christ continues to petition the Father for the Spirit to dwell not only in the disciples' hearts but also in ours today (Bede). In promising them the gift of the Holy Spirit, the Comforter, Christ calmed the troubled hearts of the disciples, who were wondering what they would do without him (Chrysostom). He refers to the Spirit as another Comforter (Gregory of Nazianzus), so that no one confuses the Spirit with the Son (Ambrose), who is also called Comforter, or Paraclete (Augustine). But he also establishes the Spirit's divinity (Augustine) so that believers know the works of the Spirit are just as efficacious as the Son's works (Leo). The Holy Spirit comforts in a different way than the Son; he is more of a consoler than a mediator, although we should infer no difference of nature (Didymus). The Holy Spirit as advocate or comforter lightens the load of the afflicted (Theodore).

The Spirit, as the consubstantial third person of the Trinity (Augustine) completes the work of the Father and the Son (Athanasius). Since the Spirit is called the Spirit of Truth, it cannot tolerate lies (Hermas). Truth is a characteristic of the Godhead as the Spirit reveals the truth of the one who sent him (Basil). The world cannot receive this kind of truth since it is caught up in its love of the things of this world (Bede). But those who have the Spirit have a unique perspective of his actions in the world that goes beyond the things of this world (Apollinaris). The Spirit is seen in the different gifts of the Spirit that Christians have (Gregory the Great), which vary according to the measure of the Spirit that is present in us, who must be present in us for us to be able to love or obey the commandments (Augustine).

14:15 *If You Love Me, You Will Keep My Commandments*

To Love Is to Submit to Christ. Chrysostom: At all times it is works and actions that we need, not a mere show of words. It is easy for anyone to say or promise something, but it is not so easy to act on that word or promise. . . . "If you love me," Christ said, "keep my commandments." . . . I have commanded you to love one another and to do to one another as I have done to you. To love me is to obey these commands and to submit to me, your beloved. Homilies on the Gospel of John 75.1.[1]

Painting a Portrait of Love. Cyril of Alexandria: Having determined and expressly declared that the enjoyment of the heavenly blessings (supplied, that is, through him by the Father) is both due to those who love him and in very truth shall be theirs, he immediately goes on to describe the power of love. He provides

[1]NPNF 1 14:273-74**.

excellent and irreproachable instruction to us for our profit with the intent that we should devote ourselves to its pursuit. For even if a person says that he loves God, he will not immediately merit credit for having true love of God, since the power of virtue does not stand on bare speech alone, nor piety on naked words. Rather, it is distinguished by performance of good deeds and an obedient disposition. Keeping the divine commandments is the best way to give living expression to our love toward God. It presents the picture of a life lived in all its fullness and truth. It is not a life sketched out in mere sounds that flow from the tongue. It gleams instead with the altogether radiant and brilliant colors that paint a portrait of good works. Commentary on the Gospel of John 9.1.[2]

There Is No Love Without the Spirit. Augustine: How, then, did the apostles love, but in the Holy Spirit? And yet they are commanded to love him and keep his commandments before they have received him and, in fact, in order to receive him. And yet, without having that Spirit, they certainly could not love him and keep his commandments. We are therefore to understand that he who loves already has the Holy Spirit, and by what he has he becomes worthy of a fuller possession, that by having more he may love more. The disciples, therefore, already had that Holy Spirit whom the Lord promised, for without him they could not call him Lord. But they had him not as yet in the way promised by the Lord. . . . He was yet to be given them in an ampler measure.[3] Tractates on the Gospel of John 74.1-2.[4]

14:16 *The Son Petitions the Father for Another Comforter*

The Son Continues to Ask for the Spirit in Us. Bede: If we too, dearly beloved, love Christ perfectly in such a way that we prove the genuineness of this love by our observance of his commandments, he will ask the Father on our behalf, and the Father will give us another Paraclete. He will ask the Father through his humanity and will give [us another Paraclete] with the Father through his divinity. We must not suppose that it was only before his passion that he was asking on behalf of the church and that now, after his ascension, he is not also asking, since the apostle speaks of him, "who is at the right hand of God who also intercedes for us."[5] Homilies on the Gospels 2.17.[6]

Christ Will Not Leave Them Alone. Chrysostom: This promise shows once again Christ's consideration. Because his disciples did not yet know who he was, it was likely that they would greatly miss his companionship, his teaching, his actual physical presence, and be completely disconsolate when he had gone. Therefore he said, "I will ask the Father, and he will give you another Counselor," meaning another like himself. . . . They received the Spirit after Christ had purified them by his sacrifice. The Spirit did not come down on them while Christ was still with them because this sacrifice had not yet been offered. But when sin had been blotted out and the disciples, sent out to face danger, were preparing themselves for the battle, they needed the Holy Spirit's coming to encourage them. If you ask why the Spirit did not come immediately after the resurrection, this was in order to increase their gratitude for receiving him by increasing their desire. They were troubled by nothing as long as Christ was with them, but when his departure had left them desolate and very much afraid, they would be most eager to receive the Spirit. Homilies on the Gospel of John 75.1.[7]

Two Different but Equal Comforters. Gregory of Nazianzus: The Spirit came after Christ so that we would not lack a Comforter.

[2]LF 48:298-99*. [3]At Pentecost. [4]NPNF 1 7:334**; CCL 36:513. [5]Rom 8:34. [6]CS 111:165*. [7]NPNF 1 14:274**.

But he is called "another" Comforter so that you might acknowledge his co-equality. For this word *another* defines an alter ego, a name of equal lordship, not of inequality. We do not use the word *another* for different kinds of things but for those that are consubstantial. On Pentecost, Oration 41.12.[8]

Do Not Confuse the Son with the Spirit. Ambrose: It was good that he said "another" so that you might not think that the Son is the Spirit, for there is a unity of the name and no Sabellian[9] confusion of the Son and of the Spirit. On the Holy Spirit 1.13.136.[10]

The Spirit and Jesus Are Both Advocates. Augustine: But when Jesus says, "I will ask the Father, and he shall give you another Paraclete," he intimates that he himself is also a Paraclete. For Paraclete is in Latin called *advocatus* [advocate]. And it is said of Christ, "We have an advocate with the Father, Jesus Christ the righteous."[11] Tractates on the Gospel of John 74.4.[12]

The Comforter Is God. Augustine: The apostle says that the Comforter—the title given to the third person of the Trinity—is God. In his epistle to the Corinthians he says, "God, who comforts those who are cast down, comforts us."[13] The Holy Spirit who comforts those who are cast down is therefore God.... Or if they rather take these words of the apostle as applying to the Father or the Son, let them no longer, then, separate the Holy Spirit from the Father and the Son or make the Holy Spirit appear less than the Son, when it is his peculiar [office] to offer comfort. Discourses Against the Arians 19.[14]

No Difference in Nature. Leo the Great: For the Only Begotten of God himself desired no difference to be felt between himself and the Holy Spirit in the faith of believers and in the efficacy of his works because there is no diversity in their nature. Letter 16.4.[15]

The Holy Spirit Comforts in a Different Way. Didymus the Blind: But the Holy Spirit was another Comforter differing not in nature but in operation. For whereas our Savior, in his office of mediator, and of messenger and as high priest, made supplication for our sins, the Holy Spirit is a Comforter in another sense, that is, as consoling our griefs. But do not infer from the different operations of the Son and the Spirit a difference of nature. For in other places we find the Holy Spirit performing the office of intercessor with the Father, as when "the Spirit himself intercedes for us."[16] . . . And the Savior . . . pours consolation into those hearts that need it, as in Maccabees, he strengthened those of the people who were brought low.[17] On the Holy Spirit 27-28.[18]

The Spirit Lightens the Load of the Afflicted. Theodore of Mopsuestia: I will confer the grace of the Holy Spirit, he says, so that you may always have it with you to teach you the truth. He speaks of another Advocate, as of another instructor, a comforter. This is a doctrine for those in dire straits because the Spirit, through its grace, will make the afflictions inflicted on them by people lighter. And, as a consolation, through its gifts, it will enable them to easily endure their afflictions. This is what actually happened. Indeed, the more his disciples feared death before, the more they rejoiced in tribulations after the descent of the Spirit. He calls it "Spirit of truth" since it teaches nothing but the truth, nor can it ever change to the contrary in order to teach anything different from the truth. He says "another" in relation to himself, for while he was among them, he certainly filled the same role for them. In addition they received from the Holy Spirit the confirmation of all those things that he had taught them when he was

[8]NPNF 2 7:383**. [9]The Sabellians, anxious to maintain the unity of God, denied the differences in persons and identified the Son with the Father. [10]FC 44:85**. CSEL 79:74. [11]1 Jn 2:1. [12]NPNF 1 7:335**; CCL 36:514. [13]2 Cor 7:6. [14]PL 42:697-98. [15]NPNF 2 12:28**. [16]Rom 8:26. [17]1 Macc 14:14. [18]PL 23:127.

present. Thus our Lord said, "But you will receive power when the Holy Spirit has come on you. And you will be my witness in Jerusalem, in all Judea and among the Samaritans, and all nations."[19] Commentary on John 6.14.15-17.[20]

14:17 *The Spirit of Truth*

The Spirit of the Trinity. Augustine: We have here, at all events, the Holy Spirit in the Trinity whom the catholic faith acknowledges to be consubstantial and coeternal with the Father and the Son. Tractates on the Gospel of John 74.1.[21]

The Spirit Completes the Trinity. Athanasius: The Lord called the Spirit "Spirit of truth" and "Paraclete," showing that the Triad[22] is complete in him. In him the Word makes glorious the creation and, by bestowing on it divine life and sonship, draws it to the Father. But that which joins creation to the Word cannot belong to the creatures. And that which bestows sonship upon the creation could not be alien from the Son. For we should have otherwise to seek another spirit, so that by him this Spirit might be joined to the Word. But that would be absurd. The Spirit, therefore, does not belong to things originated. He pertains to the Godhead of the Father, and in him the Word makes things originated divine. But he in whom creation is made divine cannot be outside the Godhead of the Father.[23] Letter to Serapion 1.25.[24]

The Spirit of Truth Cannot Abide Lies. Hermas: Again [the Shepherd] said to me, "Love the truth, and let nothing but truth proceed from your mouth,[25] so that the spirit that God has placed in your flesh may be found truthful before all. And the Lord who dwells in you [26] will be glorified, because the Lord is truthful in every word, and in him is no falsehood. They therefore who lie deny the Lord and rob him, not giving back to him the deposit that they have received. For they received from him a spirit free from falsehood. If they give him back this spirit untruthful, they pollute the commandment of the Lord and become robbers." Shepherd of Hermas 2.3.[27]

The Spirit Reveals the Truth of the Godhead. Basil the Great: Only the Spirit can adequately glorify the Lord. "He will glorify me,"[28] not as a creature, but as the Spirit of truth, since he himself is truth shining brightly. He is the Spirit of wisdom, revealing Christ, the power of God and the wisdom of God, in his own greatness. As the Paraclete he reflects the goodness of the Paraclete (the Father)[29] who sent him, and his own dignity reveals the majesty of him from whom he proceeded. . . . If we are illumined by divine power and fix our eyes on the beauty of the image of the invisible God, and [if we] through the image are led up to the indescribable beauty of its source, it is because we have been inseparably joined to the Spirit of knowledge. He gives those who love the vision of truth the power that enables them to see the image. And this power is himself. He does not reveal it to them from outside sources but leads them to knowledge personally: "No one knows the Father except the Son,"[30] and "No one can say 'Jesus is Lord' except in the Holy Spirit."[31] Notice that it does not say *through* the Spirit but *in* the Spirit. It also says, "God is Spirit, and those who worship him must worship in spirit and truth,"[32] and "in your light do we see light,"[33] through the illumination of the Holy Spirit, "the true light that enlightens every one who comes into the world."[34] He reveals the glory of the Only Begotten in himself, and he gives true worshipers the knowledge of God in

[19]Acts 1:8. [20]CSCO 4 3:271-72. [21]0CCL 36:512; NPNF 1 7:333. [22]Gk *triada*. [23]Cyril makes a similar argument for the Spirit's divinity in his *Commentary on the Gospel of John* 9.1 (LF 48:303-4). [24]MFC 3:106*; PG 26:589. [25]Eph 4:25, 29. [26]Alt. "who put the Spirit in you." [27]ANF 2:21**. [28]Jn 16:14. [29]Basil leaves ambiguous to whom "*tou othen proelthen*" in the Greek refers. It could be the Father or the Son. See note 7 in NPNF 2 8:29. [30]Mt 11:27. [31]1 Cor 12:3. [32]Jn 4:24. [33]Ps 36:9 (35:10 LXX). [34]Jn 1:9.

himself. The way to divine knowledge ascends from one Spirit through the one Son to the one Father. On the Holy Spirit 18.46-47.[35]

The World Is an Impediment to the Spirit's Indwelling. Bede: He calls "the world" the inhabitants of this world who are given over to love of it.[36] In contrast, the saints are on fire with a desire for heavenly things.... And so, anyone who is searching for consolation outwardly in the things of the world is not capable of being reformed inwardly by the favor of divine consolation. Whoever yearns after lowly delight cannot receive the Spirit of truth. The Spirit of truth flees from a heart it discerns is subject to vanity and restores by the light of his coming only those it beholds carrying out the commandments of truth out of love. Homilies on the Gospels 2.17.[37]

Seeing What Others Cannot. Apollinaris of Laodicea: Thus, his coming would not be perceived by those who think only about visible matters ... since whatever they do not see with their eyes they cannot know or even imagine to exist, whereas those who can partake of the Spirit are able to perceive him when he comes. They have a better perception of spiritual things because they are partakers of the Spirit and thus distinguish themselves from the world since they are filled with the Spirit. Through their participation with the divine [Spirit], they have a unique understanding of his art and the divine power behind it, just as someone who has wisdom or a certain art understands in himself what he has, even if it remains unknown to his neighbors. Fragments on John 104.[38]

Different Gifts and Possessions of the Spirit. Gregory the Great: But if the Holy Spirit abides in the disciples, how is it a special mark of the Mediator that [the Spirit] abides in him.... We shall better understand if we distinguish between the different gifts of the Spirit.... In respect of those gifts without which we cannot attain to salvation, the Holy Spirit ever abides in all the elect. But in respect of those that do not relate to our own salvation but to procuring that of others, [the Spirit] does not always abide in them.... For he sometimes withdraws his miraculous gifts so that his grace may be possessed with humility.... Christ ... has him without measure and always. Morals on the Book of Job 2.56.90-91.[39]

We Cannot Love or Obey Without the Spirit. Augustine: The apostle says, "The love of God is shed abroad in our hearts by the Holy Spirit who is given to us."[40] How then does the Lord say here, "If you love me, keep my commandments, and [then] I will ask the Father, and he will give you another Comforter"? Notice he says this about the Holy Spirit. But without the Spirit we can neither love God nor keep his commandments. How can we love so that we will receive him when, without him, we cannot love at all? How can we keep the commandments so that we will receive him when, without him, we have no power to keep them? Or is it the case that the love by which we love Christ has a prior place in us so that by loving Christ in this way and keeping his commandments we become worthy of receiving the Holy Spirit so that the love of God the Father (not of Christ, which we already had) may be shed abroad in our hearts by the Holy Spirit who is given to us? That kind of thinking is all wrong. For whoever believes he loves the Son without loving the Father loves some figment of his own imagination, not the Son....

We should therefore understand that whoever loves already has the Holy Spirit, and by having him he becomes worthy of having even more of him. And the more he has the Spirit the more he loves. The disciples already had the Holy Spirit

[35]*OHS* 73-75*. In *On the Holy Spirit* 19.48 (*OHS* 76), Basil further notes how the Spirit is given the same title here as the Father and the Son have, demonstrating his equality with them. See also Tertullian. *Against Praxeas* 9, 25. [36]See also Augustine *Tractates on the Gospel of John* 74.4. [37]CS 111:166*. [38]*JKGK* 42-43. [39]LF 18:128**; ODGM 11:238. [40]Rom 5:5.

whom the Lord promised. . . . But they did not yet have him in the way the Lord promised. And so they had him and did not have him inasmuch as they did not have to the extent that they would later. They had him in a more limited sense. He was later to be given to them more fully. They had him in a hidden way, but he was yet to be given to them more openly. . . . Let us admit then that without the Holy Spirit we can neither love Christ nor keep his commandments. [But it is also true that] the less experience we have of the Spirit's presence, the less we can do, while the fuller our experience of the Spirit is, the greater is our ability. And so this is no empty promise of Jesus here—either to the one who does not have the Holy Spirit or to the one who has him. For the promise is made to the one who does not have the Spirit so that he may have him, and it is made to the one who does have the Spirit so that he may have him more abundantly. Tractates on the Gospel of John 74.1-2.[41]

[41]NPNF 1 7:333-34**. On the gradual indwelling of the Spirit, see also Gregory of Nazianzus *Oration* 31.26.

14:18-24 The Promise of Christ's Presence Through the Spirit

[18]"I will not leave you desolate; I will come to you. [19]Yet a little while, and the world will see me no more, but you will see me; because I live, you will live also. [20]In that day you will know that I am in my Father, and you in me, and I in you. [21]He who has my commandments and keeps them, he it is who loves me; and he who loves me will be loved by my Father, and I will love him and manifest myself to him." [22]Judas (not Iscariot) said to him, "Lord, how is it that you will manifest yourself to us, and not to the world?" [23]Jesus answered him, "If a man loves me, he will keep my word, and my Father will love him, and we will come to him and make our home with him. [24]He who does not love me does not keep my words; and the word which you hear is not mine but the Father's who sent me."

Overview: Jesus is like a father to orphans (Augustine), not wanting to leave them alone but providing them the Spirit's presence until he comes back (Chrysostom) in order to fortify them (Cyril). But since the world cannot see the Spirit, it does not receive him (Gregory the Great), demonstrating the feeble nature of a world that does not understand spiritual things (Basil). Those who have kept inviolate the Spirit entrusted to them will behold the divine beauty of Christ without obstruction (Cyril). But first Christ must be raised from the dead, and then his disciples and we too shall be raised (Augustine). The disciples can know they will see Jesus again after the resurrection (Theodore).

Christ speaks of the indwelling of himself in the Father and of us in him. He was in the Father through the nature of his deity. We dwell in him through his birth in the body of which we partake in the mystery of the sacrament (Hilary). The union he speaks of is not simply one of mutual love but is a participation in the divine nature, which he himself enables through his incarnation (Cyril). This union is an intimate connection accomplished through the power of the Spirit (Theodore). The believer unites in himself three persons—himself; Christ, who dwells in him; and God, who dwells in Christ (Aphrahat). The apostles knew that Christ was in the Father, and they have united Christ and the Father to us through their writings (Bede).

Those who leave behind the world (Mark the Hermit) and live righteously demonstrate that they are the ones who love Jesus and thus are loved by him and the Father (Cyril). At the future judgment, they will be granted a vision of Jesus (Theodore) as they see the king in all his beauty (Bede). Jesus reveals himself to those who love him (Augustine). Such obedient love keeps our self-will in check (Gregory the Great) so that God dwells in us once we have cleaned the house of our heart from the filth of sin (Origen, Gregory the Great, Cyril). The Spirit of God and of Christ dwells in us as one, although they remain separate under the mysterious appearance of a joint indwelling (Hilary). God dwells in heaven as the first of his works and in us as the last of his works (Ambrose) in which he is pleased to dwell (Augustine). The Son is the Father's Word (Gregory the Great), and those who reject the word of the Son reject the word of the Father (Gaudentius).

14:18 *Christ Is Not Deserting the Disciples*

Jesus Speaks Like a Father to Orphans. Augustine: After the promise of the Holy Spirit, in case anyone should think that the Lord was to give the Spirit, as it were, in place of himself (implying that he himself would not be with them in the same way), he added the words, "I will not leave you orphans. I will come to you." *Orphani* [Greek] are *pupilli* [orphans] in Latin.... Accordingly, although it was not the Son of God that adopted sons to his Father or willed that we should have by grace that same Father who is his Father by nature, yet in a sense it is paternal feelings toward us that [the Son] himself displays. Tractates on the Gospel of John 75.1.[1]

The Spirit's Presence Until Christ Comes. Chrysostom: Earlier he had said, "Where I go you shall come" and "In my Father's house there are many mansions."[2] But since this was a long time off, he gives them the Spirit in the intervening time. They did not know what that [Spirit] was, however, and so they derived little comfort from what he said.... And so he promises them what they required most: his own presence. He says, "I will come to you." But he intimates at the same time that they are not to look for the same kind of presence all over again. "Yet a little while, and the world sees me no more," as if he said, I will come to you but not to live with you every day as I did before. Homilies on the Gospel of John 75.2.[3]

Fortification of the Spirit. Cyril of Alexandria: It is impossible for one's soul to accomplish anything good, or to have power over its own passions or to escape the great subtlety of the devil's snare if the soul is not fortified by the grace of the Holy Spirit and has Christ himself within it.... Christ promises nothing less than that he will be present and will help those who believe on him through the Spirit, even though he ascends into the heavens after his resurrection from the dead. Commentary on the Gospel of John 9.1.[4]

14:19 *The World Could Not See, but You Will*

Constricting the Heart with Worldly Things. Gregory the Great: This other Consoler of humanity, who himself is invisible, inflames each person that he has filled so that he too longs after invisible things. And because worldly hearts are only focused on what is seen,

[1]NPNF 1 7:335**; CCL 36:515. [2]Jn 14:2. [3]NPNF 1 14:274-75**. [4]LF 48:307**.

they do not receive him because their minds are not elevated to what is unseen. As secular minds broaden their horizons by focusing on the outward things [of this world], they constrict the ability of the arteries of the heart to admit the Spirit. Morals on the Book of Job 5.28.50.[5]

The Feeble Nature of the World. Basil the Great: [Jesus] applied the word *world* to those who, being bound by this material and carnal life and beholding the truth by material sight alone, were ordained through their unbelief in the resurrection to see our Lord no more with the eyes of the heart. . . . For the carnal person who has never trained his mind for contemplation but rather keeps it buried deep in the lust of the flesh, as in mud, is powerless to look up to the spiritual light of the truth. On the Holy Spirit 22.53.[6]

Beholding Christ's Beauty. Cyril of Alexandria: Those who love evil in the world will go down to Hades and be banished from the presence of Christ. However, the lovers of virtue who have kept inviolate the earnest of the Spirit will be with him and dwell with him. And being with him surely they shall also behold his divine beauty without any hindrance. For he says, "the Lord shall be your eternal light and God shall be your glory."[7] Commentary on the Gospel of John 9.1.[8]

First Jesus' Resurrection, Then Ours. Augustine: But why does he speak of life as present to him and future to them? Because his resurrection preceded, and theirs was to follow. His resurrection was about to take place so soon that he speaks of it as present, theirs being deferred till the end of the world. He does not say "you live" but "you shall live." . . . Because he lives, therefore we shall live: "As by man came death, by man came also the resurrection of the dead."[9] Tractates on the Gospel of John 75.3.[10]

The Disciples Will See Jesus Again. Theodore of Mopsuestia: The world, that is, all the other people, sees me for a short time only, but you will see me again after my resurrection so that this vision of yours may testify that I am living again. And you will not only see me living, but the same thing will happen to you. When you also resurrect at the right time after your death, you will live and will participate in a second life. He does not say, "because I live" casually, that is, you will see me because I live. But he means You will witness the fact that I am alive, and by seeing it you will know that I resurrected from the dead and live and that I did not remain subject to death, as many believe. Commentary on John 6.14.18-19.[11]

14:20 *Mutual Indwelling of Father, Son and You*

Different Human and Divine Indwellings. Hilary of Poitiers: If he wished to indicate a mere unity of will, why did he set forth a kind of gradation and sequence in the completion of the unity, unless it were that, since he was in the Father through the nature of deity and we on the contrary are in him through his birth in the body, he would have us believe that he is in us through the mystery of the sacraments? And thus there might be taught a perfect unity through a mediator while, we abiding in him, he abode in the Father and as abiding in the Father abode also in us. In this way we might arrive at unity with the Father, since in him who dwells naturally in the Father by birth, we also dwell naturally while he himself abides naturally in us also. On the Trinity 8.15.[12]

A Union of Divine Participation. Cyril of Alexandria: If it is merely because he loves and is loved that the Son is in God the Father, and if by the same law we are in the Son and he in us,

[5]LF 18:279*. See also Bede *Homilies on the Gospels* 2.17 (CS 111:166). [6]NPNF 2 8:34. [7]See Is 60:19. [8]LF 48:310**. [9]1 Cor 15:21. [10]NPNF 1 7:336**; CCL 36:516. [11]CSCO 4 3:264. [12]NPNF 2 9:141-42*; CCL 62A:327.

and no different bond of union is discernible—whether we consider that which binds the Son to the Father or us to him and him to us—then in what sense, or on what principle, I ask you, does Jesus say that "in that day" we shall know the mystery of this? . . .

"For in that day you shall know," he says, "that I am in the Father, and you are in me, and I am in you." For I myself live, he says, for I am life by nature and have shown the temple of my own body alive. But when you yourselves (albeit you are of a corruptible nature) also behold yourselves living in a similar way as I do, then indeed you shall know very clearly that I, being life by nature, knitted you through myself into God the Father, who is also himself life by nature, making you partakers as it were and sharers in his incorruption. For I am in the Father naturally, being the fruit of his essence and its real offspring, subsisting in it, having shone forth from it. I am life of life, and you are in me and I in you, forasmuch as I appeared as a man myself and made you partakers of the divine nature by having my Spirit dwell in you. For Christ is in us through the Spirit, converting that which has a natural tendency to corruption into incorruption and transferring it from the condition of dying to that which is otherwise. And so Paul also says that "he who raised Jesus Christ from the dead shall enliven also your mortal bodies through his Spirit that dwells in you."[13] For albeit the Holy Spirit proceeds from the Father, yet he comes through the Son and is his own. For all things are through the Son from the Father. The divine psalmist will testify that it was through the Spirit that we were recreated for eternal life when he cries as one speaking to the God of all . . . , "You shall take away their breath and they shall fail and shall turn again to their dust. You shall send forth your Spirit, and they shall be made, and you shall renew the face of the earth.[14] Do you hear how the transgression that was in Adam and the "turning away" from the divine commandments, troubled the nature of humanity and made it return to its own earth? But when God sent forth his Spirit and made us partakers of his own nature and through him renewed the face of the earth, we were transfigured to "newness of life," casting off the corruption that comes with sin and once more grasping eternal life through the grace and love toward the human race that our Lord Jesus Christ has. Commentary on the Gospel of John 9.1.[15]

Implications of Unity with Father and Son. Theodore of Mopsuestia: Then, he says, from these facts only you will learn that what I said to you was true about which you now have your doubts. I said, "I am in my Father" concerning the equality of nature and the inseparable connection when I will appear so. And I said "you are in me" concerning your faith and love for me when you will be made a participant with me in charity and also in the gift of the Spirit. "And I in you" is said with reference to what the close connection will cause when, after being regenerated by the power of the Spirit, you are with me in the body and I am with you in the head.[16] Commentary on John 6.14.20.[17]

Becoming One of Three Persons. Aphrahat: When someone sweeps clean their soul in the name of Christ, Christ dwells in them and God dwells in Christ. From that time onward, that person becomes one of three persons—himself; Christ, who dwells in him; and God, who dwells in Christ. Demonstration 4.11.[18]

14:21 *Love and Keeping the Commandments*

Love of God Leaves Love of the World Behind. Mark the Hermit: Do you see how [Jesus] has hidden his manifestation in the commandments? Of all the commandments, therefore, the most comprehensive is to love God and our neighbor. This love is made firm through abstaining from material things and through stillness of thoughts.

[13]Rom 8:11. [14]Ps 104:28-30 (103:28-30 LXX). [15]LF 48:312, 321-22*. [16]Eph 4:15-16; Col 2:19. [17]CSCO 4 3:274-75. [18]CS 101:15-16**.

Knowing this, the Lord enjoins us "not to be anxious about tomorrow,"[19] and rightly so. For if someone has not freed himself from material things and from concern about them, how can he be freed from evil thoughts? And if he is beset by evil thoughts, how can he see the reality of the sin concealed behind them? This sin wraps the soul in darkness and obscurity and increases its hold on us through our evil thoughts and actions. The devil initiates the whole process by testing a person with a provocation that the person is not compelled to accept. But the one urged on by self-indulgence and self-esteem begins to entertain this provocation with enjoyment. Even if their discrimination tells them to reject it, yet in practice they take pleasure in it and accept it. If someone has not perceived this general process of sinning, when will he pray about it and be cleansed from it? And if he has not been cleansed, how will he find purity of nature? And if he has not found this, how will he behold the inner dwelling place of Christ? For we are a dwelling place of God, according to the words of prophet, evangelist and apostle.[20] No Righteousness by Works 223-24.[21]

Not All Will Receive an Eternal Reward. Cyril of Alexandria: Jesus has added the qualification "he who loves me," clearly showing that none other than those who have chosen to live most righteously will be allowed to choose such an incomparable grace, for they are the ones who love him. While it is true that Christ raises the bodies of all—for there will be a resurrection of the evil and the good alike—a new life of glory and happiness will not be given to all without distinction. For it is clear that some only rise again to punishment and will have a life worse than any death, while others . . . will live a desirable and holy life in Christ. Commentary on the Gospel of John 10.[22]

A Vision of the Son for the Faithful. Theodore of Mopsuestia: Whoever loves me and keeps my commandments will enjoy my love and that of the Father and will obtain in addition a vision of who I really am. They will not be disadvantaged by the fact that they did not see me in body. Indeed, they will also enjoy that vision at the appropriate time as well when they see me coming down from heaven. Commentary on John 6.14.21.[23]

The King in All His Beauty. Bede: Even now the Son loves those who love him and the Father. But he loves them now so that they may live properly as a result of their faith, which works through love. Then (in the future), he will love them as well, but in such a way that they may come to the vision of the truth of which they only had a taste through faith. When he adds, "I will show myself to him," he will indeed show himself to all human beings but will show his very own being only to the elect. At the judgment even the damned will see Christ,[24] but only the just will see the king in all his beauty.[25] Homilies on the Gospels 2.17.[26]

14:22-23 *Judas's Question and Jesus' Answer*

God Reveals Himself to Those Who Love Him. Augustine: Judas the holy, not the impure, the follower, not the persecutor of our Lord, asks why Jesus will make himself known to his own but not to the world. . . . Jesus answers that is because the one loves him and the other does not. . . . The saints are distinguished from the world by that love that moves those who are of one mind to dwell together in a house. In this house Father and Son make their home and impart that very love to those whom they shall also honor at last with this promised self-manifestation that the disciple asked his master about. Tractates on the Gospel of John 76.1-2.[27]

Love Keeps Self-Will in Check. Gregory the Great: The proof of love is its manifestation

[19]Mt 6:34. [20]See Zech 2:10; Jn 14:23; 1 Cor 3:16; Heb 3:6. [21]*TP* 1:145*. [22]LF 48:324-25**. [23]CSCO 4 3:275. [24]See Zech 12:10. [25]Is 33:17. [26]CS 111:169-70*. [27]NPNF 1 7:337*.

in deeds. This is why John says in his letter, "He who says, 'I love God' and does not observe his commandments is a liar."[28] Our love is true if we keep our self-will in check according to his commandments. One who is still wandering here and there through his unlawful desires does not really love God, because he is opposing him in his self-will. Forty Gospel Homilies 30.1.[29]

God Dwells in Us After Cleaning House. Origen: God does indeed consume and utterly destroy: he consumes evil thoughts, wicked actions and sinful desires when they find their way into the minds of believers. God, with his Son, inhabits those souls that have been rendered capable of receiving his word and wisdom, in line with his saying, "I and the Father shall come and make our abode with him." After their vices and passions have been consumed, he makes them a holy temple, worthy of himself. On First Principles 1.1.2.[30]

God As Guest. Gregory the Great: Consider, dearly beloved, how great this solemnity is that commemorates the coming of God as a guest in our hearts. If some rich and powerful friend were to enter your home, you would quickly clean the entire house for fear something there might offend your friend's eyes when he entered. Let anyone then who is preparing his inner house for God cleanse away the dirt of his evil deeds. . . . He does indeed enter the hearts of some but does not make his home there because through repentance they acquire respect for God, but during a time of temptation they forget that they have repented and so return to committing sins as if they had never wept over them at all. The Lord comes into the heart and makes his home in one who truly loves God and observes his commandments, since the love of his divine nature so penetrates him that he does not turn away from it during times of temptation. That person loves truly whose heart does not consent to be overcome by wicked pleasures. Forty Gospel Homilies 30.2.[31]

God Will Not Dwell in the Filth of Sin. Cyril of Alexandria: Just as we ourselves cannot bear to live among filth and stench and are eager to rid our houses of such if there should be any, will not the pure and all-holy God even more disdain the polluted soul and abhor a heart sunk in the swamp of sin? Of this there can be no question. Commentary on the Gospel of John 10.[32]

One Mysterious Indwelling. Hilary of Poitiers: For by this he testified that while the Spirit of Christ abides in us the Spirit of God abides in us. The Spirit of him who was raised from the dead is no different from the Spirit of him who raised him from the dead. For they come and dwell in us. I ask whether they will come as strangers associated together and make their abode or in unity of nature? No, the teacher of the Gentiles contends that it is not two spirits—the spirits of God and of Christ—that are present in those who believe but the Spirit of Christ, which is also the Spirit of God. This is no joint indwelling; it is one indwelling, yet an indwelling under the mysterious semblance of a joint indwelling. For it is not the case that two spirits indwell, nor is one that indwells different from the other. For there is in us the Spirit of God and there is also in us the Spirit of Christ, and when the Spirit of Christ is in us there is also in us the Spirit of God. And so, since what is of God is also of Christ, and what is of Christ is also of God, Christ cannot be anything different from what God is. Christ, therefore, is God, one Spirit with God. On the Trinity 8.27.[33]

God Dwells Not Only in Heaven. Ambrose: It is only right that heaven is first and last in the creation of the world, for heaven also has what is beyond heaven, the God of heaven who says, "Heaven is my throne."[34] For God does not sit above the element of heaven but in the

[28] 1 Jn 4:20. [29] CS 123:236-37; PL 76:1220. [30] ANF 4:242*; GCS 22(5):17-18. [31] CS 123:237; PL 76:1220-21. [32] LF 48:333*. [33] NPNF 2 9:145*; CCL 62A:338-39. [34] Is 66:1.

heart of humankind. For this reason the Lord also says, "We will come to them and make our home with them." Heaven, therefore, is the first of the works on earth. Human beings are the close or end or last of his works. Letter 49 (to Horontianus).[35]

God Is Pleased to Dwell in Us. Augustine: God is not too grand to come, he is not too fussy or shy, he is not too proud—on the contrary he is pleased to come if you do not displease him. Listen to the promise he makes. Listen to him indeed promising with pleasure, not threatening in displeasure, "We shall come to him," he says, "I and the Father." To the one he had earlier called his friend, the one who obeys his precepts, the keeper of his commandment, the lover of God, the lover of his neighbor, he says, "We shall come to him and make our abode with him." Sermon 23.6.[36]

14:24 *My Words and the Father's Words*

The Son Is the Father's Word. Gregory the Great: You know, dearly beloved, that the one speaking, the only-begotten Son, is the Father's Word. Therefore the word that the Son speaks is not his but the Father's, because the Son himself is the Father's Word. Forty Gospel Homilies 30.[37]

Reject the Son, Reject the Father. Gaudentius of Brescia: He made known to them many things concerning the oneness of his own divinity with that of the Father. He made clear that there was no separation between them so that even the words he spoke to them were not his, he declared, but the Father's. "And the word that you have heard is not mine but the Father's who sent me." In this sentence he makes it abundantly clear that all who reject the teaching of his only-begotten Son reject the teaching of the Father also, since the Son says that the words he spoke are not his but the Father's. And from this it follows that if they are the words of the Father, they are also the words of the Son, for he declares, "All things whatever the Father has are mine."[38] . . . And this is clearly because of the oneness of the divine substance that recognizes nothing as part of it that does not belong to the divine nature. Sermon 14.[39]

[35]FC 26:257-58**; CSEL 82 1:99. [36]*WSA* 3 2:59; CCL 41:312. [37]CS 123:238*; PL 76:1221. [38]Jn 16:15; see Jn 17:10. [39]PL 20:944.

14:25-31 Christ's Departure and the Gift of the Spirit and Peace

[25]"These things I have spoken to you, while I am still with you. [26]But the Counselor, the Holy Spirit, whom the Father will send in my name, he will teach you all things, and bring to your remembrance all that I have said to you. [27]Peace I leave with you; my peace I give to you; not as the world gives do I give to you. Let not your hearts be troubled, neither let them be afraid. [28]You heard me say to you, 'I go away, and I will come to you.' If you loved me, you would have rejoiced, because I go to the Father; for the Father is greater than I. [29]And now I have told you before it

takes place, so that when it does take place, you may believe. [30]*I will no longer talk much with you, for the ruler of this world is coming. He has no power over me;* [31]*but I do as the Father has commanded me, so that the world may know that I love the Father. Rise, let us go hence."*

OVERVIEW: Christ withdrew his bodily presence from his disciples, but he would replace it by the revealed truth in his word (LEO) revealed through the Spirit, the Comforter who brings the peace that Christ promised he would leave with his disciples (CHRYSOSTOM). The Spirit is called "Paraclete," which can mean both advocate and consoler, as he prepares a hope of pardon for those grieving over their sin (GREGORY THE GREAT). He mentions his departure, foreshadowing his ascension, while his giving of the Spirit looked toward Pentecost. But this should not imply that either the Son or the Spirit were ever absent from heaven or earth (GAUDENTIUS). When the Paraclete is present in us, he makes our spirit-bearing souls spiritual, moving us beyond our nature (BASIL).

The Holy Spirit comes in the name of the Son from the Father (DIDYMUS). The name of Father, Son and Spirit is one (AMBROSE), whose persons are distinguished in Scripture by their activity of sending or being sent (GAUDENTIUS). The Spirit's presence in the heart of a listener enables the teacher to be heard (GREGORY THE GREAT) as the Son speaks and the Spirit teaches (AUGUSTINE). The Spirit provides us with the secrets of God (GREGORY THE GREAT), giving us wholesome hints to remember what has been revealed (AUGUSTINE).

The character of Christ's peace is evident in a serenity of mind and tranquility of soul (CAESARIUS) in those not easily influenced by worldly things or troubled with fear, tormented by doubt or distressed with pain (AMBROSE). Having defeated our enemies, he offers us a lasting peace (APOLLINARIS) that shines forth in those who are called to be his peacemakers (CYPRIAN). This is why we must rely on Christ who is our peace to fulfill his call to us to be at peace (AUGUSTINE). He did not even withdraw the kiss of peace from Judas (AUGUSTINE). The external peace that the world gives can be hurtful, whereas the peace with one another that Christ gives can make you stronger (CHRYSOSTOM). This is because a person who has peace will also have love (AMBROSIASTER). Despite this talk of peace, the disciples were nonetheless worried about the wolves who might seek to scatter the flock in the Shepherd's absence (AUGUSTINE).

When Jesus tells the disciples to rejoice over his departure, he teaches us that we too should rejoice rather than grieve for our loved ones who depart this world (CYPRIAN) even as he seeks to shield the souls of his saints from sorrow (CYRIL). Christ says he ascends to the Father because the Father is greater than him. But he says this according to his human nature (DIDYMUS, HILARY) because Christ is equal to the Father according to his divine nature (HILARY) and according to his whole person, as his humanity is both assumed and exalted (THEODORET, AUGUSTINE). This statement confirms that the Father and Son are of one substance, since comparisons are best done among those who are of the same substance (BASIL). This passage also demonstrates that the Son has his origin from the Father (AUGUSTINE), yet the Father is not greater than the Son in nature or in time but only by being begetter in terms of causation (JOHN OF DAMASCUS).

The faith of the disciples would be impaired by his death, which would cause them to doubt. But their faith would also be repaired by his resurrection, which would confirm what he had predicted (AUGUSTINE). When Jesus tells his disciples that the prince of this world is coming, he may be referring to the devil or someone else (ORIGEN), such as the rulers of this age (AMBROSIASTER). As a serpent cannot mark its track on a rock, so the devil could not find sin in the body of Christ (HIPPOLYTUS), who leaves no sin or fault for the devil to exploit (AUGUSTINE). In fact, the Son's every action, as well as those who follow him, will be seen to exonerate him because everything he does has been done out of love for his Father (THEODORE). As Christ is now ready for his passion, he invites his disciples, as well as each one of us, to rise up from things of the earth and to strive for what is eternal (AMBROSE). One cannot comprehend that eternal state unless he has first fled from what is earthly, transformed by the power of the Spirit (CHRYSOSTOM).

14:25 *While I Am Still with You*

VISION TO BE SUCCEEDED BY REVEALED TRUTH. LEO THE GREAT: He withdrew his bodily presence for a time, for he is to abide at the right hand of the Father until the times that have been divinely decreed for the multiplication of the children of the church are accomplished. And then in the same body in which he ascended he will come again to judge the living and the dead. And so what was visible in Christ is now veiled in mystery. And, so that faith might be more perfect and more steadfast, vision was succeeded by revealed truth whose authority the hearts of the faithful, illumined by light from above, would now begin to follow. SERMON 74.2.2.[1]

14:26 *The Comforter*

THE GIFT OF THE SPIRIT. CHRYSOSTOM: The phrase "he remains with you" is what someone who himself is leaving would say. And so, to calm their grief, he says that as long as he remains with them the Spirit won't come, which means they wouldn't come to know the greater or more sublime things to come. He wanted them, in other words, to see his departure as a blessing. Notice how he often calls [the Spirit] Comforter, because of the troubles they had to deal with. And since they were still troubled, even after hearing all this, because of their sadness, the struggles and his departure, he calms them again by saying, "Peace I leave you." . . . And because he brings up the subject of leaving again, which is enough in itself to trouble them, he again says, "Do not let your heart be troubled, neither let it be afraid." HOMILIES ON THE GOSPEL OF JOHN 75.3.[2]

THE SPIRIT ROUSES US TO PLEAD. GREGORY THE GREAT: Many of you, dearly beloved, know that the Greek word *Paraclete* means in Latin "advocate" or "consoler." He is called an advocate because he intervenes before the Father's justice on behalf of the wrongdoings of sinners. He who is of one substance with the Father, and the Son is said to plead earnestly on behalf of sinners because he causes those whom he fills to do so. This is why Paul says, "For the Spirit himself pleads for us with unutterable groanings."[3] But one who pleads is of less importance than the one receiving the plea. How is the Spirit, then, who is not less important, said to plead? The Spirit pleads, rousing those he fills to plead. The same Spirit is called a consoler because when he prepares a hope of pardon for those grieving over their sins he is lifting up their hearts from sorrow and affliction. FORTY GOSPEL HOMILIES 30.[4]

FORESHADOWING OF ASCENSION AND PENTECOST. GAUDENTIUS OF BRESCIA: He insists that we must believe that the Holy Spirit also shares in the same oneness [that the Son does], when he foretells that the fullness of his doctrine will be perfected in them by the same Paraclete. . . . He meant to forewarn the blessed apostles both of his own ascent into heaven after the passion he was to suffer and of the descent of the Holy Spirit on them from heaven. But the Holy Spirit was not only in heaven, nor was he only on the earth. And neither would the Son ascend to heaven in such a way that he left the earth behind, nor did the Father alone possess the throne of heaven where the Son was returning and from where the

[1]PL 54:398. [2]NPNF 1 14:276**. [3]Rom 8:26. [4]CS 123:238*; PL 76:1221.

Holy Spirit is said to come. Sermon 14.[5]

Spirit-Bearing Souls Become Spiritual Through the Paraclete. Basil the Great: The Spirit is simple in being. His powers are many. They are entirely present everywhere and in everything. He is distributed but does not change. He is shared yet remains whole. Consider the analogy of the sunbeam: each person on whom its kindly light falls rejoices as if the sun existed for him alone, yet it illumines land and sea and is master of the atmosphere. In the same way, the Spirit is given to each one who receives him as if he were the possession of that person alone, yet he sends forth sufficient grace to fill the entire universe. Everything that partakes of his grace is filled with joy according to its capacity—the capacity of its nature, not of his power.

The Spirit does not take up his abode in someone's life through a physical approach. How could a corporeal being approach the bodiless One? Instead, the Spirit comes to us when we withdraw ourselves from evil passions that have crept into the soul through its friendship with the flesh, alienating us from a close relationship with God. Only when a person has been cleansed from the shame of his evil and has returned to his natural beauty, and [only when] the original form of the royal image has been restored in him, is it possible for him to approach the Paraclete. Then, like the sun, he will show you in himself the image of the invisible, and with purified eyes you will see in this blessed image the unspeakable beauty of its prototype. Through him hearts are lifted up, the infirm are held by the hand, and those who progress are brought to perfection. He shines on those who are cleansed from every spot and makes them spiritual people through fellowship with himself. When a sunbeam falls on a transparent substance, the substance itself becomes brilliant and radiates light from itself. So too Spirit-bearing souls, illumined by him, finally become spiritual themselves, and their grace is sent forth to others. From this comes knowledge of the future, understanding of mysteries, apprehension of hidden things, distribution of wonderful gifts, heavenly citizenship, a place in the choir of angels, endless joy in the presence of God, becoming like God, and the highest of all desires, becoming God.[6] On the Holy Spirit 9.22-23.[7]

The Holy Spirit Comes in the Name of the Son From the Father. Didymus the Blind: The Savior affirms that the Holy Spirit is sent by the Father, in his, the Savior's, name. This name is the Son. Here an agreement of nature and propriety, so to speak, of persons is shown. The Son can come in the Father's name only, consistent with the proper relationship of the Son to the Father and the Father to the Son. No one else comes in the name of the Father, but in the name of God, of the Lord, of the Almighty, and the like. . . . As servants who come in the name of their Lord do so as being the servants of that Lord, so the Son who comes in the name of the Father bears that name as being the acknowledged only-begotten Son of the Father. That the Holy Spirit then is sent in the Son's name, by the Father, shows that he is in unity with the Son: from this he is said also to be the Spirit of the Son and to make those sons [children] by adoption who are willing to receive him. The Holy Spirit who then comes in the name of the Son from the Father shall teach those who are established in the faith of Christ all things—all things that are spiritual, that is, both the understanding of truth and the sacrament of wisdom. But he will teach, not like those who have acquired an art or knowledge by study and industry but as being the very art, doctrine, knowledge itself. As being this himself, the Spirit of truth will impart the knowledge of divine things to the mind. On the Holy Spirit 30-31.[8]

Name of Father, Son and Spirit Is One. Ambrose: For he who came in the name of the

[5]PL 20:944-45. [6]This last phrase should be understood in the context of the larger doctrine of *theōsis* that Basil is espousing here. [7]*OHS* 43-44*. [8]PL 23:129-30**.

Son surely also came in the name of the Father, for the name of the Father and of the Son is one. Thus it comes about that the name of the Father and of the Son and of the Holy Spirit is one. On the Holy Spirit 1.13.134.[9]

"Sending" Helps Distinguish Persons in the Trinity. Gaudentius of Brescia: Neither must the Holy Spirit be regarded as separated from the Father whose Spirit he is, nor should the Son be believed to be separated from him whose face he is, as well as his right hand, power and wisdom. . . . For the divinity of the ever adorable Trinity is one and the same everywhere and forever. But so that a clear faith and separate belief in the Father, Son and Holy Spirit might be given to those who believe, it is accordingly written that the Father sends both the Son and the Holy Spirit, since neither he who sends nor he who is sent can be believed to be God if there is a place where he is and a place where he is not. Let us believe in the Son speaking to us, since he is the Truth: "I am not alone," he says, "because the Father is with me."[10] And again, speaking of the Holy Spirit, he says, "But if I by the Spirit of God cast out devils."[11] . . . Accordingly, since nowhere is the divinity of the Trinity not present, it is part of the divine plan for the redemption of humankind that it is spoken of as both sending and being sent. For otherwise the human mind could not grasp that the Father is the Father, and the Son is the Son and the Holy Spirit is the Holy Spirit, unless it should learn their separateness by the naming of one as sent and one as sending. Sermon 14.[12]

Different Perceptions of Meaning via the Spirit. Gregory the Great: It is only right that Jesus promised, "He will teach you all things," because unless the Spirit is present in the heart of a listener, the teacher's utterance is useless. No one should attribute to his teacher what he understands from him, because unless there is an inner teacher, the one outside is exerting himself in vain. You all hear equally the single voice of the person speaking, and yet you each have a different perception of the meaning. The voice is not different—why do your hearts understand it differently? Is it not that through what the speaker's voice counsels generally there is an inner master who teaches each one individually about its meaning? John says this about the anointing of the Spirit: "His anointing teaches you about everything."[13] No one is instructed by a voice when his heart is not anointed by the Spirit. But why do I speak in this way about human teaching when our Creator himself does not speak for the instruction of any person unless he speaks to that person by the anointing of the Spirit? Forty Gospel Homilies 30.[14]

The Son Speaks and the Spirit Teaches. Augustine: So then the Son speaks, the Holy Spirit teaches. When the Son speaks, we take in the words; when the Holy Spirit teaches, we understand those words. . . . The whole Trinity indeed both speaks and teaches, but unless each person worked separately as well, the whole would be too much for human infirmity to take in. Tractates on the Gospel of John 77.2.[15]

The Secrets of God. Gregory the Great: We must ask why it is said of the Spirit, "He will remind you of everything," when reminding is usually the action of someone of lesser importance. We sometimes use "remind" to mean "furnish with information," and so we say that the invisible Spirit "reminds" us because he provides us with knowledge not as an inferior but as one who knows what is secret. Forty Gospel Homilies 30.[16]

Remembering by the Grace of the Spirit. Augustine: The text says the Spirit will, "Suggest," that is, "bring to your remembrance." Every wholesome hint to remember that we receive is of

[9]FC 44:84 ; CSEL 79:73. [10]Jn 8:16, 19. [11]Mt 12:28. [12]PL 20:946-47. [13]1 Jn 2:27. [14]CS 123:238-39**; PL 76:1221-22. [15]NPNF 1 7:339**; CCL 36:520. [16]CS 123:239; PL 76:1222.

the grace of the Spirit. Tractates on the Gospel of John 77.2.[17]

14:27 *Peace I Leave with You*

Peace Defines a Christian. Caesarius of Arles: Peace, indeed, is serenity of mind, tranquility of soul, simplicity of heart, the bond of love, the fellowship of charity. It removes hatred, settles wars, restrains wrath, tramples on pride, loves the humble, pacifies the discordant and makes enemies agree. For it is pleasing to everyone. It does not seek what belongs to another or consider anything as its own. It teaches people to love because it does not know how to get angry,[18] or to extol itself or become inflated with pride. It is meek and humble to everyone, possessing rest and tranquility within itself. When the peace of Christ is exercised by a Christian, it is brought to perfection by Christ. If anyone loves it, he will be an heir of God, while anyone who despises it rebels against Christ. When our Lord Jesus Christ was returning to the Father, he left his peace to his followers as their inherited good, teaching them and saying, "My peace I give to you, my peace I leave with you." Anyone who has received this peace should keep it, and one who has destroyed it should look for it, while anyone who has lost it should seek it. For if anyone is not found with it, he will be disinherited by the Father and deprived of his inheritance. Sermon 174.1.[19]

Christ Brings an Inner Peace. Ambrose: It is the part of those who have been perfected not to be easily influenced by worldly things or to be troubled with fear or tormented with suspicion or stunned with dread or distressed with pain. Rather, as if on a shore of total safety, they ought to calm their spirit, immovable as it is in the anchorage of faith against the rising waves and tempests of the world. Christ brought this support to the spirits of Christians when he brought an inner peace to the souls of those who had proved themselves, so that our heart should not be troubled or our spirit be distressed.... The fruit of peace is the absence of disturbance in the heart. In short, the life of the righteous person is calm, but the unrighteous person is filled with disquiet and disturbance. Therefore the ungodly person is struck down more by his own suspicions than most people are by the blows of others, and the stripes of the wounds in his soul are greater than those in the bodies of those who are lashed by others. Jacob and the Happy Life 2.6.28.[20]

A Lasting Peace Through Christ's Freedom. Apollinaris of Laodicea: Christ stopped those who were waging war and established peace by destroying the might of those waging war. Those opposing powers have no power against those of the household of Christ who came out of captivity as soon as they learned to know the Redeemer. Therefore, they have an unshakeable peace because it is a peace of the soul that has been led to freedom and has put off fear and shed all trouble. Since these good things of the soul have been assured and cannot be taken away, the peace of the soul has been made sure. Fragments on John 106.[21]

We Are Children of Peace. Cyprian: The person of peace ought to seek peace and follow it. The one who knows and loves the bond of charity ought to refrain his tongue from the evil of dissension. Among his divine commands and salutary teachings, the Lord, when he was now very near to his passion, added this one, saying, "Peace I leave with you, my peace I give unto you." He gave this to us as an inheritance. He promised all the gifts and rewards of which he spoke through the preservation of peace. If we are fellow heirs with Christ, let us abide in the peace of Christ. If we are children of God, we ought to be peace-

[17]NPNF 1 7:339**; CCL 36:521. [18]See also Ambrose *On Joseph* 13.78 (FC 65:233). See also Ambrosiaster's *Commentary on First Corinthians* 14.33 (CSEL 81 2:160-61), where he extols the need of patience in promoting peace. [19]FC 47:432-33*. [20]CSEL 32 2:48; FC 65:162-63. [21]*JKGK* 43.

makers. "Blessed," says he, "are the peacemakers. For they shall be called the sons of God."[22] It behooves the children of God to be peacemakers, gentle in heart, simple in speech, agreeing in affection, faithfully linked to one another in the bonds of unanimity. The Unity of the Church 24.[23]

He Is Our Peace. Augustine: And yet it is in him and from him that we have peace, whether it is the peace he leaves with us when going to the Father or that which he will give us when we ourselves are brought by him to the Father. And what is it he leaves with us, when ascending from us, other than his own presence, which he never withdraws? For he himself is our peace who has made both one.[24] It is he, therefore, who becomes our peace, both when we believe that he is and when we see him as he is.[25] For if—so long as we are in this corruptible body that burdens the soul and are walking by faith, not by sight—he does not forsake those who are sojourning at a distance from himself,[26] how much more, when we have attained to that sight, shall he fill us with himself? Tractates on the Gospel of John 77.3.[27]

Jesus Even Gives Judas the Kiss of Peace. Augustine: This peace he left, after a fashion, in his last will and testament to his disciples, our apostles. As he was about to go to the Father, you see, he said, "My peace I give, my peace I leave to you." And he did not separate Judas from himself, though he would not have been making a mistake if he had wished to separate him. I mean he would never separate an innocent person instead of a guilty one, or by separating the guilty forsake the innocent. . . . It was Judas himself who separated himself from the Lord. He was tolerated to the very end. He gave the kiss of peace, though he did not have peace in his heart. And yet he accepted the kiss of peace. That kiss did not bind him to Christ. It condemned him. Sermon 313E.3.[28]

External Peace of the World Can Be Harmful. Chrysostom: Jesus is all but saying here, "How are you harmed by the trouble of the world, provided that you are at peace with me? For this peace is not the same as the world's peace. The world's peace is external and often more hurtful than profitable, and it is of no real advantage to those who possess it. But I give you the kind of peace that calls for peace with one another. This makes you stronger." Homilies on the Gospel of John 75.3.[29]

One Who Has Peace Will Also Have Love. Ambrosiaster: The God of peace is Christ, who said, "My peace I give you, my peace I leave you." . . . But the peace of God is one thing, the peace of the world another, because even malignant and foul people have peace, but [this is] to their damnation. The peace of Christ is free from sins. For it flees faithlessness, spurns trickery and rejects evil deeds. This peace is pleasing and congenial to God, hostile to the devil. A person who has peace will also have love and the God of both to keep him safely guarded forever. Commentary on 2 Corinthians 13.11.2.[30]

Worried About the Wolf. Augustine: Though he was only going for a time, their hearts would be troubled and afraid for what might happen before he returned, lest in the absence of the Shepherd the wolf might attack the flock. Tractates on the Gospel of John 78.1.[31]

14:28a *If You Loved Me, You Would Have Rejoiced*

Going to the Father Is Joyful. Cyprian: He shows the profit of departing from the world. . . . When his disciples were grieved because he said he was now about to go away, he said, "If you loved me, you would rejoice because I go to the Father." Here he teaches and demonstrates that

[22]Mt 5:9. [23]ANF 5:429**. [24]See Eph 2:14. [25]See 1 Jn 3:2. [26]See 2 Cor 5:6-7. [27]NPNF 1 7:339*; CCL 36:521. [28]*WSA* 3 9:110-11; MiAg 1:437. [29]NPNF 1 14:276**. [30]CSEL 81 2:313-14. [31]NPNF 1 7:340**; CCL 36:523.

when the dear ones we love go out from this world, we should rejoice rather than grieve. On Mortality 7.[32]

The Comfort of Christ. Cyril of Alexandria: Jesus soothes the agony of grief he found in his disciples, and just as a beloved and good father, compelled for some legitimate reason to take his children from the nurse that bears them, and seeing a flood of tears flowing down their delicate cheeks, he coaxes them by insisting on the good that will result from her absence and arms them against grief with hope. So also our Lord Jesus Christ shields the souls of his saints from sorrow. For he knew, being truly God, that his abandonment of them would be hard for them to take, even though he would always be with them through the Spirit. This proves his love and extreme holiness. Commentary on the Gospel of John 10.[33]

14:28b *The Father Is Greater Than I*

The Father Is Greater in the Sense of Christ's Human Nature. Didymus the Blind: How then is "greater" to be understood? Does it pertain to the size of bodies? Or does it mean "more advanced" in age? Or does it mean "adorned with more virtue"? But all these things can be quantified—whatever can be perceived and measured. But in God there is nothing that can be perceived or measured. Thus, the words *greater* and *less* cannot be spoken concerning the Word of God or concerning the Father. For by nature God cannot be measured or quantified. But if you say that the Father is greater since he is unbegotten while the Son is begotten, we reply that these words speak of their natures, not of their properties of existence. And especially in the cases of those incorporeal beings one does not diminish the value of those of the same substance by granting more or less to this one or to that one. For by nature Absolute Being cannot be measured in essence or in knowledge simply by any measure or quantity of size. Then why did [Christ] say these things?

The Savior in one word set forth a double manner of teaching, for the meaning of the word he spoke is twofold. It is just as in the phrases "the one sending me" and "I depart": he alluded to the body embraced by definite locations, inasmuch as it is circumscribed by them, and he did not refer to the uncircumscribed divine nature that embraces all things. By analogy, then, when he says "greater," he indicates that his divinity can be equaled to that of the Father, since he is of the same substance with him, but the Father is greater because the Son accepted a body, since the Son's nature is understood to be less than that of the Father inasmuch as the Son has become man. And do not marvel that the Savior says that he is less than the Father since he became man, since he also has said that he became lower than the angels, as in this verse: "We see Jesus made lower than the angels for a little time because of the suffering of his death, but now crowned with glory and honor."[34] He was also said to be lower than his own disciples, for he said, "I am in your midst as your servant" and as the least.[35] Therefore, things that are compared share the same substance, but things that are undivided (whether in our knowledge or by their essence) cannot admit of "greater" and "less." Now if you wish to understand the sentence, "The Father who sent me is greater than me," to apply to the divinity of the Son apart from considering that he has taken on flesh, you will have to suppose that he is enclosed in and restricted to certain places and that he was sent where he had not previously been and removed from where he had been. But this makes no sense. Fragments on John 17.[36]

Form of Servant, Form of God. Hilary of Poitiers: We must confess the Father to be in the Son and the Son in the Father, by unity of nature, by might of power, as equal in honor as begetter and begotten. But, perhaps you say, the

[32]CCL 3A:20. [33]LF 48:343*. [34]Heb 2:9. [35]See Mt 20:26. [36]*JKGK* 184-85.

witness of our Lord himself is contrary to this declaration, for he says, "The Father is greater than I." . . . Can you be ignorant that the incarnation for your salvation was an emptying of the form of God and that the Father, unaffected by this assumption of human conditions, abode in the blessed eternity of his own incorrupt nature without taking our flesh? We confess that the only-begotten God, while he abode in the form of God, abode in the nature of God, but we do not at once reabsorb into the substance of the divine unity his unity bearing the form of a servant. Nor do we teach that the Father is in the Son, as if he entered into him bodily. . . . God, born of God, being found as man in the form of a servant but acting as God in his miracles, was at once God as his deeds proved, and yet man, for he was found in the fashion of man. On the Trinity 9.51.[37]

How the Father Is Greater and the Son Not Less. Hilary of Poitiers: The Father, therefore, is greater, because he is the Father; but the Son, because he is the Son, is not less. By the birth of the Son the Father is constituted greater: the nature that is his by birth does not suffer the Son to be less. The Father is greater, for the Son prays to him to render glory to the manhood he has assumed. The Son is not less, for he receives back his glory with the Father. Thus are consummated at once the mystery of the birth and the dispensation of the incarnation. The Father, as Father—and as glorifying him who now is Son of man—is greater. Father and Son are one in that the Son, born of the Father, after assuming an earthly body is taken back to the glory of the Father. On the Trinity 9.56.[38]

How the Father Is Greater. Theodoret of Cyr: Sometimes, therefore, I [Jesus] say that I am equal to the Father,[39] and at other times I say that the Father is greater. I am not contradicting myself, but I am showing that I am God and a human being—God through the lofty words, and a human being through the humble ones. But if you want to know how the Father is greater than I, I was talking from the flesh, not from the person of the divinity. Dialogue 1.56.[40]

Humanity Assumed and Exalted. Augustine: Let us, along with the disciples, listen to the Teacher's words, and not, with strangers, give heed to the wiles of the deceiver. Let us acknowledge the twofold substance of Christ, namely, the divine, in which he is equal with the Father, and the human, in respect to which the Father is greater. And yet at the same time both are not two, for Christ is one. And God is not a quaternity but a Trinity. For as the rational soul and the body form but one man, so Christ, while both God and man, is one. Thus Christ is God, a rational soul and a body. In all of these we confess him to be Christ. We confess him in each. Who, then, is he who made the world? Christ Jesus, but in the form of God. Who is it that was crucified under Pontius Pilate? Christ Jesus, but in the form of a servant. And this is true of the several aspects of which he consists as man. Who is he who was not left in hell? Christ Jesus, but only in respect of his soul. Who was to rise on the third day, after being laid in the tomb? Christ Jesus, but solely in reference to his flesh. In reference, then, to each of these, he is likewise called Christ. And yet, all of them are not two or three but one Christ. On this account, therefore, he said, "If you loved me, you would surely rejoice, because I go to the Father." For human nature is worthy of congratulation in being so assumed by the only-begotten Word as to be constituted immortal in heaven and, earthly in its nature, to be so sublimated and exalted that, as incorruptible dust, it might take its seat at the right hand of the Father. Tractates on the Gospel of John 78.3.[41]

---

[37]NPNF 2 9:173*; CCL 62A:428-30. See also *On the Trinity* 1.30; 3.12; 9.54; Ambrose *Of the Christian Faith* 2.8.59. [38]NPNF 2 9:175*; CCL 62A:435-36. [39]See Jn 10:30. [40]FC 106:83. [41]CCL 36:524-25; NPNF 1 7:341-42*. See also Augustine on this passage in *On Eighty-three Varied Questions* 83.69.1.

"Greater Than" Implies Being of One Substance with the Father. Basil the Great: "Greater" is used when talking about size, time, dignity, power, or the cause of something. The Father cannot be called greater than the Son in size because he is incorporeal. He cannot be called greater than the Son in time because the Son is the creator of time. You can't say that he is greater in dignity either, because he was not made into something that he had not previously been, nor can you say he is greater in power since, "whatever the Father does, the Son does as well." And finally, no one can say the Father is greater because he is the cause of the Son's existence, because he is also the cause of our existence, and this would place the Son on a similar footing with us. Instead, see the words as expressing the honor that is given by the Son to the Father instead of devaluing the Son who speaks these words. You should also realize that what is greater is not necessarily of a different essence. One human being is called greater than another human being, just like one horse is called greater than another horse. If the Father is called greater, it does not immediately follow that he is of another substance. In a word, the comparison lies between beings of one substance, not between those of different substances. A human being is not properly said to be greater than a brute or an inanimate thing. Human beings are compared to human beings, just as brutes are compared with other brutes. The Father is therefore of one substance with the Son, even though he is called greater. Against Eunomius 4.[42]

"Less Than" Implies Origin. Augustine: Whenever . . . it seems that the Son is shown to be less than the Father, interpret it as spoken . . . not to show one is greater or less than the other but . . . that one has his origin from the other. Answer to Maximus 2.14.8.[43]

The Father Is Greater in Terms of Causation. John of Damascus: If we say that the Father is the origin of the Son and greater than the Son, we do not suggest any precedence in time or superiority in nature of the Father over the Son (for through his agency he made the ages) or superiority in any other respect except causation. And we mean by this that the Son is begotten of the Father and not the Father of the Son, and the Father naturally is the cause of the Son. So then, whenever we hear it said that the Father is the origin of the Son and greater than the Son, let us understand it to mean in respect of causation.[44] Orthodox Faith 1.8.[45]

14:29 *Forewarned for Faith*

Faith Impaired by Death, Repaired by Resurrection. Augustine: If faith is in things that are believed and in things that are not seen,[46] what does our Lord mean when he says, "And now I have told you before it happens, so that when it does happen you might believe"? Shouldn't he rather have said, And now I have told you before it happens so that you may believe what you shall see when it happens? For even [Thomas], who was told, "Because you have seen, you have believed," did not believe only what he saw. But he saw one thing and believed another. For he saw [Jesus] as man and believed him to be God. . . . But though we may be said to believe what we see, just as everyone says that he believes his own eyes, yet that is not to be mistaken for the faith that is built up by God in our souls. Rather, from things that are seen, we are brought to believe in those that are invisible. Wherefore, beloved, in the passage before us, when our Lord says, "And now I have told you before it happens, that when it happens you might believe," by the words "when it happens" he certainly means that they would yet see him after his death, alive and ascending to his Father. And when they saw this, they would then be compelled to believe that he was indeed the Christ, the Son of the living God, seeing he could do such a thing

[42]NPNF 2 8:xxxviii*; PG 29:693-96. [43]PL 42:775. [44]But see Basil above. [45]NPNF 2 9:8-9. Irenaeus also speaks of the Father being greater because he has greater knowledge than the Son since he alone knows the time of judgment. See *Against Heresies* 2.28.2. [46]Heb 11:1.

even after predicting it and also could predict it before he did it. And this then they would believe, not with a new but with an increased faith—or at least [with a faith] that had been impaired by his death and was now repaired by his resurrection. TRACTATES ON THE GOSPEL OF JOHN 79.1.[47]

14:30 *The Ruler of This World Holds Nothing over Jesus*[48]

THE IDENTITY OF THE RULER. ORIGEN: Also mentioned is a prince of this world, but it is not yet clear whether this is the devil himself or someone else.[49] There are also certain princes of this world spoken of as possessing a kind of wisdom that will come to nothing. ON FIRST PRINCIPLES 1.5.2.[50]

THE RULERS OF THIS AGE. AMBROSIASTER: The rulers of this age are not to be understood as merely people of the Jews and Romans but also those princes and powers referred to above,[51] to whom this saying pertains and against whom is our struggle.... The rulers of this age crucified the Lord of majesty through their ignorance. For how can the rulers of this age be understood as the rulers of the Jews who were subject to the Roman Empire? COMMENTARY ON 1 CORINTHIANS 2.8.1-2.[52]

CHRIST LEAVES NO TRAIL OF SIN. HIPPOLYTUS: As a serpent cannot leave a trail on a rock, so the devil could not find sin in the body of Christ. For the Lord says, "Behold, the prince of this world comes and will find nothing in me." For as a ship, sailing in the sea, leaves no traces of her way behind it, so neither does the church, which is situated in the world as in a sea, leave its hope on the earth, because it has its life reserved in heaven. And as [the church] holds its way here only for a short time, it is not possible to trace out its course. FRAGMENTS ON PROVERBS 22-23.[53]

THERE IS NO FAULT IN JESUS THAT SATAN CAN EXPLOIT. AUGUSTINE: Why be surprised that Christ died, although Christ committed no sin whatever? He wanted to pay back for you what he did not owe himself, in order to deliver you from debt. The devil, having taken in the human race, was in possession of it by right. He possessed what he had taken; he had taken what he had taken in. Christ brought along in his mortal flesh his blood to be shed, with which to cancel the bill of our sins. That other one would still be holding the guilty if he had not put the innocent to death. But now see with what justice he is told, "You have put to death one who had no debt. Now hand over the debtors." "Behold," he says, "the prince of this world is coming, and in me he will find nothing." "How nothing? Haven't you got a soul, haven't you got flesh? Aren't you also the Word? Is all that nothing?"

Of course not. Nothing of his[54] own, because [I have] no sin. He is the prince of sinners. The prince of sinners will find nothing in me. I have not sinned, I have contracted nothing from Adam, because I came to you from the Virgin. I did not add anything, because I did not have anything to add it to, and by living a just life I committed no sin. Let him come and find something of his own in me, if he can. But he will find nothing of his own in me. I have no sin. Born innocently, I have led an innocent life. Let him come, he will find nothing. "So why are you dying, if he is coming and will find nothing?" And he gives the reason why he must die: "Behold, the prince of this world is coming, and he will find nothing in me." And if we might hypothetically ask, "So then, why are you dying?" he would answer, "So that all might know that I am doing the will of my Father. Arise, let us go from here";[55] That is, let us go to [my] passion. He was willing to die because if was the will of his good Father, not because he owed it to the evil prince. SERMON 265D.4.[56]

---

[47]NPNF 1 7:342**; CCL 36:525-26. [48]The Latin text on which Hippolytus and Augustine comment reads, "*in me nihil inveniet,*" lit. "He will find nothing in me." [49]1 Cor 2:6. [50]ANF 4:257**; GCS 2(5):70. [51]See Rom 8:38. [52]CSEL 81 2:24-25. [53]ANF 5:174; GCS 1 2:165. [54]The devil's. [55]Jn 14:30-31. [56]*WSA* 3 7:257; MiAg 1:661-62. See also Hilary *On the Trinity* 9.55.

14:31a *The World Will Know Jesus' Love for the Father*

The Father's Will Is for the Salvation of All. Theodore of Mopsuestia: Great and powerful things will happen to me in the course of my passion. Similar things will happen to those who believe in me after my passion. They will cast out demons with a mere word, heal the sick, perform numerous signs, command the removal of all human tribulations through my name. Any number of different punishments will befall sinners. From all these things it will be clear that I was unjustly executed. But because of my love for the Father I accomplish his [primordial] will that all would be saved. The defeat of death that I will justly accomplish through the intervention of the omnipotent one will be the destiny for all humanity by grace. Commentary on John 6.14.30-31.[57]

14:31b *Rise, Let Us Go*

Each One, Following Jesus, Should Arise from the Earth. Ambrose: Let us withdraw from the bond of the body and leave everything earthly so that when the adversary comes he may find nothing of his in us. Let us strive for the eternal and fly up to the divine on the wings of love and the oars of charity. Let us rise up from here, that is, from the things of the age and those of the world. For the Lord has said, "Rise, let us be on our way," teaching that each one should arise from the earth, raise up his soul that lies on the ground, lift it to the things that are above and call forth his eagle, the eagle of whom it is said, "Your youth will be renewed like the eagle's."[58] Death as a Good 5.16.[59]

The Transforming Power of the Spirit. Chrysostom: For they who now trembled and feared, after they had received the Spirit sprang into the midst of dangers and stripped themselves for the contest against steel, and fire, and wild beasts, and seas, and every kind of punishment. And they, the unlettered and ignorant, spoke so boldly as to astonish their hearers. For the Spirit made them men of iron instead of men of clay, gave them wings and allowed them to be cast down by nothing human. For such is that grace: if it finds despondency, it disperses it; if evil desires, it consumes them; if cowardice, it casts it out and does not allow one who has partaken of it to be afterward a mere person but, as it were removing him to heaven itself, causes him to imagine to himself all that is there.[60] Homilies on the Gospel of John 75.5.[61]

[57]CSCO 4 3:279-80. [58]Ps 103:5 (102:5 LXX, Vg). [59]FC 65:82; CSEL 32 1:717-18. See also Ambrose *Flight from the World* 1.4 (FC 65:283). [60]Acts 4:32, 2:46. [61]NPNF 1 14:277*.

15:1-3 The True Vine and His Branches

[1]I am the true vine, and my Father is the vinedresser. [2]Every branch of mine that bears no fruit, he takes away, and every branch that does bear fruit he prunes, that it may bear more fruit. [3]You are already made clean by the word which I have spoken to you.

Overview: Christ rises quickly from the table where he has sat with his disciples for the Last Supper in order to perform the sacrament of his final passion in the mystery of his flesh (Hilary).

Like a grapevine hung on the wood of the cross for us (Ambrose), the true vine (Augustine) of David is put through the winepress of the cross (Gaudentius). He lets the juice from his veins flow in support of its branches (Clement) in the Eucharist as an antidote to our grief (Theophilus of Alexandria). As the vine, he joins himself to our nature that we might become partakers in his nature through the Holy Spirit as branches attached to and supported by him (Cyril).

The vine nourishes the fruit while the vinedresser tends the soil (Cyril) as he cultivates the field of the church (Augustine). As we praise God, he cultivates us (Augustine). Jerusalem was pruned because of its lack of fruit (Irenaeus), teaching us that spiritual fruit will be realized in concrete action (Cyril). Some natural pruning takes place too as the wind on the vines tests the grapes of the church (Ephrem). The Word prunes our impulses (Clement) as spiritual circumcision prunes the bodily passions (Cyril). Persecution too prunes the church, getting rid of dead wood in order to bring about growth both in the Christian and in the church (Justin, Chrysostom). There is a cleansing power in the Word of Jesus (Basil), which as a double-edged sword prunes our souls (Cyril) and cleanses us through its connection with the water in the sacrament of baptism (Augustine).

15:1a *I Am the True Vine*

The Vine As Christ's Assumption of Flesh. Hilary of Poitiers: Jesus rises and hurries to complete the mystery of his bodily passion. But the next moment, he unfolds the mystery of his assumption of flesh. Through this assumption we are in him, as the branches are in the vine. And unless he had become the vine, we could have borne no good fruit. He encourages us to abide in him through faith in his assumed body, that, since the Word has been made flesh, we may be in the nature of his flesh, as the branches are in the vine. He separates the form of the Father's majesty from the humiliation of the assumed flesh by calling himself the vine, the course of unity for all the branches. He calls the Father the careful husbandman who prunes away its useless and barren branches to be burned in the fire. On the Trinity 9.55.[1]

The Grapevine Hanging on the Cross. Ambrose: Jacob spoke of [our Lord as] a grape,[2] because Christ hung on the wood like a grape. He is the vine; he is the grape. He is the vine because he cleaves to the wood and the grape because, when his side was opened by the soldier's lance, he sent forth water and blood[3]. . . water for baptism, blood for redemption. The water washed us; the blood redeemed us.[4] On the Patriarchs 4.24.[5]

The True Vine Bears Fruit. Augustine: When he says, "I am the true vine," it is no doubt to distinguish himself from that [vine] to which the words are addressed, "How are you turned into the degenerate plant of a strange vine to me?"[6] For how could that be a true vine that was expected to bring forth grapes and brought forth thorns?[7] Tractates on the Gospel of John 80.1.[8]

The Holy Vine of David. Didache: Now, concerning the Eucharist, give thanks as follows.

First, concerning the cup:
We give you thanks, our Father,
for the holy vine of David your servant,
which you have made known to us
through Jesus, your servant;
to you be the glory forever.

Didache 9.1-2.[9]

The Winepress of the Cross. Gaudentius of Brescia: The wine of his blood, gathered from the many grapes of the vine planted by him,

[1]NPNF 2 9:174-75*; CCL 62A:434. [2]Gen 49:11. [3]Jn 19:34. [4]See also Ambrose *On the Sacraments* 5.14. [5]FC 65:255-56; CSEL 32 2:138. See also Eusebius *Proof of the Gospel* 8.1.379. [6]Jer 2:21. [7]Is 5:4. [8]NPNF 1 7:344**. [9]*AF* 259-61.

is pressed out in the winepress of the cross, and of its own power it begins to ferment in the capacious vessels of those who receive it with faithful heart. Two Tractates on Exodus.[10]

Wine of the Vine, Blood of the Word. Clement of Alexandria: The vine produces wine as the Word produces blood, and both are drunk for the health of men and women—wine for the body, blood for the spirit. Christ the Educator 1.5.[11]

The Vine As Antidote to Grief. Theophilus of Alexandria: I am the true vine. Drink my joy, the wine I have mixed for you. For my cup is intoxicating for me,[12] intoxicating like the most powerful antidote—like joy against the grief that sprouted in Adam. . . . I have given you a table, life-giving and joy-creating, that offers in exchange for distress unspeakable joy before those who have envied you. Eat the bread that renews your nature. Drink the wine, the exultation of immortality. Eat the bread that purges away the old bitterness, and drink the wine that eases the pain of the wound. This is the healing of your nature; this is the punishment of the one who did the injury. . . . I became the true vine in your race, that in me you might bear sweet-smelling fruit. Sermon on the Mystical Supper.[13]

Attached to the Vine Through the Spirit. Cyril of Alexandria: He wants to show us how important it is to love, to hold fast to our love toward him and how much we gain from our union with him. This is why he says that he is the vine, by way of illustration. Those united, anchored and rooted in him, who are already partakers in his nature through their participation in the Holy Spirit, are branches. For it is his Holy Spirit who has united us with the Savior Christ since connection with the vine produces a choice of those things that belong to it. And our connection[14] with the vine holds us fast. From a firm resolve in goodness we proceed onward by faith and we become his people, obtaining from him the dignity of sonship. . . . He says that he is a vine, the mother and nourisher, as it were, of its branches. For we are begotten of him and in him, in the Spirit, to produce the fruits of life. Commentary on the Gospel of John 10.2.[15]

15:1b *The Father Is the Vinedresser*

The Vine Nourishes, the Vinedresser Tends the Soil. Cyril of Alexandria: For it is the function of the vine to nourish the branches, and of the tiller of the soil to tend them. And if we think about this in the right way, we will see that neither the one function if performed apart from the Father, nor the other function if performed apart from the Son or Holy Spirit, could sustain the whole. For everything proceeds from the Father by the Son in the Spirit. And so it is only appropriate now that the Savior called the Father a vinedresser so that no one might think that the Only Begotten is the only one who exercised care over us.[16] This is why he represents God the Father as cooperating with him, calling himself the vine that enlivens his own branches with life and the power to produce, and the Father as the vinedresser, thereby teaching us that providential care over us is a sort of distinct activity of the divine substance. Commentary on the Gospel of John 10.2.[17]

God Is the Tiller of the Field, the Church. Augustine: Not only is the church a field, but God is the tiller of the field. Listen to the Lord himself: "I am the vine, you the twigs, and my Father is the vinedresser." Toiling in this

---

[10]MFC 7:93; CSEL 68:32. [11]ANF 2:213. [12]Ps 23:5 (22:5 LXX). [13]MFC 7:152. See also Origen *Commentary on John* 1.205-6 (FC 80:74-75). [14]Achieved through the Spirit. [15]LF 48:363**. [16]In Athanasius's account of the vine and the vinedresser, he records Dionysius of Alexandria's distinction between vine and vinedresser as akin to the distinction between Father and Son (NPNF 2 4:180-81). This passage occasioned much discussion in Cyril concerning how the analogy cannot be pressed too far, however, in equating the relationship among the vine, vinedresser and branches with the relationship between Father, Son and us, especially in an ontological sense. [17]LF 48:365**.

field as a laborer and hoping for an eternal reward, the apostle claims no credit for himself, except a laborer's due. "I planted," he says, "Apollos watered, but God gave the increase. And so neither the one who plants is anything, nor the one who waters, but God who gives the increase."[18] Sermon 4.26.[19]

God Cultivates Us. Augustine: For we [through praise] cultivate God, and God cultivates us. But our cultivating of God does not make him better: our cultivating is that of adoration, not of plowing. . . . His cultivating of us makes us better. . . . His cultivating consists in getting rid of all the seeds of wickedness from our hearts, in opening our heart to the plow, as it were, of his word, in sowing in us the seeds of his commandments, and in waiting for the fruits of godliness. Sermon 87.1.[20]

15:2a *Dead Branches Are Taken Away*

Jerusalem Forsaken for Lack of Fruit. Irenaeus: Concerning Jerusalem and the Lord, they[21] venture to assert that if it had been "the city of the great King,"[22] it would not have been deserted. This is like someone saying that if the stalk were a creation of God, it would never part company with the wheat. And that the vine twigs, if made by God, never would be lopped away and deprived of the clusters. But these [vine twigs] were not originally made for their own sake but for that of the fruit growing on them. When that fruit comes to maturity and is taken away, the twigs are left behind, and those that are not fruitful are lopped off altogether. It was the same way with Jerusalem, which had in itself borne the yoke of bondage . . . when the fruit of liberty had come, and reached maturity, and been reaped and stored in the barn, and when those which had the power to produce fruit had been carried away from it [i.e., from Jerusalem] and scattered throughout all the world. . . . Once the fruit, therefore, had been sown throughout all the world, it [Jerusalem] was deservedly forsaken, and those things that had formerly brought forth fruit abundantly were taken away. For from these, according to the flesh, were Christ and the apostles enabled to bring forth fruit. Against Heresies 4.4.1.[23]

Spiritual Fruit Realized in Concrete Action. Cyril of Alexandria: If we demonstrate what kind of union we have by only a mere barren confession of faith—without sealing the bond of our union by the good works that proceed from love—we will be branches indeed, but still dead and without fruit. Faith without works is dead, as the saint says.[24] Accordingly, if the branch hangs fruitlessly, so to speak, from the trunk of the vine, know that such a person will encounter the pruning knife of the husbandman. He will entirely cut it off and burn it as worthless rubbish. Commentary on the Gospel of John 10.2.[25]

Wind Tests the Grapes of the Church. Ephrem the Syrian:

The sons of truth grow large on this Branch of Truth;[26] they have been perfected and have become fruits fit for the kingdom.
But, although the Branch is living, on it are also dead fruits that only seem to blossom.
The wind[27] tested them and shook down the wild grapes. Blessed is he who crowned by [the Spirit] those who held fast in him! . . .

Jesus, bend down to us your love that we may grasp this Branch that bent down her fruits for the ungrateful;
they ate and were satisfied, yet they demeaned her who had bent down as far as Adam in Sheol.
She ascended and lifted him up and with him returned to Eden.

[18]1 Cor 3:6-7. [19]WSA 3 1:199; CCL 41:39. [20]PL 38:530-31. [21]I.e., the Gnostics. [22]Mt 5:35. [23]ANF 1:465-66; SC 100:416-18. [24]See Jas 2:20. [25]LF 48:375**. [26]McVey notes that the Branch of Truth is grammatically feminine, representing the church but also Christ in this passage. [27]Or "spirit."

Blessed is he who bent her down toward us
that we might seize her and ascend on her.
Who indeed will not weep that although the
Branch is great, the weakness of one unwill
ing to seize her greatness maintains that
she is a feeble branch—
she who has conquered all kings and cast a
shadow upon the entire world! By suffering
her power has increased.
Blessed is he who made her greater than that
vine from Egypt![28]
Who will not hold fast to this Branch of
Truth.
She bore the true ones; she shed the false.
Not because they were too heavy for her did
she shed them.
For our sake she tested them in the breeze;
it shook down the shriveled; it ripened the
firm.

Hymn Against Julian: On the Church 5, 8-10.[29]

15:2 *Pruning That Produces More Fruit*

The Word Prunes Our Impulses. Clement of Alexandria: The Lord clearly reveals himself when describing figuratively his many and various ways of service.... For the vine that is not pruned grows to wood. It is the same way with humankind. The Word—the knife—clears away the wanton shoots, compelling the impulses of the soul to become fruitful, not to indulge in lust. Now, reproof addressed to sinners has their salvation for its aim, the word being harmoniously adjusted to each one's conduct, now with tightened, now with relaxed cords. Christ the Educator 1.8.[30]

Spiritual Circumcision Prunes Bodily Passions. Cyril of Alexandria: God works with those who have chosen to live the best and most perfect life and to do good works as far as they are able, having elected to seek perfection as citizens of God. God uses the working power of the Spirit as a pruning hook, sometimes circumcising in them the pleasures that are always calling us to fleshly lusts and bodily passions. Other times, God circumcises all those temptations that are likely to assail the souls of people, defiling the mind by diverse kinds of evils. We say that this circumcision is not the work of hands but is truly that of the Spirit.[31]... If the branches of the vine suffer any purging, that purging cannot take place, I suppose, without suffering. For it is painful insofar as wood can suffer pain.... For our God who loves virtue instructs us by pain and tribulation.... But while divine wrath will bring about the complete severance of the barren branches that are consigned to punishment, a [less severe] judgment—one that is out of consideration and mercy—will purge those who bear fruit, bringing only a little pain while accelerating their fertility and occasioning a greater number of blossoms springing up.... Therefore let the fervor that shows itself in works be combined with the confession of the faith, and let it unite action with the doctrines concerning God. For then we shall be with Christ and experience the secure and safe power of fellowship with him, escaping the peril that results from being cut off from him. Commentary on the Gospel of John 10.2.[32]

Persecution as Pruning for Growth. Justin Martyr: It is evident that no one can terrify or subdue us who have believed in Jesus over all the world. For it is plain that, though beheaded, and crucified, and thrown to wild beasts, and chains, and fire, and all other kinds of torture, we do not give up our confession. But the more such things happen, the more do others—and in larger numbers—become faithful and worshipers of God through the name of Jesus. For just as if one should cut away the fruit-bearing parts of a vine, it grows up again, and yields other branches flourishing and fruitful. Even so the same thing

[28]Ps 80:8 (79:9 LXX). [29]*ESH* 222-23. [30]ANF 2:226. [31]See Rom 2:28-29. [32]LF 48:377-79**.

happens with us. For the vine planted by God and Christ the Savior is his people. Dialogue with Trypho 110.[33]

Purging Is a Type of Pruning. Chrysostom: "And every branch that bears fruit, he purges," that is, "causes it to enjoy great care." Yet the root requires even more care than the branches. It needs to be dug around and cleared. And yet everything here is spoken about the branches. Jesus is saying then that he is sufficient unto himself but that the disciples need considerable help from the husbandman even though they are quite excellent already. Therefore he says, "that which bears fruit, he purges." The one branch, because it is fruitless, cannot even remain in the vine, but the other, because it bears fruit, he makes even more fruitful. This, some might assert, was said concerning the persecutions then coming upon them. For the purging is a type of pruning that makes the branch bear better. This implies that persecutions rather make people stronger. Then, in case they might ask about whom he said these things and become anxious again, he says, "Now you are clean through the word that I have spoken to you." Homilies on the Gospel of John 76.1.[34]

15:3 *Cleansed by Jesus' Word*

The Sanctifying Power of Jesus' Teaching. Basil the Great: The world, that is, life enslaved by the affections of the flesh, can no more receive the grace of the Spirit than a weak eye the light of a sunbeam. But the Lord, who by his teaching bore witness to purity of life, gives to his disciples the power of now both beholding and contemplating the Spirit. For "now," he says, "you are clean through the word that I have spoken to you," wherefore "the world cannot receive him, because it does not see him . . . but you know him. For he dwells with you." And this is what Isaiah says, "He who spread forth the earth and that which comes out of it; he who gives breath to the people on it, and Spirit to them that trample on it."[35] For those who trample down earthly things and rise above them are shown to be as worthy of the gift of the Holy Spirit. On the Holy Spirit 22.53.[36]

The Purifying Power of the Gospel Word. Cyril of Alexandria: He makes his disciples a palpable and convincing demonstration of the art of the purifier of their souls. For already, he says, they are purged not by participating in anything else but merely by the word spoken to them, that is, the divine guidance of the gospel. And this word proceeds from Christ. What man or woman of sense, then, can any longer call into question that the Father has, as it were, a pruning knife and hand through whose instrumentality everything exists, that is, the Son, fulfilling the activity of that husbandry in us which he attributes to the person of the Father, teaching us that all things proceed from the Father by the instrumentality of the Son? For it is the Word of the Savior that purges us; the husbandry of our souls is attributed to God the Father. For this is his living Word, sharp as a sword, "piercing even to the dividing of soul and spirit, of both joints and marrow, and quick to discern the thoughts and intents of the heart."[37] For, reaching into the depths of each person's inmost soul and having every person's hidden purpose revealed before it as God, it brings its keen edge to bear on our vain pursuits by the working of the Spirit. For this is what our purification consists in, I suppose. And all things that are for our profit in the attainment of virtue it increases and multiplies to bear the fruit that is conceived in righteousness. Commentary on the Gospel of John 10.2[38]

The Power of the Word in the Sacrament. Augustine: "Now you are clean through the word that I have spoken to you." Why doesn't

[33]ANF 1:254*. [34]NPNF 1 14:279**; PG 59:411. [35]Is 42:5. [36]NPNF 2 8:34. [37]Heb 4:12. [38]LF 48:381-82*.

he say, You are clean through the baptism with which you have been washed, rather than "through the word that I have spoken to you," except for the fact that in the water also it is the word that cleanses? Take away the word, and the water is neither more nor less than water. The word is added to the element, and there results the sacrament, as if it itself is also a kind of visible word. For he had said also the same thing when washing the disciples' feet: "He who is washed needs not to wash, except for his feet, but is altogether clean."[39] And how does water have so great an efficacy, as in touching the body to cleanse the soul, if not by the operation of the word—and that not because it is uttered but because it is believed? For even in the word itself, the passing sound is one thing, the abiding efficacy another.[40] . . . For Christ, who is the vine with us, and the husbandman with the Father, "loved the church and gave himself for it."[41] But read the apostle and see what he adds: "That he might sanctify it, cleansing it with the washing of water by the word."[42] The cleansing, therefore, would on no account be attributed to the fleeting and perishable element were it not for what is added: "by the word." This word of faith possesses such power in the church of God that through the medium of him who in faith presents and blesses and sprinkles it, he cleanses even the tiny infant, although itself unable as yet with the heart to believe unto righteousness and to make confession with the mouth unto salvation. All this is done by means of the word about which the Lord says, Now you are clean through the word that I have spoken to you." Tractates on the Gospel of John 80.3.[43]

[39]Jn 13:10. [40]Augustine cites Rom 10:10; Acts 15:9; 1 Pet 3:21; Rom 10:8. [41]Eph 5:25. [42]Eph 5:26. [43]NPNF 1 7:344-45*; CCL 36:529.

15:4-11 Abiding in the Vine Through Love

[4]Abide in me, and I in you. As the branch cannot bear fruit by itself, unless it abides in the vine, neither can you, unless you abide in me. [5]I am the vine, you are the branches. He who abides in me, and I in him, he it is that bears much fruit, for apart from me you can do nothing. [6]If a man does not abide in me, he is cast forth as a branch and withers; and the branches are gathered, thrown into the fire and burned. [7]If you abide in me, and my words abide in you, ask whatever you will, and it shall be done for you. [8]By this my Father is glorified, that you bear much fruit, and so prove to be my disciples. [9]As the Father has loved me, so have I loved you; abide in my love. [10]If you keep my commandments, you will abide in my love, just as I have kept my Father's commandments and abide in his love. [11]These things I have spoken to you, that my joy may be in you, and that your joy may be full.

Overview: The vine is a living parable (Ambrose) of the life-giving nourishment the Spirit provides for those who remain attached to that vine by remaining in intimate union with Christ (Cyril). This union is of more advantage to the fruit than to the vine (Augustine). The vine of the cross was planted in Golgotha, but its branches have spread far beyond there to the world through the Spirit coursing through the branches of the apostles and the church (Anonymous). In the Old Testament, Jacob had prophesied of a spreading vine in his son Naphtali, foreshadowing the vine of Christ and his spreading church (Ambrose). Christ's body, which is the vine, serves as the root for our bodily resurrection and salvation (Theodoret).

Our weakness ensures that we can do nothing good apart from the vine (Maximus). We should stop relying on the decorative foliage of our good works (Prosper) since everything we are able to do is only by grace (Augustine). When we do accomplish something good, we should remember the words "without me you can do nothing" (Mark the Hermit). The Father, as vinedresser, is both cultivator and judge (Theodore). Christ tells us first to abide in the Word and then to ask since the Word is a possession that lacks nothing (Clement). To abide in the Word, however, is more than just acknowledging God's existence (Cyril). Abiding in Christ governs what we desire (Augustine), which in turn brings glory to God as we live out the faith and life given to us by God (Augustine). Love is the underlying motivation for such living (Basil). As we abide in Christ's love, we become like him (Irenaeus) and enjoy the security that comes with obeying his call to love through keeping the commandments (Chrysostom). Jesus speaks of the joy we can have through him as we face life's trials (Cyril) as well as the joy he has over us through the grace he has given us (Augustine).

15:4 *Reciprocal Abiding of Branch and Vine*

The Vine as a Living Parable. Ambrose: It seems clear, therefore, that the example of the vine is designed, as this passage indicates, for the instruction of our lives. It is observed to bud in the mild warmth of early spring, and next to produce fruit from the joints of the shoots from which a grape is formed. This gradually increases in size, but it still retains its bitter taste. When, however, it is ripened and mellowed by the sun, it acquires its sweetness. Meanwhile, the vine is decked in green leaves by which it is protected in no slight manner from frosts and other injuries and is defended from the sun's heat. Is there any spectacle that is more pleasing or any fruit that is sweeter?[1] What a joy to behold the rows of hanging grapes like so many jewels of a beautiful countryside, to pluck those grapes gleaming in colors of gold and purple! . . . Let them praise you who behold you, and let them admire the marshaled bands of the church like the serried rows of vine branches. Let everyone among the faithful gaze on the gems of the soul. Let them find delight in the maturity of prudence, in the splendor of faith, in the charm of Christian affirmation, in the beauty of justice, in the fecundity of pity, so that it may be said of you, "Your wife is a fruitful vine on the sides of your house,"[2] because you imitate by the exercise of your abundant and generous giving the bountiful return of a fruit-bearing vine. Six Days of Creation 3.12.52.[3]

The Spirit Nourishes the Fruit. Cyril of Alexandria: Unless the branch is provided with the life-producing sap from its mother the vine, how will it bear grapes or what fruit will it bring forth—and from what source? . . . For no fruit of virtue will spring up anew in those of us who have fallen away from intimate union with Christ. To those, however, who are joined to the one who is able to strengthen them and who nourishes them in righteousness, the capacity to bear fruit will readily be added by the provision and grace of the Spirit, which is like a life-producing water. Commentary on the Gospel of John 10.2.[4]

Christ Nourishes with the Spirit. Cyril of Alexandria: Just as the root of the vine administers and distributes to the branches the benefit of its own natural and inherent qualities, so too the only-begotten Word of God imparts

[1]See Cicero *De senectute* 15.53. [2]Ps 128:3 (127:3 LXX, Vg). [3]FC 42:106-7*; CSEL 32 1:94-95. [4]LF 48:386**.

to the saints, as it were, a likeness to his own nature and the nature of God the Father by giving them the Spirit, insomuch as they have been united with him through faith and perfect holiness. Christ nourishes them in piety and works in them the knowledge of all virtue and good works. Commentary on the Gospel of John 10.2.[5]

The Branches Benefit More Than the Vine. Augustine: Jesus said, "Abide in me, and I in you." They are not in him in the same kind of way that he is in them. And yet both ways tend to their advantage, not to his. For the relation of the branches to the vine is such that they contribute nothing to the vine but derive their own means of life from it, while that of the vine to the branches is such that it supplies their vital nourishment and receives nothing from them. And so their having Christ abiding in them and abiding themselves in Christ are in both respects advantageous not to Christ but to the disciples. For when the branch is cut off, another may spring up from the living root. But that which is cut off cannot live apart from the root. Tractates on the Gospel of John 81.1.[6]

15:5a *I Am the Vine, You Are the Branches*

The Branches of the Single-Stemmed Cross. Anonymous:

There is a place, we believe, at the center of the world,
Called Golgotha by the Jews in their native tongue.
Here was planted a tree cut from a barren stump:
This tree, I remember hearing, produced wholesome fruits,
But it did not bear these fruits for those who had settled there;
It was foreigners who picked these lovely fruits.
This is what the tree looked like: it rose from a single stem
And then extended its arms into two branches
Just like the heavy yardarms on which billowing sails are stretched
Or like the yoke beneath which two oxen are put to the plough.
The shoot that sprung from the first ripe seed
Germinated in the earth and then, miraculously,
On the third day it produced a branch once more,
Terrifying to the earth and to those above, but rich in life-giving fruit.
But over the next forty days it increased in strength,
Growing into a huge tree which touched the heavens
With its topmost branches and then hid its sacred head on high.
In the meantime it produced twelve branches of enormous
Weight and stretched forth, spreading them over the whole world:
They were to bring nourishment and eternal life to all
The nations and to teach them that death can die.
And then after a further fifty days had passed,
From its very top the tree caused a draught of divine nectar
To flow into its branches, a breeze of the heavenly spirit.
All over the tree the leaves were dripping with sweet dew.
And look! Beneath the branches' shady cover
There was a spring, with waters bright and clear
For there was nothing there to disturb the calm. . . .
Around this spring countless races and peoples gathered,
Of different stock, sex, age and rank,
Married and unmarried, widows, young married women,

[5]LF 48:364*. [6]NPNF 1 7:345*; CCL 36:530.

Babies, children and men, both young and old. The Tree of the Cross 1-33.[7]

The Vine of Naphtali Foreshadowed Christ and the Cross. Ambrose: [The spreading vine of Naphtali][8] is a beautiful reference to a shoot clinging to a spiritual vine, of which we are the branch and can bear fruit if we remain on the vine. But otherwise we are cut off. The holy patriarch Naphtali was an abundant shoot.[9] This explains why Jacob had called him a spreading vine. That is, through the grace of faith he was stripped of the bonds of death, and the people of God are foreshadowed in him, called to the liberty of faith and to the fullness of grace and spread over the whole world. It clothes the crossbeam of Christ with good fruit and encompasses the wood of that true vine, that is, the mysteries of the Lord's cross. It does not fear the danger of acknowledging him, but rather, even amid persecutions, it glories in the name of Christ. On the Patriarchs 10.42-3.[10]

Christ's Body the Root. Theodoret of Cyr: Just as the branches are of the same substance as the vine and [come] from it, so we, who have the same kind of body as the Lord's body, receive from his fullness and have it as a root for resurrection and salvation. And the Father is called the vinedresser, because through the Word he took care of the vine, which is the Lord's body. Dialogue 1.36.[11]

15:5b *Apart from Me You Can Do Nothing*

We Could Do Nothing Without God. Maximus the Confessor: The Lord told us, "Outside of me you can do nothing." This is because our weakness, when moved to do good things, is unable to bring anything to completion without the giver of good things. The one who has come to understand the weakness of human nature has had experience of the divine power. And such a person who because of divine power has succeeded in some things and is eager to succeed in others never looks down on anyone. For he knows that in the same way that God has helped him and freed him from many passions and hardships, so can he help everyone when he wishes, especially those who are striving for his sake. The Four Hundred Chapters on Love 2.38-39.[12]

Branches Do Nothing Apart from the Vine. Prosper of Aquitaine:

Our hope lies not in the flower of the field that withers.
For just as the vine branch is unable to produce any fruit
Unless it remains on the vine which helps to bring the sap
From the root into the leaves and fills the grapes with must,
So those who are barren of virtues and bear no fruit
Will feed the everlasting fires: those who abandon the vine
And dare to trust in the immoderate freedom of the foliage
So that their fertility is not dependent on the fruitfulness of Christ
Believe that they can excel by means of their own efforts
Better than if God is the source of the virtues that please him. . . .
[But] why are they ashamed even in this vale of tears to have their powers
From God, to have very little of human effort
Because it is nothing but sin which destroys
Freedom and to freedom alone do wicked deeds return?
And yet when we focus our minds on holy acts,

---

[7]*ECLP* 137-38. This poem, which in total is sixty-nine lines long, is also known as *On Easter*, or *The Tree of Life*. It has been variously attributed to Tertullian, Cyprian and Marius Victorinus. It presents us with an allegorical description of a vining tree representing the cross on which Christ was crucified. The tree that grows up from the stem (the rod of Jesse) and its connecting branches provide life-giving fruit that is meant to benefit not just the local inhabitants but all who are drawn to its nourishment. [8]Gen 49:21 (LXX). [9]Deut 33:23. [10]FC 65:265*; CSEL 32 2:148-49. [11]FC 106:75-76. [12]*MCSW* 52*.

When a chaste mind resists the desires of the flesh,
When we refuse to yield to the tempter and when tormented
By painful punishments, our mind remains unaffected,
Then we are acting with freedom. But with a freedom redeemed
And guided by God who is light from the highest light,
Life, health, virtue, wisdom. It is the grace of Christ that allows freedom
To run, rejoice, endure, beware, choose, press on,
To have faith, hope, love, to be purified and justified.
For if anything we do is right, O Lord, we do it
With your help; you inspire our hearts, you grant the wishes—
Those you wish to grant—of one who asks; you preserve what you bestow,
Create rewards from favors granted, adding prizes to your gifts.
But one must not imagine that our efforts can therefore be diminished,
Our striving toward virtue relaxed or our mental efforts grow dull,
Because the good qualities of holy people are yours and whatever
Is healthy and strong in these people depends on you for its power;
So it might seem that the human will can do nothing, while you do all.
For what does the will achieve without you, but to be exiled far from you?
The paths are always steep and when the will moves along them
On its own impulse it goes astray unless you in your goodness take it up.
When it is tired and weak, bring it back, care for it, protect and adorn it.
Then it will make rapid progress, its eyes will be clear-sighted,
Its freedom free, its wisdom wise and its justice just,
Strong its virtue and its powers effective.
On the Ungrateful People 954-97.[13]

Grace. Augustine: A great encomium on grace, my brothers—one that will instruct the souls of the humble and stop the mouths of the proud! Let those now answer it, if they dare, who, ignorant of God's righteousness and going about to establish their own, have not submitted themselves to the righteousness of God. Let the self-complacent answer who think they have no need of God for the performance of good works. . . . They say, It is of God that we have our existence as human beings, but it is of ourselves that we are righteous. What is it you say, you who deceive yourselves and, instead of establishing free will, cast it headlong down from the heights of its self-elevation through the empty regions of presumption into the depths of an ocean grave? Why, your assertion that a person of himself works righteousness, *that* is the height of your self-elation. . . . For whoever imagines that he is bearing fruit of himself is not in the vine, and whoever is not in the vine is not in Christ, and whoever is not in Christ is not a Christian. Such are the ocean depths into which you have plunged.

Look further into what the Truth has to say. . . . For just to keep anyone from supposing that the branch can bear at least some little fruit of itself, after saying, "the same brings forth much fruit," his next words are not, without me you can do but little, but "you can do nothing." Whether then it is a little or a lot, without him it is impracticable. For without him nothing can be done. For although, when the branch bears little fruit, the husbandman purges it that it may bring forth more, yet if it does not abide in the vine and draw its life from the root, it can bear no fruit whatever of itself. And although Christ would not have been the vine had he not been man, yet he could not have supplied such grace to the branches had he not also been God. Tractates on the Gospel of John 81.2-3.[14]

[13]*ECLP* 116-17. [14]NPNF 1 7:345-46**.

In the Face of Pride. Mark the Hermit: When you have done something good, remember the words, "without me you can do nothing." On the Spiritual Law 41.[15]

15:6 *Destroying Dead Branches*

Vinedresser As Cultivator and Judge. Theodore of Mopsuestia: The Father is like the vinedresser, for, if he sees some who do not love me, he cuts them off like fruitless branches and sends them off to the fire, but if he sees the opposite, he takes care of them so that they may bring forth even more fruit through the spiritual gifts he gives. Commentary on John 6.15.1-6.[16]

15:7 *Abide in the Word, Then Ask*

The One Who Has the Word Lacks Nothing. Clement of Alexandria: He who has the almighty God, the Word, lacks nothing and never is in dire straits for what he needs. For the Word is a possession that lacks nothing and is the cause of all abundance. If someone says that he has often seen the righteous person in need of food, this is rare, and it happens only where there is not another righteous person. Notwithstanding, let him read what follows: "For the righteous one shall not live by bread alone but by the word of the Lord,"[17] who is the true bread, the bread of the heavens. The good person, then, can never be in difficulties so long as he keeps intact his confession toward God. For it belongs to him to ask and to receive whatever he requires from the Father of all and to enjoy what is his own if he keeps the Son. And he also should feel that he lacks nothing. Christ the Educator 3.7.[18]

Abiding Is More Than Acknowledging God's Existence. Cyril of Alexandria: Shall we say that faith bare and alone is sufficient for one to attain the fellowship that is from above—will even the band of demons rise up to fellowship with God, since they acknowledge God's unity and have believed that God exists? How could this be? For the mere knowledge that the one God is the creator and producer of all things is useless. But I think it necessary that the confession of piety toward God should accompany faith. For one who does this abides in Christ and will be seen to possess his words, according to the text in the book of Psalms, "I have laid up your word in my heart, that I might not sin against you."[19] Commentary on the Gospel of John 10.2.[20]

Abiding in Christ Governs What You Desire. Augustine: "If you abide in me," he says, "and my words abide in you, you shall ask what you will, and it shall be done unto you." For when someone abides in Christ in this way, is there anything he or she can wish for besides what will be agreeable to Christ? When they abide in the Savior in this way, can they wish for anything that is inconsistent with salvation? Some things, indeed, we wish for because we are in Christ, and other things we desire because we are still in this world. For at times, in connection with our present living quarters, we are inwardly prompted to ask what we know would not be expedient for us to receive. But God forbid that such a thing should be given to us if we abide in Christ, who, when we ask, only does what will be for our advantage. Abiding in him when his words abide in us, we shall ask what we will, and it shall be done unto us. For if we ask, and the doing does not follow, what we ask must not be connected with our abiding in him or with his words that abide in us. Instead they must be connected with that craving and infirmity of the flesh that are not in him and do not have his words abiding in them. For to his words, at all events, belongs that prayer that he taught and in which we say, "Our Father, who art in heaven."[21] Let us only not fall away from the words and meaning of this prayer in our petitions, and whatever we ask shall be done unto us. For his words may only be

[15]TP 1:113. [16]CSCO 4 3:282. [17]Deut 8:3; Mt 4:4. [18]ANF 2:281*. [19]Ps 119:11 (118:11 LXX). [20]LF 48:390**. [21]Mt 6:9.

said to abide in us when we do what he has commanded us and love what he has promised. But when his words abide only in the memory and have no place in your life, the branch is not in the vine because it does not draw its life from the root. TRACTATES ON THE GOSPEL OF JOHN 81.4.[22]

15:8 *Bearing Much Fruit*

OUR LIVES BY GOD'S GRACE BRING GLORY TO GOD. AUGUSTINE: The Savior, in thus speaking to the disciples, commends still more and more the grace whereby we are saved when he says, "By this is my Father glorified, that you bear much fruit and be made my disciples." Whether we say glorified or made bright,[23] both are the translation of one Greek verb, namely, *doxazein*. For what is *doxa* in Greek is "gloria" in Latin. I have thought it worthwhile to mention this because the apostle says, "If Abraham was justified by works, he has glory, but not before God."[24] For this is the glory before God, whereby God, and not man [humankind], is glorified, when man is justified, not by works, but by faith, so that even his doing well is imparted to him by God. Just as the branch, as I have stated above,[25] cannot bear fruit of itself. For if God the Father is glorified in this, that we bear much fruit and are made the disciples of Christ, let us not credit this to our own glory, as though we had it from ourselves. For such grace is from him, and the glory in this is therefore not ours but his. And so, in another passage, after saying, "Let your light so shine before people that they may see your good works"—to keep them from the thought that such good works were of themselves—he immediately added, "and may glorify your Father who is in heaven."[26] For here is where the Father is glorified, that we bear much fruit and are made the disciples of Christ. And by whom are we so made, but by him whose mercy has preceded us? For "we are his workmanship, created in Christ Jesus unto good works."[27] TRACTATES ON THE GOSPEL OF JOHN 82.1.[28]

15:9-10 *Abiding in Jesus' Love*

LOVE AS AN UNDERLYING MOTIVATION. BASIL THE GREAT: Now, if observing the commandments is the essential sign of love, it is very greatly feared that without love even the most effective action of the glorious gifts of grace—even of the most sublime powers and even of faith itself and the commandment that make a person perfect—will not be of help. . . . It is evident, therefore, and undeniable that without charity—even though ordinances are obeyed and righteous acts are performed, even though the commandments of the Lord have been observed and great wonders of grace effected—they will be considered as works of iniquity . . . because those who perform these acts have as their aim the gratification of their own will. CONCERNING BAPTISM 1.2.[29]

ABIDE IN CHRIST AND BECOME LIKE HIM. IRENAEUS: Whoever holds, without pride and boasting, to the true glory regarding created things and the Creator (who is the Almighty God of all and who has granted existence to all) and continues in his [i.e., God's] love and subjection and continues to give thanks shall also receive from [God] the greater glory of promotion, looking forward to the time when he shall become like him who died for him. AGAINST HERESIES 3.20.2.[30]

JESUS' LOVE BRINGS SECURITY. CHRYSOSTOM: Again, Jesus' discourse proceeds in a human way. For certainly the lawgiver himself would not be subject to commandments. Here again, as I keep on saying, this is spoken because of the infirmity of his hearers. He is primarily speaking to their suspicions, and by every means he tries to show them that they are safe and that their enemies are

[22]NPNF 1 7:346**; CCL 36:531. [23]Glorified = *glorificatus*; made bright = *clarificatus*. [24]Rom 4:2. [25]See his *Tractates on the Gospel of John* 81.2. [26]Mt 5:16. [27]See Eph 2:10. [28]NPNF 1 7:346-47**; CCL 36:532. [29]FC 9:381-82. [30]ANF 1:450**; SC 34:342.

being lost. He is showing them that everything, whatever they have, they have from the Son and that, if they demonstrate a pure life, no one can prevail against them. And observe how authoritative he is with them. He did not say, "Abide in the love *of my Father*," but "in *my* love." Then, in case they should say, "When you have put us at war with everyone, that is when you leave us and depart," he shows that he does not leave them but is as joined to them as the branch is to the vine. Then, in case they get so confident that they become lazy, he tells them the blessing can be removed if they are not vigilant. And, so that he does not refer the action to himself and make them even more apt to fall, he says, "Herein is my Father glorified." For everywhere he demonstrates his own and his Father's love toward them. HOMILIES ON THE GOSPEL OF JOHN 76.2.[31]

15:11 *Fullness of Joy*

THE POWER OF CHRISTIAN JOY. CYRIL OF ALEXANDRIA: Here it is as though when Jesus says, "All this I have spoken to you that my joy may be in you," he's saying that those things which encourage me may give you encouragement as well. You can face danger bravely, fortifying yourselves with the hope of those who will be saved. And, if suffering comes upon you in this work, don't be brought down into the feebleness of apathy, but rejoice more abundantly when you fulfill the will of him that wills that all should be saved and come to the knowledge of truth.[32] For I too rejoiced at this, [Jesus says], and thought my sufferings very sweet. COMMENTARY ON THE GOSPEL OF JOHN 10.2.[33]

JOY IN REJOICING OVER US. AUGUSTINE: And what else is Christ's joy in us except that he is pleased to rejoice over us? And what is this joy of ours that he says is to be made full, but our having fellowship with him? . . . His joy, therefore, in us is the grace he has bestowed on us, and that is also our joy. But he rejoiced over this joy even from eternity when he chose us before the foundation of the world.[34] Nor can we rightly say that his joy was not full. For God's joy was never at any time imperfect. But that joy of his was not in us. For we, in whom that joy could exist, had as yet no existence. And even when our existence commenced, it began not to be in him. But in him it always was, who in the infallible truth of his own foreknowledge rejoiced that we should yet be his own. Accordingly, he had a joy over us that was already full when he rejoiced in foreknowing and foreordaining us. And there could hardly be any fear intermingling in that joy of his that might imply a possible failure in what he foreknew would be done by himself. TRACTATES ON THE GOSPEL OF JOHN 83.1.[35]

[31]NPNF 1 14:280**; PG 59:412. [32]1 Tim 2:4. [33]LF 48:400**. [34]Eph 1:4. [35]NPNF 1 7:348**; CCL 36:534-35.

15:12-17 A FRIEND'S LOVE

[12]*This is my commandment, that you love one another as I have loved you.* [13]*Greater love has no man than this, that a man lay down his life for his friends.* [14]*You are my friends if you do what I command you.* [15]*No longer do I call you servants,*[h] *for the servant*[h] *does not know what his master is doing; but I have called you friends, for all that I have heard from my Father I have made*

known to you. [16]*You did not choose me, but I chose you and appointed you that you should go and bear fruit and that your fruit should abide; so that whatever you ask the Father in my name, he may give it to you.* [17]*This I command you, to love one another.*

h Or *slaves* **i** Or *slave*

OVERVIEW: God reveals himself in our charity, as we love one another as God has loved us (CYPRIAN). This is why we should hold on to his commandment of love (BASIL). When we love one another, we love God and, in effect, keep all that he has commanded (AUGUSTINE), since love encompasses all the other commandments (EPHREM). It is love of God that motivates us to love one another as God's love is intertwined with our own (CHRYSOSTOM). When you love your enemy as Christ did, you may even make a friend (GREGORY THE GREAT) as Christ did when he died for them (AUGUSTINE). This is all the more reason to cultivate the virtue of love in tranquil times so that it will be unconquerable in times of disorder (GREGORY THE GREAT).

Friends obey what Christ commands while enemies disobey (CLEMENT). We are called to move beyond being simply servants to being friends and sons of God (CASSIAN). As such, we serve freely (IRENAEUS), rather than out of fear (AUGUSTINE). Wisdom bursts the bonds of fear, rising up to love (GREGORY OF NAZIANZUS). Christ having made us into his friends gives his friends the crown of glory (AUGUSTINE). But with great dignity comes great responsibility (GREGORY THE GREAT). Jesus is spelling out how true friends act toward one another, with all that friendship entails (AMBROSE). Because he is the creator of all, Jesus speaks about the future with his disciples as though it were already the past (AUGUSTINE). Since we did not choose God but were instead chosen by him, he shows that we are his friends by grace (GREGORY THE GREAT, AUGUSTINE). It is our glory not that we followed him but rather that, in following the Son of God, we are glorified by him (IRENAEUS). Christ's presence with us ensures that the fruit we produce is abiding fruit (CHRYSOSTOM), and it is to our benefit to work for that fruit that endures (GREGORY THE GREAT). The Father wants us to entreat him through his Son, and it is the Son's desire that we entreat the Father (AMBROSE) as we help others obtain blessing by our prayers of faith (CYRIL). Jesus' repeated call for love is really a call to demonstrate all the concrete things that love is (AUGUSTINE).

15:12 *Loving One Another As Jesus Loved Us*

GOD REVEALS HIMSELF IN CHARITY. CYPRIAN: Discord cannot attain to the kingdom of heaven. The one who has done violence to the love of Christ by faithless dissension will not attain to the reward of Christ, who said, "This is my commandment, that you love one another." Whoever does not have charity does not have God. THE UNITY OF THE CHURCH 14.[1]

HOLD TO THE COMMANDMENT OF LOVE. BASIL THE GREAT: Do we fail to love according to the commandment of the Lord? Then we lose the distinctive mark imprinted on us. Are we puffed up till almost bursting with empty pride and arrogance? Then we fall into the inevitable condemnation of the devil. LETTER 56.[2]

IS LOVE THE ONLY COMMANDMENT? AUGUSTINE: But when he said in this way here, "This is my commandment," as if there were no other, what are we to think? Is, then, the commandment about that love with which we love one another his only one? Is there not another that is still greater, that we should love God? Or did God in truth give to us such a commandment about love

[1]ANF 5:426**. [2]NPNF 2 8:158-59.

alone that we have no need of searching for others? There are three things at least that the apostle commends when he says, "But now abide faith, hope, charity, these three. But the greatest of these is charity."[3] And although in charity, that is, in love, the two commandments are contained, yet it is here declared to be the greatest, not the only one. Accordingly, what a host of commandments are given to us about faith, what a multitude about hope! Who is there that could collect them together or suffice to number them? But let us ponder the words of the same apostle: "Love is the fulfillment of the law."[4] And so, where there is love, what can be lacking? And where it is not, what is there that can possibly be profitable? The devil believes[5] but does not love: no one loves who does not believe. One may, indeed, hope for pardon who does not love, but he hopes in vain. But no one can despair who loves. Therefore, where there is love, there will necessarily be faith and hope. And where there is the love of our neighbor, there also will necessarily be the love of God. For one that does not love God, how does he love his neighbor as himself, seeing that he does not even love himself? Such a person is both impious and iniquitous. And he who loves iniquity clearly does not love but hates his own soul.[6] Let us, therefore, hold fast to this precept of the Lord, to love one another, and then we will be doing all else that is commanded, for we have all else contained in this. Tractates on the Gospel of John 83.3.[7]

Love Encompasses the Other Commandments. Ephrem the Syrian: "This is my commandment." Have you then only one precept? This is sufficient, even if it is unique and so great. Nevertheless he also said, "Do not kill,"[8] because the one who loves does not kill. He said, "Do not steal,"[9] because the one who loves does even more—he gives. He said, "Do not lie,"[10] for the one who loves speaks the truth, against falsehood. "I give you a new commandment."[11] If you have not understood what "This is my commandment" means, let the apostle be summoned as interpreter and say, "The goal of his commandment is love."[12] What is its binding force? It is that of which [the Lord] spoke, "Whatever you want others to do to you, you should do also."[13] "Love one another" in accordance with this measure, "as I have loved you." That is not possible, for you are our Lord who loves your servants. But we who are equals, how can we love one another as you have loved us? Nevertheless, he has said it. . . . His love is that he has called us his friends. If we were to give our life for you, would our love be equal to yours? . . . How then can what he said be explained, "As I have loved you"? "Let us die for each other," he said. As for us, we do not even want to live for one another! "If I, who am your Lord and God, die for you, how much more should you die for one another." Commentary on Tatian's Diatessaron 19.13.[14]

God's Love Intertwined with Our Own. Chrysostom: "Love one another as I have loved you." Do you see that the love of God is intertwined with our own and connected like a sort of chain? Thus, it sometimes says that there are two commandments, sometimes only one. For it is not possible that the one who has taken hold of the first should not possess the second also. Homilies on the Gospel of John 77.1.[15]

15:13 *A Friend's Greatest Love*

Love Your Enemy and Make a Friend. Gregory the Great: The unique, the highest proof of love is this, to love the person who is against us. This is why Truth himself bore the suffering of the cross and yet bestowed his love on his persecutors, saying, "Father, forgive them for they know not what they do."[16] Why should we wonder that his living disciples loved their enemies, when their dying master loved his? He

[3]1 Cor 13:13. [4]Rom 13:10. [5]Jas 2:19. [6]See Ps 11:5 (10:5 LXX, 10:6 Vg). [7]NPNF 1 7:349*; CCL 36:535-36. [8]Mt 19:18. [9]Mt 19:18. [10]Mt 19:18. [11]Jn 13:34. [12]1 Tim 1:5. [13]Mt 7:12. [14]*ECTD* 288. See also Gregory the Great *Forty Gospel Homilies* 27 (CS 123:212). [15]NPNF 1 14:282*; PG 59:415. [16]Lk 23:34.

expressed the depth of his love when he said, "No one has greater love that this, than that he lay down his life for his friends." The Lord had come to die even for his enemies, and yet he said he would lay down his life for his friends to show us that when we are able to win over our enemies by loving them, even our persecutors are our friends. Forty Gospel Homilies 27.[17]

Christ Died for Us, the Ungodly. Augustine: But "greater love has no one than this, that he should lay down his life for his friends." No one, you think? Absolutely no one. It is true; Christ said it. Let us question the apostle, and let him answer us: "Christ," he says, "died for the ungodly." And again he says, "While we were enemies, we were reconciled with God through the death of his Son."[18] So there you are. In Christ we do find greater love, seeing that he gave up his life not for his friends but for his enemies. How great must be God's love for humanity and what extraordinary affection, so to love even sinners that he would die for love of them! "For God emphasizes his love toward us"—they are the apostle's words—"because while we were still sinners Christ died for us."[19] Sermon 215.5.[20]

Give Up Possessions, Then Yourself. Gregory the Great: Cultivate the virtue of love in tranquil times by showing mercy, so that it will be unconquerable in times of disorder. Learn first to give up your possessions for almighty God, and then yourself. Forty Gospel Homilies 27.[21]

15:14 *You Are My Friends If You Do What I Command You*

Friends Obey, Enemies Disobey. Clement of Alexandria: Now sinners are called enemies of God—enemies, that is, of the commands that they do not obey, just as those who obey become friends. The latter are named so from their fellowship; the former from their estrangement, which is freely chosen. For there is neither enmity nor sin without the enemy and the sinner. Stromateis 4.13.[22]

Moving from "Servant" to "Friend" to "Son." John Cassian: "The one who fears is not yet perfect in love."[23] And again, though it is a grand thing to serve God, and it is said, "Serve the Lord in fear," and "It is a great thing for you to be called my servant," and "Blessed is that servant whom his Lord, when he comes, shall find working,"[24] yet it is said to the apostles, "I no longer call you servants, for the servant does not know what his Lord does. But I call you friends, for everything I have heard from my Father I have made known to you." And once more, "You are my friends if you do what I command you." You see then that there are different stages of perfection and that we are called by the Lord from high things to still higher in such a way that he who has become blessed and perfect in the fear of God—going, as it is written, "from strength to strength"[25] and from one perfection to another, that is, mounting with an eager soul from fear to hope—is summoned in the end to that still more blessed stage, which is love. And whoever has been "a faithful and wise servant"[26] will pass to the companionship of friendship and to the adoption of sons. Conference 2.11.12.[27]

15:15 *No Longer Servants, but Friends*

Friends Freely Serve. Irenaeus: Inasmuch as all natural commandments are common to both Christians and Jews, the Jews indeed had the beginning and origin of the commandments, but [those commandments] received their growth and completion in us. For to yield assent to God, and to follow his Word, and to love him above all and one's neighbor as one's self (now people are neighbors to one another), and to

[17]CS 123:213; PL 76:1205-6. [18]Rom 5:6, 10. [19]Rom 5:8. [20]*WSA* 3 6:163; *RB* 68:22. [21]CS 123:214*; PL 76:1206. [22]ANF 2:426. [23]1 Jn 4:18. [24]Ps 2:11; Is 49:6; Mt 24:46. [25]Ps 84:7 (83:8 LXX). [26]Mt 24:45. [27]NPNF 2 11:420*.

abstain from every evil deed, and all other things of a similar nature that are common to both [covenants]—all of this reveals one and the same God. But this is our Lord, the Word of God, who in the first instance certainly drew slaves to God, but afterward he set those free who were subject to him, as he himself declares to his disciples, "I will not now call you servants, for the servant does not know what his lord does. But I have called you friends, for all things that I have heard from my Father I have made known." For when he says, "I will not now call you servants," he indicates in the most marked manner that it was he who originally appointed for men and women that bondage with respect to God through the law and then afterward conferred on them freedom. And, in that he says, "For the servant does not know what his lord does," he points out, by means of his own advent, the ignorance of a people in a servile condition. But when he terms his disciples "the friends of God," he plainly declares himself to be the Word of God whom Abraham also followed voluntarily and under no compulsion[28] because of the noble nature of his faith—and who thus became "the friend of God."[29] Against Heresies 4.13.4.[30]

Two Kinds of Servants. Augustine: Just as there are two kinds of fear that produce two classes of fearers, so there are two kinds of servitude that produce two classes of servants. There is a fear that perfect love casts out,[31] and there is another fear, which is virtuous[32] and endures forever.[33] . . . In that fear that love casts out, servitude also needs to be cast out along with it. For both were joined together by the apostle, that is, the servitude and the fear, when he said, "For you have not received the spirit of servitude again to fear."[34] . . . Since, therefore, he has given us power to become the children of God,[35] let us not be servants but children, so that, in some wonderful and indescribable but real way, we may as servants have the power not to be servants. Let us be servants, indeed, with that virtuous fear that distinguishes the servant that enters into the joy of his lord,[36] but not servants with the fear that has to be cast out and that characterizes one who does not abide in the house forever.[37] Tractates on the Gospel of John 85.3.[38]

Wisdom Bursts Bonds of Fear. Gregory of Nazianzus: The fear of the Lord is the beginning of wisdom, and, so to say, its first swathing band. But, when wisdom bursts the bonds of fear and rises up to love, it makes us friends of God and children instead of slaves. On the Great Athanasius, Oration 21.6.[39]

He Made You into His Friends. Augustine: He made human beings into his friends. Won't he be making them angels? "I no longer call you slaves, but friends." It was to people still carrying flesh, still subject to death, still living this poor fragile life that he said that. "I no longer call you slaves, but friends." And what is he going to give friends? What he manifested in himself as he rose again. They shall be crowned and transfigured into heavenly glory and shall be equal to the angels of God. Sermon 45.10.[40]

Great Dignity, Great Responsibility. Gregory the Great: How great is our Creator's mercy! We were unworthy servants, and he calls us friends. How great is our human value, that we should be friends of God! You have heard your glorious dignity—now listen to what the struggle costs: "If you do whatever I command you." Forty Gospel Homilies 27.[41]

How Friends Act Toward One Another. Ambrose: God himself made us friends instead of servants. . . . He gave us a pattern of friendship to follow. We are to fulfill the wish of a friend, to unfold to him our secrets that we hold in our own hearts, and are not to disregard his confidences.

[28]Lat *sine vinculis*. [29]Jas 2:23. [30]ANF 1:478**; SC 100:534-36. [31]See 1 Jn 4:18. [32]Lat *castus*, which might also be translated as "pure." [33]See Ps 19:9 (18:10 LXX, Vg). [34]Rom 8:15. [35]See Jn 1:12. [36]See Mt 25:21. [37]See Jn 8:35. [38]NPNF 1 7:351-52*; CCL 36:539-40. [39]NPNF 2 7:271. [40]*WSA* 3 2:259; CCL 41:526. [41]CS 123:214*; PL 76:1206.

Let us show him our heart, and he will open his to us. . . . A friend, then, if he is a true one, hides nothing. He pours forth his soul as the Lord Jesus poured forth the mysteries of his Father. DUTIES OF THE CLERGY 3.22.135.[42]

PAST PERFECT. AUGUSTINE: How are we to understand that [Jesus] made known to the disciples all that he had heard from the Father when there are many things that he did not say because he knows that they cannot bear them now? Doubtless, what he is yet to do, he says that he has done as the same Being who has made those things which are yet to be.[43] For he says by the prophet, "They pierced my hands and my feet,"[44] and not, "They will yet pierce." He speaks as though it were in the past and yet predicting what was still in the future. So also in the passage before us he declares that he has made known to the disciples all that he knows he will yet make known in that fullness of knowledge about which the apostle says, "But when that which is perfect is come, then that which is in part shall be done away."[45] For in the same place he adds, "Now I know in part, but then shall I know even as also I am known. And now as through a glass in a mystery, but then face to face."[46] TRACTATES ON THE GOSPEL OF JOHN 86.1.[47]

15:16a *You Did Not Choose Me, but I Chose You*

FRIEND OF GOD BY GRACE. GREGORY THE GREAT: But let one who has attained the dignity of being called a friend of God observe that the gifts he perceives in himself are beyond him. Let him attribute nothing to his own merits so that he becomes an enemy. The Lord adds, "You have not chosen me, but I have chosen you and appointed you to go and bring forth fruit. I have appointed you for grace. I have planted you to go willingly and bring forth fruit by your works." FORTY GOSPEL HOMILIES 27.[48]

TRULY AMAZING GRACE. AUGUSTINE: "You did not choose me, but I chose you." That is amazing grace! . . . For what were we before Christ had chosen us besides being wicked and lost? We did not believe in him, so as to be chosen by him. For if he chose those who already believed, then he was [in effect] chosen himself prior to his choosing [them]. . . . This passage refutes the vain opinion of those who say that we were chosen before the foundation of the world[49] because God foreknew that we should be good, not that he himself would make us good. For if he had chosen us because he foreknew that we should be good, he would have foreknown also that we should first choose him. For without choosing him we cannot be good, unless indeed someone can be called good who has not chosen good. What then has he chosen in those who are not good? . . . You cannot say, I am chosen because I believed. For if you believed in him, you had already chosen him. Nor can you say, Before I believed I did good works and therefore was chosen. For what good work is there before faith when the apostle says, "Whatever is not of faith is sin"?[50] What is there for us to say, then, but that we were wicked and were chosen, that by the grace of having been chosen we might become good? TRACTATES ON THE GOSPEL OF JOHN 86.2.[51]

OUR GLORY IS TO SERVE. IRENAEUS: As much as God lacks nothing, so much do we stand in need of fellowship with God. For this is the glory of humanity: to continue and remain permanently in God's service. This is also why the Lord said to his disciples, "You did not choose me, but I chose you," indicating that they did not glorify him when they followed him but that, in following the Son of God, they were glorified by him. AGAINST HERESIES 4.14.1.[52]

---

[42]NPNF 2 10:89**. [43]See Is 45:11. [44]Ps 22:16 (21:17 LXX, Vg). [45]1 Cor 13:10. [46]1 Cor 13:12. [47]NPNF 1 7:352-53*; CCL 36:541. See also *Sermon* 27.5 (*WSA* 3 2:106). [48]CS 123:216; PL 76:1207. [49]Eph 1:4. [50]Rom 14:23. [51]NPNF 1 7:353**; CCL 36:542. [52]ANF 1:478*; SC 100:540.

15:16b *Abiding Fruit that Entreats the Father*

Christ's Presence Ensures Abiding Fruit. Chrysostom: Now if your fruit remains, much more shall you. For I have not only loved you, [he says], but I have given you the greatest benefits by extending your branches through the entire world. Do you see in how many ways he shows his love? He shows his love by telling them secrets, by having in the first instance run to meet their friendship, by granting them the greatest blessings, by suffering for them what then he suffered. After this, he shows that he also remains continually with those who shall bring forth fruit. For it is needful to enjoy his help and so to bear fruit. Homilies on the Gospel of John 77.1.[53]

Work for Fruit That Endures. Gregory the Great: I have appointed you for grace. I have planted you to go willingly and bring forth fruit by your works. I have said that you should go willingly, since to will to do something is already to go in your heart. Then he adds the quality their fruit is to have: "And your fruit is to endure." Everything we labor for in this present world scarcely lasts until death. Death intervenes and cuts off the fruit of our labor. But what we do for eternal life remains even after death. It begins to appear only when the fruits of our physical labors cease to be visible. The reward of the one begins when the other is ended. Let one who recognizes that he now bears eternal fruit within his soul think little of the temporal fruits of his labors. Let us work for the fruit that endures; let us work for the fruit that begins at death since death destroys all others. Forty Gospel Homilies 27.[54]

Father and Son Both Entreated. Ambrose: Let us then with faithful spirit and devout mind call on Jesus our Lord. Let us believe that he is God, to the end that whatever we ask of the Father, we may obtain in his name. For the Father's will is that he be entreated through the Son. The Son's will is that the Father be entreated. On the Christian Faith 1.2.12.[55]

Help Others Obtain the Blessing of the Believer's Prayer. Cyril of Alexandria: Since therefore you follow in the path of my words and ministry and have the mind that my true disciples should have, it follows that you should not, by your own delay, throw obstacles in the way of someone who of his own will seeks the faith and is self-called to a life of piety. Rather, you should attach yourselves as guides to those who are still ignorant and wandering and bring the gospel of salvation to those who do not yet want to learn it and eagerly encourage them to attain to the true knowledge of God, even though the mind of your hearers may be hardened into disobedience. In other words, bring them more in line with your own condition so they will advance and return to fruit bearing in God by gradually growing in what is better for them. Then they too can have fruit that always remains and is preserved, and they can also have that most desirable object of prayer—the bestowal of whatever they wish, if only they "ask in my name." Commentary on the Gospel of John 10.2.[56]

15:17 *Love One Another*

Love Is the Fruit We Are to Bear. Augustine: This [love] is our fruit about which he said, "I have chosen you, that you should go and bring forth fruit and that your fruit should remain." And what he added, "That whatever you shall ask of the Father in my name, he may give it you," he will certainly give us if we love one another, seeing that this is the very thing he has also given us in choosing us when we had no fruit, because we had not chosen him. He appointed us that we should bring forth fruit—that is, that we should love one another—a fruit that we cannot have apart from him, just as the branches can do noth-

[53]NPNF 1 14:282**; PG 59:415. [54]CS 123:216*; PL 76:1207. [55]NPNF 2 10:203*. [56]LF 48:409**.

ing apart from the vine.

Our fruit, therefore, is charity, which the apostle explains to be "out of a pure heart, and a good conscience and sincere faith."[57] When we love one another, we love God. For it would be with no true love that we loved one another, if we did not love God. For everyone loves his neighbor as himself if he loves God. And if he does not love God, he does not love himself. For on these two commandments of love hang all the law and the prophets:[58] this is our fruit. And it is in reference, therefore, to such fruit that he gives us this commandment when he says, "These things I command you, that you love one another." In the same way also the apostle Paul, when wishing to commend the fruit of the Spirit in opposition to the deeds of the flesh, posited this as his principle, saying, "The fruit of the Spirit is love." And then, as if springing from and bound up in this principle, he wove the others together, which are "joy, peace, patience, kindness, goodness, faith, meekness, temperance."[59]

For who can truly rejoice who does not love the good as the source of his joy? Who can have true peace, if he does not have it with one whom he truly loves? Who can be long-enduring through persevering continually in good, except through fervent love? Who can be kind, if he does not love the person he is helping? Who can be good, if he is not made so by loving? Who can be sound in the faith without that faith that works by love? Whose meekness can be beneficial in character, if not regulated by love? And who will abstain from that which is debasing, if he does not love that which dignifies? Appropriately, therefore, the good Master frequently commends love as the only thing needing to be commended. Without love, everything else that is good is no help, and you cannot have love without bringing with it all those other good things that make a person truly good. Tractates on the Gospel of John 87.1.[60]

[57]1 Tim 1:5. [58]See Mt 22:40. [59]Gal 5:22. [60]NPNF 1 7:354-55*; CCL 36:543-44.

15:18-21 Hatred of the World

[18]If the world hates you, know that it has hated me before it hated you. [19]If you were of the world, the world would love its own; but because you are not of the world, but I chose you out of the world, therefore the world hates you. [20]Remember the word that I said to you, "A servant[i] is not greater than his master." If they persecuted me, they will persecute you; if they kept my word, they will keep yours also. [21]But all this they will do to you on my account, because they do not know him who sent me.

i Or *slave*

Overview: Jesus prepares his disciples for persecution by speaking first from personal experience (Cyprian). Preaching the gospel is not always popular (Cyril), evident in the fact that the world that stands condemned persecutes, while the world that is reconciled is persecuted (Augustine). The hatred of the world is evidence of a person's goodness while the world's admiration is more than likely evidence of wickedness (Chrysostom). This world lays hold on us but is not able to keep us (Ambrose). No one can please God and God's enemies (Gregory the Great). The disciples should realize this and that the humiliation Jesus will undergo is also what is in store for them (Cyril). But this should also serve as their consolation (Chrysostom). Those who suffer with Christ reign with him. We can also take solace in the fact that we are only called upon to sow the seed of the Word; God will bring forth the fruit (Cyril). When persecutors attack us, it is Christ they are attacking (Augustine).

15:18 *The World Hated Me First*

Prepare for Persecution. Cyprian: How grave is the case of a Christian if, as a servant, he is unwilling to suffer when his master first suffered! How serious it is that we should be unwilling to suffer for our own sins, when he who had no sin of his own suffered for us! The Son of God suffered that he might make us sons [children] of God, and yet we who are human sons will not suffer so that we may continue to be sons of God! If we suffer from the world's hatred, Christ first endured the world's hatred. If we suffer reproaches in this world, if exile, if tortures, the maker and Lord of the world experienced harder things than these. And he also warns us, saying, "If the world hates you, remember that it hated me before you. If you were of the world, the world would love its own. But because you are not of the world, but I have chosen you out of the world, therefore the world hates you. Remember the word that I said to you, 'The servant is not greater than his lord. If they have persecuted me, they will also persecute you.' " Whatever our Lord and God taught, he also did, so that the disciple might not be excused if he learns but then does not put into practice what he learned.

Let none of you, beloved, be so terrified by the fear of future persecution or the coming of the threatening antichrist that you are not found armed for all things by the preaching of the gospel and its commands—and by the heavenly warnings. Antichrist is coming, but above him Christ comes also. The enemy goes about and rages, but the Lord immediately follows to avenge our sufferings and our wounds. The adversary is enraged and threatens, but there is One who can deliver us from his hands. Letter 55.6-7.[1]

Preaching the Gospel Is Not Always Popular. Cyril of Alexandria: The word that speaks to the pleasure of the listeners will flatter rather than benefit the world. But those who obey the words of the Savior will not conduct their ministry in this way. Such a minister will prefer rather to please the Savior, and if the minister incurs hatred from those who have chosen to treat virtue with the utmost hostility, it shall be considered spiritual wealth. Commentary on the Gospel of John 10.2.[2]

World Condemned Persecutes, World Reconciled Suffers. Augustine: But look here, the one that persecutes is called the world. Let us find out whether the one that suffers persecution is also called the world. Or are you completely deaf to the voice of Christ saying—or rather of holy Scripture testifying, "God was in Christ reconciling the world to himself"[3]? "If the world hates you," he said, "know that it first hated me." There you are, the world hates. . . . Which world? "God was in Christ reconciling the world to himself." The world condemned persecutes; the world reconciled suffers persecution. The world condemned includes whatever is outside and apart from the church; the world reconciled is the church. "For the Son of man," he says, "did not come to judge the world, but that the world might be saved through him."[4] Sermon 96.8.[5]

Evidence of Goodness. Chrysostom: As if Christ's suffering were not consolation enough,

[1]ANF 5:349**; *Letter* 58.6-7 in CCL 3C:328-29. [2]LF 48:413. [3]2 Cor 5:19. [4]Jn 3:17. [5]*WSA* 3 4:33; PL 38:588.

he consoles them still further by telling them that the hatred of the world would be an evidence of their goodness. They ought rather to grieve . . . if they were loved by the world, as that would be evidence of their wickedness. Homilies on the Gospel of John 77.2.[6]

15:19 *Belonging to the World*

Of This World, Yet Not in It. Ambrose: That which is promised to us is already present with you, and the object of your prayers is with you. You are of this world and yet not in this world. This age has held you but has not been able to retain you. Concerning Virgins 1.9.52.[7]

God and His Enemies. Gregory the Great: For the disparaging of the perverse [toward us] is our praise. There is nothing wrong in not pleasing those who do not please God. For no one can by one and the same act please God and the enemies of God. He proves himself no friend to God who pleases his enemy. And he whose soul is in subjection to the Truth will have to contend with the enemies of that Truth. Homilies on Ezekiel 1.9.14[8]

15:20a *A Servant Is Not Greater Than His Master*

Jesus' Humiliation Will Be His Disciples' Humiliation. Cyril of Alexandria: Jesus indicates to his disciples that they will encounter every kind of disgrace, saying, "The slave is not above his lord." "For," he says, "wicked people attacked me with their unbridled tongues. And leaving no kind of insult untried, they called me a man possessed of a devil and a drunkard and the fruit of fornication. Yet I did not immediately seek their punishment, but not being cut to the heart by their insults, I granted to my hearers the word of salvation." Do not, then, seek out of reason your own aggrandizement or scorn the limits within which your Lord was bound, who lowered himself to such humiliation for us to benefit all. Commentary on the Gospel of John 10.2.[9]

Consolation That Their Lord Suffered. Chrysostom: He showed that in this point they would be his most ardent imitators. For while Christ was in the flesh, people made war against him, but when he was translated [to heaven], the battle next came on them. Then because they were so few, they were terrified at being about to encounter the attack of so great a multitude. And so he raises their souls by telling them that it was a special subject of joy that they were hated by them, "For you shall share my sufferings. You should not therefore be troubled, for you are not better than I." As I told you before, "The servant is not greater than his lord." Then there is also a third source of consolation, that the Father also is insulted together with them. Homilies on the Gospel of John 77.2.[10]

15:20b *Persecution and the Fruitful Word*

Sufferers with Christ Reign with Christ. Cyril of Alexandria: It is just as if Jesus said, "I, the creator of the universe, who have everything under my hand, both in heaven and on earth, did not bridle their rage or restrain . . . their inclinations. Rather, I let each one choose their own course and permitted all to do what they wanted. Therefore, when I was persecuted, I endured it even though I had the power of preventing it. When you too follow in my wake and pursue the same course I did, you also will be persecuted. You're going to have to momentarily endure the aversion of those who hate you without being overly troubled by the ingratitude of those whom you benefit. This is how you attain my glory, for those who suffer with me shall also reign with me." Commentary on the Gospel of John 10.2.[11]

---

[6]NPNF 1 14:283**; PG 59:416. [7]NPNF 2 10:371*. [8]CCL 142:130. [9]LF 48:416-17*. [10]NPNF 1 14:283*; PG 59:416. [11]LF 48:419**.

GOD BRINGS FORTH THE FRUIT. CYRIL OF ALEXANDRIA: Just as those who have been trained in agriculture . . . cut up the land with the plough, and then bury the seed in the furrow and do not rely any further on their own skill but rather leave the rest to the power and favor of God—I mean the germination of the seed that is buried in the earth and nourishing it up to perfect fruit—so too I think the interpreter of the noblest truths ought only to sow the Word and leave the rest to God. The Savior therefore gives his advice in this matter to his disciples as a medicine for lack of spirit and a cure for listlessness. For, he says, do not ever choose to shy away from continuing to teach, even if some of those who have once been admonished should nullify the teaching that has been given to them. Rather, finding that even my words are often not received by many, do not strive to surpass my reputation. Instead, follow in my footsteps and do not become discouraged. COMMENTARY ON THE GOSPEL OF JOHN 10.2.[12]

15:21 *All These Things for My Name's Sake*

IN YOU THEY WILL ATTACK ME. AUGUSTINE: "All these things" that "they will do to you" refers to what he had just said, namely, that the world would hate and persecute you and despise your word. . . . "for my name's sake." In other words, in you they will hate me, in you they will persecute me. They will not keep your word because it is my word. TRACTATES ON THE GOSPEL OF JOHN 88.2.[13]

[12]LF 48:420**. [13]NPNF 1 7:356**; CCL 36:546

15:22-25 HATING FATHER AND SON

[22]If I had not come and spoken to them, they would not have sin; but now they have no excuse for their sin. [23]He who hates me hates my Father also. [24]If I had not done among them the works which no one else did, they would not have sin; but now they have seen and hated both me and my Father. [25]It is to fulfil the word that is written in their law, "They hated me without a cause."

OVERVIEW: Jesus' enigmatic statement, "If I had not come, they would not have sin," has been understood in a number of ways: some believe it refers to those who have not yet come to the age of reason (ORIGEN). Others see Jesus pointedly challenging the world about its sin of unbelief (AUGUSTINE), implying that ignorance is now no excuse because he has become incarnate (AMBROSE).

Christ calls the Father "*my* Father," not only asserting a claim to a type of sonship no one else can claim, but also demonstrating that anyone who hates him also hates his Father (HILARY). Even though Jesus had just said that the Jews did not know his Father, their hatred of the Father is still evident because they have constructed a picture of the Father that has no basis in reality—a reality that is evident in the Son and his works (AUGUSTINE). Jesus' words and works testify to his close relationship with the Father (CHRYSOSTOM). By saying he did works that no one else had done before him, he meant that the scope and breadth of his works were much greater than anything that had happened before (Augustine). Notice how Jesus here extends the preaching of salvation to those who insulted him; we should do no less (Cyril). And yet, his opponents display an irrational ignorance of the prophecy regarding the Gentiles (Theodore) and even descend into deliberate and willful sin in their denial of the gospel to the Gentiles (Gregory the Great).

15:22 *If I Had Not Come, They Would Not Have Sin*

The Age of Reason. Origen: That declaration in the Gospel, "If I had not come and spoken to them, they would not have had sin, but now they have no excuse for their sin," makes it clear to all who are rational just how long a time a person is without sin and just when he is liable to sin. By participating in the word or reason, people are said to have sinned, that is, from the time they are capable of understanding, from the time that the reason implanted within them suggests to them the difference between good and evil. After they have begun to know what evil is, they are liable for any sin they commit.

This is the meaning of the expression that "people have no excuse for their sin," namely, that from the time the divine word or reason has begun to show them internally the difference between good and evil, they ought to avoid and guard against evil: "For to the one who knows to do good and does not do it, to him it is sin."[1] On First Principles 1.3.6.[2]

Jesus Refers to the Sin of Unbelief. Augustine: Christ spoke to the Jews only, not to any other nation. In them then was that world that hated Christ and his disciples. And not only in them, but even these latter [i.e., the Gentiles] were shown by him to belong to the same world. What, then, does he mean by the words "If I had not come and spoken unto them, they would not have sin"? Were the Jews then without sin before Christ came in the flesh, because Christ had not spoken to them? Only the greatest fool would think so. By sin here he means not every sin but a certain great sin which includes everyone and which alone hinders the remission of other sins, that is, the sin of unbelief. They did not believe in Christ, who came that they might believe in him. This is the sin, then, they would not have had if Christ had not come. His advent has become as much fraught with destruction to unbelievers as it is with salvation to those who believe. . . .

"But now they have no excuse for their sin." If those to whom Christ had not come or spoken had no excuse for their sin, why is it said here that these had no excuse, because Christ had come and spoken to them? If the first had excuse, did it do away with their punishment altogether or only mitigate it? I answer that this excuse did not cover all their sin but only this one, that is, that they did not believe in Christ. But they are not of this number to whom Christ came by his disciples and to whom he spoke by them, as he also does at present. For by his church he has come, and by his church he speaks to the Gentiles. Tractates on the Gospel of John 89.1-2.[3]

Those Who Have Not Heard the Gospel Have No Excuse. Augustine: It remains for us to inquire whether those who, prior to the coming of Christ in his church to the Gentiles and to their hearing of his gospel, have been or are now being overtaken by the close of this life—can they have such an excuse? Evidently they can, but this is no reason for them to escape damnation. "For as many as have sinned without the law, shall also perish without the law. And as many as have sinned in the law, shall be judged by the law."[4] . . . Such an excuse not only brings them no help but even becomes an additional aggrava-

[1]Jas 4:17. [2]ANF 4:254*; GCS 22(5):57. [3]NPNF 1 7:357-58**; CCL 36:548-49. [4]Rom 2:12.

tion. For those who excuse themselves because they did not hear are the ones who "shall perish without the law."

Paul's discourse was not distinguishing between unbelievers and believers, but between Jews and Gentiles, both of whom are most certainly lost if they do not find salvation in the Savior who came to seek what was lost.[5] Although, one might say that some will have lighter, others more severe punishments in their damnation. Whoever is punished with an exclusion from that happiness that is given to the saints is lost to God. But there is as great a diversity of punishments as there is of sins—although how this is settled is a matter known only to divine Wisdom, something too deep for human conjecture to examine or express. Tractates on the Gospel of John 89.3-4.[6]

Ignorance Is No Excuse. Ambrose: The mystery of Christ is so great that even angels stood amazed and bewildered before it. This is why, then, it is your duty to worship him and, as a servant, this is why you should not detract from your Lord. You cannot plead ignorance because establishing your faith is why he came down in the first place. If you do not believe, he has not come down for you or suffered for you. "If I had not come," says the Scripture, "and spoken to them, they would not have sin. But now they have no excuse for their sin. Whoever hates me hates my Father also." Who, then, hates Christ, if not the one who speaks to his dishonor? For just as it is love's part to render honor, so it is hate's part to withdraw honor. The one who hates calls into question Christ's honor; the one who loves, pays reverence. On the Christian Faith 4.2.27.[7]

15:23 *Whoever Hates the Son Hates the Father*

The Son Is from the Father by His Birth. Hilary of Poitiers: "Hates my Father also." This *my* is the assertion of a relation to the Father that is shared by no one else. . . . He condemns the man who claims God as his Father and does not love the Son as using a wrongful liberty with the Father's name, since he who hates him, that is, the Son, must hate the Father also. And none can be devoted to the Father except those who love the Son. For the one and only reason that he gives for loving the Son is his origin from the Father. The Son, therefore, is from the Father, not by his advent but by his birth. And love for the Father is only possible to those who believe that the Son is from him. On the Trinity 6.30.[8]

Those Who Hate the Son. Augustine: He had just said a little before, "They will do these things to you because they do not know him who sent me."[9] A question arises here that cannot be overlooked: How can they hate someone they do not know? If they hated God, believing him to be something else instead of God, this was not hatred of God. . . . If the Jews were asked whether they loved God, they would have replied that of course they loved him, not intentionally lying but only erroneously thinking they did. For how could those who hated the Truth love the Father of the Truth? They had no desire to have their conduct condemned, and yet it is the task of truth to condemn such conduct. And so, they hated the Truth even though at the time, they did not know he was the truth who came to condemn them. Therefore, they hate what they do not know. And hating it, they certainly cannot do anything else but hate him from whom he was born. Because they do not know the truth who is condemning them as the one who is born of God the Father, it is certain that they not only do not know the Father but also hate the Father himself. Tractates on the Gospel of John 90.1, 3.[10]

15:24 *Unique Works Testify*

[5]Lk 19:10. [6]NPNF 1 7:358**; CCL 36:549-50. See also his *Sermon* 143.2 (*WSA* 3 4:426). [7]NPNF 2 10:265**; CSEL 78:165 (*On the Christian Faith* 4.2.26). See also *Jacob and the Happy Life* 1.4.14; FC 65:129). [8]NPNF 2 9:109*; CCL 62:233. [9]Jn 15:21. [10]NPNF 1 7:359-60**.

WORDS AND WORKS TESTIFY FOR JESUS. CHRYSOSTOM: Jesus proclaims ahead of time that there will be no small punishment against them. For, since they continually pretended that they persecuted him on account of the Father, to deprive them of this excuse he says: I gave them doctrine, I added miracles, which, according to Moses' law, should convince all if the doctrine itself is good also. If I had not done among them the works that no one else had ever done, they would have had no sin. HOMILIES ON THE GOSPEL OF JOHN 77.2.[11]

HAD NO ONE ELSE DONE THESE THINGS? AUGUSTINE: Their [i.e., those who hate Christ] sin was in the fact that they did not believe him, notwithstanding his doctrine and his miracles. . . . But why does he add, "which no one else ever did"? Christ did no work greater than the raising of the dead, which we know the ancient prophets did before him.[12] . . . Is it that he did some things that no one else did? But others also did what neither he nor anyone else did. . . . True. Yet none of the ancient prophets that we read of healed so many bodily defects, sicknesses, infirmities. For to say nothing of single cases, Mark says . . . that wherever he entered, into villages, or cities or country, they laid the sick in the streets and asked that they might touch just the border of his garment. And any who touched him were made whole.[13] . . . Such works as these no one else had done in them. In them, he says, meaning not among them or before them but directly in them because he healed them . . . for which they surely ought to have returned him with love and not with hatred. . . . The wicked hate the Lord, but he is loved by the righteous gratuitously [*gratis*, freely,] inasmuch as they expect no other gifts beyond himself, for he himself will be all in all. . . . But even where particular works, like some of these, had been done before, whoever worked such things did not really do them, for he [i.e., Jesus] did them through them, whereas Jesus performs these miracles by his own power. TRACTATES ON THE GOSPEL OF JOHN 91.1-4.[14]

15:25 *Hate Without Cause*

PREACHING TO THOSE WHO HATE US. CYRIL OF ALEXANDRIA: Here our Lord clearly shows that he is not unaware of the stubborn temper of the Jews[15] but rather, he had foretold and knew in advance how they would respond. However, he still treated them with mildness and forgiveness as was befitting his divine nature. For he set before them the Word that called them to salvation even though they were ill disposed to receive it. And if any of them did have a good and suitable disposition, he even confirmed their faith by miracles. Here too he gives his disciples considerable benefit, with the goal that in a forgiving spirit they might extend the preaching of salvation even to those who offered them insults and might even in this be seen to walk in the path of excellence which was first revealed in Christ. COMMENTARY ON THE GOSPEL OF JOHN 10.2.[16]

IGNORING THE PROPHECY IS IRRATIONAL. THEODORE OF MOPSUESTIA: [Jesus says], If I was not engaged in dialogue with them in deed and in word, they would have something to say. But now, since they do not accept my words, they are clearly condemned for their enmity toward me and the Father. Through the prophecy[17] he also shows that their hatred of him was irrational. COMMENTARY ON JOHN 6.15.25.[18]

DELIBERATE, WILLFUL SIN. GREGORY THE GREAT: It is one thing not to do good, another to hate the teacher of goodness since there is a difference between sudden and deliberate sins. Our state generally is that we love what is good but from infirmity cannot perform it. But to sin on

[11]NPNF 1 14:283**; PG 59:416. [12]Augustine then cites many examples of miracles in both the Old and New Testament. [13]Mk 6:56. [14]NPNF 1 7:361-62**; CCL 36:553-55. [15]Cyril is referring to those Jews, specifically, with whom Jesus is interacting. [16]LF 48:429-30**. [17]See Ps 35:19 (34:19 LXX); 69:4 (68:5 LXX). [18]CSCO 4 3:287.

purpose means not doing or desiring what is good. As, then, it is sometimes a heavier offense to love sin than to do it, so is it more wicked to hate justice than not to do it. There are some in the church who not only do not do what is good but even persecute it and hate in others what they neglect to do themselves. The sin of these people is not that of infirmity or ignorance but deliberate, willful sin. MORALS ON THE BOOK OF JOB 25.11.28.[19]

[19]LF 23:119-20**.

15:26-27 THE COMFORTER SENT FROM THE FATHER

[26]But when the Counselor comes, whom I shall send to you from the Father, even the Spirit of truth, who proceeds from the Father, he will bear witness to me; [27]and you also are witnesses, because you have been with me from the beginning.

OVERVIEW: Jesus calls the Holy Spirit "Comforter," giving him a name taken from his office, which is not only to relieve sorrow (CYRIL OF JERUSALEM) but to fill with joy (DIDYMUS). The Son is our Paraclete as intercessor while the Spirit is our Paraclete in bestowing consolation (ORIGEN). As the life-giving water from heaven, the Spirit binds us who are the many dry particles of wheat flour into the one loaf of bread (IRENAEUS).

The Spirit proceeds from the Father (COUNCIL OF CONSTANTINOPLE) and rests in the Son (JOHN OF DAMASCUS). It is not generated from the Father like the Son was (DIDYMUS, GREGORY OF NAZIANZUS) but rather is distinguished in the Trinity by his procession (GREGORY OF NAZIANZUS)—albeit not from a place (AMBROSE). The Spirit proceeds from the Word, who himself is from the Father (ATHANASIUS) and so in this way may also be said to proceed from the Father and the Son (AUGUSTINE) as the Son sends the Spirit from the Father (HILARY, AUGUSTINE). This demonstrates that the Spirit is not inferior in any way in the Godhead, having been sent both by the Father and the Son (AMBROSE, CHRYSOSTOM). But Christ refers to the Spirit as proceeding from the Father alone because he always refers all that he has to the Father from whom he has received everything (AUGUSTINE).

The Spirit floods our souls with holiness (AMBROSE), bearing witness to the Father and the Son, having the same knowledge of the Father as the Son has (AMBROSE). This knowledge in turn was bestowed on the faithful at Pentecost when the Holy Spirit was given (THEODORE). The Spirit empowers the witness of the apostles (THEODORE), whose later eyewitness testimony was important for the life of the church (CHRYSOSTOM).

15:26a *The Coming of the Comforter*

THE COMFORTER IS WITH US IN OUR TROUBLES. CYRIL OF JERUSALEM: He is called the

Comforter because he comforts and encourages us and helps our infirmities. We do not know what we should pray for as we should, but the Spirit himself makes intercession for us, with groanings that cannot be uttered,[1] that is, he makes intercession to God. Very often, someone has been outraged and dishonored unjustly for the sake of Christ. Martyrdom is at hand; tortures on every side, and fire, and sword, and savage beasts and the pit. But the Holy Spirit softly whispers to him, "Wait on the Lord."[2] What is now happening to you is a small matter; the reward will be great. Suffer a little while, and you will be with angels forever. "The sufferings of this present time are not worth comparing to the glory that shall be revealed in us."[3] He portrays to the person the kingdom of heaven. He gives him a glimpse of the paradise of delight. CATECHETICAL LECTURES 16.20.[4]

THE OFFICE OF THE HOLY SPIRIT IS "COMFORTER." DIDYMUS THE BLIND: He calls the Holy Spirit the Comforter, a name taken from his office, which is not only to relieve the sadness of the faithful but also to fill them with unspeakable joy. Everlasting gladness is in those hearts in which the Spirit dwells. The Spirit, the Comforter, is sent by the Son, not as angels, or prophets or apostles are sent, but as the Spirit must be sent, which is of one nature with the divine wisdom and power that sends him. The Son, when sent by the Father, is not separated from him but abides in the Father and the Father in him. In the same way the Holy Spirit is not sent by the Son and proceeds from the Father, in the sense of change of place. For as the Father's nature, being incorporeal, is not local, so neither does the Spirit of truth, who is incorporeal also, and superior to all created things, have a local nature. ON THE HOLY SPIRIT 25.[5]

SON IS INTERCESSOR, SPIRIT IS COMFORTER. ORIGEN: The name Paraclete seems to be understood in the case of our Savior as meaning intercessor. For he is said to intercede with the Father because of our sins.[6] In the case of the Holy Spirit, the Paraclete must be understood in the sense of comforter because he bestows consolation on the souls to whom he openly reveals the apprehension of spiritual knowledge. ON FIRST PRINCIPLES 2.7.4.[7]

THE SPIRIT AS LIFE-GIVING WATER FROM HEAVEN. IRENAEUS: The Lord promised to send the Comforter who would join us to God. For as a compacted lump of dough cannot be formed of dry wheat without liquid, nor can a loaf possess unity, so, in the same way, neither could we, being many, be made one in Christ Jesus without the water from heaven. And as dry earth does not produce fruit unless it receives moisture, in the same way we also, being originally a dry tree, could never have produced life-bearing fruit without the voluntary rain from above. AGAINST HERESIES 3.17.2.[8]

15:26b *The Spirit of Truth Proceeds from the Father*

CREEDAL STATEMENT. COUNCIL OF CONSTANTINOPLE 381:

And [we believe] in the Holy Spirit,
the Lord and giver of life,
who proceeds from the Father,[9]
who with the Father and Son
together is worshiped and glorified;
who spoke by the prophets.

NICENE-CONSTANTINOPOLITAN CREED, THIRD ARTICLE (GREEK TEXT).[10]

PROCEEDS FROM THE FATHER, RESTS IN THE SON. JOHN OF DAMASCUS: We believe also in one Holy Spirit, the Lord and Giver of life, who proceeds from the Father and rests in the Son, the object of equal adoration and glorification with the

[1]Rom 8:26. [2]Ps 27:14 (26:14 LXX). [3]Rom 8:18. [4]NPNF 2 7:120**. [5]PL 23:125-26. [6]1 Jn 2:1-2. [7]ANF 4:286*; GCS 22(5):152. [8]ANF 1:444-45; SC 34:304. [9]Western Latin churches later added the word *filioque*, which eventually brought about schism between Eastern and Western Christianity that continues today. [10]ACO 1.1.7:66.

Father and Son, since he is co-essential and co-eternal;[11] the Spirit of God, direct, authoritative, the fountain of wisdom, and life and holiness; God existing and addressed along with Father and Son; uncreated, full, creative, all-ruling, all-effecting, all-powerful, of infinite power, Lord of all creation and not under any lord; deifying, not deified; filling, not filled; shared in, not sharing in; sanctifying, not sanctified; the intercessor, receiving the supplications of all; in all things like to the Father and Son: proceeding from the Father and communicated through the Son, participated in by all creation, through himself creating and investing with essence and sanctifying and maintaining the universe: having subsistence, existing in its own proper and peculiar subsistence, inseparable and indivisible from Father and Son, possessing all the qualities that the Father and Son possess, except that of not being begotten or born. For the Father is without cause and unborn; since he is derived from nothing but derives from himself his being, nor does he derive a single quality from another. Rather, he is himself the beginning and cause of the existence of all things in a definite and natural manner. But the Son is derived from the Father after the manner of generation, and the Holy Spirit likewise is derived from the Father, yet not after the manner of generation but after that of procession. And we have learned that there is a difference[12] between generation and procession, but the nature of that difference we in no wise understand. Further, the generation of the Son from the Father and the procession of the Holy Spirit are simultaneous. Orthodox Faith 1.8.[13]

The Spirit Proceeds from the Father. Didymus the Blind: He does not say, "from God" or "from the Almighty" but "from the Father," because though the Father and God Almighty are the same, yet the Spirit of truth properly proceeds from God as the Father, the Begetter. . . . The Father and the Son together send the Spirit of truth: He comes by the will both of the Father and the Son. On the Holy Spirit 26.[14]

The Spirit Proceeds. Gregory of Nazianzus: The Holy Spirit is truly Spirit, coming forth from the Father indeed, but not after the manner of the Son, for it is not by generation but by procession. . . . There is then one God in three, and these three are one. On the Holy Lights, Oration 39.12.[15]

Procession Belongs to the Spirit. Gregory of Nazianzus:

The Holy Spirit always existed, and exists and always will exist,
who neither had a beginning nor will have an end . . .
ever being partaken but not partaking;
perfecting, not being perfected;
sanctifying, not being sanctified;
deifying, not being deified . . .
Life and Lifegiver;
Light and Lightgiver;
Absolute Good and Spring of Goodness . . .
By whom the Father is known and the Son is glorified. . . .

Why make a long discourse of it? All that the Father has the Son has also; except the being unbegotten. And all that the Son has the Spirit has also, except the generation. On Pentecost, Oration 41.9.[16]

The Relationship of the Trinity. Gregory of Nazianzus: Tell me, what position will you assign to that which proceeds, which has started up between the two terms of your distinctions [i.e., the terms *begotten* and *unbegotten*] and is introduced by a better theologian than you, namely, our Savior himself? Or perhaps you have taken that word out of your Gospels for the sake of your third testament: "The Holy Spirit, who proceeds from the Father." Because he proceeds from that source, he is no creature. And because he is not begotten, he is no son. And because he is

[11]See Gregory of Nazianzus *Oration* 37. [12]See Gregory of Nazianzus *Oration* 29.35. [13]NPNF 2 9:9*. [14]PL 23:126-27. [15]NPNF 2 7:356*. [16]NPNF 2 7:382.

between the unbegotten and the begotten, he is God. And so, escaping the labors of your syllogisms, he [i.e., the Spirit] has manifested himself as God, stronger than your distinctions. What then is procession? Tell me what the unbegottenness of the Father is, and I will explain to you the physiology of the generation of the Son and the procession of the Spirit, and we shall both of us be frenzy-stricken for prying into the mystery of God![17] And who are we to do these things, we who cannot even see what lies at our feet or number the sand of the sea, or the drops of rain, or the days of eternity, much less enter into the depths of God and supply an account of that nature that is so unspeakable and transcending all words?

What then, they say, is there lacking to the Spirit that prevents him from being a Son, for if there were not something lacking he would be a Son? We assert that there is nothing lacking—for God has no deficiency. But the difference of manifestation, if I may so express myself, or rather of their mutual relations one to another, has caused the difference of their names. For indeed, there is no deficiency in the Son that prevents his being Father (for sonship is not a deficiency), and yet he is not Father. According to this line of argument there must be some deficiency in the Father, in re-spect of his not being Son. For the Father is not Son, and yet this is not due to either deficiency or subjection of essence. But the very fact of being unbegotten or begotten or proceeding has given the name of Father to the first, of the Son to the second, and of the third, him of whom we are speak-ing, of the Holy Spirit that the distinction of the three persons may be preserved in the one nature and dignity of the Godhead. For neither is the Son Father, for the Father is one, but he is what the Father is. Nor is the Spirit Son because he is of God, for the Only Begotten is one, but he is what the Son is. The three are one in Godhead, and the one three in properties, so that neither is the unity a Sabellian one,[18] nor does the Trinity countenance the present evil distinction. What then? Is the Spirit God? Most certainly. Well then, is he consubstantial? Yes, if he is God. On the Holy Spirit, Theological Oration 5(31).8-10.[19]

The Spirit's Procession Is Not from a Place. Ambrose: If the Spirit proceeds from a place and passes to a place, the Father also will be found in a place, and so will the Son. If he goes out of a place, whom the Fathers sends, or the Son, surely the Spirit passing and proceeding from a place seems to leave both the Father and the Son as a body, according to impious interpretations. I declare this with reference to those who say that the Spirit has motion by descending. But neither is the Father circumscribed in any place, who is over all things not only of a corporeal nature but also of invisible creation, nor is the Son enclosed by the places and times of his works, who as the worker of all creation is over every creature. Nor is the Spirit of truth, namely, the Spirit of God, circumscribed by any corporeal boundaries,[20] who, since he is incorporeal, is over all rational creation by the ineffable fullness of the Godhead, having the power of breathing where he wishes and of inspiring as he wishes over all things. On the Holy Spirit 1.11.117-18.[21]

The Spirit Proceeds from the Word, Who Is from the Father. Athanasius: As the Son is an only-begotten offspring, so also the Spirit, being given and sent from the Son, is himself one and not many, nor one from among many, but Only Spirit. As the Son, the living Word, is one, so must the vital activity and gift by which he sanctifies and enlightens be one, perfect and complete. This [activity and gift] is said to proceed from the Father because it is from the Word, who is confessed to be from the Father, that it shines forth, is sent and is given. The Son is sent from the Father. For he says, "God so loved the world that he gave his only begotten Son."[22] The Son sends the Spirit. "If I go away," he says, "I will

[17]Sir 1:2. [18]That is, they are not three manifestations, or modes, of the Godhead. [19]NPNF 2 7:320-21**. [20]See Wis 7:23. [21]FC 44:77-78*; CSEL 79:65-66. [22]Jn 3:16. [23]Jn 16:7.

send the Paraclete."[23] The Son glorifies the Father, saying, "Father, I have glorified you."[24] The Spirit glorifies the Son, for he says, "He shall glorify me."[25] The Son says, "The things I heard from the Father I speak unto the world."[26] The Spirit takes of the Son. "He shall take of mine," he says, "and shall declare it unto you."[27] The Son came in the name of the Father. "The Holy Spirit," says the Son, "whom the Father will send in my name."[28] Letter to Serapion 1.20.[29]

The Son Sends the Spirit from the Father. Hilary of Poitiers: The Advocate shall come, and the Son shall send him from the Father, and he is the Spirit of truth who proceeds from the Father. . . . He will send from the Father the Spirit of truth who proceeds from the Father. [The Son] therefore cannot be the recipient, since he is revealed as the sender. It only remains to make sure of our conviction on the point, whether we are to believe an egress of a co-existent being or a procession of a being begotten. . . . If one believes that there is a difference between receiving from the Son and proceeding from the Father, surely to receive from the Son and to receive from the Father will be regarded as one and the same thing. . . . For when he says that all things whatever the Father has are his and that for this cause he declared that it must be received from his own, he teaches also that what is received from the Father is yet received from himself, because all things that the Father has are his. On the Trinity 8.19-20.[30]

The Spirit of the Father and the Son. Augustine: That he is the Spirit of the Father is what the Son himself says: "He proceeds from the Father," and in another place, "For it is not you who speak, but the Spirit of your Father who speaks in you."[31] That he is also the Spirit of the Son is what the apostle tells us: "God sent the Spirit of his Son into our hearts, crying Abba, Father,"[32] that is, "making us cry." It is, after all, we who cry out but in him, that is to say, through his pouring out charity in our hearts, without which anyone who cries out, cries out in vain. That is why he also says, "Whoever does not have the Spirit of Christ is not one of his."[33] So to which person of the Trinity would communion in this companionship properly belong, if not to that Spirit who is common to Father and Son? Sermon 71.29.[34]

The Spirit Sent by Father and Son. Ambrose: When you hear that the Son sends the Spirit, you might believe that the Spirit is of inferior power. So both the Father and the Spirit sent the Son. Also, the Father and the Son sent the Spirit. The Father sent him because it is written, "But the Paraclete, the Holy Spirit, whom the Father will send in my name." The Son sent him, because he said, "When the Advocate comes, whom I will send to you from the Father, the Spirit of truth." If, then, the Son and the Spirit send each other, as the Father sends, there is no affront of subjection but a community of power. On the Holy Spirit 3.1.7-8.[35]

Both Father and Son Send the Spirit. Chrysostom: [The Spirit] shall be worthy of belief because he is the Spirit of truth. This is why he called it not the Holy Spirit but the "Spirit of truth." But when he says it "proceeds from the Father," he shows that [the Spirit] knows all things precisely, just as Christ also says of himself, "I know from where I come and where I am going."[36] He also was speaking in that place about truth. "Whom I will send" indicates that it is no longer the Father alone but the Son also who sends. Homilies on the Gospel of John 77.3.[37]

Not the Spirit of One, but of Both Father and Son. Augustine: If it is asked here whether the Holy Spirit proceeds from the Son also, we may answer in this way: The Son is

[24]Jn 17:4. [25]Jn 16:14. [26]Jn 8:26. [27]Jn 16:14. [28]Jn 14:26. [29]*LAHS* 116-18; PG 26:577-80. [30]NPNF 2 9:142-43*; CCL 62A:330-32. [31]Mt 10:20. [32]Gal 4:6. [33]Rom 8:9. [34]*WSA* 3 3:264; *RB* 75:97. [35]FC 44:156; CSEL 79:152-53. [36]Jn 8:14. [37]NPNF 1 14:284**.

the Son of the Father alone, and the Father is the Father of the Son only. But the Holy Spirit is not the Spirit of one but of both, since Christ himself said, "The Spirit of your Father which speaks in you."[38] And the apostle says, "God has sent the Spirit of his Son into your hearts."[39]... This indeed, I think, is the reason why he is called peculiarly the Spirit. For both of the Father and the Son separately we may say that each is a Spirit. For God is a Spirit,[40] that is, God is not carnal but spiritual. But what each is separately in a general sense, he who is not either one separately, but the union of both, is spiritually. But if the Holy Spirit is the Spirit of the Son, why shouldn't we believe that he proceeds from the Son seeing that he is also the Spirit of the Son? Indeed, if he did not proceed from the Son, Christ would not after the resurrection have breathed on his disciples and said, "Receive the Holy Spirit."[41] ... This too is what is meant by the virtue that went out of him and healed all. If the Holy Spirit then proceeds both from the Father and the Son, why does the Son say, "Who proceeds from the Father"? He says this because it agrees with his general way of referring all that he has to him from whom he is. TRACTATES ON THE GOSPEL OF JOHN 99.6-8.[42]

15:26c *The Spirit Testifies on the Son's Behalf*

COME HOLY SPIRIT.[43] AMBROSE:

Come, Holy Spirit, who ever One
Are with the Father and the Son,
It is the hour, our souls possess
With your full flood of holiness.

Let flesh, and heart, and lips and mind,
Sound forth our witness to humankind;
And love light up our mortal frame,
Till others catch the living flame.

Grant this, O Father, ever One
With Christ, your sole begotten Son
And Holy Spirit we adore,
Reigning and blest forevermore. Amen.

LITURGY OF HOURS, TERCE.[44]

THE SPIRIT KNOWS WHAT THE SON KNOWS. AMBROSE: So the Holy Spirit proceeds from the Father and bears witness of the Son. A witness, both faithful and true, bears witness also of the Father. There is no more complete expression of the divine majesty, nothing more clear regarding the unity of divine power than this, since the Spirit knows the same as the Son, who is the witness and the inseparable sharer of the Father's secrets. ON THE HOLY SPIRIT 1.1.25.[45]

SIGNS OF PENTECOST WILL VINDICATE JESUS. THEODORE OF MOPSUESTIA: Through the descent of the Spirit, he says, there will be a confirmation of what I said, that is, that they committed a serious offense against me and my Father. When in my name signs happen through the power of the Spirit, then the truth of my words will appear. It will be evident that the Father was despised with me because of the iniquity of my enemies. And then Jesus, wanting to emphasize their fault on the basis of the person who will testify, says, "who comes from the Father," that is, the one whose essence is from the nature of the Father. In fact, if the natural procession [of the Spirit] were not understood from the word *comes* but, for instance, a certain external sending, there would be uncertainty about the spirit he is talking about, because many spirits are sent on missions, as also the apostle Paul said, "Are not all angels spirits in the divine service, sent to serve?"[46] Here also the fact that he mentions it by itself is sufficient to signify the one who proceeds from the Father and appropriately is called by the name of Spirit in the Holy Scripture. COMMENTARY ON JOHN 6.15.26.[47]

[38]Mt 10:20. [39]Gal 4:6. [40]Jn 4:24. [41]Jn 20:22. [42]NPNF 1 7:383-84**; CCL 36:585-87. [43]Hymn used for the office of Terce (mid-morning prayer, about 9:00 A.M.) from the Liturgy of the Hours. It is particularly appropriate for Terce, for it was at that hour the Holy Spirit came on the apostles on Pentecost (Acts 2:15). [44]*HBM* 35. [45]FC 44:45*; CSEL 79:26-27. [46]Heb 1:14. [47]CSCO 4 3:287-88.

15:27 *You Also Are Witnesses*

The Spirit Empowers the Witness of the Apostles. Theodore of Mopsuestia: When you speak, the Spirit, through its testimony, will confirm your words with evident signs, as also the apostle said, "My speech and my proclamation were not with plausible words of wisdom but with a demonstration of the Spirit and of power."[48] The signs that happened through the power of the Spirit in the name of the Lord showed the greatness of him who underwent passion and, at the same time, the foolishness of those who dared crucify him. Commentary on John 6.15.27.[49]

The Apostles' Eyewitness Testimony Is Important. Chrysostom: In matters of belief, the very thing that gives one a right to be believed is the fact of having learned what you believe from eyewitnesses. . . . Therefore John also says, "I saw and bore record that this is the Son of God."[50] . . . Accordingly, Jesus gave them permission to rest many details of their testimony on the fact of their having seen them when he said, "And you also are witnesses because you have been with me from the beginning." The apostles themselves also often speak in a similar way.[51] . . . For they more readily received the testimony of people who had been his companions because the notion of the Spirit was as yet very much beyond them. Therefore John also at that time, in his Gospel, speaking of the blood and water, said, he himself saw it, making the fact of his having seen it equivalent to the highest testimony for them, although the witness of the Spirit is more certain than the evidence of sight, but not so with unbelievers. Homilies on the Acts of the Apostles 1.[52]

[48]1 Cor 2:4. [49]CSCO 4 3:288. [50]Jn 1:34. [51]Acts 2:32; 10:41. [52]NPNF 1 11:3**.

16:1-4 WARNING OF COMING PERSECUTION

[1]I have said all this to you to keep you from falling away. [2]They will put you out of the synagogues; indeed, the hour is coming when whoever kills you will think he is offering service to God. [3]And they will do this because they have not known the Father, nor me. [4]But I have said these things to you, that when their hour comes you may remember that I told you of them.

I did not say these things to you from the beginning, because I was with you.

Overview: Jesus prepares his disciples for tribulation through prophesying about what would happen (Theodore). They are to endure the hatred they receive, understanding that it is misplaced zeal (Bede). Christ's warning foretells the disciples' ultimate success (Augustine). Those who thought they were offering service to God in killing Jesus went up to Jerusalem to "purify themselves" for this supposed service (Origen). Jesus as well as the disciples would be cast out of the synagogue by them, but if the Jews had instead acknowledged and received Christ, the churches of Christ would have been no different from the synagogue (Augustine). Those who partake in Christ's suffering should realize these persecutions are to test us (Cyprian). But those who persecute the ones who are sent also persecute the sender (Cyril). There is an ultimate reward for their endurance (Chrysostom). In the same way, we too should remember Jesus' words when tested (Chrysostom). He gives these words of comfort to his disciples because he is about to leave them (Augustine). He had warned them earlier but now is more specific (Chrysostom).

16:1 *To Keep You from Falling Away*

Training Through Difficulties. Theodore of Mopsuestia: I predicted these things to you, he says, so that when sudden unexpected tribulations would occur, your resolve might not turn and fail but instead, through constant meditation, you might be trained through these difficulties. Commentary on John 6.16.1.[1]

Misdirected Zeal. Bede: The Savior warned his disciples ahead of time that they would not only be driven away from fellowship with their fellow citizens but also that they would suffer death at their hands. The Jews thought that they were doing a service to God in pursuing the ministers of the new covenant with hatred and death. The apostle says, "For I bear witness to them that they have zeal for God, but not according to full knowledge."[2] Here, it is as if he were saying, "You are going to suffer battles and tribulations from your fellow citizens, but accept them the more steadfastly in the realization that you are afflicted with them not so much out of hatred toward yourselves as out of zeal for the divine law." Mindful of this advice, the blessed martyr Stephen prayed for his slayers. Those zealous for the Law thought that they were doing a service to God when they were murdering the heralds of grace. Homilies on the Gospels 2.16.[3]

16:2 *Persecution and Misdirected Service to God*

Christ's Warning Foretells the Disciples' Success. Augustine: On the whole, I do not think Jesus wanted to convey any further meaning than that they might understand and rejoice that they themselves would gain so many to Christ. When they were being driven out of the Jewish congregations, ultimately it would be found insufficient to expel them, and the Jews would not allow them to live, fearing that everyone would be converted by their preaching to the name of Christ and turned away from the observance of Judaism, as if what they were preaching were the very truth of God. This is how we should understand his reference to the Jews, when he said of them, "They will put you out of the synagogues." For the witnesses, in other words, the martyrs of Christ, were similarly slain by the Gentiles. The Gentiles, however, did not think that it was to the true God but to their own false deities that they were doing service when they acted. But every Jew who killed the preachers of Christ considered that he was serving God, believing as he did that all who were converted to Christ were deserting the God of Israel. Tractates on the Gospel of John 93.3.[4]

Prior to "Service," Jews Purified Themselves. Origen: What the Savior said in prophesying to the disciples . . . was originally fulfilled in his own case. For those who required that he should die thought they were offering a service to God and had gone up to Jerusalem before the Passover to purify themselves. Commentary on the Gospel of John 28.235-36.[5]

Churches Might Have Been Synagogues. Augustine: But what harm was it for the apostles to be expelled from the Jewish synagogues, as if they were not going to separate themselves from it soon enough, although no one expelled them? No doubt he meant to announce that the Jews would refuse to receive Christ while the disciples . . . were not going to desert him. And so, the disciples, who could not exist without him, would also be thrown out along with him by those who would not have him as their dwelling

[1]CSCO 4 3:289. [2]Rom 10:2. [3]CS 111:152**. [4]NPNF 1 7:365-66**; CCL 36:560. [5]FC 89:339-40*; SC 385:172.

place. For certainly there were no other people of God than the seed of Abraham. And if they would only acknowledge and receive Christ, they would have remained as the natural branches in the olive tree.[6] The churches of Christ also would have been no different from the synagogues of the Jews. They would have been one and the same if they had also desired to remain in him. But since they refused, continuing to keep Christ outside, there was nothing left to do but put out of the synagogues those who would not abandon Christ. Tractates on the Gospel of John 93.2.[7]

Purpose in Partaking in Christ's Suffering. Cyprian: No one should wonder that we are harassed with constant persecutions and continually tried with increasing afflictions when the Lord before predicted that these things would happen in the last times. He has instructed us for the warfare through his teaching and exhortation. Peter also, his apostle, has taught that persecutions occur to test us. We are to look to the example of the righteous who have gone before us and are to be joined to the love of God by death and sufferings. For he wrote in his epistle, "Beloved, do not be surprised at the fiery ordeal that comes on you to prove you, as though something strange were happening to you. But rejoice in so far as you share Christ's sufferings, that you may also rejoice and be glad when his glory is revealed. If you are reproached for the name of Christ, you are blessed, because the spirit of glory and of God rests on you."[8] The name of Christ is indeed blasphemed by them but is glorified by us. Letter 55.2.[9]

16:3 *Persecuting the Son and the Father*

Those Who Persecute the Sent Persecute the Sender. Cyril of Alexandria: In these words the Lord Jesus Christ defends himself and also accuses the audacity of the Jews ... censuring those who dishonor him by their cruelty toward the holy apostles. For the charge of transgression will not merely have reference to their treatment of the saints but also will bear on the one who laid on them the service of apostleship. Just as God said to the holy Samuel concerning the children of Israel, "They have not rejected you, but they have rejected me."[10] Commentary on the Gospel of John 10.2.[11]

Endurance and Reward. Chrysostom: He says to them, in effect: It is sufficient comfort that you endure these things for my sake and the Father's. Here he reminds them of the blessedness of which he spoke at the beginning, "Blessed are you when people shall revile you, and persecute you and shall say all kinds of evil against you falsely, for my sake. Rejoice, and be exceeding glad. For great is your reward in heaven."[12] Homilies on the Gospel of John 77.3.[13]

16:4a *Remember What I Told You*

Remember Jesus' Words When Tested. Chrysostom: Let us also consider these things in our temptations when we suffer anything from wicked people, "looking to the Beginner and Finisher of our faith."[14] Let us consider that it is by wicked people and for virtue's sake and for his sake [that we suffer]. For if we reflect on these things, everything will be easier and more tolerable. Since one is even proud when suffering for those he loves, what kind of feeling will such a person have who suffers for the sake of God? For if Jesus, for our sake, calls that shameful thing, the cross, "glory,"[15] how much more should we think that way! And if we can so despise sufferings, much more shall we be able to despise riches and covetousness. We ought then, when about to endure anything unpleasant, to think not of the toils but of the crowns. For as merchants take into account not the seas only but also the profits, so should we count on heaven and confidence in

[6]Rom 11:17. [7]NPNF 1 7:364-65**; CCL 36:558-59. [8]1 Pet 4:12-14. [9]ANF 5:347-48; *Letter* 58.2 in CCL 3C:321-22. [10]1 Sam 8:7. [11]LF 48:437*. [12]Mt 5:11-12. [13]NPNF 1 14:284**. [14]Heb 12:2. [15]Jn 13:31.

God. If acquiring things seems pleasant, simply remember that this is not what Christ called us to, and it will immediately appear displeasing. And if it is hard for you to give to the poor, do not keep adding things up in your mind, but rather immediately transport your thoughts to the harvest that results from the sowing. And when it is hard to despise the love of a strange woman, think of the crown that comes after the struggle, and you shall easily bear the struggle. For if fear diverts a person from unseemly things, much more should the love of Christ. Virtue is difficult. But let us cast around its form the greatness of the promise of things to come. Indeed, those who are virtuous, even apart from these promises, see [virtue] beautiful in itself. This is why they go after it and work for it, because it seems good to God and not because it is a job they have to do. Homilies on the Gospel of John 77.4.[16]

16:4b *I Did Not Say These Things at the Beginning*

Proper Things at the Proper Time. Augustine: In the other three Evangelists, these predictions occur before the supper.[17] John implies the supper was over.... Still, if the other Evangelists relate them as given very near his passion, what John records here is strictly true as well when it says, "And I said these things to you at the beginning." Matthew, however, relates these prophecies as given by the Lord not only on the evening of the Passover, when he sat with his disciples, but also at the beginning, when the twelve apostles are named and sent on their work from God.[18] How do we reconcile this with our Lord's words here? ... We apply these words to the promise of the Holy Spirit and the testimony he would give amid their suffering. Jesus had not spoken of [the Comforter] at the beginning because he himself was with them.... And his presence was a sufficient consolation. But on the eve of his own departure, it was proper that he should tell them of the Spirit's coming by whom the love of God would be shed abroad in their hearts to preach the word of God with all boldness. Tractates on the Gospel of John 94.1-2.[19]

Reasons for Withholding Information. Chrysostom: "And these things," says he, "I did not tell you at the beginning." Why didn't he tell them at the beginning? He did not tell them so that no one might say that he was guessing based on the ordinary course of events. And why did he enter into a matter of such unpleasantness? I knew these things, he says, from the beginning and did not speak of them—not because I did not know them but "because I was with you." And this again was spoken after a human manner, as though he had said, I didn't tell you because you were in safety, and it was in your power to question me when you wanted to, and all the storms blew on me [not you], and so it was superfluous to tell you these things at the beginning. But did he not tell them this? Did he not call the Twelve and say to them, "You shall be brought before governors and kings for my sake," and, "they shall scourge you in the synagogues"?[20] How then can he say, "I did not tell you these things at the beginning"? He can say this because he had foretold their scourging and their being brought before princes, but not that their death should appear so desirable that the action should even be deemed a service to God. For this more than anything was enough to terrify them—that they were to be judged as impious and corrupters. We might also add that in that earlier place he spoke of what they should suffer from the Gentiles, but here he has added in a stronger way the acts of the Jews also, and told them that it was almost at their doors. Homilies on the Gospel of John 78.1.[21]

[16]NPNF 1 14:284-85**. [17]Mt 24:9; Mk 8:9-13; Lk 21:12-17. [18]Mt 10:1-15. [19]NPNF 1 7:366-67**; CCL 36:562. [20]Mt 10:17. [21]NPNF 1 14:286**.

16:5-11 The Coming of the Spirit

[5]But now I am going to him who sent me; yet none of you asks me, "Where are you going?" [6]But because I have said these things to you, sorrow has filled your hearts. [7]Nevertheless I tell you the truth: it is to your advantage that I go away, for if I do not go away, the Counselor will not come to you; but if I go, I will send him to you. [8]And when he comes, he will convince[x] the world concerning sin and righteousness and judgment: [9]concerning sin, because they do not believe in me; [10]concerning righteousness, because I go to the Father, and you will see me no more; [11]concerning judgment, because the ruler of this world is judged.

x Or *convict*

Overview: When Jesus speaks of his return to the Father, it is a reference to his ascension (Bede). The disciples are afflicted with paralyzing grief not only contemplating Jesus' absence but also the painful events that await them (Chrysostom, Augustine). And thus, his absence would create faith in those who would enjoy the blessing of not seeing and yet believing (Augustine). Christ's presence would impede the Spirit's coming since, as the Holy Spirit did not humble himself as the Son did, it was necessary that the form of the servant should be removed from their eyes; otherwise they would never think Christ was more than they saw him to be in his humiliation (Augustine). Jesus leaves so that we may be glorified (Cyril) and eligible to receive the gifts of the Spirit (Theodore), which were delayed until sin had been done away with (Chrysostom).

The Paraclete whom Jesus will send comforts the disciples and us (Bede). The most fitting and appropriate time for the mission of the Spirit, which is to unite us to the divine nature, was the occasion of our Savior's departure to heaven (Cyril). Jesus' departure helps faith move beyond the flesh of Christ (Augustine) as bodily vision gives way to spiritual vision (Gregory the Great) and the form of a servant gives way to the form of God (Augustine). His departure also enables the threefold spiritual presence of the Trinity within us (Augustine).

When the Spirit descends, he will show the power he has in exposing sinners through his threefold judgment (Ammonius).The Spirit convicts concerning sin since whatever is not of faith is sin (Augustine). As it is, there is a great difference between believing in Christ and believing that Jesus is the Christ (Augustine). The Spirit also convicts concerning righteousness by the mighty works he did, which were done in the name of the Savior condemned by the world (Ambrosiaster). Christ's return to the Father, who welcomes him, demonstrates his vindication (Chrysostom). When our hope is fulfilled or completed, as it is in our resurrection, that is also when our justification will be fully realized (Augustine). Unbelievers, who have heard the word of life in the same way as believers but still are unwilling to believe, are convicted of this righteousness because of their lack of faith (Bede). Our faith in him whom we have not seen, which is our righteousness, is what convicts the world of its own lack of righteousness (Augustine). The Spirit convicts concerning judgment when the prince of this world is judged, and in doing so, the Spirit brings freedom for all those oppressed by the devil (Origen). Because of Pentecost and the overwhelming power of the Spirit on display there (Theodore), the devil sees his defeat as he is forced to watch those souls going instead from hell to heaven (Ambrosiaster).

Satan is only a pretender to the title "ruler of this world" (Cyril), ruling over those who, in a perverse way, love the world rather than the world's maker (Bede).

16:5 *Returning to the Father*

Reference to Ascension. Bede: It is as if he were clearly saying, "By my ascension I shall return to him who determined that I was to become incarnate. And so great and so evident will be the honor of this ascension that there will be no need for any of you to ask where I am going, since all of you will see that I am on my way to heaven." But it is good that when he had said regarding his ascension, "I am going to him who sent me," he added, "And none of you asks me, 'Where are you going?' " Earlier on, when he was testifying publicly about his passion and saying, "You are not able to come where I am going,"[1] Peter questioned him saying, "Lord, where are you going?"[2] He received the answer, "Where I am going you cannot follow me now, but [you will follow me] later on." This was undoubtedly because they were not yet able to understand, not yet able to imitate the mystery of his passion and death. Yet they truly recognized the majesty of his ascension as soon as they saw it, and they wished with the entire capacity of their minds that they might deserve to follow [him]. Homilies on the Gospels 2.11.[3]

16:6 Sorrow over Jesus Leaving

Paralyzing Grief. Chrysostom: Great is the tyranny of despondency. We need great courage in order to stand strong against it and, after gathering from it what is useful, to let go of what is superfluous. And so, it has a purpose at times. When we ourselves or others sin, that is a good time to grieve. But when we fall into human difficulties, then despondency is useless. And now when it has overthrown the disciples, who were not yet perfect, see how Christ raises them again by his rebuke. They who before this had asked him ten thousand questions[4]. . . —these men, I say, now hearing, "they will put you out of the synagogues" and "will hate you" and "whoever kills you will think that he does God's service"—were so cast down as to be struck dumb, so that they say nothing to him. And so he reproaches them and says, "These things I did not say to you at the beginning, because I was with you. But now I go to him that sent me, and none of you asks me, 'Where are you going?' But because I have said these things to you, sorrow has filled your heart." Immoderate sorrow is a horrible thing, dreadful and even deadly, as Paul said, "Lest perhaps such a one should be swallowed up by too much sorrow."[5] Homilies on the Gospel of John 78.1.[6]

Afraid of Losing Jesus' Outward Presence. Augustine: Or, whereas they had asked him before where he was going and he had replied that he was going where they would not come, now he promises that he will go in such a way that no one will ask him where he goes. For a cloud received him [in broad daylight]. When he ascended up to heaven, they questioned him not in words but followed with their eyes.[7] . . . But our Lord saw what effect his words would produce on their minds. Not having yet that inward consolation that the Holy Spirit was to impart, they were afraid to lose the outward presence of Christ. And so, when they could no longer doubt from his own words that they were going to lose him, their human affections were saddened by the loss of their visible object. But he knew that it would be for their good because that inward sight that the Holy Spirit would use to console them was the better sight. Tractates on the Gospel of John 94.3-4.[8]

Absence Creates Faith. Augustine: So

[1]Jn 13:33. [2]Jn 13:36. [3]CS 111:98-99; CCL 122:253-54. [4]See Jn 13:36; 14:5, 8. [5]2 Cor 2:7. [6]NPNF 1 14:286**. [7]Acts 1:9-11. [8]NPNF 1 7:367**; CCL 36:563.

since we could in no way enjoy this blessing of not seeing and yet believing, unless we had received it from the Holy Spirit, it was very properly said, "It is to your advantage that I should go. For if I do not go away, the Advocate will not come to you. But if I do go away, I will send him to you."[9] In his divinity, of course, he is always with us. But unless he went away from us in the body, we would always be able to see his body in the flesh and would never believe in a spiritual way. And that is the only kind of faith by which we can be justified and made blessed and earn the right to contemplate this very Word who is God with God, through whom all things were made and who became flesh in order to dwell among us. Sermon 143.4.[10]

16:7a *If Christ Stays, the Counselor Will Not Come*

Christ's Presence Would Impede the Spirit's Coming. Augustine: This he says not because of any inequality between the Word of God and the Holy Spirit but because the presence of the Son of man among them would impede the coming of the [Spirit]. For the Holy Spirit did not humble himself, as the Son did, by taking on him the form of a servant.[11] It was necessary therefore that the form of the servant should be removed from their eyes. For so long as they looked on that form, they thought that Christ was no more than what they saw him to be. On the Trinity 1.9 [.18].[12]

Jesus Leaves So We May Be Glorified. Cyril of Alexandria: Jesus places us in the sight of the Father by departing into heaven as the firstfruits of humanity. . . . For he ascended to heaven as our forerunner, as the inspired Paul also says.[13] There, as man, he is truly the high priest of our souls, our comforter and the propitiation for our sins. And as God and Lord by his nature, Jesus sits on his own Father's throne, and this glory is reflected even on us. Commentary on the Gospel of John 10.2.[14]

Eligible for Gifts of the Spirit. Theodore of Mopsuestia: "If I do not go away, the Advocate will not come to you. But if I go, I will send him to you." This indeed is the order of things, so that when I am in glory but you are still anticipating participation in that glory, you may receive the grace of the Spirit. Therefore, if I go, you will also necessarily receive through the gift of the Spirit the participation in the gifts that I enjoy. But if I do not enjoy them first, you cannot expect them either. And since he, by leaving them, shows that he will invite them to receive those gifts, he proves in many ways that the gift of the grace of the Spirit is great. And this is only right, because the Spirit provides all the gifts given to people. Commentary on John 6.16.7.[15]

The Spirit's Delay Explained. Chrysostom: But why didn't the Spirit come before he departed? He could not come because the curse had not yet been taken away, sin had not yet been forgiven, and everything was still subject to the penalty for it. "It is necessary then," Jesus says, "that the enmity be put away, that we be reconciled to God and then receive that gift." But why does he say, "I will send him"? It means, "I will prepare you beforehand to receive him." For how can that which is everywhere be "sent"? In addition, he shows the distinction of the persons. Moreover, he speaks in this way for two reasons: first, because they were finding it hard to be separated from him, to persuade them to hold fast to the Spirit. And second, in order that they might cherish the Spirit. For Christ himself could have accomplished these things, but he concedes to the Spirit the working of miracles so that they might understand his dignity. For as the Father could have brought into being things that are, but it was the Son who did so in order that we might understand his power, so also is it in this case.

---

[9]Jn 16:7. [10]*WSA* 3 4:427; PL 38:786. [11]See Phil 2:7. [12]NPNF 1 3:27**; CCL 50:53-54. See also Bede *Homily* 2.11. [13]See Heb 9:24. [14]LF 48:442**. [15]CSCO 4 3:292. See also Gregory the Great *Morals on the Book of Job* 8.13.

For this reason he himself was made flesh by delegating the performing of this work to the Spirit, thus silencing those who take the argument of his ineffable love for an occasion of impiety. Homilies on the Gospel of John 78.3.[16]

16:7b *Jesus Will Send the Counselor*

The Paraclete Comforts the Disciples and Us. Bede: It is evident, and there is no need of a lengthy explanation why he calls this Spirit "the Paraclete," that is, "the Consoler." [The Spirit's] coming consoled and refreshed the hearts of the disciples when [Christ's] departure had caused them to be sad. But also, when [the Spirit] inspires a hope of pardon and heavenly mercy in any individual believers who are saddened about the commission of sin or are laboring under the ordinary afflictions of this life, he unquestionably relieves them of the anguish of their sorrow by enlightening their minds. Homilies on the Gospels 2.11.[17]

We Become Partakers of the Divine Nature Through the Spirit. Cyril of Alexandria: After Christ had completed his mission on earth, it still remained necessary that we should become partakers and sharers of the divine nature of the Word. We had to give up our own life and be so transformed that we would begin to live an entirely new kind of life that would be pleasing to God. However, this was something we could do only by sharing in the Holy Spirit. And the most fitting and appropriate time for the mission and descent of the Holy Spirit to us was . . . the occasion of our Savior's departure to heaven. As long as Christ was with them in the flesh, the believers would have thought that they possessed all the blessings he had to offer. But when the time came for him to ascend to his Father in heaven, it was necessary for him to be united through his Spirit to those who worshiped him and to dwell in our hearts through faith. Only by his presence within us in this way could he give us the confidence to cry out, "Abba, Father," and enable us to grow in holiness and, through our possession of the all-powerful Spirit, strengthen us to become invincible against the traps of the devil and the assaults of our fellow human beings.[18] . . .

You see that the Spirit changes those in whom he comes to dwell and alters the whole pattern of their lives. . . . With the Spirit within them it is quite natural for people who had been absorbed by the things of this world to become entirely other-worldly in their outlook and for cowards to become people of great courage. There is no question that this is what happened to the disciples. The strength they received from the Spirit enabled them to hold firmly to the love of Christ, facing the violence of the persecutors without fear. What our Savior said, then, was very true, that is, that it was to their advantage that he return to heaven. For that return was the occasion for the descent of the Spirit. Commentary on the Gospel of John 10.2.[19]

Faith Moves Beyond Christ in the Flesh. Augustine: For what does this mean, "If I do not go away, the Comforter will not come to you. But if I depart, I will send him to you"? Was it that he could not send him while located here himself? Who would venture to say so? Neither was it that the other [i.e., the Spirit] had withdrawn from where he was or that he had come from the Father in such a way that he did not still remain with the Father. And still further, how could he, even when having his own dwelling on earth, be unable to send him, who we know came and remained upon him at his baptism?[20] And even more so, how could this be the case when we know that the Son was never separable from [the Spirit]? What does it mean, then, "If I do not go away, the Comforter will not come to you?" It means that you cannot receive the Spirit so long

[16]NPNF 1 14:288**. [17]CS 111:100. [18]Cyril goes on to cite 1 Sam 10:6 and 2 Cor 3:17-18 as examples of how the Spirit changes the disposition of those in whom he dwells. [19]LF 48:443-44**. [20]See Jn 1:32.

as you continue to know Christ after the flesh. Tractates on the Gospel of John 94.4.[21]

Bodily Vision Gives Way to Spiritual Vision. Gregory the Great. It is as if he said plainly, If I do not withdraw my body from your eyes, I cannot lead you to the understanding of the invisible through the comforting Spirit. Morals on the Book of Job 8.24.41.[22]

The Form of Servant Gives Way to the Form of God. Augustine: The Holy Spirit the Comforter has brought us this blessing: that the form of the servant, received from the Virgin's womb, being once removed from the sight of our bodily eyes, we might start to focus the attention of purified minds on the very form of God in which he remained equal to the Father even when he had graciously appeared in the flesh. Sermon 143.3.[23]

The Spiritual Presence of the Trinity Enabled Within Us. Augustine: But with Christ's bodily departure, both the Father and the Son, as well as the Holy Spirit, were spiritually present with them. For if Christ had left them so that the Holy Spirit replaced him rather than dwelling along with him, what would have become of his promise, "Lo, I am with you always, even to the end of the world"[24] and, I and the Father "will come to him and will make our dwelling with him"?[25] He had also promised that he would send the Holy Spirit in such a way that he would be with them forever. Jesus knew, however, that though they were presently in a carnal condition, they would undoubtedly possess in a more comprehensive way both the Father, and the Son and the Holy Spirit. But we should in no way think that the Father is present without the Son and the Holy Spirit or [vice versa]. . . . Wherever any one of them is, there also is the Trinity, one God. Tractates on the Gospel of John 94.5.[26]

16:8 *When the Spirit Comes*

The Power of the Spirit's Descent Revealed. Ammonius: This is the power of the descent of the Holy Spirit, that "then the sin of those who have erred against me will be revealed." Whoever after the descent of the Holy Spirit did not believe in the Christ remained in their sins. Whoever did not believe in the sinless One will be condemned as a sinner. Fragments on John 538.[27]

16:9 *The Spirit Convicts Concerning Sin*

Whatever Is Not of Faith Is Sin. Augustine: When the Lord said of the Holy Spirit, "He shall convict the world of sin," he meant unbelief. For this is what he meant when he said, "Of sin because they believed not on me." And he means the same when he says, "If I had not come and spoken to them, they should not have sin."[28] He was not talking about [a time] before they had no sin. Rather, he wanted to indicate that very lack of faith by which they did not believe him even when he was present to them and speaking to them. These were the people who belonged to "the prince of the power of the air, who now works in the children of unbelief."[29] Therefore those in whom there is no faith are the children of the devil because they have nothing in their inner being that would cause them to be forgiven for whatever is committed either by human infirmity, ignorance or any evil will whatever. But the children of God are those who certainly, if they should "say that they have no sin, deceive themselves, and the truth is not in them," but immediately (as it continues) "when they confess their sins" (which the children of the devil do not do, or do not do according to the faith which is peculiar to the children of God), "he is faithful and just to forgive them their sins and to cleanse them from all unrighteousness."[30] Against Two Letters of the Pelagians 3.4.[31]

[21]NPNF 1 7:368*. [22]LF 18:447**. [23]*WSA* 3 4:426-27**. [24]Mt 28:20. [25]Jn 14:23. [26]NPNF 1 7:368**. [27]*JKGK* 329. [28]Jn 15:22. [29]Eph 2:2. [30]1 Jn 1:9. [31]NPNF 1 5:403**.

Belief in Christ. Augustine: Now there is a great difference between believing in Christ and in believing that Jesus is the Christ. For even the devils believe that he was the Christ. But the one who believes in Christ both loves Christ and puts his hope in him. Sermon 144.2.[32]

The World Reproved by the Spirit's Mighty Works. Ambrosiaster: In this way too the Holy Spirit reproved the world of sin, that is, by the mighty works he did in the name of the Savior who was condemned by the world. Questions on the Old and New Testament 89.2.[33]

16:10 *The Spirit Convicts Concerning Righteousness*

Going to the Father Vindicates Christ's Righteousness. Chrysostom: Jesus is saying here, "My going to the Father will prove that I have led an irreproachable life." For since they continually accused him of not being from God because he was a sinner and transgressor, the Spirit will take away from them this accusation as well. . . . Again when he says that the Spirit will convict the world, "of judgment, because the prince of this world is judged," he makes their argument concerning righteousness moot as well, inasmuch as he conquered the devil. If he had been a sinner, he could not have overthrown the devil. Not even a righteous person would have been strong enough to do that. "But those who trample on him afterward shall know that he has been condemned through me. And my resurrection, which is the mark of [my Father] who condemned the devil, will clearly show that the devil was not able to detain me. And so they can no longer say that I had a devil or that I was a deceiver." Homilies on the Gospel of John 78.1.[34]

Our Justification Is Complete. Augustine: And therefore we ought not to think of ourselves as having no part in that justice that the Lord himself is referring to, when he speaks "about justice, because I am going to the Father." After all, we too have risen again with Christ, and with our head we are Christ, for the time being in faith and hope. But our hope will be fulfilled in the final resurrection of the dead. But when our hope is fulfilled or completed, that is when our justification will be completed too.[35] It is the Lord who is going to complete it, and he showed us what we should hope for in his own flesh (that is, in our head), in which he rose again and ascended to the Father. Because this is what Scripture says: "He was handed over for our transgressions and rose again for our justification."[36] So the world is challenged about sin, in those who do not believe in Christ, and about justice, in those who rise again among the members of Christ. Sermon 144.6.[37]

Righteousness of Disciples, Believers and Unbelievers. Bede: The righteousness of Christ's disciples consisted in this, that they believed that the Lord, whom they discerned was a true human being, was also the true Son of God, and that they worshiped always with a definite love the one whom they knew had been taken away bodily from them. The righteousness of the believers, that is, of those who have not seen the Lord in his human body, consists in this, that with their hearts they believe and love him whom they have never seen with their bodily vision as true God and man. Unbelievers are convicted of this righteousness, [which arises from] faith because, when they hear the word of life in the same way [as believers], they are unwilling to believe [in a way that leads] to righteousness. Homilies on the Gospels 2.11.[38]

Our Faith, Our Righteousness, Convicts an Unbelieving World. Augustine: By what means, then, is the world to be

[32]*WSA* 3 4:431**. [33]CSEL 50:150. [34]NPNF 1 14:287**. [35]Lat *complebitur*. Our justification is complete now, but its full effects will not be seen until our resurrection. [36]Rom 4:25. [37]*WSA* 3 4:433; PL 38:790. [38]CS 111:101*.

reproved of righteousness, if not by the righteousness of believers? Accordingly, it is convinced of sin because it does not believe on Christ, and it is convinced of the righteousness of those who do believe. For the very comparison with believers is itself a reproving of unbelievers. . . . And since the cry of unbelievers usually is, "How can we believe what we do not see?" the righteousness of believers lies in this very definition [of faith]: "Because I go to the Father you will see me no more." For blessed are those who do not see and yet believe.[39] Those who saw Christ were not commended for what they saw, namely, the Son of man, but for believing what they did not see, namely, the Son of God. But after his servant form was itself also withdrawn from their view, then in every respect was the word truly fulfilled, "The just shall live by faith."[40]. . . This, then, he says, will be your righteousness by which the world shall be reproved . . . seeing that you shall believe in me as in one whom you shall not see. . . . In the future you will see me, not in my humility but in my exaltation; not in my mortality but in my eternity; not at the bar of justice but on the throne of judgment. And by this faith of yours, in other words, your righteousness, the Holy Spirit will reprove an unbelieving world. Tractates on the Gospel of John 95.2-3.[41]

16:11 *The Spirit Condemns the Prince of This World*

Freedom for the Oppressed. Origen: Jesus came to free all those oppressed by the devil and said of him with some befitting depth, "Now is the prince of this world judged." Against Celsus 8.54.[42]

The Overwhelming Power of the Spirit. Theodore of Mopsuestia: So awesome is the descent of the Spirit—because it is so great and powerful—that through its coming down on men and women the "sin" appears of those who made attempts on my life. They planned to kill him who was worthy of such honor and greatness, as the gift of the Spirit among those who believe in me, will clearly show. Also my "righteousness" will be known, which I preached among them with works and words and with great righteousness and performed with equity. From all this, in addition, it will become evident that the divine plan concerning my passion was not useless and vain. Its purpose was to condemn Satan. Indeed, when through the power of the gift of the Spirit ill people are healed, dead people resurrected, demons exorcised, then through all these works the condemnation of Satan will appear. If I did evil actions or taught false doctrine, I would receive a just punishment according to my actions. And especially after my death I would be despised. And my disciples would also necessarily share with me the same contempt. But when the presence of the Spirit, with the accomplishment of miracles, shows the contrary, when it places my disciples also in great glory, then the condemnation of Satan will appear and the manifestation of my glory will be evident, whereas the sin of my enemies will be condemned. He referred all these actions to the Spirit in order to reveal its nature and power through the things that it does. Commentary on John 6.16.8-11.[43]

Pentecost Proves Satan's Defeat. Ambrosiaster: The devils, seeing souls go from hell to heaven, knew that the prince of this world was judged. They saw that once he was brought to trial in the Savior's cause, he had lost all right to what he held. This was seen on our Savior's ascension but was declared plainly and openly in the descent of the Holy Spirit on the disciples. Questions on the Old and New Testaments 89.1-2.[44]

Satan Merely a Pretender to the Title. Cyril of Alexandria: God has called the devil

[39]Jn 20:29. [40]Rom 1:17; Hab 2:4. [41]NPNF 1 7:369-70**. [42]ANF 4:660**; SC 150:296. [43]CSCO 4 3:293. [44]CSEL 50:150.

the ruler of this world not as though it was actually true, or as though this overruling power were a dignity inherent in his being, but rather because he obtained the glory of ruling through fraud and covetousness. The devil is still influencing and ruling over those who are astray by reason of the wicked purpose that is in them that binds their minds in error and inextricably entangles them in the noose of captivity, even though it is in their power to escape by being converted through faith in Christ to a recognition of the one who is truly God. Satan is merely a pretender to the title of ruler and has no natural right to it as opposed to God, and he maintains it only through the abominable wickedness of those who are astray. Commentary on the Gospel of John 10.2.[45]

Satan Judged As Ruler of Those Who Love the World. Bede: He calls the devil "the ruler of this world" because he rules over those who, in a perverse way, love the world rather than the world's Maker. He was judged by the Lord when he said, "I saw Satan falling like lightning from heaven."[46] He was judged by [the Lord] when he was casting out demons and when he gave his disciples the power of treading on all the power of the enemy.[47] Accordingly, the world is convicted of the judgment by which the devil is judged when human beings are frightened by the example of the archangel who was condemned because of his pride, lest they presume to resist the will of God. The Holy Spirit convicts the world of the judgment by which the ruler of the world has been judged when the apostle Jude, speaking in the Holy Spirit, in order to correct the wickedness of evil human beings records the punishment of the proud angels, saying, "The angels who did not preserve their place of leadership but left their dwelling place, he has kept in eternal chains in darkness for the judgment of the great day."[48] Homilies on the Gospels 2.11.[49]

[45]LF 48:447-48**. [46]Lk 10:18, [47]Lk 10:19. [48]Jude 6. [49]CS 111:102*.

16:12-15 Gifts of the Spirit

[12]I have yet many things to say to you, but you cannot bear them now. [13]When the Spirit of truth comes, he will guide you into all the truth; for he will not speak on his own authority, but whatever he hears he will speak, and he will declare to you the things that are to come. [14]He will glorify me, for he will take what is mine and declare it to you. [15]All that the Father has is mine; therefore I said that he will take what is mine and declare it to you.

Overview: The Holy Spirit is able to overcome the inability of the apostles to bear Christ's words (Origen), which are divine mysteries still waiting to be revealed (Gregory of Nazianzus, Hilary). He has put these words off to a future time but has not cut them out altogether, preferring to have them revealed by the Spirit (Augustine), whose own divinity was to be more fully revealed (Gregory of Nazianzus). But there is to be no speculation on what remains hidden. The Spirit will instruct the heart through the spiritual light and Word that enlightens the inward eyesight and hearing. This does not mean that we will have full knowledge, since there are still things yet to be revealed in eternity (Augustine). Before the Spirit was given, the disciples were still slaves to the shadows of the Law, but afterward they were led by his teaching and discipline into all truth (Didymus). Christ here speaks of the Spirit's procession from both Father and Son, not of the Spirit being taught, since just because the Spirit hears and receives something does not imply additional knowledge is imparted to it (Apollinaris). The Spirit serves as the Lord's vicar in his absence (Tertullian) as the Spirit does not speak on its own but in the voice of the Trinity (Didymus, Ambrose). The fact that the Spirit speaks what he hears shows that he is not "of himself"; it is the Father only who is not of another (Augustine). The Spirit's words are nonetheless the same as his (Chrysostom).

The prophets, in turn, spoke what they heard from the Spirit (Didymus), and the faithful now declare the joys of heaven and their relief from anxiety through the gift of the Spirit into their lives (Bede, Chrysostom). The Spirit proclaims the glory of the Son by pouring love into believers' hearts and making them spiritual, enabling them to see the Son whom they had formerly known only in the flesh as equal to the Father (Augustine). In Christ's words here he demonstrates a close cohesion between the persons of the Trinity (Tertullian). In that giving and receiving that occurs in the Trinity there is no diminution or inferiority in either the giver or the receiver (Didymus, Augustine).

Although the Spirit of truth proceeds from the Father, this does not mean that the Spirit is a thing or possession that the Father and Son have (Didymus). There is a reciprocal sharing between the Father and the Son (Gregory of Nazianzus), since receiving from the Son is the same as receiving from the Father (Hilary).

16:12 *Many Things You Cannot Yet Bear*

The Holy Spirit Overcomes Their Inability. Origen: The Gospel shows him [the Paraclete] to be of such power and majesty that the apostles could not yet receive those things that the Savior wished to teach them until the advent of the Holy Spirit, who, pouring himself into their souls, might enlighten them regarding the nature and faith of the Trinity. On First Principles 2.7.3.[1]

Divine Mysteries. Gregory of Nazianzus: The Word himself intimated that there were things that could not now be borne but that should be borne and cleared up hereafter, and that John the forerunner of the Word and great voice of the truth declared even the whole world could not contain.[2] On Theology, Theological Oration 2(28).20.[3]

The Mystery of the Spirit. Hilary of Poitiers: According to the apostle, Lord, your Holy Spirit fully understands and penetrates your inmost depths. He also intercedes on my behalf, saying to you things for which I cannot find the words. Nothing can penetrate your being but what is divine already. Nor can the depths of your immense majesty be measured by any power that itself is alien or extrinsic to you. So, whatever enters into you is yours already, nor can anything that has the power to search your very depths ever have been other than your own. . . .

Your Holy Spirit proceeds through your Son from you. Though I may fail to grasp the full meaning of that statement, I give it nonetheless the firm assent of my mind and heart.

I may indeed show dullness and stupidity in my understanding of these spiritual matters. It is as your only Son has said: "Do not be surprised if I have said to you: 'You must be born again.' Just as the wind blows where it pleases and you hear the sound of it without knowing where it is coming from or going to, so will it be with everyone who is born again of water and the Holy Spirit."[4] By my regeneration I have received the faith, but I am still ignorant. And yet I have a firm hold on something that I do not understand. I am born again, capable of rebirth but without conscious

[1]ANF 4:285*; GCS 22(5):150. [2]Jn 21:25. [3]NPNF 2 7:295-96. [4]Jn 3:7-8.

perception of it. The Spirit abides by no rules. He speaks when he pleases, what he pleases and where he pleases. We are conscious of his presence when he comes, but the reasons for his approach or his departure remain hidden from us.

John tells us that all things came into being through the Son who is God the Word abiding with you, Father, from the beginning. Paul in his turn enumerates the things created in the Son, both visible and invisible, in heaven and on earth. And while he is specific about all that was created in and through Christ, of the Holy Spirit he considers it enough simply to say that he is your Spirit.

Therefore I concur with those chosen men in thinking that just as it is not expedient for me to venture beyond my mental limitation and predicate anything of your only-begotten Son except that, as those witnesses have assured us, he was born of you, so it is not fitting for me to go beyond the power of human thought and the teaching of those same witnesses by declaring anything regarding the Holy Spirit other than that he is your Spirit. Rather than waste time in a fruitless war of words, I would prefer to spend it in the firm profession of an unhesitating faith.

I beg you therefore, Father, to preserve in me that pure and reverent faith and to grant that to my last breath I may testify to my conviction. May I always hold fast to what I publicly professed in the creed when I was baptized in the name of the Father and of the Son and of the Holy Spirit. May I worship you, the Father of us all, and your Son together with you, and may I be counted worthy to receive your Holy Spirit who through your only Son proceeds from you. For me there is sufficient evidence for this faith in the words "Father, all that I have is yours, and all that is yours is mine," spoken by Jesus Christ my Lord who remains, in and from and with you, the God who is blessed for endless ages. Amen. On the Trinity 12.55-57.[5]

I Still Have Much to Say to You. Augustine: So that is how we must take what the Lord says to the disciples, when he says, "Everything I have heard from my Father I have made known to you."[6] If this had already happened, why does he tell them somewhere else, "I have still many things to say to you, but you cannot bear them now"? Certainly, everything I have heard from my Father I have made known to you. But when he says, "You cannot bear them now," and says, "I still have to say to you," he is putting things off, not cutting them off altogether. So because of the certainty of his hope, by which he knew without a doubt that he would do this, it was in his reckoning already as good as done. And that is why he could say, "I have made known to you." Sermon 27.5.[7]

The Deity of the Spirit to Be Revealed. Gregory of Nazianzus: Our Savior had some things that, he said, could not be borne at that time by his disciples (though they were filled with many teachings) . . . and therefore they were hidden. And again he said that all things should be taught by the Spirit when he would come to dwell among us.[8] Of these things, one, I take it, was the deity of the Spirit himself, made clear later on when such knowledge should be seasonable and capable of being received after our Savior's restoration. . . . For what greater thing than this did either he promise, or the Spirit teach? On the Holy Spirit, Theological Oration 5(31).27.[9]

No Speculation on What Is Hidden. Augustine: Now, however, you are perhaps wishing to know what those things were that the apostles were then unable to bear. But which of us would venture to assert his own present capacity for what they lacked in ability to receive? And this is why you are neither to expect me to tell you things that perhaps I could not comprehend myself were they told me by another; nor would

[5]*JFC* 66-67*; PL 10:468-72. See NPNF 2 9:233. [6]Jn 15:15. [7]*WSA* 3 2:106. [8]Jn 14:26. [9]NPNF 2 7:326*.

you be able to bear them even if I were talented enough to let you hear of things that are above your comprehension. It may be, indeed, that some among you are fit enough already to comprehend things that are still beyond the grasp of others. . . But what they were that he himself thus omitted to tell, it would be rash to have even the wish to presume to say. . . . Therefore, one may say that Christian people, even when desiring to hear, ought not to be told what those things are of which the Lord said here. . . . If the apostles were still unable, much more so are you. . . . For surely if we had read any such thing in the books confirmed by canonical authority, which were written after our Lord's ascension, it would not have been enough to have read such a statement, had we not also read in the same place that this was actually one of those things that the Lord was then unwilling to tell his disciples because they were unable to bear them. Tractates on the Gospel of John 96.1-2.[10]

16:13a *The Spirit Will Guide You into All Truth*

Taught by God the Spirit. Augustine: Beloved, you should not expect to hear from us what the Lord refrained from telling his disciples because they were still unable to bear them. Rather, seek to grow in the love that is shed abroad in your hearts by the Holy Spirit who is given to you[11] so that, fervent in spirit and loving spiritual things, you may be able—not by any sign apparent to your bodily eyes or any sound striking on your bodily ears but by the inward eyesight and hearing—to become acquainted with that spiritual light and that spiritual word that carnal people are unable to bear. For that cannot be loved that is altogether unknown. But when what is known, in however small a measure, is also loved, by the same love, one is led on to a better and fuller knowledge. If, then, you grow in the love that the Holy Spirit spreads abroad in your hearts, "He will teach you all truth," or, as other codices have it, "He will guide you in all truth"; as it is said, "Lead me in your way, O Lord, and I will walk in your truth."[12] So shall the result be, that not from outward teachers will you learn those things that the Lord at that time declined to utter, but you will all be taught by God,[13] so that the very things that you have learned and believed by means of lessons and sermons supplied from without . . . your minds themselves may have the power to perceive. Tractates on the Gospel of John 96.4.[14]

Knowledge Yet to Come in Eternity. Augustine: Accordingly, when he says, "He will teach you all truth" or "will guide you into all truth," I do not think the fulfillment is possible in anyone's mind in this present life. For who is there, while living in this corruptible and soul-oppressing body,[15] that can know all truth when even the apostle says, "We know in part"? But it is effected by the Holy Spirit, of whom we have now received the promise,[16] that we shall attain also to the actual fullness of knowledge that the same apostle references when he says, "But then face to face" and "Now I know in part, but then shall I know even as also I am known."[17] He is not talking about something he knows fully in this life but about something that would still be in the future when he would attain that perfection. This is what the Lord promised us through the love of the Spirit, when he said, "He will teach you all truth" or "will guide you unto all truth." Tractates on the Gospel of John 96.4.[18]

Still Slaves to the Shadows of the Law. Didymus the Blind: He means that his hearers had not yet attained to all those things that for his name's sake they were able to bear. And so, revealing more minor things, he puts off the greater for a future time. These were things they could not understand because the Spirit had not

[10]NPNF 1 7:371-72**. [11]Rom 5:5. [12]Ps 86:11 (85:11 LXX, Vg). [13]Jn 6:45. [14]NPNF 1 7:372-73**. [15]See Wis 9:15. [16]See 2 Cor 1:21. [17]1 Cor 13:12. [18]NPNF 1 7:373**.

yet been given, as the Evangelist says, "For the Spirit had not been given because Jesus had not yet been glorified,"[19] intimating the glory of Jesus was in his tasting death for all. And after the resurrection, when he appeared to his disciples, he breathed on them and said, "Receive the Holy Spirit" and again "You will receive the power of the Holy Spirit when he comes on you." Where the Spirit entered into their believing hearts, they were filled with wisdom and knowledge and other effects of the Spirit that would lead them into all truth. But, as yet, they were slaves to the types, and shadows and images of the Law, and they could not bear the truth of which the Law was the shadow. But when the Holy Spirit came, he would lead them by his teaching and discipline into all truth, transferring them from the dead letter to the quickening Spirit in whom alone all scriptural truth resides. On the Holy Spirit 33.[20]

16:13b *The Spirit Will Not Speak on His Own*

The Lord's Vicar. Tertullian: The Lord sent the Paraclete because, since human weakness could not receive everything at once, it might gradually be directed and regulated and brought to perfection of discipline by the Lord's vicar, the Holy Spirit. . . . And so, he declared the work of the Spirit. This, then, is the Paraclete's guiding office: the direction of discipline, the revelation of the Scriptures, the reforming of the intellect and the progress in us toward "better things." On the Veiling of Virgins 1.[21]

Speaking in the Trinity. Didymus the Blind: "He will not speak on his own," that is, not without me or without the Father's and my will. This is because he is not of himself but is from the Father and me. The fact that he exists and that he speaks he has from the Father and me. "I speak the truth," that is, I inspire as well as speak by him, since he is the Spirit of truth. To say and to speak in the Trinity must not be understood according to our usage but according to the usage of incorporeal natures, and especially the Trinity, which implants its will in the hearts of all of those believers who are worthy to hear it. . . . For the Father then to speak and the Son to hear, or vice versa, is a mode of expressing the identity of their nature and their agreement. Again, the Holy Spirit, who is the Spirit of truth and the Spirit of wisdom, cannot hear from the Son what he does not know, seeing he is the very thing that is produced from the Son, that is, truth proceeding from truth, Comforter from Comforter, God from God. And finally, in case anyone should separate him from the will and company of the Father and the Son, it is written, "Whatever he shall hear, that shall he speak." On the Holy Spirit 34, 36.[22]

The Spirit Does Not Speak Without Father and Son. Ambrose: The Son of God says concerning the Holy Spirit that "he will not speak from himself," that is, not without the participation of the Father and myself. For the Spirit is not divided and separated but speaks what he hears. . . . This means he shall not speak without me. For he speaks the truth, he breathes wisdom. He does not speak without the Father, for he is the Spirit of God. He does not hear from himself, for all things are of God. . . . Therefore what the Spirit says is the Son's, what the Son has given is the Father's. So neither the Son nor the Spirit speaks anything of himself. For the Trinity speaks nothing external to itself. On the Holy Spirit 2.12.131, 133, 134.[23]

16:13c *The Spirit Speaks What He Hears*

The Spirit Hears and Knows from the Father. Augustine: When it says that the Holy Spirit "shall not speak of himself; but whatever he hears, that shall he speak," we should

[19]Jn 7:39. [20]PL 23:132-33. [21]ANF 4:27**. See also *Prescription of Heretics* 28.6. [22]PL 23:133-34. [23]NPNF 2 10:131-32**. See also *On the Christian Faith* 5.11.133.

understand this as saying that he is not of himself. It is the Father only who is not of another. For the Son is born of the Father, and the Holy Spirit proceeds from the Father. But the Father is neither born of, nor proceeds from, another. And yet this should not occasion in human thought any idea of disparity in the supreme Trinity. For the Son is equal to him of whom he is born just as the Holy Spirit is equal to him from whom he proceeds. But what difference there is in such a case between proceeding and being born would be too lengthy to make the subject of inquiry and dissertation. It would also make our definition liable to the charge of rashness, even after we had discussed it. For such a thing is of the utmost difficulty, both for the mind to comprehend in any adequate way—even if it had reached the level of such comprehension—and for the tongue to explain no matter how capable the one that presides as a teacher or he that is present as a hearer are. . . . Because, then, [the Spirit] is not of himself, but of him from whom he proceeds and of whom he has essence, it is of him [i.e. the Father] that he has knowledge. From the Father, therefore, the Spirit has hearing, which is nothing else than knowledge. Tractates on the Gospel of John 99.4.[24]

The Words Are the Same. Chrysostom: Here most of all Christ shows his dignity, for to foretell things to come is especially the property of God. Now if he also learned this from others, he will have nothing more than the prophets. But here Christ declares a knowledge brought into exact agreement with God so that it is impossible that he should speak anything else. But "shall receive of mine" means "shall receive, either of the grace that came into my flesh or of the knowledge that I also have, not as needing it or as learning it from another, but because it is one and the same." And why did he speak this way and not otherwise? Because they do not yet understand the word concerning the Spirit, which is why he provides for one thing only, that the Spirit should be believed and received by them and that they should not be offended. For since he had said, "One is your Teacher, even Christ"[25]—so that they might not think that they disobeyed him in obeying the Spirit—he says, "his teaching and mine are one. Whatever I would have taught is what he also will speak. Do not suppose his words are other than mine, for those words are mine and confirm my opinion. For the will of the Father, and of the Son and of the Holy Spirit is one." He also wants this for us, which is why he says, "that they may be one, as you and I are one."[26] Homilies on the Gospel of John 78.3.[27]

16:13d *Declaring the Things to Come*

Prophets Foresee by the Spirit. Didymus the Blind: By the Spirit of truth too the knowledge of future events has been granted to holy people. Prophets filled with this Spirit foretold and saw things to come, as if they were present: "And he will show you things to come." On the Holy Spirit 38.[28]

Declaring the Joys of Heaven. Bede: It is true that a countless number of the faithful have foreknown and proclaimed coming events as a result of the gift of the Spirit. There are some who, filled with the grace of the Spirit, cure the sick raise, raise the dead, command demons and shine forth with many virtues. They lead an angelic life on earth. Nevertheless they do not know by a revelation of the Spirit the things that are to come about there. We can also take these words of the Lord to mean that when the Spirit comes, he may announce to us "the things that are to come" when he brings back to our memory the joys of the heavenly fatherland, when he makes known to us the feasts of the commonwealth on high through the gift of his breathing on [us]. He announces to us "the things that are to come" when he draws us away from the delights of present things and kindles within us

[24]NPNF 1 7:382-83. [25]Mt 23:10. [26]See Jn 17:11. [27]NPNF 1 14:289*. [28]PL 23:143.

the desire for the kingdom that has been promised us in heaven. Homilies on the Gospels 2.11.[29]

Relief from Anxiety. Chrysostom: In this way, then, he raised their spirits. For there is nothing for which people so long as the knowledge of the future.... He relieves them from all anxiety by showing them that dangers would not fall on them unawares. Homilies on the Gospel of John 78.2.[30]

16:14 *Glory and Mutual Declaration*

Christ's Fame Proclaimed. Augustine: He will make me clearly known[31] by pouring love into the hearts of believers and making them spiritual and thus able to see that the Son whom they had known before only according to the flesh—and who they thought was only a man like themselves—was equal to the Father. Or at least, when his love filled them with boldness and cast out fear, they would proclaim Christ to men and women, and in this way they would spread Christ's fame throughout the whole world.... For what they were going to do in the power of the Holy Spirit, this the Holy Spirit says he does himself. Tractates on the Gospel of John 100.1.[32]

Christ Speaking of the Spirit's Procession. Apollinaris of Laodicea: The work and teaching of the Spirit will redound to my glory, for the Spirit also proceeds from me. For when he says "from me," it is clear that he is also from the Father, for "what belongs to me belongs to the Father." Then he hears again in the same manner the phrase "he will take from what is mine." It is not as if some knowledge comes on the Spirit—and that at the present time. It would be a horrible thing, indeed, almost an evil conjecture, to state that the Spirit received his instruction when he was about to bring it to humankind. Indeed, it would be a horrible suggestion if someone should say that the Spirit was taught at all. Then he would no longer be believed to dwell in people and bring all wisdom to them, if he did not have some innate wisdom in him but rather needed to be taught. Thus, when he said, "he will take from what is mine and announce it to you," he meant simply to say that the Spirit would proceed from him. The statements speak of lesser things since they are adapted to what is well known to people, but the real glory of the Spirit is greater since it pertains to divinity. Moreover, it is said that God listens to a person's words. However, it is clear that nothing is added at that time to the knowledge of God but that even before we spoke our words, he knew our prayers and had created everything according to his knowledge from the very beginning of his creation, knowing full well the changes in emotions that would take place in his creatures. Nonetheless, it is still said, "Hear, O Lord" and "The Lord heard." And yet it is not necessary for God to wait for anything in time, as if there would be some change in God because of the prayers of human beings, or as if God would gain some knowledge from what is being said. Rather, these words are being spoken in a human fashion, so to speak, while among the godly they are understood in a divine fashion. In your suppositions the unchanging and unchangeable nature of the glory of God is not purified because he hears people speaking. So then simply because the Spirit hears and receives something does not mean that he will receive any additional knowledge or a change to the unchanging nature of the Spirit. Fragments on John 120.[33]

---

[29]CS 111:103-4*. [30]NPNF 1 14:288**. [31]Augustine notes a little later on in this same section that the Greek word *doxasei* has been rendered by the Latin interpreters in their respective translations as either *clarificabit* ("shall make clearly known") or *glorificabit* ("shall glorify"). He chose the former sense here, noting that *doxa,* from which *doxasei* derives, could be interpreted as both *claritas* ("brightness") and *gloria* ("glory"). According to Augustine, he is within the stream of the older Latin writers who defined glory as "the generally diffused and accepted fame of anyone accompanied with praise," although, in this case, it is not Christ but the world that receives benefit from this glory. [32]NPNF 1 7:385**. [33]*JKGK* 48-49.

Close Cohesion in the Trinity. Tertullian: He says, "He will take of mine," as I myself have taken of the Father's. So the close series of the Father in the Son and the Son in the Paraclete makes three who cohere, the one attached to the other. Against Praxeas 25.[34]

Names of God Are Christ's. Tertullian: "All things that the Father has," he says, "are mine"—and why not also the names? When therefore you read of God Almighty, and the Most High, and the God of hosts, and the King of Israel and "I am," beware lest by these the Son also is shown to be of his own right God Almighty, as being the Word of God Almighty, and as having received power over all.[35] Against Praxeas 17.[36]

No Diminution of Giver or Receiver. Didymus the Blind: To "receive" [or "take"] must be taken here in a sense agreeable to the divine nature. As the Son in giving is not deprived of what he gives or imparts to others with any loss of his own, so too the Holy Spirit does not receive what before he did not have. For if he received what before he did not have—the gift being transferred to another—the giver would be thereby a loser. We must understand then that the Holy Spirit receives from the Son that which belonged to his nature and that there are not two substances implied, one giving and the other receiving, but one substance only. In the same way, the Son too is said to receive from the Father that wherein he himself subsists. For neither is the Son anything but what is given him by the Father, nor is the Holy Spirit any substance but that which is given him by the Son. On the Holy Spirit 36-37.[37]

16:15 *All That the Father Has Belongs to the Son*

The Holy Spirit Not Inferior. Augustine: For the Holy Spirit is not inferior to the Son, as certain heretics have imagined, as if the Son received from the Father and the Holy Spirit received from the Son in reference to some kind of gradation of natures. . . . He himself immediately solves this difficulty and explains his own words: "All things that the Father has are mine; therefore said I, that he shall take of mine and shall show it to you." Tractates on the Gospel of John 100.4.[38]

The Spirit Not a Thing or Possession. Didymus the Blind: As if he said, Although the Spirit of truth proceeds from the Father, yet all things that the Father has are mine, and even the Spirit of the Father is mine and receives of mine. But beware, when you hear this, that you do not think it is a thing or possession that the Father and the Son have. That which the Father has according to his substance, that is, his eternity, immutability, goodness, the Son has also. Away with the cavils of logicians who say, Therefore the Father is the Son. If he had indeed said, "All that God has are mine," impiety might have taken occasion to raise its head. But when he said, "All things that the Father has are mine," by using the name of the Father, he declares himself the Son, and being the Son, he does not usurp the paternity, though by the grace of adoption he is the Father of many saints. On the Holy Spirit 38.[39]

Reciprocal Sharing. Gregory of Nazianzus: All things that the Father has are the Son's. And . . . all that belongs to the Son is the Father's. Nothing then is peculiar [to any person] because all things are in common. For their being itself is common and equal, even though the Son receives it from the Father. On the Son, Theological Oration 4(30).11.[40]

Are Receiving and Proceeding the Same? Hilary of Poitiers: Our Lord therefore has not left it uncertain whether the Paraclete is from the Father or from the Son. . . . For he is sent by the Son and proceeds from the Father; both these he

[34]*TTAP* 169. [35]Mt 28:20. [36]*TTAP* 155. [37]PL 23:134-35. [38]NPNF 1 7:386**. [39]PL 23:135-36. [40]NPNF 2 7:313*.

receives from the Son. You ask whether to receive from the Son and to proceed from the Father are the same thing. . . . Certainly, to receive from the Son must be thought one and the same thing with receiving from the Father. For when he says, "All things that the Father has are mine, therefore I said that he shall receive of mine" . . . he shows here that these things are received from him because all things the Father has are the Son's, but also that they are received from the Father. . . . This unity has no diversity, nor does it matter from whom the thing is received, since that which is given by the Father is counted also as given by the Son. ON THE TRINITY 8.20.[41]

[41]NPNF 2 9:143**.

16:16-22 THE GRIEF OF THE DISCIPLES

[16]"A little while, and you will see me no more; again a little while, and you will see me." [17]Some of his disciples said to one another, "What is this that he says to us, 'A little while, and you will not see me, and again a little while, and you will see me'; and, 'because I go to the Father'?" [18]They said, "What does he mean by 'a little while'? We do not know what he means." [19]Jesus knew that they wanted to ask him; so he said to them, "Is this what you are asking yourselves, what I meant by saying, 'A little while, and you will not see me, and again a little while, and you will see me'? [20]Truly, truly, I say to you, you will weep and lament, but the world will rejoice; you will be sorrowful, but your sorrow will turn into joy. [21]When a woman is in travail she has sorrow, because her hour has come; but when she is delivered of the child, she no longer remembers the anguish, for joy that a child[j] is born into the world. [22]So you have sorrow now, but I will see you again and your hearts will rejoice, and no one will take your joy from you."

j Greek *a human being*

OVERVIEW: Jesus speaks of what will happen "in a little while," alluding to his betrayal, crucifixion and burial (BEDE) but also to his resurrection (AUGUSTINE).These are words of consolation for the disciples, since they indicate Jesus' death is only a translation to his future resurrected state (CHRYSOSTOM), although he is also vague in many details in order, for the moment, to spare the disciples the fear they would soon enough undergo (CYRIL). The grief and subsequent joy the disciples experience mirrors that of those in the church today who rightly lament and weep over the present time, being as yet incapable of seeing their Lord face to face (BEDE). But just as suffering is a time for weeping, the resurrection will be a time for laughter (DIONYSIUS). Those who are of the world may laugh now (CYRIL), but it is Christians who will later rejoice as the world mourns (TERTULLIAN). Jesus likens these temporary sufferings to the pains of childbirth (CHRY-

SOSTOM), looking toward the faithful who are birthed into heaven at their death (BEDE). The joy that Christ offers is much more lasting than that of the world (CYPRIAN). It is a joy that will find its full completion in the life that is yet to come (AUGUSTINE).

16:16 *In a Little While*

ALLUDING TO BETRAYAL, CRUCIFIXION AND BURIAL. BEDE: Since he spoke these words on the night on which he was betrayed,[1] it was "a little while," that is, the [remaining] time of that same night and that of the following day, until the hour [came] when they would begin not to see him. For he was arrested on that night by the Jews, and he was crucified the next day when it was late. He was taken down from the cross and shut off from human sight within the confines of the sepulcher. "And again" it was "a little while" until they saw him again, for he rose from the dead on the third day and appeared to them with many proofs throughout forty days.[2] As to why there had to be "a little while" when they would not see him, "and again a little while" and they would see him, he added the reason, saying, "Because I am going to the Father," as if he were saying unmistakably, "After a little while I am going to be hidden from your sight within the closed space of the grave, and again after a little while I am going to appear for you to look at, after the sovereignty of death has been destroyed. This is so that I may now return to the Father, since the divinely arranged plan of my taking mortality on myself has been fulfilled, together with the triumph of my resurrection." HOMILIES ON THE GOSPELS 2.13.[3]

THE NEARNESS AND THEIR IGNORANCE TROUBLE THEM. AUGUSTINE: What troubled them is that he said, "A little while and you shall not see me, and again a little while and you shall see me." For in the words that preceded this Gospel, he had not said, "A little while" but had said, "I go to the Father. And you shall see me no longer."[4] And he appears as though he is speaking quite plainly, nor did they need to ask each other anything regarding this saying. But now, what was obscure to them and was soon after made plain to them is very plain to us also. For after a little while he suffered, and they did not see him. And again after a little while he arose, and they saw him. TRACTATES ON THE GOSPEL OF JOHN 101.1.[5]

WORDS OF CONSOLATION. CHRYSOSTOM: But then, if one examines, these are words of consolation: "Because I go to the Father." For they show that his death was only a translation. And more consolation follows, for he does not say merely, "A little while and you will see me no longer" but adds, "A little while and you shall see me." In this way he shows that he would return, that his departure would be for a brief time only and that his presence with them would be everlasting. HOMILIES ON THE GOSPEL OF JOHN 79.1.[6]

DELIBERATELY VAGUE. CYRIL OF ALEXANDRIA: Since he had said a little before this that he would reveal to them through his Holy Spirit all things that were necessary and profitable to them, he also tells them of his passion and that then would come his ascension into heaven. After this would follow the most necessary descent of the Holy Spirit. Returning now to the Father, there would be no more mutual conversing in the flesh with his holy apostles. He uses only a few words, lessening in this way the sharpness of their sorrow. For he knew that the fear his disciples were going to face would not be easy and that they were going to be tested by the most piercing grief, awaiting in dread grave and unendurable evils after the Savior had ascended to his Father in heaven, leaving them alone. Because of this, I believe, he does not openly tell them that he is about to die and that the fury of the Jews was about to break on him. Rather, sympathetically

[1] 1 Cor 11:23. [2] Acts 1:3. [3] CS 111:117-18. [4] Jn 16:10. [5] NPNF 1 7:387*. [6] NPNF 1 14:291**.

and mingling great delicacy with his words, he shows them that the sufferings of his passion will swiftly be followed by the joy of his resurrection, saying to them, "A little while and you shall not see me, and again a little while and you shall see me." For the time of his death was now at hand, when the Lord would be taken from the sight of his disciples. And indeed, it would be for a little time until he destroyed the power of hell and opened the gates of darkness to those who dwelled there. Then he would again raise up his temple.[7] Once he accomplished this, he would again appear to his disciples, promising that he would remain with them all the days of this world, as it is written.[8] For though absent in the flesh, having placed himself before the Father for our sake and sitting at the right hand of his begetter, he dwells in the just through his Spirit and remains forever one with his saints. For he has promised that he will not leave them as orphans.[9] Commentary on the Gospel of John 11.2.[10]

16:17-20 *Sorrow and Joy for Believers*

Sorrow and Joy, Then and Now. Bede: What he added by way of explanation to those inquiring of him, "Truly, truly, I say to you that you will lament and weep, but the world will rejoice. You will be sorrowful, but your sorrow will be changed to joy" is fitting to their condition and to that of the entire church. Those who loved Christ lamented and wept when they saw him apprehended by his enemies, bound, led before the Sanhedrin, condemned [to death], scourged, exposed as an object of derision and finally crucified, his side pierced with a lance and buried. Those who loved the world . . . rejoiced when they condemned to a shameful death one who was troubling for them even to look at. The disciples were sorrowful when their Lord was put to death, but when they acknowledged his resurrection, their sorrow was changed to joy. And when they saw the mighty power of his ascension, they were raised up to an even higher level of joy, praising and blessing God.[11] . . .

But this discourse of the Lord is also appropriate to all believers who are striving to arrive at eternal joys through the tears and distress of the present [life]. They rightly lament and weep and are sorrowful during the present [time], since they are not yet capable of seeing him whom they love. As long as they are in their body, they recognize that they are on a journey and [absent] from their fatherland and kingdom. They have no doubt that they must reach their crown by labors and contests. Their sorrow will be changed to joy when, after the struggle of this present life is over, they receive the prize of everlasting life, about which it is said in the psalm, "Those who sow in tears will reap in joy."[12] Homilies on the Gospels 2.13.[13]

Laughing at the Time of Resurrection. Dionysius of Alexandria: "A time to weep, and a time to laugh."[14] A time to weep, when it is the time of suffering, as when the Lord also says, "Truly I say to you, that you shall weep and lament."[15] But to laugh at the resurrection: "For your sorrow," he says, "shall be turned into joy." Fragment 1.[16]

The Worldly Shall Not Always Rejoice. Cyril of Alexandria: When Christ died according to the flesh, his disciples mourned, but the world rejoiced at his passion. If, however, the mourning of the saints was turned into joy when death and corruption were rendered powerless by Christ our Savior's resurrection from the dead, then surely in a similar way the joy of the worldly minded was lost in sorrow. Commentary on the Gospel of John 11.2.[17]

Mourn While the World Rejoices. Tertullian: If we rejoice with the world, it is to be feared that we shall also mourn with the world. But let us mourn while the world rejoices, and we

[7]Jn 2:19. [8]Mt 28:20. [9]See Jn 14:18, or "comfortless." [10]*LF* 48:459-60**. [11]Lk 24:53. [12]Ps 126:5 (125:5 LXX, Vg). [13]CS 111:119*. [14]Eccles 3:4. [15]See also Lk 6:25. [16]ANF 6:114. [17]LF 48:463**.

shall afterward rejoice when the world mourns. On Idolatry 13.[18]

16:21 *Pains of Childbirth Bring Joy*

Birth Pangs of Death Loosed. Chrysostom: And he has used a comparison that the prophets frequently employed, comparing sufferings with the excessive pains of childbirth. What he meant is something like this: "Sufferings like birth pangs will lay hold of you, but the pain of childbirth is a cause of joy." This confirms his words about the resurrection and shows that his departure from them was like passing from the womb into the light of day. It is as though he had said, "Don't be amazed that I bring you to what is profitable for you by way of such sorrow, since even a mother, to become a mother, passes in a similar way through pain." Here also he implies something mystical, that he has removed the birth pangs of death and caused a new person to be born of them. Furthermore, he not only said that the pain shall pass away but also that "she does not even remember it," so great is the joy that follows; so also shall it be with the saints. And yet the woman does not rejoice because "a human being has come into the world" but because a child has been born to her. For if the former had been the case, nothing would have hindered the barren woman from rejoicing over another who gives birth to a child. Homilies on the Gospel of John 79.1.[19]

Martyrs' Birthdays. Bede: Just as a woman is glad when a human being has been born into the world, so the church is filled with fitting exultation when a multitude of the faithful are born into the life to come. [The church] labors and groans greatly at the present [time] over their birth, and it sorrows like [a woman] in travail. It should not seem odd to anyone that a person's departure from this life is said to be his birth. Just as it is customary to say that a person "is born" when he comes forth from his mother's womb and emerges into the light here [on earth], so also can someone be perfectly appropriately referred to as "born" when he is released from the bonds of the flesh and raised up to eternal light. Hence church practice has been that the day on which blessed martyrs or confessors of Christ departed from the world we call their birthday, and their solemn festival is not spoken of as their "funeral" but as their "birthday." Homilies on the Gospels 2.13.[20]

16:22 *No One Will Take Your Joy from You*

True Joy Is in Christ. Cyprian: Does it delight us to stand here long among the swords of the devil when we should rather long for and choose to hurry toward Christ? . . . Who would not choose to be free from sorrow? Who would not speed toward joy? But our sorrow is indeed to be turned into joy, as our Lord makes clear. . . To see Christ is to rejoice, and we cannot have joy unless we see him. What blindness of mind or what foolishness is it to love the world's afflictions, and punishments and tears, and not rather to rush to the joy that can never be taken away! On Mortality. 5.[21]

Joy Future. Augustine: Now the church is in travail, longing for this fruit of all its labor. Then [i.e., in the future] it will bring it to birth in its actual contemplation. Now it is groaning and in labor; then it will bring forth in joy. Now it brings forth in prayer; then it will bring forth in praise. And accordingly it is a male child since it is toward this fruit of [the church's] eager longing that all the tasks of its activity are directed. For he alone is free of every bond, for he is desired of himself and not for any other end. All its actions are in service to him. For what is worthily done is directed toward him because it is done for his sake. He is to be had and to be held because of himself, not because of another beyond him. Here then is the end that contents us. Therefore

[18]ANF 3:69**. [19]NPNF 1 14:291**. [20]CS 111:121*. [21]ANF 5:470**.

it shall be eternal, for no end will suffice for us if it is not the One of which there is no end. It was this thought that inspired Philip when he said, "Show us the Father, and it is enough for us."[22] And in that showing the Son promises us himself also. . . . This is the joy that "no one shall take from you." Tractates on the Gospel of John 101.5.[23]

[22]Jn 14:8. [23]NPNF 1 7:388**.

16:23-28 Asking in the Name of the Son

[23]In that day you will ask nothing of me. Truly, truly, I say to you, if you ask anything of the Father, he will give it to you in my name. [24]Hitherto you have asked nothing in my name; ask, and you will receive, that your joy may be full.

[25]I have said this to you in figures; the hour is coming when I shall no longer speak to you in figures but tell you plainly of the Father. [26]In that day you will ask in my name; and I do not say to you that I shall pray the Father for you; [27]for the Father himself loves you, because you have loved me and have believed that I came from the Father. [28]I came from the Father and have come into the world; again, I am leaving the world and going to the Father.

Overview: Christ says that in that day when we see him face to face, we will no longer ask anything of him because all our longings and questions will be answered (Augustine). But while we are still here, our petitions are important, and one who is scrupulous about prayer will not address prayer to the Father without the Son (Origen). Having Christ as our Advocate with the Father, we can be confident in our prayers (Cyprian) because of the power of his name (Chrysostom). And so, we can ask for "anything" in his name, although "anything" should be understood of those things that have to do with the life of blessedness and salvation (Bede). Our joy, then, becomes complete when we enjoy God in the Trinity in whose image we were made (Augustine). We should pray for what can truly satisfy (Augustine) through the name of the Son, for we can draw near to God the Father in no other way (Cyril). We can count on God's provision just as he cares for the halcyon (Basil).

In saying he will speak to the disciples plainly of the Father, Jesus is either referring to the time when face to face (Augustine) they will be enlightened through the Spirit (Cyril), or to that time after the end of the world when we shall clearly behold the glory of God. Jesus is alluding to the manifestation of his equality with the Father (Gregory the Great) as it is Father and Son who together hear those who ask (Augustine); although insofar as he is man, Christ is also said to intercede for us and can do so because he is consubstantial with the Father (Theodore). It is a gift of God that we are able to love him since he would not have created in us something he could love unless he loved us before he created that something (Augustine). When we pray to him, God places himself as our debtor, placing himself under obligation to hear our requests (Chrysostom).

Christ says, "I came forth from the Father and am come into the world," referring first to his oneness with the Father and then to his incarnation (Hilary). His being from the Father was by generative, not creative, means (John of Damascus). He left his Father and then us, in one sense, but in neither case is he ever far away (Cyril). He came forth from the Father because he is of the Father, and he returns to him by his ascension when he withdraws his bodily presence from his, but he is still here ruling the world (Augustine). When he tells them he is leaving the world and going to the Father, he affirms that his disciples' faith is not in vain and that they would still be under his protection (Chrysostom). But when Christ returns to his Father, he brings our human nature along with him into heaven (Bede).

16:23 *In That Day You Will Ask Nothing of Me*

All Our Longings and Questions Will Be Satisfied. Augustine: The verb "to ask" used here means not only to entreat but also to question. And the Greek Gospel, of which this is a translation, has a word that may also be understood in both senses, so that by it the ambiguity is not removed.[1] Even if we could remove the ambiguity, it still would not remove every difficulty. For we read that the Lord Christ, after he rose again, was both questioned and petitioned. He was asked by the disciples, on the eve of his ascension into heaven, when he would be manifested and when the kingdom of Israel would come.[2] And even when he was already in heaven, he was petitioned [asked] by Stephen to receive his spirit.[3] And who dares either to think or say that Christ ought not to be asked, sitting as he does in heaven, and yet was asked while he lived here on earth? Or that he ought not to be asked in his state of immortality, although it was our duty to ask him while still in his state of subjection to death? . . .

For by his going to the Father, they soon would not see him. And for this reason, therefore, his words did not mean that he was about to die and to be withdrawn from their view till his resurrection. But [it meant] that he was about to go to the Father, which he did do after his resurrection when . . . after forty days he ascended into heaven.[4] He therefore addressed the words "a little while, and you shall no more see me" to those who saw him at the time in bodily form because he was about to go to the Father and was never thereafter to be seen in that mortal state wherein they now beheld him when he was addressing them at that moment. But the words that he added, "And again a little while, and you shall see me," he gave as a promise to the church universal, just as he gave another promise, "Lo, I am with you always, even to the end of the world."[5] The Lord is not slow concerning his promises. And so, in a little while, we shall see him, but we will have no further requests to make, no questions to put forward. For nothing shall remain to be desired, nothing will lie hidden that needs to be inquired about. This little while appears long to us, because it is still going on. But when it is over, we shall then feel what a little while it was. So let us not make our joy then be like that of the world. Tractates on the Gospel of John 101.4, 6.[6]

Ask the Father Through Christ. Origen: And so, when the saints give thanks to God in their prayers, they acknowledge through Christ Jesus the favors he has done. And if it is true that one who is scrupulous about prayer ought not to pray to someone else who prays but rather to the Father whom our Lord Jesus taught us to address in prayers, it is especially true that no prayer should be addressed to the Father without him, who clearly points this out himself when he says, "Truly, truly, I say to you, if you ask anything of the Father, he will give it to you in my name. Up till now you have asked nothing in my name. Ask, and you will receive, that your joy may be full." Now he did not say "ask me" or simply "ask the Father." On the contrary, he said, "If you ask any-

[1]Gk *erōtēsete*. [2]Acts 1:6. [3]Acts 7:59. [4]Acts 1:3, 9. [5]Mt 28:20. [6]NPNF 1 7:388-89**

thing of the Father, he will give it to you in my name." For until Jesus taught this, no one asked the Father in the name of the Son. And what Jesus said was true, "Up till now you have asked nothing in my name." And also true was his saying, "Ask, and you will receive, that your joy may be full." On Prayer 15.2.[7]

Ask, and He Will Give. Cyprian: Let Christ, who dwells within our heart, also dwell in our voice. And since we have him as an advocate with the Father for our sins, let us, when as sinners we petition on behalf of our sins, put forward the words of our advocate. For since he says that "whatever we shall ask of the Father in his name, he will give us," how much more effectually shall we obtain what we ask in Christ's name, if we ask for it in his own prayer! The Lord's Prayer 3.[8]

The Power of the Name. Chrysostom: He shows the power of his name when—even if it is neither seen nor called on but only named—he even gains our approval with the Father. But when has this taken place? When they said, "Lord, behold their threats, and grant to your servants to speak your word with boldness and work miracles in your name. And the place was shaken where they were."[9] Homilies on the Gospel of John 79.1.[10]

Ask for What Pertains to Salvation. Bede: It can disturb hearers with weak [faith] that, at the beginning of this reading from the Gospel, the Savior promises his disciples, "If you ask anything of the Father in my name, he will give it to you." Not only do people like us not receive many things we seek to ask of the Father in Christ's name, but even the apostle Paul himself asked the Lord three times that the angel of Satan with which he was tormented might depart from him, and he was not able to obtain what he asked.[11] But the perplexity caused by this question has already been resolved by the old explanation of the Fathers.[12] They understood truthfully that those people alone ask in the name of the Savior who ask for those things that pertain to eternal salvation. They understood, therefore, that the apostle did not ask in the Savior's name [when he asked] to be relieved of the temptation that he had received as a protection for his humility. If he had been relieved of it, he could not have been saved. . . . Whenever we are not listened to when we ask, it happens either because we are asking [for something] contrary to what would aid our salvation, and for this reason the grace of his kindness is denied us by our merciful Father because we are unsuitably asking . . . or [it happens because] we are asking for things that are indeed useful for and connected with true salvation, but we ourselves by our evil lives divert away from us the voice of the just Judge, falling into what was said by Solomon, "The person who turns away his ear from hearing the law, his prayer will be an abomination."[13] Or [it happens because] when we pray for certain sinners, that they may recover their senses and return to themselves, that although we are asking [for something] pertaining to salvation, and we deserve to be heard for our own merit, yet their obstinacy stands in the way of our obtaining what we ask. Homilies on the Gospels 2.12.[14]

16:24 *Ask, That Your Joy May Be Full*

Enjoying God in the Trinity. Augustine: Our fullness of joy—and there is nothing greater than this—is to enjoy God in the Trinity, in the image of whom we are made. On the Trinity 1.8.18.[15]

Ask for What Can Satisfy. Augustine: So what should we pray for? "Ask in my name." And he did not say what for, but in his words we can understand what we ought to ask for. "Ask, and

[7]*OSW* 113*; GCS 3(2):334-35. [8]ANF 5:448**. [9]A reference to Pentecost, see Acts 4:29-31. [10]NPNF 1 14:292**. [11]2 Cor 12:8. [12]See Augustine *Tractate* 73.2-4. [13]Prov 28:9. [14]CS 111:108-9*. [15]NPNF 1 3:26**.

you will receive, that your joy may be full." Ask, and you will receive, in my name. But what? Not nothing. What though? "That your joy may be full," which means, ask for what can finally satisfy you. Because sometimes you ask for nothing. "Whoever drinks of this water will be thirsty again."[16] You lower the bucket of greed into the well, you pull up something to drink, and you will again be thirsty. "Ask, so that your joy may be full," that is, so that you may be permanently satisfied, not just so as to enjoy yourselves for a time. Ask for what can satisfy you. Utter Philip's words, "Lord, show us the Father, and that suffices us." The Lord says to you, "Have I been with you such a long time, and you do not know me? Philip, whoever sees me also sees the Father."[17] So give thanks to Christ who took our humanity to himself for you in your weakness. And get your stomachs ready to be satisfied with Christ's divinity. Sermon 145.6.[18]

Prayer in Christ's Name. Cyril of Alexandria: He urges the disciples to seek for spiritual gifts and at the same time gives them confidence that, if they ask for them, they will not fail to obtain them. He adds the word *Amen,* that he might confirm their belief that if they ask the Father for anything they would receive it from him. He would act as their mediator and make known their request and, being one with the Father, grant it. For this is what he means by "in my name." For we cannot draw near to God the Father in any other way than through the Son. For it is by him that we have access in the one Spirit to the Father.[19] It was because of this that he said, "I am the door. I am the way. No one comes to the Father but by me."[20] For as the Son is God, he being one with the Father provides good things for his sanctified people and is found to be generous of his wealth to us. . . . Let us then offer our prayers in Christ's name. For in this way, the Father will most readily consent to them and grant his graces to those who seek them, that receiving them we may rejoice. Commentary on the Gospel of John 11.2.[21]

An Example of Provision for the Halcyon. Basil the Great: We should give thanks to God for the good things he gives us and not bear it with bad grace because he measures his giving. Should he grant us to be in union with him, this we shall receive as a most perfect and joyful gift. Should he delay this, let us suffer the loss in patience since he disposes of our lives more perfectly than we could ever order them.

The halcyon is a sea bird that nests by the shore, laying its eggs in the sand and bringing forth its young in the middle of winter when the sea beats violent and frequent storms. But during the seven days while the halcyon broods—for it takes but seven days to hatch its young—all winds sink to rest and the sea grows calm. And as it then is in need of food for its young ones, the most bountiful God grants this little creature another seven days of calm so that it may feed its young. Since all sailors know of this, they give this time the name of the *halcyon days.*

These things are ordered by the providence of God for the creatures that are without reason so that you may be led to seek of God the things you need for your salvation. And when for this small bird he holds back the great and fearful sea and bids it be calm in winter, what will he not do for you made in his own image? And if he should so tenderly cherish the halcyon, how much more will he not give you [what you need] when you call on him with your heart? Sermon 9.5, On Prayer.[22]

16:25 *I Will Tell You Plainly of the Father*

All Revealed in Due Time. Cyril of Alexandria: What the time would be, Jesus did not tell them very clearly. We must surmise that he either meant that time when we are enriched with the knowledge that comes to us through the Spirit, whom Christ himself brought down to us after his resurrection from the dead. Or it may be

[16]Jn 4:13. [17]Jn 14:8-9. [18]*WSA* 3 4:441. [19]See Eph 2:8. [20]Jn 10:7; 14:6. [21]LF 48:465-66**. [22]PG 32:1244.

the time to come after the end of the world, in which we shall clearly behold the glory of God, that God will impart to us directly. . . . In the darkness of the night the bright beauty of the stars shines forth, each casting abroad its own ray of light, but when the sun rises with its own radiant beams . . . the luster of the stars waxes feeble and ineffective. In a similar manner I think also that the knowledge we now have will cease, and that which is partial will vanish away at the moment when the perfect light has come on us and sheds forth its radiance, filling us with perfect knowledge of God. Then, when we are enabled to approach God in confidence, Christ will tell us the things that concern his Father. Commentary on the Gospel of John 11.2.[23]

He Will Manifest His Equality with the Father. Gregory the Great: When he declares that he will show them plainly of the Father, he alludes to the manifestation about to take place of his own majesty that would show his own equality with the Father and the procession of the co-eternal Spirit from both. For we shall then openly see how what has its existence from something else is not subsequent to him from whom it springs and how he who is produced by procession is not preceded by those from whom he proceeded. We shall then see openly how both the One is divisibly Three and the Three indivisibly One. Morals on the Book of Job 30.4.17.[24]

Blessedness in Seeing God Face to Face. Augustine: Ask in my name so that your joy may be full and you shall receive. For his saints who persevere in asking for such a good thing as this will never be defrauded by the mercy of God. Then he continues, "These things have I spoken to you in proverbs. But the hour is coming when I shall no more speak to you in proverbs, but I shall show you plainly of my Father." The hour of which he speaks may be understood of that future period of life when we shall see him openly, as the apostle said, "face to face." Thus, when Jesus says, "These things I have spoken to you in proverbs" agrees with what the apostle said, "Now we see as in a glass darkly."[25] But "I will show you" that the Father shall be seen through the instrumentality of the Son, which is akin to what Jesus says elsewhere, "For no one knows the Father except the Son and the one to whom the Son shall reveal him."[26] Tractates on the Gospel of John 102.2-3.[27]

16:26 *I Do Not Say That I Will Pray the Father for You*

Father and Son Both Intercede. Augustine: But this sense seems to be interfered with by what follows: "At that day you shall ask in my name." In that future world, when we have reached the kingdom where we shall be like him . . . what will we have to ask for when all our desires will already be satisfied with good things?[28] . . . Asking implies the lack of something, which can hardly be the case where there will be such an abundance. It remains then that we understand Jesus as having promised to change his disciples from being carnal and natural beings to making them spiritual beings. . . . The natural person does not perceive the things of the Spirit of God, and so when he hears something about the nature of God, he can conceive of nothing else but some bodily form, however spacious or immense, however lustrous and magnificent, yet still as a body. And so, whatever Wisdom said of the incorporeal, immutable substance are proverbs to him, not that he considers them as proverbs but understands them as if they were proverbs. But when the spiritual person begins to discern all things, . . . though in this life he see but through a glass and in part, still he perceives—not through his bodily senses or by an idea of the imagination but by the clearest understanding of the mind—that God is not material but spiritual. This is how the Son shows us so plainly of the Father,

[23]LF 48:467*. [24]LF 31:375**. [25]1 Cor 13:12. [26]Mt 11:27. [27]NPNF 1 7:390**. [28]Ps 103:5 (102:5 LXX, Vg).

that [the Son] who shows is seen to be of the same nature with [the Father] who is shown. Then, those who ask, ask in his name, because by the sound of that name they understand nothing else than the reality itself that is expressed by that name. . . . They are able, to a certain extent, to perceive that our Lord Jesus Christ, in so far as he is human, intercedes with the Father on our behalf. But in so far as he is God, they also recognize that he hears [and answers] us together with the Father. This is what I think he means when he says, "And I say not that I will pray the Father for you." To understand this, that is, how the Son does not ask the Father but Father and Son together hear those who ask, is beyond the reach of any but the spiritual vision. TRACTATES ON THE GOSPEL OF JOHN 102.3-4.[29]

THE SON IS CONSUBSTANTIAL WITH THE FATHER. THEODORE OF MOPSUESTIA: Knowing that the Son is consubstantial with the Father, they would, therefore, petition from the Son what he was asking from the Father. By saying, "I do not ask," he indicated that he is God, able also to give "whatever you may ask," without petitioning the Father. You see, when he said above, "And I will ask the Father and he will give you another Paraclete," he spoke as a human, according to the divine plan.[30] After all, why would he ask for that which the Father already intended? COMMENTARY ON JOHN, FRAGMENT 132.16.26-27.[31]

16:27 *The Father Himself Loves You*

LOVE FROM LOVE. AUGUSTINE: "For the Father himself," he says, "loves you because you have loved me." Is it the case, then, that he loves because we love or, rather, that we love because he loves? Let this same Evangelist give us the answer out of his own epistle: "We love him," he says, "because he first loved us."[32] This, then, was the efficient cause of our loving, that we were loved. And certainly to love God is the gift of God. He is the one who gave us the grace to love him, who loved while still unloved. Even when we displeased him, we were loved so that there might be that in us whereby we should become pleasing in his sight. For we could not love the Son unless we also loved the Father. The Father loves us because we love the Son, seeing it is of the Father and Son we have received the power to love both the Father and the Son: for love is shed abroad in our hearts by the Spirit of both,[33] by which Spirit we love both the Father and the Son and whom we love along with the Father and the Son. It was God, therefore, who created this religious love of ours whereby we worship God, and he saw that it is good, and for this reason he himself loved what he had made. But he would not have created in us something he could love if it were not for the fact that he loved us before he brought about that something. TRACTATES ON THE GOSPEL OF JOHN 102.5.[34]

GOD AS OUR DEBTOR. CHRYSOSTOM: When we ask God for something, there is no need for intermediaries. And he is no more disposed to help us because he is asked by others than if we ourselves ask. For he wants us to seek things from him often. This pleases him very much. For it is in this alone that he becomes our debtor: Every time we pray to him, he is pleased and freely gives us what we have not loaned him. And should he see someone who is in need fervently praying to him, he will himself pay down for us what he has not received from us. But if we pray in an indifferent manner, he will be indifferent to our request—not because he does not want to give but because our prayer is acceptable only when we pray to him with all our hearts.

Nor does God put off the granting of our prayers because he detests them or because he is against us. But he does clearly wish, by delaying his giving, to keep us close to himself; just as fathers who love their children tenderly will withhold a gift from children who are lazy and indifferent in order to teach them to persevere.

[29]NPNF 1 7:390-91**. [30]Or, "he spoke incarnationally." [31]ECS 7:128. [32]1 Jn 4:19. [33]See Rom 5:5. [34]NPNF 1 7:391**.

And have your prayers been heard? Then give thanks because your prayers have been heard. And have your prayers not been heard? Keep praying so that they may be heard. . . . For, though you may be helpless and without a protector, if you cry out to God himself you shall most certainly be heard. Poem on Prayer, Homily 2.[35]

16:28 *Coming and Going of the Son*

First His Generation from the Father, Then His Incarnation. Hilary of Poitiers: A perfect faith in the Son, which believes and loves the fact that he has come forth from God, has access to the Father without any need of his intervention. The confession that the Son was born and sent from God entitles such a person to a direct audience with God and to love from him. And so the narrative of Jesus' birth and coming must be taken in the strictest and most literal sense. He says, "I went forth from God,"[36] conveying the fact that his nature is exactly what was given to him by his birth. For what being other than God could go forth from God, that is, could enter upon existence by being born from him? And then he continues, "And I have come from the Father into this world." In order that he might assure us that this going forth from God means his birth from the Father, he tells us that he came from the Father into the world, referring here to his incarnation. When he said prior to this that he "went forth from God," however, there he was referring to his [birth by] nature. Since he put on record first the fact of his going forth from God, and then his coming from the Father, we cannot say that the going and the coming are the same thing. Coming from the Father and going forth from God are not synonymous. Perhaps we might paraphrase them instead as "birth" and "presence," knowing that they are as different in meaning as these two words. It is one thing to have gone forth from God, entering into a substantial existence [with him] by birth. It is quite another, however, to have come from the Father into this world [by birth] in order to accomplish the mysteries of our salvation. On the Trinity 6.31.[37]

The Father As Cause of Christ's Origin. John of Damascus: Some of the things said concerning Christ make known the fact of his origin from the Father as cause. . . . For from him he derives both his being and all that he has. His being was by generative and not by creative means, as, "I came forth, and I have come," and "I live because of the Father."[38] But all that he has is not by free gift or by teaching, but in a causal sense, as "the Son is not able to do anything of himself, unless he sees the Father doing anything."[39] For if the Father does not exist, neither does the Son. For the Son is *of* the Father and *in* the Father and *with* the Father, and not *after* the Father. In a similar way also what he does is of him and with him. For there is one and the same—not similar but the same—will and energy and power in the Father, Son and Holy Spirit. Orthodox Faith 4.18.[40]

Christ Is Never Far Away. Cyril of Alexandria: When Jesus says that he came into this world and again left the world and went to the Father, he does not mean that he either abandoned the Father when he became man or that he abandoned the human race when, in the flesh, he went to the Father. For he is truly God and with his ineffable power fills all things and is not far from anything that exists. Commentary on the Gospel of John 11.2.[41]

He Does Not Abandon His Father or Us. Augustine: In coming to the world, he came forth in such a sense from the Father that he did not leave the Father behind. And when he leaves the world, he goes to the Father in such a sense that he does not forsake the world. For he came

[35]PG 63:580-81. [36]The RSV has "Father" here at the end of verse 27, but the Greek and Latin have "God," which for Hilary is an important distinction. [37]NPNF 2 9:109**. [38]Jn 6:57. [39]Jn 5:19. [40]NPNF 2 9:90*. [41]LF 48:472*.

forth from the Father because he is of the Father. And he came into the world in showing to the world his bodily form that he had received from the Virgin. He left the world by a bodily withdrawal, he proceeded to the Father by his ascension as man, but he did not forsake the world in the ruling activity of his presence. Tractates on the Gospel of John 102.6.[42]

The Disciples' Faith in Christ Validated. Chrysostom: Since his teaching about his resurrection and how he came from God and went to God did not, at the time, cheer them up, he dwells on these subjects again and again. The first was proof that their faith in him was not vain; the second that they would still be under his protection. Homilies on the Gospel of John 79.2.[43]

Christ Brings Human Nature into Heaven. Bede: He came forth from the Father and came into the world because he made himself visible to the world in his humanity, who in his divinity was invisible along with the Father. He came forth from the Father, because he appeared not in that form in which he is equal to the Father but in the lesser one of a created being that he took on himself. And he came into the world because, in the form of a servant that he accepted, he offered himself to be seen even by those who love this world. Again, he left the world behind and returned to the Father because he removed from the sight of those who love the world what they had seen, and he taught to those who love him that he should be believed to be equal to the Father. He left the world behind and returned to the Father because by his ascension he brought the humanity that he had put on to the place of invisible realities. Homilies on the Gospels 2.12.[44]

[42]NPNF 1 7:391**. [43]NPNF 1 14:292**. [44]CS 111:114*. See also Augustine *Tractates on the Gospel of John* 102.6.

16:29-33 Peace in Overcoming the World

[29]His disciples said, "Ah, now you are speaking plainly, not in any figure! [30]Now we know that you know all things, and need none to question you; by this we believe that you came from God." [31]Jesus answered them, "Do you now believe? [32]The hour is coming, indeed it has come, when you will be scattered, every man to his home, and will leave me alone; yet I am not alone, for the Father is with me. [33]I have said this to you, that in me you may have peace. In the world you have tribulation; but be of good cheer, I have overcome the world."

Overview: The disciples say that Jesus speaks plainly, but they do not even understand that they do not understand. Jesus asked questions to teach, not to learn (Augustine). His works testify to his origin (Hilary). When Jesus questions the disciples as to whether they now believe, it is a reminder of the tender age of their inner man (Augustine). Jesus foretells their betrayal (Chrysostom), when they would desert him not only with their bodies but also with their minds of faith, but he was never separated from his Father because he had come forth from the Father (Augustine).

In Christ our flesh is capable of overcoming suffering, death and corruption (Gregory Thaumaturgus). The suffering believers undergo is not because they have done evil but simply on account of the name (Eusebius). The disciples' peace comes in not rejecting Christ in the midst of tribulations (Chrysostom). They will have Christ within them even as they have the world outside (Gregory the Great). Tribulation begins with scattering, but they would later return and remain in him and have peace with him (Augustine). And so, Jesus tells them to be of good cheer and at peace because their Master is victorious (Chrysostom). In fact, the object of this entire discourse is to bring peace to their troubled hearts and minds (Augustine). These are words of comfort and love that no one should try to denude of power by dragging them down into doctrinal arguments (Chrysostom). Jesus wants us to know that we are not alone in our struggles and that the world is only as strong as Christ allows it to be (Origen). We overcome the world and all its opposition as we fight it with the virtue that comes from being united with God (Maximus).

16:29 *Now You Speak Plainly*

Disciples Do Not Even Know They Do Not Understand. Augustine: But how can they say, "Now you speak plainly and do not utter proverbs"? Had the hour, indeed, already come—the hour when he had promised that he would no longer speak to them with proverbs? Certainly such an hour had not yet come, as is shown by how he continues speaking to them.[1]... They say this then because, although our Lord's communications to them still continue as proverbs to them, they are so far from understanding them that they do not even understand their own lack of understanding his words. They were still infants who had no spiritual discernment concerning what they heard. Tractates on the Gospel of John 103.1.[2]

16:30 *No One Need Question Jesus*

Questions for Our Benefit. Augustine: Why do they say this to someone who knew all things, instead of saying, "you don't need for anyone to ask you"? It would have been more appropriate to have said, You don't need to ask anyone. And yet we know that both of these were done, that is, that our Lord both asked questions and was asked. But this is soon explained. For both were for the benefit not of himself but of those whom he asked questions or by whom he was asked. He asked questions of people not in order to learn himself but to teach them. And in the case of those who asked questions of him, such questions were necessary for them in order to gain the knowledge they wanted. But they were not necessary for him to tell him what that was, because he knew what the inquirer wanted before the question was put to him.... And so, to know people's thoughts beforehand was no great thing for the Lord, but to the minds of babes it was a great thing: "By this we know that you came forth from God." Tractates on the Gospel of John 103.2.[3]

Works Testify to Origin. Hilary of Poitiers: They believe that he came forth from God because he does the works of God.... Notice how, on the one hand, they are not at all amazed when he says, "I am come into the world from the Father." In fact, these are words which they had often heard before. But their reply shows a belief in and appreciation of the previous words when he had said, "I came forth from the Father." They, in fact, make specific mention of this in their reply: "By this we believe that you came forth from God." They didn't add the phrase, "and are come into the world," because they knew already that he was sent from God. But they had not yet

[1]See Jn 16:25-28. [2]NPNF 1 7:392**. [3]NPNF 1 7:392-93**.

received anything concerning the doctrine of his eternal generation. That unutterable doctrine they now began to see for the first time in consequence of these words and therefore reply that he spoke no longer in parables. For God is not born from God after the manner of human birth. His is a *coming forth from*, rather than *a birth from* God. He is one from one. He is not a portion, not a defection, not a diminution, not a derivation, not a pretension, not a passion. He is the birth of living nature from living nature. He is God coming forth from God, not a creature appointed to the name of God. He did not begin to be from nothing, but he came forth from a nature that has always existed. To come forth has the signification of birth, not of beginning. On the Trinity 6.34-35.[4]

16:31-32 *Faith and the Hour of Desertion*

Reminder of the Tender Age of the Inner Man. Augustine: Finally, he reminds them of their weak tender age in respect of the inner man. Jesus answered them, "Do you now believe?" Tractates on the Gospel of John 103.2.[5]

Betrayal Foretold. Chrysostom: He tells them, "You still have a long way to go to reach perfection. Nothing, as of yet, has been achieved by you. In fact, you will soon betray me to my enemies, and you will be so afraid that you will not even be able to flee together. But I will not be harmed because of this."... He shows them that now, when they say they believe, they really do not yet believe, nor does he accept their words. Homilies on the Gospel of John 79.2.[6]

Jesus Never Separated from the Father. Augustine: He replied, "The Father is with me," so that they would not think that the Son had come forth from the Father in any sense that would lead them to suppose that [the Father] had also withdrawn from his presence. Tractates on the Gospel of John 103.2.[7]

Physical and Spiritual Desertion. Augustine: But when he was taken, not only did [the disciples] outwardly abandon his bodily presence, but they mentally abandoned their faith. This is what he is talking about when he says, "Do you now believe?" ... This was as if he had said, Afterward, you will be so confused that you will leave behind even what you now believe. It is apparent that this is indeed what happened because they did fall into such despair and such a death, so to speak, of their old faith. For instance, Cleopas, after Jesus' resurrection, and unaware that he was speaking with Jesus, narrated what had happened to him, saying, "We trusted that he was the one who was going to redeem Israel."[8] They left him, in other words, by abandoning the very faith that had formerly believed in him. Tractates on the Gospel of John 103.3.[9]

16:33 *In the World You Have Tribulation*

In Christ We Are Capable of Eternal Life. Gregory Thaumaturgus: [Christ] says, "Be of good cheer, I have overcome the world." And he said this not as holding before us any contest proper only to God but as showing our own flesh in its capacity to overcome suffering, and death and corruption. Twelve Topics on the Faith 12.[10]

For His Name's Sake. Eusebius of Caesarea: When the Master gave them gloomy prophecies, if they paid attention to the things he said to them ... they demonstrated the strength and depth of their nature, since it is evident they had no fear of disciplining the body, nor did they run after pleasure. And their master too, as one who himself would not soothe them by deceit, was like them in renouncing his property. And so, when he prophesied about the future in such an open and honest way, he convinced them to choose his way of life. These were prophecies of

[4]NPNF 2 9:110-11**. [5]NPNF 1 7:392**. [6]NPNF 1 14:292-93**. [7]NPNF 1 7:393*. [8]Lk 24:21. [9]NPNF 1 7:393*. [10]ANF 6:52**.

what would happen to them for his name's sake that told how they would be brought before rulers and kings and undergo all sorts of punishments, not for any wrong they had done due to any reasonable charge, but solely for this: his name's sake. And we who see it now fulfilled ought to be struck by the prediction. For the confession of the name of Jesus always inflames the minds of rulers. And even though one who confesses Christ has done no evil, they still punish him with every kind of contempt "for his name's sake," as the worst of evildoers. But if someone else swears away the name and denies that he is one of Christ's disciples, he is let off scot-free, even if he has been convicted of many crimes. PROOF OF THE GOSPEL 3.5.[11]

PEACE IN NOT REJECTING CHRIST. CHRYSOSTOM: "These things have I said to you so that you might have peace," that is, that you may not drive me from your thoughts but receive me. No one should drag these words down into some type of doctrinal argument. They are spoken for our comfort and love. "For," [Jesus might say], "not even when you suffer such things as I have mentioned will your troubles come to an end, but as long as you are in the world you will have sorrow, not only when I am betrayed but also afterward. However, raise up your spirits, for you will suffer no serious harm. When the Master is victorious, the disciples should not be dejected." "And how," tell me, "have you conquered the world?" "I have already said that I have cast down its ruler, but you shall know later when everything yields and obeys you." HOMILIES ON THE GOSPEL OF JOHN 79.2.[12]

CHRIST WITHIN, WORLD WITHOUT. GREGORY THE GREAT: As if he said, Have me within you to comfort you because you will have the world without you. MORALS ON THE BOOK OF JOB 26.16.26.[13]

TRIBULATION BEGINS WITH SCATTERING. AUGUSTINE: The scattering of everyone to his own home was the beginning of the tribulation. ... For in adding, "and you shall leave me alone," he did not mean that they would do this in the subsequent tribulation that they would have to endure in the world after his ascension. They were not going to desert him then. That is when they would abide and have peace in him. ... In the tribulation that they encountered after his glorification when they had received the Holy Spirit they did not leave him. Even though they fled from city to city, they never fled from him. Rather, while they did indeed have tribulation in this world, they made him their refuge so that they would have peace in him, instead of being fugitives from him. When the Holy Spirit was given to them, they were joyful then and victorious in his strength. For he would not have overcome the world if the world had still overcome his members. TRACTATES ON THE GOSPEL OF JOHN 103.3.[14]

THE OBJECT OF THE ENTIRE DISCOURSE IS PEACE. AUGUSTINE: When he says, "These things have I spoken to you, that in me you might have peace," he refers not only to what he has just said but also to what he had said all along, either from the time that he first had disciples, or since the supper, when he began this long and wonderful discourse. ... He declares this to be the object of his whole discourse, that is, that in him they might have peace. And this peace will have no end but is itself the end of every godly action and intention. TRACTATES ON THE GOSPEL OF JOHN 104.1.[15]

WE ARE NOT ALONE IN OUR STRUGGLES. ORIGEN: We are not to suppose that each individual must contend with all these adversaries, which would be impossible for anyone .... For I think that human nature has definite limitations, even though there is a Paul, of whom it is said, "He is a chosen vessel unto me,"[16] or a Peter against whom "the gates of hell shall not pre-

[11]*POG* 1:136-37**. [12]NPNF 1 14:293**. [13]LF 23:151**. [14]NPNF 1 7:393**. [15]NPNF 1 7:393-94**. [16]Acts 9:15.

vail,"[17] or a Moses, "the friend of God."[18] For not even one of these could face the whole crowd of opposing powers at once without destruction to himself, except perhaps on the condition that there was working within him the power of him who said, "Be of good cheer, I have overcome the world." . . .

I do not think that human nature alone can maintain a contest with angels and with the powers of the "height" and of the "depth" or with "any other creature."[19] But when it feels the presence of the Lord dwelling within it, confidence in the divine help will lead it to say, "The Lord is my light and my salvation; whom shall I fear? The Lord is the protector of my life; of whom shall I be afraid?"[20] On First Principles 3.2.5.[21]

The World Is Only As Strong As Christ Allows. Origen: We are persecuted when God allows the tempter the power to persecute us. But when God does not want us to suffer this, even in the world that hates us, we wondrously have peace and are of good cheer because of him who said, "Be of good cheer, I have overcome the world." And truly he has overcome the world, because the world is strong only insofar as its Victor wants it to be. He has received from the Father the victory over the world. And because of his victory we can indeed be of good cheer. Against Celsus 8.70.[22]

Victory over the World Means to Be with God. Maximus the Confessor: Rebelling as we do against God through the passions and agreeing to pay tribute in the form of evil to that cunning tyrant and murderer of souls, the devil, we cannot be reconciled with God until we have first begun to fight against the devil with all our strength. For even though we assume the name of faithful Christians, until we have made ourselves the devil's enemies and fight against him, we continue by deliberate choice to serve the shameful passions. And nothing of profit will come to us from our peace in the world, for our soul is in an evil state, rebelling against its own maker and unwilling to be subject to his kingdom. It is still sold into bondage to hordes of savage masters who urge it toward evil and treacherously contrive to make it choose the way that leads to destruction instead of that which brings salvation.

God made us so that we might become "partakers of the divine nature"[23] and sharers in his eternity, and so that we might come to be like him[24] through deification by grace. It is through deification that all things are reconstituted and achieve their permanence. And it is for its sake that what is not is brought into being and given existence. If we desire to belong to God in both name and reality, let us struggle not to betray the Word[25] to the passions.[26] . . . To deny the Word is to fail through fear to do what is good. To betray him is deliberately to choose and commit sin. The outcome of every affliction endured for the sake of virtue is joy, the outcome of every labor is rest, and the outcome of every shameful treatment is glory. In short, the outcome of all sufferings for the sake of virtue is to be with God, to remain with him forever and to enjoy eternal rest. Various Texts on Theology, First Century 41-44.[27]

[17]See Mt 16:18. [18]See Ex 33:11. [19]Rom 8:38-39. [20]Ps 27:1 (26:1 LXX). [21]ANF 4:332-33*; GCS 22(5):252-53. [22]ANF 4:666**; SC 150:336-38. [23]2 Pet 1:4. [24]See 1 Jn 3:2. [25]Or, "Logos." [26]He cites the examples of Judas and Peter; see Mt 26:14-16, 69-75. [27]*TP* 2:172-73*.

17:1-5 Jesus' Prayer for Himself: Humble Glory

[1]*When Jesus had spoken these words, he lifted up his eyes to heaven and said, "Father, the hour has come; glorify thy Son that the Son may glorify thee,* [2]*since thou hast given him power over all flesh, to give eternal life to all whom thou hast given him.* [3]*And this is eternal life, that they know thee the only true God, and Jesus Christ whom thou hast sent.* [4]*I glorified thee on earth, having accomplished the work which thou gavest me to do;* [5]*and now, Father, glorify thou me in thy own presence with the glory which I had with thee before the world was made."*

Overview: Tribulation should drive us to prayer as it did Jesus (Chrysostom). And when we pray, our prayer should first seek to bring glory to our Father, and then we can bring our concerns to God (Cyril). The prayer Jesus offers is as effective a source of edification as his discourse (Augustine). He speaks of the hour that has come, indicating that anything he did or allowed to be done to him was by his own arrangement (Augustine). He asks the Father to glorify him, but the glory Jesus is going to experience is that of the cross, whose humiliation seems anything but glorious (Chrysostom). When those who nailed him to the cross confess that he truly is the Son of God, his prayer has been answered (Hilary). But if he was glorified in his passion, he was even more so in his resurrection (Augustine). The Son glorifies the Father, demonstrating mutual glorification and mutual divinity (Hilary). The Father's eternal glory is not increased, but his glory among the world is increased as the gospel is spread throughout the world (Augustine). In asking to be glorified, Jesus is asking his Father not to give him glory so much as to reveal the honor the Father had already given him (Theodore). The Son's willing obedience and his glorious deeds, then, reflect well on his Father who begat him and are passed on to us as we enjoy the benefits of the salvation won for us (Didymus).

The Father had given Christ the power over all flesh, the power to give eternal life, which is a power given to Christ's human nature (Augustine) as his flesh restores our flesh (Hilary). The fact that Christ receives power to give life in no way diminishes his divinity; rather, it posits the fatherhood of the giver and the divinity of the receiver (Hilary). The Son speaks of giving life to all flesh, which he always could do. But now he also includes the Gentiles when he says "all flesh." If there are some who did not believe, however, that is not the fault of the teacher (Chrysostom). To be ignorant of the Father is death (Clement of Alexandria), but to truly know him and the Son is eternal life because it brings us into participation with the divine in the Eucharist (Cyril). In this way, we are moved to worship of the Trinity (Theodore), which, in turn leads ultimately to an eternal life spent contemplating the great "I am." Our faith then sees its object while eternity possesses our changed mortality (Augustine).

Eternal life is to know "the only true God," (Origen), thus distinguishing him from the false gods of the Gentiles to whom the apostles would be sent (Chrysostom). "Only," however, does not preclude the divinity or honor of the Son (Athanasius), nor is it a barrier to the sharing of attributes since Christ evidences the properties of divinity in the works he does, such as creation (Hilary). Further, in adding the words "and Jesus Christ whom you have sent," Christ in fact asserts his divinity since, while linking the statement to the Father, he nowhere offers any further qualification with reference to his humanity

(Novatian). The hope of life, then, rests in the Father and the Son (Hilary), as well as the Spirit (Augustine).

Knowledge of God is eternal life, and the more we grow in his knowledge the greater the advances we make toward a life that most fully glorifies God (Augustine). His name had already been glorified in heaven and by the worship of the angels, but this glorification was accomplished on earth when he came to serve humankind by doing the work that had been given him to do by the Father (Chrysostom). He speaks of having finished the work already in the sense that he has done his part and is now already looking toward the future when it will have been accomplished; or he implies that at least the roots have been laid for the fruits that will follow (Chrysostom).

When Christ asks his Father to glorify him, he is not abdicating his divine position but elevating ours (Hilary) as his human nature receives the glory that the Word always had (Didymus). The glory that was Christ's before the creation of the world now seeks to restore once again what had fallen through Adam's sin (Ephrem). Christ also speaks here of the order of glorification, that is, that the Father was first to be glorified by the Son on earth by preaching about him to the nations, and then the Son is to be glorified by the Father when he is placed at the Father's right hand (Augustine). He was predestined to glorification before the world began and now prays for the consummation of that glorification when he sits at the right hand of the Father (Augustine).

17:1a *Jesus Faces the Hour of Tribulation with Prayer*

He Teaches How to Rely on the Father in Trials. Chrysostom: Christ not only speaks about the endurance of evil but puts himself forward as an example. After his admonition that "in the world you will have tribulation," he himself turns to prayer in order to teach us that in our testing we are to leave everything behind and flee to God. He had shaken their souls in his admonition but raised them up again by this prayer. Homilies on the Gospel of John 80.1.[1]

How We Should Pray. Cyril of Alexandria: When an occasion calls us to prayer, it is fitting for us to pray for that which increases God's glory before we pray for that which concerns ourselves.... The Savior indeed spoke these words to show how very necessary his own glory was to the Father so that he might be known to be consubstantial with him ... for the Father is glorified in the glory of his offspring. Commentary on the Gospel of John 11.3.[2]

Prayer Teaches As Well As Discourse. Augustine: Our Lord, the only begotten who is co-eternal with the Father but who also took the form of a servant, could have prayed in silence if need be. But by praying out loud he wanted to show himself as one who prayed to the Father; he remembered that he not only had to pray but to teach. And so, the prayer that he offered for us, he also made known to us. For it was not only his discourse but also his prayers that were a source of edification for his disciples—and for us who read it today. Tractates on the Gospel of John 104.2.[3]

Christ Selected the Time to Be Born and Die. Augustine: In saying, "Father, the hour is come; glorify your Son," he showed that all time, and every occasion when he did anything or suffered anything to be done, was arranged by him who was subject to no time ... Let no one think that this hour came through any urgency of fate but rather by divine appointment. It was no necessary law of the heavenly bodies that tied the passion of Christ to its timetable. How could anyone think that the stars compelled their own maker to die? It was not the time, therefore, that drove Christ to his death, but Christ who

[1]NPNF 1 14:296**. Theodore of Mopsuestia believes this chapter is not a prayer but only in the form of a prayer. [2]LF 48:479, 481*. [3]NPNF 1 7:394**; CCL 36:602.

selected the time to die. He also fixed the time when he was born of the Virgin, with the Father, of whom he was born independently of time. . . . He then may say, "Father, the hour is come," who has arranged every hour with the Father saying, as it were, "Father, the hour," which we fixed together for the sake of humanity and of my glorification among them, "is come; glorify your Son, that your Son also may glorify you." Tractates on the Gospel of John 104.2.[4]

17:1b *Mutual Glorification*

Glory and the Cross. Chrysostom: Again he shows us that he willingly comes to the cross. For how could someone who prayed that this might happen be unwilling, calling what would happen "glory" not only for himself the crucified but also for the Father? This was indeed the case, since not only the Son but also the Father too was glorified. For before the crucifixion, not even the Jews knew him. "Israel," it says, "has not known me."[5] But after the crucifixion, the whole world flocked to him. Then he also speaks of how the glory would take place and how [the Father] will glorify him. Homilies on the Gospel of John 80.1.[6]

Proved As Son by Nature, Not Adoption. Hilary of Poitiers: He does not say that the day or the time but that the hour has come. An hour contains a portion of a day. What was this hour? . . . He was now to be spit on, scourged, crucified. But the Father glorifies the Son. The sun, instead of setting, fled, and all the other elements felt that same shock of the death of Christ. The stars in their courses, to avoid complicity in the crime, escaped by self-extinction from beholding the scene. The earth trembled under the weight of our Lord hanging on the cross and testified that it did not have the power to hold within it him who was dying. . . . The centurion proclaimed, "Truly this was the Son of God." Creation is set free by the mediation of this sin offering. The very rocks lose their solidity and strength. Those who had nailed him to the cross confess that truly this is the Son of God. The outcome justifies the assertion. Our Lord had said, "Glorify your Son," testifying that he was not the Son in name only but properly the Son. "Your Son," he said. Many of us are sons [children] of God. But he is Son in another sense. He is the proper, true Son by nature, not by adoption; in truth, not in name; by birth, not by creation. After he was glorified, that centurion's confession touched on the truth. And so, when the centurion confesses him to be the true Son of God, none of his believers might doubt what one of his persecutors could not deny. On the Trinity 3.10-11.[7]

Glorified in His Resurrection. Augustine: But if he was glorified by his passion, how much more was he glorified by his resurrection? For his passion showed his humility more than his glory. . . . Humility is the earning of glory. Glory is the reward of humility.[8] . . . So we must understand "Father, the hour is come, glorify your Son" to mean, the hour is come for sowing the seed—humility. Do not defer the fruit—glory. Tractates on the Gospel of John 104.3.[9]

Mutual Glorification, Mutual Divinity. Hilary of Poitiers: But perhaps this proves weakness in the Son. He waited to be glorified by one superior to himself. And who does not confess that the Father is superior, seeing that he himself said, "The Father is greater than I"? But beware that you do not let the honor of the Father impair the glory of the Son. . . . But the prayer, "Father glorify your Son," is completed by "that your Son also may glorify you." So then the Son is not weak, inasmuch as he gives back in his turn glory for the glory that he receives. . . . This petition for glory to be given and paid back is nei-

[4]NPNF 1 7:394**; CCL 36:602. [5]Is 1:3. [6]NPNF 1 14:296**. [7]NPNF 2 9:64-65**; CCL 62:81-83. [8]See Phil 2:5-11. [9]NPNF 1 7:395**; CCL 36:602-3.

ther a robbery of the Father nor a depreciation of the Son. Rather, it shows the same power of divinity to be in both. On the Trinity 3.12.[10]

Increased Glory Among Us, Not in the Father. Augustine: It is worthy of inquiry how the Son can glorify the Father when the eternal glory of the Father neither suffered diminution in any human form nor could be increased in respect of its own divine perfection. In itself, indeed, the glory of the Father could neither be diminished nor enlarged. But without any doubt it was less among people when God was known only in Judea.[11] . . . Therefore the Son glorified the Father when the gospel of Christ spread the knowledge of the Father among the Gentiles. Had the Son, however, only died, and not risen again, he would without doubt have neither been glorified by the Father nor have glorified the Father. But now, having been glorified through his resurrection by the Father, he glorifies the Father by the preaching of his resurrection. "Glorify your Son so that your Son also may glorify you." In other words, raise me from the dead, that by me you may be known to the whole world. Tractates on the Gospel of John 105.1.[12]

Reveal My Glory. Theodore of Mopsuestia: Jesus says, in effect, You gave the Son the kind of honor that accorded him universal dominion—although he would have received such honor later. And what a great honor it was already being the one chosen by God! Nonetheless, he says, you gave me this [honor], so glorify me, that is, in a way fitting to the honor of which you made me worthy. Reveal me before everyone at the time of my passion so that through the events that will happen on the cross everyone may know the greatness of my honor. They will recognize that I did not deserve to suffer, nor did I do so unwillingly, but I did it for the greater benefit of all people. So the words "glorify me" do not mean "give me glory." Rather, they mean "reveal my glory" that was given to me by you. With the same meaning he added, "So that the Son may glorify you," that is, from those things that were done to me [i.e., the Son], you also will be seen to be great and glorious through me. The more my works appear to be admirable, the more your dignity becomes known. Commentary on John 6.17.1.[13]

The Glory Passes to Us. Didymus the Blind: The Father glorified his own Son, having put everything under the sun under his rule. The Father in turn was glorified through the Son. The Son was glorified by the Father, for he was entrusted with all things, because he is the Son and offspring of the one who can do everything. The Father in turn was glorified, just as a father is glorified by his own son [child]. When the Son was known to have accomplished willingly every mighty deed, the favor of his reputation passes on to the one who begat him. . . . This glory, then, passes on to us. That which is altogether subordinate, which has been put under the hand of the Word of God (who is mightier than all things) and which has been saved once and for all must remain for the good, since it is no longer ruled by death or governed by corruption or made subject to sins and ancient evils. Fragments on John 18.[14]

17:2 *The Power to Give Eternal Life*

Power Given to Human Nature. Augustine: The fact that power over all flesh was given to Christ by the Father is to be understood in respect of his humanity. For in respect of his Godhead all things were made by himself, and in him all things were created in heaven and on earth, visible and invisible.[15] Tractates on the Gospel of John 105.2.[16]

Flesh Restores Flesh. Hilary of Poitiers: The glory [that the Son would give to the Father]

[10]NPNF 2 9:65**; CCL 62:83-84. [11]Ps 76:1 (75:2 LXX, Vg). [12]NPNF 1 7:395-96**; CCL 36:603-4. [13]CSCO 4 3:307. [14]*JKGK* 185. [15]Col 1:16. [16]NPNF 1 7:396**; CCL 36:604.

was that the Son, being made flesh, received power over all flesh from the Father, along with the charge of restoring eternal life to ephemeral beings like us who are burdened with the body. On the Trinity 3.13.[17]

Fatherhood of Giver, Divinity of Receiver. Hilary of Poitiers: Perhaps the Son is weak in that he receives power over all flesh. And indeed the receiving of power might be a sign of weakness if he were not able to give eternal life to those whom he receives. Yet the very fact of receiving is used to prove inferiority of nature. It might prove such is the case if Christ were not true God by birth as truly as is the Unbegotten. But if the receiving of power signifies neither more nor less than the birth by which he received all that he has, that gift does not degrade the Begotten, because it makes him perfectly and entirely what God is. God Unbegotten brought God only-begotten to a perfect birth of divine blessedness. It is, then, the mystery of the Father to be the author of the birth, but it is no degradation to the Son to be made the perfect image of his author by a real birth. The giving of power over all flesh—and this giving is done in order that eternal life might be given to all flesh—postulates the fatherhood of the giver and the divinity of the receiver. For giving signifies that the One is the Father and, in receiving the power to give eternal life, the other remains God the Son. All power is therefore natural and congenital to the Son of God. And though it is given, that does not separate him from his author. For that which is given is the property of his author, that is, power to bestow eternal life and to change the corruptible into the incorruptible. The Father gave all; the Son received all. On the Trinity 9.31.[18]

Mission to Gentiles Is No Innovation on Jesus' Part. Chrysostom: But what is the meaning of "you have given him power over all flesh"? I will ask the heretics, "When did he receive this power? Was it before he formed them, or after?" He himself says that it was after he had been crucified and had risen again. At least it was then that he said, "All power is given unto me. Therefore go and make disciples of all nations."[19] What then? Didn't he have authority over his own works? Did he make them and yet not have authority over them after having made them? Yet he is seen doing everything in times of old, punishing some as sinners[20] . . . and honoring others as righteous. Is it that he had the power at that time but now had lost it, but was going to receive it again? What devil could assert this? But if his power was the same both then and now—for he says, "as the Father raises up the dead and gives them life, even so the Son gives life to whom he will"[21]—what is the meaning of the words? The answer lies in the fact that he was about to send them to the Gentiles. In order therefore that they might not think that this was an innovation, because he had said, "I am not sent, except unto the lost sheep of the house of Israel,"[22] he shows that this seemed good to the Father also. . . .

But what does he mean by "of all flesh"? For certainly not all believed. Yet, as far as his mission was concerned, all could have believed. And if some did not listen to his words, the fault was not in the teacher but in those who did not receive his words. Homilies on the Gospel of John 80.1-2.[23]

17:3a *Eternal Life Is Knowing Father and Son*

We Know Through Participation in Divinity. Clement of Alexandria: One who does not have the knowledge of good is wicked: for there is one good, the Father. And to be ignorant of the Father is death, just as to know him is eternal life, through participation in the power of the incorrupt One. And to be incorruptible is to participate in divinity. But revolt from the knowl-

[17]NPNF 2 9:65**; CCL 62:84. [18]NPNF 2 9:165-66**; CCL 62A:404-5. [19]Mt 28:18-19. [20]Gen 18:17. [21]Jn 5:21. [22]Mt 15:24. [23]NPNF 1 14:296-97**.

edge of God brings corruption. Stromateis 5.10.[24]

Knowledge of the True God Nurtures Us to Eternal Life. Cyril of Alexandria: Are we saying that knowledge is eternal life? Are we saying that to know the one true and living God will suffice to give us complete security for the future without need of anything else? Then how is "faith apart from works dead"?[25] When we speak of faith, we mean the true knowledge of God and nothing else, since knowledge comes by faith. The prophet Isaiah tells us this: "If you do not believe, neither shall you understand."[26] But he is not talking about a knowledge that consists in barren speculations, which is entirely worthless. For one of the holy disciples said, "You believe that God is one; you do well. Even the demons believe—and shudder."[27] What then shall we say to this? How is it that Christ speaks the truth when he says that eternal life is the knowledge of God the Father, the one true God, and with him of the Son? I think, indeed, we must answer that the saying of the Savior is completely true. For this knowledge is life, laboring as it were in birth of the whole meaning of the mystery and granting to us participation in the mystery of the Eucharist, whereby we are joined to the living and life-giving Word. And for this reason, I think, Paul says that the Gentiles are made fellow members of the body and fellow partakers of Christ,[28] inasmuch as they partake in his blessed body and blood. And our members may in this sense be conceived of as being members of Christ.[29] This knowledge, then, which also brings to us the Eucharist by the Spirit, is life. For it dwells in our hearts, reshaping those who receive it into sonship with him and molding them into incorruption and piety toward God through life, according to the Gospel. Our Lord Jesus Christ, then, knowing that the knowledge of the one true God brings to us and promotes our union with the blessings of which we have spoken, says that it is eternal life. It is the mother and nurse of eternal life, being in its power and nature pregnant with those things that cause life and lead to life. Commentary on the Gospel of John 11.5.[30]

Eternal Life Is True Knowledge of the Trinity. Theodore of Mopsuestia: The cause of eternal life is steadfast faith, and to believe in one God, and to not attribute to others the title of God but to believe not only in the Father but also in the Son who was incarnated for us and was sent for the salvation of humankind. This doctrine expels the lie of the polytheistic error. It admits only one God while also surpassing the Jewish belief—inasmuch as the Jews worship only the Father. They surely do not understand that from the Father, by means of an unspoken word, his Son was born. It also teaches Christians to worship both the God begotten from the Father and the Spirit that is provided from the Father through the Son[31] and is in its own existence consubstantial with the Father and the Son—the very one who is perfect life and the cause of eternal life. Commentary on John, Fragment 132.17.3.[32]

We Will Contemplate the "I Am." Augustine: What he said to his servant Moses, "I am that I am," . . . this is what we shall contemplate when we live in eternity. On the Trinity 1.8.17.[33]

Eternity Will Be Ours When Faith Sees. Augustine: We are distanced from eternity to the extent that we are changeable. But eternal life is promised to us through the truth. Our faith, however, stands as far apart from the clear knowledge of the truth as mortality does from eternity. At the present we put faith in things done in time on our account, and by that faith itself we are cleansed. In this way, when we have come to sight, as truth follows faith, so eternity may fol-

[24]ANF 2:459. [25]Jas 2:26. [26]Is 7:9. [27]Jas 2:19. [28]See Eph 3:6. [29]See 1 Cor 6:15. [30]LF 48:488-89*. [31]As the editors note, in the West, the *filioque* clause and Augustine's *On the Trinity* are introduced about the same time as Theodore's commentary. [32]ECS 7:130. [33]NPNF 1 3:26*.

low on mortality. Our faith will become truth, then, when we have attained to that which is promised to us who believe. And that which is promised to us is eternal life. And the Truth—not that which shall come to be according to how our faith shall be, but that truth that always exists because eternity is in it—the Truth then has said, "And this is life eternal, that they might know you the only true God, and Jesus Christ, whom you have sent." When our faith sees and comes to be truth, then eternity shall possess our now changed mortality. ON THE TRINITY 4.18.24.[34]

17:3b *The Only True God*

PARTAKERS OF THE GODHEAD. ORIGEN: God,[35] accompanied by the article [in Greek], is very God.[36] Therefore also the Savior says in his prayer to the Father, "That they may know you the only true God." But everything made divine[37] because of the very God by partaking of his divinity would be most properly called not God[38] but god.[39] COMMENTARY ON THE GOSPEL OF JOHN 2.17.[40]

WHY "ONLY" TRUE GOD? CHRYSOSTOM: He says "the only true God" in order to distinguish [the true God] from those which are not gods, since he was about to send them to the Gentiles. But if they[41] will not allow this, but on account of this word "only" reject the Son as being true God, then they are denying that he is God at all. For he also says, "You do not seek the glory that is from the only God." Well then, shall not the Son be God? But if the Son is God and the Son of the Father who is called the only God, it is clear that he also is true, and the Son of him who is called the only true God. Why, when Paul says, "or I only and Barnabas,"[42] surely he was not excluding Barnabas? Not at all. For the "only" is to distinguish him from others. And if he is not true God, how is he "Truth"? For truth far surpasses what is true. What shall we call the condition of not being a "true" one, tell me? Shall we not call it "the not being a person at all?" So if the Son is not true God, how is he God? And how does he make us gods and sons [children], if he is not true God? HOMILIES ON THE GOSPEL OF JOHN 80.2.[43]

"ONLY" CONTRASTS THE FATHER WITH FALSE GODS, NOT WITH THE SON. ATHANASIUS: The one who believes in the Son believes also in the Father, for he believes in what is proper to the Father's essence. And thus the faith is one in one God. And the one who worships and honors the Son, in the Son worships and honors the Father. For the Godhead is one. And therefore the honor is one[44] and the worship is one that is paid to the Father in and through the Son. And the one who worships in this way worships one God. For there is one God and none other. . . . Therefore, these passages[45] are not written in order to deny the Son or with reference to him at all, but to overthrow falsehood. Notice how God did not speak these kinds of words to Adam at the beginning, although his Word was with him by whom all things came to be. For there was no need before idols came in. But when human beings made insurrection against the truth and named for themselves gods such as they did, then the need arose for such words in order to deny the gods that were not.[46] . . . If then the Father is called the only true God, this is said not to the denial of him who said, "I am the Truth"[47] but of those . . . who by nature are not true, as the Father and his Word are. And so the Lord himself added at once, "And Jesus Christ whom you have sent." Now had he been a creature, he would not have added this and ranked himself with his creator. For what fellowship is there between the True and the not true? But as it is,

[34]NPNF 1 3:81-82**; CCL 50:191-92. [35]Gk *ho theos.* [36]Gk *auto theos.* [37]Gk *theopoioumenou.* [38]Gk *ho theos.* [39]Gk *theos.* [40]FC 80:98-99**; SC 120:216-18. [41]The Arians. [42]1 Cor 9:6. [43]NPNF 1 14:297**. [44]Athanasius *On the Incarnation* 19; see also Ambrose *On the Faith* 3.12, 13; Gregory Nazianzus *Oration* 23. [45]He had just cited Mk 12:29; Ex 3:14; Deut 32:39 (LXX); Is 44:6 as well as Jn 17:2. [46]On this point, see also Gregory of Nazianzus *Oration* 30.13. [47]Jn 14:6.

by including himself with the Father, he has shown that he is of the Father's nature. And he has given us to know that of the true Father he is true offspring. Discourses Against the Arians 3.23.6-24.8-9.[48]

Is "Only" a Barrier to Sharing of Attributes? Hilary of Poitiers: For when the [Arians] say that [the Father] alone is true, alone is righteous, alone is wise, alone is invisible, alone is good, alone is mighty, alone is immortal, they are raising up this word *alone* as a barrier to cut off the Son from his share in these attributes. He who is alone, they say, has no partner in his properties. But if we suppose that these attributes reside in the Father only, and not in the Son also, then we must believe that God the Son has neither truth nor wisdom. We must believe that he is a bodily being composed of visible and material elements, ill-disposed and feeble and void of immortality. For we exclude him from all these attributes of which we make the Father the solitary possessor. On the Trinity 4.9.[49]

The Son's Nature and Powers Evidence His Divinity. Hilary of Poitiers: But it must be clear to everyone that the truth or genuineness of something is evidenced in its nature and powers. For instance, true wheat is what grows to maturity with the beard bristling around it which is then purged from the chaff and ground into flour, baked into a loaf and taken for food. [Wheat] demonstrates the nature and uses that bread is known for. . . . What element of the Godhead, then, is lacking in the Son who possesses both the nature and power of God? For he had at his disposal the powers of the divine nature to bring into being the nonexistent and to create whenever he wanted.[50] On the Trinity 5.3-4.[51]

17:3c *Jesus Christ, the Sent One*

Christ Asserts His Deity. Novatian: If Christ is only a man, why did he lay down for us such a rule of faith as to say, "But this is life eternal, that they may know you the one and true God, and Jesus Christ whom you have sent"? If he had not wanted himself to be understood also as God, why did he add, "And Jesus Christ whom you have sent" unless it is because he wanted to be accepted as also God? Because, if he had not wanted himself to be understood as God, he would have added "and the man Jesus Christ whom you have sent." But as it is, neither Christ added this nor did he hand down to us that he is only man. Rather, he joined [himself] to God so that he might also by this union be understood as God, as indeed he is. On the Trinity 16.4.[52]

Hope of Life Rests in Father and Son. Hilary of Poitiers: But in what does eternal life consist? His own words tell us: "That they may know you, the only true God, and Jesus Christ whom you have sent." Is there any doubt or difficulty here, or any inconsistency? It is life to know the true God. But the bare knowledge of him does not give life. What, then, does he add? "And Jesus Christ whom you have sent." In you, the only true God, the Son pays the honor due to his Father. By the addition "and Jesus Christ whom you have sent," he associates himself with the true Godhead. The believer in his confession draws no line between the two, for his hope of life rests in both. And indeed, the true God is inseparable from him whose name follows in the creed. Therefore when we read, "That they may know you, the only true God, and Jesus Christ whom you have sent," these terms of sender and of sent are not intended, under any semblance of distinction either in name or interval[53] [of time], to convey a difference between the true Godhead of Father and of Son. Rather, they are meant to be a guide to the devout confession of them as begetter and begotten. On the Trinity 3.14.[54]

[48]NPNF 2 4:397-98**; PG 26:337-39. [49]NPNF 2 9:73*; CCL 62:110. [50]Col 1:16. [51]NPNF 2 9:86*. [52]ANF 5:626**; CCL 4:40. [53]Lat *significationis aut dilationis diversitate*. [54]NPNF 2 9:65-66**. CCL 62:85-86. See also Hilary *On the Trinity* 5.3.

CATHOLIC FAITH CONFESSES THAT FATHER AND SON ARE TRULY GOD. HILARY OF POITIERS: But perhaps by saying "you the only," Christ severs himself from communion and unity with God. Yes, but after the words "you the only true God," does he not immediately continue, "and Jesus Christ whom you have sent"? I appeal to the sense of the reader: what must we believe Christ to be when we are commanded to believe in him also, as well as the Father the only true God? Or, perhaps, if the Father is the only true God, there is no room for Christ to be God. It might be so, if, because there is one God the Father, Christ were not the one Lord.[55] The fact that God the Father is one leaves Christ nonetheless the one Lord. And similarly the Father's one true Godhead makes Christ nonetheless true God. For we can obtain eternal life only if we believe in Christ, as well as in the only true God. . . . But the faith of the church, while confessing the only true God the Father, confesses Christ also. It does not confess Christ true God without the Father the only true God. Nor does it confess the Father as the only true God without Christ. It confesses Christ true God, because it confesses the Father the only true God. Thus the fact that God the Father is the only true God constitutes Christ also as true God. The only-begotten God suffered no change of nature by his natural birth. And he who, according to the nature of his divine origin was born God from the living God, is, by the truth of that nature, inalienable from the only true God. ON THE TRINITY 9.34, 36.[56]

KNOWING THE TRINITY. AUGUSTINE: Passing by [the Arians], however, we must see whether, when it is said to the Father, "that they may know you the one true God," we are forced to understand it as if he wished to intimate that the Father alone is the true God—in case we should not understand any to be God except the three together, the Father, Son and Holy Spirit. Are we therefore, from the testimony of the Lord, both to call the Father the one true God, and the Son the one true God, and the Holy Spirit the one true God, and the Father, the Son, and the Holy Spirit together, that is, the Trinity itself together, not three true Gods but one true God? Or because he added, "And Jesus Christ whom you have sent," are we to supply "the one true God," so that the order of the words is this, "That they may know you, and Jesus Christ whom you have sent, the one true God"? Why then did he omit to mention the Holy Spirit? Is it because it follows that whenever we name One who cleaves to One by a harmony so great that through this harmony both are one, this harmony itself must be understood, although it is not mentioned?[57] ON THE TRINITY 6.9.10.[58]

17:4 *God's Glory on Earth Accomplished*

FULL KNOWLEDGE BRINGS FULL GLORY. AUGUSTINE: If knowledge of God is eternal life, the more we grow in this knowledge, the greater the advances we make toward life. And we shall not die in the eternal life that is to come. For then, when there shall be no death, the knowledge of God shall be perfected. Then God will be most fully glorified because then it will be the completed glory, as expressed in Greek by *doxa*. . . . But glory was defined among the ancients as fame accompanied with praise. But if one's praise depends on what is said of him, how will God be praised when he himself shall be seen? And so it is said in Scripture, "Blessed are they who dwell in your house. They will be praising you forever and ever."[59] There, where there shall be full knowledge of God, his praise will continue without end. And because it is full knowledge, the glorification will also be full and complete. TRACTATES ON THE GOSPEL OF JOHN 105.3.[60]

THE EARTHLY GLORY OF SERVICE. CHRYSOSTOM: He says "on the earth," because in heaven he

[55]See 1 Cor 8:6; see also Hilary *On the Trinity* 9.32. [56]NPNF 2 9:166-67*; CCL 62A:408-10. [57]See also *Tractate* 105.3; NPNF 1 7:396; CCL 36:604 on the Spirit's inclusion. [58]NPNF 1 3:102**; CCL 50:239-40. [59]Ps 84:4 (83:5 LXX, Vg). [60]NPNF 1 7:396**; CCL 36:605.

had been already glorified in respect to his own natural glory and to his being worshiped by the angels. Christ then speaks not of that glory that is bound up with his essence—for he always possesses that glory in its fullness even if no one glorified him—but of that which comes from the worship given him by humankind. And so, "Glorify me" also has this meaning. And listen to what follows so that you may understand that he speaks of this kind of glory: "I have finished the work that you gave me to do." Homilies on the Gospel of John 80.2.[61]

The Meaning of "I Have Finished." Chrysostom: And yet the action was still in its beginning, or rather had not even yet begun. What did he mean by "I have finished" then? Either he means that "I have done all my part" or he speaks of the future, as having already happened. Or, the most likely explanation is that all had already been accomplished by anticipation because the root of blessings to come had been laid and its fruits would inevitably follow. This is so because Jesus would be present at and assisting in those things that would take place after these did. Homilies on the Gospel of John 80.2.[62]

17:5 *The Once and Future Glory*

Let Mortal Become Immortal. Hilary of Poitiers: And so, he had not abdicated his own position. And yet, he had taken ours. He prays, then, that the nature that he had assumed may be promoted to the glory that he had never renounced.[63] . . . This Son, now incarnate, prayed that flesh might be to the Father what the Son had been. He prayed that flesh, born in time, might receive the splendor of the everlasting glory, that the corruption of the flesh might be swallowed up, transformed into the power of God and the incorruption of the Spirit. On the Trinity 3.16.[64]

The Divine Word Is the Glory. Didymus the Blind: The splendid glory of the Son of God—what else would it be other than the divine Word himself, the "true Light" itself? He is not glorified by another glory through the agency of another person as if he were someone else other than the glory. No, he is himself the "Lord of glory" and King of glory, as I said previously. But since "he emptied himself, taking the form of a servant"—for he says, "the Word became flesh" and "we saw him"[65] and "he did not have any comeliness or beauty"[66]—and many did not believe that this descent had taken place, since many did not believe that God became man to reveal his divinity to those who had not recognized him, he said, "Father, glorify your Son," that is, "reveal me to those who have not recognized me, manifest my glory that I had with you as the divine Word." Therefore, Paul says, "God considered it good to reveal his Son to me, so that I might proclaim him among the Gentiles." Fragments on John 20.[67]

Creator of Old and New. Ephrem the Syrian: The Lord also said, "Give me glory in your presence from that which you gave me before the world was made." [This was] when the Father was fashioning creatures through his Son, according to the psalmist's account, "He is clothed with glory and magnificence,"[68] after which he drew them out of nothingness and established them as spotless creatures. "Lord God," he said, "you are exceedingly great. You are clothed with glory and magnificence, and you have covered yourself with light as with a cloak." . . . Following Adam's fall, [however], creatures were clothed in [Adam's] humiliation[69]. . . and the Son of the Creator came to heal them so as to remove, at the moment of his coming, all uncleannesses through the baptism of his death, as he himself has said, "The hour has come and is at hand; glorify your Son that your Son may glorify you." He asked this not as a beggar wishing to receive something, but wishing to restore and accom-

[61]NPNF 1 14:297**. [62]NPNF 1 14:297**. [63]Novatian *On the Trinity* 13, 16 (ANF 5:622, 626) notes this as another passage that proves Christ's divinity. [64]NPNF 2 9:66*; CCL 62:88. [65]Jn 1:14. [66]Is 53:2. [67]*JKGK* 186. [68]Ps 104:1 (103:1 LXX). [69]Rom 8:20.

plish the first order of creation. [He asked] for the glory with which he was clothed at the time when creatures were clothed [with glory].

For just as he formed the first essence [of creatures] through grace so that [they would be] without stain, in the glory and magnificence with which he himself was clothed, [so] too, by the mercy of God, there will be a new creation of all things, without any stain, in the glory with which he is clothed. What he said, "Give me," is to be understood of the glory that he possessed before creatures, with the Father and in the Father's presence. For the Greek text says clearly, "Glorify me with that glory that I possessed in your presence, before the world was made." Even more, in saying, "Glorify your Son, that your Son may glorify you," he did not reveal a need but a desire. The Father does not receive glory from the Son as though he had need of it, and the Son is not glorified by his Father as if he were lacking this [glory]. Commentary on Tatian's Diatessaron 19.17.[70]

The Order of Glorification. Augustine: For he had said above, "Father, the hour is come; glorify your Son, that your Son may glorify you." In this arrangement of the words, he had shown that the Father was first to be glorified by the Son, in order that the Son might glorify the Father. But now he says, "I have glorified you on the earth: I have finished the work which you gave me to do. And now glorify me." This seems to be saying that the Son himself had been the first to glorify the Father by whom he then demands to be glorified. We are therefore to understand that he used both words above in accordance with what was future and in the order in which they were future: "Glorify your Son, that your Son may glorify you." But now, he uses the word in the past tense of what was still in the future when he said, "I have glorified you on the earth: I have finished the work that you gave me to do."... For in saying that the Father was glorified by [the Son] on the earth but that he himself was glorified by the Father with the Father's very self, the Son showed them how both glorifications took place. For the Son himself glorified the Father on earth by preaching him to the nations. But the Father glorified the Son with his own self in setting him at his own right hand. But for that very reason, when the Son says afterward in reference to the glorifying of the Father, "I have glorified you," he preferred putting the verb in the past tense, in order to show that it was already done in the act of predestination, and what was with perfect certainty yet to take place was to be accounted as already done—namely, that the Son, having been glorified by the Father with the Father, would also glorify the Father on the earth. Tractates on the Gospel of John 105.5.[71]

Predestination and Consummation. Augustine: The proper order of the words is "[the glory] that I had with you before the world was."... Some have imagined that this should be understood of the human nature assumed by the Word in such a way that it would be converted into the Word and the man were changed into God, or as if the humanity were lost in the Godhead. For no one would say that the Word of God would by that change be doubled or increased.... But we [avoid this error] if we understand [he is speaking of] the predestination of the glory of his human nature, as previously being mortal, becoming immortal with the Father. And we also understand that this had already been done by predestination before the world was, as also in its own time it was done in the world.... Accordingly, when the Son saw that the time of this, his predestined glorification, had now arrived—in order that what had already been done in predestination might also now actually be accomplished—he prayed, "And now, O Father, glorify me with your own self with the glory that I had with you before the world was," that is, it is time now for me to have that glory at your right hand that I had with you by your predestination. Tractates on the Gospel of John 105.6-8.[72]

[70]*ECTD* 290-91. [71]NPNF 1 7:397**; CCL 36:605-6. [72]NPNF 1 7:397-98**; CCL 36:606-8.

17:6-10 PRAYER FOR DISCIPLES' SAFETY

[6]I have manifested thy name to the men whom thou gavest me out of the world; thine they were, and thou gavest them to me, and they have kept thy word. [7]Now they know that everything that thou hast given me is from thee; [8]for I have given them the words which thou gavest me, and they have received them and know in truth that I came from thee; and they have believed that thou didst send me. [9]I am praying for them; I am not praying for the world but for those whom thou hast given me, for they are thine; [10]all mine are thine, and thine are mine, and I am glorified in them.

OVERVIEW: The Son is now the Father's new name (TERTULLIAN) as he reveals God not only as God but also as Father (CYRIL). Such is the close relationship between Father and Son that the Father chooses not to keep the glory only for himself but also desires belief in his Son (CHRYSOSTOM). Jesus speaks these words not only to the disciples but to all who would believe (AUGUSTINE). But when he speaks of those who "were yours and you gave them to me," he does not mean there was a time when the Father had something that the Son did not have (AUGUSTINE). The Father gave the Son all things when, having all things, he begat his Son (AUGUSTINE). Christ takes what is ours, such as our infirmities and hunger, and gives us in return the gifts that come from God ([Pseudo]-ATHANASIUS). They have learned from Jesus' words that he has come from the Father (CHRYSOSTOM). Even though they may not have fully learned this at the time, Jesus anticipates his disciples' later confident faith (AUGUSTINE).

As our high priest and mediator, Jesus prays for us as man even as he also cooperates in distributing the good gifts of the Father as God (CYRIL). When Jesus says he does not pray for the world, he means those who live according to the lust of the world (AUGUSTINE). And when he again further speaks of those "you have given me," he emphasizes that everything that he does is according to the Father's will (CHRYSOSTOM). All that belongs to the Father also belongs to the Son because the Son himself is also God (AUGUSTINE), but he carries out the plan of his Father (BASIL). The Son does not somehow divide his glory with the Father (GREGORY OF NYSSA), nor is there any part of creation that is not the Son's since he is the one "by whom all things were made" (CYRIL OF JERUSALEM). Christ is the "glory of God" in that he is the almighty one for whom every knee shall bow (ORIGEN). Believers will glorify Father and Son equally (CHRYSOSTOM).

17:6 *The Father's Name*

THE SON IS NOW THE FATHER'S NEW NAME. TERTULLIAN: The name "God the Father" had been published to no one. Even Moses, who had interrogated him on that very point, had heard a different name. To us it has been revealed in the Son, for the Son is now the Father's new name. . . . That name, therefore, we pray "may be hallowed." ON PRAYER 3.[1]

"FATHER" MORE ACCURATE THAN "GOD." CYRIL OF ALEXANDRIA: When the Savior declares that he has made known the name of God the Father, it is the same as saying that he has shown the whole world his glory. How did he do this? By making himself known through his wonderful works. The Father is glorified in the Son as

[1]ANF 3:682; CCL 1:258-59. On their shared titles, see also Tertullian *Against Praxeas* 17.

in an image and type of his own form, for the beauty of the archetype is seen in its image. The only Son then has made himself known, and he is in his essence wisdom and life, the artificer and creator of the universe. He is immortal and incorruptible, pure, blameless, merciful, holy, good. His Father is known to be like him, since he could not be different in nature from his offspring. The Father's glory is seen, as in an image and type of his own form, in the glory of the Son. . . .

The Son made known the name of God the Father to teach us and make us fully comprehend not that he is the only God—for inspired Scripture had proclaimed that even before the coming of the Son—but that besides being truly God he is also rightly called "Father." This is so because in himself and proceeding from himself he has a Son possessed of the same eternal nature as his own: it was not in time that he became the Father of the Creator of the ages!

To call God "Father" is more exact than to call him "God." The word *God* signifies his dignity, but the word *Father* points to the distinctive attribute of his person. If we say "God," we declare him to be Lord of the universe. If we call him "Father," we show the way in which he is distinct as a person, for we make known the fact that he has a Son. The Son himself gave God the name of Father, as being in some sense the more appropriate and truer appellation, when he said not "I and God" but "I and the Father are one,"[2] and also, with reference to himself, "On him has God the Father set his seal."[3] And when he commanded his disciples to baptize all nations, he did not tell them to do this in the name of God but expressly ordained that they were to do it in the name of the Father and of the Son and of the Holy Spirit. Commentary on the Gospel of John 11.7.[4]

The Father Desires Belief in the Son. Chrysostom: His desire here is to teach that he is greatly loved by the Father since it is clear that he did not need to receive the [disciples] since he made them and cares for them continually. How then did he receive them? This, as I said before, shows his oneness with the Father. Now one could interpret this to mean, humanly speaking and according to its literal meaning, that the disciples will no longer belong to the Father. For if when the Father had them, the Son did not have them, it is evident that when he gave them to the Son, he relinquished his dominion over them. An even more unseemly conclusion would be that the disciples were found to have been imperfect while they were yet with the Father but then became perfect when they came to the Son. But it is ridiculous even to say such things. What then does he mean by this? He means that it seemed good to the Father also that they should believe on the Son. Homilies on the Gospel of John 81.1.[5]

Not Only Twelve, but All Who Would Believe. Augustine: If he speaks of the disciples only with whom he had eaten supper, this has nothing to do with that glorifying of which he spoke above and whereby the Son glorified the Father. For what glory is it to be known to twelve or eleven mortal creatures? But if by the men who were given to him out of the world, he means all those who should believe in him afterward and populate his great church, which was to be made up of all nations, this is without doubt the glory whereby the Son glorifies the Father. . . . "I have made known your name" . . . is similar to what he had said a little earlier, "I have glorified you on the earth," where the past is used for the future both there and here. . . . But what follows shows that he is speaking here of those who were already his disciples, not of all who should afterward believe on him. . . . At the beginning of his prayer then . . . our Lord is speaking of all believers, all to whom he should make known the Father, and this is how he would glorify him. For after saying, "that your Son also may glorify you," he immediately showed how that was to be done by adding, "As you have given him power over all

[2]Jn 10:30. [3]Jn 6:27. [4]LF 48:499-500**. [5]NPNF 1 14:299**.

flesh that he should give eternal life to as many as you have given him." Tractates on the Gospel of John 106.1-3.[6]

How the Father Gives to the Son. Augustine: But what are we to make of the words "whom you have given me out of the world," for it was said that they were not of the world? But this they were by regeneration, not by generation [i.e., by nature]. And what is meant by "they were yours, and you gave them to me"? Was there a time when they belonged to the Father and not to his only-begotten Son? Did the Father ever have anything without the Son? God forbid. But there was a time when the Son of God possessed something which that same Son as man did not possess. For he had not yet become man when he possessed all things in common with the Father. And so, by saying "they were yours," the Son of God does not separate himself from the Father but only attributes all his power to him from whom he is and has this power.... In saying, therefore, "and you gave them to me," he intimated that he had received as man the power to have them, seeing that he who was always omnipotent, was not always man. And so, while he seems rather to have attributed his receiving of them to the Father, since [Christ] is whatever he is because his existence is from [the Father], yet Christ also gave them to himself, that is, Christ, God with the Father, [gave them] to Christ as man who is not with the Father. ... Those whom God the Son chose along with the Father out of the world, the very same Son as man received out of the world from the Father. For the Father would not have given them to the Son if he had not chosen them. Tractates on the Gospel of John 106.5.[7]

17:7 *All Things Given Are the Father's*

All Things Given. Augustine: Whatever God the Father gave to God the Son, he gave in the act of begetting. For the Father gave those things to the Son without which he could not be the Son, in the same way that he gave him being itself. Tractates on the Gospel of John 106.7.[8]

Christ Takes What Is Ours and Gives What He Receives. (Pseudo-)Athanasius: He takes our infirmities without himself being infirm and hungers without hungering. He sends up what is ours that it may be abolished. As he does this, in the same way, the gifts that come from God instead of our infirmities he also receives so that we, being united to him, may be able to partake of them. This is how the Lord says, "All things whatever you have given me, I have given them," and again, "I pray for them." For he prayed for us, taking on himself what is ours and giving what he received. Since then, the Word was united to man himself and the Father purposed for us to be exalted and have power, therefore all things that we receive through him [i.e., the Son] are referred to the Word himself. For as he for our sake became man, so we for his sake are exalted. It is no absurdity then, if, as for our sake he humbled himself, so also for our sake he is said to be highly exalted. So "he gave to him" means, in essence, "[he gave] to us for his sake." And "he highly exalted him"[9] means essentially "[he exalted] us in him." And the Word himself—when we are exalted and receive and are helped as if he himself were exalted and received and were helped—gives thanks to the Father, referring what is ours to himself and saying, "All things, whatever you have given me, I have given unto them." Fourth Discourse against the Arians 7.[10]

17:8 *They Received the Words You Gave Me*

They Kept the Words Jesus Taught. Chrysostom: And from where have they learned? They have learned from my words, ... for I taught them that I came forth from you. For

[6]NPNF 1 7:399-400**; CCL 36:608-10. [7]NPNF 1 7:400-401**; CCL 36:611. [8]NPNF 1 7:402*; CCL 36:613. [9]Phil 2:9. [10]NPNF 2 4:435-36**.

this was what he has been anxious to prove throughout the whole of the Gospel. Homilies on the Gospel of John 81.1.[11]

Jesus Anticipates the Disciples' Confident Faith. Augustine: He says, "They have received them," that is, they have understood and remembered his words. For a word is received when the mind perceives it. Then he adds, "And they have known truly that I came out from you, and they have believed that you sent me."... What they truly believed was what they truly knew, just as "I came out from you" is the same as "You sent me." And, so that no one might imagine that that knowledge was one of sight and not of faith, he adds, "And they have [truly][12] believed that you did send me." They truly believed, that is, not as he said they believed when he spoke earlier ... when they were afraid of being scattered and would desert him,[13] but truly, that is, how they would soon believe [in the future]—firmly, steadily, unwaveringly, never again to be scattered to their own people while leaving Christ behind. The disciples as yet were not the way he describes them to be here in the past tense, but it was how they would be when they had received the Holy Spirit, who would teach them all things. Tractates on the Gospel of John 106.6.[14]

How the Father Gave His Words. Augustine: The question of how the Father gave those words to the Son is easier to solve if we suppose him to have received them from the Father as Son of man.... But if we understand it to be as the Begotten of the Father that he received them, let there be no time supposed previous to his having them, as if he once existed without those words. For whatever God the Father gave God the Son, he gave in the act of begetting. Tractates on the Gospel of John 106.7.[15]

17:9 *I Pray for Them, Not the World*

Our High Priest Prays As God and Man. Cyril of Alexandria: Christ, who manifested himself in the last times above the types and figures of the Law, at once our high priest and mediator, prays for us as man. And at the same time he is ever ready to cooperate with God the Father, who distributes good gifts to those who are worthy. Paul showed us this most plainly in the words "grace to you and peace from God our Father and the Lord Jesus Christ."[16] Christ, then, prays for us as man and also unites in distributing good gifts to us as God. For he, being a holy high priest, blameless and undefiled, offered himself—not for his own weakness, as was the custom of those to whom was allotted the duty of sacrificing according to the Law, but rather for the salvation of our souls. Commentary on the Gospel of John 11.8.[17]

"World" Evidences Not Being Chosen. Augustine: When the Lord was speaking to the Father of those whom he already had as disciples, he said this also among other things: "I pray for them. I pray not for the world but for those whom you have given me." By the world, he now wishes to be understood those who live according to the lust of the world and who do not stand in the gracious lot of those who were to be chosen by him out of the world. And so he says he prays not for the world but for those whom the Father has given him. For by the very fact of their having already been given to him by the Father, they have ceased belonging to that world for which he refrains from praying. And then he adds, "For they are yours." The Father did not lose those whom he gave when he gave them to the Son. After all, the Son still goes on to say, "And all mine are yours, and yours are mine." Tractates on the Gospel of John 107.1-2.[18]

Christ Acts According to the Father's Will. Chrysostom: He often repeats "you have

[11]NPNF 1 14:300**. [12]"Truly" is understood, Augustine says. [13]Jn 16:31-32. [14]NPNF 1 7:401**; CCL 36:612-13. [15]NPNF 1 7:402**; CCL 36:612-13. [16]2 Cor 1:2. [17]LF 48:506-7*. [18]NPNF 1 7:402**; CCL 36:613.

given me" to impress on them that it was all according to the Father's will. Then . . . to show them that this authority was not recent or that he had just now received them, he adds, "All things that are mine are yours, and yours are mine." . . . Do you see the equality of honor? By speaking this way, he removes any suspicion that they are either separated from the Father's power or that, before this, they had been separate from the power of the Son. Homilies on the Gospel of John 81.1.[19]

17:10a *Yours and Mine*

Christ Equal to the Father. Augustine: It is sufficiently apparent how it is that all that belongs to the Father belongs also to the Son because the Son himself is also God and, born of the Father, is the Father's equal. It is not in the sense in which the elder son is told, "You are always with me, and all that I have is yours."[20] For that was said of all those creatures that are inferior to the holy rational creature[21] and are certainly subordinate to the church. . . . But here it means that even the rational creature itself is included, which is subject only to God, so that all beneath the rational heavenly creature are also subject to him. Since then such a creature belongs to God the Father, it would not at the same time be the Son's unless he were equal to the Father. . . . For it is impossible that the saints, of whom this is said, should belong to anyone except the one who created and sanctified them. And for the same reason, everything also that is theirs must of necessity be the Son's also to whom they themselves belong. Since, then, they belong both to the Father and to the Son, they demonstrate the equality of those to whom they equally belong. But when he says, speaking of the Holy Spirit, "All things that the Father has are mine; therefore I said that he shall take of mine and shall show it unto you,"[22] he referred to those things that pertain to the divinity of the Father and in which he is equal to him in having all that he has because he adds, "he [the Holy Spirit] shall receive of mine." And the Holy Spirit would never receive from a creature what was subject to the Father and the Son. Tractates on the Gospel of John 107.2.[23]

Christ Carries Out His Father's Plan. Basil the Great: The Lord says "all mine are yours," as if he were submitting his lordship over creation to the Father, but he also adds "yours are mine," to show that the creating command came from the Father to him. The Son did not need help to accomplish his work, nor are we to believe that he received a separate commandment for each portion of his work. Such extreme inferiority would be entirely inadequate to his divine glory. Rather, the Word was full of his Father's grace. He shines forth from the Father and accomplishes everything according to his parent's plan. He is not different in essence, nor is he different in power from his Father, and if their power is equal, then their works are the same. Christ is the power of God and the wisdom of God.[24] All things were made through him,[25] and all things were created through him and for him,[26] not as if he were discharging the service of a slave, but instead he creatively fulfills the will of his Father. On the Holy Spirit 8.19.[27]

The Son Does Not Divide Glory with the Father. Gregory of Nyssa: For if the Son were not of the same nature as the Father, how could he have had in himself that which was different? Or how could he have shown in himself what was dissimilar if the foreign and alien nature did not receive the stamp of what was of a different kind from itself? But [Eunomius][28] says, "Neither does he have a divider of his glory." Here he speaks truly even though he does not know what he is saying. For the Son does not divide the glory with the Father but has the glory of the

[19]NPNF 1 14:300**; PG 59 438-39. [20]Lk 15:31. [21]The holy angels, for example. [22]Jn 16:15. [23]CCL 36:613-14; NPNF 1 7:402-3**. [24]1 Cor 1:24. [25]Jn 1:3. [26]Col 1:16. [27]*OHS* 39-40*. [28]An Arian opponent of orthodoxy

Father in its entirety, even as the Father has all the glory of the Son. For this is what he said to the Father, "All mine are yours and yours are mine." Notice how Christ also says that he will appear on the judgment day "in the glory of the Father,"[29] when he will render to every one according to his works. And by this phrase he shows the unity of nature that subsists between them. For as "there is one glory of the sun and another glory of the moon,"[30] because of the difference between the natures of those luminaries (since if both had the same glory we would think there was any difference in their nature), so he who foretold of himself that he would appear in the glory of the Father indicated by the identity of glory their community of nature. Against Eunomius 2.6.[31]

All of Creation Is the Son's. Cyril of Jerusalem: Angels did not create the world, but the only-begotten Son, begotten, as I have said, before all ages, by whom all things were made,[32] nothing having been excepted from his creation. ... "For all mine are yours and yours are mine," the Lord says in the Gospels. And this we may certainly know from the Old and New Testaments. For he who said, "Let us make man in our image and after our likeness"[33] was certainly speaking to someone present. But clearest of all are the psalmist's words, "He spoke, and they were made; he commanded, and they were created,"[34] as if the Father commanded and spoke and the Son made all things at the Father's bidding. Catechetical Lectures 11.22-23.[35]

17:10b *I Am Glorified in Them*

Glory of Omnipotence of Father and Son. Origen: Now, if all things that are the Father's are also Christ's, certainly among those things that exist is the Father's omnipotence. Of course, the only-begotten Son ought to be omnipotent, that the Son also may have all things that the Father possesses. "And I am glorified in them," he declares. For "at the name of Jesus every knee shall bow."[36] ... Therefore he is the effluence of the glory of God in this respect, that he is Almighty—the pure and vivid Wisdom itself—glorified as the effluence of omnipotence or glory.

So that it may be more clearly understood what the glory of omnipotence is, we shall add the following: God the Father is omnipotent because he has power over all things, namely, over heaven and earth, sun, moon and stars and all things in them. And he exercises his power by means of his Word. ... Now if every knee is bent to Jesus, then, without doubt, it is Jesus to whom all things are subject, and he it is who exercises power over all things and through whom all things are subject to the Father. For through wisdom, that is, by word and reason, not by force and necessity, all things are subject. On First Principles 1.2.10.[37]

Believers Will Glorify Father and Son. Chrysostom: "And I am glorified in them," that is, either that "I have power over them" or that "they shall glorify me, believing in you and me. And they shall glorify us alike." But if he is not glorified equally in them, what the Father has is no longer his. For no one is glorified in those over whom he has no authority. Yet how is the Son glorified equally? All die for him equally as they do for the Father. They preach him as they do the Father. And as they say that all things are done in his name, so also are they done in the name of the Son. Homilies on the Gospel of John 81.2.[38]

[29]Mk 8:38. [30]1 Cor 15:41. [31]NPNF 2 5:107**. [32]See the Nicene Creed. [33]Gen 1:26. [34]Ps 148:5. [35]NPNF 2 7:70**. [36]Phil 2:10-11; Origen quotes both verses. [37]ANF 4:250**; GCS 22(5):43-44. [38]NPNF 1 14:300*.

17:11-13 Prayer for Unity Amid Opposition

[11]And now I am no more in the world, but they are in the world, and I am coming to thee. Holy Father, keep them in thy name, which thou hast given me, that they may be one, even as we are one. [12]While I was with them, I kept them in thy name, which thou hast given me; I have guarded them, and none of them is lost but the son of perdition, that the scripture might be fulfilled. [13]But now I am coming to thee; and these things I speak in the world, that they may have my joy fulfilled in themselves.

Overview: Jesus was not speaking metaphorically when he said, "I am no more in the world," but rather he was already anticipating his departure from it (Augustine). As the soul dwells in the body but is not of the body, Christians dwell in the world but are not of the world (Letter to Diognetus). And so, Jesus asks the Father to keep them in the Father's name, which he has also caused to dwell in our hearts through the Eucharist. It is a prayer Jesus is so certain will be answered that he allows the disciples to sleep in the Garden of Gethsemane in the face of the approaching danger (Hilary).

Jesus prays that in the face of this danger his disciples may be one, a word that can be taken in a number of ways, including likeness of nature and harmony of will (Origen) such as is found in the bond of Christian unity expressed through love (Cyril). One becomes many through harmony (Chrysostom). The Arians, however, misunderstand Jesus' words as implying that Jesus is one with the Father in the same way that we are one with him (Athanasius). However, it is as "sons" that we become one with God, not as the Son; we become as gods, but we do not become God himself (Athanasius).

Judas fulfills the prophecy of Psalm 109 (Augustine) as he is bent on his own destruction (Leo). And so, even as he was numbered among the disciples as a child of God, he did not persevere unto the end (Augustine). Why some persevere and others do not, however, is a divine mystery (Augustine). But God will not compel his children to stay in him (Chrysostom). Christ also prays for his disciples' joy—a joy that will be fulfilled in the unity shown now and in the peace and blessedness that will be theirs in the world to come (Augustine). He also wants them to know that even as he had kept them in his care while physically present, he would still be present with them and care for them when away, because he is God (Cyril).

17:11a *No More in the World*

Jesus Already Anticipating His Departure. Augustine: "And now," he adds, "I am no more in the world, and these are in the world." If your thoughts turn to the very hour in which he was speaking, both [he and his disciples] were still in the world. And yet, we must not understand "I am no more in the world" metaphorically of the heart and life. . . . For there is one word used here that makes any such understanding altogether inadmissible, because he does not say, "And I am not in the world" but "I am no more in the world." In this way he shows that he himself had been in the world but was no more so. And so are we then at liberty to believe that he at one time savored the world, but, delivered from such a mistake, no longer retained such a disposition? Who would venture to shut himself up in so profane a meaning? It remains, therefore, that in the same sense in which he himself also was previously in the world, he declared that he was no longer in the world, that is to say, in his bodily presence. In other words, he was showing that his own absence from the world was now in the immediate future, and his disciples' absence would be later when he said that he was no longer here but they were—although both he and they were still present. He was using the prevailing custom of human speech. Do we not say every day, "he is no longer here," about someone who is on the very point of departure? And we talk this way especially about those who are at the point of death. And besides all else, the Lord himself, as if foreseeing the thoughts that might possibly be excited in those who were afterward to read these words, added, "And I come to you," explaining at least in some measure why he said, "I am no more in the world." Tractates on the Gospel of John 107.4.[1]

17:11b *They Are in the World*

Christians Are to the World What the Soul Is to the Body. Letter to Digonetus: In a word, what the soul is to the body, Christians are to the world. The soul is dispersed through all the members of the body, and Christians throughout the cities of the world. The soul dwells in the body but is not of the body. Likewise, Christians dwell in the world but are not of the world. The soul, which is invisible, is confined in the body, which is visible. In the same way, Christians are recognized as being in the world, and yet their religion remains invisible. The flesh hates the soul and wages war against it, even though it has suffered no wrong, because it is hindered from indulging in its pleasures. Similarly, the world also hates the Christians, even though it has suffered no wrong, because they set themselves against its pleasures. The soul loves the flesh that hates it and its members, and Christians love those who hate them. The soul is enclosed in the body, but it holds the body together. And though Christians are detained in the world as if in a prison, they in fact hold the world together. The soul, which is immortal, lives in a mortal dwelling. In a similar way, Christians live as strangers amid perishable things, while waiting for the imperishable in heaven. The soul, when poorly treated with respect to food and drink, becomes all the better. And so Christians when punished daily increase more and more. Such is the important position to which God has appointed them, and it is not right for them to decline it. Letter to Diognetus 6.[2]

17:11c *Holy Father, Keep Them in Your Name*

A Prayer of Thanks for the Holy Name. Didache:

We give you thanks, Holy Father,
For your holy name which you
have caused to dwell in our hearts,
And for the knowledge and faith and immortality
Which you have made known to us
Through Jesus your servant;
To you be the glory forever. . . .
Remember your church, Lord,
To deliver it from all evil
And to make it perfect in your love;
And gather it, the one that has been sanctified,
From the four winds into your kingdom,
Which you have prepared for it;
For yours is the power and the glory forever.

Didache 10.2-5.[3]

Jesus Is Certain His Prayer Will Be Answered. Hilary of Poitiers: John, who especially brings out the working of spiritual causes in the Gospel, preserves this prayer of the Lord for the apostles that all the others passed over. Notice how he prayed, namely, "Holy Father, keep them in your name. . . . While I was with them, I kept them in your name: those whom you gave me I have kept." That prayer was not for himself but for his apostles. He was

[1]NPNF 1 7:403**; CCL 36:614. [2]*AF* 541-43. [3]*AF* 261-63.

not in sorrow for himself[4] since he asks them to pray that they won't be tempted. . . . And when he prays, he prays for those whom he preserved, so long as he was with them, whom he now hands over to the Father to preserve. Now that he is about to accomplish the mystery of death, he begs the Father to guard them. The presence of the angel who was sent to him (if this explanation is true) is no doubt significant. Jesus showed his certainty that the prayer was answered when, at its close, he commands the disciples to sleep.[5] The effect of this prayer and the security that prompted the command, "sleep," is noticed by the Evangelist in the course of the passion, when he says of the apostles just before they escaped from the hands of the pursuers, "That the word might be fulfilled which he had spoken, 'Of those whom you have given me, I lost not one of them .' " He himself fulfills the petition of his prayer, and they are all safe. But he asks that those whom he has preserved the Father will now preserve in his own name. And they are preserved; the faith of Peter does not fail: it cowered, but repentance followed immediately. On the Trinity 10.42.[6]

17:11d *That They May Be One*[7]

The Meanings of "One." Origen: "One" has many meanings, including that of likeness. It is used both of harmony[8] and likeness.[9] "All the believers were of one heart and mind,"[10] and in the same way, "by one Spirit we were all baptized into one body."[11] According to likeness of nature and having Adam as the natural origin and head of our birth, we are all said to have one body. So also we are inscribed as having Christ as head through our new birth, which has become to us a figure of the death and resurrection of him who rose as the firstborn from the dead. We inscribe him as head according to the prefiguring of his resurrection, of whom we are individually members and a body, through the Spirit, begotten unto incorruption.[12] Fragment 140 on the Gospel of John.[13]

The Bond of Christian Unity in Love. Cyril of Alexandria: Christ wishes the disciples to be kept in a state of unity by maintaining a like-mindedness and an identity of will, being mingled together as it were in soul and spirit and in the law of peace and love for one another. He wishes them to be bound together tightly with an unbreakable bond of love, that they may advance to such a degree of unity that their freely chosen association might even become an image of the natural unity that is conceived to exist between the Father and the Son. That is to say, he wishes them to enjoy a unity that is inseparable and indestructible, which may not be enticed away into a dissimilarity of wills by anything at all that exists in the world or any pursuit of pleasure, but rather reserves the power of love in the unity of devotion and holiness. And this is what happened. For as we read in the Acts of the Apostles, "the company of those who believed were of one heart and soul,"[14] that is, in the unity of the Spirit. This is also what Paul himself meant when he said "one body and one Spirit."[15] "We who are many are one body in Christ for we all partake of the one bread,"[16] and we have all been anointed in the one Spirit, the Spirit of Christ.[17] Commentary on the Gospel of John 11.9.[18]

Love Is a Multiplier. Chrysostom: "For the will of the Father, and of the Son and of the Holy Spirit is one." This is what he wants us to be as well when he says, "That they may be one, as you and I are one." There is nothing that can equal unanimity and concord, for this is how one becomes many. If two or ten are of one mind, the one is no longer one, but each one is multiplied tenfold, and you will find the one in the ten and

[4]Hilary here speaking of the cup Jesus asked to pass from him. [5]Hilary may be reflecting a variant in Matthew's and Mark's accounts of Jesus' prayer. [6]NPNF 2 9:193*; CCL 62A:495-96. [7]See also comments under Jn 17:20-26. [8]Gk *symphōnian*; see 1 Cor 7:5; 2 Cor 6:15; Lk 5:36. [9]Gk *homoiotēta*; see Heb 4:15; 7:15. [10]Acts 4:32. [11]1 Cor 12:13. [12]See 1 Cor 15:49-54. [13]AEG 5:315**; GCS 10(4):574. [14]Acts 4:32. [15]Eph 4:4. [16]1 Cor 10:17; see Rom 12:5. [17]See 1 Cor 12:13. [18]COA 128.

the ten in the one. And if they have an enemy, he who attacks the one (as having attacked the ten) is defeated, for he is the target of ten opponents instead of one. Is someone in need? No, he is not in need, for he is wealthy in his greater part, that is, in the nine. And the needy part, the lesser, is concealed by the wealthy part, the greater. Each of these has twenty hands, twenty eyes and as many feet. For he does not see with his own eyes alone but with those of the others as well. He does not walk with his own feet alone but with those of the others. He does not work with his own hands alone but with theirs. He has ten souls, for not only does he think about himself, but those souls also think about him. And if they are made into a hundred, it will still be the same, and their power will be extended even more. Don't you see how the excess of love makes the one both irresistible and multiplied? See how one can even be in many places, the same both in Persia and in Rome? Don't you see that what nature cannot do, love can? . . . See what a multiplier love is when it can even make one a thousand. Why then do we not acquire this power and place ourselves in safety? This is better than all power or riches. This is more than health, than light itself. It is the groundwork for courage. HOMILIES ON THE GOSPEL OF JOHN 78.3-4.[19]

ARIAN MISUNDERSTANDING OF "ONE." ATHANASIUS: The Arians, however, reply . . . the Son and the Father are one as the Father is in the Son and the Son in the Father—just as we too may become one in him. For this is written in the Gospel according to John.[20] . . . Then, as having found an evasion, these crafty ones add [to John's Gospel], "If, as we become one in the Father, so also the Son and the Father are one, and thus the Son too is in the Father, how do you pretend that 'I and the Father are One,' and 'I in the Father and the Father in Me,' mean that the Son is proper and like the Father's essence? For it follows either that we too are proper to the Father's essence or the Son is foreign to it as we are foreign." This is how they idly babble. But they are, in fact, devilishly reckless. . . . For what is given to humankind by grace is what they would make equal to the Godhead of the giver. And so, hearing that human beings are called sons, they considered themselves equal to the true Son who is by nature [a Son of God]. And now again hearing from the Savior, "that they may be one as we are," they deceive themselves and are arrogant enough to think that they may be such as the Son is in the Father and the Father in the Son—not considering the fall of their father the devil who thought the same thing. DISCOURSES AGAINST THE ARIANS 3.25.17.[21]

A TRUE UNDERSTANDING OF "ONE." ATHANASIUS: For it is as "sons" [that we become one with God], not as the Son. We become *as* "gods"—we do not become God himself. We are not *as* the Father but "merciful as the Father." And, as has been said, by becoming one in this way, that is, as the Father and the Son are one, we shall be one. We shall be so, however, not as the Father is by nature in the Son and the Son in the Father, but according to our own nature. And in this way it is possible for us then to be molded and to learn how we ought to be one, just as we learned also to be merciful. For similar things are naturally one with other similar things. And so, all flesh is ranked together in kind.[22] But the Word is unlike us, although it is like the Father. And therefore, while the Son is in nature and truth one with his own Father, we—as being of one kind with each other (for from one were all made, and one is the nature of all men and women)—become one in our good disposition toward each other.[23] We have as our copy the Son's natural unity with the Father. For he taught us meekness from himself, saying, "Learn from me, for I am meek and lowly in heart."[24] He taught us this not so that we may become equal to him (which is impossible) but so

[19]NPNF 1 14:289-90**. [20]Athanasius quotes the Arian usage of Jn 17:11, 20-23. [21]NPNF 2 4:403**. [22]See *Against the Arians* 2.23, 42. [23]Gk *diathesei*. See also Hippolytus *Against Noetus* 7 on this point. [24]Mt 11:29.

that when we look toward his [example], we may continually remain meek. So also here he desires that our good disposition toward each other should be true and firm and indissoluble, taking himself as the pattern. And so he says, "that they may be one as we are," whose oneness is indivisible. And so, when they learn from us of that indivisible nature, they may preserve agreement with each other in a similar way. Discourses against the Arians 3.25.20.[25]

17:12 *None of Them Was Lost but the Son of Perdition*

Prophecy of Psalm 109 Fulfilled. Augustine: The betrayer of Christ was called the son of perdition, as foreordained to perdition, according to the Scripture, where it is specially prophesied of him in Psalm 109.[26] Tractates on the Gospel of John 107.7.[27]

Judas Bent on His Own Destruction. Leo the Great: But O ungodliest of people, "seed of Canaan and not of Judah,"[28] and no longer "a vessel of election" but "a son of perdition" and death! You thought the devil's instigations would profit you better so that, inflamed with the torch of greed, you were ablaze to gain thirty pieces of silver without seeing the riches you would lose. For even if you did not think the Lord's promises were to be believed, what reason was there for preferring so small a sum of money to what you had already received? You were allowed to command the evil spirits, to heal the sick, to receive honor with the rest of the apostles. And that you might satisfy your thirst for gain, you had the opportunity to steal from the box that was in your charge. But your mind, which lusted after forbidden things, was more strongly stimulated by what was less allowed. It was not the amount of the price that pleased you so much as the enormity of the sin. And so your wicked bargain is not so detestable merely because you valued the Lord so cheaply but because you sold him who was the redeemer, yes, even yours, and yet you asked for no pity for yourself.[29] And justly was your punishment put into your own hands because none could be found more cruelly bent on your destruction than yourself. Sermon 67.4.[30]

Why God Grants Perseverance to Some and Not Others Is a Mystery. Augustine: Here, if I am asked why God should not have given them perseverance to whom he gave that love by which they might live in a Christian way, I answer that I do not know. I am not speaking arrogantly but rather with an acknowledgment of my own small capabilities when I hear the apostle saying, "O man, who are you that makes a reply against God?"[31] . . . Insofar as he condescends to make his judgments known to us, let us give thanks. However, insofar as he thinks it is fitting to conceal them, let us not murmur against his counsel. Rather, let us believe that this also is the most wholesome for us. But whoever of you are in opposition to his grace and ask [concerning this question of perseverance], what do you yourself say? It is well that you do not deny yourself to be a Christian and boast of being a catholic. If, therefore, you confess that to persevere to the end in good is God's gift, I think that equally with me you are ignorant why one person should receive this gift and another should not receive it. And in this case we are both unable to penetrate the unsearchable judgments of God. On Rebuke and Grace 17.[32]

A Son of Promise Does Not Perish. Augustine: When, therefore, God's children say of those who did not have perseverance, "They went out from us, but they were not of us," and add, "Because if they had been of us, they would assuredly have continued with us,"[33] what else are they saying than that they were not children,

[25]NPNF 2 4:405**. [26]Ps 108 Vg. [27]NPNF 1 7:404; CCL 36:615. [28]Sus 56, said by Daniel to one of the two elders; see also Acts 9:15. [29]*Redemptorem etiam tuum ne tibi parceres, vendidisti.* See also *Sermon* 58.3, 4; *Sermon* 62.4. [30]NPNF 2 12:179**; CCL 138A:410-11. [31]Rom 9:20; he also cites Rom 11:33. [32]PL 44:925-26; NPNF 1 5:478**. [33]1 Jn 2:19.

even when they were called and professed to be children? It is not because they simulated righteousness but because they did not continue in it. For he does not say, "If they had been of us, they would assuredly have maintained a real and not a feigned righteousness with us." Rather, he says, "If they had been of us, they would assuredly have continued with us." Beyond a doubt, he wanted them to continue in goodness. Therefore they were in goodness. However, because they did not remain in it—that is, they did not persevere to the end—he says, "They were not of us, even when they were with us." In other words, they were not of the number of children even when they were in the faith as children because those who are truly children are foreknown and predestined as conformed to the image of his Son. They are called according to his purpose so as to be elected, as is evident in the fact that the son of promise does not perish, but the son of perdition does. On Rebuke and Grace 20.[34]

No Compulsion to Stay. Chrysostom: In another place he says, "Of all that you gave me, I will surely lose nothing."[35] Yet not only was [Judas] lost, but also many afterward were lost too. So how then can he say, "I will not lose any?" [He means], "At least for my part, I will not lose them." So in another place, declaring the matter more clearly, he said, "I will not reject anyone who comes to me."[36] In other words, [Jesus is saying], it is not through any fault on my part. They will not be lost at my instigation or because I abandon them. But if they start going away on their own, I will not force them back. Homilies on the Gospel of John 81.2.[37]

17:13 *Christ Does Not Leave Them Without Joy*

Their Joy Is Their Unity. Augustine: But he tells what this joy is when he says, "That they may have my joy fulfilled in themselves." This has already been elucidated above where he says, "That they may be one, even as we are." This joy of his that is bestowed on them by him was to be fulfilled, he says, in them. And for that very end he declared that he had spoken in the world. This is that peace and blessedness in the world to come. If we want to attain it, we must live temperately and righteously and godly in the present. Tractates on the Gospel of John 107.8.[38]

Christ Works in Them. Cyril of Alexandria: Showing himself to them simultaneously as God and man, Christ induces his disciples to reflect that he would work to accomplish their salvation in God whether present or absent. And that as he had them in his keeping while he was with them on the earth in the form of man, so also would he keep them while absent from them as God.... For that which is divine is not bounded by space and is not far from anything that exists but fills and pervades the universe. And though it is present in all things, it is contained by none. When addressing his own Father, Christ says, "Holy Father, keep them," referring ... to the universal working of the power of the Father. And at the same time showing that he does not stand apart from the nature of the Father but being in it and proceeding from it, Christ is indivisibly united with it, though he is conceived of as independently existing. Commentary on the Gospel of John 11.9.[39]

[34]PL 44:928; NPNF 1 5:480**. See also *Letter* 159.4. [35]Jn 6:39. [36]Jn 6:37. [37]NPNF 1 14:301**. [38]NPNF 1 7:404**; CCL 36:616. [39]LF 48:521*.

17:14-19 SANCTIFIED BY TRUTH IN A WORLD OF HATE

[14]I have given them thy word; and the world has hated them because they are not of the world, even as I am not of the world. [15]I do not pray that thou shouldst take them out of the world, but that thou shouldst keep them from the evil one.[k] [16]They are not of the world, even as I am not of the world. [17]Sanctify them in the truth; thy word is truth. [18]As thou didst send me into the world, so I have sent them into the world. [19]And for their sake I consecrate myself, that they also may be consecrated in truth.

k Or *from evil*

OVERVIEW: The world hates those who no longer look at it but begin to look beyond to what is unseen (ORIGEN). The moment the mind stops thinking about the affairs of the world, it encounters God (JOHN THE ELDER). The disciples were of the world by generation but were taken out of the world through regeneration (AUGUSTINE). The world hates Christ because it is in conflict with his words and teaching (CYRIL). It is only as we imitate Christ's detachment from the world that we become strangers to the world (APHRAHAT). But even as Christ was taken out of the world, he left his apostles in the world to keep his message alive and guide others to the virtues of a godly life (CYRIL). In praying that they be kept from evil, he calls on us to pray like this as well (DIDACHE). He is also praying for their growth in sanctification (AUGUSTINE), preparing them and us for a worthy participation in heaven (CHRYSOSTOM). Experience itself teaches us to look beyond this world (CASSIAN) to our citizenship in heaven (CAESARIUS). We are to be reborn, leaving the world as a baby leaves the womb (JOHN THE ELDER).

Jesus' prayer for his disciples calls on us to imitate Christ, who is the truth, so that we become virtuous just as he is (ATHANASIUS). In this prayer we also learn that not only does the Spirit sanctify but the Father and Son do as well (GREGORY OF NYSSA). To sanctify them in the truth is to make them holy by the gift of the Spirit and cause them to hold right and true doctrine (CHRYSOSTOM). The word of the Father, which is truth, is his own Word, his only-begotten in whom we believe (AUGUSTINE).

Having been sanctified from sin (AUGUSTINE), Jesus' disciples are now sent out into the world for mission as he equips them with the power of the Spirit (THEODORE). Christ offers himself as a holy sacrifice in order to sanctify his disciples (THEODORE, CHRYSOSTOM). His consecration means our consecration (CYRIL) as we the members of his body are sanctified in Christ our head (AUGUSTINE). Christ is sanctified as a human being even as he also sanctifies us as God (AMBROSE).

17:14 *The World Hates Those Not of the World*

CHANGE OF PERSPECTIVE CAN ELICIT HATE. ORIGEN: "And the world hated them, because they are not of the world," for it hated us from the time when we no longer looked "at the things that are seen but at the things that are not seen,"[1] because of the teaching of Jesus. COMMENTARY ON MATTHEW 13.20.[2]

[1]2 Cor 4:18. [2]ANF 9:487*.

Leave the World Behind. John the Elder: He said that his friends were not of the world and that the world has hated them. The fulfillment of his commandments[3] is the cross, that is to say, the forgetting and obliteration of all desire for the world and a yearning desire to depart from it in the flame of love, as was the case with Paul. In openness of speech toward my God and in confidence I truly say that the moment the mind strips off the world, it puts on Christ. The moment it departs from thinking about the affairs of the world, it encounters God. The moment the soul cuts off from itself associating with the world, the Spirit starts singing within it of its ineffable mysteries. It is a "mystery for me"[4] here, and a cause for fear. But to the true, truth is revealed. Letter 5.2.[5]

Otherworldly Generation. Augustine: And then, adding the reason for their being hated by the world, he says, "Because they are not of the world, even as I am not of the world." This was conferred on them by regeneration. For by generation they were of the world, as he had already said to them, "I have chosen you out of the world."[6] It was therefore a gracious privilege bestowed on them, that they, like himself, should not be of the world, through the deliverance that he was giving them from the world. He, however, was never of the world. For even in respect of his servant form he was born of that Holy Spirit of whom they were born again. For if they were no more of the world, because they were born again of the Holy Spirit, he too was never of the world because he was born of the Holy Spirit. Tractates on the Gospel of John 108.1.[7]

Why the World Hates Christ. Cyril of Alexandria: The world indeed hates Christ because it is in conflict with his words and does not accept his teaching. People's minds entirely yield to base desires. And even as the world hates our Savior Christ, it has also hated the disciples who carry through him his message. Commentary on the Gospel of John 11.9.[8]

Imitate Christ's Detachment. Aphrahat: Let us hate ourselves and love Christ as he loved us and gave himself up for our sakes.[9] Let us honor the spirit of Christ that we may receive grace from him. Let us be strangers to the world, even as Christ was not of it. Let us be humble and mild that we may inherit the land of life. Let us be unflagging in his service that he may cause us to serve in the abode of the saints. Let us pray his prayer in purity that it may have access to the Lord of majesty. Let us be partakers in his suffering so that we may also rise up in his resurrection.[10] Let us bear his sign on our bodies that we may be delivered from the wrath to come. Demonstration 6.[11]

17:15a *Do Not Take Them Out of the World*

Why the Apostles Should Stay in the World. Cyril of Alexandria: Christ does not wish for the apostles to be set free of human affairs or to be rid of life in the body when they have not yet finished the course of their apostleship or distinguished themselves by the virtues of a godly life. Rather, his desire is so see them live their lives in the company of people in the world and guide the footsteps of those who are his to a state of life well pleasing to God. After they have done this, then at last, with the glory they have achieved, they will be carried into the heavenly city and dwell with the company of the holy angels. Commentary on the Gospel of John 11.9.[12]

17:15b *Keep Them from Evil*

Pray to Be Kept from Evil. Didache: "And do not lead us into temptation, but deliver us from the evil one;[13] for yours is the power and the glory forever."[14] Pray like this three times a day. Didache 8.2-3.[15]

---

[3]Jn 14:15, 23. [4]Is 24:16 (Syriac). [5]CS 101:331. [6]Jn 15:19. [7]NPNF 1 7:404*; CCL 36:616. [8]LF 48:526*. [9]Jn 12:25; Eph 5:2. [10]See 2 Tim 2:11-12. [11]NPNF 2 13:362-63**. [12]LF 48:527*. [13]Or, possibly, "evil." [14]See Mt 6:13, textual variant. [15]*AF* 259.

Sanctification Keeps Them from Evil. Augustine: "I pray not," he adds, "that you should take them out of the world but that you should keep them from the evil." For they still thought it was necessary to be in the world, although they were no longer of it. Then he repeats the same statement: "They are not of the world, even as I am not of the world. Sanctify them in the truth." For they are kept from the evil, as he had previously prayed that they might be. But it may be inquired how they were no longer of the world if they were not yet sanctified in the truth. Or, if they already were, why does he request that they should be sanctified? Isn't it because even those who are sanctified still continue to make progress in the same sanctification and grow in holiness? And they do not do so without the aid of God's grace but by his sanctifying of their progress, even as he sanctified them at the outset [of their sanctification]. Tractates on the Gospel of John 108.2.[16]

Preparation for Worthy Participation in Heaven. Chrysostom: Christ came not to put us to death and deliver us from the present life in that sense but to leave us in the world and prepare us for a worthy participation in our heavenly home. This is why he said to the Father, "And these are in the world, and I come to you. I pray not that you should take them from the world but that you should keep them from the evil," that is, from sin. Further, those who insist that the present life is evil ... would have to agree that murderers would deserve a crown for rescuing us from evil. ... Miserable, wretched person! What are you saying? Is this life evil, a life where we have learned to know God, and meditate on things to come, and have become angels instead of humans and take part in the choirs of the heavenly powers? ... In calling the present world evil, he[17] has accommodated himself to our usage. Commentary on Galatians 1.4.[18]

17:16 *Foreign to the World*

Experience Teaches Us to Look Beyond. John Cassian: The Lord speaks to his Father in the Gospel as follows: "They are not of the world, as I am not of the world." ... No one can understand the truth and force of this except one who has gone through the trials of what [Jesus] was talking about—one who has been under the teacher of experience. This is someone the eyes of whose soul the Lord has turned away from all things present, so that he no longer considers them as things that will soon pass away but as things that are already over and done with, and he sees them vanish into nothing, like misty smoke. ... And so, if we are anxious to attain true perfection, we ought to ensure that we have outwardly with the body made light of parents, home, the riches and pleasures of the world, so that we may also inwardly with the heart forsake all these things and never be drawn back by any desires to what we have forsaken. Conference 3.7.2, 4-5.[19]

Christians Look to Another City. Caesarius of Arles: There are two cities, dearest brothers. ... The first is the city of this world, the second, the city of paradise. The first city is full of labor, the second is restful. The first is full of misery, the second is blessed. If a person lives sinfully in the first, he cannot arrive in the second. We must be pilgrims in this world in order to be citizens of heaven. If one wants to love this world and remain a citizen of it, he has no place in heaven, for we prove our pilgrim status by our longing for our true country. Let no one deceive himself, beloved brothers. The true country of Christians is in heaven, not here. ... The angels are our fellow citizens. Our parents are the patriarchs, prophets, apostles and martyrs. Our King is Christ. May we live, therefore, in this earthly sojourn in a manner that will enable us to long for such a country during our stay here. Sermon 151.2.[20]

---

[16]NPNF 1 7:404-5**; CCL 36:616-17. [17]Paul, commenting on Gal 1:4, makes the same point as Christ in Jn 17:15. [18]NPNF 1 13:5-6**. [19]ACW 57:125-26**. Origen uses this passage to speculate on whether there are other worlds besides ours. See *On First Principles* 2.3.6. [20]MFC 4:185*; CCL 104:618.

Leave the World as a Baby Leaves the Womb. John the Elder: Do you want Christ to appear to you in prayer as he would to his friend? Let love for him be within you without a moment's break. Do you want this love to be continually inflamed in your soul? Then remove from your soul love for the world. Do you want your home to be in that place which is without place, being in God? Leave the world, as a baby leaves the womb. Then you will have seen reality. For Christ cannot live with the world. I beg you, listen to him as he demonstrates to you with his own words, "I am not of the world." This is why it chases me away from where I would live, and also why I cannot live with it, "because it hates me."[21] But he is continuously overshadowing the soul and visiting it, so that if it empties itself of the things of the world he can dwell in it. Letter 5.1.[22]

17:17 *Sanctify Them in Your Word, Which Is Truth*

Imitating the Truth, We Become Sons. Athanasius: We are made sons through Christ by adoption and grace, partaking of his Spirit. For "as many as received him," he says, "to them he gave power to become children of God, even to them that believe on his name."[23] And therefore, he is also the Truth, saying, "I am the Truth,"[24] and in his address to his Father, he said, "Sanctify them through your Truth, your Word is Truth." We, by imitation[25] [of this truth], become virtuous and sons. Therefore, he did not say "that they may be one as we are" so that we might become such as he is, but that as he, being the Word, is in his own Father, we too, seeing him as our example, might become one toward each other in concord and oneness of spirit, nor be at variance as the Corinthians, but be of one mind as those five thousand in the Acts of the Apostles who were as one.[26] Discourses Against the Arians 3.25.19.[27]

Not Only the Spirit Sanctifies. Gregory of Nyssa: The Father, the Son and the Holy Spirit alike give sanctification, life, light, comfort, and any other similar graces. And let no one attribute the power of sanctification in a special sense to the Spirit when he hears the Savior in the Gospel saying to the Father concerning his disciples, "Father, sanctify them in your name."[28] So too all the other gifts are produced in those who are worthy alike by the Father, the Son and the Holy Spirit: every grace and power, guidance, life, comfort, the change to immortality, the passage to liberty, and every other boon that exists, which descends to us. On the Holy Trinity.[29]

Set Apart for the Word and Preaching. Chrysostom: "Make them holy by the gift of the Spirit and right doctrines." As when he says, "You are clean through the word that I spoke to you,"[30] so now he says the same thing, "Instruct them, teach them the truth." "And yet he says that the Spirit does this. Why then does he now ask it from the Father?" He asks so that you may again learn their equality of honor. For right doctrines concerning God sanctify the soul. And if he says that they are sanctified by the word, do not be amazed. And to show that he speaks of doctrines, he adds, "Your word is truth," that is, "there is no falsehood in it, and all that is said in it must happen." Again, it signifies nothing purely figurative or material. Paul says something similar concerning the church that he has sanctified by the Word. For the Word of God is also used to cleanse.[31] Moreover, "sanctify them" seems to me to signify something else, namely, "set them apart for the Word and for preaching." And this is made plain from what follows. For, he says, "as you have sent me into the world, even so have I also

[21]Jn 7:7; 15:18. [22]CS 101:330-31. [23]Jn 1:12. [24]See Jn 14:6. [25]Gk *kata mimēsin*. On this point of imitating the truth, see also Clement of Alexandria *The Instructor* 1.3; Gregory of Nazianzus *Letter* 102; Irenaeus *Against Heresies* 5.1; Augustine *Sermon* 101.6; *On the Trinity* 4.17; 9.21; Eusebius *Ecclesiastical Theology* 3. [26]Acts 4:4, 32. [27]NPNF 2 4:404-5**. [28]Jn 17:11 and 17 are here conflated. [29]NPNF 2 5:328**. See also Basil *Letters* 189.7; Ambrose *On the Holy Spirit* 3.4.25. [30]See Jn 15:3. [31]Eph 5:26.

sent them into the world." Homilies on the Gospel of John 82.1.[32]

The Logos Is Truth. Augustine: "Your speech (*sermo*) is truth." What else did he mean than "I am the truth?"[33] For the Greek Gospel has *logos*, which is also the word that is found in the passage where it is said, "In the beginning was the Word, and the Word was with God, and the Word was God."[34] And that Word at least we know to be the only begotten Son of God, which "was made flesh and dwelt among us." And so, there also might have been put here (as it actually has been put in certain copies) "Your Word is truth," just as in some copies that other passage is written, "In the beginning was the speech." But in the Greek without any variation it is *logos* in both cases. The Father therefore sanctifies in the truth—that is, in his own Word, in his Only Begotten—his own heirs and his [Son's] co-heirs. Tractates on the Gospel of John 108.3.[35]

17:18 *I Send Them into the World*

Sanctified from Sin, Now Sent. Augustine: But now he still goes on to speak of the apostles, for he proceeds to add, "As you have sent me into the world, even so have I also sent them into the world." Whom did he send in this way but his apostles? For even the very name of apostles, which is a Greek word, signifies in Latin nothing more than, those that are sent. God, therefore, sent his Son, not in sinful flesh but in the likeness of sinful flesh.[36] And his Son sent those who (born themselves in sinful flesh) were sanctified by him from the defilement of sin. Tractates on the Gospel of John 108.4.[37]

The Power of the Spirit for Mission. Theodore of Mopsuestia: The participation in the Spirit will not only give them the power to be freed from evil but will make them so strong that they will travel throughout the world and preach as I have preached. Commentary on John 6.17.18.[38]

17:19 *For Their Sakes, I Sanctify Myself*

Disciples Empowered Through Christ's Passion. Theodore of Mopsuestia: [Christ says], "The reason I bring myself to the passion is so that through me they may obtain the sanctification that comes through the Spirit, and be sanctified and be empowered to preach the truth, being certain of the hope of the resurrection." He says that he sanctifies himself because, after the passion, he would hurry to heaven along with his own body and be in holiness.[39] Commentary on John 6.17.19.[40]

Christ Offers Himself or His Disciples As a Sacrifice. Chrysostom: What does he mean by "I sanctify myself"? He means, "I offer to you a sacrifice." Now all sacrifices are called "holy." But those that are specially called "holy" are reserved for God. In [Old Testament times], sanctification was typologically indicated by the sheep. But now it is not in type but in truth itself. Therefore he says, "That they may be sanctified in your truth." "For I both dedicate them to you and make them an offering." He says this either because the disciples' Head was being made so, or because they too would be sacrificed. For it says elsewhere, "Present your bodies as a living sacrifice, holy,"[41] and "We were counted as sheep for the slaughter."[42] And he makes them a sacrifice and offering apart from death. For it is clear from what follows that he was alluding to his own sacrifice when he said, "I sanctify." Homilies on the Gospel of John 82.1.[43]

His Consecration Means Our Consecration. Cyril of Alexandria: Christ called down on us the ancient gift of humanity,[44] that is, sanctification through the Spirit and communion with the divine nature, his disciples being the

[32]NPNF 1 14:303*. [33]See Jn 14:6. [34]Jn 1:1. [35]NPNF 1 7:405*; CCL 36:617. [36]See Jn 1:1, 14. [37]NPNF 1 7:405*; CCL 36:617. [38]CSCO 4 3:318. [39]Note again the separation of the two natures in Theodore. [40]CSCO 4 3:318-19. [41]Rom 12:1. [42]Ps 44:22 (43:22 LXX). [43]NPNF 1 14:303**. [44]See Eph 2:10.

first to receive it. For the saying is true that the hard-working farmer ought to have the first share of the crops.[45] But, in order for him to have preeminence[46] in this—for it is fitting that . . . he is seen as the beginning and the gate and the way of every good thing for us—he is inspired to add what follows, namely, the words "for their sake I consecrate myself." Commentary on the Gospel of John 11.10.[47]

The Members Sanctified in the Head. Augustine: But since, on the ground that the Mediator between God and humanity, the man Christ Jesus, has become head of the church, they are his members. Therefore he says in the words that follow, "And for their sakes I sanctify myself." For what does he mean by the words "and for their sakes I sanctify myself" but I sanctify them in myself, since they also are myself? For those of whom he speaks in this way are, as I have said, his members. And the head and body are one Christ.[48]. . . And to be assured of the certainty of this in the present passage, listen to what follows. For after saying, "and for their sakes I sanctify myself"—to let us understand that he thereby meant that he would sanctify them in himself—he immediately added, "that they also may be sanctified in the truth." And what else is this but in me, in accordance with the fact that the truth is that Word in the beginning that is God? Tractates on the Gospel of John 108.5.[49]

Christ Is Sanctified and Sanctifies. Ambrose: Let us pay attention to the distinction of the Godhead from the flesh. In each there speaks one and the same Son of God, for each nature is present in him. And yet, while it is the same person who speaks, he does not always speak in the same way. At one time you see in him the glory of God, at another time human characteristics. As God he speaks the things of God because he is the Word. As man he speaks in a human way because he speaks in my nature. . . . Even the letter itself [here] teaches us that it is not the Godhead but the flesh that needed sanctification. For the Lord himself said, "And I sanctify myself for them," in order that you may acknowledge that he is both sanctified in the flesh for us and sanctifies by virtue of his divinity. On the Christian Faith 2.9.77-78.[50]

[45]See 2 Tim 2:6. [46]See Col 1:18. [47]LF 48:536*. [48]Augustine quotes Gal 3:16, 29; Col 1:24. [49]NPNF 1 7:405**; CCL 36:617-18. [50]NPNF 2 10:233-34**; CSEL 78:84-85.

17:20-26 PRAYER FOR ALL BELIEVERS: UNITY

[20]I do not pray for these only, but also for those who believe in me through their word, [21]that they may all be one; even as thou, Father, art in me, and I in thee, that they also may be in us, so that the world may believe that thou hast sent me. [22]The glory which thou hast given me I have given to them, that they may be one even as we are one, [23]I in them and thou in me, that they may become perfectly one, so that the world may know that thou hast sent me and hast loved them even as thou hast loved me. [24]Father, I desire that they also, whom thou hast given me, may be with me where I am, to behold my glory which thou hast given me in thy love for me before the foundation

of the world. [25]*O righteous Father, the world has not known thee, but I have known thee; and these know that thou hast sent me.* [26]*I made known to them thy name, and I will make it known, that the love with which thou hast loved me may be in them, and I in them.*

OVERVIEW: In Christ's prayer for the unity of all who believe, we see not only an exhortation for unity in the church (CYPRIAN) but also look forward to the time when humanity is restored to the unity it once had with God (ORIGEN). This is a unity not of nature, however, but according to grace (JEROME). Jesus speaks here of a unity of will that binds us together (HILARY). The unity of the church is modeled on that of the Trinity (JEROME, AMBROSE). When believers are united in faith and confession, they are enabled by God's grace to become one even as our Lord is able to bring unity from diversity through participation in the Spirit and his gifts (CYRIL). When there is peace and unity, it is a powerful witness to the world (CHRYSOSTOM).

Christ both received and gave glory as he took on human nature so that it might be exalted, and thus we receive his glory (ATHANASIUS). The Father bestowed his glory on the Son and through the Son onto us (HILARY) by means of the Spirit, who is the glory that binds us together; this glory Christ later bestowed on his disciples so that they might be one (GREGORY OF NYSSA). This glory may also be understood as Christ's immortality, which human nature would afterward receive from him (AUGUSTINE). He also speaks of the perfect oneness we have with him and the Father, a oneness achieved as he unites himself to us in the sacrament (CYRIL). As we are cleansed from the sin that separates us, we become fused together by the Spirit into our one mediator Jesus Christ (AUGUSTINE). The result is that the Father loves us as he sees in us the likeness of his own Son and so calls us his sons and daughters by adoption (AMBROSE), but loves us like his own Son (CYRIL). When we look on the Son of God, we are glorified by that sight just as those who look on the bright beams of the sun on a clear day rejoice in its rays (CHRYSOSTOM).

Christ prays to his Father that we may be where he is. Our concern should not be about where Christ resides but that we be found where he is (AUGUSTINE). When we are fully united with him in that age that is yet to come, everything we feel, understand, think or do will be wholly of God, since there will no longer be any evil to corrupt these things (ORIGEN). Christ allows us to share in his glory for our benefit, not his (IRENAEUS). It is a glory we look forward to as we struggle under present-day persecution (CYPRIAN). Jesus here expresses his frustration with the world's ignorance (CHRYSOSTOM) of this future glory that is ours because of his descent to be among us to restore our human nature (CYRIL). Christ made his Father's name known to the world and is counting on us to continue making his name known through our actions of love (CHRYSOSTOM), which are in us because we are in Christ, even as he is in us (AUGUSTINE).

17:20 *Prayer of Unity for All Who Believe*

CALL FOR UNITY. CYPRIAN: The Lord's loving-kindness, no less than his mercy, is great in respect of our salvation in that, not content to redeem us with his blood, he in addition prayed for us. See now what the desire of his petition was, that just as the Father and Son are one, so also we should abide in absolute unity. From this, it may be evident how greatly someone sins who divides unity and peace, since even the Lord himself petitioned for this same thing. He no doubt desired that his people should in this way be saved and live in peace since he knew that discord cannot come into the kingdom of God. THE LORD'S PRAYER 30.[1]

[1]ANF 5:455*; CCL 3A:108-9.

In the Future, the World Restored to Initial Unity. Origen: I am of the opinion, so far as I can see, that this order of the human race has been appointed in order that in the future world—or in ages to come, when there shall be the new heavens and new earth spoken of by Isaiah[2]—that unity may be restored that was promised by the Lord Jesus in his prayer to God the Father on behalf of his disciples.[3] And this is further confirmed by the language of the apostle Paul: "Until we all come in the unity of the faith to a perfect man, to the measure of the stature of the fullness of Christ."[4] And in keeping with this is the declaration of the same apostle when he exhorts us—who even in the present life are placed in the church, which is a form of that kingdom that is to come—to this same similitude of unity, "That you all speak the same thing and that there be no divisions among you. But that you be perfectly joined together in the same mind and in the same judgment."[5] On First Principles 1.6.2.[6]

As Christ Is Loved, So We Are Loved and United. Jerome: He reminds us that the whole Christian people are one in God, and, as his well-beloved children, are "partakers of the divine nature."[7] We have already said (and the truth must now be inculcated more in detail) that we are not one in the Father and the Son according to nature but according to grace. For the essence of the human soul and the essence of God are not the same, as the Manichaeans constantly assert. But, says our Lord, "You have loved them as you have loved me." You see, then, that we are privileged to partake of his essence, not in the realm of nature but of grace. And the reason why we are beloved of the Father is that he has loved the Son—and the members of the body are loved.[8] Against Jovinianus 2.29.[9]

17:21a *That They May All Be One*

Unity of Will Makes Us One. Hilary of Poitiers: [This passage] shows that since human beings cannot, so to speak, be fused back into God or themselves coalesce into one undistinguished mass, this oneness must arise from unity of will, as all perform actions pleasing to God and unite with one another in the harmonious agreement of their thoughts. Therefore, it is not nature that makes them one but will. On the Trinity 8.5.[10]

The Church Assembly Is One in Many. Jerome: "As we are Father, Son and Holy Spirit, one God," [Jesus might say], "so may they be one people in themselves, that is, like dear children and partakers of the divine nature." Call the church what you will—bride, sister, mother—its assembly is but one and never lacks husband, brother or son. [The church's] faith is one, and it is not defiled by variety of doctrine or divided by heresies. [The church] continues a virgin. Wherever the Lamb goes, it follows him. It alone knows the song of Christ. Against Jovinianus 2.19.[11]

Our Unity and the Godhead's Unity Compared. Ambrose: No separation, then, is to be made of the Word from God the Father, no separation in power, no separation in wisdom because of the unity of the divine substance. Again, God the Father is in the Son, as we often times find it written, yet not as sanctifying one who lacks sanctification or as filling a void, for the power of God knows no void. Nor, again, is the power of the one increased by the power of the other, for there are not two powers but one power. Nor does Godhead entertain Godhead, for there are not two Godheads but one Godhead. We . . . shall be one in Christ through power received [from another] and dwelling in us. The letter[12] [of the unity] is common, but the substance of God and the substance of humanity

[2]Is 66:22. [3]He cites Jn 17:22, 23. [4]Eph 4:13. [5]1 Cor 1:10. [6]ANF 4:261**; GCS 22(5):82. [7]2 Pet 1:4. [8]See Jn 1:12, 13. [9]NPNF 2 6:410**; PL 23:340. [10]NPNF 2 9:139**; CCL 62A:318-19. [11]NPNF 2 6:403**; PL 23:328. [12]Lat *littera*.

are different. We shall be one. The Father and the Son [already] are one. We shall be one by grace; the Son is so by substance. Again, unity by conjunction is one thing, unity by nature another. Finally, observe what it is that Scripture has already recorded: "That they may all be one, as you, Father, are in me, and I in you." Now notice that he did not say, "You in us, and we in you" but "You in me, and I in you." In this way he sets himself apart from his creatures. Further, he added "that they also may be in us," in order to separate here his dignity and his Father's dignity from us so that our union in the Father and the Son may appear the result not of nature but of grace, while the unity of the Father and the Son is the Son's, not by grace but by natural right of sonship. On the Christian Faith 4.3.36-38.[13]

Unity from Diversity in God. Cyril of Alexandria: Our Lord Jesus Christ did not pray for the twelve apostles alone. He prayed for all who were destined in every age to yield to and obey the words that call them to be holy by believing and to be purified through participation in the Holy Spirit. . . . "May they all be one," he prayed. "As you Father are in me and I am in you, may they also be one in us." . . . The only Son shines out from the very substance of the Father and possesses the Father completely in his own nature. He became man, according to the Scriptures, blending himself, so to speak, with our nature by an inexplicable union with an earthly body. . . . In himself he somehow united totally disparate natures to make us sharers in the divine nature.

The communion and abiding presence of the Spirit has passed even to ourselves. This was experienced first through Christ and in Christ when he was seen to have become like us, that is, a human being anointed and sanctified. By nature, however, he was God, for he proceeded from the Father. It was with his own Spirit that he sanctified the temple of his body and also, in a way befitting it, the world of his creation. Through the mystery of Christ, then, sharing in the Holy Spirit and union with God has become possible also for us, for we are all sanctified in him.

By his own wisdom and the Father's counsel he devised a way of bringing us all together and blending us into a unity with God and one another, even though the differences between us give us each in both body and soul a separate identity. For in Holy Communion he blesses with one body, which is his own, those who believe in him, and he makes them one body with himself and one another. Who could separate those who are united to Christ through that one sacred body or destroy their true union with one another? If "we all share one loaf," we all become one body, for Christ cannot be divided.

So it is that the church is the body of Christ, and we are its members. For since we are all united to Christ through his sacred body, having received that one indivisible body into our own, our members are not our own but his. Commentary on the Gospel of John 11.11.[14]

17:21b *The World Will Believe You Sent Me*

Peace in Unity Is a Witness. Chrysostom: This is similar to what he said earlier, "By this shall all know that you are my disciples, if you love one another."[15] And how will they believe this? "Because," he says, "you are a God of peace." And, if therefore the [disciples] keep that same peace that they have learned [from me], their hearers will know the teacher by the disciples. But if they quarrel, people will deny that they are the disciples of a God of peace and will not allow that I, not being peaceable, have been sent from you. Do you see how he proves his unanimity with the Father to the very end? Homilies on the Gospel of John 82.2.[16]

17:22 *The Glory That Unifies*

[13]NPNF 2 10:266-67**; CSEL 78:169-70 (*On the Christian Faith* 4.3.35-37). [14]LF 48:546, 549-50**. [15]Jn 13:35. [16]NPNF 1 14:304*

He Asked for Glory Because of Us. Athanasius: What advantage then was it for the immortal to have assumed the mortal? Or what improvement[17] does the everlasting one get by putting on the temporal? How great can any reward be for the everlasting God and King in the bosom of the Father? Don't you see that this too was done and written because of us and for us? The Lord became man for us, we who are mortal and temporal, so that he might make us immortal and bring us into the everlasting kingdom of heaven. . . . It is not the Word then (viewed as the Word) that is improved. For he had all things and has them always. But it is the human race, which has its origin[18] in him and through him, that is the one who receives the improvement. For when he is now said to be anointed according to human terms, it is we who in him are anointed, since also when he is baptized, it is we who in him are baptized. But on all these things the Savior throws significant light when he says to the Father, "And the glory that you gave me, I have given to them, that they may be one, even as we are one." Because of us, then, he asked for glory. And the words "took" and "gave" and "highly exalted" occur so that we might take, and to us might be given and we might be exalted in him. He also sanctifies himself for us so that we might be sanctified in him. Discourses Against the Arians 1.12.48.[19]

All Are One in the Glory of the Father. Hilary of Poitiers: Now I ask whether glory is identical with will, since will is an emotion of the mind while glory is an ornament or embellishment of nature. So then, it is the glory received from the Father that the Son has given to all who shall believe in him, and certainly not *will*. Had *will* been given, faith would carry with it no reward, for a necessity of will attached to us would also impose faith on us. However, he has shown what is effected by the bestowal of the glory received: "that they may be one, even as we are one." It is then with this object that the received glory was bestowed, that all might be one. So now all are one in glory, because the glory given is none other than that which was received; nor has it been given for any other reason than that all should be one. And since all are one through the glory given to the Son and by the Son bestowed on believers, I ask how the Son can be of a different glory from the Father's, since the glory of the Son brings all that believe into the unity of the Father's glory. Now it may be that the utterance of human hope in this case may be somewhat immoderate, yet it will not be contrary to faith. For though to hope for this were presumptuous, yet not to have believed it is sinful, for we have one and the same author both of our hope and of our faith. On the Trinity 8.12.[20]

The Glory That Unifies Is the Holy Spirit. Gregory of Nyssa: In giving "all power" to his disciples by his blessing, in his prayer here to the Father he grants many other favors to those who are holy. And he adds this, which is the crown of all blessings, that in all the diversity of life's decisions they should never be divided greatly in their choice of the good. And so he prays that all "may be one," united in a single good so that linked "in the bond of peace,"[21] as the apostle says, through "the unity of the [Holy] Spirit," all might become "one body and one spirit," through the "one hope" to which they have all been called.

But it would be better here if we would quote the actual words of the Gospel. "That they all may be one," he says, "as you, Father, are in me, and I in you; that they also may be one in us." Now the bond of this unity is glory, and no one who would consider seriously the Lord's words would deny that this glory is the Holy Spirit. For he says, "The glory that you have given me, I have given to them." He gave his disciples this glory when he said to them, "Receive the Holy Spirit."[22] And he himself received this glory when he put on human nature, though he had indeed

[17]Gk *beltiōsis*. [18]Gk *archē*. [19]NPNF 2 4:334-35**; PG 26:112. [20]NPNF 2 9:140-41**; CCL 62A:324. [21]Eph 4:3. [22]Jn 20:22.

always possessed it since before the beginning of the world. And now that his human nature has been glorified by the Spirit, this participation in the glory of the Spirit is communicated to all who are united with him, beginning with his disciples. Homilies on the Song of Songs 15.[23]

The Glory of Immortality Is Given. Augustine: "And the glory that you gave me, I have given them." And what was that glory but immortality, which human nature was afterward to receive in him? For not even he himself had as yet received it, but in his own customary way, because predestination is so absolutely inflexible, he intimates what is future in verbs of the past tense. He does this because he is now on the point of being glorified, or in other words, raised up again by the Father, knowing that he himself is going to raise us up to the same glory in the end. Tractates on the Gospel of John 110.3.[24]

17:23 *Perfect Oneness Evidences Love to the World*

The Sanctification of Human Nature. Cyril of Alexandria: The Son dwells in us in a corporeal sense as man, commingled and united with us by the mystery of the Eucharist. And also [he dwells with us] in a spiritual sense as God, by the effectual working and grace of his own Spirit, building up our spirit into newness of life and making us partakers of his divine nature. Christ, then, is seen to be the bond of union between us and God the Father. He is seen as human, making us, as it were, his branches,[25] and is seen as God because he is by nature inherent in his own Father. For in no other way could that nature which is subject to corruption be elevated to incorruption, except by the coming down to it of that nature that is high above all corruption and changeability. . . .We have, therefore, been made perfect in unity with God the Father, through the mediation of Christ. For by receiving in ourselves (both in a corporeal and spiritual sense, as I said just now) him who is the Son by nature and who has essential union with the Father, we have been glorified and become partakers in the nature of the Most High. Commentary on the Gospel of John 11.12.[26]

Cleansed, We Become One. Augustine: He did not say, "I and they are one,"[27] although inasmuch as he is the head of the church and the church is his body,[28] he could not only say, "I and they are one but also one person,"[29] because the head and the body are the one Christ. But when he reveals that his own Godhead is consubstantial with the Father (for which reason he also says in another place, "I and the Father are one"[30]), then it is rather his will that his own in their own kind, that is to say, in the consubstantial equality of the same nature, should be one, but be one in him. For they could not be one in themselves, since they were separated from one another by conflicting inclinations, desires and unclean sins. They are, therefore, purified through the Mediator, in order that they may be one in him. And indeed [they are one] not only through the same nature in which all mortals become equal to the angels, but also [they are one] by the same will working together most harmoniously toward the same blessedness, and [they are] fused together in some way by the fire of charity into one spirit. On the Trinity 4.9.12.[31]

Can We Be Loved by God As the Son Is? Ambrose: There are some . . . who in their desire to deny the unity of the divine substance try to make light of the love of the Father and the Son, because it is written, "You have loved them, as you have loved me." But when they say this, what else do they do but adopt a likeness of comparison between the Son of God and human beings? Can we indeed be loved by God as the Son is, in whom the Father is well-pleased?[32] The Son is

[23]FGTG 286-87. [24]NPNF 1 7:409**; CCL 36:623-24. [25]See Jn 15:1. [26]LF 48:554-55*. See also Hilary *On the Trinity* 8.13 (NPNF 2 9:141). [27]Lat *unum*. [28]Eph 1:22- 23. [29]Lat *unus*. [30]Lat *unum*, Jn 10:30. [31]FC 45:146*; CCL 50:177. [32]Mt 3:17.

well-pleasing in himself; we are well-pleasing through him. For those in whom God sees his own Son after his own likeness, he admits through his Son into the favor of sons [children]. As we go through likeness unto likeness, in the same way, we are called to adoption through the generation of the Son. The eternal love of God's nature is one thing; that of grace is another. And if they start a debate on the words that are written, "And you have loved them, as you have loved me," and think a comparison is intended, they must think that the following also was said by way of comparison, "Be merciful, as your Father who is in heaven is merciful."[33] It is also elsewhere said, "Be perfect, as my Father who is in heaven is perfect."[34] But if he is perfect in the fullness of his glory, we are but perfect according to the growth of virtue within us. The Son also is loved by the Father according to the fullness of a love that always remains in him, but in us growth in grace merits the love of God. You see, then, how God has given grace to humankind, and do you want to separate the natural and indivisible love of the Father and the Son? And do you still strive to make nothing of words, where you note the mention of a unity of majesty? On the Christian Faith 5.7.88-91.[35]

17:24a *That They Also Be with Me Where I Am*

We Are Loved As the Son Is Loved. Cyril of Alexandria: He shows that to live with him and to be considered worthy to see his glory is something that belongs only to those who have been already united to the Father through him and have obtained his love—a love that he must be conceived to enjoy from the Father. For we are loved by God the Father as children inasmuch as we are like him who is actually the Son of God by nature. For although it is not dealt out to us in equal measure, it still is a complete resemblance of the love the Father has for the Son and, intersecting with it, images forth the glory of the Son. Commentary on the Gospel of John 11.12.[36]

Beholding and Reflecting Christ's Glory. Chrysostom: This again is a sign of his being of one mind with the Father and of a higher character than those who lived in former times. For he says "before the foundation of the world." And yet, there is also a certain humility evident when Jesus says, "You have given me." Now if this is not the case, I would gladly ask those who do not think so a question: The one that gives is considered superior to the one who receives the gift. Did the Father, then, having first begotten the Son, afterward give him glory, having allowed him to be without glory until then? How can this be reasonable? See that the "he gave" really means "he begot"? But why didn't he say, "That they may share my glory" instead of "that they may behold my glory"? Here he implies that what they are doing is looking on the Son of God. This certainly is what causes them to be glorified, as Paul says, "with open face mirroring the glory of the Lord."[37] For as they who look on the sunbeams and enjoy a very clear atmosphere draw their enjoyment from their sight, so then also our sight will cause us greater pleasure. At the same time also he shows that what they should behold was not the body then seen but something awesome. Homilies on the Gospel of John 82.2-3.[38]

Presence and Vision. Augustine: Let us not be making inquiries as to where the Son, the Father's co-equal, is, since no one has yet found out where he is not. But if anyone would inquire, let him inquire rather how he may be with him—not everywhere, as he is, but wherever he may be. For when he said to the [thief] . . . "Today you will be with me in paradise,"[39] in respect to his human nature his own soul was on that very day to be in hell, his flesh in the sepulcher. But as respected his Godhead he was certainly also in paradise. And therefore the soul of the thief, absolved from his past crimes and already in the

[33]Lk 6:36. [34]Mt 5:48. [35]NPNF 2 10:295**; CSEL 78:248-50 (*On the Christian Faith* 5.7.89-92). [36]LF 48:556-57*. [37]2 Cor 3:18. [38]NPNF 1 14:304-5**. [39]Lk 23:43.

blessed enjoyment of his grace, although his soul could not be everywhere as Christ was, yet could on that very day be also with him in paradise, from which he, who is always everywhere, had not withdrawn. On this account, doubtless, it was not enough for him to say, "I will that they also be where I am," but he added, "with me." For to be with him is the chief good. For even the miserable can be where he is, since wherever any are, there is he also. But the blessed are only with him because it is only of him that they can be blessed. Was it not truly said to God, "If I ascend into heaven, you are there. And if I go down into hell, you are present"?[40] Or is not Christ after all that Wisdom of God that "penetrates everywhere because of its purity"?[41] But "the light shines in the darkness, and the darkness does not comprehend it."[42] Let us take a similar illustration from what is visible, even if it is only remotely similar. The blind person—even when there is light where he is—does not really experience the light but is, in reality, absent from its presence. In the same way, because someone who is an unbeliever and ungodly (or even a believer who is godly) is not yet competent to gaze on the light of wisdom—although there is nowhere he or she could be where Christ is not—yet that person still cannot experience Christ with actual sight. For there is no doubt that a true believer is with Christ by faith, because in reference to this he says, "He that is not with me is against me."[43] But when he said to God the Father, "I will that they also whom you have given me be with me where I am," he spoke exclusively of that sight that will see him as he is.[44] Tractates on the Gospel of John 111.2.[45]

Future Implications of Unity in God. Origen: The Lord himself, in the Gospel, not only declares that these same results will occur in the future but that they are to be brought about by his own intercession when he himself decides to obtain them from the Father for his disciples, saying, "Father, I will that where I am, they also may be with me. And as you and I are one, may they also be one in us." In this, the divine likeness itself already appears to advance (if we may so express it) from being merely similar to becoming the same, because, undoubtedly, in the consummation, or the end, God is "all and in all."[46] . . .

I am of the opinion that the expression by which God is said to be "all in all" means that he is "all" in each individual person. Now he will be "all" in each individual when all those with any rational understanding—cleansed from the dregs of every sort of vice and with every cloud of wickedness completely swept away—either feel, understand or think in terms wholly divine. He will be "all" in each person when that person's understanding will no longer behold or retain anything else other than God, but God alone will be the measure and standard of all his or her movements. This is when God will be "all," for there will no longer be any distinction of good and evil, since evil will no longer exist. For God is, then, all things, and no evil can be present where he is. Nor will there be a desire any longer to eat from the tree of the knowledge of good and evil on the part of one who is always in the possession of good and to whom God is everything. On First Principles 3.6.1, 3.[47]

17:24b *Sharing Christ's Glory*

Our Glory Is Received, Not Given. Irenaeus: Service [rendered] to God brings no profit to God, nor does God need our obedience. However, he grants life, incorruption and eternal glory to those who follow and serve him, bestowing gifts on those who serve [him] because they do serve him and on his followers because they do follow him. But he does not receive any benefit from them because he is already rich, perfect and in need of nothing. Still, God demands service from men and women so that he can benefit those who continue in his service, since he is so good

[40]Ps 139:8 (138:8 LXX). [41]Wis 7:24. [42]Jn 1:5. [43]Mt 12:30. [44]See 1 Jn 3:2. [45]NPNF 1 7:413-14**; CCL 36:629-30. [46]1 Cor 15:28. [47]ANF 4:344-45**; GCS 22(5): 280-81, 283-84.

and merciful. For as much as God lacks nothing, that is how much we stand in need of fellowship with God, because our glory consists in continuing and remaining permanently in God's service. Against Heresies 4.14.1.[48]

Looking Forward to Future Glory. Cyprian: When we die, we are passing over to immortality by death; nor can eternal life follow, unless we depart from this life. It is not an ending but a transit, and this journey of time that we are traveling on is a passage to eternity. Who would not want to hurry on to something better? Who would not crave being changed and renewed into the likeness of Christ and to arrive more quickly to the dignity of heavenly glory, since Paul the apostle announces and says, "For our [citizenship] is in heaven, from where also we look for the Lord Jesus Christ who shall change the body of our humiliation, and conform it to the body of his glory"?[49] Christ the Lord also promises that this is how we shall be when—in order that we may be with him and that we may live with him in eternal mansions and rejoice in heavenly kingdoms—he prays to the Father for us, saying, "Father, I will that they also whom you have given me may be with me where I am and may see the glory that you have given me before the world was made." The person who is allowed to go up to the throne of Christ, to the glory of the heavenly kingdoms, should not mourn or lament, but rather, in keeping with the Lord's promise and his faith in the truth, he should rejoice in this his departure and translation. On Mortality 7.22.[50]

17:25 *The World Is Ignorant of the Father*

Jesus Frustrated with the Unbelief of the Jews. Chrysostom: What does he mean when he says, "O righteous Father, the world has not known you"? What is the connection with what preceded? Here he shows that no one knows God except those who have come to know the Son. And what he says, then, is like this: "I wanted everyone to know you, and yet they have not known you, although they can find no fault with you." For this is the meaning of "O righteous Father." And here he seems to me to speak these words as one who is frustrated that they refused to know someone who is so just and good. For since the Jews had said that they knew God but that Jesus did not, he takes aim at this perception, saying, "For you [the Father] loved me before the foundation of the world." In this way he put together a defense against the accusations of the Jews. For how could he who had received glory, who was loved before the foundation of the world, who desired to have them as witnesses of that glory—how could he be opposed to the Father? And so, he is in effect saying, "What the Jews say then is not true when they say they know you and I don't. On the contrary, I know you, and they don't." Homilies on the Gospel of John 82.3.[51]

The World Ignorant of Christ's Purpose to Restore Humanity. Cyril of Alexandria: Christ calls the Father righteous with good reason. For by the Father's approval and consent the Son became man that he might endow human nature, which was created for good works,[52] with sanctification through the Spirit, and union with God and an abiding place in the mansions above where he will live and reign with him. For God did not create humanity at the beginning to do wickedness. But their nature was perverted into vice by the impious schemes of the devil, and they were led astray from the guidance of old that they had received at the hands of God. They were uprooted, as it were, from its moorings. In truth, it seemed good to the righteous Father to lift up again that human nature that had been cast down through the devil's malice and to establish in its former position what had been unduly debased. He wanted to rid the human nature of the foulness of sin and, as it were, transform it into its original image as it had

[48]ANF 1:478**; SC 100:538-40. [49]Phil 3:20-21. [50]ANF 5:474**; CCL 3A:28-29. [51]NPNF 1 14:305**. [52]See Eph 2:10.

been at first created. He also sought to subject the adversary, that is, Satan, who assaulted humanity and impiously dared to make its ruin complete, to the vengeance that was fitting for him. Although I personally think any kind of chastisement was slight for someone who exhibited such madness against God. Therefore he says, "O righteous Father," "for you are righteous and good, and your judgment is true,"[53] because you have sent me down, your own true Son, to the world to help and renew it. But the world is blind to all this! He says, For though you are exactly as I described you, "the world did not know you." Otherwise they would have surely seen the loving-kindness of your judgment and your merciful will. In that case, they should have hurried to welcome their Savior and provided him with willing service. Commentary on the Gospel of John 11.12.[54]

17:26 *The Name Made Known*

Our Actions of Love Make the Name Known. Chrysostom: For, [Jesus says], if they learn who you are, O Father, then they will know that I am not separated from you. They will know that I am one of your most dearly loved, a true Son and someone who is closely knit to you. And those who are rightly persuaded of this will keep their faith focused on me and remain in perfect love. And as long as they exercise their love as they should, I remain in them. Isn't it great how he finishes off this discourse on the note of love, the mother of all blessings? Let us then believe and love God, that it may not be said of us, "They profess that they know God, but in their works they deny him."[55] And again, "He has denied the faith and is worse than an infidel."[56] For when he helps his workers and family and strangers, while you do not even help those who are related to you by family, what will be your excuse later on when God is blasphemed and insulted because of you? Consider what opportunities of doing good God has given to us. "Have mercy on one," he says, "as a family member, on another as a friend, on another as a neighbor, on another as a citizen, on another as a fellow human being." Homilies on the Gospel of John 82.3-4.[57]

The Father Loves Us As Members of Christ's Body. Augustine: But how else is the love with which the Father has loved the Son in us as well, except because of the fact that we are his members and are loved in him—since he is loved in the totality of his person as both head and members? Therefore he added, "and I in them," as if he were saying, "Since I am also in them." For in one sense he is in us as in his temple. But in another sense, he is also in us because we are also [part of] him, since, when he became man and our head, we became his body. And so, the Savior's prayer is finished, his passion begins. Let us, therefore, also finish the present discourse, that we may treat his passion, as he grants us grace.
Tractates on the Gospel of John 111.6.[58]

---

[53]Ps 119:137 (118:137 LXX). [54]LF 48:561*. [55]Tit 1:16. [56]1 Tim 5:8. [57]NPNF 1 14:305**. [58]NPNF 1 7:415**; CCL 36:632-33

18:1-11 THE ARREST OF JESUS

[1]When Jesus had spoken these words, he went forth with his disciples across the Kidron valley, where there was a garden, which he and his disciples entered. [2]Now Judas, who betrayed him, also knew the place; for Jesus often met there with his disciples. [3]So Judas, procuring a band of soldiers and some officers from the chief priests and the Pharisees, went there with lanterns and torches and weapons. [4]Then Jesus, knowing all that was to befall him, came forward and said to them, "Whom do you seek?" [5]They answered him, "Jesus of Nazareth." Jesus said to them, "I am he." Judas, who betrayed him, was standing with them. [6]When he said to them, "I am he," they drew back and fell to the ground. [7]Again he asked them, "Whom do you seek?" And they said, "Jesus of Nazareth." [8]Jesus answered, "I told you that I am he; so, if you seek me, let these men go." [9]This was to fulfil the word which he had spoken, "Of those whom thou gavest me I lost not one." [10]Then Simon Peter, having a sword, drew it and struck the high priest's slave and cut off his right ear. The slave's name was Malchus. [11]Jesus said to Peter, "Put your sword into its sheath; shall I not drink the cup which the Father has given me?"

Overview: After delivering the mysteries of his body and blood to his disciples (Apostolic Constitutions), Jesus willingly enters into the garden that holds certain death for him (Chrysostom) in order to deliver us from Adam's death in the first garden of paradise (Cyril). John omits the name of that garden, but we know from the other Gospels that it is Gethsemane (Augustine). John also has left out certain other details, but there is nothing written by one Evangelist that would contradict any of the other Evangelists for the believer (Augustine).

Knowing that Judas would be there with the armed guard, as a sheep in wolf's clothing (Augustine), Jesus places himself in the garden as though it were a prison (Chrysostom). It was a place Jesus often frequented with his disciples, so Judas knew he would be there (Chrysostom). Those who come for Jesus are a band of soldiers, not the Jews (Augustine) who previously had been unsuccessful in apprehending Jesus; they are now able to seize him, but only because he voluntarily surrenders (Chrysostom). One might ask, however, why so many were needed to apprehend so few (Origen). We should also remember Jesus' steadfastness in the face of the swords that came against him so that we too are steadfast and will not have to feel the eternal sword (Cyril of Jerusalem).

The crowd with Judas carried torches for fear of stumbling in the dark, but they ended up stumbling on the rock of offense (Cyril). Jesus' question to them, "Whom do you seek?" exposes their blindness, not Jesus' ignorance (Cyril). No one, in fact, sees unless he or she is permitted to by Jesus (Chrysostom). In his reply to them of "I am," he not only confirms he is the one they are looking for but also gives them a foretaste of his divinity as they are cast to the ground at the sound of his name (Augustine). One little word can fell them (Augustine) because darkness cannot stand up in the face of the Light (Quodvultdeus). They do not know it, but they are accomplishing Christ's will in seizing him (Augustine). But even as they seize him, Jesus does not forget about the care of his disciples (Chrysostom, Augustine). He was concerned for their eternal loss (Chrysostom), although the

Evangelist here understood he was concerned for their physical lives as well (AUGUSTINE).

In the skirmish that follows, one might question why the disciples were armed (CHRYSOSTOM), since the gospel does not permit vengeance (CYRIL). Peter, however, is defending his master, not himself, and is not therefore seeking vengeance (CHRYSOSTOM). When Malchus was injured in the struggle, Jesus healed him, demonstrating love for one's enemy (CHRYSOSTOM), mercy (GREGORY OF NAZIANZUS), compassion and forgiveness (GREGORY OF NAZIANZUS), and patience (TERTULLIAN). He gave him a new ear to hear the freedom of the gospel (AUGUSTINE).

The disciples had brought their swords, which they may have been using during the previous meal. But they may have also heard rumors that there were those who wanted to arrest Jesus (CHRYSOSTOM). Judea also was a dangerous place, and they may have been carrying them for self-defense (CYRIL). Nonetheless, Jesus commands them and us to replace the sword of violence with the sword of the Spirit (ORIGEN). Christ does not want them preventing him from drinking the cup of his passion that would fulfill his Father's will (THEODORE). Can we also drink such a cup when we face the prospect of suffering (CLEMENT OF ALEXANDRIA)? To "drink the cup" meant Christ was to go through with the suffering the Father had planned for him in order to spare his children from drinking the cup of his wrath (DIONYSIUS). Jesus demonstrates that he was not afraid to suffer (HILARY) since saving the world had always been the plan (LEO). It is also helpful to remember, however, when facing persecution, that Jesus did not give himself up but waited until they came to him with their swords and spears (PETER OF ALEXANDRIA).

18:1 *Jesus Enters the Garden*

SEQUENCE OF EVENTS. APOSTOLIC CONSTITUTIONS: And when he had delivered to us the representative mysteries of his precious body and blood, Judas not being present with us, he went out to the Mount of Olives, near the brook Kidron, where there was a garden. CONSTITUTIONS OF THE HOLY APOSTLES 5.3.14.[1]

JESUS WILLINGLY ENTERS THE GARDEN THAT HOLDS HIS DEATH. CHRYSOSTOM: An awful thing is death, and very full of terror, but not to those who have learned the true wisdom that is above ... who consider death as only a departure to another ... far better and brighter place that has no end. This is what Christ teaches us when he goes to his passion, not out of constraint or necessity but willingly. HOMILIES ON THE GOSPEL OF JOHN 83.1.[2]

THE GARDEN OF PARADISE, THE GARDEN OF SUFFERING. CYRIL OF ALEXANDRIA: The place was a garden, typifying the paradise of old. For in this place, as it were, all places were recapitulated and our return to humanity's ancient condition was consummated. For the troubles of humanity began in paradise, while Christ's suffering, which brought us deliverance from all the evil that happened to us in times past, began in [this] garden. COMMENTARY ON THE GOSPEL OF JOHN 11.12.[3]

THE GARDEN OF GETHSEMANE. AUGUSTINE: Matthew proceeds with his narrative ... as follows: "Then Jesus came with them to a place called Gethsemane."[4] This is mentioned also by Mark.[5] Luke, too, refers to it, although he does not mention the piece of ground by name.... There, we understand, was also the garden that John brings into notice when he gives his narrative. HARMONY OF THE GOSPELS 3.4.10.[6]

JOHN'S OMISSIONS AND THE INTEGRITY OF THE CANONICAL GOSPELS. AUGUSTINE: What John here relates of the Lord entering the garden with his disciples did not take place immediately after Jesus had brought the prayer to a close, of which he says, "When Jesus had spoken these

[1]ANF 7:444**. [2]NPNF 1 14:306**. [3]LF 48:566**. [4]Mt 26:36-46. [5]Mk 14:32-42. [6]NPNF 1 6:182**; CSEL 43:281.

words." Rather, certain other incidents were interposed that are passed over by the present Evangelist and found in the others, just as in this one are found many things on which the others are similarly silent in their own narratives. But anyone who desires to know how they all agree together—and the truth that is advanced by one is never contradicted by another—may seek for what he wants, not in these present discourses but in other more elaborate treatises.[7] But he will master the subject not by standing and listening but rather by sitting down and reading or by giving his closest attention and thought to one who does so. Yet let him believe (before he knows whether he is able also to come to such a knowledge in this life or finds it impossible because of some existing entanglements) that there is nothing written by any one Evangelist, as far as regards those who have been received by the church into canonical authority, that can be contrary to his own or another's equally veracious narrative. Tractates on the Gospel of John 112.1.[8]

18:2 *Judas Also Knew the Place*

Judas the Wolf in Sheep's Clothing. Augustine: There the wolf in sheep's clothing, permitted by the deep counsel of the Master of the flock to go among the sheep, learned in what way to disperse the slender flock and ensnare the Shepherd. Tractates on the Gospel of John 112.2.[9]

In the Garden As in a Prison. Chrysostom: Jesus travels at midnight, and crosses a river and hurries to come to a place known to the traitor, lessening the labor of those who plotted against him and freeing them from all trouble. He also comforts the disciples by showing them that he came to this action willingly when he placed himself in the garden as in a prison. Homilies on the Gospel of John 83.1.[10]

How Did Judas Know Where to Find Them? Chrysostom: How did Judas get to the garden, or from where did he get his information when he came? It is evident from this circumstance that Jesus generally passed the night out of doors. For if he had been in the habit of spending time at home, Judas would not have come to that lonely spot but to the house, expecting there to find him asleep. And, in case when you hear a "garden" you should think that Jesus hid himself, it adds that "Judas knew the place." Not only did he know about it, but Jesus "often went there with his disciples." For he often spent time with them alone, talking about important matters that it was not permitted for others to hear. And he did this especially in the mountains and gardens, seeking a place free from distraction so that their attention might be fixed on what he had to say. Homilies on the Gospel of John 83.1.[11]

18:3 *Soldiers Come for Jesus*

A Band of Soldiers. Augustine: It was a band not of Jews but of soldiers who were given legal authority by the governor to take the so-called criminal and crush any opposition that might be made. Tractates on the Gospel of John 112.2.[12]

Previously Unsuccessful, They Now Seize Jesus. Chrysostom: These men had often at other times sent to seize him but had not been able. And so it is plain that this time Jesus voluntarily surrendered. And how did [the Jewish leaders] persuade the band to accompany Judas? They were soldiers[13] who had made it their practice to do anything for money. Homilies on the Gospel of John 83.1.[14]

Why So Many? Origen: It may be asked why a great multitude was gathered against him with

[7]Augustine is referring to his own *Harmony of the Gospels*, loc. cit. [8]NPNF 1 7:416**; CCL 36:633. [9]NPNF 1 7:416**; CCL 36:634. [10]NPNF 1 14:306-7**. [11]NPNF 1 14:307**. [12]NPNF 1 7:416*; CCL 36:634. [13]Gk *stratiōtai*, "mercenaries." [14]NPNF 1 14:307**.

swords and staves. According to John, this great multitude was a contingent of soldiers and officials sent by the chief priests. Maybe it was because there were so many now that believed in him that so many also assembled against him. They were afraid that a great number of believers would snatch him out of their hands. But I think there was another reason for a multitude being gathered against him. Those who thought that he could cast out demons through Beelzebub[15] thought he could by some sorcery or magic escape from the midst of those who sought to hold him. And perhaps some of them had heard how once, when he was just about to be cast headlong from the brow of the mountain, he escaped the hands of those who held him—not by ordinary human flight but by one beyond human nature.[16] . . . There are many even now fighting against Jesus with spiritual swords and staves of evil spirits in the same way as these did. Jesus always gets the better of their plots, although for a time he receives their attacks on him in order that the sins of those who plot against him may be complete and the wickedness of their will against the truth of God's only-begotten, the Word, may be made known. Commentary on Matthew 99.[17]

The Witnesses of Denial Will Testify. Cyril of Jerusalem: Take the cross first, therefore, as an indestructible foundation, and build on it the other articles of the faith. Do not deny the crucified. For if you deny him, you have many to arraign you. Judas the traitor will arraign you first. For he who betrayed him knows that Jesus was condemned to death by the chief priests and elders. The thirty pieces of silver bear witness. Gethsemane bears witness, where the betrayal occurred. I am not even speaking yet of the Mount of Olives on which they were with him at night, praying. The moon in the night bears witness; the day bears witness, and the sun, which was darkened. For it endured not to look on the crime of the conspirators. The fire will arraign you by which Peter stood and warmed himself. If you deny the cross, the eternal fire awaits you. I speak harsh words so that you may not experience harsh pains. Remember the swords that came against him in Gethsemane so that you do not feel the eternal sword. Catechetical Lectures 13.38.[18]

Real Danger. Cyril of Alexandria: The crowd that accompanied the traitor when they made their attack on Christ carried lanterns and torches. They would seem to have guarded against stumbling in the dark and accidentally falling into holes, for such accidents often happen in the dark. But, how unfortunate for their blindness! The miserable men, in their extreme ignorance, did not perceive that they were stumbling on the stone concerning which God the Father says, "Behold, I lay in Zion a stumbling block and a rock of offense."[19] They who happened to be afraid of falling into a small hole did not see that they were rushing into the depths of the abyss and the very bowels of the earth. And they who were cautious in the twilight of evening took no account of perpetual and endless night. For those who impiously plotted against the light of God, that is, Christ, were doomed to walk in darkness and the dead of night,[20] as the prophet says. And not only this, but they were also doomed to vanish away into outer darkness, there to give an account of their impiety against Christ and to be consigned to bitter and endless punishment. Commentary on the Gospel of John 11.12.[21]

18:4 *Whom Do You Seek?*

Those Who Persecute Jesus Are Blind. Cyril of Alexandria: Jesus inquires of those who come to capture him. He asks them whom they have come in search of, not because he did not know (for how could that be?) but that he might prove that those who had come to capture him and were gazing on him were not even able to recognize the very person they were searching for, and

[15]Mt 12:24. [16]Mt 4:6. [17]AEG 6:3-4**; GCS 38 2 (11):217. [18]NPNF 2 7:92**. [19]See Rom 9:33. [20]See Is 59:9. [21]LF 48:568*.

thus confirming in us the true conviction that he would never have been taken if he had not of his own will gone to those who sought him. For observe, when he openly asks, "Whom do you seek?" they did not at once reply, "We are here to take you who have just spoken." But rather, they reply, as though he was not present or before their very eyes, saying, "Jesus of Nazareth." Commentary on the Gospel of John 11.12.[22]

No Seeing Unless Permitted by Jesus. Chrysostom: Do you see his invincible power, how being in the midst of them he disabled their eyes? For that the darkness was not the cause of their not knowing him, the Evangelist has shown by saying that they also had torches. And even had there been no torches, they ought at least to have known him by his voice. Or if they did not know it, how could Judas be ignorant, who had been so continually with him? For he too stood with them and knew him no more than they, but with them he fell backward. Now Jesus did this to show that not only could they not seize him but that they could not even see him when he was in their midst, unless he himself permitted. Homilies on the Gospel of John 83.1.[23]

18:5-6 *I Am*

One Little Word Can Fell Them. Augustine: With no other weapon than his own solitary voice uttering the words "I am," he knocked down, repelled and rendered helpless that great crowd, even with all their ferocious hatred and terror of arms. For God lay hidden in that human flesh, and eternal day was so obscured in those human limbs that he was looked for with lanterns and torches to be slain in the darkness. "I am," he says, and throws the wicked to the ground. What will he do when he comes as judge, who did this when giving himself up to be judged? What will his power be like when he comes to reign, who had this kind of power when he came to die? And now even at the present time Christ is still saying through the Gospel, "I am." And . . . the result is the same, as people go backward and fall to the ground because they have abandoned what is heavenly in favor of what is earthly. Tractates on the Gospel of John 112.3.[24]

Light Looks at Darkness, and It Falls Down. Quodvultdeus: They come with their torches, lanterns and weapons. The many seek the one, and the sons of darkness come, bearing in their hands light, through which they would reveal the true Light to others, the true Light that they themselves, blinded, were not able to hold in their heart. . . . Behold, the true Light, who lies hidden here under the cloud of flesh, looks at the darkness, and it fell to the ground. . . . In order that the Light might accomplish what it came for, however, the darkness gets back up. He gives [the darkness] power over himself. Darkness seizes the Light, not to follow but to kill it. The Light permits himself to be seized by darkness, to be led away, to be hung, to be killed, in order that, stripped of the cloud of flesh, he might restore the splendor of his majesty. Third Homily on the Creed 5.14-17.[25]

18:7-8 *They Asked Him Again*

Unconscious Agents of Christ's Will. Augustine: They had heard him the first time when he said, "I am he." But they did not comprehend what he said. Why then did they go backward and fall unless the one who could do whatever he wanted did not want them to understand at first? But had he never permitted himself to be taken by them, they would not have done indeed what they came to do. However, he also would not have been able to do what he came to do. So now that he had shown his power to them when they wanted to take him and could not, he lets them seize him and thereby makes them unconscious agents of his will. Tractates on the Gospel of John 112.3.[26]

[22]LF 48:569*. [23]NPNF 1 14:307*. [24]NPNF 1 7:417; CCL 36:634. [25]ACW 60:75-76. See also Gregory the Great *Homilies on Ezekiel* 1.9. [26]NPNF 1 7:417**; CCL 36:634-35.

He Shows His Love for His Own to the End. Chrysostom: "If you seek me, let these go their way," is like saying, "Even though you are looking for me, you should have nothing to do with them. Look, I am giving myself up." And so, even to the last hour he shows his love for his own. Homilies on the Gospel of John 83.1.[27]

18:9 *Jesus Loses No One*

Foreknowledge and God's Kindness. Augustine: Will any one dare to say that God did not foreknow those to whom he would give faith? Or [would anyone dare to say] that God did not foreknow those whom he would give to his Son—those of whom he should lose none? And certainly, if he foreknew these things, he just as certainly foreknew his own kindnesses with which he condescends to deliver us. This is the predestination of the saints—nothing else. In other words, this is the foreknowledge and the preparation of God's kindnesses whereby they are most certainly delivered—whoever they are that are delivered. On the Gift of Perseverance 14.35.[28]

Opposition Restrained by the Power of Christ. Chrysostom: When Jesus says, "I have not lost one," he was not referring to temporal but eternal death here, although the Evangelist also understood him to be talking about temporal death. And one might wonder why they did not seize the disciples with him and cut them to pieces, especially when Peter had roused their anger by what he did to the servant. Who then restrained them? It was no other than that power that cast them backward. And so the Evangelist, to show that it did not happen through their intention but by the power and decree of him whom they had seized, has added, "That the saying might be fulfilled which he spoke, 'Of those which you have given me, I have lost none.' " Homilies on the Gospel of John 83.1.[29]

The Disciples' Faith Not Yet Strong Enough. Augustine: But were the disciples not going to die later? How then was he going to lose them if they died now, unless it was because they did not believe in him yet in such a way as all do who believe and do not perish?[30] Tractates on the Gospel of John 112.4.[31]

18:10 *Peter's Act of Defense with Malchus*

Why Were the Disciples Armed? Chrysostom: But this other point is worth inquiry: Why were they carrying swords? For it is evident that they had them, not only here, but also from replying when asked [if they had swords], "here are two."[32] But why did Christ even allow them to have swords? . . . He did so to assure them that he was to be betrayed. Therefore he says to them, "Let him buy a sword,"[33] not that they should arm themselves; far from it. Rather, by this he was indicating that he was being betrayed. Homilies on the Gospel of Matthew 84.1[34]

The Gospel Does Not Permit Vengeance. Cyril of Alexandria: Peter's violence was lawful according to the Old Testament, but our Lord Jesus Christ, when he came to give us teaching superior to the Law and to reform us to his meekness of heart, rebukes those passions that are in accordance with the Law as being incompatible with the perfect accomplishment of true virtue. For perfect virtue consists not in retaliation of like for like but is rather seen in perfect forbearance. Commentary on the Gospel of John 11.12.[35]

Peter Defends His Master, Not Himself. Chrysostom: Peter, therefore, taking courage from his master's voice and from what had already happened, arms himself against the assailants. "And how," someone says, "does he who was told not to have money, not to have two

[27]NPNF 1 14:307**. [28]NPNF 1 5:539**; PL 45:1014. [29]NPNF 1 14:307-8**. [30]Jn 3:16. [31]NPNF 1 7:417**. [32]Lk 22:38. [33]Lk 22:36. [34]NPNF 1 10:501-2**. [35]LF 48:574*.

coats—how does he come to possess a sword?" I think he had prepared it long before because he was afraid this very thing would happen. But you might say, "How does he, who was forbidden even to strike a blow with the hand, become a [potential] killer?" He certainly had been commanded not to defend himself, but here he did not defend himself but his master. And besides, they were not as yet perfect or complete. But if you want to see Peter endued with heavenly wisdom, you shall after this see him wounded and bearing it meekly, suffering ten thousand dreadful things and not once moved to anger. Homilies on the Gospel of John 83.2.[36]

Jesus Heals an Enemy. Chrysostom: He therefore restored the servant's ear and said to Peter, "All they that take the sword shall perish by the sword."[37] And as he did at the washing of the feet, when he checked his impetuosity by a reproof, he does the same here as well. The Evangelist adds the name of the servant, because what was done was very great, not only because he healed him but because he healed one who had come against him and who shortly after would strike him, and because he prevented the hostility that would probably have been kindled against the disciples by this deed. For this reason the Evangelist has given the name: so that the people of that time might search and inquire diligently as to whether these things had really happened. And not without a cause does he mention the "right ear," but as I think desiring to show the impetuosity of the apostle, that he almost beheaded the man. Yet Jesus not only restrains him by a threat but also calms him by other words, saying, "The cup that my Father has given me, shall I not drink it?" Homilies on the Gospel of John 83.2.[38]

The Ultimate Example of Mercy. Gregory of Nazianzus: We think it is an important matter to obtain penalties from those who have wronged us: an important matter, I say. . . . But it is far greater and more godlike to put up with injuries. For the former course of action curbs wickedness, but the latter makes people good, which is much better and more perfect than merely not being wicked. Let us consider that the great pursuit of mercifulness is set before us, and let us forgive the wrongs done to us that we also may obtain forgiveness, and let us by kindness lay up a store of kindness. Letter 77.[39]

Jesus' Compassion and Forgiveness. Gregory of Nazianzus: Is Jesus suddenly arrested? He reproaches indeed, but follows. And if through zeal you cut off the ear of Malchus with the sword, he will be angry and will restore it. . . . And if you ask for the fire of Sodom on his captors, he will not pour it forth. And if he takes a thief hanging on the cross for his crime, he will bring him into paradise through his goodness. Against the Arians and on Himself, Oration 33.14.[40]

Jesus' Patience Wounded in the Wound of Malchus. Tertullian: While Jesus was betrayed, he nonetheless did not approve of the avenging sword of even one disciple. And this is someone who, if he wanted to, had legions of angels who would at one word have presented themselves from the heavens. The patience of the Lord was wounded in [the wound of] Malchus. And so, too, he cursed for the time to come the works of the sword. And, by the restoration of health, made satisfaction to him whom himself had not hurt, through patience, the mother of mercy. On Patience 3.[41]

Destined to Reign. Augustine: This is the only Evangelist who has given us the very name of this servant, as Luke is the only one who tells us that the Lord touched his ear and healed him.[42] The interpretation of Malchus is "one who is destined to reign." What, then, is signified by the ear that was cut off in the Lord's behalf and healed by the Lord, but the renewed hearing that

[36]NPNF 1 14:308**. [37]Mt 26:52. [38]NPNF 1 14:308. [39]NPNF 2 7:471. [40]NPNF 2 7:333. [41]ANF 3:708*; CCL 1:301. [42]See Lk 22:51.

has been pruned of its oldness, that it may from that point on be in the newness of the spirit and not in the oldness of the letter?[43] Who can doubt that he, who had such a thing done for him by Christ, was yet destined to reign with Christ? And his being found a servant pertains also to that oldness that generates bondage, which is Hagar.[44] But when healing came, liberty was also signified. Tractates on the Gospel of John 112.5.[45]

18:11 *The Sword and the Cup*

Where Did the Swords Come From? Chrysostom: But where did the swords come from? They came from the supper and from the table. It was likely also there should be swords because of the lamb and that the disciples, hearing that certain people were coming out against Jesus, took the swords for defense. They meant to fight on behalf of their Master—but this they thought on their own. This is why Peter also is rebuked for using it—and with a severe threat. For he was resisting the servant who came, warmly indeed, yet Peter was not defending himself but his Master. Christ, however, allowed no harm to ensue. For he healed him and demonstrated a great miracle. It was enough to indicate at once both his forbearance and his power and the affection and meekness of his disciple. For then Peter acted from affection, now with dutifulness. For when he heard "Put up your sword into its sheath," he immediately obeyed and never does this again [i.e., take up the sword]. Homilies on the Gospel of Matthew 84.1.[46]

Judea Was Dangerous. Cyril of Alexandria: Someone may now, perhaps, raise the question and ask himself: Why did Peter carry a sword? We reply that the duty of repelling the assaults of evildoers, according to the Law, brought the need of a sword. For if one of the disciples had chosen to strike the innocent with a sword, how could the same issue have been tried? It is likely, too, that the holy disciples, as they were hurrying at midnight from their place of rest and expected to find woods and gardens in their way, were suspicious of the attacks of wild beasts. Judea had many of these. Commentary on the Gospel of John 11.12.[47]

Replace Sword of Violence with Sword of Spirit. Origen: Jesus at once speaks to him who had used the sword and cut off the servant's right ear. He does not, however, say "withdraw your sword" but "return the sword into its place." There is therefore some place for the sword from which it may be taken by one who does not want to perish, especially by the sword. For Jesus wants his disciples to be peaceful so that, laying aside this warlike sword, they may take another peaceful sword that Scripture calls "the sword of the Spirit." Commentary on Matthew 102.[48]

Jesus Declares His Intent. Theodore of Mopsuestia: The [sword] is not necessary, he says. I must suffer my passion because the Father wants this for the redemption of the whole of the human race. Therefore the words "am I not to drink the cup" must accurately be read in a declarative sense, that is, it is necessary that I drink it. Commentary on John 7.18.11.[49]

Can We Also Drink the Cup? Clement of Alexandria: Alone, therefore, the Lord "drank the cup," for the purification of the people who plotted against him and disbelieved him. The apostles also imitated this so that they might be . . . perfected, suffering for the churches that they founded. So then, also those . . . who tread in the footsteps of the apostles ought to be sinless and, out of love to the Lord, they should also love their brother. In this way, if the occasion calls for it, "they may drink the cup," enduring afflictions for the church without stumbling. Those who witness in their life by deed and at the tribunal by

[43]See Rom 7:6. [44]See Gal 4:24. [45]NPNF 1 7:417*; CCL 36:635. [46]NPNF 1 10:502**. [47]LF 48:575**. [48]*AEG* 6:7*; GCS 38 2 (11):221. [49]CSCO 4 3:325.

word (whether entertaining hope or imagining fear) are better than those who confess salvation by their mouth alone. But if one ascends also to love, he is a really blessed and true martyr who makes a confession perfectly both to the commandments and to God. He demonstrates his love for the Lord, acknowledging him as a brother and giving himself up wholly for God, giving himself up with love and without struggle as one who is asked to return a deposit. Stromateis 4.9.[50]

"Drink the Cup" Means Discharge the Ministry. Dionysius of Alexandria: Now, to drink the cup was to discharge the ministry and the whole divine plan of trial with fortitude. It meant to follow and fulfill the Father's determination and to surmount any apprehension. And the exclamation "Why have you forsaken me?" fits in with the requests he had previously made. In other words, Why is it that death has been with me all along up until now, but I have not yet borne the cup? This I judge to have been the Savior's meaning in this concise utterance. Fragment 2.[51]

Was Jesus Afraid to Suffer? Hilary of Poitiers: Could fear induce him to pray for the removal of what, in his zeal for the divine plan, he was hurrying to fulfill? To say he shrank from the suffering he desired is not consistent. You allow that he suffered willingly. Would it not be more reverent to confess that you had misunderstood this passage than to rush with blasphemous and headlong folly to the assertion that he prayed to escape suffering, although you allow that he suffered willingly? And yet, I suppose, you will arm yourself also for your godless contention with these words of the Lord, "My God, my God, why have you forsaken me?"[52] Perhaps you think that after the disgrace of the cross, the favor of his Father's help departed from him, and this is why he cried out that he was left alone in his weakness. But if you regard the contempt, the weakness, the cross of Christ as a disgrace, you should remember his words, "Truly I say unto you, from now on you shall see the Son of man sitting at the right hand of power and coming with the clouds of heaven."[53] On the Trinity 10.30-31.[54]

Saving the World Has Always Been the Plan. Leo the Great: It is not to be thought that the Lord Jesus wished to escape the passion and the death, the sacraments of which he had already committed to his disciples' keeping. This is obvious, seeing that he himself forbids Peter, when he was burning with devoted faith and love, to use the sword. He says, "The cup that the Father has given me, shall I not drink it?" The Lord also most certainly says, according to John's Gospel, "For God so loved the world that he gave his only begotten Son, that everyone who believes in him may not perish but have eternal life."[55] Similarly, the apostle Paul says, "Christ loved us and gave himself for us, a victim to God for a sweet-smelling savor."[56] For the saving of all through the cross of Christ was the common will and the common plan of the Father and the Son. Nor could that by any means be disturbed that before eternal ages had been mercifully determined and unchangeably foreordained. Therefore in assuming true and entire manhood Jesus took the true sensations of the body and the true feelings of the mind. And it does not follow because everything in him was full of sacraments, full of miracles, that therefore he either shed false tears or took food from pretended hunger or feigned slumber. It was in our humility that he was despised, with our grief that he was saddened, with our pain that he was racked on the cross. For his compassion underwent the sufferings of our mortality with the purpose of healing them, and his power encountered them with the purpose of conquering them. And this Isaiah has most plainly prophesied, saying, "He carries our

[50]ANF 2:422**. [51]ANF 6:115**. [52]Mt 27:46; Mk 15:34. [53]Mt 26:64; cf 16:27. [54]NPNF 2:9:189-90*; CCL 62A:484-85. [55]Jn 3:16. [56]Eph 5:2.

sins and is pained for us, and we thought him to be in pain and in stripes and in affliction. But he was wounded for our sins and was stricken for our offenses, and with his stripes we are healed."[57] Sermon 58.4.[58]

Do Not Needlessly Surrender to Persecutors. Peter of Alexandria: Those Christians who deliver themselves up to persecution forget that the Savior taught us to pray not to enter into temptation. They forget his many retreats from those who sought to plot against him . . . and how when the time of his passion was at hand he did not give himself up but waited until they came upon him with swords and spears. Canonical Epistle 9.[59]

[57]Is 53:4-5 LXX. [58]CCL 138A:345-47; NPNF 2 12:170**. [59]ANCL 14:304**.

18:12-14 JESUS BEFORE ANNAS

[12]So the band of soldiers and their captain and the officers of the Jews seized Jesus and bound him. [13]First they led him to Annas; for he was the father-in-law of Caiaphas, who was high priest that year. [14]It was Caiaphas who had given counsel to the Jews that it was expedient that one man should die for the people.

Overview: Jesus' captors bound their liberator (Augustine) with the chains of our freedom (Cyril). They present Jesus to Annas as if they were presenting him with a trophy (Chrysostom). They brought him to the high priest Annas first, since he was the prime mover behind the scenes in hatching the plot against Jesus; then they bring him to Caiaphas, who was the instigator of his slaughter (Cyril). In explaining the priesthood of Annas and Caiaphas, it is helpful to remember that Jesus passed the entire time of his ministry under four high priests who each served one year, according to Josephus, beginning with Annas and ending with Caiaphas under whom Jesus suffered (Eusebius).

18:12 *They Bound Him*

They Bound Their Liberator. Augustine: They took him: someone to whom they had never found access. For he continued [as] the day while they remained as darkness. Neither had they listened to the words "Come unto him, and be enlightened."[1] For if they had approached him in this way, they would have taken him, not with their hands for the purpose of murder but with their hearts for the purpose of a welcome reception. Now, however, when they laid hold of him in this way, their distance from him was vastly increased. And they bound the one who could have freed them. And perhaps there were those among them who then fastened their fetters on Christ, and yet were afterward delivered by him and could say, "You have loosed my bonds."[2] Tractates on the Gospel of John 112.6.[3]

Chains of Freedom. Cyril of Alexandria: Now that all obstacles had been overcome and Peter had put away his sword, and Christ had, as it were, surrendered himself to the hand of the Jews (though he did not have to die) and it was

[1]Ps 34:5 (33:6 LXX). [2]Ps 116:16 (115:7 LXX). [3]CCL 36:635-36; NPNF 1 7:417-18**.

easier for him to escape, the soldiers and servants together with their guide give way to cruel rage and are transported with the ardor of victory. They took the Lord, who gave himself up wholly to their will, and put chains upon him, even though he came to us to release us from the bondage of the devil and to loose us from the chains of sin. Commentary on the Gospel of John 11.13.[4]

18:13-14 *Annas and Caiaphas*

Jesus the Trophy. Chrysostom: In their exultation, they took him to Annas to show what they had done, as if they were bringing home the trophy. Homilies on the Gospel of John 83.2.[5]

Jesus Brought First to Annas Because He Is the Instigator. Cyril of Alexandria: They bring Jesus to Annas, who was the father-in-law of Caiaphas. From this we may conclude that he was the prime mover and planner of the iniquity against Christ. . . . Jesus is, therefore, taken away to him first of all. . . . Having been captured by the malice of Annas and the services of his hirelings and ensnared within the net, Jesus was then led to the one who encompassed and instigated the slaughter of the innocent. This was Caiaphas, and he was adorned with the office of the priesthood. . . . This miserable man committed the most impious act ever committed. For what can be worse than impiety against Christ? Commentary on the Gospel of John 11.13.[6]

Jesus' Ministry Under Annas and Caiaphas. Eusebius of Caesarea: The divine Scripture[7] says that he completed the entire time of his teaching while Annas and Caiaphas were high priest, showing that the entire time of his teaching was included within the years of their administration. Since he began in the high priesthood of Annas and continued until the reign of Caiaphas, the entire intervening time does not amount to four years. For, since the regulations of the law of that time were already being destroyed, somehow, there was a relaxation of the rule by which the duties of the service of God were for life and by hereditary descent, and different men at different times were entrusted with the high priesthood by the Roman governors and continued in this office for no more than one year.[8] Josephus relates that four high priests intervened in succession from Annas to Caiaphas, speaking as follows in the same text of the *Antiquities*: "Valerius Gratus[9] put an end to the priesthood of Annas[10] and appointed Ishmael[11] the son of Phabi as high priest, and after a short time he removed this one and named as high priest Eliezer, the son of Annas the high priest. And after a year had passed he removed this one also and passed over the high priesthood to Simon,[12] the son of Kamithus. But no more than a year passed with him in office when Josephus, known also as Caiaphas,[13] became his successor."[14] So, the entire period of our Savior's teaching is shown to be not even a complete period of four years, since four high priests from Annas to the appointment of Caiaphas fulfilled an annual service over a period of four years. The Gospel, therefore, has rightly indicated Caiaphas as the high priest of the year in which the events of the Savior's passion were fulfilled, and from this we also can see that the time of Christ's ministry does not disagree with the foregoing investigation. Ecclesiastical History 1.10.2-7.[15]

---

[4]LF 48:578**. [5]NPNF 1 14:308**. [6]LF 48:578**. [7]See Lk 3:2; also, Jn 11:49, 51; 18:13. [8]The high priests were frequently changed by the Roman governors, and there was no regularly prescribed interval. Some continued in office for many years. Thus, Caiaphas was high priest for more than ten years, having been appointed by Pilate and also by his predecessor, Valerius Gratus, and his successor, the Proconsul Vitellius. [9]Made procurator by Tiberius early in his reign. He ruled about eleven years, when he was succeeded by Pilate in A.D. 26. [10]Also known as Annas; he was appointed high priest by Quirinius, governor of Syria, in A.D. 6 or 7. He remained in office until 14 or 15, when he was removed by Valerius Gratus. [11]Either Ishmael or Caiaphas must have held the office of high priest for eight or ten years, or Gratus's period would not be filled up. Eusebius seems to be wrong in limiting his period of office to one year, although Eusebius may be assuming some facts not in evidence. [12]This Simon is otherwise unknown, except by Josephus here. [13]Joseph Caiaphas, son-in-law of Annas, well known for his prominence in gospel history. [14]Josephus *Jewish Antiquities* 18.34, 35. [15]FC 19:70-72**.

18:15-18 Peter's Trial and First Denial

[15]Simon Peter followed Jesus, and so did another disciple. As this disciple was known to the high priest, he entered the court of the high priest along with Jesus, [16]while Peter stood outside at the door. So the other disciple, who was known to the high priest, went out and spoke to the maid who kept the door, and brought Peter in. [17]The maid who kept the door said to Peter, "Are not you also one of this man's disciples?" He said, "I am not." [18]Now the servants[l] and officers had made a charcoal fire, because it was cold, and they were standing and warming themselves; Peter also was with them, standing and warming himself.

l Or *slaves*

Overview: John begins his account of Jesus' contemptible treatment with the temptation of Peter (Augustine). He also includes himself in the narrative, although not by name but rather self-effacingly as the one "whom Jesus loved" (Augustine, Chrysostom). In contrast to the other disciples, Peter and John are quite brave in seeking out what was happening to Jesus (Cyril). Since John was known to the high priest, he is able to get Peter inside the courtyard (Chrysostom, Theodore).

Just as Peter took his eyes off Jesus when he attempted walking on water, so now when Peter is questioned about Jesus, he denies knowing him and stumbles into the sea (Romanus), in effect denying his own Christianity (Augustine). The humbling he undergoes here, however, prepares him for humility later in dealing with others who have sinned (Chrysostom). He later recovers his footing through tears of repentance (Origen). The coldness at the time of the vernal equinox (Augustine), when it normally would not have been cold (Ambrose), contributes to the smothering of the fire of love in Peter's heart (Gregory the Great). The cold and darkness that accompanied our Lord's passion was indicative of the love that had grown cold and the spiritual darkness that enveloped the earth (Eusebius).

18:15 *Peter and the Other Disciple*

John Begins with Peter's Temptations. Augustine: The temptation of Peter, which took place during the time that the Lord was enduring these injuries, is not placed by all Evangelists in the same order. Matthew and Mark first narrate the injuries inflicted on the Lord and then this temptation of Peter.[1] Luke first describes Peter's temptation, and only after this does he record the reproaches borne by the Lord.[2] John begins with Peter's temptation but then introduces some verses that record what the Lord had to bear, appending the statement that the Lord was sent away from Annas to Caiaphas the high priest, and then at this point he resumes and sums up what he had been relating about Peter's temptation in the house to which Jesus was first conducted. He then gives a full account of that incident and thereafter reverts to the succession of events that happened to the Lord, telling us how Jesus was brought to Caiaphas.[3] Harmony of the Gospels 3.6.21.[4]

Who Is the Other Disciple? Augustine: Who that other disciple is we cannot affirm with confidence because it is left unnoticed here. But it

[1]See Mt 26:57-75; Mk 14:53-72. [2]Lk 22:54-23:12. [3]The Evangelists indicate three distinct episodes of recognition and denial with Peter and Jesus, respectively, but do not refer to the same facts in detail. [4]NPNF 1 6:187**; CSEL 43:292-93.

is in this way that John usually refers to himself, with the addition "whom Jesus loved."[5] Perhaps, therefore, it is he also in the present case. Tractates on the Gospel of John 113.2.[6]

John Is Again Self-Effacing. Chrysostom: Who is that other disciple? It is the writer himself. And why doesn't he name himself? When he lay on the bosom of Jesus, he with reason concealed his name. But now why does he do this? He does it for the same reason. Here also he mentions a deed greatly to his credit, that when all had run away, John followed. Therefore John conceals himself and puts Peter before him. He was obliged to mention himself so that you might understand that he narrates more exactly than the rest what took place in the hall since he was there inside. But observe how he detracts from his own praise. For, in case anyone should ask, "How, when all had retreated, did this man enter in farther than Simon?" he says that he "was known to the high priest," so that no one should wonder that he followed, or admire him for his courage. Homilies on the Gospel of John 83.2.[7]

The Bravery of Peter and John. Cyril of Alexandria: While the other disciples, it seems, were panic-stricken and fled from the present wrath of the murderers, Peter (who was always moved by a more fervent passion) clings to his love for Christ and follows him at the peril of his own life, as he watched the chain of events unfold. The other disciple accompanying him (and with similar courage) sustained a similar resolution. This was John, the truly pious writer of this divine work. For he calls himself that other disciple without giving himself a definite name. He did not want to seem boastful, and he abhorred the appearance of being better than the rest. For the crowning achievements of virtue, if shown by any of the righteous, are never trumpeted to the world by their own mouth. For it very ill becomes someone to win praise out of his own mouth rather than the conversation of other people. Commentary on the Gospel of John 11.12.[8]

18:16 *Peter Is Brought In*

Peter, Though Afraid, Still Follows. Chrysostom: But the wonder is that Peter, even though he was so afraid, still came even as far as the hall when the others had retreated. His coming this far was caused by love. He did not enter, however, because he was distressed and afraid. For the Evangelist has recorded these things to pave the way for excusing his denial. But with regard to himself, he does not set it down as any great matter that he was known to the high priest. And yet, since he had said that he alone went in with Jesus (in case you might think he was bragging), he also gives the reason why he went in. And that Peter would have also entered, had he been permitted, he shows by what happens next. For when John went out and asked the servant girl who kept the door to bring in Peter, he immediately came in. But why didn't John bring him in himself? It was because he clung to Christ and followed him. This is why he asked the woman to bring Peter in. Homilies on the Gospel of John 83.2.[9]

Peter Afraid to Go in Alone. Theodore of Mopsuestia: After he had showed his power through these things, our Lord surrendered voluntarily and was bound. First they took him to Annas, who was the father-in-law of Caiaphas the high priest. His disciples Simon Peter and John, who wrote this Gospel, followed him. John, who was known to the high priest, went into the courtyard without fear. Simon . . . stayed alone outside the gate because he lacked the courage to go in alone and knew no one on the inside. John, when he saw that Simon did not get in, went out and told the woman guarding the gate to let him in. Actually, John's frankness allowed him to be

[5]See Jn 13:23; 19:26. [6]NPNF 1 7:418; CCL 36:636. [7]NPNF 1 14:308**. [8]LF 48:579**. [9]NPNF 1 14:308-9**

familiar with the high priest. Commentary on John 7.18.16.[10]

18:17 *I Am Not*

The Maiden and the Waves. Romanus Melodus:

Forgetful of the fearful waves[11]
And changed by the remark of the maiden,
Peter said, "Christ, God,
When I was sinking in the waves, I was frightened, and with reason.
Calling out to Thee, I have fallen, through my denial;
But weeping, I cry to Thee:
Hasten, Holy One, save Thy Sheep."

Another kind of deep water is here on land, the maidservant;
But as I find a pilot for the future
I flee to Thee for refuge as to a harbor.
Lord, I shall shed my tears of intercession to you,
And hence I shall cry out to you:
"Hasten, Holy One, save Thy sheep."

O Good Shepherd, Thou who hast placed His Spirit in the flocks,
Hasten, Holy One, save Thy sheep.

Kontakion on Peter's Denial 18, Prooimion 1-3.[12]

Peter Denies His Christianity. Augustine: See how the pillar of greatest strength has at a single breath of air trembled to its foundations. Where now is all that boldness of the one who made promises and who had such overweening confidence in himself beforehand? What now of those words when he said, "Why can't I follow you now? I will lay down my life for your sake."[13] Is this the way to follow the Master—to deny his own discipleship? Is this the way one lays down his life for the Lord—frightened at a maidservant's voice that might compel us to the sacrifice? But is it any wonder that God foretold what was true, and human beings presumptuously imagined what was false? Assuredly in this denial of the apostle Peter, which had now entered on its first stage, we ought to take notice that not only is Christ denied by one who says that he is not Christ, but by someone also who, while really a Christian, himself denies that he is so. For the Lord did not say to Peter, "You shall deny that you are my disciple" but "you shall deny me."[14] He denied him, therefore, when he denied that he was his disciple. And what else did such a form of denial imply but a denial of his own Christianity?[15] . . . How many afterward, not only old men and women who have had long lives already, but even boys and girls—along with an innumerable company of holy martyrs with brave hearts who by a violent death entered the kingdom of heaven—how many end up doing what at that moment Peter was unable to do who received the keys of that kingdom? It is here we see why it was said, "Let these go their way," when Jesus, who has redeemed us by his own blood, gave himself for us. It was so that the saying that he spoke might be fulfilled, "Of those whom you have given me, I have lost none." For assuredly, if Peter had gone away after denying the Christ, what else would have awaited him but destruction? Tractates on the Gospel of John 113.2.[16]

Peter Humbled for the Future. Chrysostom: Peter was permitted to be the first to fall, in order that he might be less severe to sinners from the remembrance of his own fall. . . . Peter, the teacher and master of the whole world, sinned, and he obtained pardon in order that judges might from there on out have that rule to go by in dispensing pardon. . . . For this reason I suppose the priesthood was not given to angels. Otherwise, being without sin themselves, they would punish the sins of the people without pity.

[10]CSCO 4 3:326. [11]Mt 14:28-33. Romanus parallels Peter's fear of the waves with his fear of the maiden. [12]*KRBM* 1:181. [13]Jn 13:37. [14]Mt 26:34. [15]Augustine then speaks of the legitimacy of using the anachronistic term *Christian*. [16]CCL 36:636-37; NPNF 1 7:418-19**.

Rather, man [a human being] is placed over man in order that remembering his own sin, he may be merciful to others who are sinners. Sermon on St. Peter and Elijah 1.[17]

Peter Later Recovers His Footing Through Weeping. Origen: Peter had once almost been lost and taken away from the consecration of the apostolic number by the instigation of the devil through the mouth of the maidservant of the high priest. But when Jesus simply looked on him and turned toward him the lines of his gentle face, he immediately came to himself and, recovering his footing, wept bitterly. Peter, looked on by God in this way, recovered by weeping his place that he had lost by denying. Homilies on Leviticus 16.7.3.[18]

18:18 *Because It Was Cold*

Cool During the Vernal Equinox. Augustine: It was not winter, and yet it was cold, as it often is at the vernal equinox.[19] Tractates on the Gospel of John 113.3.[20]

Peter Frozen in His Denial. Ambrose: The Evangelist John says, "It was cold." If we consider the season, it could not have been cold.[21] But it was cold where Jesus was not acknowledged, where there was none to see the light, where the consuming fire[22] was denied. Peter stood beside the brazier, because he felt he was freezing. Evil is the . . . flame [that night]. It burns but does not warm. Evil is the hearth that scatters a soot of error even on the minds of the saints because even the inner eyes of Peter were darkened. Exposition on the Gospel of Luke 10.76.[23]

The Fire of Love Smothered. Gregory the Great: The fire of love was smothered in Peter's breast, and he was warming himself before the coals of the persecutors, that is, he was warming himself with the love of this present life, which only increased his weakness. Morals on the Book of Job 2.2.2.[24]

Love Grows Cold. Eusebius of Caesarea: See how clearly this description of the day of our Savior's passion, a day in which "there shall be no light,"[25] was fulfilled, since "from the sixth hour to the ninth hour there was darkness over all the earth."[26] And also the "frost and cold,"[27] since according to Luke: "They led Jesus to the palace of the high priest. And Peter followed afar off. And while they kindled a fire in the midst of the hall, he sat down,"[28] according to Mark, with the others to warm himself. And John, too, especially mentions the cold, saying, "The servants and the ministers stood, having made a fire of coals, for it was cold, and they warmed themselves." And this day, he says, was known to the Lord and was not night. It was not day, because, as has been said already, "there shall be no light."[29] This was fulfilled when "from the sixth hour there was darkness over all the earth until the ninth hour."[30] Nor was it night, because "at eventide it shall be light"[31] was added, which also was fulfilled when the day regained its natural light after the ninth hour. Proof of the Gospel 6.18.[32]

[17]PG 50:728. [18]FC 83:275-76**; GCS 29(6):505. [19]But see Ambrose below. [20]CCL 36:637; NPNF 1 7:419*. [21]Ambrose uses what he perceives as a deliberate incongruity in a detail of John's account to launch into a spiritual interpretation of the cold. [22]Deut 4:24; Heb 12:29. [23]CCL 14:368. [24]LF 18:68**; ODGM 1 1:162. [25]Zech 14:6. [26]Mt 27:45. [27]Zech 14:6. [28]Lk 22:54-55. [29]Zech 14:6. [30]Mt 27:45. [31]Zech 14:6. [32]*POG* 2:34-35**.

18:19-24 JESUS' TRIAL

[19]The high priest then questioned Jesus about his disciples and his teaching. [20]Jesus answered him, "I have spoken openly to the world; I have always taught in synagogues and in the temple, where all Jews come together; I have said nothing secretly. [21]Why do you ask me? Ask those who have heard me, what I said to them; they know what I said." [22]When he had said this, one of the officers standing by struck Jesus with his hand, saying, "Is that how you answer the high priest?" [23]Jesus answered him, "If I have spoken wrongly, bear witness to the wrong; but if I have spoken rightly, why do you strike me?" [24]Annas then sent him bound to Caiaphas the high priest.

Overview: In the questioning of Jesus that follows, the high priest searches for evidence of sedition (Chrysostom). But Jesus' reply demonstrates that he has never had anything to hide the whole time he has been with them (Augustine). Having spoken "openly to the world" indicates not only that he has nothing to hide but that what was formerly hidden in shadows in the Law is now fully revealed in him (Cyril).

Jesus talks back to the one who strikes him instead of turning the other cheek, but in reality he goes further in preparing not only his other cheek but his entire body to be struck with the nails of the cross (Augustine). His humility and patience are evident in calling his interrogator a priest who he knew in reality made a sacrilege out of the priesthood (Cyprian). It is obvious that what Jesus experienced was not a trial but a conspiracy (Chrysostom). Christ the Lord of all truly is a pattern for us of humility, gentleness and forbearance (Cyril). They had taken Jesus to Annas first because he was Caiaphas's father-in-law and because his house may have been on the way. But now they bind Jesus and send him to Caiaphas, who was high priest that year, a position he occupied in alternate years with his father-in-law (Augustine).

18:19 *Caiaphas Asks About Jesus' Disciples and Teaching*

Seeking to Prove Sedition. Chrysostom: O the wickedness! Though he had continually heard him speaking in the temple and teaching openly, he now wants to be informed. For since they had no charge to bring, they inquired concerning his disciples—perhaps where they were, why he had collected them, with what intention and on what terms. And this he said because he wanted to prove that Jesus was a seditious person and a rebel since no one listened to him except them alone, as though his were some factory of wickedness. Homilies on the Gospel of John 83.3.[1]

18:20-21 *Nothing to Hide*

Had Jesus Spoken Openly? Augustine: A question occurs that ought not to be passed over: Why did the Lord Jesus say, "I spoke openly to the world" and in particular what he afterward added, "In secret have I said nothing"? Even in the latest discourse that he had delivered to the disciples after supper, didn't he say to them, "These things have I spoken unto you in proverbs. But the hour is coming when I shall no more speak to you in proverbs, but I shall show you plainly of my Father"?[2] If, then, he did not speak openly even to the more intimate company of his disciples but gave the promise of a time when he

[1]NPNF 1 14:309**. [2]Jn 16:25.

would speak openly, how was it that he spoke openly to the world? And still further, as is also testified on the authority of the other Evangelists, to those who were truly his own, in comparison with others who were not his disciples, he certainly spoke with much greater plainness when he was alone with them at a distance from the multitudes. For then he unfolded to them the parables that he had uttered in obscure terms to others. What then is the meaning of the words "in secret have I said nothing"? It is . . . as if he had said, There were many who heard me. And . . . he spoke out in the open where many heard him. But then again it was not so openly spoken that they understood him, because they did not. And even what he spoke to his disciples when he was alone with them was certainly not in secret. For who is going to speak in secret in front of that many people? . . . And so, the very things that they had heard without understanding were the kinds of things that could not with any justice or truth be turned into a criminal charge against him. And as often as they tried by their questions to find something to accuse him of, he gave them such replies as utterly upset all their plots, leaving no ground for the calumnies they devised. Tractates on the Gospel of John 113.3.[3]

The Law Was Obscure, Christ Is Clear. Cyril of Alexandria: It would be fruitless, Christ says, to consider as obscure something universally known. And how can it be right to set up a pretence of ignorance when something is fully known? This is what Christ seems to us to be saying, with the object of releasing himself from the charges that had been fabricated and maliciously devised against him by the malice of the leaders of the people. But I think, also, that there is a suggestion of another meaning. For he says, "I have spoken openly to the world," that is to say, the words given to you by the mediation of Moses come in types and shadows and do not teach expressly the will of God but rather create a vision of the actual truth beyond themselves. And, wrapped up in the obscurity of the letter, they do not completely reveal the knowledge of those things that we need. "I have spoken openly to the world." And, apart from riddles and the shadow of the form of that which is good, I set before you the right way and pointed out the straight path of a life directed toward God without any tortuous turnings. I spoke to the world—not, he says, to the one nation of the Israelites. If the whole world does not yet know me, it will know in due time. "I always taught in the synagogues." We can scarcely fail to see what he means here. He reminds those of the Jews who were in his presence, I think—however reluctant they were—of the prophecies that spoke about him. For what did the divine Isaiah say, putting the words in Christ's mouth? "I have not spoken in secret, in a dark place of the earth."[4] And again: "I have spread out my hands all the day unto a disobedient and rebellious people."[5] For what else can "not speaking in secret, in a dark place" mean, but teaching openly and speaking in places where there is no small gathering of hearers? Commentary on the Gospel of John 11.13.[6]

18:22 *One of the Officers Struck Jesus*

Jesus Goes Further Than What He Commands. Augustine: If we consider who it was that received the blow, might we not well feel the wish that he who struck it were either consumed by fire from heaven, or swallowed up by the gaping earth, or seized and carried off by devils or visited with some other or still heavier punishment of this kind? For couldn't the one who made the world have commanded any one of these to happen by his power, unless he wanted rather to teach us the patience that overcomes the world? Someone will say here, Why didn't he do what he himself commanded?[7] He should not have answered the one who struck him but should have instead turned to him the other cheek. But he actually goes further than this. Didn't he

[3]CCL 36:638**; NPNF 1 7:419. [4]Is 45:19. [5]Is 65:2. [6]LF 48:583**. [7]See Mt 5:39.

answer truthfully, meekly and righteously, and at the same time prepare not only his other cheek for him who was going to strike it again, but in fact his whole body to be nailed to the tree? In this way he showed what needed to be shown, namely, that those great precepts of his are to be fulfilled not outwardly or ostentatiously but by the preparation of the heart. For even an angry person may visibly hold out his other cheek. How much better, then, is it for one who is peaceful to make a truthful answer and with tranquil mind hold himself ready for the endurance of heavier sufferings to come? Happy is the one who, in all that he suffers unjustly for righteousness' sake, can truthfully say, "My heart is ready, O God, my heart is ready." For this is what makes it possible to say, "I will sing and give praise."[8] Tractates on the Gospel of John 113.4.[9]

18:23 *What Was Wrong?*

True and False Priests. Cyprian: With that humility that taught us also to he humble, he still called him a priest whom he knew to be sacrilegious. Also under the very sting of his passion, when he had received a blow and it was said to him, "Do you answer the high priest in this way?" he said nothing reproachfully against the person of the high priest. Rather, he maintained his own innocence saying, "If I have spoken evil, bear witness of the evil. But if well, why do you hit me?" All of the things, therefore, were done by him humbly and patiently so that we might have an example of humility and patience. For he taught that true priests were lawfully and fully to be honored, in showing himself such as he was in respect of false priests. Letter 64.2.[10]

Not a Trial, but a Conspiracy. Chrysostom: See how the judgment hall is full of commotion, trouble, passion and confusion? The high priest deceitfully and treacherously questions Jesus. Christ answers in a straightforward way, which was only right. And so what should be done next? They should either disprove or admit what he said. And yet, this is not what they do. Instead, a servant hits him. It is not a trial they are carrying on but a conspiracy and a tyranny. Not knowing what else to do, they send him to Caiaphas. Homilies on the Gospel of John 83.3.[11]

What If Someone Offends Us? Cyril of Alexandria: When a brother happens to have words with us and lets fall some troublesome expression, we often think that we are justified to be enraged with the fury of dragons and ceaselessly pelt him with a storm of words in return for one. We neglect to grant forgiveness to human littleness, or to consider the frailty of our common humanity, or to bury the passions that arise in brotherly love. We neglect to look to Jesus himself, the author and perfecter of our faith.[12] Instead, we eagerly seek to avenge ourselves even though holy Scripture declares in one place, "He who pursues vengeance pursues it to his own death,"[13] and in another place, "Let none of you harbor resentment in your heart against your brother."[14] Rather, let Christ the Lord of all be a pattern for us of gentleness to one another and exceedingly great forbearance. For he said to us concerning this very thing, "A disciple is not above his master, nor a servant above his lord."[15] Commentary on the Gospel of John 11.13.[16]

18:24 *Bound and Sent to Caiaphas*

Annas and Caiaphas as High Priests. Augustine: "And Annas sent him bound unto Caiaphas the high priest." To Caiaphas, according to Matthew's account,[17] he was led at the outset because he was the high priest that year. For both the pontiffs are to be understood as in the habit of acting year by year alternately, that is, as chief priests. And these were at that time Annas and Caiaphas, as recorded by the Evangelist Luke,

[8]Ps 57:7 (56:8 LXX). [9]NPNF 1 7:419-20*; CCL 36:639. [10]ANF 5:366; *Letter* 3.2 in CCL 3B:13. [11]NPNF 1 14:309**. [12]See Heb 12:2. [13]Prov 11:19. [14]Zech 7:10. [15]Mt 10:24. [16]LF 48:588*. [17]Mt 26:57.

when telling of the time when John, the Lord's forerunner, began to preach the kingdom of heaven and to gather disciples. For he says, "Under the high priests Annas and Caiaphas, the word of the Lord came on John, the son of Zachariah, in the wilderness."[18] . . . Accordingly, these two pontiffs fulfilled their years in turn, and it was the year of Caiaphas when Christ suffered. And so, according to Matthew, when Jesus was apprehended, he was taken to him. But first, according to John, they came with him to Annas, not because he was his colleague but his father-in-law. And we must suppose that it was by Caiaphas's wish that it was so done or that their houses were so situated that Annas could not properly be overlooked by them as they passed on their way. Tractates on the Gospel of John 113.5.[19]

[18]Lk 3:2. [19]NPNF 1 7:420**; CCL 36:639.

18:25-27 Peter's Final Denials

[25]Now Simon Peter was standing and warming himself. They said to him, "Are not you also one of his disciples?" He denied it and said, "I am not." [26]One of the servants[1] of the high priest, a kinsman of the man whose ear Peter had cut off, asked, "Did I not see you in the garden with him?" [27]Peter again denied it; and at once the cock crowed.

1 Or *slaves*

Overview: As Jesus is being led away, Peter remains and chooses to stay by the fire, but he denies Jesus a second time, demonstrating how weak human nature is without God (Chrysostom, Augustine). In Peter we see how the prediction of the Great Physician is fulfilled, while the presumption of the sick man is shown for what it is (Augustine). But the example of Peter in his threefold denial is recorded for our consolation to show how God changed his weakness into power (Cyril) and how great an evil it is to trust in ourselves instead of committing everything to God (Chrysostom). All of Peter's denials were made in the night and in the darkness before the coming of the Sun of righteousness (Origen).

18:25 *Peter's Second Denial*

Weakness of Human Nature Exposed. Chrysostom: The once fervid disciple was now lethargic when Jesus was being led away! After such things as had taken place, he does not move but still warms himself. This happened so that you might learn how great the weakness of our nature is if God abandons us. And, being questioned, he denies again. Homilies on the Gospel of John 83.3.[1]

Who Are Peter's Questioners? Augustine: Here we find that Peter's second denial occurred, not when he was at the door but as he was standing by the fire. This, however, could not have been the case, so that he must have returned after he had gone out of doors, where Matthew says he was. It was not that he went out, and then another woman sees him on the outside. Rather,

[1]NPNF 1 14:309-10**

another woman saw him as he was getting up to go out, and she made a remark about him. She told those who were near, that is, those who were standing with her at the fire inside the hall, "This fellow also was with Jesus of Nazareth." He heard this outside and returned and swore, "I do not know the man." . . . Then John continues, "They said, 'Are not you also one of his disciples?'" These words were probably said to him when he had come back and was standing at the fire. And this explanation is confirmed by the fact that, besides the other woman mentioned by Matthew and Mark in the second denial, there was another person mentioned by Luke who also questioned him. So John uses the plural. "They said therefore to him." . . . When we compare all the Evangelists on this, we come clearly to the conclusion that Peter's second denial took place not when he was at the door but when he was within, by the fire in the court. It becomes evident, therefore, that Matthew and Mark, who have told us how he went outside, have left the fact of his return unnoticed simply with a view to brevity. . . . And then follows the third denial. Harmony of the Gospels 3.6.24-25.[2]

18:26-27 *Peter Denies a Third Time*

Jesus Fulfills Promises, Peter Cannot. Augustine: See how the prediction of the Physician is fulfilled and the presumption of the sick man is brought to the light. For there is no performance of what Peter had asserted, "I will lay down my life for your sake." Instead, we see a fulfillment of what Jesus had predicted, "You shall deny me three times."[3] Tractates on the Gospel of John 113.6.[4]

Expedient for Us to Record Peter's Frailty. Cyril of Alexandria: For just as iron, though naturally strong, cannot encounter without injury the harder kinds of stone if it is not strengthened in the forge, so a person's soul may be buoyed up with unwavering enthusiasm for everything that is good. However, it can never be triumphant in the conflicts that come up unless it is first perfected by the grace of the Spirit of God. Even the disciples, therefore, themselves were frail at first. But when they had received the Spirit of Almighty God, they cast aside their native weakness and by communion with him attained to great boldness. It was expedient that the frailty of the saints should be recorded to the praise and glory of God, who changed their weakness into power, and like a strong tower, raised up their spirits, which were easily daunted even by slight dangers and at times were broken down by the mere apprehension of suffering. And that which happened to a single one, or a few of the saints, may afford us at the same time a lesson and a consolation. For we are taught through this example not to slacken in God's service by inconsiderately dwelling on our own infirmities. We are, rather, to trust in him who is able to make all of us strong, and we are to boast in God's miraculous works and favor shown to us who were beyond hope. Commentary on the Gospel of John 12.[5]

What Happens When You Cannot Commit. Chrysostom: But neither did the garden cause him to remember what had been said there, nor the great affection that Jesus had there shown by those words. Instead, he banished all of these from his mind due to the pressure of anxiety. But why have all the Evangelists written the same thing about him? They did so not to accuse the disciple but because they wanted to teach us how great an evil it is to trust in ourselves instead of committing everything to God. But you have to admire the tender care of his master, who, though a prisoner and bound, took great forethought for his disciple. He raises Peter up when he was down, by his look, and launches him into a sea of tears. Homilies on the Gospel of John 83.3.[6]

Peter Still in Darkness. Origen: Con-

[2]CSEL 43:296-98; NPNF 1 6:188**. [3]Jn 13:38. [4]CCL 36:640; NPNF 1 7:420**. [5]LF 48:592**. [6]NPNF 1 14:310**.

sider that when Peter sat outside, separated from Jesus while he was in the court of the high priest, he denied Jesus before everyone. And again a second time he denied him in the same way, not having gone outside the door but wanting to go out, yet still not having gone out. But also the third time, when those who stood by said, "Truly you are one of them" and he began to call a curse on himself and swore, "I do not know the man," he was still not outside. And notice that all of his denials were made in the night and in the darkness before the coming of the day and the sign of day, that is, the rooster crowing, which wakes up those who are willing from their sleep. And I may say that if Peter had denied after the rooster crowed—when it might be said "the night is far spent, the day is at hand, let us walk honorably as in the day"[7]—Peter would have deserved no excuse. But perhaps when anyone denies Jesus in such a way that the sin of denial may admit of healing, that person too appears to deny him before the rooster crows, since the Sun of righteousness has not yet been born to them, nor have they drawn near to his rising. Commentary on Matthew 114.[8]

[7]Rom 13:12. [8]*AEG* 6:12-13*; GCS 38 2 (11):237-38

18:28-32 Jesus Is Taken Before Pilate

[28]Then they led Jesus from the house of Caiaphas to the praetorium. It was early. They themselves did not enter the praetorium, so that they might not be defiled, but might eat the passover. [29]So Pilate went out to them and said, "What accusation do you bring against this man?" [30]They answered him, "If this man were not an evildoer, we would not have handed him over." [31]Pilate said to them, "Take him yourselves and judge him by your own law." The Jews said to him, "It is not lawful for us to put any man to death." [32]This was to fulfil the word which Jesus had spoken to show by what death he was to die.

Overview: John mentions the Praetorium, which seems out of place if they are taking Jesus to Caiaphas, since the Praetorium would belong to the Romans (Augustine). One possible explanation is either that there was some urgent reason for Caiaphas to leave the questioning of Jesus to his father-in-law Annas and hurry to the governor's Praetorium, or it may have been that Pilate had made his Praetorium in the house of Caiaphas because it was big enough to house Caiaphas's residence as well as the Praetorium (Augustine). John demonstrates how even with a number of different judges hearing the case and the extended examination, in the end they could prove nothing, which is why they had to send him to Pilate (Chrysostom). They refuse, however, to enter themselves in case they might become polluted, thereby demonstrating their distorted view of what truly pollutes when they themselves were bent on killing an innocent man (Chrysostom). They wanted to remain pure to celebrate what later became a day of mourning for them (Tertullian). All Scripture agrees that the Passover was to be the day Jesus would die and that he would rise on the first day of the week of harvest, when the priest was to offer the sheaf of grain (Clement).

Pilate still does not assume they have incontrovertible evidence against Jesus (Chrysostom). But instead of asking the Jewish leaders what Jesus had done, Pilate should have been asking the blind who see, the dead who were made alive and those freed from unclean spirits (Augustine). Instead, it seems, according to John, that the Jews simply expected Pilate to condemn Jesus on the basis of their testimony and authority (Augustine) while avoiding any direct accusations (Chrysostom). Pilate directs them to judge Jesus according to their own law, in essence telling them that Jesus is one of their own (Tertullian). They in turn reply that they are not allowed to put anyone to death, although they must be referring either to the festival prohibitions against killing or the manner of killing, since they did carry out summary executions in other cases such as Stephen (Chrysostom, Augustine). But Jesus had earlier prophesied that he would be delivered up to the Gentiles (Augustine).

18:28 *The Jews Refuse to Enter the Praetorium Because of Passover*

Inclusion of the Praetorium Explained. Augustine: If they took him to Caiaphas, how is it then that it mentions the Praetorium, the place where the governor Pilate resided? Either, for some urgent reason, Caiaphas went from the house of Annas (where both had met to give Jesus a hearing) to the governor's Praetorium and had left the hearing of Jesus to his father-in-law. Or Pilate had made his Praetorium in the house of Caiaphas, which was so large as to be able to house both its owner and the governor at the same time. Tractates on the Gospel of John 114.1.[1]

Attempted Explanation of Time Discrepancies. Augustine: Here we might suppose either that there had been something imperative requiring Caiaphas's presence in the hall of judgment and that he was absent on the occasion when the other chief priests held an inquiry on the Lord, or else that the hall of judgment was in his house. So then, from the beginning of this scene they had only been leading Jesus away to the personage in whose presence he was at last actually conducted. But since they brought the accused person in the character of one already convicted, and since it had previously approved itself to Caiaphas's judgment that Jesus should die, there was no further delay in delivering him over to Pilate with a view to his being put to death.[2] And so it is that Matthew here relates what took place between Pilate and the Lord. Harmony of the Gospels 3.7.27.[3]

They Prove Nothing. Chrysostom: "They lead him therefore from Caiaphas to Pilate." This was done in order that the number of his judges might show, even against their will, how fully tested his truth was. "And it was early." He was led to Caiaphas before the rooster crowed, but early in the morning to Pilate. By this the Evangelist shows that though he was questioned all during half the night, he was proved guilty in nothing and that as a result he was sent to Pilate. But leaving what passed then to the other Evangelists, he goes to what followed. Homilies on the Gospel of John 83.3.[4]

A Distorted View of What Pollutes. Chrysostom: John speaks of what follows next. Observe the ridiculous conduct of the Jews. They who had seized the innocent and taken up arms do not enter into the hall of judgment "lest they should be polluted." And tell me, what kind of pollution was it to set foot in a judgment hall where wrongdoers suffer justice? Those who paid tithes of mint and anise did not think they were polluted when bent on killing unjustly, but they

[1]NPNF 1 7:421**; CCL 36:640-41. [2]See *Tractates on John* 114, where Augustine also attempts to grapple with the difficulty created by reading *to* Caiaphas instead of *from* Caiaphas. (The Greek text is "from Caiaphas.") [3]NPNF 1 6:191**; CSEL 43:303. [4]NPNF 1 14:310**.

thought that they polluted themselves by even treading in a court of justice. And why did they not kill him instead of bringing him to Pilate? In the first place, the greater part of their rule and authority had been cut away when their affairs were placed under the power of the Romans. And besides, they feared lest they should be punished later if they were accused by him. But what does it mean, "that they might eat the Passover"? He had already done this on the first day of unleavened bread. Either he calls the whole feast "the Passover" or means that they were then keeping the Passover, while Jesus had done so one day sooner, reserving his own sacrifice for the preparation day, when the Passover was celebrated of old. But they, though they had taken up arms, which was unlawful, and were shedding blood, are scrupulous about the place and summon Pilate to themselves. HOMILIES ON THE GOSPEL OF JOHN 83.3.[5]

THE PREDICTION OF CHRIST'S PASSOVER DEATH. TERTULLIAN: We will prove that it may suffice that the death of the Christ had been prophesied, in order that, from the fact that the nature of the death had not been specified, it may be understood to have been affected by means of the *cross* and that the passion of the cross is not to be ascribed to any but him whose death was constantly being predicted. . . . For that you would do such a thing at the beginning of the first month of your new [years] even Moses prophesied when he was foretelling that all the community of the children of Israel were to sacrifice a lamb when evening came and were to eat this solemn sacrifice of this day [that is, of the Passover of unleavened bread] with bitterness." And then he added that "it was the Passover of the Lord,"[6] that is, the passion of Christ. This prediction was in this way also fulfilled that "on the first day of unleavened bread"[7] you killed the Christ.[8] AN ANSWER TO THE JEWS 10.[9]

ALL OF SCRIPTURE AND THE GOSPELS AGREE. CLEMENT OF ALEXANDRIA: Accordingly therefore, on the fourteenth day, when also Jesus suffered, the chief priests and scribes, bringing him early in the morning to Pilate, did not enter the Praetorium so that they might not be defiled but instead might without hindrance eat the Passover in the evening. By this precise reckoning of the days all the Scriptures agree, and the Gospels are harmonious. The resurrection also bears further witness. He rose on the third day, which is the first day of the weeks of harvest on which it was ordained that the priest should offer the sheaf. FRAGMENT 28, PASCHAL CHRONICLE.[10]

18:29 *Pilate Asks About the Accusations*

INCONTROVERTIBLE EVIDENCE? CHRYSOSTOM: Pilate, however, seeing him bound and led by so many captors, still did not assume that they had incontrovertible evidence against him. Instead, he questions them, thinking it absurd that they seize the right to try Christ and yet entrust to him the punishment without a trial. What reply, then, did they make? "If he were not a malefactor, we would not have delivered him up to you." HOMILIES ON THE GOSPEL OF JOHN 83.4.[11]

ASKING THE WRONG WITNESSES. AUGUSTINE: Ask those freed from unclean spirits, the blind who saw, the dead who came to life again, and, what is greater than all, the fools who were made wise, and let them answer whether Jesus was a malefactor. But they spoke, of whom he had himself prophesied in the psalms, "They rewarded me evil for good."[12] TRACTATES ON THE GOSPEL OF JOHN 114.3.[13]

HOPE FOR CONDEMNATION ON THE JEWISH LEADERS' AUTHORITY. AUGUSTINE: But is not this account contradictory to Luke's, who mentions certain positive charges. . . . "And they

[5]NPNF 1 14:310.** [6]See Ex 12:6-11. [7]See also Mt 26:17; Mk 14:12; Lk 22:7. [8]See 1 Cor 5:7. [9]ANF 3:166-67**; CCL 2:1379-80. [10]GCS 17(3): 217. [11]NPNF 1 14:310**. [12]Ps 35:12 (34:12 LXX). [13]NPNF 1 7:421**; CCL 36:641.

began to accuse him, saying, 'We found this fellow perverting the nation, and forbidding giving tribute to Caesar, saying that he himself is Christ a King.' "[14] . . . According to John, the Jews seem to have been unwilling to bring actual charges, . . . in order that Pilate might condemn him simply on their authority, asking no questions but taking it for granted that if Jesus was delivered up to him, he was certainly guilty. Both accounts are, however, compatible. Each Evangelist only inserts what he thinks sufficient. And John's account implies that some charges had been made, when it comes to Pilate's answer: 'Then Pilate said to them, "Take him, and judge him according to your law.'" Harmony of the Gospels 3.8.35.[15]

18:30 *Insistence on Jesus' Criminal Status*

They Avoid Direct Accusations. Chrysostom: What madness! Why don't you mention his evil deeds instead of concealing them? Why don't you prove the evil? See how they always avoid direct accusations that would amount to nothing anyway. Annas questioned him about his doctrine, and having heard him, sent him to Caiaphas. After Caiaphas questioned him and discovered nothing, he sent him to Pilate. Pilate asks, "What accusation do you bring against this man?" Here too they have nothing to say but again employ conjectures. Homilies on the Gospel of John 83.4.[16]

18:31 *Jewish Law and Permission to Execute*

Jesus Was One of Their Own. Tertullian: It was not as if he belonged to another god that they conceived an aversion against Christ and persecuted him, but simply as a man whom they regarded as a wonder-working juggler and an enemy because of his teaching. They brought him therefore to trial as a mere man, and one of their own too—that is, a Jew (only they saw him as a renegade and a destroyer of Judaism)—and punished him according to their law. If he had been a stranger, indeed, they would not have sat in judgment over him. Against Marcion 3.6.[17]

They Killed Others, Why Not Now? Chrysostom: And how did the expression "It is not lawful for us to put any man to death" declare this? Either the Evangelist means that Jesus was about to be slain not by the Jews only but by the Gentiles also, or that it was not lawful for them to crucify. But if they say, "It is not lawful for us to put anyone to death," they say it with reference to that season. For they did put people to death, but they did so in a different way, as is evident in the case of Stephen, who was stoned.[18] But they desired to crucify [Jesus] so that they might make a spectacle of the manner of his death. Homilies on the Gospel of John 83.4.[19]

Remain Clean While Others Do the Dirty Work? Augustine: What is this that their insane cruelty says? Did not they put him to death whom they were here presenting for that very purpose? Or does the cross perhaps fail to kill? This is the kind of foolishness of those who persecute wisdom instead of pursuing it. What then do the words mean, "It is not lawful for us to put any person to death"? If he is a malefactor, why is it not lawful? Didn't the law command them not to spare malefactors, especially those who tried to seduce them away from their God—which is what they considered Jesus was doing? We are, however, to understand that they said that it was not lawful for them to put anyone to death because of the sanctity of the festal day that they had just begun to celebrate and on account of which they were afraid of being defiled even by entering the Praetorium. Has your excessive malice so blinded you, false Israelites, that you imagined that you are unpolluted by the blood of the innocent because you gave it up to be shed by someone else? Tractates on the Gospel of John 114.4.[20]

[14]Lk 23:2. [15]NPNF 1 6:195**; CSEL 43:315-16. [16]NPNF 1 14:310**. [17]ANF 3:326*; CCL 1:516. [18]See Acts 7:58-60. [19]NPNF 1 14:310**. [20]CCL 36:641-42; NPNF 1 7:421-22**.

18:32 *Jesus Foretold How He Would Die*

Death by the Gentiles. Augustine: If it were so [i.e., that they could judge him according to their law], couldn't they have taken him and crucified him themselves if they wanted to avoid putting him to death by such a punishment [as the cross]? But who is there that may not see the absurdity of allowing those to crucify anyone who were not allowed to put anyone to death? In fact, didn't the Lord himself call that same death of his, that is, the death of the cross, a putting to death, as we read in Mark, where he says, "Behold, we go up to Jerusalem. And the Son of man shall be delivered unto the chief priests, and unto the scribes. And they shall condemn him to death and shall deliver him to the Gentiles"?[21] . . . There is no doubt, therefore, that in speaking in this way, the Lord signified what death he should die: not that he meant here the death of the cross but that the Jews were to deliver him up to the Gentiles, or, in other words, to the Romans. For Pilate was a Roman and had been sent by the Romans into Judea as governor. And so, this saying of Jesus was fulfilled. . . . Therefore when Pilate, who was the Roman judge, tried to hand him back to the Jews so that they might judge him according to their law, they refused to receive him, saying, "It is not lawful for us to put any person to death." Tractates on the Gospel of John 114.5.[22]

[21] Mk 10:33-34. [22] CCL 36:642-43; NPNF 1 7:422**.

18:33-38a Pilate Questions Jesus

[33]Pilate entered the praetorium again and called Jesus, and said to him, "Are you the King of the Jews?" [34]Jesus answered, "Do you say this of your own accord, or did others say it to you about me?" [35]Pilate answered, "Am I a Jew? Your own nation and the chief priests have handed you over to me; what have you done?" [36]Jesus answered, "My kingship is not of this world; if my kingship were of this world, my servants would fight, that I might not be handed over to the Jews; but my kingship is not from the world." [37]Pilate said to him, "So you are a king?" Jesus answered, "You say that I am a king. For this I was born, and for this I have come into the world, to bear witness to the truth. Every one who is of the truth hears my voice." [38]Pilate said to him, "What is truth?"

Overview: Pilate's inquiry of Jesus shows he was worried that Caesar's rule in the region could become endangered if he did not find a satisfactory solution (Cyril). Jesus' kingdom, however, is not of this world, as he rejects the kind of dignity and power the world seeks (Tertullian, Eusebius) in favor of where real strength lies (Chrysostom). In the same way, he calls on us to be in the world but not of it (Augustine). The inadvertent title of "king" that Jesus receives (Gregory of Nazianzus) is a title Jesus neither confirms nor denies (Augustine). But his kingdom is surely not limited by earthly rule as it extends through the whole world enlightening souls through his divine and heavenly teaching (Eusebius). Christ bears witness to the truth, which is himself (Augustine). The Psalms speak of truth springing from the earth, which is what the

Truth, the Son of God, did when he took on our flesh, which was made out of the dust of the earth (Augustine). Truth, by its nature, is not derivative (Melito). Those who are not of the truth are handed over to the governor of death, who is also the father of lies (Augustine). Pilate, the governor of Judea, had himself lost any perception of truth, which is why he asks Jesus, "What is truth?" (Cyril).

18:33-35 *The King of the Jews*

Pilate Worried That Caesar's Rule Is Endangered. Cyril of Alexandria: Having nothing at all of which to accuse him, and none of those crimes to allege against him that normally bring with them just punishment—and Pilate persisting in inquiring why they had brought him—they assert that Jesus had sinned against Caesar in assuming the dominion that Caesar had acquired over the Jews and in changing the glory of his kingdom to suit his personal aspirations. Great was the malice that suggested this device and caused the false accusation to assume this shape. For they knew that Pilate, however reluctant he might be, would think first about his own safety and would swiftly and precipitously punish the man against whom any such outcry was raised. For, as the inhabitants of Judea were always moved to riots and civil strife and were easily provoked to revolt, Caesar's officers were proportionally vigilant in this respect and were more careful guardians of order. To this end, they inflicted the most summary penalties on people who had this charge brought against them, sometimes groundlessly. The Jews, therefore, make it a charge against Christ that he ruled over Israel. ... Pilate, then, speaks out plainly what he heard the Jews muttering and bids Jesus answer him, whether he was in truth the King of the Jews. Pilate was full of anxiety, it would appear, and thought Caesar's rule was endangered. Therefore he was anxious to learn the truth in order to meet what had been done with appropriate retribution and acquit of blame the office entrusted to him by the Romans. Commentary on the Gospel of John 12.[1]

18:36 *My Kingdom Is Not of This World*

Jesus Rejects Dignity and Power. Tertullian: If he exercised no right of power even over his own followers, to whom he discharged menial tasks—if, in short, though conscious of his own kingdom, he shrank back from being made a king —he in the fullest way possible gave his own an example for turning coldly from all the pride and outward trappings, as well of dignity as of power. On Idolatry 18.[2]

Christ and His Kingdom. Eusebius of Caesarea: And when they were asked about Christ and his kingdom, of what nature it was, and where and when it would appear, they answered that it was neither of the world, nor earthly, but heavenly and angelic, and would appear at the end of the world when he would come in glory to judge the living and the dead and to give to every one according to his works. Ecclesiastical History 3.20.3-4.[3]

Where Real Strength Lies. Chrysostom: Here Jesus shows the weakness of kingship among us. He demonstrates that its strength lies in servants. But that which is above is sufficient of itself. It needs nothing.... And so, he also says that his kingdom is not from this world—not depriving the world of his providence and governance but rather showing, as I said, that his power was not human or perishable. Homilies on the Gospel of John 83.4.[4]

In the World, but Not of It. Augustine: Listen, everyone, Jews and Gentiles, circumcised and uncircumcised. Listen, all kings of the earth. I am no hindrance to your rule in this world, for "my kingdom is not of this world." Banish the

[1]LF 48:597-98**. [2]CCL 2:1119-20; ANF 3:73*. [3]FC 19:167. [4]NPNF 1 14:311**.

groundless fear that filled Herod the Great on hearing that Christ was born. More cruel in his fear than in his anger, he put many children to death,[5] so that Christ would also die. But "my kingdom is not of this world," says Christ. What further reassurance do you seek? Come to the kingdom that is not of this world. Do not be enraged by fear, but come by faith. In a prophecy Christ also said, "He," that is, God the Father, "has made me king on Zion his holy mountain."[6] But that Zion and that mountain are not of this world.

What in fact is Christ's kingdom? It is simply those who believe in him, those to whom he said, "You are not of this world, even as I am not of this world." He willed, nevertheless, that they should be in the world, which is why he prayed to the Father, "I ask you not to take them out of the world but to protect them from the evil one."[7] So here also he did not say, "My kingdom is not" *in* this world but "is not *of* this world." And when he went on to prove this by declaring, "If my kingdom were of this world, my servants would have fought to save me from being handed over to the Jews," he concluded by saying not "my kingdom is not here" but "my kingdom is not from here."

Indeed, his kingdom is here until the end of time, and until the harvest it will contain weeds. The harvest is the end of the world, when the reapers, who are the angels, will come and gather out of his kingdom all causes of sin.[8] And this could not happen if his kingdom were not here. But even so, it is not from here, for it is in exile in the world. Christ says to his kingdom, "You are not of the world, but I have chosen you out of the world."[9] They were indeed of the world when they belonged to the prince of this world, before they became his kingdom. Though created by the true God, everyone born of the corrupt and accursed stock of Adam is of the world. [But] everyone who is reborn in Christ becomes the kingdom that is no longer of the world. For God has snatched us from the powers of darkness and brought us into the kingdom of his beloved Son.[10] This is that kingdom of which he said, "My kingdom is not of this world; my kingly power does not come from here." Tractates on the Gospel of John 115.2.[11]

18:37a *Jesus Is Called a King*

The Title of King Is One of Jesus' Many Names. Gregory of Nazianzus: Who is the person who has never, by experience and contemplation, traversed the entire series of titles and powers of Christ, both those more lofty ones that originally were his and those more lowly ones that he later assumed for our sake: God, the Son, the Image, the Word, the Wisdom, the Truth, the Light, the Life, the Power . . . , the Maker, the King. . . . Who is the person who hears but pays no attention to these names so pregnant with reality and has never yet held communion with or been made partaker of the Word in any of the real relations signified by each of these names Christ bears? In Defense of His Flight to Pontus, Oration 2.98.[12]

Jesus Neither Confesses Nor Denies Kingship. Augustine: It was not that Jesus was afraid to confess himself a king, but the phrase "you say" is nuanced enough that he neither denies himself to be a king (for he is a king whose kingdom is not of this world), nor does he confess that he is such a king as to warrant the supposition that his kingdom is of this world. For, since this was the very idea in Pilate's mind when he said, '"Are you a king then?" the answer Pilate received was, "You say that I am a king." For it was said, "You say," as if it had been said, since you are worldly, you say it in a worldly way. Tractates on the Gospel of John 115.3.[13]

Jesus' Rule Not Limited. Eusebius of Caesarea: His kingdom and throne were not human. They were not of this world. Therefore he said be-

[5]See Mt 2:3, 16. [6]Ps 2:6. [7]Jn 17:15-16. [8]See Mt 13:38-41. [9]Jn 15:19. [10]See Col 1:13. [11]*JFB* 136-37*; CCL 36:644-45. [12]NPNF 2 7:224. [13]CCL 36:645; NPNF 1 7:424**.

fore Pilate, "My kingdom is not of this world." And when he was asked by him if he were a king, Jesus answered, "For this also I have been born." So if he has been born for this, he will remain for this . . . for the kingdom of this world is not able to endure forever, nor is it endless as if extended indefinitely. Commentary on Psalm 88 [89]. 39-46.[14]

Jesus' Kingdom Continues. Eusebius of Caesarea: The throne of the kingdom conferred on Jesus is nothing mortal or temporal. Rather, it truly extended throughout the whole world like light shining as the moon established forever, enlightening understanding souls through his divine and heavenly teaching. To Stephanus 15.4.[15]

18:37b *Born to Witness to the Truth*

Christ Bears Witness to Himself. Augustine: It is evident that Jesus here referred to his own birth in time when, by becoming incarnate, he came into the world. He is not referring to what had no beginning whereby he was God through whom the Father created the world. For this then, that is, because [he was referring to his birth in time], he declared that he was born, and to this end he came into the world, in other words, that by being born of the Virgin he might witness to the truth. But because not everyone has the truth[16] he further adds, "Everyone who is of the truth hears my voice." One hears, that is to say, with the ears of the inward person, or, in other words, he obeys my voice, which is equivalent to saying, he believes me. When Christ, therefore, witnesses to the truth, he witnesses, of course, to himself. . . . For if our thoughts turn to the nature wherein we have been created—inasmuch as we were all created by the Truth—who is there that is not of the truth? But it is not given to everyone to hear, that is, to obey the truth and to believe in the truth. At any rate, in no case certainly is there any preceding of merit; otherwise grace should cease to be grace. For if he had said, "Everyone who hears my voice is of the truth," then it would be supposed that someone was declared to be of the truth because that person conforms to the truth. This is not what he says however, but, "Everyone who is of the truth hears my voice." And in this way no one is of the truth simply because he or she hears his voice. They only hear because they are of the truth, that is, because this is a gift of the truth bestowed on them. And what else is this, but that by Christ's gracious bestowal they believe on Christ? Tractates on the Gospel of John 115.4.[17]

Truth Springs from the Earth. Augustine: "Truth has sprung up from the earth, and righteousness has looked down from heaven."[18] Yes, "truth has sprung up from the earth" because Christ was born from a woman. "Truth has sprung up from the earth" because the Son of God has come forth from the flesh. What is Truth? The Son of God. What is the earth? Our flesh. Inquire where Christ was born, and you will see that "truth has sprung up from the earth." Yet this Truth that has sprung up from the earth existed before the earth, for heaven and earth were made through him. But in order that righteousness might look down from heaven, that is, that human beings might be made righteous through divine grace, Truth was born from the Virgin Mary, that he might be in a position to offer sacrifice for those who needed justification, the sacrifice of his passion, the sacrifice of the cross. How could he offer his sacrifice for our sins, except by dying? But how could he die, unless he took from us what could die? Had he not taken mortal flesh from us, Christ could not have died, for the Word does not die, the Godhead does not die, the Power and Wisdom of God[19] does not die. How could he offer himself as a saving victim, if he did not die? But how could he die without clothing himself in flesh? And how could he put on flesh unless Truth sprang up from the earth? Explanation of Psalm 84.13.[20]

[14]PG 23:1112. [15]PG 22:932. [16]2 Thess 3:2. [17]NPNF 1 7:424-25**; CCL 36:645-46. [18]Ps 85:11 (84:12 LXX). [19]See 1 Cor 1:24. [20]*WSA* 3 18:216**; CCL 39:1173.

18:38a *What Is Truth?*

TRUTH IS NOT DERIVATIVE. MELITO OF SARDIS: Who is this God? It is he who is himself truth and whose word is truth. And what is truth? That which is not fashioned or made or represented by art, that is, that has never been brought into existence and is on that account called truth.[21] If, therefore, someone worships that which is made with hands, it is not the truth that he worships or yet the word of truth. A DISCOURSE WITH ANTONINUS CAESAR.[22]

THE GOVERNOR OF DEATH IS OUTSIDE THE TRUTH. AUGUSTINE: You are righteous, O Lord, but we have sinned and committed iniquity and have done wickedly.[23] Your hand has grown heavy on us, and it is only right that we are handed over to that ancient sinner, the governor of death. For he has persuaded our wills to be like his will because he does not remain in your truth.[24] What will wretched people like us do? "Who shall deliver us from the body of this death?"[25] It is only your grace through Jesus Christ our Lord, who was begotten co-eternal by you and was created in the beginning of your ways.[26] The prince of this world found nothing worthy of death in him. Yet he killed him, and the handwriting of the decree against us was blotted out. CONFESSIONS 7.21.27.[27]

IT IS DIFFICULT FOR TRUTH TO PENETRATE WARPED MINDS. CYRIL OF ALEXANDRIA: In order that he might show that the difficulty in Pilate's perception came from his stubborn heart and from his reluctance to admit the truth, Christ appropriately adds, "Everyone who is of the truth hears my voice." For the word of truth is readily accepted by those who have already learned and love it. But it is not the same for everyone. In fact, the prophet Isaiah said to some, "If you will not believe, neither shall you understand."[28] Pilate showed at once how true this was when he said, "What is truth?" For there are those whose sight has been injured or who have entirely lost the use of their eyes and their sense of color has been entirely annihilated. They would not even be able to tell if someone placed gold before them or a brilliant precious stone. In fact, even the very light of the sun's rays does not engage them in any kind of wonder since they have lost all perception and can gain no profit from any of these things. In the same way, to people whose minds have become warped, truth seems a foul and ugly thing even as it instills a spiritual and divine brilliance into the minds of those who behold it. COMMENTARY ON THE GOSPEL OF JOHN 12.[29]

[21]Or "that which is fixed and invariable." [22]ANF 8:753**. [23]The Song of the Three Children 4ff. [24]Jn 8:44. [25]Rom 7:24. [26]Prov 8:22. Augustine understood this passage of the incarnation, not that Christ was a creature. [27]NPNF 1 1:114-15**; CCL 27:111. [28]Is 7:9 LXX. [29]LF 48:601-2**.

18:38b-40 RELEASE JESUS OR BARABBAS

After he had said this, he went out to the Jews again, and told them, "I find no crime in him. [39]But you have a custom that I should release one man for you at the Passover; will you have me release for you the King of the Jews?" [40]They cried out again, "Not this man, but Barabbas!" Now Barabbas was a robber.

Overview: Pilate leaves quickly after asking Jesus his question because he believed there still might be a chance to save him (Augustine), and he knew this question required time to answer (Chrysostom). He shows his prudence in having first acquitted Jesus and then going the extra mile in seeking Jesus' release on account of the season (Chrysostom). The custom of releasing prisoners is difficult to trace but can perhaps be found in Numbers 35 (Cyril). One might also ask whether such a custom could find its way back into today's church for someone who has sinned and seeks release (Origen). Pilate calls Jesus the king of the Jews, despite the Jews' protestations—almost as if it had been inscribed on his heart as it would later be inscribed on the cross (Augustine). Perhaps Pilate spoke in jest in a feeble attempt to abate the fury of the mob (Cyril). He seeks to release Barabbas, whose name appears similar to Jesus' name in certain texts and thus occasions a comparison between the two (Origen). They tried to defame Jesus by lumping him together with known criminals (Chrysostom, Origen). But the one who did not consider his equality with God as robbery took the place of the robber and us in order to deliver both from the true criminal, Satan (Cyril).

18:38b *No Fault Can Be Found in Jesus*

Pilate Leaves. Augustine: I believe when Pilate said, "What is truth?" there immediately occurred to his mind the custom of the Jews of releasing one prisoner at the Passover. Therefore he did not wait to hear Jesus' answer to his question, "What is truth?" in order to avoid delay on the chance that Jesus might be released to them during the Passover—something he clearly desired. Tractates on the Gospel of John 115.5.[1]

The Question Needed Time to Be Answered. Chrysostom: For the present, he applies himself to what was most pressing, for he knew that this question needed time. He wanted to rescue Jesus from the violence of the Jews. And so he went out. Homilies on the Gospel of John 84.1.[2]

18:39a *Passover Custom of Prisoner Release*

Pilate Goes the Extra Mile. Chrysostom: Consider how prudently Pilate acted. He did not say, "Since he has sinned and is deserving of death, forgive him on account of the feast."[3] Rather, having first acquitted him of all guilt, Pilate goes the extra mile and asks them if they are willing to allow him the benefit of the season, even though they are unwilling to let him go as innocent.[4] Homilies on the Gospel of John 84.1.[5]

Custom Found in Numbers 35. Cyril of Alexandria: As I was considering and meditating in my mind how the custom arose for the Jews to ask for one man to be released to them (a robber, it might be, or a murderer), the idea occurred to me that they no longer regulated their actions altogether according to the Law, but, choosing rather to use their own customs, they fell into a decayed state of manners not altogether in agreement with the law of Moses. But while I was searching the divine Scriptures and hunting everywhere for the origin of this custom,[6] I came on one of the divine dictates that caused me to suspect that when the Jews sought the release of a malefactor, they were, in fact, in however mistaken a way, fulfilling one of the customs of the Law. At the end of the book called Numbers we find recorded the law concerning voluntary and involuntary homicide. When the penalty in the case of premeditated murder has been clearly laid down, the book goes on to speak of involuntary homicide, and, after other remarks, makes the

[1]NPNF 1 7:425**. [2]NPNF 1 14:313*. [3]Lit. "grant him to the feast." [4]This favorable view of Pilate is common among many patristic commentators. [5]NPNF 1 14:313**. [6]Interpreters over the centuries have wrestled with the difficulty of finding a reference either in the Old Testament or extracanonical sources, such as Josephus, who is silent on this custom.

following declaration: "But if he stabbed him suddenly without enmity, or hurled anything on him without lying in wait or used a stone, by which a man may die, and without seeing him cast it on him, so that he died, though he was not his enemy and did not seek his harm, then the congregation shall judge between the manslayer and the avenger of blood, and the congregation shall restore him to the city of his refuge, to which he had fled."[7]

Since this was the written commandment when any, as it happened, were involved in such a calamity, the Jews, when they were congregated together (and so that they might not appear altogether to neglect this enactment), sought the release of one of them. For the Law laid down that it was to be the act of the entire assembly. Since, then, they were permitted by the Law to ask for the release of a prisoner, they make this request of Pilate. For after they had once accepted the Roman yoke, from then on they were, for the most part, ruled by their laws in the administration of their affairs. We might say even further that, although it was lawful for them to put to death anyone convicted of a crime, they brought Jesus to Pilate as a criminal, saying, "It is not lawful for us to put any man to death." For, though they alleged as a plea their purification by the sacrifice of the Passover, yet they showed themselves flatterers of Rome in entrusting to the laws of the Romans the duty that the divine commandment from heaven laid on themselves. Commentary on the Gospel of John 12.[8]

Similar Custom in the Church Possible? Origen: Do not wonder that the Roman government, holding sway over the Jews who had recently become their subjects, thought it was appropriate to grant them something acceptable at the feast of the Passover. They allowed them to ask for anyone they wanted [to be freed] even though he might appear guilty of many murders. For in this way nations sometimes grant favors to those whom they have conquered, until their rule is established. Yet this custom of releasing a prisoner existed at one time among the Jews also.[9] . . . Let us inquire whether anything like this may take place also in God's judgment where the whole church may ask for any sinner to be released from the condemnation of sin especially if, while having other evil works, he is eager to do good for the church. Commentary on Matthew 120.[10]

18:39b *Release the King of the Jews?*

Truth Inscribed on Pilate's Heart. Augustine: It could not, however, be torn from Pilate's heart that Jesus was the king of the Jews, but it was inscribed there, as in the superscription, by the truth itself about which he had just inquired. Tractates on the Gospel of John 115.5[11]

Pilate Speaks in Jest. Cyril of Alexandria: When he called Jesus king of the Jews, he spoke in jest and tried to abate by ridicule the anger of the furious mob. He also clearly showed that this particular accusation was brought in vain. A Roman officer would never have thought a man condemned of plotting for a kingdom and revolution against Rome worthy to be released. He bore witness, then, to Jesus' utter innocence by the very reasons he gave for Jesus' release. Commentary on the Gospel of John 12.[12]

18:40 *Barabbas*

Barabbas and Jesus Compared. Origen: There is a likeness between the names of Barabbas and Jesus that is nothing short of a true mystery.[13] Barabbas is appointed for making sedition and wars and murders in the souls of people, but Jesus is appointed for all good things as the Son of God and Peace and Word and Wisdom. These

[7]Num 35:22-25. [8]LF 48:603-4**. [9]Origen quotes 1 Sam 14:43-45, where the people sought to spare Jonathan's life from Saul's hand. [10]AEG 6:41-42*; GCS 38 2 (11):253-54. [11]NPNF 1 7:425**; CCL 36:646. [12]LF 48:605*. [13]Origen's text on Matthew reads "Jesum Barabbam."

two therefore are bound in both human things and bodies. Here the people [of the Jews] asked for Barabbas to be released to them. Therefore, that nation [i.e., Israel] does not cease from having seditions and murders and robberies, as regards some of their own race in outward things but also as regards all the Jews who do not believe in Jesus who have also struggles within their own souls. For where Jesus is not, there are seditions and quarrels and battles. But where Jesus is . . . all good things, and innumerable spiritual riches, along with peace, rest in their hands. For he is our peace who made both one. And if anyone sees the opposite take place, he will recognize in them all that notable prisoner, Barabbas, whose release is craved not only then by sinful Israel according to the flesh but also by all like them in either doctrine or life. Whoever, therefore, does evil things in his body frees Barabbas and binds Christ. But whoever does good things frees Christ and binds Barabbas. Commentary on Matthew 121.[14]

Seeking to Defame Christ. Chrysostom: How many were offended . . . when they made that dreadful and monstrous assertion that the robber and housebreaker, the man laden with the crime of murder, deserved to be released rather than Jesus. How many were offended when, having received permission from the judge to make their choice, they preferred Barabbas, desiring not only to crucify Christ but also to involve him in infamy? For they thought that by these means they should be able to manufacture the belief that he was worse than the robber and such a great transgressor that neither on the plea of mercy nor the privilege of the festival was it possible to save him. For they did everything for the purpose of slandering his fame. This is also why they crucified the two robbers with him. Nevertheless the truth was not obscured but shone forth all the more clearly. Letters to Olympias, To My Lady 4.[15]

Christ Equated with Robbers. Origen: Celsus's comparison of Christ to a robber or murderer . . . is anticipated in the Gospels since God was numbered with the transgressors by wicked people who wanted a murderer (one who had been cast into prison for sedition and murder) to be released to them and wanted Jesus to be crucified. And they crucified him between two robbers. Jesus, indeed, is always being crucified with robbers among his genuine disciples and witnesses to the truth, and he suffers the same condemnation they do among people—if indeed we grant that those people have any resemblance to robbers who because of their godly lives suffer all kinds of injury and death so that they may keep their lives clean and pure. . . . But neither Jesus . . . nor they were . . . put to death according to any form of justice, and so it is his persecutors who are the ones who should incur the charge. Against Celsus 2.44.[16]

One Robber Not Exchanged for Another. Cyril of Alexandria: For they preferred a robber to him who did not regard his equality with God the Father [as robbery][17] and took our poverty upon him for this very end, that is, that he might deliver us from the true murderer, that is, Satan. . . . For the assembly, by its clamor, put him to death, though Pilate invited them to choose his release. In this way, even those who had not yet learned the divine law might be proved better than those instructed in the Law. Commentary on the Gospel of John 12.[18]

[14]AEG 6:43**; GCS 38 2 (11):256-57. [15]NPNF 1 9:292**. [16]ANF 4:448**; SC 132:384. [17]Cyril surely has in mind parallels occasioned by the Gk *harpagmos* ("robbery," or "something to be grasped") in Phil 2:6, a word that he often uses elsewhere in the commentary, although it is not found here. [18]LF 48:605*.

19:1-8 JESUS BEFORE PILATE

[1]Then Pilate took Jesus and scourged him. [2]And the soldiers plaited a crown of thorns, and put it on his head, and arrayed him in a purple robe; [3]they came up to him, saying, "Hail, King of the Jews!" and struck him with their hands. [4]Pilate went out again, and said to them, "See, I am bringing him out to you, that you may know that I find no crime in him." [5]So Jesus came out, wearing the crown of thorns and the purple robe. Pilate said to them, "Behold the man!" [6]When the chief priests and the officers saw him, they cried out, "Crucify him, crucify him!" Pilate said to them, "Take him yourselves and crucify him, for I find no crime in him." [7]The Jews answered him, "We have a law, and by that law he ought to die, because he has made himself the Son of God." [8]When Pilate heard these words, he was the more afraid;

Overview: The rock on which the church stands is hewn by Pilate on a pillar of stone (Romanus) where Jesus was scourged before Pilate delivered him up to be crucified (Augustine). He was scourged unjustly so that he might deliver us from the punishment we deserved (Cyril). The crown of thorns placed on Jesus serves as a type and reminder to us that there is no approaching the Word without blood (Clement). His crown, if you dare to wear it (Tertullian), is a garland of thorns and thistles (Tertullian) that needs no further thorns from us (Origen). Christ's blood is our purple robe (Tertullian). Therefore, the mocking intended by the crown and robe fulfilled God's purpose in crowning the dignity of the chosen king's humility (Cyril of Jerusalem) even as the treatment of the King of creation by the soldiers caused utter amazement among the heavenly hosts (Anonymous). Pilate, as the prince of this world, presents Jesus' innocence, thereby implicating both himself and the people in the wrongful scourging (Cyril). He presents to them "the man" who, as the second Adam, would defeat the sin that condemned his fellow human beings (Cyril). The Jewish leaders then hand the Judge over to a judge who himself already stands condemned for his actions (Romanus). Their purpose, however, was to shame Jesus into oblivion through the most ignominious death they could find so that Jesus would soon be forgotten (Chrysostom). The devil would much rather Jesus die in secret in order to persuade people that Jesus did not die at all (Chrysostom).

Pilate sees the sentence pronounced on Jesus for what it is (Cyril), so that, although they brought Jesus to be condemned, instead Pilate acquits him (Chrysostom). Those who deny that Jesus is the Son of God should see that even the Jews understood Jesus was claiming to be the Son of God (Hilary). And so, their charges should have elicited worship instead of condemnation (Chrysostom). When Pilate hears that Jesus is the Son of God, his reaction demonstrates more concern than did that of the Jewish leaders (Chrysostom). There may even be a hint that Pilate may have believed in Jesus' divinity as one of the gods (Cyril).

19:1 *Pilate Has Jesus Scourged*

The Rock of the Church Is Hewn on the Pillar of Stone. Romanus Melodus:

> Like a lion they roared to seize the life of the lamb, Christ.
> Pilate, fulfilling their will, flogged Thee, the gentle One.
> So he set to work on Thy back....

The Redeemer endured the lash; the Deliverer was in chains;
Nude and stretched out on a pillar,
Is He who in a pillar of cloud formerly spoke to Moses and Aaron.[1]
He who established the pillars of the earth, as David said,[2] is fastened to a pillar.
He who showed the people the road in the desert,
(For the pillar of fire appeared before them),[3] He has been attached to a pillar;
The rock is on a column and the church is hewn in stone for me.

Kontakion on the Passion of Christ 20.13-14.[4]

When Did the Scourging Take Place? Augustine: Previous to stating how Pilate delivered him up to be crucified, John has introduced the following passage: "Then Pilate therefore took Jesus and scourged him." . . . This makes it evident that Matthew and Mark have reported this incident in the way of a recapitulation and that it did not take place after Pilate had delivered him up to be crucified. For John informs us distinctly enough that these things took place when he yet was with Pilate. Therefore, we conclude that the other Evangelists have introduced the occurrence at that particular point, just because, having previously passed it by, they recollected it there. Harmony of the Gospels 3.9.36.[5]

Christ's Suffering for Us. Cyril of Alexandria: Jesus was scourged unjustly so that he might deliver us from the punishment we deserved. He was beaten and struck so that we might beat Satan, who had beaten us, and that we might escape from the sin that cleaves to us through the original transgression. For if we think correctly, we shall believe that all of Christ's sufferings were for us and on our behalf and that they have power to release and deliver us from all those calamities we have deserved because of our rebellion against God. Commentary on the Gospel of John 12.[6]

19:2 *Crown of Thorns and Purple Robe*

The Crown of Thorns As Type. Clement of Alexandria: The Lord's crown of thorns prophetically pointed to us who once were barren but are placed around him through the church of which he is the head. But it is also a type of faith, of life in respect to the substance of the wood, of joy in respect to the appellation of crown, of danger in respect to the thorn. For there is no approaching the Word without blood. . . . They crowned Jesus raised up high, testifying to their own ignorance. . . . This crown is the flower of those who have believed on the glorified One, but it covers with blood and chastises those who have not believed. It is a symbol, too, of the Lord's successful work, he having borne on his head (the princely part of his body) all our iniquities by which we were pierced. For he by his own passion rescued us from offenses and sins and other thorns. And having destroyed the devil, deservedly said in triumph, "O Death, where is your sting?"[7] Christ the Educator 2.8.[8]

Christ's Crown in Contrast to All Other Crowns. Tertullian: What patriarch, what prophet, what Levite, or priest or ruler, or at a later period what apostle, or preacher of the gospel or bishop do you ever find the wearer of a crown? . . . If, perhaps, you object that Christ himself was crowned, to that you will get the brief reply: Go ahead and be crowned like he was. You have my full permission. The Chaplet 9.[9]

Do Not Add More Thorns. Origen: There are those who still have thorns with which they crown and dishonor Jesus, those, namely, who are

[1]Ex 33:8-11. [2]Asaph said this in Ps 75:3 (74:4 LXX). [3]Ex 13:21; Num 9:15-23. [4]*KRBM* 1:212. [5]CSEL 43:320; NPNF 1 6:197**. [6]LF 48:606*. [7]1 Cor 15:55. [8]ANF 2:256-57*; CCL 2:1052. [9]ANF 3:98. Tertullian is here contrasting the world's idea of glory with that of humble faith, which will not wear the crown that the heathen and their deities wear.

choked by the cares and riches and pleasures of life and, though they have received the word of God, do not bring it to perfection.[10] We must beware, therefore, lest we also, as crowning Jesus with thorns of our own, should be entered in the Gospel . . . and read how he is dishonored and mocked and beaten [by us]. COMMENTARY ON THE GOSPEL OF JOHN 1.72-73.[11]

CHRIST'S BLOOD IS OUR PURPLE ROBE. TERTULLIAN: You belong to Christ for you have been enrolled in the books of life.[12] There the blood of the Lord serves for your purple robe, and your broad stripe is his own cross. THE CHAPLET 13.[13]

19:3 *Mockery from the Soldiers*

EVEN MOCKERY FULFILLS THE PROPHECY. CYRIL OF JERUSALEM: They dressed him in a purple robe in mockery, of course. But they also fulfilled the prophecy, doing so under inspiration. For he *was* a King. However much they did it in a spirit of derision, still they did it. His royal dignity was emblematically heralded. So, likewise, though it was with thorns they crowned him, it was still a crown. And it was soldiers who crowned him. Kings are proclaimed by soldiers. SERMON ON THE PARALYTIC 12.[14]

HEAVEN WONDERS AT ITS KING'S TREATMENT. ANONYMOUS: When the soldiers mocked you, O Lord, before your death on the precious cross, the heavenly hosts were struck with wonder. For you who have adorned the earth with flowers were arrayed in a crown of shame. You who have wrapped the firmament in clouds were clothed in a robe of mockery. And so, O Christ, in your providence you have made known your compassion and great mercy. STICHERA FOR THE THIRD HOUR OF HOLY FRIDAY.[15]

19:4 *Pilate Presents an Innocent Man*

PILATE ADMITS TO SCOURGING AN INNOCENT MAN. CYRIL OF ALEXANDRIA: He confesses the wrong he had done and is not ashamed. For he admitted that he had scourged him without cause and declares that he will show him to them supposing that would satisfy their savage passion by so pitiable a spectacle. In fact, he practically accuses them as well—and that publicly—of putting him to death unjustly and of compelling him openly to be a lawbreaker who, if he transgressed his own laws, could not escape without repercussions. The saying was fulfilled in Christ and shown to be true, that "the prince of this world comes and he will find nothing in me."[16] COMMENTARY ON THE GOSPEL OF JOHN 12.[17]

19:5 *Behold the Man*

SIN AND SATAN DEFEATED BY A MAN. CYRIL OF ALEXANDRIA: Just as in Adam Satan subdued the whole human race demonstrating its subjection to sin, so now Satan is vanquished by humanity. For the one who was truly God and without sin was still also human. And just as all of humanity was condemned under the sentence of sin through one man, the first Adam, in the same way, the blessing of justification by Christ is extended to all through one man, the second Adam.[18] COMMENTARY ON THE GOSPEL OF JOHN 12.[19]

19:6 *Crucify Him!*

JUDGING THE JUDGE. ROMANUS MELODUS:

Abel was envied by Cain and was later murdered.
That is what Christ endured:
Though He loved envious people, He moved them to anger, even as He showed affection;
He healed those who were ill, and instead of gratitude, He suffers, and is crucified,
In order that Adam might exult.

---

[10]See Lk 8:14. [11]FC 80:48**; SC 120:96. [12]Phil 4:3. [13]CCL 2:1060; ANF 3:101*. [14]FC 64:217**. [15]LT 604*. [16]Jn 14:30. In the present context, this could refer either to Pilate or to Satan. [17]LF 48:607*. [18]Rom 5:18. [19]LF 48:608**.

The crowd of the lawless, feeling aversion for the multitude of miracles
Cried out: "Kill him, crucify him!"
As they handed over to Pilate the One who created all things;
They handed over to the court of justice the One who will judge kings and peasants;
The condemned judges the just Judge;
The one who lives unknown[20] threatened to kill like a thief the Redeemer!
Meanwhile He, in order to suffer, endures in silence, standing speechless,
In order that Adam might exult.
KONTAKION ON THE PASSION OF CHRIST 20.5-6.[21]

TRUTH IS EXALTED BY HINDRANCES. CHRYSOSTOM: Pilate, because of hearing just a few words, wanted to let Jesus go, but they pressed on, saying, "Crucify him." And why did they push for killing him in this way? It was a shameful death. They were afraid that afterward someone might remember him, and so they wanted to bring him to a punishment that came with a curse. They did not know that truth is exalted by hindrances. HOMILIES ON THE GOSPEL OF JOHN 84.2.[22]

THE DEVIL WOULD RATHER JESUS DIE IN SECRET. CHRYSOSTOM: The devil has never been in as shameful a plight as he was that day. For while he expected to have Christ, he lost even those he had, because when that body was nailed to the cross, the dead arose. There death received his wound, being met with a death stroke from a dead body. . . . For the devil would have done everything to persuade people that Jesus did not die and that instead he [Satan] had the power. For one can see that the time following his resurrection was indeed proof positive [that he had risen from the dead]. But, concerning his death, no other time except when it actually happened could ever furnish proof. Therefore Jesus had to die publicly in the sight of everyone, but [the event] of his resurrection was not public, knowing that the time following it would bear witness to the truth. It is a marvel that, while the world was looking on, the serpent was slain on high on the cross. For look at what the devil did to try to have Christ die in secret. Hear Pilate saying, "Take him away and crucify him, for I find no fault in him," and withstanding them in a thousand ways. And again the Jews said to him, "If you are the Son of God, come down from the cross."[23] Then further, when he had received a mortal wound and did not come down, he was buried. And yet, it was in his power to have risen immediately—but he did not so that the fact [of his death] might be believed. And yet in cases of private death, indeed, it is possible to say they only swooned, but here, it is not possible to say such a thing. HOMILIES ON COLOSSIANS 6.[24]

PILATE PERCEIVES AN UNJUST SENTENCE. CYRIL OF ALEXANDRIA: Here, we may imagine Pilate as saying, "If you have a law that subjects the sinless to so fearful a penalty, that chastises the guiltless, execute it with your own hands. I will not endure being a part of it." COMMENTARY ON THE GOSPEL OF JOHN 12.[25]

BROUGHT FOR CONDEMNATION, ACQUITTAL IS RESULT. CHRYSOSTOM: See in how many ways the judge makes his defense, continually acquitting Jesus of the charges. . . . For "You take him and crucify him" is the expression of one clearing himself of the guilt and thrusting them forward to an action not permitted to them. They had brought Jesus in order to have the matter decided by the governor. But the contrary happened, and Jesus was acquitted rather than condemned by the governor's decision. HOMILIES ON THE GOSPEL OF JOHN 84.2.[26]

19:7 *Claims to Be the Son of God*

[20]Referring to Pilate's relative obscurity compared with Jesus and his blindness to the truth. [21]*KRBM* 1:209. [22]NPNF 1 14:315**. [23]Mt 27:40. [24]NPNF 1 13:286**. [25]LF 48:610**. [26]NPNF 1 14:314**.

Jews Understood He Claimed to Be the Son of God. Hilary of Poitiers: If you [Arians] will not learn who Christ is from those who know him, learn it at least from those who do not. . . . Can't you see your fellowship with the . . . Jews [of Jesus' day] in which your denial of the divine Sonship has involved you! For they have put on record the reason of their condemnation: "And by our law he ought to die because he made himself the Son of God." Isn't this the same charge that you are blasphemously bringing against him, that, while you pronounce him a creature, he calls himself the Son? He confesses himself the Son, and they declare him guilty of death. You too deny that he is the Son of God. What sentence do you pass on him? You have the same repugnance to his claim as had the Jews. You agree with their verdict. I want to know whether you will quarrel about the sentence. Your offense, in denying that he is the Son of God, is exactly the same as theirs, though their guilt is less, for they sinned in ignorance. On the Trinity 6.50.[27]

Their Charges Should Have Elicited Worship. Chrysostom: How then, when the judge said, "You take him, and judge him according to your law," did you reply, "It is not lawful for us to put any man to death," while here you flee to the Law? And consider the charge, "He made himself the Son of God." Tell me, is this the ground of your accusation, that is, that he who performed the deeds of the Son of God should call himself the Son of God? And so what does Christ do? While they held this dialogue with each other, he held his peace, fulfilling that saying of the prophet that "he opens not his mouth. In his humiliation his judgment was taken away."[28] Homilies on the Gospel of John 84.2.[29]

19:8 *Pilate's Reaction*

Pilate More Worried Than the Jewish Leaders. Chrysostom: Then Pilate is alarmed when he hears from them that he made himself the Son of God, worrying that he might be administering justice improperly if the assertion might possibly be true. But these men who had learned this, both by his deeds and words, did not shudder. Instead, they are putting him to death for the very reasons for which they ought to have worshiped him. Homilies on the Gospel of John 84.2.[30]

Pilate May Have Believed Christ Was Divine. Cyril of Alexandria: The malicious design of the Jews had a result they little expected. They wanted to build up an indictment against Christ by saying that he had ventured to sin against the person of God himself. But the weighty character of the accusation itself increased Pilate's caution, and he was more alarmed and more careful concerning Christ than before. He became more particular in his questions: what Jesus was and where he came from. I think he believed that, though Jesus was a man, he might also be the Son of God. This idea and belief of his was not derived from holy Scripture but the mistaken notions of the Greeks. Greek fables call many men demi-gods and sons of gods. The Romans, too, who in such matters were still more superstitious, gave the name of god to the more distinguished of their own monarchs, and set up altars to them, and allotted them shrines and put them on pedestals. Therefore Pilate was more earnest and anxious than before in his inquiry of who Christ was and where he came from. Commentary on the Gospel of John 12.[31]

---

[27]NPNF 1 9:116**. [28]Is 53:7-8 (LXX). [29]NPNF 1 14:314**. [30]NPNF 1 14:314**. [31]LF 48:614**.

19:9-16 TWO KINGDOMS COLLIDE

[9] *[Pilate] entered the praetorium again and said to Jesus, "Where are you from?" But Jesus gave no answer.* *[10]* *Pilate therefore said to him, "You will not speak to me? Do you not know that I have power to release you, and power to crucify you?"* *[11]* *Jesus answered him, "You would have no power over me unless it had been given you from above; therefore he who delivered me to you has the greater sin."*

[12] *Upon this Pilate sought to release him, but the Jews cried out, "If you release this man, you are not Caesar's friend; every one who makes himself a king sets himself against Caesar."* *[13]* *When Pilate heard these words, he brought Jesus out and sat down on the judgment seat at a place called The Pavement, and in Hebrew, Gabbatha.* *[14]* *Now it was the day of Preparation of the Passover; it was about the sixth hour. He said to the Jews, "Behold your King!"* *[15]* *They cried out, "Away with him, away with him, crucify him!" Pilate said to them, "Shall I crucify your King?" The chief priests answered, "We have no king but Caesar."* *[16]* *Then he handed him over to them to be crucified.*

Overview: Jesus is silent in the face of Pilate's further inquiry. The silence of the lamb Jesus (Augustine) was not a sign of weakness (Origen) as the Word stood without a word (Romanus). In the face of such silence, Pilate tries waving his wand of power (Cyril), but the state's authority comes from God (Augustine). Jesus appeals to the power that is from above, which allows Pilate to put him to death, since it is true that nothing happens without God (Origen), although just because Pilate had been given the power does not mean that he had to use it (Augustine). Christ did have power, but chose not to use it, instead giving himself to suffer for us (Cyril). Although those who handed Jesus over were guilty of a greater sin, Pilate is still not exempt from blame for his complicity in Jesus' death (Augustine). The Jews' implicit accusation that Jesus made himself a king agrees with what we find in Luke's account (Augustine). But if this was really true, then Pilate should have investigated further (Chrysostom). Instead, he chooses to be an enemy of the Almighty instead of being an enemy to Caesar (Romanus).

At this point John is specific about the time of events and chronology, which introduces its own difficulties that have received various solutions (Theodore, Augustine, Ignatius, Eusebius). The fact, however, that our Lord was offered up on the day of preparation for the Passover should enable us to see how the Passover as type was giving way to the true Passover that is found in Christ our Passover lamb (Peter of Alexandria). By specifying the day and the hour, John also makes clear Jesus' fulfillment of the prophecy of Jonah (Cyril of Alexandria). Once John has established the chronology of events, he records Pilate's presentation of Jesus to the people as their king. But Israel rejects its king in favor of Caesar (Irenaeus, Chrysostom). And so Pilate hands Jesus over to be crucified, but neither Pilate nor the Jewish leaders are without guilt in this (Cyril, Augustine).

19:9 *No Answer for Pilate*

Silence of the Lamb. Augustine: It is found, in comparing the narratives of all the Evangelists, that this silence on the part of our Lord Jesus Christ took place more than once, both before the chief priests and before Herod, to whom, as Luke intimates, Pilate had sent him for a hearing, and before Pilate himself.[1] So it was not in vain that the prophecy regarding him had preceded, "As the lamb before its shearer was dumb, so he opened not his mouth,"[2] especially on those occasions when he did not answer his questioners. For although he frequently replied to questions addressed to him, yet because of those questions where he made no reply, the metaphor of the lamb is supplied in order that in his silence he might be accounted not as guilty but innocent. When, therefore, he was passing through the process of judgment, wherever he "opened not his mouth" it was in the character of a lamb that he did so. In other words, he did so not as one with an evil conscience who was convicted of his sins but as one who in his meekness was sacrificed for the sins of others. Tractates on the Gospel of John 116.4.[3]

Silence Not a Sign of Weakness. Origen: Since he willed to suffer on behalf of the world, he is silent when examined and beaten by Pilate. For if he had spoken, he would not have been crucified from weakness,[4] since there is no weakness in the words that the Word speaks. Commentary on the Gospel of John 19.61.[5]

The Word Without a Word. Romanus Melodus:

The Thunderer stood voiceless—the Word, without a word;
For if He had spoken out, He would not have been overpowered,
And as victor, He would not have been crucified, and Adam would not have been saved.
Therefore, He who had caught the wise,[6] conquered by His silence.
The judge on seeing that He did not utter a sound
Was overcome with embarrassment and said: "What am I to do with one who does not speak?"
But they answered: "He is liable for those things which we question, hence his silence. . . ."

"Death is a debt I owed," said my Savior
To the lawless people—as for Pilate,
[Jesus] did not consider the unspeakable animal[7] worthy of a word.

Kontakion on the Passion of Christ 20.7-8.[8]

19:10 *The Power to Crucify?*

Pilate Tries Waving His Wand of Power. Cyril of Alexandria: Pilate thought this silence of Jesus was the silence of a madman. Therefore, he stretches over him, as it were, the wand of his official power and thought that he could, through fear, induce Jesus to return a fruitless answer against his will. For he says that nothing could hinder his inclining whichever way he chose, either to punish him or to take compassion on him. He [implies] that there was nothing that could make him give a verdict against his will since it was with him alone that the fate of the accused rested. He rebukes Jesus, therefore, as though he felt himself insulted by untimely silence. Commentary on the Gospel of John 12.[9]

The State's Authority Comes from God. Augustine: "There is no authority but God's."[10] Jesus also taught that someone is a greater sinner who maliciously delivers up the innocent to be killed by such an authority than the authority itself, if that authority kills him through fear of another authority that is greater still. This was the kind of authority that God had given to Pilate, since Pilate was under the authority of Caesar. Tractates on the Gospel of John 116.5.[11]

---

[1]See Mt 26:63; 27:14; Mk 14:61; 15:5; Lk 23:7-9; Jn 19:9. [2]Is 53:7. [3]NPNF 1 7:426*. [4]2 Cor 13:4. [5]FC 89:182**; SC 290:84-86. [6]Job 5:13. [7]Pilate is both a brute animal and unspeakable; the Gk word *alogon* implies both. [8]*KRBM* 1:209-10. [9]LF 48:615**. [10]Rom 13:1. [11]NPNF 1 7:426**.

19:11 *Power from Above and Pilate's Guilt*

Nothing Happens Without God. Origen: As with Job . . . it is not by accidental attacks that we are assailed, whenever we are visited with any such loss of property. It is not by chance when one of us is taken prisoner or when those who are dear to us are crushed to death in their houses[12] that fall in ruins. For in each one of these circumstances every believer ought to say, "You could have no power at all against me, except it were given you from above." For observe that the house of Job did not fall on his children until the devil had first received power against them. Nor would the horsemen have made a raid in three bands to carry away his camels and oxen and cattle unless they had been instigated by that spirit to whom they had delivered themselves up as servants of his will. On First Principles 3.2.6.[13]

Ability Does Not Imply Necessity. Augustine: But still, when the ability is given, surely no necessity is imposed. Therefore, although David had received ability to kill Saul, he preferred sparing to striking him.[14] From this, we understand that bad people receive ability for the condemnation of their depraved will, while good people receive ability for the trying of their good will. On the Spirit and the Letter 54.[15]

The Consent of Father and Son. Cyril of Alexandria: When Jesus says that power was given to Pilate from above, he does not mean that God the Father inflicted crucifixion on his own Son against his will. Rather, he means that the Only-Begotten himself gave himself to suffer for us and that the Father suffered the fulfillment of the mystery in him. It is, then, plainly the consent and approval of the Father that is here said to have been given, and the pleasure of the Son is also clearly signified. For no doubt the force of numbers could never have overcome the power of the Savior. Commentary on the Gospel of John 12.[16]

Pilate Not Exempt from Blame. Augustine: Jesus told Pilate, "You would have no power against me," that is, even the little measure you really have, "except" this very measure, whatever its amount, "were given to you from above." But knowing as I do its amount, for it is not so great as to render you altogether independent, "therefore he that delivered me unto you has the greater sin." He, indeed, delivered me to your power at the bidding of envy, while you exercise your power on me through the impulse of fear. And yet not even through the impulse of fear should one person kill another, especially the innocent. Nevertheless to do so by an officious enthusiasm is a much greater evil than under the constraint of fear. And therefore the truth-speaking teacher does not say, "Only the one who delivered me to you has sin," as if the other had none. Rather, he says that he "has the greater sin," letting him understand that Pilate himself was not exempt from blame. The sin of the latter is not reduced to nothing because the other sin is greater. Tractates on the Gospel of John 116.5.[17]

19:12 *No Friend of Caesar*

This Charge Agrees with Luke's Version. Augustine: This [charge] may very well agree with what Luke records in connection with the said accusation brought by the Jews. For after the words "we found this fellow perverting our nation," he has added the clause, "and forbidding to give tribute to Caesar and saying that he himself is Christ a king."[18] This will also offer a solution for the difficulty previously referred to, namely, the occasion that might seem to be given for supposing John to have indicated that no specific charge was laid by the Jews against the Lord, when they answered and said to him, "If he were not a malefactor, we would not have delivered him up unto you." Harmony of the Gospels 3.8.35.[19]

[12]Job 1:6-19. [13]ANF 4:333-34*; GCS 22(5):254. [14]1 Sam 24:7; 26:9. [15]NPNF 1 5:107**. [16]LF 48:616**. [17]NPNF 1 7:426**. [18]Lk 23:2. [19]NPNF 1 6:196**.

Pilate Should Have Investigated. Chrysostom: Pilate ought therefore to have accurately inquired whether Jesus had aimed at sovereignty and set his hand to expel Caesar from the kingdom. But he makes no such exact inquiry, and therefore Christ answered him nothing, because he knew that he asked all the questions idly. Besides, since his works bore witness to him, he would not prevail by word or compose any defense, showing that he came voluntarily to this condition. . . . Pilate, thinking that he might now incur some danger if he were to overlook these words, comes forth as though to inquire into the matter (for the "sitting down" showed this), but without making any inquiry, he gave Jesus up to them, thinking to shame them. Homilies on the Gospel of John 84.2.[20]

An Enemy of the Almighty Instead of Caesar. Romanus Melodus:

"Crucify!", the murderer heard the impious cry out,
And he fulfilled their will,
Handing over, without being compelled to, the One whom he wished to be crucified.
For having heard that he would be the enemy of Caesar, the coward was frightened;
He wished to be the enemy of the Almighty
Rather than the enemy of Caesar, preferring his life to Life.
He will certainly not be blameless, since in answer to the lawless, he killed the Living One.

Kontakion on the Passion of Christ 20.16.[21]

19:13-14 *Pilate at Noon on the Day of Preparation*

Mark's Account Is More General Than John's. Theodore of Mopsuestia: It was the day of preparation, that is, the sixth holy day of the week,[22] and it was about the sixth hour. For those who think that the words of the Evangelists are in contradiction, as some say at the third hour, others at about the sixth, it is necessary that we say something in this regard. Matthew and Luke, like John, said that there was darkness at about the sixth hour.[23] Indeed, Pilate went out immediately and sat at the tribunal and handed Jesus over to be crucified. And after he was fixed to the cross, the dark-ness began to spread, as the Evangelists said. There are any number of reasons why it is not surprising that Mark said that it was the third hour.[24] He said this, first of all, because he was not present. Second, he was not a disciple of our Lord but learned these facts from Peter or some other apostle. And finally, everyone has different opinions about times and hours,[25] and the doubt about the hours does not affect in any way the reported facts. In addition, we especially must notice that Mark did not say that it was the third hour about any specific and well-known fact. But by relating in a simple and general way the things that happened, he rightly said that they took place at the third hour and so designated the entire interval of time in which these facts happened. Then he added, "They crucified him."[26] Therefore the sentence, "It was nine in the morn-ing" refers to the account of all those events, which happened in the meantime. "They crucified him" is added concerning the pre-vious events. Commentary on John 7.19.14.[27]

Time Discrepancy? Augustine: What else, then, is the meaning of the Evangelist Mark saying, "And it was the third hour, and they crucified him,"[28] but this, that the Lord was crucified at the third hour by the tongues of the Jew, at the sixth

[20]NPNF 1 14:314-15**. [21]*KRBM* 1:213. [22]*Hebdomas.* [23]That is, noon. See Mt 27:45; Lk 23:44 [24]Mk 15:25. Theodore assumes that the third hour mentioned by Mark is 9:00 in the morning. [25]Theodore here reflects another solution that has been put forward to this problem of chronology, that is, that the different Gospel writers may have been writing with different conceptions as to when to begin counting the hours of the day. [26]Mk 15:25. [27]CSCO 4 3:333-34. [28]Mk 15:25.

hour by the hands of the soldiers?[29] Tractates on the Gospel of John 117.1.[30]

One Possible Timeline. Ignatius of Antioch: On the day of the preparation, then, at the third hour,[31] Jesus received the sentence from Pilate, the Father permitting that to happen. At the sixth hour he was crucified. At the ninth hour he gave up the ghost. And before sunset he was buried. Epistle to the Trallians 9 (longer version).[32]

Copyist Error? Eusebius of Caesarea: Mark says Christ was crucified at the third hour. John says that it was at the sixth hour that Pilate took his seat on the tribunal and tried Jesus. This discrepancy is a clerical error or an earlier copyist. *Gamma* (Γ) signifying the third hour is very close to the *episemon* (ϛ́)[33] denoting the sixth. As Matthew, Mark and Luke agree that the darkness occurred from the sixth hour to the ninth, it is clear that Jesus, Lord and God, was crucified before the sixth hour, i.e. about the third hour, as Mark has recorded. John similarly signified that it was the third hour, but the copyists turned the *gamma* (Γ) to the *episemon* (ϛ́). Minor Supplements to Questions to Marinus 4.[34]

Passover As Type Gives Way to True Passover. Peter of Alexandria: After his public ministry, Jesus did not eat of the lamb, but he himself suffered as the true Lamb in the Paschal feast, as John, the divine and Evangelist teaches us in the Gospel written by him. ". . . And it was the preparation of the Passover, and about the third hour,"[35] as the correct books render it and the copy itself that was written by the hand of the Evangelist, which by divine grace has been preserved in the most holy church of Ephesus and is there adored by the faithful. . . . On that day, therefore, on which the Jews were about to eat the Passover in the evening, our Lord and Savior Jesus Christ was crucified. He was made the victim to those who were about to partake by faith of the mystery concerning him. This is what is written by the blessed Paul, "For even Christ our Passover is sacrificed for us."[36] It is not the case, as some who, carried along by ignorance, confidently affirm that after he had eaten the Passover, he was betrayed. We neither learn this from the holy Evangelists, nor has any of the blessed apostles handed it down to us. At the time, therefore, in which our Lord and God Jesus Christ suffered for us, according to the flesh, he did not eat of the legal Passover. Rather, as I have said, he himself, as the true Lamb, was sacrificed for us in the feast of the typical Passover on the day of the preparation, the fourteenth of the first lunar month. The typical Passover, therefore, then ceased, the true Passover being present: "For Christ our Passover was sacrificed for us," as was said earlier. And he was that chosen vessel, as the apostle Paul teaches. Fragment 1.7.[37]

The First of Three Days. Cyril of Alexandria: The inspired Evangelist is induced to signify, for our benefit, the day and hour because of the resurrection itself and his three days' sojourn among the departed, that the truth of our Lord's saying to the Jews might appear: "For as Jonah was three days and three nights in the belly of the whale, so also shall the Son of man be three days and three nights in the heart of the earth."[38] Commentary on the Gospel of John 12.[39]

[29]Augustine's chronological solution in his *Harmony of the Gospels* 3.13.40-50 (especially par. 42) extends Theodore's thought by asserting that Mark has a hidden agenda when he mentions the third hour. For Mark, the crucifixion technically begins when the Jews first cried out that Jesus should be crucified and extends to the later crucifixion by the Roman soldiers. Mark, Augustine says, did this so that the reader would understand who was truly responsible for Jesus' death, noting that while the soldiers were the executioners, it was the cry to crucify him, which took place at the third hour and was inspired by the Jewish leaders, that was the cause of his death. [30]NPNF 1 7:428*. [31]Ignatius or, more likely, his editors in this case reflect a tradition that seems to contradict John but fits in with the broader Synoptic timetable. [32]ANF 1:70**. [33]See *PGL* 530-31. [34]PG 22:1009. [35]Peter here seems to give some credence to the belief of Eusebius and others, such as Severus and Theophylact, that there was an early error among the copies of John's Gospel. See Eusebius above. [36]1 Cor 5:7. [37]ANF 6:282**. [38]Mt 12:40. [39]LF 48:619*. Irenaeus reflects the tradition that Jesus died on the same day as Adam; see *Against Heresies* 5.23.2.

19:15 *We Have No King but Caesar*

The Jews Give Away Their Blessing to the Christians.[40] Irenaeus: [Jacob] received the rights of the firstborn when his brother looked on them with contempt. In the same way, the younger nation [i.e., the Christians] received Christ, the first-begotten, when the elder nation [i.e., the Jews] rejected him, saying, "We have no king but Caesar." But in Christ every blessing [is summed up], and therefore the latter people has snatched away the blessings of the former from the Father, just as Jacob took away the blessing of this Esau. This is why his brother suffered the plots and persecutions of a brother, just as the church suffers this self-same thing from the Jews. Against Heresies 4.21.3.[41]

Israel Rejects God's Rule. Chrysostom: Of their own will they subjected themselves to punishment. Therefore God also gave them up, because they were the first to cast themselves out from his providence and governance. And since with one voice they rejected his rule, he allowed them to fall by their own expressed wish. Homilies on the Gospel of John 84.2.[42]

19:16 *Jesus Handed Over to Be Crucified*

Pilate Is Not Without Guilt. Cyril of Alexandria: We cannot acquit Pilate of his complicity in the iniquity of those who committed this impious crime against Christ. Pilate shared their responsibility inasmuch as when he might have delivered and rescued him from the madness of his murderers, he did not merely refrain from releasing him but even gave him up to them to be crucified. Commentary on the Gospel of John 12.[43]

Jewish Leaders Are Not Without Guilt. Augustine: It was not said "then he delivered him to them" so that they might crucify him but "so that he might be crucified," that is, that Jesus might be crucified by the judicial sentence and power of the governor. But the Evangelist has said that Jesus was delivered to them so that he might show that they [i.e., the Jewish leaders] were implicated in the crime from which they tried to hold themselves aloof. For Pilate would have done no such thing except to implement what he perceived was their determined desire. Tractates on the Gospel of John 116.9.[44]

---

[40]This passage was used often in polemics of Christians against Jews in the patristic period. [41]ANF 1:493*. [42]NPNF 1 14:315*. [43]LF 48:622-23**. [44]NPNF 1 7:427**.

19:17-22 THE CRUCIFIXION OF JESUS

[17]So they took Jesus, and he went out, bearing his own cross, to the place called the place of a skull, which is called in Hebrew Golgotha. [18]There they crucified him, and with him two others, one on either side, and Jesus between them. [19]Pilate also wrote a title and put it on the cross; it read, "Jesus of Nazareth, the King of the Jews." [20]Many of the Jews read this title, for the place where Jesus was crucified was near the city; and it was written in Hebrew, in Latin, and in Greek. [21]The chief priests of the Jews then said to Pilate, "Do not write, 'The King of the Jews,' but, 'This man said, I am King of the Jews.'" [22]Pilate answered, "What I have written I have written."

Overview: John tells us that Jesus carried his own cross that is later taken up by Simon of Cyrene, as we learn from the other Evangelists, (Theodore) and ultimately taken up by us (Origen). Abraham was willing to give up his son Isaac, who carried the wood for his own sacrifice, but was not called on to do so. Our heavenly Father, however, did give up his own Son, having him also carry the wood for his sacrifice for us (Romanus, Clement). Jesus goes further, however, in finishing what Isaac was spared (Chrysostom), thus fulfilling the type of the ram who is sacrificed while caught in the thorns of his crown and cross (Tertullian). He carried a cross that was rightfully ours, not his, and so it is fitting not only that our Savior carried his own cross but that we should do so as well (Cyril). The cross is the scepter of Jesus' power as he carries the trophy of victory (Leo). He came to the place of the skull, which, according to Hebraic tradition (although its veracity may be questioned) was the place where the body of Adam was buried (Origen, Jerome). The blood of the second Adam thus washes away the sin of the first Adam (Jerome). The naming of the place of the skull is indeed prophetic since Christ, the true head, began his headship from this place (Cyril of Jerusalem).

Jesus is crucified between two thieves as the Jews seek to discredit Jesus, but instead of infamy, they bring glory to Jesus (Chrysostom). The two thieves who are crucified with him are a type of Israel and the Gentiles (Cyril) with Jesus in the middle foreshadowing his future seat of judgment (Augustine). The cause of Jesus' death was contained in the inscription above his head, that is, that he was king of the Jews (Origen). The Jews could not keep him from being their king even in death (Augustine).

In posting this notice on the cross, Pilate proclaims Jesus' victory as well as his innocence (Chrysostom). This very public record (Chrysostom), written in the most conspicuous languages of the day (Augustine), amounted to a declaration that Christ would not only rule over the Jews but over all nations and languages (Cyril). The chief priests object to the title King of the Jews, but it remains an accurate description of Jesus, who reigns over all nations but does so, nonetheless, as the King of the Jews (Augustine). Pilate wrote what he wrote because the Lord said what he said (Augustine). The Gentile Pilate ends up bearing witness to Jesus at his death just as the Gentile magi had done at his birth (Augustine).

19:17a *Carrying His Own Cross*

Christ Carried First, Simon Second. Theodore of Mopsuestia: When Christ was condemned, they laid his cross on him. However, on the way out to Golgotha, they met Simon of Cyrene and transferred it on to him.[1] In this way there is no disagreement among the Evangelists. Commentary on John 7.19.17.[2]

Let Us Also Bear the Cross. Origen: But it was fitting not only that the Savior should take his own cross but that we also should bear it, fulfilling our being pressed into service in the cause of salvation. But yet again, we do not profit from taking his cross as much as we do when Jesus himself takes his cross and bears it. Commentary on Matthew 126.[3]

Abraham and the Father, Isaac and Christ. Romanus Melodus:

"In you [Abraham] I foreshadow my plans,[4]
For indeed, O just man, you are clearly my figure in relief.[5]
Do you wish to know what is to come after you as a result of your deeds?
It is for this reason that I had you ascend here, to show you.

[1]Mt 27:32. [2]CSCO 4 3:335. [3]AEG 6:53*; GCS 38 2 (11):263. This is a common solution to John omitting mention of Simon of Cyrene, that is, that Jesus first carried the cross and then Simon. See, for instance, Theodore on this point. Irenaeus alludes to a possible Gnostic proposal that it was Simon of Cyrene and not Christ who was crucified, implying a theological reason for Simon's omission by John. See *Against Heresies* 1.24.4. [4]Gen 22:15-19. [5]Gen 1:26; 22:12, 16.

Just as you did not spare your son because of me,
Just so, I shall not spare my son because of all men;
But I shall give him to be slain for the sake of the world."[6]. . .

"In the same way that your Isaac has carried the wood on his shoulders,
In the same way, my son will bear the cross on His shoulders.
Your great love has revealed to you the future.
See now the battering ram attached to the wood;
As you see the source of its support, you will understand the mystery.
It is by the horns that it holds in the bonds;
The horns signify the hands of my son.
Set the seal of approval on Him, and I shall guard your son."
KONTAKION ON ABRAHAM AND ISAAC 41.22-23.[7]

THE SACRIFICE OF ISAAC PREFIGURED CHRIST'S SACRIFICE. CLEMENT OF ALEXANDRIA: Isaac (for the narrative may be interpreted otherwise) is a type of the Lord, a child as a son. For he was the son of Abraham, as Christ was the Son of God, and a sacrifice as the Lord, but he was not immolated as the Lord. Isaac only bore the wood of the sacrifice, as the Lord the wood of the cross. And he laughed mystically,[8] prophesying that the Lord should fill us with joy, who have been redeemed from corruption by the blood of the Lord. Isaac did everything but suffer, as was right, yielding the precedence of suffering to the Word. Furthermore, there is an intimation of the divinity of the Lord with his not being slain. For Jesus rose again after his burial, having suffered no harm, like Isaac released from sacrifice. CHRIST THE EDUCATOR 1.5.[9]

JESUS FINISHES WHAT ISAAC WAS SPARED. CHRYSOSTOM: And now, [the Jews] laid the cross on him as a malefactor. For they even abhorred the wood and would not even touch it. This was also the case in the type. For Isaac bore the wood, but then the matter stopped because his father wanted it to, for it was the type. Here there was no stopping it because it was the reality [and not the type]. HOMILIES ON THE GOSPEL OF JOHN 85.1.[10]

ISAAC AND CHRIST CARRIED THEIR OWN WOOD. TERTULLIAN: Isaac the son of Abraham personally carried the wood for his own sacrifice when God had enjoined that he should be made a victim to God himself. But these had been mysteries that were being kept for perfect fulfillment in the times of Christ. Therefore Isaac, with his wood, was preserved when the ram that was caught by the horns in the bramble was offered in his place.[11] Christ, however, carried his wood on his own shoulders, adhering to the horns of the cross with a thorny crown encircling his head. For he chose to be made a sacrifice on behalf of all. AN ANSWER TO THE JEWS 13.[12]

HE BECAME A CURSE FOR US. CYRIL OF ALEXANDRIA: They led away the author of life to die—to die for our sake. In a way beyond our understanding, the power of God brought from Christ's passion an end far different from that intended by his enemies. His sufferings served as a snare for death and rendered it powerless. The Lord's death proved to be our restoration to immortality and newness of life. Condemned to death though innocent, he went forward bearing on his shoulders the cross on which he was to suffer. He did this for our sake, taking on himself the punishment that the law justly imposed on sinners. He was cursed for our sake according to the saying of Scripture: "A curse is on everyone who is hanged on a tree."[13] . . . We who

[6]Rom 8:32. [7]*KRBM* 2:69. For a further sampling among the many comparisons between Isaac and Christ in the patristic literature, see J. Cavadini, "Exegetical Transformations: The Sacrifice of Isaac in Philo, Origin, and Ambrose," in *Dominico Eloquio*, ed. Paul Blowers et. al. (Grand Rapids: Eerdmans, 2002), 35-49. [8]The name Isaac means "laughter." [9]ANF 2:215*. For further parallels between Isaac and Christ here see also Tertullian *An Answer to the Jews* 10 and *Against Marcion* 3.18 and the commentaries, *loc. cit.* [10]NPNF 1 14:317**. [11]Gen 22:1-14. [12]ANF 3:170-71**. [13]Gal 3:13.

have all committed many sins were under that ancient curse for our refusal to obey the law of God. To set us free he who was without sin took that curse on himself. Since he is God who is above all, his sufferings sufficed for all, his death in the flesh was the redemption of all. And so, Christ carried the cross, a cross that was rightfully not his but ours, who were under the condemnation of the law. . . . Indeed, our Lord Jesus Christ has warned us that anyone who does not take up his cross and follow him is not worthy of him.[14] And I think taking up the cross means simply renouncing the world for God's sake and, if this is required of us, putting the hope of future blessings before the life we now live in the body. Our Lord Jesus Christ was not ashamed to carry the cross we deserved, and he did so because he loved us. Commentary on the Gospel of John 12.[15]

The Cross Is the Scepter of Jesus' Power. Leo the Great: When our Lord was handed over to the will of his cruel foes, they ordered him, in mockery of his royal dignity, to carry the instrument of his own torture. This was done to fulfill the prophecy of Isaiah: "A child is born for us, a son is given to us; sovereignty is laid on his shoulders."[16] To the wicked, the sight of the Lord carrying his own cross was indeed an object of derision. But to the faithful a great mystery was revealed, for the cross was destined to become the scepter of his power. Here was the majestic spectacle of a glorious conqueror mightily overthrowing the hostile forces of the devil and nobly bearing the trophy of his victory. On the shoulders of his invincible patience he carried the sign of salvation for all the kingdoms of the earth to worship, as if on that day he would strengthen all his future disciples by the symbol of his work and say to them, "Anyone who does not take up his cross and follow me is not worthy of me."[17] Sermon 8.4.[18]

19:17b *The Place of the Skull*

Adam and the Place of the Skull. Origen: The place of the skull is said to have some special appropriateness for the death of him who was to die for humankind. A Hebraic tradition has come down to us that says that the body of Adam the first man was buried just where Christ was crucified. And so, as in Adam all die, so in Christ all should be made alive. In the place that is called the place of the skull or head, the head of the human race should find resurrection along with the whole people through the resurrection of the Lord and Savior who suffered there and rose again. For it was unfitting that when many born from him received remission of sins and attained the blessing of resurrection, the very father of all people should not also attain this grace. Commentary on Matthew 126.[19]

The Tradition of Adam Questionable. Jerome: [The tradition that Adam died at Calvary is] an apt connection and smooth to the ear but not true. For the place where they cut off the heads of people condemned to death, called in consequence Calvary, was outside the city gates, whereas we read in the book of Jesus [i.e., Joshua] the son of Nave [Nun], that Adam was buried by Hebron and Arbah.[20] Commentary on Matthew 4.[21]

The Blood of the Second Adam Washes the Sin of the First Adam. Jerome: Well, then, to bring forward something still more out of place, we must go back to yet remoter times. Tradition has it that in this city, in fact, on this very spot, Adam lived and died. The place where our

[14]See Mt 10:38. [15]LF 48:623-24**. [16]Is 9:6. [17]Mt 10:38. [18]NPNF 2 12:172; *JFB* 44; PL 54:339-40. [19]*AEG* 6:54-55*; GCS 38 2 (11):264-65. [20]Jerome makes a somewhat dubious assertion here on the basis of the Hebrew text of Josh 14:15, which contains the Hebrew word *Adam*, but the context would suggest its translation as "man" rather than "Adam." He more than likely knew the rabbinic tradition preserved in *Genesis Rabbah* 58.4 and based his assertion on that explanation which gave the name of Kiriath Arbah as the burial place of Adam and Eve as well as the patriarchs and their wives. At any rate, he still cites the tradition in one of his own letters, *Letter* 46, which follows. [21]CCL 77:270.

Lord was crucified is called Calvary,[22] because the skull of the first man was buried there. So it came to pass that the second Adam, that is, the blood[23] of Christ, as it dropped from the cross, washed away the sins of the buried one who was first formed,[24] the first Adam, and thus the words of the apostle were fulfilled: "Awake, you who sleep, and arise from the dead, and Christ shall give you light."[25] Letter 46.3.[26]

The Prophetic Name of Golgotha. Cyril of Jerusalem: Now Golgotha is interpreted "the place of a skull." Who were they, then, who prophetically named this spot Golgotha in which Christ the true head endured the cross? The apostle calls him "the image of the invisible God," and a little after, "the head of the body, the church."[27] And again, "The head of every man is Christ."[28] And again, "[He] is the head over all principalities and powers."[29] The head suffered in "the place of the skull." O wondrous prophetic appellation! The very name also reminds you, saying, "Do not think of the Crucified as a mere man." He is "the head of all principalities and powers." That head that was crucified is the head of all power and has for his head the Father, "for the head of the man is Christ, and the head of Christ is God."[30] Catechetical Lectures 13.23.[31]

19:18 *Crucified with Two Others*

Three Crucified, Only One Attributed Glory. Chrysostom: Who cares if the Jews did these things with a different intent? They crucified him too with thieves, in this also unintentionally fulfilling prophecy. For what they did for insult contributed to the truth, that you may learn how great its power is, since the prophet of old had foretold, "He was numbered with the transgressors."[32] The devil therefore wished to cast a veil over what was done but was unable. For the three were crucified, but Jesus alone was glorious, that you may learn that his power affected all. Yet the miracles took place when the three had been nailed to the cross. But no one attributed anything of what was done to either of those others but to Jesus only. This is how the plot of the devil was rendered so entirely impotent and how everything rained back on his own head. For even of these two, one was saved. He therefore did not insult the glory of the cross but contributed to it not a little. For it was not a lesser matter than shaking the rocks to change a thief on the cross and to bring him into paradise. Homilies on the Gospel of John 85.1.[33]

The Two Thieves Are a Type of Israel and the Gentiles. Cyril of Alexandria: The two criminals who hung by Christ's side symbolize the two nations who were about to be brought into close contact with him, namely, the children of Israel and the Gentiles. And why do we take condemned criminals as the type? Because the Jews were condemned by the Law, for they were guilty of transgressing it. And the Greeks were condemned by their idolatry, for they worshiped the creature more than the Creator. . . . Therefore, the crucifixion of the two robbers, side by side with Christ, signifies . . . the juxtaposition of the two nations, dying together, as it were, with the Savior Christ by bidding farewell to worldly pleasures, refusing any longer to live after the flesh and preferring to live with their Lord, as far as possible, by fashioning their lives according to him and consecrating them to his service. And the meaning of the figure is in no way affected by the fact that the men who hung by his side were criminals. For we were by nature children of wrath[34] before we believed in Christ and were all doomed to death. Commentary on the Gospel of John 12.[35]

---

[22]The place of a skull (Lat. *Calvaria*). [23]One of Jerome's fanciful ideas. *Haddam* is the Hebrew for "the blood." [24]Gk *protoplastos*. See Wis 7:1. [25]Eph 5:14. [26]NPNF 2 6:61**. [27]Col 1:15, 18. [28]1 Cor 11:3. [29]Col 2:10. [30]1 Cor 11:3. [31]NPNF 2 7:88**. Sozomen records in his *Ecclesiastical History* 2.26 the completion of the "Great Martyrium," which was built on the site during Constantine's reign as a focal point for Christian piety and pilgrimage. [32]Is 53:12. [33]NPNF 1 14:317*. [34]Eph 2:3. [35]LF 48:626-27*.

The Middle Cross Foreshadows the Judgment Seat. Augustine: Even the cross, if you consider it well, was a judgment seat. For the Judge was set up in the middle with the thief who believed and was pardoned on one side and the thief who mocked and was damned on the other. Already then he signified what he would do with the living and the dead: some he will place on his right hand, others on his left. Tractates on the Gospel of John 31.11.[36]

19:19 *The Inscription*

The Cause of Jesus' Death and His Crown. Origen: Whether in pretence or in truth, Christ is proclaimed king, and every letter bears witness of his reign, whether of Greeks, or Romans, or Hebrews. And for a crown above his head was written, "This is Jesus the King of the Jews." And since no other cause is found for his death (for there was none), this alone is put forward, "He was king of the Jews."[37]... And the high priest according to the letter of the law used to carry on his head the form of the sign and the sanctification of the Lord written on the plate. But the true high priest and king, Jesus, on the cross has it written, "This is the King of the Jews." But ascending to the Father and receiving the Father into himself, he has for letters and for a name what he [God] is named and has him [the Father] as a crown. Commentary on Matthew 130.[38]

Their King Even in Death. Augustine: The title placed over his cross, on which was written "The King of the Jews," showed that they could not keep him from being their king even by his death. Sermon 218.5.[39]

Pilate Proclaims Jesus' Victory and Innocence. Chrysostom: Pilate wrote a title that both requited the Jews and made a defense for Christ. They had given him up as worthless and attempted to confirm his sentence by making him share the punishment of the robbers. He does this in order that, in the future, it might be in no one's power to bring evil charges against Jesus or accuse him of being a worthless and wicked person. He closes their mouths and the mouths of all who might desire to accuse him and shows that they had risen up against their own king. Pilate, however, places those letters almost as if he were placing them on a trophy—letters that proclaim in a clear voice Jesus' victory and kingdom. Homilies on the Gospel of John 85.1.[40]

19:20 *Written in Hebrew, Latin and Greek*

A Very Public Record. Chrysostom: He wrote this title not in a single tongue but in three languages. It was likely that there would be a mixed crowd among the Jews because of the feast. And so, in order that no one might be ignorant of the defense, he publicly recorded[41] the charges ... in all the languages. Homilies on the Gospel of John 85.1.[42]

The Most Conspicuous Languages of the Day. Augustine: These three languages were conspicuous in that place beyond all others: the Hebrew because of the Jews who gloried in the law of God; the Greek, because of the wise people among the Gentiles; and the Latin, because of the Romans who at that very time were exercising sovereign power over many, in fact, over almost all countries. Tractates on the Gospel of John 117.4.[43]

The Title Is Fulfillment of Prophecy. Cyril of Alexandria: It was providential and the fruit of God's inexpressible purpose that the title was written in three languages: one in Hebrew, another in Latin and another in Greek. For it lay in plain view, proclaiming the kingdom of our Savior Christ in the most widely known of all languages ... fulfilling the prophecy that had

[36]NPNF 1 7:193**. [37]See also Ps 2:6. [38]*AEG* 6:57-58*; GCS 38 2 (11):267. [39]*WSA* 3 6:184**. [40]NPNF 1 14:317**. [41]Lit. "inscribed on a pillar." [42]NPNF 1 14:317**. [43]NPNF 1 7:429*.

been spoken concerning him. For the wise Daniel said that there was given him glory and a kingdom and that all nations and languages shall serve him.[44] Similarly the holy Paul teaches us, crying out that "every knee shall bow; of things in heaven and things on earth and things under the earth. And every tongue shall confess that Jesus Christ is Lord, to the glory of God the Father."[45] Therefore the title proclaiming Jesus "king" was, as it were, the true firstfruits of the confession of tongues.[46] Commentary on the Gospel of John 12.[47]

19:21 *Objection by the Chief Priests*

King of the Jews and the Gentiles. Augustine: The leaders of the Jews urged Pilate not to write without qualification that he is the king of the Jews, but that he himself said he was the king of the Jews, to which he replied, "What I have written, I have written." This had Pilate representing the wild olive to be grafted on, while the leaders of the Jews represented the broken-off branches. He was, you see, a man of the nations, writing for the nations their confession of faith, convicting the Jews of their denial of it, so that the Lord himself rightly said to them, "The kingdom shall be taken away from you and given to a nation that does justice."[48] . . . Pilate, certainly, wrote "king of the Jews," not "king of the Greeks or the Latins," although Jesus was going to reign over the nations. And what he has written, he has written, and he did not change it at the urging of unbelievers, as had been foretold such a long time before in the psalm, "Do not corrupt the inscription of the title."[49] All the nations believe in the king of the Jews. He reigns over all the nations but reigns nonetheless as the king of the Jews. Such was the worth and potency of that root that it could change the engrafted wild olive into itself, while the wild olive could not eliminate the name of the olive. Sermon 218.7.[50]

19:22 *What I Have Written, I Have Written*

Truth Cannot Be Altered. Augustine: What Pilate has written, he has written. But the high priests, who wanted it to be corrupted, what did they say? "Do not write, 'The King of the Jews.' But that he said, 'I am King of the Jews.' " What is it you are saying, madmen? Why do you oppose the doing of what you are utterly unable to alter? Will it become any less true that Jesus said, "I am King of the Jews"? If that cannot be tampered with which Pilate has written, can that be tampered with which the truth has uttered? Tractates on the Gospel of John 117.5.[51]

The Magi and Pilate Acknowledge the King. Augustine: The magi were from the Gentiles. Pilate too was a Gentile. They saw a star in the sky; he wrote a title on the tree. Both, however, were looking for or acknowledging the king, not of the Gentiles but of the Jews. Thus already there was a prefiguring of what the Lord himself spoke about later, "Many will come from the east and the west and sit down with Abraham and Isaac and Jacob in the kingdom of heaven. But the children of the kingdom will go into outer darkness."[52] The magi, you see, had come from the east, Pilate from the west. So they bore witness to the king of the Jews rising, that is, to his being born. Pilate bore witness to the king of the Jews setting, that is, to his dying. In this way, they could take their seats in the kingdom of heaven with Abraham and Isaac and Jacob, from whom the Jews derived their descent. They were not descended from them, of course, in the flesh but grafted into them by faith. Thus the wild olive the apostle talks about, that was to be grafted into the olive, was already being prefigured. Sermon 201.2.[53]

---

[44]Dan 7:14. [45]Phil 2:10-11. [46]See Acts 2:1-12. [47]LF 48:628-29*. See also Augustine *Sermon* 218.6. [48]Mt 21:43. [49]See the superscriptions to Ps 57 (56:1 LXX) and Ps 58 (57:1 LXX). [50]*WSA* 3 11:240. [51]NPNF 1 7:429**. [52]Mt 8:11-12. [53]*WSA* 3 6:88.

19:23-24 THE SEAMLESS GARMENT

[23]When the soldiers had crucified Jesus they took his garments and made four parts, one for each soldier; also his tunic. But the tunic was without seam, woven from top to bottom; [24]so they said to one another, "Let us not tear it, but cast lots for it to see whose it shall be." This was to fulfil the scripture,

"They parted my garments among them,
and for my clothing they cast lots."

Overview: Jesus' cloak is divided into four parts symbolizing the gospel's spread to the four corners of the world (Ephrem). But his other garment, the tunic, is left intact by the soldiers—if only we could do the same with divisions in the church (Augustine)! One cannot possess the garment of Christ as a whole who parts and divides the church of Christ (Cyprian). The church's seamless garment of unity (Augustine) is woven and clothed throughout in charity (Augustine). The seamless woven garment also symbolizes the unity of God and man in Christ (Chrysostom). And lest one think that such evil deeds could not have such beautiful symbolism, one need only look at the cross to see how an instrument of torture has become the symbol of God's grace (Augustine).

19:23 *Dividing the Clothing*

The Gospel's Spread to the Four Corners. Ephrem the Syrian: "His tunic was not torn" since it represented his divinity, which was undivided because it was not composite. "His clothing, divided into four parts," symbolized his gospel, which was to go forth into the four parts of the world. Share then, for love of him, the body of him who, for love of you, shared his garment between those who were crucifying him. Take it, all of you, absorb it in its entirety, just as he, on his own, took and absorbed your death for everyone. Open the doors of your hearts to him who opened the doors of his kingdom to you. Commentary on Tatian's Diatessaron 20.27.[1]

The Soldiers Showed Restraint. Augustine: Even the men who parted the garment of Christ among them did not rudely tear in pieces the seamless robe—and these were men who at that time had no faith in Christ's resurrection. In fact, they were witnessing his death. If, then, persecutors stopped themselves from tearing the clothing of Christ when he was hanging upon the cross, why should Christians destroy the sacrament of his institution now when he is sitting in heaven on his throne? Letter 23.4.[2]

19:24 *The Seamless Coat and the Soldiers' Actions*

The Sacrament of Unity of Christ's Church. Cyprian: This sacrament of unity, this bond of a unity inseparably cohering, is set forth where in the Gospel the coat of the Lord Jesus Christ is not at all divided or cut. Rather, it is received as an entire garment, and it is possessed as an uninjured and undivided robe by those who cast lots for Christ's garment who should instead put on Christ. Holy Scripture says, "But of the coat, because it was not sewn but woven from the top throughout, they said one to another, Let us

[1]*ECTD* 307-8. [2]NPNF 1 1:243**.

not tear it but cast lots whose it shall be." That coat bore with it a unity that came down from the top, that is, that came from heaven and the Father, which was not to be at all torn by the receiver and the possessor, but without separation we obtain a whole and substantial completeness. He cannot possess the garment of Christ who parts and divides the church of Christ. . . . His robe, woven and united throughout, is not divided by those who possess it. Undivided, united and connected, it shows the coherent harmony of our people who put on Christ. By the sacrament and sign of his garment, he has declared the unity of the church. THE UNITY OF THE CHURCH 7.[3]

THE TUNIC WITHOUT SEAM. AUGUSTINE: That they cast lots for his tunic alone, "woven from the top without seam," rather than dividing it, demonstrated clearly enough that the visible sacraments, even though they too are the garments of Christ, can still be had by anybody, good or bad. But that sincere and genuine faith, which "works through love"[4] to achieve the integrity of unity—because "the love of God has been poured out in our hearts through the Holy Spirit who has been given to us"[5]—that this faith does not belong to anybody at all but is given by God's hidden grace as by lot. Thus to Simon, who had baptism but did not have this, Peter could say, "You have no lot or part in this faith."[6] SERMON 218.9.[7]

CLOTHED IN CHARITY. AUGUSTINE: Someone, perhaps, may inquire what is signified by the division that was made of his garments into so many parts and of the casting of lots for the coat. The clothing of the Lord Jesus Christ divided into four symbolized his fourfold church. This church is spread abroad over the whole world, consisting of four equal quarters, that is to say, harmoniously distributed over all these quarters. This is why he says elsewhere that he will send his angels to gather his elect from the four winds[8]—and what is that, but from the four quarters of the world: east, west, north and south? But the coat, for which lots were cast, signifies the unity of all the parts that is contained in the bond of charity. . . . If, then, charity is both a more excellent way[9] and far surpasses knowledge[10] and is enjoined above all things,[11] it is with great propriety that the garment, by which it is signified, is represented as woven from above. And it was without seam so that it can never become unsewn. And it is in one piece because he gathers all into one. . . . And by the casting of lots, what else is commended but the grace of God? . . . When the lot is cast, the award is decided not by the merits of each individual but by the secret judgment of God. TRACTATES ON THE GOSPEL OF JOHN 118.4.[12]

UNITY OF GOD AND MAN SYMBOLIZED IN WOVEN GARMENT. CHRYSOSTOM: The soldiers parted the garments but not the coat. See how the prophecies in every instance are fulfilled by their wickedness. This also had been predicted of old. And yet, there were three crucified, but the matters of the prophecies were fulfilled only in Christ. For why didn't they do this in the case of the others also? Consider too, I pray you, the exactness of the prophecy. For the prophet says not only that they "parted" but that they "did not part." The rest therefore they divided, the coat they did not divide, but instead they committed the matter to a decision by lot. And "woven from the top" is not mentioned without purpose. Some say that a figurative assertion is declared by it: that the Crucified was not simply man but had also the divinity from above. Others say that the Evangelist describes the very form of the coat. For since in Palestine they put together two strips of cloth and so weave their garments, John, to show that the coat was of this kind, says "woven from the top." And to me he seems to say this, alluding to the poorness of the garments, and that

[3]ANF 5:423*. [4]Gal 5:6. [5]Rom 5:5. [6]Acts 8:21. [7]*WSA* 3 6:185. [8]See Mt 24:31. [9]1 Cor 12:31. [10]Eph 3:19. [11]Col 3:14. [12]NPNF 1 7:431**.

as in all other things, so in dress also, he followed a simple fashion. Homilies on the Gospel of John 85.2.[13]

Wicked Deeds, but Beautiful Symbols. Augustine: And yet, let no one say there could be no positive significance for what happened just because they were done by wicked people. . . . For if that were the case, what would be left to say about the cross itself, which everyone knows was made to nail Christ to by his enemies and sinners? And yet the words of the apostle apply to it: "what is the breadth and length and height and depth."[14] For its breadth lies in the cross beam, on which the hands of the crucified are extended that signify the breadth of love and good he accomplished on it. Its length extends from the cross beam to the ground on which the back and feet are affixed and signifies perseverance through the whole length of time up to the end. Its height is its top, which rises upward above the cross beam and signifies the ultimate goal toward which everything is oriented. . . . Its depth is found in the part that is fixed into the ground, for there it is both concealed and invisible. And yet, from there all the parts of the cross spring up and are seen and experienced by us. In the same way, all that is good in us springs from the depths of God's grace. . . . But even though the cross of Christ signified no more than what was said by the apostle, "And they who are Jesus Christ's have crucified the flesh with the passions and lusts,"[15] how great a good it is! . . . And finally, as everyone knows, what else is the sign of Christ but the cross of Christ? For unless that sign is applied, whether on the foreheads of believers, or to the very water out of which they are regenerated, or to the oil of chrism or to the sacrament that nourishes them, none of these is profitable for life. How then can it be that no good is signified by what is done by the wicked? Tractates on the Gospel of John 118.5.[16]

[13]NPNF 1 14:317-18*. [14]Eph 3:18. [15]Gal 5:24. [16]NPNF 1 7:431-32**.

19:25-27 Jesus Cares for His Mother

[25]So the soldiers did this. But standing by the cross of Jesus were his mother, and his mother's sister, Mary the wife of Clopas, and Mary Magdalene. [26]When Jesus saw his mother, and the disciple whom he loved standing near, he said to his mother, "Woman, behold, your son!" [27]Then he said to the disciple, "Behold, your mother!" And from that hour the disciple took her to his own home.

Overview: While the soldiers divide up Jesus' last remaining possession, his only concern is for the care of his mother (Chrysostom). John is the only Evangelist who tells us of Mary's presence at her son's cross (Ambrose). Part of her must have wondered why he hurried to the cross, though, when it meant he would be leaving her to suffer (Romanus). But the storm that must have overtaken her soul at that moment had been prophesied by Simeon years earlier (Basil). While the apostles had fled (Chrysostom), she was there with Mary the mother of

James the less (JEROME) and the wife of Clopas, who was Joseph's brother (EUSEBIUS). Mary Magdalene is there as well, along with the other women (AUGUSTINE).

Jesus honors the beloved disciple by entrusting the virgin mother into the virgin disciple's care and protection that, as Jesus' mother, she would need (CHRYSOSTOM, BEDE). Since Christ lives in John, even as he lives in us, Jesus is in effect presenting himself to Mary when he tells her to behold John "your son" (ORIGEN). In caring for his earthly mother here, the hour that had not yet come at Cana when Jesus spoke with Mary has now arrived, and the earlier harsh treatment he had given her at Cana gives way to affection and love (GREGORY THE GREAT). He provides her, to a certain degree, a son in place of himself (AUGUSTINE) and also honors the fourth commandment in ensuring her care (CYRIL). And so, John took Mary into the house of his parents near Mount Olivet (THE PASSING OF MARY) or later to Ephesus, according to allusions in the Council of Ephesus.[1] John renounced the wealth and rank he enjoyed in his association with the high priest in order to serve his Lord and his Lord's mother (JEROME).

19:25 *Jesus' Mother at the Cross of Her Son*

JESUS' ACTIONS CONTRASTED WITH THE SOLDIERS'. CHRYSOSTOM: The soldiers did these things to him, but while on the cross, he commits his mother to the disciple, teaching us to show every care for our parents even to our last breath. When indeed she unseasonably troubled him, he said, "Woman, what have I to do with you?"[2] and "Who is my mother?"[3] But here he shows how much he loves his mother and commits her to the disciple whom he loved. HOMILIES ON THE GOSPEL OF JOHN 85.2.[4]

ONLY JOHN INCLUDES MARY'S PRESENCE. AMBROSE: Mary, the mother of the Lord, stood by her Son's cross. No one has taught me this but the holy Evangelist John. Others have related how the earth was shaken at the Lord's passion, the sky was covered with darkness, the sun withdrew itself[5] and how the thief was, after a faithful confession, received into paradise.[6] John tells us what the others have not told, how the Lord while fixed on the cross called to his mother. He thought it was more important that, victorious over his sufferings, Jesus gave her the offices of piety than that he gave her a heavenly kingdom. For if it is the mark of religion to grant pardon to the thief, it is a mark of much greater piety that a mother is honored with such affection by her Son. "Behold," he says, "your son."... "Behold your mother." Christ testified from the cross and divided the offices of piety between the mother and the disciple....

Nor was Mary below what was becoming the mother of Christ. When the apostles fled, she stood at the cross and with pious eyes beheld her Son's wounds. For she did not look to the death of her offspring but to the salvation of the world. Or perhaps, because that "royal hall"[7] knew that the redemption of the world would be through the death of her Son, she thought that by her death she also might add something to that universal gift. But Jesus did not need a helper for the redemption of all, who saved all without a helper.[8] This is why he says, "I am counted among those who go down to the pit. I am like those who have no help."[9] He received indeed the affection of his mother but sought not another's help. Imitate her, holy mothers, who in her only dearly beloved Son set forth so great an example of maternal virtue. For neither have you sweeter children, nor did the Virgin seek the consolation of being able to bear another son.[10] LETTER 63.109-11.[11]

---

[1]See footnote on *The Passing of Mary* in quote below. [2]See Jn 2:4. [3]Mt 12:48. [4]NPNF 1 14:318**. [5]Mt 27:45. [6]Lk 23:43. [7]A favorite expression of Ambrose emphasizing Mary as the bearer of the divine king. [8]Ambrose here seems to speak against the idea of Mary as co-redeemer with Christ that developed within later Marian piety. For further discussion, see Paula Bowes, "Mary and the Early Christian Fathers," *Epiphany* 4.4 (summer 1984):45-55. [9]Ps 88:4-5 (87:5-6 LXX). [10]See note 23 on perpetual virginity under Jn 19:27. [11]NPNF 2 10:472-73**.

Mary Questions Her Son's Haste to the Cross. Romanus Melodus:

The lamb, beholding her lamb advancing to the slaughter,
Followed Him wearily with the other women, saying,
"Where dost Thou go, O my son?
Is there another wedding in Cana,
And dost Thou hasten there to turn water into wine?
Shall I go with Thee, my child, or shall I wait for Thee?
Give me word, O Word, some word, and do not pass me by in silence,
O Thou who hast kept me pure,
My son and my God. . . .

"Thou dost advance, my child, to an unjust death,
And no one suffers with Thee. Peter does not accompany Thee—he who said to Thee,
'I shall never deny Thee, even if I die.'[12]
Thomas has left Thee—he who said: 'Let us all die with Him.'[13]
And again the others, well-known and intimate friends,
Destined to judge the tribes of Israel, where are they now?
No one of all of them is here. But the One above all,
Thou, alone, O Son art to die in return for all whom Thou hast gratified,
My son and my God." . . .

[Jesus replies] "Bear up for a short time, O Mother, and thou shall shalt see
How, like a physician, I strip and come where they lie dead
And cure their wounds,
Cutting their callousness and hardness with the spear;
And I take the vinegar and use it as an astringent on the wound;
And when I have opened up the cut with the surgical lancet of the nails, I shall use my cloak as dressing,
Using my cross as remedy,
I use it, O Mother, so that thou mayest sing with understanding:[14]
'He has redeemed suffering by suffering,
My son and my God.'

"Lay aside thy grief, Mother,
And advance with joy; for I now hasten to that for which I came,
To do the will of Him who sent me;
For, from the first this was ordained for me by my Father,
And it was not displeasing to my spirit
That I should assume human form and suffer for the fallen.
Then, O Mother, hastening, tell all people
That by suffering He strikes down the one who hates Adam
And, having conquered, He comes,
My son and my God."

Kontakion on Mary at the Cross 19.1, 3, 13-14.[15]

Mary's Apprehension About the Inevitable. Basil the Great: Simeon . . . prophesies about Mary herself, that when standing by the cross and seeing what is being done and hearing the voices, after the witness of Gabriel, after her secret knowledge of the divine conception, after the great exhibition of miracles, she shall feel about her soul a mighty tempest. The Lord was bound to taste of death for every human being—to become a propitiation for the world and to justify all people by his own blood. Letters 260.9.[16]

The Women Remain As the Disciples Flee. Chrysostom: The women stood by the cross [as the disciples fled], and the weaker appeared the stronger. From that point, everything was entirely transformed. Homilies on the Gospel of John 85.2.[17]

---

[12]Mt 26:35; Mk 14:31. [13]Jn 11:16. [14]Ps 47:7 (46:8 lxx). [15]*KRBM* 1:196-97, 201-2. [16]NPNF 2 8:299. [17]NPNF 1 14:318**.

IS MARY, WIFE OF CLOPAS, JAMES'S MOTHER? JEROME: The Mary who is described as the mother of James the less was the wife of Alphaeus and sister of Mary the Lord's mother, the one who is called by John the Evangelist "Mary of Clopas," whether after her father or family or for some other reason. But if you think they are two persons because elsewhere we read, "Mary the mother of James the less," and here, "Mary of Clopas," you have still to learn that it is customary in Scripture for the same individual to bear different names. THE PERPETUAL VIRGINITY OF MARY 15.[18]

TRADITION'S IDENTIFICATION OF CLOPAS. EUSEBIUS OF CAESAREA: Hegesippus relates that Clopas was the brother of Joseph. ECCLESIASTICAL HISTORY 3.11.2.[19]

MARY MAGDALENE IN TWO PLACES? AUGUSTINE: If Matthew and Mark had not mentioned by name Mary Magdalene, we might have thought that there were two parties, one who stood far away and the other near.... But how can we account for the same Mary Magdalene and the other women standing far off, as Matthew and Mark say, and being near the cross, as John says? We can do so by supposing that they were within such a distance as to be within sight of our Lord and yet sufficiently far off to be out of the way of the crowd and centurion and soldiers who were immediately around him. Or we may suppose that after our Lord had commended his mother to the disciple, they retired to be out of the way of the crowd and saw what took place afterward at a distance. In this way, those Evangelists who do not mention them till after our Lord's death describe them as standing far away. That some women are mentioned by all alike, others not, makes no difference. HARMONY OF THE GOSPELS 3.21.58.[20]

19:26 *Behold Your Son*

WHAT AN HONOR! CHRYSOSTOM: Jesus teaches us to show the utmost care for our parents even to our last breath.... He commits her to the disciple whom he loved. Again, John modestly conceals himself. If he had wanted to boast, he would have also told us why he was loved since it was most likely some great and wonderful thing he had done. But why doesn't Jesus mention anything else or try to comfort him in his despondency? Because this was no time for comforting words. Besides, it was no small thing for him to be honored in such a way.... And what an honor it was that Jesus gave to the disciple! He entrusts his mother to him to take care of her now that he himself was departing. It was likely that she would need protection in her grief and because she was his mother, and so Jesus entrusted her to the beloved. HOMILIES ON THE GOSPEL OF JOHN 85.2-3.[21]

THE VIRGIN COMMENDED TO THE VIRGIN. BEDE: Beyond the others, Jesus loved the one who, being a virgin when chosen by him, remained forever a virgin. Now stories handed down say the [Christ] called [John] from his marriage ceremony when he wished to marry, and on that account he granted the more desirable sweetness of his own love to one whom he had withdrawn from fleshly pleasures. Accordingly, when [Christ] was about to die on the cross, he commended his mother to [John], so that virgin might watch over virgin, and when he himself ascended to heaven after his death and resurrection, a son would not be lacking to his mother, whose chaste life would be protected by his chaste services. HOMILIES ON THE GOSPELS 1.9.[22]

CHRIST'S GIFT OF HIMSELF IN JOHN AND US. ORIGEN: The Gospels are the firstfruits of all the Scriptures. But the firstfruits of the Gospels is the Gospel according to John whose meaning no one can understand who has not leaned on Jesus' breast or received Mary from Jesus to be his mother also. But whoever wants to become another "John" must also become such as John

[18]NPNF 2 6:341**. [19]NPNF 2 1:146*. [20]NPNF 1 6:207-8**. [21]NPNF 1 14:318**. [22]CS 110:87.

was. In other words, he must be shown to be Jesus, so to speak. For Mary had no son except Jesus (in accordance with those who hold a sound opinion of her).[23] But Jesus says to his mother, "Behold your son," and not, "Behold, this man also is your son." If this is so, then Jesus has in effect said, "Behold, this is Jesus whom you bore" [when he presents John to her]. For indeed, everyone who has been perfected "no longer lives, but Christ lives in him."[24] And, since "Christ lives" in him [i.e., John], it is said of him to Mary, "Behold your son," the Christ. Commentary on the Gospel of John 1.23.[25]

19:27 *Behold Your Mother*

Now the Hour Has Come. Gregory the Great: The virgin mother, when wine was lacking, wanted Jesus to do a miracle. She was at once answered, "Woman, what have I to do with you?" as if to say plainly, The fact that I can do a miracle comes to me from my Father, not my mother. For it was from the nature of his Father that he could do miracles but from the nature of his mother that he could die. When he was on the cross, then, in dying he acknowledged his mother whom he commended to the disciple, saying, "Behold your mother." And so, when he says, "Woman, what have I to do with you? My hour is not yet come,"[26] he is in effect saying, In the miracle, which I did not from your nature, I do not acknowledge you. When the hour of death shall come, however, I shall acknowledge you as my mother, since it is from you that I can die. Letter 10.39.[27]

A Devoted Son. Augustine: The good teacher does what he thereby reminds us ought to be done, and by his own example he instructed his disciples that care for their parents ought to be a matter of concern to pious children, as if that tree to which the members of the dying One were affixed were the very chair of office from which the Master was imparting instruction. From this salutary doctrine it was that the apostle Paul had learned what he taught in turn, when he said, "But if any does not provide for his own, and especially for those of his own house, he has denied the faith and is worse than an infidel."[28] And what are so much home concerns to anyone, as parents to children or children to parents? Of this most wholesome precept, therefore, the very Master of the saints set the example from himself, when—not as God for the handmaid whom he had created and governed but as a man for the mother of whom he had been created and whom he was now leaving behind—he provided to a certain degree another son in place of himself. Tractates on the Gospel of John 119.2.[29]

Honoring One's Parents. Cyril of Alexandria: Christ here wanted to confirm the commandment that is clearly emphasized in the Law: "Honor your father and mother that it may be well with you."[30]. . . Honoring one's parents is surely a very precious virtue. And how else would we learn the importance of that love—even when we are overwhelmed by a flood of intolerable calamities—except by this primary example that Christ offers us? It is one thing to be mindful of the holy commandments in times of peace and quietness and quite another to fulfill your duty during the storms and troubles of life. Commentary on the Gospel of John 12.[31]

A Tradition[32] About Mary Living with John. The Passing of Mary: Therefore, when

[23]The perpetual virginity of Mary was the consensus of the ancient church, although the church today has not reached such consensus. A helpful discussion between Roman Catholics and Protestants on this issue is Raymond E. Brown, *Mary in the New Testament: A Collaborative Assessment by Protestant and Roman Catholic Scholars* (Philadelphia: Fortress, 1978). See also Istvan Benko, "The Perpetual Virginity of the Mother of Jesus," *Lutheran Quarterly* 16 (May 1964):147-63. [24]See Gal 2:20. [25]FC 80:38**; SC 120:70-72. [26]Jn 2:4. [27]NPNF 2 13:48**. See also Augustine *Tractates on the Gospel of John* 119.1; *On Faith and Creed* 4.9. [28]1 Tim 5:8. [29]NPNF 1 7:432-33*. [30]Ex 20:12. [31]LF 48:634-35**. [32]*The Passing of Mary* is part of the Apocrypha of the New Testament. It is cited here to provide a glimpse of the tradition on Mary. Other tradition places Mary in Ephesus with John. This is inferred from allusions in the records of the Council of Ephesus in 431, where a church is dedicated to Mary and we see Marian piety especially strong in Ephesus.

the Lord and Savior Jesus Christ was hanging on the tree fastened by the nails of the cross for the life of the whole world, he saw about the cross his mother standing, and John the Evangelist, whom he peculiarly loved above the rest of the apostles because he alone of them was a virgin in the body. He gave him, therefore, the charge of holy Mary, saying to him, "Behold your mother!" And he said to her, "Behold your son!" From that hour the holy mother of God remained especially in the care of John, as long as she lived. And when the apostles had divided the world by lot for preaching, she settled in the house of his parents near Mount Olivet. The Passing of Mary 1.[33]

John Renounced Wealth and Rank to Serve. Jerome: For we judge people's virtue not by their sex but by their character, and we hold those to be worthy of the highest glory who have renounced both rank and wealth. It was for this reason that Jesus loved the Evangelist John more than the other disciples. For John was of noble birth and known to the high priest, yet he was so little intimidated by the plotting of the Jews that he introduced Peter into his court[34] and was the only one of the apostles bold enough to take his stand before the cross. For it was he who took the Savior's parent to his own home. It was the virgin son[35] who received the virgin mother as a legacy from the Lord. Letter 127.5.[36]

[33]ANF 8:595**. [34]See Jn 18:15-16. [35]Tertullian goes so far as to call him a "voluntary celibate" (*On Monogamy* 17). [36]NPNF 2 6:255**. See also *Against Jovinianus* 1.26.

19:28-30 The Death of Jesus

[28]After this Jesus, knowing that all was now finished, said (to fulfil the scripture), "I thirst." [29]A bowl full of vinegar stood there; so they put a sponge full of the vinegar on hyssop and held it to his mouth. [30]When Jesus had received the vinegar, he said, "It is finished"; and he bowed his head and gave up his spirit.

Overview: Although Jesus is suffering in agony, this seems not to affect his enemies (Chrysostom). Just as he thirsted for the faith of the Samaritan woman at the well, so he thirsts here at the cross for those who have rejected him (Augustine). The fact of his physical thirst proves his humanity (John of Damascus). But the one who changed water into wine—all he is given for his thirst is vinegar. He who is sweetness and desire destroys its bitter taste (Gregory of Nazianzus). The wine that turned sour indicated the abrupt change that would soon occur in Jesus' circumstances (Dionysius). Jesus asks for fruit of the vine, which he had planted in Israel, but receives only a sponge filled with the vinegar (Cyril of Jerusalem) of unfaithfulness (Augustine). Having tasted the wine of his vineyard that had gone sour, he proclaims his work finished, that is, that the Scriptures are fulfilled (Leo) and sins are forgiven (Cyril of Jerusalem).

Jesus lays down his life showing that he was God (Augustine). Death had only the power that had been given to it (Hilary). It was not long before he had completed everything he had been waiting to complete (Augustine). He freely gave up his spirit then. He did not wait for death to take him; rather, he freely received death (Eusebius). But no one should think that it was a death in appearance only (Adamantius). It is simply that he gave up his spirit rather than his spirit being taken away against his will (Augustine). He went to sleep "like a lion," in full control of his death (Augustine). The good Shepherd does indeed lay down his life for the sheep (Peter Chrysologus).

19:28 *I Thirst*

Jesus' Suffering Has No Effect on Enemies. Chrysostom: "I thirst." Jesus here again fulfills a prophecy.[1] But consider, I ask you, the cursed nature of the bystanders. Though we have ten thousand enemies and have suffered intolerable things at their hands, yet when we see them perishing, we relent. But these people made no such peace with Jesus, nor were they tamed by what they saw. In fact, they became more savage and increased their mockery. They brought to him vinegar on a sponge, as one would bring it to someone condemned, and they gave it to him to drink. It is also on this account [of the prophecy] that the hyssop is added. Homilies on the Gospel of John 85.3.[2]

Jesus Thirsted for Their Faith. Augustine: The Samaritan woman at the well found the Lord thirsting, and by him thirsting, she was filled. She first found him thirsting in order that he might drink from her faith. And when he was on the cross, he said, "I thirst," although they did not give him that for which he was thirsting. For he was thirsting for them. Explanation of Psalm 62.5.[3]

By Christ's Humility, We Are Cleansed. Augustine: Jesus said, "I thirst," as if he were saying, There is one thing still you have failed to do, that is, to give me what you are. For the Jews were themselves the vinegar, degenerated as they were from the wine of the patriarchs and prophets and filled like a full vessel with the wickedness of this world, with hearts like a sponge, deceitful in the formation of its cavernous and tortuous recesses. But the hyssop, on which they placed the sponge filled with vinegar, being a lowly herb and purging the heart, we rightly take for the humility of Christ himself. This humility is what they enclosed and imagined that they had completely ensnared. And so we have it said in the psalm, "You shall purge me with hyssop, and I shall be cleansed."[4] For it is by Christ's humility that we are cleansed because, if he had not humbled himself and became obedient unto the death of the cross,[5] his blood certainly would not have been shed for the remission of sins or, in other words, for our cleansing. Tractates on the Gospel of John 119.4.[6]

Jesus Thirsted As Man. John of Damascus: If, on the one hand it was as God that Jesus suffered thirst and when he had tasted would not drink, surely he must be subject to passion[7] also as God. For thirst and taste are passions.[8] But if it was not as God but altogether as man that he was thirsty, similarly as man he must be endowed with will. Orthodox Faith 3.14.[9]

19:29 *Vinegar on a Branch of Hyssop*

Humiliation of the Exalted One. Gregory of Nazianzus: He is given vinegar to drink mingled with gall. Who? He who turned water into wine,[10] the destroyer of the bitter taste who is sweetness and altogether desire. On the Son, Theological Oration 3(29).20.[11]

Wine Turned Sour Indicates Changed Circumstances. Dionysius of Alexandria: The sour wine perhaps signified the sharp turn and change that happened to Jesus—freedom from suffering instead of suffering, immortality

[1]See Ps 69:21 (68:22 LXX); 22:15 (21:16 LXX). [2]NPNF 1 14:318-19**. [3]NPNF 1 8:253-54. [4]Ps 51:7 (50:9 LXX). [5]Phil 2:8. [6]NPNF 1 7:433-34**. [7]Gk *empathēs*. [8]Gk *pathos*. [9]NPNF 2 9:59**. [10]Jn 2:1-11. [11]NPNF 2 7:309.

instead of death, incorruption instead of corruption, judging instead of being judged, reigning as king instead of suffering from tyranny. For the sponge, as I think, signified the entire and complete infusion of the Holy Spirit that was in him. The reed implied the royal scepter and the divine law. The hyssop showed his living and saving resurrection through which he restored us also to health. FRAGMENT 42.[12]

THE VINE OF ISRAEL OFFERS JESUS VINEGAR. CYRIL OF JERUSALEM: Jesus says, "I thirst"—he who had brought forth water for them out of the craggy rock. Then he asked for fruit of the vine that he had planted. But what does the vine do? When the Lord was thirsty, this vine . . . having filled a sponge and put it on a reed, offers him vinegar. "They gave me also gall for my food, and in my thirst, they gave me vinegar to drink."[13] See how clear the prophet's description is. But what sort of gall did they put into my mouth? "They gave him," it says, "wine mingled with myrrh."[14] Now myrrh tastes a lot like gall, and very bitter. Are these things how you reward the Lord? Are these your offerings, O vine, for your master? The prophet Isaiah was right when in times past he wailed, "My beloved had a vineyard in a hill in a fruitful place . . . and I waited for it to bring forth grapes." I thirsted, and it should have given me wine "but sprouted thorns instead."[15] CATECHETICAL LECTURES 13.29.[16]

THE VINEGAR OF FAITHLESSNESS. AUGUSTINE: When he said, "I thirst," he was looking for faith from his own people. But because "he came to his own possessions, but his own people did not receive him,"[17] instead of the sweetness of faith, they gave him the vinegar of faithlessness—and that in a sponge! They are indeed comparable to a sponge, a thing not solid but swollen; not open with straight access of confession but hollow with the tortuous twists and turns of treachery. It is true that that drink also contained hyssop, which is a lowly herb, said to have an extremely strong root with which to cling to the rock. There were some, that is to say, among that people, for whom this dark deed was kept as a means of humbling their souls by their repudiation of it later on and their repentance. The one who accepted the hyssop with the vinegar knew who they were. After all, as the other Evangelist bears witness, he even prayed for them when hanging on the cross. He said, "Father, forgive them, because they do not know what they are doing."[18] SERMON 218.11.[19]

19:30 *It Is Finished*

THE SCRIPTURES ARE FULFILLED. LEO THE GREAT: Having now tasted the vinegar, the produce of that vineyard that had degenerated in spite of its divine planter and had turned to the sourness of a foreign vine,[20] the Lord says, "It is finished," that is, the Scriptures are fulfilled. There is nothing more to endure from these raging people. I have endured all that I foretold I should suffer. The mysteries of weakness are completed. Let the proofs of power be produced. And so he bowed the head and yielded up his spirit and gave that body that would be raised again on the third day the rest of peaceful slumber. SERMON 55.4.[21]

SCRIPTURE FULFILLED, SINS FORGIVEN. CYRIL OF JERUSALEM: When he had drunk the wine mingled with myrrh and vinegar, he said, "It is finished." For the mystery has been fulfilled. The things that are written have been accomplished. Sins are forgiven. CATECHETICAL LECTURES 13.32.[22]

CHRIST FREELY GIVES UP HIS SPIRIT. TERTULLIAN: Nailed upon the cross, he exhibited many notable signs by which his death was distinguished from all others. By his own free will, he dismissed from him his spirit with a word, anticipating the executioner's work. APOLOGY 21.[23]

[12]*AEG* 6:79; *LDA* 240-41. [13]Ps 69:21 (68:22 LXX). [14]Mk 15:23. [15]Is 5:1, 2. [16]NPNF 2 7:90**. [17]Jn 1:11. [18]Lk 23:34. [19]*WSA* 3 6:186*. [20]See Is 5:1-5. [21]NPNF 2 12:168**. [22]NPNF 2 7:91**. [23]ANF 3:35

Death Had No Power. Hilary of Poitiers: The only-begotten God had the power of laying down his life and of taking it up again.[24] After the drought of vinegar, when he had shown that his work of human suffering was finished and in order to accomplish in himself the mystery of death, he bowed his head and gave up his spirit. If it has been granted to our mortal nature of its own will to breathe its last breath and seek rest in death—if the buffeted soul may depart without the breaking up of the body and the spirit burst forth and flee away without being as it were violated in its own home by the breaking and piercing and crushing of limbs—then fear of death might have seized the Lord of life. This is true if, that is, when he gave up the ghost and died, his death was not an exercise of his own free will. But if he died of his own will and through his own will gave back his spirit, death had no terror, because it was in his own power. On the Trinity 10.11.[25]

A Powerful Death. Augustine: Who can sleep like this when he pleases, as Jesus died when he pleased? Who is there that puts off his garment like this when he pleases, as he put off his flesh at his pleasure? Who is there who leaves like this when he pleases, as he left this life at his pleasure? How great the power, to be hoped for or dreaded, that must be his as judge, if such was the power he exhibited as a dying man! Tractates on the Gospel of John 119.6.[26]

Jesus Does Not Wait for Death. Eusebius of Caesarea: He cried out with a loud voice to the Father, "I commend my spirit" and freely departed from the body. He did not wait for death, which was lagging behind as it were in fear to come to him. Instead, he pursued it from behind and drove it on and trampled it under his feet as it was fleeing. He burst the eternal gates of death's dark realms and made a road of return back again to life for the dead bound there with the bonds of death. Proof of the Gospel 4.12.3.[27]

A Real Death, Not in Appearance Only. Adamantius (Origen): It was not in appearance only that he died. It was a true death. . . . The spirit did not expire since it was eternal and incorruptible. But there was one who had the spirit who indeed expired who, while expiring, commended the spirit to the Father. He is the one whom Joseph wrapped in the linen cloth and buried. He did not wrap up and bury a shadow but him who was nailed to the tree. Concerning Right Faith in God 4.[28]

The Spirit Does Not Leave Against Christ's Will. Augustine: The spirit is to be preferred to the body. The death of the spirit means that God has abandoned it, but the death of the body means that the spirit has abandoned it. The punishment in the death of the body lies in this, that the spirit abandons the body unwillingly because it has willingly abandoned God. Therefore, the spirit must abandon the body, even though it does not want to, because by its will it has abandoned God. Nor may it abandon the body when it wants to, unless it inflicts some form of violence on itself by which the body itself is destroyed. The spirit of the Mediator has shown how it was not any punishment for sin that brought about the death of his flesh because he did not abandon it unwillingly. Rather, the spirit left because he willed it to, and it left at the time in the manner that he wanted it to leave. For since he is so commingled with the flesh by the Word of God as to be one with it, he says, "I have the power to lay down my life, and I have the power to take it up again. No one takes it from me, but I therefore lay it down of myself, and I take it up again."[29] On the Trinity 4.13.16.[30]

He Goes to Sleep Like a Lion. Augustine: He had the authority to lay down his life, as he himself had declared. And he gave up the spirit in

[24]Jn 10:18. [25]NPNF 2 9:185*. [26]NPNF 1 7:434*. [27]POG 1:186**. [28]PG 11:1848-49; TLG 2950.001,198.7. [29]Jn 10:17-18. [30]NPNF 1 3:77**.

humility, that is, with a bowed head. He would receive it back again by rising again with a raised head. This death and bowing of the head were acts of great power, as was shown by that ancestor Jacob when he blessed Judah and said, "You have gone up lying down; you have slept like a lion."[31] By "going up" he signified his death; by "like a lion" he signified his power. SERMON 218.12.[32]

THE GOOD SHEPHERD LAYS DOWN HIS LIFE FOR HIS SHEEP. PETER CHRYSOLOGUS: But what do the sheep gain from the death of their shepherd? We can see from Christ's own death that it leaves the beloved flock a prey to wild beasts, exposed to depredation and slaughter, as indeed the apostles experienced after Jesus had laid down his life for his sheep, consenting to his own murder, and they found themselves uprooted and scattered abroad. The same story is told by the blood of martyrs shed throughout the world, the bodies of Christians thrown to wild beasts, burned at the stake or flung into rivers: all this suffering was brought about by the death of their shepherd, and his life could have prevented it.

But it is by dying that your shepherd proved his love for you. When danger threatens his sheep and he sees himself unable to protect them, he chooses to die rather than to see calamity overtake his flock. What am I saying? Could Life himself die unless he chose to? Could anyone take life from its author against his will? He himself declared, "I have power to lay down my life, and I have power to take it up again; no one takes it from me."[33] To die, therefore, was his own choice. Immortal though he was, he allowed himself to be put to death.

By allowing himself to be taken captive, he overpowered his opponent. By submitting, he overcame him. By his own execution, he penalized his enemy, and by dying he opened the door to the conquest of death for his whole flock. And so the good Shepherd lost none of his sheep when he laid down his life for them. He did not desert them but kept them safe. He did not abandon them but called them to follow him, leading them by the way of death through the lowlands of this passing world to the pastures of life. SERMON 40.[34]

[31]Gen 49:9. [32]*WSA* 3 6:186*. [33]Jn 10:18. [34]*JFC* 44; PL 52:313-14. See also Romanus Melodus *Kontakion on the Victory of the Cross*, where he records the dialogue between Hades and the serpent lamenting their defeat at the hands of the cross (TLG 2881.1: 38.1-18).

19:31-37 THE DAY OF PREPARATION AND JESUS' BODY

[31]*Since it was the day of Preparation, in order to prevent the bodies from remaining on the cross on the sabbath (for that sabbath was a high day), the Jews asked Pilate that their legs might be broken, and that they might be taken away.* [32]*So the soldiers came and broke the legs of the first, and of the other who had been crucified with him;* [33]*but when they came to Jesus and saw that he was already dead, they did not break his legs.* [34]*But one of the soldiers pierced his side with a spear, and at once there came out blood and water.* [35]*He who saw it has borne witness—his testimony is true, and he knows that he tells the truth—that you also may believe.* [36]*For these things took place*

that the scripture might be fulfilled, "Not a bone of him shall be broken." [37]*And again another scripture says, "They shall look on him whom they have pierced."*

Overview: The day of preparation received its name from the time of Israel's wanderings in the desert when, on the day before the sabbath, they prepared twice as much manna in preparation for the sabbath (Origen). But it is also the sixth day of the week when the world is created anew as Christ finishes his work on the cross, just as the work of creation was finished on the sixth day; he then rests in the tomb on the seventh day to be resurrected on the eighth day (Bede). At the time of Jesus' crucifixion, the Jews were careful in observing the sabbath, even as the most outrageous crime was being carried out against God (Cyril). In order not to revile the high Sabbath, which would soon be at hand, the soldiers would break the legs, which would hasten death (Augustine). Those who witnessed it were amazed that Jesus had already died, since those sentenced to suffer on the cross normally were tortured by a prolonged death (Augustine).

They pierced his side, which was an act of mercy (Origen), or at least expediency (Origen). Blood normally congeals (Origen), but in this case the Lord's body, though dead, poured forth life both in the sacred blood and the holy water that poured out to the world (Hippolytus), washing us in the tide of the Paschal victim sacrificed for us (Ambrosian Hymn). Christ, the rock that sustained Israel in the wilderness, is struck on the cross in order to bring forth the refreshing waters of the New Testament (Origen). Just as Moses began his ministry with blood and water, so Jesus ends his ministry in the same way as he experiences the second baptism of martyrdom (Cyril of Jerusalem). Christ's earlier prophecy concerning the living streams that would pour forth from his belly[1] are here fulfilled (Rufinus) as his earthly ministry begins and ends with water (Jerome). The cross opens up baptism through Christ's opened side so that it becomes the mother of life in place of Eve who came from the side of Adam (Jacob).

Noah was commanded to make a door in the side of the ark to save the animals, prefiguring the door opened from Christ's side, which brought salvation (Augustine). And, just as Eve came from the rib of Adam, so the church was born from the side of Christ (Ephrem) through the water and blood that poured forth in the mysteries of baptism and Eucharist (Chrysostom). John seems to intimate that the blood and water were not seen by all, but he insists that his testimony is true (Theodore).

Because Jesus' side was pierced, there was no need to break his bones, thus rendering him a perfect sacrificial lamb as prophesied by Moses (Augustine, Chrysostom). "Pierced," which is found in the Hebrew text of Zechariah (Jerome), along with the Septuagint's "insulted," both capture the essence of what was done to Christ (Augustine). In either case, when Christ comes again for judgment, everyone, whether Jew or Gentile, will recognize him for who he is (Apostolic Constitutions, Theodoret). The prophecy of the pierced Christ can also be traced back to Genesis 49 and the prophecy of the hamstrung bull who voluntarily submits to death (Hippolytus).

19:31 *The Day of Preparation and Removal of Bodies*

Israel Gathered Double the Manna. Origen: What do they [i.e., the Jews] take it to mean when it says, "For six consecutive days you shall gather. On the sixth day, however, you shall gather double"?[2] It appears that that day that is placed before the sabbath is called the sixth day, which we call the Day of Preparation.[3] Homilies on Exodus 7.5.[4]

[1]See Jn 7:37-38. [2]See Ex 16:26, 5. [3]Lat *Parasceve*. [4]FC 71:307-8; GCS 29(6):211.

The Sixth Day of Creation and the Day of Preparation. Bede: *Parasceve* is interpreted as preparation. . . . They called it this as the day when it was necessary that they prepare for the sabbath according to the command they had received concerning the manna, "On the sixth day you shall gather double, etc." . . . Therefore, because it was on the sixth day that human beings were made and the whole creation of the world completed, but on the seventh day it was required that he rested from his work and this is the sabbath, that is, rest—so it is only right to call that the day on which our Lord was crucified the sixth day fulfilling the reparation of humanity back to what it was at the beginning. [And we read], "And when he received the strong drink, he said 'It is finished,'" that is, the work of the sixth day is perfect as I have totally accomplished the restoration of the world. But on the sabbath he rests in the sepulcher awaiting the event of the resurrection, which will occur on the eight day. Exposition on the Gospel of Luke 6.23.54.[5]

A Gross Misinterpretation of the Law. Cyril of Alexandria: The Jews strained out the gnat while they swallowed the camel.[6] They completely discounted the most outrageous and awful of all crimes against God, while they exercised the greatest diligence with reference to the most paltry and insignificant matters, showing their folly in either case. Commentary on the Gospel of John 12.[7]

Broken Legs Hastened Death. Augustine: [The breaking of the legs] was not so that their legs might be taken away. Rather, their legs were broken in order to bring about their death, which then allowed for them to be detached from the tree. Otherwise, their continuing to hang on the crosses would defile the great festal day by the horrible spectacle of their day-long torments. Tractates on the Gospel of John 120.1.[8]

19:32-33 *Legs of Criminals Broken, but Not of Jesus*[9]

Jesus Was Already Dead. Augustine: The Gospel declares those who were present especially marveled at this, that after the lament in which he expressed the figure of sin, he immediately gave up his spirit. For those who were suspended on the cross were tortured by a lingering death. Consequently, the legs of the thieves were broken, in order that they might quickly die and be taken down from the cross before the sabbath. But that he was found to be dead was a cause for amazement. And we read that Pilate also wondered at this when the body of the Lord was asked of him for burial.[10] On the Trinity 4.13.16.[11]

19:34 *Blood and Water from Pierced Side*

Piercing As an Act of Mercy. Origen: Pilate sought to gratify the whole people who had said, "Crucify, crucify him." He also feared a riot among the people and so did not give orders (according to the usual practice of the Romans with those who are crucified) for Jesus to be stabbed under his armpits. This is sometimes done by those who condemn people guilty of greater crimes, because greater suffering is endured by those who are not stabbed after crucifixion who end up living in very great torment sometimes even the whole night and still the whole day after. Jesus therefore, since he had not been stabbed and was expected to hang a long time on the cross and endure greater torments, prayed to the Father and was heard. Immediately on crying to the Father, he was taken. Or, as one who had the power to lay down his life, he laid it down when he wanted to. Commentary on Matthew 140.[12]

Mercy or Expediency? Origen: John also makes clear that some such thing took place at the time of Christ's condemnation and that Pilate

[5]CCL 120:409. [6]See Mt 23:24. [7]LF 48:644*. [8]NPNF 1 7:434**. [9]See also comments on Jn 19:36. [10]See Mk 15:43-44. [11]FC 45:151. [12]*AEG* 6:94-95*; GCS 38 2(11):290.

did not order the practice to be observed by Christ's body being stabbed. He writes that they asked Pilate for their legs to be broken and that they then be taken away. But why would it have been necessary to ask for this if it would have been done according to custom? The Jews then pitied after their cruel condemnation those who they thought were still living in fearful torment. They broke the legs of the first and likewise the second. But Jesus had no need of their intercession with Pilate. Therefore coming to Jesus, and since he was already dead, they did not break his legs. Or, perhaps the Jews did not do this out of mercy but primarily because of the sabbath so that the bodies might not remain on the cross on the Sabbath, since that sabbath day was a high day. Commentary on Matthew 140.[13]

Blood Normally Congeals. Origen: Celsus asks whether the blood in the body of the crucified Jesus was the same as that which flows in the bodies of the immortal gods.[14] He asks in jest, but we shall show that it was no mythic or Homeric blood that flowed from the body of Jesus. . . .With other dead bodies the blood congeals and pure water does not flow. But in the case of Jesus' dead body, the miraculous feature was that both blood and water flowed forth from his side. Against Celsus 2.36.[15]

From This Dead Body Comes Life. Hippolytus: The Lord's body furnished both sacred blood and holy water to the world. . . . This body, clinically dead, still has a great power of life in it. For what [normally] does not flow from dead bodies flowed from this one, that is, blood and water. This happened so that we might know the great power for life possessed by the power that inhabited this body that, even while dead, was able to pour forth to us the causes of life. Fragment on the Two Robbers 1-2.[16]

The Tide from His Pierced Side. Ambrosian Hymn Writer:

At the Lamb's high feast we sing
Praise to our victorious King,
Who has washed us in the tide
Flowing from his pierced side.

Praise we him whose love divine
Gives the guests his blood for wine,
Gives his body for the feast,
Love the victim, love the priest.

Where the Paschal blood is poured,
Death's dark angel sheathes his sword;
Israel's hosts triumphant go
Through the wave that drowns the foe.

Christ, the Lamb whose blood was shed,
Paschal victim, Paschal bread;
With sincerity and love
Eat we manna from above.

Mighty victim from the sky,
Powers of hell beneath you lie;
Death is conquered in the fight;
You have brought us life and light.
Alleluia!

Easter Hymn, At the Lamb's High Feast 1-5.[17]

Striking Christ the Rock. Origen: If there is anyone who, when he reads Moses, murmurs against him, and the Law which has been written according to the letter is displeasing to him because it seems incoherent in many things, Moses shows him the rock which is Christ and leads him to it that he may drink from it and quench his thirst. But this rock will not give water unless it has been struck, but when it has been struck it brings forth streams.[18] For after Christ had been struck and crucified, he brought forth the streams of the New Testament. This is why it was said of him, "I will the strike the shepherd and the sheep will be scattered."[19] He had to be struck, therefore, for unless he had been struck and unless "water

[13] *AEG* 6:95*; GCS 38 2(11):291-92. [14] *Iliad* 5.340. [15] ANF 4:446**; SC 132:372. [16] AEG 6:96**; GCS 1 2:211. [17] *HBM* 144-45*. [18] See Jn 7:37. [19] See Zech 13:7.

and blood had gone out from his side," we all would suffer "thirst for the word of God."[20] This, therefore, is what the Apostle also understood when he said, "They all ate the same spiritual food and drank the same spiritual drink. For they drank of the spiritual rock which followed, but the rock was Christ."[21] Homilies on Exodus 11.2.[22]

Martyrs' Baptism and Jesus' Side. Cyril of Jerusalem: The beginning of signs under Moses was blood and water. And the last of all Jesus' signs was the same. First, Moses changed the river into blood. And Jesus at the last gave forth from his side water with blood.... In the Gospels, the power of saving baptism happens in two ways: one is granted through water to the illuminated, a second is granted to holy martyrs in persecutions through their own blood. Since this is so, blood and water[23] came out of that saving Side to confirm the grace of the confession made for Christ, whether in baptism or martyrdom. Catechetical Lectures 13.21.[24]

Streams of Living Water. Rufinus of Aquileia: It is written that when the side of Jesus was pierced, "he poured out blood and water." This has a mystical meaning. For Jesus himself had said, "Out of his belly shall flow rivers of living water."[25] Commentary on the Apostles' Creed 23.[26]

The Cross Opens Baptism. Jacob of Sarug: Christ came and opened up baptism by his cross, so that it should be a mother of life for the world in place of Eve, water and blood for the fashioning of spiritual infants flowed forth from it, and baptism became the mother of life. No previous baptism [i.e., of Moses or of John] ever gave the Holy Spirit. Only the baptism that was opened by the Son of God on the cross did so. It gives birth to children spiritually with the "water and the blood," and, instead of a soul, the Holy Spirit is breathed into them. Homily on Three Baptisms.[27]

The Door of the Ark Is Opened. Augustine: The Evangelist has expressed himself cautiously. He does not say "struck" or "wounded" but "opened his side." Here was opened the gate of life from which the sacraments of the church flowed without which we cannot enter into that life that is the true life: "And there came out blood and water." That blood was shed for the remission of sins. That water tempers the cup of salvation. This was prefigured when Noah was commanded to make a door in the side of the ark by which the animals that were not to perish by the deluge entered. These animals prefigured the church. To foreshadow this, the woman was made out of the side of the sleeping man. For this second Adam bowed his head and slept on the cross, so that out of that which came, there might be formed a wife for him. Tractates on the Gospel of John 120.2.[28]

The Bride from Adam's Rib and Christ's Side. Ephrem the Syrian: "There came forth blood and water," which is his church, and it is built on him, just as [in the case of] Adam, whose wife was taken from his side.[29] Adam's rib is his wife, and the blood of our Lord is his church. From Adam's rib there was death, but from our Lord's rib, life. The olive tree [symbolizes] the mystery of Christ, from which spring forth milk, water and oil; milk for the children, water for the youths and oil for the sick. The olive tree gave water and blood through its death, [just as] the Messiah gave these through his death.[30] Commentary on Tatian's Diatessaron 20.11.[31]

The Beginning of the Sacraments. Chrysostom: Yet the soldiers, in order to gratify the Jews, pierced his side with a spear and now insulted the dead body. O abominable and accursed purpose! Yet, beloved, do not be confused

[20]See Amos 8:11. [21]1 Cor 10:3-4. [22]FC 71:356-57. [23]See also Cyril of Jerusalem *Catechetical Lecture* 3.10. Origen also speaks of this martyr baptism in his *Homily on the Book of Judges* 7.2 and *On the Gospel of Matthew* 16.6. [24]NPNF 2 7:88**. See also Tertullian *On Modesty* 22; *On Baptism* 16; Jerome *Letter* 69.6; *Commentary on the Apostles' Creed* 23. [25]Jn 7:38. [26]NPNF 2 3:552*. [27]OrChrAn 197:212*. [28]NPNF 1 7:434-35**. [29]See Gen 2:21-22. [30]See Mt 3:1-12. [31]*ECTD* 323*.

or despondent. What these men did from a wicked will fought on the side of the truth, since there was a prophecy that spoke concerning this very circumstance: "They shall look on him whom they pierced."[32] And not only this, but this deed would become evidence to confirm the faith of those who should afterward disbelieve, as it was for Thomas and those like him. With this too an ineffable mystery was accomplished. For "there came forth water and blood." Not without purpose or by chance did those fountains spring forth. Rather, it is because the church consists of these two together. And those who have been initiated know this, being regenerated indeed by water and nourished by the blood and the flesh. And so, the mysteries take their beginning. In this way, when you approach that awesome cup, you may so approach as though you were drinking from his very side. Homilies on the Gospel of John 85.3.[33]

Eucharistic Mixture. Clement of Alexandria: The sacred vine produced the prophetic cluster. This was a sign to them, after they had been trained from wandering to [find] their rest. The sacred vine represented the great cluster of the Word, bruised for us. For the blood of the grape—that is, the Word—desired to be mixed with water, as his blood is mingled with salvation. And the blood of the Lord is twofold. For there is the blood of his flesh, by which we are redeemed from corruption. And there is the spiritual blood, that by which we are anointed. And to drink the blood of Jesus is to become a partaker of the Lord's immortality with the Spirit as the enervating principle of the Word, as blood is of flesh. Accordingly, as wine is blended with water, so is the Spirit with humankind. And the one, the mixture of wine and water, nourishes the faith; while the other, the Spirit, brings us to immortality. And the mixture of both, of the water and of the Word, is called Eucharist, renowned and glorious grace. And they who by faith partake of it are sanctified both in body and soul. For the Father's will has mystically compounded the divine mixture, man, by the Spirit and the Word. For in truth, the spirit is joined to the soul, which is inspired by it. And the flesh, by reason of which the Word became flesh, is joined to the Word. Christ the Educator 2.2.[34]

The Blood of the Grape Flows. Theodoret of Cyr: When the soldiers pierced the Savior's side with the lance, what flowed out of it according to the Gospel writers? Blood and water. He called the Savior's blood, therefore, the blood of a grape. For if the Lord was called a vine, and if the fruit of the vine is called wine, and if springs of blood and water poured from the Lord's side and ran over the rest of his body to the ground, then the patriarch's prophecy was reasonable and appropriate: "He will wash his robe in wine and his garment in blood of the grape."[35] For just as we call the sacramental fruit of the vine the Lord's blood after the consecration, so he called the blood of the true vine blood of the grape. Dialogue 1.[36]

19:35 *Evangelist As Witness*

John the Only Witness of Blood and Water? Theodore of Mopsuestia: The Evangelist alludes to himself, because he always talks about himself without mentioning his name. From this it is clear that John was present at these events. It seems also that he wants to suggest the emission of blood and water did not occur so that everybody might see it but that it remained invisible to many. Indeed, he points out this by saying, "He who saw this has testified," and he means that he only saw and testified to this event. But he was worthy to be believed about this, even though he said that he only saw and testified. Therefore he also recalled the words of Scripture. Indeed, those events happened just like they had been written. So the death of our Lord happened in this manner. Commentary on John 7.19.35.[37]

[32]Zech 12:10. [33]NPNF 1 14:319**. See also Theodore and Cyril, *loc cit.* [34]ANF 2:242-43**. [35]Gen 49:11. [36]FC 106:46. [37]CSCO 4 3:338.

19:36 *Prophecy of No Broken Bones*

No Broken Bones with a Passover Lamb. Augustine: In the Passover a lamb is killed, representing Christ of whom it is said in the Gospel, "Behold the Lamb of God, who takes away the sin of the world!"[38] In the Passover the bones of the lamb were not to be broken. And on the cross the bones of the Lord were not broken. The Evangelist, in reference to this, quotes the words "a bone of him shall not be broken."[39] The posts were marked with blood to keep away destruction, as people are marked on their foreheads with the sign of the Lord's passion for their salvation. Reply to Faustus the Manichaean 12.30.[40]

John Enlists Moses' Testimony. Chrysostom: For even if this was said with reference to the lamb of the Jews, still it was for the sake of the reality that the type preceded and was fulfilled in this event. On this account the Evangelist brought forward the prophet. For John would have cast doubt on himself if he continually produced only himself as a witness. Therefore, he brings Moses to help him and says that this did not happen without purpose but was written about long ago. And this is the meaning of the words "a bone of him shall not be broken."[41] Again he confirms the prophet's words by his own witness. These things, he says, I have told you so that you might learn the close relationship between the type and its reality. He goes to great lengths to create faith in what might otherwise be a matter of reproach and shame. . . . Let no one then be unbelieving, [John is saying], or through shame do injury to our cause. For the things that appear to be most shameful are the very venerable records[42] of our good things. Homilies on the Gospel of John 85.3.[43]

19:37 *Prophecy of the Pierced Body*

Comparing Hebrew, Greek and Latin Texts. Jerome: Look at this instance from Zechariah where the Evangelist John quotes from the Hebrew, "They shall look on him whom they pierced." We read in the Septuagint, "And they shall look on me because they have mocked me." In the Latin version, we read, "And they shall look on me for the things that they have mocked or insulted." Here the Evangelist, the Septuagint and our own version[44] all differ. And yet, the divergence of language is atoned for by oneness of spirit. Letter 57.7.[45]

"Insult" and "Pierced" Are Both Apt Descriptions. Augustine: Certainly the words that the Septuagint has translated, "They shall look on me because they insulted me," stand in the Hebrew, "They shall look on me whom they pierced."[46] And by this word the crucifixion of Christ is certainly more plainly indicated. But the Septuagint translators preferred to allude to the insult that was involved in his whole passion. For in point of fact they insulted him both when he was arrested and when he was bound, when he was judged, when he was mocked by the robe they put on him and the homage they did on bended knee, when he was crowned with thorns and struck with a rod on the head, when he bore his cross and when at last he hung upon the tree. And therefore we recognize more fully the Lord's passion when we do not confine ourselves to one interpretation but combine both and read both "insulted" and "pierced." When, therefore, we read in the prophetical books that God is to come to do judgment at the last, from the mere mention of the judgment, and although there is nothing else to determine the meaning, we must gather that Christ is meant. For though the Father will

[38]Jn 1:29. [39]Num 9:12. [40]NPNF 1 4:193**. A less satisfactory answer as to why there were no broken bones is given by Lactantius *Divine Institutes* 4.26: "lest his body, being injured and broken, should be rendered unsuitable for rising again. But see also Origen *Commentary on the Gospel of John* 10.94, which anticipates Augustine's interpretation. [41]See Ex 12:46; Num 9:12. [42]Gk *semnologēmata*. [43]NPNF 1 14:319**. [44]The Italic, for the Vulgate, which was not then published, accurately represents the Hebrew. [45]NPNF 2 6:115**. [46]See the Vulgate.

judge, he will judge by the coming of the Son. For he himself, by his own manifested presence, "judges no one but has committed all judgment to the Son."[47] For as the Son was judged as a man, he shall also judge in human form. City of God 20.30.[48]

Seeing Jesus at the Judgment. Apostolic Constitutions: Jesus will come at the consummation of the world with power and great glory to judge the living and the dead and to reward every one according to his works. And then shall they see the beloved Son of God whom they pierced, and when they know him, they shall mourn for themselves tribe by tribe. Constitutions of the Holy Apostles 5.19.[49]

Two Audiences at Christ's Second Coming. Theodoret of Cyr: He promised to come again. And so, he will be seen both by those who have believed and those who have crucified, for it is written, "They shall look on him whom they pierced." Letter 151.[50]

Christ the Hamstrung Bull. Hippolytus: "In their anger they killed men, in their passion they hamstrung a bull."[51] This he says regarding the conspiracy into which they were to enter against the Lord. . . . By the "strong bull" he means Christ whom "they hamstrung," since, when he was suspended on the tree, they pierced through his sinews. Again, "in their anger they hamstrung a bull." And mark the appropriateness of the expression when it says, "They killed men, and hamstrung a bull." For they killed the saints, and they remain dead, awaiting the time of the resurrection. But as a young bull, so to speak, when hamstrung, sinks down to the ground, such was Christ in submitting voluntarily to the death of the flesh. But he was not overcome by death. But though as man he became one of the dead, he remained alive in the nature of divinity. For Christ is the bull—an animal, above all, strong and sleek and devoted to sacred use. And the Son is Lord of all power, who did not sin but rather offered himself for us, a savor of a sweet smell to his God and Father. Fragment on Genesis 49.6.[52]

[47]Jn 5:22. [48]NPNF 1 2:450*. [49]ANF 7:448**. Constitutions of the Holy Apostles 5.20, according to Greek source. [50]NPNF 2 3:331**. See also *Dialogues* (NPNF 2 3:200). [51]Gen 49:6. [52]ANF 5:164**. ANF provides incorrect referencing.

19:38-42 The Burial of Jesus

[38]After this Joseph of Arimathea, who was a disciple of Jesus, but secretly, for fear of the Jews, asked Pilate that he might take away the body of Jesus, and Pilate gave him leave. So he came and took away his body. [39]Nicodemus also, who had at first come to him by night, came bringing a mixture of myrrh and aloes, about a hundred pounds' weight. [40]They took the body of Jesus, and bound it in linen cloths with the spices, as is the burial custom of the Jews. [41]Now in the place where he was crucified there was a garden, and in the garden a new tomb where no one had ever been laid. [42]So because of the Jewish day of Preparation, as the tomb was close at hand, they laid Jesus there.

Overview: The outstretched arms of Jesus remain so on the cross till evening, just as Moses' arms remained outstretched at the crossing of the Red Sea until all were safely across (Justin). Jesus is taken down from the cross by the pious and worthy Joseph of Arimathea (Tertullian, Bede) and Nicodemus (Augustine). Joseph means "increased" while Nicodemus is a combination of "victory" and "people," both of which are fitting descriptions of Christ's work (Augustine). Notice that it is Nicodemus, who seems to have been a repeat visitor to Jesus after his first encounter (Augustine), and Joseph of Arimathea who bury Jesus, rather than one of the twelve (Chrysostom). Notice also how the Evangelist ensures the reader understands what happened to the body of Christ, lest anyone think that either the soul or the Godhead was buried (Theodoret) in the tomb that Isaiah prophesied would be a glorious resting place (Jerome).

John speaks of wrapping Jesus' body in linen cloths as opposed to a single cloth (Augustine), which has since become a custom of the church at the Eucharist of consecrating the Lord's body not on silk or gold cloth but a clean linen cloth (Bede). If we seek to be buried with Christ, we must leave all that is unclean behind us as we enter the new tomb clothed in the clean linen cloth of righteousness (Origen). Christ was, so to speak, a new dead man buried in a new clean tomb, his burial to new life thus parallel to his pure and virgin birth (Origen). The new tomb, in other words, is like a new womb awaiting the new life contained in it (Jerome, Augustine). Christ earnestly desired that his burial should be confessed no less than his resurrection, since the veracity of the two is intimately connected (Chrysostom). Jesus' burial in a garden hearkens back to what took place in the garden in Genesis (Cyril of Jerusalem). The true vine is planted in the garden (Cyril of Jerusalem), and we are planted with him when we are buried with Christ in baptism even as we shall also rise with him (Origen).

19:38 *After the Crucifixion, Joseph Asks for Jesus' Body*

Jesus and Moses. Justin Martyr: For, it was not without design that the prophet Moses, when Hur and Aaron upheld his hands, remained in this form until evening. For, indeed, the Lord remained upon the tree almost until evening, and they buried him that evening. Then on the third day he rose again. Dialogue with Trypho 97.[1]

Joseph Rewarded for His Piety. Tertullian: Surely Joseph knew that what he handled with full respect[2] was a body. This is that Joseph who had not consented with the Jews in their crime, the blessed man who did not enter the counsel of the ungodly or stand in the way of sinners, nor did he sit in the seat of mockers.[3] It was right for him who buried the Lord to have been a subject of prophecy and now to be deservedly blessed. Against Marcion 4.42-43.[4]

Joseph Ideally Suited to Bury Jesus. Bede: It was providentially ordered that he should be rich, in order that he might have access to the governor, and righteous, in order that he might merit the charge of our Lord's body. Exposition on the Gospel of Mark 4.15.[5]

Body Language. Theodoret of Cyr: Observe how often mention is made of the body. See how often the Evangelist shows that it was the body that was nailed to the cross, the body begged by Joseph of Pilate, the body taken down from the tree, the body wrapped in linen clothes with the myrrh and aloes, and then the name of the person given to it. And Jesus is said to have been laid in a tomb. Thus the angel said, "Come see the place where the Lord lay,"[6] naming the part by the name of the whole. And we constantly do just the same. In this place, we say, such a person was buried; not the body of such a person. Every one in

[1]ANF 1:247**. [2]Or, piety. [3]Ps 1:1. [4]ANF 3:421**. [5]CCL 120:637-38. [6]Mt 28:6.

his senses knows that we are speaking of the body, and such a mode of speech is customary in divine Scripture. Dialogue 2.[7]

19:39 *Nicodemus Brings Spices for Burial*

Nicodemus a Repeat Visitor. Augustine: For Nicodemus had at first come to Jesus by night, as recorded by this same John in the earlier portions of his Gospel.[8] By the statement given us here, therefore, we are to understand that Nicodemus came to Jesus, not only then, but he might that he was a regular visitor afterward in order, by hearing, to become a disciple. Tractates on the Gospel of John 120.4.[9]

The Meaning of Joseph and Nicodemus. Augustine: Joseph and Nicodemus buried him. As some people have explained their names, Joseph means "increased." Because Nicodemus is a Greek name, many will know that it is a compound of "victory" and "people," since *nikos* means "victory" and *demos* means "people." So, who was increased by dying if not the one who said, "If the grain of wheat does not die, it remains alone. But if it dies, it is multiplied"?[10] And who by his very dying won a victory over the people who were persecuting him, if not the one who by his rising will sit in judgment on them? Sermon 218.15.[11]

Jesus Receives a Burial Befitting Him. Chrysostom: Not one of the Twelve, but perhaps one of the seventy—for now, deeming that the anger of the Jews was quenched by the cross—approached without fear and took charge of his funeral. Joseph therefore came and asked the favor from Pilate, which he granted. And why should he not? Nicodemus also assists him and furnishes a costly burial. For they were still disposed to think of him as a mere man. And they brought those spices whose special nature is to preserve the body for a long time and not allow it quickly to yield to corruption, which was an act of people imagining nothing great respecting him. Nonetheless, they exhibited very loving affection. But how is it that not one of the Twelve came, neither John, nor Peter nor any other of the more distinguished disciples? Nor does the writer conceal this point. If anyone says that it was from fear of the Jews, these men also were occupied by the same fear. For Joseph too was, it says, "A secret [disciple] for fear of the Jews." And no one can say that Joseph acted this way because he now had no fear of their power. Rather, he came despite his fear. But John, who was present and had seen him expire, did nothing of the kind. It seems to me that Joseph was a man of high rank (as is clear from the funeral) and known to Pilate, which is why he obtained the favor. And then he buried him, not as a criminal, but magnificently after the Jewish fashion, as some great and admirable person. Homilies on the Gospel of John 85.3.[12]

Prophecy of Tomb. Jerome: Long before this sepulcher was hewn out by Joseph, its glory was foretold in Isaiah's prediction, "His rest shall be glorious,"[13] meaning that the place of the Lord's burial should be held in universal honor. Letter 46.5.[14]

19:40 *Jesus' Body Wrapped in Linen Cloths*

John Speaks of More Than One Linen. Augustine: For those Evangelists who have left Nicodemus unnoticed have not affirmed that the Lord was buried by Joseph alone, although he is the only one introduced into their records. Neither does the fact that these three are all at one in informing us how the Lord was wrapped in the linen cloth by Joseph, preclude us from entertaining the idea that other linens may have been brought by Nicodemus and added to what was given by Joseph. So John may be perfectly correct in his narrative, especially as what he tells us is that the Lord was wrapped not in a linen cloth

[7]NPNF 2 3:227**. [8]Jn 3:1-2. [9]NPNF 1 7:435*. [10]Jn 12:24. [11]*WSA* 3 6:187*. [12]NPNF 1 14:320**. [13]Is 11:10. [14]NPNF 2 6:62*.

but in linen clothes.[15] At the same time, when we take into account the handkerchief that was used for the head and the bandages with which the whole body was wrapped, and consider that all these were made of linen, we can see how, even though there was really but a single linen cloth [of the kind referred to by the first three Evangelists] there, it could still have been stated with the most perfect truth that "they wound him in linen clothes." For the phrase "linen clothes" is one applied generally to all textures made of flax. HARMONY OF THE GOSPELS 3.23.60.[16]

LINEN CLOTH USED IN THE EUCHARIST. BEDE: It has come down as the custom of the church of consecrating the Lord's body not on silk or gold cloth but in a clean linen cloth. EXPOSITION ON THE GOSPEL OF MARK 4.15.[17]

A CLEAN LINEN CLOTH, A CLEAN LIFE. ORIGEN: If you still live to sin, you cannot be buried with Jesus or laid in his new tomb because your old self still lives and cannot walk in newness of life. Therefore the Holy Spirit was careful to hand down through the Scriptures that it was a new sepulcher in which Jesus was buried and that he was wrapped in a clean linen cloth. He did this so that everyone who wants to be buried with Jesus by baptism might know that nothing of the old state should be brought to the new tomb, nothing of uncleanness to the clean linen cloth. COMMENTARY ON THE EPISTLE TO THE ROMANS 5.8.4.[18]

19:41 *A New Tomb in the Garden*

A NEW DEAD MAN IN A NEW TOMB. ORIGEN: Observe whether the harmony of the three Evangelists here is not fitted to make an impression: for they have thought it right to describe the tomb as one that was "quarried or hewn out of the rock." Whoever examines the words of the narrative will see something worthy of consideration, both in them and in the newness of the tomb—a point mentioned by Matthew[19] and John—and in the statement of Luke[20] and John, that no one had ever been interred there before. For it became him, who was unlike other dead people (but who even in death manifested signs of life in the water and the blood) and who was, so to speak, a new dead man, to be laid in a new and clean tomb, in order that, as his birth was purer than any other (because he was born not in the way of ordinary generation but of a virgin), his burial also might have the purity symbolically indicated in his body being deposited in a sepulcher that was new, not built of stones gathered from various quarters and having no natural unity, but quarried and hewn out of one rock, united together in all its parts. AGAINST CELSUS 2.69.[21]

THE VIRGIN TOMB. JEROME: Christ himself is a virgin.[22] His mother is also a virgin. In fact, although she is his mother, she is still a virgin. For Jesus has entered in through the closed doors,[23] and in his sepulcher—a new one hewn out of the hardest rock—no one is laid either before him or after him. LETTER 48.21.[24]

NEW WOMB, NEW TOMB. AUGUSTINE: As in the womb of the Virgin Mary no one was conceived before him and no one after him, so in this sepulcher there was no one buried before him and no one after him. TRACTATES ON THE GOSPEL OF JOHN 120.5.[25]

TESTIFY TO THE TRUTH OF THE BURIAL. CHRYSOSTOM: It is providentially ordered that he should be placed in a new tomb where no one had been placed before, so that his resurrection might not be deemed to be that of someone else who was lying there with him. And, because the place was near, the disciples would easily be able to

[15]John uses the Greek term *othoniois*, which the Latin renders *linteis*. Augustine's discussion is not intelligible unless this variation is recognized. [16]NPNF 1 6:209**. [17]CCL 120:638 [18]FC 103:355**; AGBL 33:424. [19]See Mt 27:60. [20]Lk 23:53. [21]ANF 4:459**; SC 132:448-50. [22]See Jerome *Against Jovinianus* 1.31. [23]Jn 20:19. [24]NPNF 2 6:78**. [25]NPNF 1 7:435*.

come and be spectators of what happened. And not they alone, but also his enemies, should be witnesses of his burial. For when they placed seals on the tomb and stationed soldiers to watch it, these were the actions of people testifying to the burial. For Christ earnestly desired that this burial should be confessed no less than the resurrection. This is also why the disciples are very earnest about showing that he died. For all succeeding ages would confirm the resurrection. But Jesus' death, if at that time it had been partially concealed or not made entirely evident, would be likely to harm the account of the resurrection. Nor was it for these reasons only that he was laid nearby, but also that the story about the stealing might be proved false. Homilies on the Gospel of John 85.4.[26]

In Paradise the Fall, in a Garden Our Salvation. Cyril of Jerusalem: And since we have touched on things connected with paradise, I am truly astonished at the truth of the types. In Paradise was the fall, and in a garden was our salvation. From the tree came sin, and until the tree, sin lasted. In the evening, when the Lord walked in the garden, they hid themselves.[27] And in the evening the robber is brought by the Lord into paradise. Catechetical Lectures 13.19.[28]

The Vine Planted in the Garden. Cyril of Jerusalem: A garden was the place of his burial, and a vine was what was planted there, as he said, "I am the vine."[29] He was planted therefore in the earth in order that the curse that came because of Adam might be rooted out. The earth was condemned to thorns and thistles; the true Vine sprang up out of the earth, that the saying might be fulfilled, "Truth sprang up out of the earth, and righteousness looked down from heaven."[30] And what will he that is buried in the garden say? "I have gathered my myrrh with my spices"; and again, "myrrh and aloes, with all chief spices ."[31] Now these are the symbols of burial. Catechetical Lectures 14.11.[32]

19:42 *They Laid Jesus There*

Buried with Christ in Baptism. Origen: Surely if no one had as yet been laid there, men and women were afterward laid there. For this is the meaning for those who consider carefully. . . . He who said, "We have been buried with Christ through baptism and have risen with him,"[33] has himself been after Christ buried together with Christ in a new and spiritual tomb hewn in the rock. It is the same for all who have been buried together with Christ in baptism so that they may rise with him from the new tomb of the Firstborn from the dead who holds the preeminence in all things. Commentary on Matthew 143.[34]

[26]NPNF 1 14:320**. [27]Gen 3:8. [28]NPNF 2 7:87*. [29]See Jn 15:1. [30]Ps 85:11 (84:12 LXX). [31]Song 5:1; 4:14. [32]NPNF 2 7:96-97**. [33]Rom 6:4. [34]AEG 6:101*; GCS 38 2 (11):296-97.

20:1-9 THE EMPTY TOMB

[1]Now on the first day of the week Mary Magdalene came to the tomb early, while it was still dark, and saw that the stone had been taken away from the tomb. [2]So she ran, and went to Simon Peter and the other disciple, the one whom Jesus loved, and said to them, "They have taken the Lord out of the tomb, and we do not know where they have laid him." [3]Peter then came out with

the other disciple, and they went toward the tomb. [4]*They both ran, but the other disciple outran Peter and reached the tomb first;* [5]*and stooping to look in, he saw the linen cloths lying there, but he did not go in.* [6]*Then Simon Peter came, following him, and went into the tomb; he saw the linen cloths lying,* [7]*and the napkin, which had been on his head, not lying with the linen cloths but rolled up in a place by itself.* [8]*Then the other disciple, who reached the tomb first, also went in, and he saw and believed;* [9]*for as yet they did not know the scripture, that he must rise from the dead.*

Overview: Our Lord was delivered from the womb of the tomb early on the first day of the week on what is now known as the Lord's day (Augustine, Chrysostom), a day of victory and triumph over death (Hesychius). The exact time of when the resurrection occurred is not given (Dionysius), although "early dawn" and "late night" would seem to indicate around the same time, albeit from different starting points (Theodore, Cyril). The text says "it was dark," which is also an apt description of Mary's faith when she first came to the tomb, ignorant of Jesus' resurrection (Gregory the Great). The women, who demonstrate more faith than the disciples, perhaps send Mary to the tomb on their behalf (Romanus). Mary comes looking for consolation (Chrysostom) and may have also been accompanied later by the other women, although these women are not included in John's account (Augustine). John records that Mary is the first witness, showing his high regard for her and for women (Chrysostom) as he captures the ardor of her faith (Augustine, Cyril). He tells us that Mary reported what she had witnessed only to the chief apostles, who believed, while Luke records the initial skepticism of the other disciples (Eusebius). The Gospel next records how Peter and John came to the tomb in broad daylight so that no one could suspect them of having stolen the body of Jesus, as the chief priests had alleged (Eusebius). We too should hurry to the tomb as they did (Gregory of Nazianzus).

The disciples looked in the tomb, noting the neatness of the folded linens, which would not have been the case had someone stolen the body (Chrysostom, Eusebius). When John looked into the tomb, it is said that he believed. It is unclear from the text what it is John believed, however. Did he simply believe Mary's words, that is, that they had taken the body away (Augustine)? Or, did John infer from the neatly folded linen cloths and the prophecies he knew, that Jesus had indeed risen from the dead (Cyril)?

20:1 *Early on the First Day of the Week*

The Lord's Day. Augustine: The first of the week[1] is what Christian practice now calls the Lord's day, because of the resurrection of the Lord. Tractates on the Gospel of John 120.6.[2]

The Womb and the Tomb. Chrysostom: How can I recount for you these hidden realities or proclaim what goes beyond any word or concept? How can I lay open before you the mystery of the Lord's resurrection, the saving sign of his cross and of his three days' death? For each and every event that happened to our Savior is an outward sign of the mystery of our redemption. Just as Christ was born from his mother's inviolate virginal womb, so too he rose again from the closed tomb. As he, the only-begotten Son of God was made the firstborn of his mother, so, by his resurrection, he became the firstborn from the dead. His birth did not break the seal of his mother's virginal integrity. Nor did his rising from the dead break the seals on the sepulcher. And so, just as I cannot fully express his birth in words, neither can I wholly encompass

[1]Lat *una Sabbati*. [2]NPNF 1 7:435.

his going forth from the tomb. Homily on Holy Saturday 10.[3]

The Womb of the Earth Gives Birth. Hesychius of Jerusalem: Hidden first in a womb of flesh, he sanctified human birth by his own birth. Hidden afterward in the womb of the earth, he gave life to the dead by his resurrection. Suffering, pain and sighs have now fled away. For who has known the mind of God, or who has been his counselor if not the Word made flesh who was nailed to the cross, who rose from the dead and who was taken up into heaven? This day brings a message of joy: it is the day of the Lord's resurrection when, with himself, he raised up the race of Adam. Born for the sake of human beings, he rose from the dead with them. On this day paradise is opened by the risen one, Adam is restored to life and Eve is consoled. On this day the divine call is heard, the kingdom is prepared, we are saved and Christ is adored. On this day, when he had trampled death under foot, made the tyrant a prisoner and despoiled the underworld, Christ ascended into heaven as a king in victory, as a ruler in glory, as an invincible charioteer. He said to the Father, "Here am I, O God, with the children you have given me." And he heard the Father's reply, "Sit at my right hand until I make your enemies your footstool."[4] To him be glory, now and for ever, through endless ages. Amen. Easter Homily 5-6.[5]

No Exact Time Recorded of When Jesus Arose. Dionysius of Alexandria: No very exact account seems to be offered in the Scriptures of the hour at which Jesus rose. For the Evangelists have given different descriptions of the parties who came to the sepulcher one after another, and all have declared that they found the Lord risen already. It was "in the end of the sabbath," as Matthew has said.[6] It was "early, when it was yet dark," as John writes. It was "very early in the morning," as Luke puts it. And it was "very early in the morning, at the rising of the sun," as Mark tells us. And so, no one has shown us clearly the exact time when he rose. It is admitted, however, that those who came to the sepulcher in the end of the sabbath found him no longer lying in it, as it began to dawn toward the first day of the week. And let us not suppose that the Evangelists disagree or contradict each other. But even though there may seem to be some small difficulty as to the subject of our inquiry, if they all agree that the light of the world, our Lord, rose on that one night, while they differ with respect to the hour, we may well seek with wise and faithful mind to harmonize their statements. Fragment 5.1.[7]

In Hebraic Thought, Day Begins with Night. Theodore of Mopsuestia: It seems to those who dissent that here also the words of the Evangelists do not agree with one another. On the contrary, it seems to me that on the basis of their accounts their words are perfectly consistent. . . . Indeed, John says, "Early . . . while it was dark." The word *early* is not referred here to the morning. In fact, he does not say while it was "still" dark, which should have been said with regard to morning. But he wrote, "while it was dark," that is, on the next day when the night began, by designating with the term *early* the entire day so that he might say the day after the sabbath. The holy Scripture usually defines both day and night with the word *day*, because the sun, after its course throughout the night and the day, makes the beginning of the next day by returning to its place in the west. And this is confirmed by Moses, who says, "And there was evening and there was morning, the first day,"[8] which he also says about the second and third days, and all the rest. . . . John says, "Early on the first day of the week," indicating the next day, that is, "on the first day of the week, when it was dark," in order to signify that when the night began, the women came, in order

[3]*JFA* 54*; PG 88:1860-61. PG offers an alternate attribution of this work to Gregory of Antioch. See *EEC* 1:363. [4]Ps 110:1 (109:1 LXX). [5]*JFA* 56-57*; SC 187:66-68. [6]Mt 28:1. [7]ANF 6:94-95*. [8]Gen 1:5.

to perform the proper honor according to customs. Commentary on John 7.20.1.[9]

The Evangelists Agree It Was the Dead of Night. Cyril of Alexandria: No one, I suppose, will imagine that the inspired writers disagree or that they fix the time of the resurrection differently. But anyone who chooses to investigate the meaning of the indications they give of the time will find that their accounts add up. For early dawn and late night fix the same point of time, that is, the very dead of night, so to say. There is, therefore, no discrepancy between them. For the one, taking as his starting point the end of night, and the other the beginning, both reach the middle watch and meet at the same point, that is, as I just now said, the dead of night. Commentary on the Gospel of John 12.[10]

Darkened Faith. Gregory the Great: Mary Magdalene came to the sepulcher when it was still dark. We note the hour historically, but we who seek understanding must find what is mystically intended. Mary was looking for the creator of all things in the tomb whom she had seen physically dead in the sepulcher. Because she did not find any trace of him, she believed that he had been stolen away. Truly it was still dark when she came to the sepulcher. Forty Gospel Homilies 22.[11]

Mary Goes to the Tomb on Behalf of the Women. Romanus Melodus:

To the Sun before sun who had then sunk in the tomb[12]
The young women bearing incense hastened toward the dawn,
As though seeking day, and saying to one another,
"O friends, come let us anoint with spices
The body, life-bringing and buried,
The flesh which resurrects the fallen Adam which lies here in the tomb.
Let us go, let us hasten like the Magi,
And let us kneel down and bring with us
The spices as gifts—not to Him in swaddling clothes
But to Him wrapped in a shroud;
And let us weep and cry out: 'O Master, arise,
Thou who dost offer resurrection to the fallen.' "

When the holy women were saying these things to each other,
They considered another idea, which is full of wisdom,
And they said to one another: "Women, why are we self-deceived?
For surely the Lord is not in the tomb!
Up until now, would it have held in subjection
One who controls the breath of living beings?
Would He still be a buried corpse? . . .
Let Mary leave and go see the tomb
And let us act in conformity with what she says,
For most certainly, as He foretold, the Immortal One has arisen,
He who offers resurrection to the fallen."

The wise women, having made arrangements according to this plan,
No doubt sent forward Mary Magdalene
To the tomb, as the Theologian[13] says.
It was dark, but love lighted the way for her;
And so she saw the great stone rolled away
From the entrance of the tomb.

Kontakion on the Resurrection 29.1-3.[14]

Mary Comes Looking for Consolation. Chrysostom: For he arose while both stone and seals lay over him. But because it was necessary that others should be fully satisfied, the tomb was

[9]CSCO 4 3:340-44. See also Augustine *Harmony of the Gospels* 3.24.65 for further discussion. [10]LF 48:651**. [11]CS 123:165*. [12]Ps 72:17 (71:17 LXX). The comparison between Christ in the tomb and the setting sun occurs in the offices of Saturday of Holy Week. [13]The Theologian is John and is a reference to his Gospel. [14]*KRBM* 1:314-15. Romanus offers one solution to the Synoptic problem. See Augustine below for another.

opened after the resurrection and what had happened was confirmed. This then was what startled Mary. For being entirely full of loving affection toward her Master, when the sabbath was past, she could not bear to rest but came very early in the morning, desiring to find some consolation from the place. Homilies on the Gospel of John 85.4.[15]

All the Women Were with Mary. Augustine: It was in the early morning of the first day of the week that the women came to the sepulcher, as all the Evangelists are at one in attesting. By that time, all that is recorded by Matthew alone had already taken place, that is to say, in regard to the quaking of the earth, and the rolling away of the stone and the terror of the guards who were so frightened that they lay there like dead men. Then, as John informs us, Mary Magdalene came. She was unquestionably more ardent in her love than these other women who had ministered to the Lord. And so, it was not unreasonable in John to only mention her, leaving the other women unnamed who, however, were with her, as we gather from the reports given by other Evangelists. Harmony of the Gospels 3.24.69.[16]

20:2 *Mary's Report*

Women Favored in Mary As First Witness. Chrysostom: Do you see how she did not yet know anything clearly concerning the resurrection? Instead, she thought the body had been removed, which is what she simply tells to the disciples. And the Evangelist has not deprived the woman of such praise, nor did he think it shameful that they should have learned these things first from her who had passed the night in watching. This shows how his love of the truth is on display everywhere. Homilies on the Gospel of John 85.4.[17]

"They Have Taken My Lord." Augustine: Some of the Greek codices have, "They have taken my Lord," which may likely enough have been said by someone with a stronger than ordinary affection of love than simply that of a relationship of a handmaid. However, we have not found it in the several codices to which we have had access.[18] Tractates on the Gospel of John 120.6.[19]

Mary's Ardor of Faith. Cyril of Alexandria: This excellent and pious woman would never have endured remaining at home and leaving the sepulcher [after the burial] if she had not had respect for sabbath law and the penalty that was incurred by those who transgressed it. This fear curbed her excessive zeal, allowing ancient custom to prevail, and to withdraw her thoughts from the object of her most earnest longings for awhile. But when the sabbath was already past and the dawn of the next day was appearing, she hurried back to the spot. And then, when she saw the stone rolled away from the mouth of the tomb, well-grounded suspicions seized her mind and, calling to mind the ceaseless hatred of the Jews, she thought that Jesus had been carried away. And so she accuses them of this crime in addition to their other misdeeds. While she was thus engaged and mulling over the possibilities in her mind, the woman returned to the men who loved the Lord, anxious to obtain the cooperation of the most intimate of his disciples in her quest. And so deep-rooted and impregnable was her faith that she thought no less of Christ because of his death on the cross but even when he was dead called him Lord, as she had always done, thereby showing a truly God-loving spirit. Commentary on the Gospel of John 12.[20]

Mary's Secret and the Disciples' Examination. Eusebius of Caesarea: Question: How is it that in John the disciples hearing Mary, and then coming to the sepulcher, believed. But

[15]NPNF 1 14:320*. [16]NPNF 1 6:213**. [17]NPNF 1 14:320*. [18]Modern sources would agree with Augustine, since it remains unclear which Greek codices may have had this variant, since no textual variant is listed in Nestle Aland. Swanson ("John," 272) records the variant in MSS 037 in St. Gall, but this is a ninth-century manuscript. However, Tatian's *Diatessaron* preserves the reading "my Lord" and could have been the source. [19]NPNF 1 7:435**. [20]LF 48:650*.

in Luke it is said that "their words appeared in their sight as an idle tale and they did not believe?

Answer: Mary, in John, told what she had seen to the chief apostles Peter and John alone, as declaring some secret. And they again, unknown to the other disciples, ran to the sepulcher, saw and believed. And there was nothing strange in the chief apostles having seen and believed while the rest to whom the women reported, not having received with their own eyes, did not believe them. Indeed, when the Savior appeared to the assembled disciples themselves, according to John, those who saw him rejoiced. But Thomas, since he was not with them and did not see, was not persuaded. But if he disbelieved the apostles, one would scarcely blame the rest because, not having as yet beheld him, they disbelieved the women. The Scripture shows much examination and carefulness on the part of the disciples, not readily assenting to their words but at first suspending judgment until they recognized the truth fully and clearly. TO MARINUS, SUPPLEMENT 3.[21]

DID THE DISCIPLES BELIEVE MARY? EUSEBIUS OF CAESAREA: The passage may have another meaning. It may be said that the women reporting the Savior's resurrection from the message of the two men who appeared to them, according to Luke, were not believed by the Eleven, among whom were even Peter and John, who themselves had not believed. But Mary saying, according to John, "They have taken my Lord away from the tomb," was not believed by the two disciples on this very point, that is, that the Savior had been taken away, until they came to the place and found it actually so. TO MARINUS, SUPPLEMENT 3.[22]

20:3-4 *Peter and John's Race to the Tomb*

PETER AND JOHN COME IN BROAD DAYLIGHT. EUSEBIUS OF CAESAREA: Peter and John seem to come to the sepulcher in broad daylight (an opportune time). By not coming during the night and in darkness, no one can suspect them of what the chief priests falsely accused them, that is, that they came by night and stole him. Therefore the men did not come by night or while it was still dark but while it was broad daylight. But if the Gospel says that the disciples were gathered together for fear of the Jews, someone may object, "How then did those who were shut up visit the sepulcher in broad daylight?" We respond that it was natural that those who were living in the city in the midst of the Jews would be closed in, gathered together in one house. But those who came to the tomb, since they were outside the city, were far from fear of the Jews since they were going to a place deserted and empty of people. But perhaps it may also be the case that Peter and John, being above the fear of the other disciples, ventured more boldly to go out from the house while the others were too scared. In other matters it was recorded that they were considered worthy of more honor than the other apostles. TO MARINUS, SUPPLEMENT 2.[23]

ALONG WITH PETER AND JOHN. GREGORY OF NAZIANZUS:

Be a Peter or a John;
Hasten to the sepulcher,
Running together,
Running against one another,
Vying in the noble race.
And even if you are beaten in speed,
Win the victory of showing who wants it more—
Not just looking into the tomb, but going in.

ON HOLY EASTER, ORATION 45.24.[24]

20:5-7 *Detail of the Linens and Tomb*

NEATNESS OF LINENS PROVES NO THEFT. CHRYSOSTOM: When [Mary] came and said these things, the apostles heard them and drew near to the sepulcher with great eagerness. They see the linen clothes lying there, which was a sign of the

[21] *AEG* 6:119-20**; PG 22:988. [22] *AEG* 6:120**; PG 22:988-89. [23] *AEG* 6:122-23**; PG 22:988. [24] NPNF 2 7:432**.

resurrection. For if they had removed the body, they would not have stripped it first, nor, if any had stolen it, would they have taken the trouble to remove the napkin and roll it up and lay it in a place by itself apart from the linens. They would have taken the body as it was. Therefore, John tells us by anticipation that it was buried with much myrrh, which glues linen to the body not less firmly than lead. He tells us this so that when you hear that the napkin lay apart from the linens, you may not endure those who say that he was stolen. For a thief would not have been so foolish as to expend so much effort on a trifling detail. HOMILIES ON THE GOSPEL OF JOHN 85.4.[25]

PROOF NO THEFT OCCURRED. EUSEBIUS OF CAESAREA: The cloths lying within seem to me at once to furnish also a proof that the body had not been taken away by people, as Mary supposed. For no one taking away the body would leave the linens, nor would the thief ever have stayed until he had undone the linens and so be caught. And at the same time they establish the resurrection of the body from the dead. For God, who transforms the bodies of our humiliation so as to be conformed to the body of Christ's glory, changed the body as an organ[26] of the power that dwelt in it, changing it into something more divine. But he left the linen cloths as superfluous and foreign to the nature of the body. TO MARINUS, SUPPLEMENT 2.[27]

20:8-9 *What Did John Believe?*

JOHN BELIEVED MARY'S REPORT. AUGUSTINE: Here some, by not giving due attention, suppose that John believed that Jesus had risen again.[28] But there is no indication of this from the words that follow. For what does he mean by immediately adding, "For as yet they knew not the Scripture, that he must rise again from the dead"? He could not then have believed that Jesus had risen again when he did not know that he had to rise again. What then did he see? What was it that he believed? It was nothing else but this, that is, that he saw the sepulcher empty and believed what the woman had said, that is, that Jesus had been taken away from the tomb. "For as yet they knew not the Scripture, that he must rise again from the dead." In the same way also, when they heard of it from the Lord himself—although uttered in the plainest of terms—yet from their custom of hearing him speaking by parables they did not understand and believed that he meant something else. TRACTATES ON THE GOSPEL OF JOHN 120.9.[29]

PETER AND JOHN TESTIFY TO THE RESURRECTION. CYRIL OF ALEXANDRIA: When these men (I mean Peter and John, the writer of this book, for he gives himself the name of the other disciple) heard this news from the woman's mouth, they ran with all the speed they could and hurried to the sepulcher. They saw the marvel with their own eyes, being in themselves competent to testify to the event, for they were two in number as the Law enjoined.[30] As yet they did not meet Christ risen from the dead, but they infer his resurrection from the bundle of linen clothes, and from that time on they believed that he had burst the bonds of death, as holy Scripture had long ago proclaimed that he would do. When, therefore, they looked at the issues of events in the light of the prophecies that turned out true, their faith was from that time forward rooted on a firm foundation. COMMENTARY ON THE GOSPEL OF JOHN 12.[31]

---

[25]NPNF 1 14:320-21*. [26]Gk *organon*. [27]*AEG* 6:122; PG 22:985-88. [28]See Cyril's comments below where he says John believed in the resurrection. Chrysostom affirms this as well. [29]NPNF 1 7:436**. [30]See Deut 19:15. [31]LF 48:650-51*.

20:10-16 Jesus Appears to Mary Magdalene

[10]*Then the disciples went back to their homes.*

[11]*But Mary stood weeping outside the tomb, and as she wept she stooped to look into the tomb;* [12]*and she saw two angels in white, sitting where the body of Jesus had lain, one at the head and one at the feet.* [13]*They said to her, "Woman, why are you weeping?" She said to them, "Because they have taken away my Lord, and I do not know where they have laid him."* [14]*Saying this, she turned round and saw Jesus standing, but she did not know that it was Jesus.* [15]*Jesus said to her, "Woman, why are you weeping? Whom do you seek?" Supposing him to be the gardener, she said to him, "Sir, if you have carried him away, tell me where you have laid him, and I will take him away."* [16]*Jesus said to her, "Mary." She turned and said to him in Hebrew, "Rabboni!" (which means Teacher).*

Overview: After looking inside the tomb, the disciples go home, but Mary remains (Chrysostom). By leaving, the disciples avoided unnecessary risk (Cyril), but Mary's love causes her to remain (Gregory the Great) and to take a second look into the tomb (Augustine). There were two angels inside, one at the head and the other at the foot, symbolizing the preaching of the gospel from beginning to end (Augustine) and representing the two testaments (Gregory the Great).The angels are initially silent about the resurrection (Chrysostom), but Mary's tears soon receive their reward (Cyril), and our tears too are wiped away with the promise of seeing our Lord again (Gregory the Great). Mary's love was foretold in the Song of Songs (Rufinus). Although all that remained of Jesus to human eyes was his body, Mary nonetheless refers to this body as the Lord who has been taken (Gregory of Nyssa, Augustine).

When Mary turns from the tomb, she sees Jesus but does not recognize him because he did not want his appearance to overwhelm her (Chrysostom). But her eyes were also still closed to the resurrection (Jerome), and by her doubting, she turned her back, as it were, on our Lord (Gregory the Great). But then Jesus speaks to her, spurring her longing for him even more (Gregory the Great). He gradually reveals himself to her (Theodore) so that at this point she still assumes he is the gardener, which he was in a spiritual sense, as he tended to her heart (Gregory the Great) and was indeed the Gardener of paradise (Jerome). In her reply to him, she initially uses the title Lord out of courtesy, a title that she had earlier used in a different sense (Augustine). When she does finally recognize Jesus, it is because it is the voice of her Shepherd who calls her to come and take her place among the other ninety-nine lambs (Romanus). She then calls him Rabboni, because she still seeks to learn more from her teacher at whose feet she had sat while Martha busied herself (Severus).

20:10 *The Disciples Return Home*

The Disciples Go Home, Mary Stays. Chrysostom: As a woman, Mary was full of feeling and more inclined to pity. I say this in case you might wonder how it was that Mary wept bitterly at the tomb, while Peter was in no way affected. For "the disciples," it says, "went away to their own home." But she stood shedding tears. This was because hers was a tender nature, and she as yet did not have an accurate account of the resurrection. They . . . saw the linen clothes and believed and then left for their own homes in astonishment. And why didn't they immediately go to Galilee as they were commanded to do before the passion? They waited for the others, perhaps, and besides they were yet at the height of their amazement. These then went their way, but she remained there. Homilies on the Gospel of John 86.1.[1]

The Disciples Avoid Unnecessary Risk. Cyril of Alexandria: The wise disciples, after having gathered sufficiently satisfactory evidence of the resurrection of our Savior, were unsure, as it were, what to do with their confirmed and unshaken faith. Comparing the events as they had actually occurred with the prophecies of holy Scripture, they went back home and most likely hurried to see their fellow workers to recount the miracle and afterward consider what course should be pursued. They may have also had another motive in doing what they did. For the passion of the Jews was at its height, and the rulers were thirsting eagerly for the blood of every person who marveled at the teaching of the Savior and confessed his divine and ineffable power and glory. But most of all they thirsted for the blood of the holy disciples themselves, who then had good reason for shrinking from an encounter with them. This is why they left the sepulcher before it was quite light, since they could not have done so without risk if they were seen leaving in the daytime—the sun's rays revealing them to everyone. We are far from saying that they were cowards as a reason for their cautious flight. Rather, it is more likely that the knowledge of what was expedient for them was instilled in the minds of the saints by Christ who did not permit these who were destined to be lights and teachers of the world to run unnecessary risks.[2] Commentary on the Gospel of John 12.[3]

20:11 *Mary Stays*

Why Does Mary Take a Second Look? Augustine: What then does it mean, that, as she wept, she stooped down and looked again into the sepulcher? Was it because her grief was so excessive that she hardly thought she could believe either their eyes or her own? Or was it rather by some divine impulse that her mind led her to look within? Tractates on the Gospel of John 121.1.[4]

Mary's Love Causes Her to Remain. Gregory the Great: Mary Magdalene, who had been a sinner in the city,[5] loved the Truth and so washed away with her tears the stains of wickedness.[6] Her sins had kept her cold, but afterward she burned with an irresistible love. . . . We must consider this woman's state of mind whose great force of love inflamed her. When even the disciples departed from the sepulcher, she did not depart. She looked for him whom she had not found. . . . But it is not enough for a lover to have looked once, because the force of love intensifies the effort of the search. She looked for him a first time and found nothing. She persevered in seeking, and that is why she found him. As her unfulfilled desires increased, they took possession of what they found.[7] . . . Holy desires, as I have told you before, increase by delay in their fulfillment. If delay causes them to fail, they were not desires. . . . This was Mary's kind of love as she turned a second time to the sepulcher she had already looked into. Let us see the result of her search, which had been redoubled by the power of love. Forty Gospel Homilies 25.[8]

20:12 *Two Angels in White*

From Beginning to End. Augustine: Why is it that one was sitting at the head and the other at the feet? Was it because those who in Greek are called angels are in Latin newsbearers [*nuntii*]? In this way they signified that the gospel of Christ was to be preached from head to foot, from the

[1]NPNF 1 14:323**. [2]See Phil 2:15. [3]LF 48:651-52**. [4]NPNF 1 7:436-37*. [5]Lk 7:37. [6]Gregory cites Lk 7:47. [7]Gregory cites Song 3:1-4. [8]CS 123:187-90**.

beginning even to the end? Tractates on the Gospel of John 121.1.[9]

The Two Testaments. Gregory the Great: An angel sits at the head, so to speak, when the apostles preach, "In the beginning was the Word."[10] And an angel sits at his feet when he says that "the Word was made flesh and dwelt among us."[11] We can also recognize the two testaments in the two angels, one earlier and the other later. These angels are brought together at the place of the Lord's body because, while both testaments proclaim equally the message that the Lord became a man and died and rose, the Old Testament sits at his head, so to speak, and the New Testament at his feet. Forty Gospel Homilies 25.[12]

20:13 *Mary's Sorrow at Losing Her Lord*

Angels Initially Silent About the Resurrection. Chrysostom: The angels who appear say nothing about the resurrection. But by degrees the subject is entered on. First of all they address her compassionately, to prevent her from being overpowered by a spectacle of such extraordinary brightness. And they say to her, "Woman, why are you weeping?" Homilies on the Gospel of John 86.1.[13]

No Occasion for Tears. Cyril of Alexandria: Observe that the tears shed for Christ do not lose their reward, nor is it long before love for him bears fruit. Rather, his grace and rich restitution will follow closely in the wake of pain. Notice how—as Mary was sitting there, her cheeks bedewed with mourning for her beloved Lord whom she had lost—notice how the Savior granted to her the knowledge of the mystery about him through the mouth of holy angels. They tell her to stop crying because this was no occasion for tears. She was making a subject for rejoicing a cause of grief. Why, indeed, they say, when death has been subdued, and corruption has lost its power and our Savior Christ has risen again and made a new pathway for the dead back to incorruption and to life—why would you misunderstand what is going on now? Why are you so distraught with pain when what is actually going on calls for rejoicing? You should be glad, even ecstatic! And so, why then are you crying and, in effect detracting from the honor due to what amounts to a celebration? Commentary on the Gospel of John 12.[14]

Our Tears Wiped Away Too. Gregory the Great: The very declarations of Scripture that excite our tears of love wipe away those very tears by promising us the sight of our Redeemer again. Forty Gospel Homilies 25.[15]

Mary's Love Foretold in the Song of Songs. Rufinus of Aquileia: This was foretold in the Song of Songs: "On my bed I sought the one my soul loves. I sought him in the night and did not find him."[16] Of those also who found him and held him by the feet, it is foretold, in the same book, "I will hold the one my soul loves and will not let him go."[17] Commentary on the Apostles' Creed 30.[18]

Jesus' Body Is Called Lord. Gregory of Nyssa: His body too is called "the Lord" on account of the inherent Godhead. Letter 17.[19]

Mary Calls Jesus' Inanimate Body "Her Lord." Augustine: Mary calls her Lord's inanimate body her Lord, meaning a part for the whole. It is the same as when all of us acknowledge that Jesus Christ, the only Son of God, our Lord, who of course is at once both the Word and soul and flesh, was nevertheless crucified and buried, while it was only his flesh that was laid in the sepulcher. Tractates on the Gospel of John 121.1.[20]

---

[9]NPNF 1 7:437*. [10]Jn 1:1. [11]Jn 1:14. [12]CS 123:191**. On the question of harmonizing the different Gospel accounts concerning the angels at the tomb, see Augustine *Harmony of the Gospels* 3.24.67-69. [13]NPNF 1 14:323**. [14]LF 48:653**. [15]CS 123:191**. [16]Song 3:1. [17]Song 3:4. [18]NPNF 2 3:555**. See also Cyril of Jerusalem *Catechetical Lectures* 14.12. [19]NPNF 2 5:544*. [20]NPNF 1 7:437**.

20:14 *Mary Turns but Does Not Recognize Jesus*

Jesus Does Not Want His Appearance to Overwhelm Mary. Chrysostom: But why, after speaking with the angels and not having yet heard anything from them, did Mary turn back? I think that while she was speaking, Christ suddenly appeared behind her and struck the angels with awe. And when they saw their ruler, they showed immediately by their attitude, their gaze and their movements that they saw the Lord. This is what drew the woman's attention and caused her to turn around. This is how he appeared to them, but this is not how he appeared to the woman in order not to terrify her at the first sight of him. Rather, he appears to her in a more humble and ordinary form, as is clear from her reaction, supposing that he was the gardener. It was appropriate to lead one of so lowly a mind to higher matters not all at once but gently. He therefore in turn asks her, "Woman, why are you weeping? Whom do you seek?" Homilies on the Gospel of John 86.1.[21]

Mary's Eyes Closed to the Resurrection. Jerome: Was he one person when he was not known and another when he was known? He was surely one and the same. Whether, therefore, they knew him or not depended on their sight. It did not depend on him who was seen. And yet, it did depend on him in this sense, that he held their eyes so that they might not know him. And finally, in order that you may see that the mistake that held them was not to be attributed to the Lord's body but to the fact that their eyes were closed, we are told, "Their eyes were opened, and they knew him." This is why, as long as Mary Magdalene did not recognize Jesus and sought the living among the dead, she thought he was the gardener. Afterward she recognized him, and then she called him Lord. Against John of Jerusalems 35.[22]

Still Doubting, She Turned Her Back. Gregory the Great: Mary, who was still in doubt about the Lord's resurrection, turned around to see Jesus. By this doubt she had turned her back to the face of the Lord whom she did not believe had risen. Because she loved and doubted, she saw and did not recognize him. Her love revealed him to her, and her doubt prevented her from knowing him. Forty Gospel Homilies 25.[23]

20:15 *Jesus Speaks to Mary*

Along with Mary Magdalene. Gregory of Nazianzus: Be the first to see the stone taken away, and perhaps you will see the angels and Jesus himself. Say something. Hear his voice. If he says to you, "Do not touch me,"[24] stand far away. Reverence the Word, but do not grieve because he knows those to whom he appears first. On Holy Easter, Oration 45.24.[25]

Jesus Spurs Mary's Desire Still More. Gregory the Great: Jesus says to her, "Woman, why do you weep?" He asked the reason for her sorrow to increase her longing still more, so that when he asked whom she was seeking she might feel a more fervent love for him. Forty Gospel Homilies 25.[26]

Jesus Avoids Frightening Mary. Theodore of Mopsuestia: And our Lord acted this way so that when she suddenly sees the one who she thought was beyond hope of ever seeing again because she still thought he was dead, she might not be overcome with emotion and think that he was some demonic apparition. He also wanted her first to speak to him gradually, as to a man, and after she had realized that she was speaking to a real man, she might finally understand who he was and at the same time might believe and admire the greatness of the event. Commentary on John 7.20.11-14.[27]

[21]NPNF 1 14:323**. [22]NPNF 2 6:442-43**. [23]CS 123:192**. [24]Jn 20:17. [25]NPNF 2 7:432*. [26]CS 123:192**. [27]CSCO 4 3:348.

Jesus the Spiritual Gardner. Gregory the Great: Perhaps this woman was not as mistaken as she appeared to be when she believed that Jesus was a gardener. Was he not spiritually a gardener for her when he planted the fruitful seeds of virtue in her heart by the force of his love? But why did she say to the one she saw and believed to be the gardener, when she had not yet told him whom she was seeking, "Sir, if you have taken him away"? She had not yet said who it was who made her weep from desire or mentioned him of whom she spoke. But the force of love customarily brings it about that a heart believes everyone else is aware of the one of whom it is always thinking. . . . After he had called her by the common name of "woman," he called her by her own name, as if to say, "Recognize him who recognizes you.". . . And so because Mary was called by name, she acknowledged her creator and called him at once "Rabboni," that is, "teacher." He was both the one she was outwardly seeking and the one who was teaching her inwardly to seek him. Forty Gospel Homilies 25.[28]

The Gardener of Paradise. Jerome: When Mary Magdalene had seen the Lord and thought that he was the gardener . . . she was mistaken, indeed, in her vision, but the very error had its prototype. Truly, indeed, Jesus was the gardener of his paradise, of his trees of paradise. "She thought that he was the gardener" and wanted to fall at his feet. What does the Lord say to her? "Do not touch me, for I have not yet ascended to my Father." Do not touch me. You do not deserve to touch the one you looked for in a grave. Do not touch me whom you only suppose, but do not believe, has arisen. Do not touch me, for to you I have not yet ascended to my Father. When you believe that I have ascended to my Father, then, it will be your privilege to touch me. Homily 87, On John 1:1-14.[29]

20:16 *Rabboni*

Sir and Master. Augustine: Let no one think bad of the woman because she called the gardener "sir" *(domine)* and Jesus "Master" *(magistrum)*. . . . In the first instance she was honoring a person from whom she was asking a favor. In the second she was recalling the teacher from whom she was learning to distingush the divine from the human. She called one *lord* (sir) even when she was not his servant so that through him she could come to the Lord whose [servant] she was. She used the word *lord* in one sense when she said "They have taken away my Lord," and in anoher sense when she said, "Sir [i.e., lord], if you have carried him away." Tractates on the Gospel of John 121.2.[30]

Mary Recognizes the Voice of Her Shepherd. Romanus Melodus:

He who searches the hearts and reins and watches over them,[31]
Knowing that Mary would recognize His voice;
Like a shepherd, called His crying lamb,
Saying, "Mary." She at once recognized Him and spoke:
"Surely my wonderful shepherd calls me;
In order that from this time forward He may number me among the nine and ninety lambs;[32]
For I see behind Him who calls me
The bodies of the saints, the ranks of the just,
And so, I do not say, 'Who art Thou who callest me?'
For I know clearly who He is who calls me;
It is my Teacher and my Lord,
He who offers resurrection to the fallen."

Kontakion on the Resurrection 29.10.[33]

Mary Wants to Hold to the Divine, but Also to Learn. Severus of Antioch: Some indeed say that because this woman approached him and touched him just as she had done before,

[28]CS 123:192-93**. [29]FC 57:220*. See also Jerome *Letter* 39.6. [30]NPNF 1 7:437**. [31]Ps 7:9 (7:10 LXX); Jer 11:20; 20:12. [32]Mt 18:12-14; Lk 15:4-6. [33]*KRBM* 1:318-19.

without thinking anything of it, that she did not believe that this act of resurrection was worthy of the glorious and sublime divinity. Rather [they say] she still thought the same as she did earlier, that he would be characterized by his humility and humanity as when he was with his disciples. And so when our Savior asks why she is acting this way, as if he was still earthbound, because he had not yet ascended to his Father, it is as if he said, Do not touch me with too much curiosity. . . . Perhaps indeed he also knew that every fiber of her being wanted to hold on to these divine feet with joy and emotion as a friend of God because Matthew also records others, besides Mary, who seized his feet and adored him.[34] But others say that he was raising her to a higher and more sublime way of thinking. Because [they say] when Mary approached him with more fervent desire and to ask something concerning the divine, she did so because she wanted the reason for his resurrection revealed to her and so she returned to touch him. . . . And so Jesus, as one who knows the hidden things of the heart, says to her, "Do not touch me, because I have not yet ascended to my Father." [He says this] because he had promised to his disciples, once he had ascended into heaven, that the Holy Spirit would come who would lead them to perfection by teaching and revealing to them what was hidden. . . . Then [i.e., at that time] he had said, "I still have many things to teach you but you cannot bear them now, but when the Spirit of truth comes, he will lead you into all truth."[35] This is why [now] he says, "Do not touch me," that is, do not probe, do not seek the reason for what you came to ask. Do not touch me. The time has not yet come because I have not yet ascended to the Father. But I will ascend, and when I do, the Spirit will come and teach you as he also promised to me. It is obvious that Mary, [once she recognized him], wanted to learn, because she addressed him not as "Lord" [as she had done earlier] but as "Rabboni," that is, teacher. . . . She was anxious to learn. But, as one who directs his words with understanding to teach, Jesus deflects her [question] as being inappropriate. . . . [The Gospel] testifies to this desire of Mary, the sister of Martha, to know when, instead of listening to Martha's instruction, she should remain close to Jesus, who said concerning her, "Mary has chosen the better share, which will not be taken away from her."[36] Cathedral Homilies 45.[37]

[34]Mt 28:9. [35]Jn 16:12-13. [36]Lk 10:42. [37]PO 36 (167):118-22.

20:17-18 Ascending to the Father

[17]Jesus said to her, "Do not hold me, for I have not yet ascended to the Father; but go to my brethren and say to them, I am ascending to my Father and your Father, to my God and your God." [18]Mary Magdalene went and said to the disciples, "I have seen the Lord"; and she told them that he had said these things to her.

Overview: Jesus' request to Mary to not hold on to him has been understood in various ways. There is the thought that Jesus needed purification after the battle of his passion, a purification that could only come when his resurrection was perfected by the Father (Origen). Or this was only spoken of his human nature (Theodoret). It is possible that Jesus is telling Mary that their relationship has changed because in her joy she had not perceived the change so that she might regard him now with more reverence (Chrysostom) as one might approach a king (Ephrem). This must have been said figuratively, however, since elsewhere after the resurrection he allows himself to be touched by Thomas and others; therefore he is speaking of the church (Leo). It is better not to touch Christ with the hand but rather by faith (Augustine) to touch him as God (Augustine). And so Jesus is not so much reproaching her as telling her to look beyond the human to his divinity, which he shares with the Father (Romanus).

When Jesus told Mary of his need to ascend to the Father, he was telling her the good news that the one from whom we were formerly alienated has become our Father and our God (Gregory of Nyssa). Jesus restricts Mary from touching him just as the church restricts those who are impure and lacking the Spirit from touching the divine mysteries (Cyril). He wanted to teach her and his disciples the fact of his resurrection and ascension (Theodore).

As Christ ascends into heaven, he paves the way for us (Ambrose). He is, in effect, announcing to Mary that he is the firstfruit of the resurrection with all that this means for humankind's relationship to the Father (Gregory of Nyssa). This passage also shows again the distinction between Father and Son as persons in the Godhead (Tertullian). Jesus clearly delineates his nature from ours when he speaks of "my father" and "your father" (Cyril of Jerusalem). Christ's Father is our creator (Ambrose) and his Father by nature, our Father by adoption (Cyril of Jerusalem). In his humility, Christ here ranks himself with us (John of Damascus). The two natures must, however, be distinguished if this passage is to be interpreted properly (Gregory of Nazianzus).

When Mary makes the announcement that she has seen the Lord, she is most likely accompanied by the other women who were at the tomb (Augustine). Just as a woman had previously delivered the words of the serpent that brought death, so now a woman brings the words that bring life (Gregory the Great).

20:17a *Do Not Hold Me*

Purification Needed After Battle. Origen: But after he had destroyed his enemies through his passion, the Lord, who is mighty in battle and strong,[1] required a purification that could be given to him by his Father alone. And this is why he forbids Mary to touch him. Commentary on the Gospel of John 6.287.[2]

Perfection of the Resurrection Comes with the Father. Origen: It belongs to the resurrection that one should be on the first day in the paradise of God,[3] and it belongs to the resurrection when Jesus appears and says, "Do not touch me. For I am not yet ascended to my Father," but the perfection of the resurrection was when he came to the Father. Commentary on the Gospel of John 10.245.[4]

Jesus Speaks According to Human Nature. Theodoret of Cyr: For the human being who died rises up on the third day. But when Mary strives with longing to touch his holy limbs, he objected and says to her, "Do not touch me, for I have not yet ascended to my Father; go to my brothers and tell them, 'I am ascending to my Father and your Father, my God and your God.' " God the Word, who comes from heaven and lives in the bosom of the Father, did not utter the phrase "I have not yet ascended to my Father." The Wisdom that embraces all things that exists did not say it either. This was spoken by the very human being who was formed out of all kinds of limbs, who had been raised from the dead and who after death had not yet ascended to his Father but reserved for himself the firstfruit of his passage. Dialogue 3.12.[5]

[1]Ps 24:8 (23:8 LXX). [2]SC 157:528; FC 80:246**. [3]Lk 23:43. [4]FC 80:309**; SC 157:528. [5]FC 106:225-26.

The Relationship Has Changed. Chrysostom: Some assert that she asked for spiritual grace because she had heard him say to the disciples, "If I go to the Father, 'I will ask him, and he shall give you another Comforter.' "[6] But how could she who was not present with the disciples have heard this? Besides, such an interpretation is far from the meaning here. And how should she ask such a thing when he had not yet gone to the Father? What, then, does it mean? I think that she still wanted to talk with Jesus like she used to and that in her joy she perceived nothing out of the ordinary in him, although he had become far more excellent in bodily appearance. To lead her therefore from this idea, and so that she might speak to him with more awe (for he no longer appears so familiar with the disciples either), he raises her thoughts so that she is more reverent toward him. To have said, "Do not approach me as you did before, for matters are not in the same state, nor shall I any longer be with you in the same way" would have been harsh and high-sounding. But by saying, "I am not yet ascended to the Father," it was not as painful to hear, although he was basically saying the same thing. For by saying, "I am not yet ascended," he shows that he is hurrying and pressing on. He was saying that it was not right for one about to leave for [heaven] and who would no longer converse with human beings to be looked on with the same feelings as before. Homilies on the Gospel of John 86.2.[7]

Approaching the King. Ephrem the Syrian: He said, "Do not touch me," first of all, because this body was [like] a first-flowering fruit from Sheol that our Lord, as priest, was preserving carefully from contact with any [human] hand, so as to offer it to the [only] hand capable of receiving such a gift and capable of paying the price for an offering such as this. Second, [he did not want anyone to touch him] in order to show that this body was [already] glorified and magnified. Thus he showed them that, while he had been a servant, everyone had power over him, since even tax collectors and sinners used to come and touch him. But when he was made Lord, fear of him was over everyone like [the fear of] God.[8] Even kings and nobles convince us [of this], for those who see [them] are afraid to touch them. Commentary on Tatian's Diatessaron 21.26.[9]

Mary Lacks Spiritual Understanding. Leo the Great: The Son of man and Son of God, therefore, dearly beloved, then attained a more excellent and holier fame when he returned to the glory of the Father's majesty. In an incomprehensible way, he began to be nearer to the Father in respect of his Godhead after having become distanced in respect of his manhood. A better instructed faith then began to draw closer to a conception of the Son's equality with the Father without the necessity of handling the corporeal substance in Christ. As a result of this [substance], he is less than the Father, since, while the nature of the glorified body still remained, the faith of believers was called on to touch not with the hand of flesh but with the spiritual understanding the Only Begotten, who was equal with the Father. And this is why the Lord said to Mary Magdalene (who represents the church),[10] when she hurriedly approached and touched him, "Do not touch me, for I have not yet ascended to my Father," that is, I would not have you come to me as to a human body or recognize me by fleshly perceptions. I want you to wait for higher things. I prepare greater things for you. When I have ascended to my Father, then you shall handle me more perfectly and truly, for you shall grasp what you cannot touch and believe what you cannot see. Sermon 74.4.[11]

Touch Christ by Faith. Augustine: What does this mean, "Do not touch me, for I have not yet ascended to the Father"? If she could not

[6]Jn 14:3, 16. [7]NPNF 1 14:324**. [8]The fear of God was one of the spiritual dispositions on which Syrian theologians insisted most. [9]*ECTD* 329. [10]See also Augustine *Sermon* 5.7 (*WSA* 3 1:222). [11]NPNF 2 12:188-89**.

touch him as he was standing on earth, would she be able to touch him seated in heaven? As though he was saying, "Do not touch me now; touch me then, when I have ascended to the Father." Your graces will recall yesterday's reading, when the Lord appeared to the disciples and they thought they were seeing a spirit. But wishing to relieve them of this mistaken idea, he offered himself to their touch. What did he say? It was yesterday. There was a sermon about it.[12] "Why are you troubled, and why are thoughts coming up into your hearts? See my hands and my feet; feel and see."[13] He had not already ascended to the Father, had he, when he said feel and see, offering himself to his disciples to be touched, not just touched but felt, to produce faith in the real flesh of his real body, to present the solid reality of truth even to the human touch? So he offers himself to the hands of the disciples to be felt, but he says to the woman, "Do not touch me, for I have not yet ascended to my Father." What can it mean? Could men only touch him on earth, while women had to touch him in heaven, "for I have not yet ascended to my Father"?

So what can touching be, but believing? We touch Christ, you see, by faith, and it is better not to touch him with the hand and to touch him with faith than to feel him with the hand and not touch him with faith. It was not a great matter to touch Christ; the Jews touched him when they seized him, they touched him when they bound him, touched him when they hung him up; they touched him, and by touching him in a bad way, they lost what they touched. Just you touch by faith, O Catholic church; see that you touch by faith. If you have thought of Christ only as a man, you have touched him on earth. If you have believed Christ is Lord, equal to the Father, then you have touched him when he has ascended to the Father. Sermon 246.4.[14]

Touch Me As God. Augustine:

What is "Touch me as I ascended to the Father"?
Touch me as equal to the Father.
What is "Touch me as equal to the Father"?
Touch me as God, that is believe in me as God.

Sermon 375c.4.[15]

20:17b *I Have Not Yet Ascended to the Father*

Move Beyond the Human to the Divine. Romanus Melodus:

Carried away by the warmth of her affection, and by her fervent love,
The maiden hastened and wished to seize Him,
The One who fills all creation without being confined by boundaries;
But the Creator did not find fault with her eagerness;
He lifted her to the divine when He said,
"Do not touch me; or do you consider me merely human? I am God, do not touch me.
O holy woman, lift up your eyes
And consider the heavenly spheres;
Seek me there, for I ascend
To my Father, whom I have not left;
For I share His throne, and with Him I am without time and beginning,
I who offer resurrection to the fallen."

Kontakion on the Resurrection 29.11.[16]

Formerly Estranged, We Become Children. Gregory of Nyssa: Now that the words addressed to Mary are not applicable to the Godhead of the Only Begotten, one may learn from the intention with which they were uttered. For he who humbled himself to a level with human littleness is the one who spoke these words.[17] . . . He from whom we were formerly alienated by our revolt has become our Father and our God. Accordingly in the passage cited above the Lord

[12]Here we see Augustine's interaction with his audience characteristic of many of his sermons and tractates. [13]Lk 24:38-39. [14]*WSA* 3 7:104-5. [15]*WSA* 3 10:342*. [16]*KRBM* 1:319. [17]Gregory goes on to speak of our alienation from God and how Christ took that alienation into his own body.

brings the good news of this benefit. And the words are not a proof of the degradation of the Son but the good news of our reconciliation to God. For that which has taken place in Christ's humanity is a common boon bestowed on humankind generally. For as when we see in him the weight of the body that naturally gravitates to earth ascending through the air into the heavens, we believe according to the words of the apostle that we also "shall be caught up in the clouds to meet the Lord in the air."[18] Even so, when we hear that the true God and Father has become the God and Father of our Firstfruits, we no longer doubt that the same God has become our God and Father too, inasmuch as we have learned that we shall come to the same place where Christ has entered for us as our forerunner.[19] Against Eunomius 12.1.[20]

Holy Things for the Holy Ones. Cyril of Alexandria: What is the difference if he was not yet ascended to his Father? How could this reason suffice to render it improper for those that loved him to touch his holy body? Would it not be blameworthy for anyone to imagine that the Lord shrank from the pollution of the touch and said this so that he might be pure when he ascended to the Father in heaven?[21] Would not such a person stand convicted of great foolishness and madness? For the nature of God can never be polluted. For just as the light of the sun's ray, when it strikes on a manure pile or any other earthly impurities, suffers no stain, for it remains as it is, that is, undefiled, and it partakes in no degree of the ill odor of the objects that it encounters, even so the all-holy nature of God can never admit of the blemish of defilement. Why then was Mary prevented from touching him when she drew near and yearned to do so? . . .

We say that the reasons for our Savior dwelling among us were many and diverse, but there is one overriding principle, indicated in his own words: "For I came not to call the righteous but sinners to repentance."[22] Therefore, before the saving cross and the resurrection from the dead, while as yet his providential scheme had not received its appropriate fulfillment, he mingled both with the just and the unjust, and ate with publicans and sinners and allowed any that wanted to come to him and touch his holy body so that he might sanctify all who came and call them to a knowledge of the truth and might bring back to health those who were diseased and enfeebled by the constant practice of sin.[23] . . .

At that time, by his providence, people who were still unclean and who were polluted both in mind and body were allowed without hindrance to touch the holy flesh itself of our Savior Christ and to gain every blessing from it. But after he completed the plan of our redemption, having suffered death on the cross and rising to life again, he showed that his nature was superior to death. And so, from then on, instead of granting them access, he hinders those who come to him from touching the very flesh of his holy body. In this way he gives us a type of the holy churches and the mystery concerning himself, just as also the law given by the all-wise Moses itself did when it represented the slaughter of the lamb as a figure of Christ. For "no uncircumcised person," said the Law, "shall eat thereof,"[24] meaning by uncircumcised someone who is "impure." And humanity may justly be deemed impure in its own nature. For what is the nature of a human being, as compared with God's inherent purity? We may not, therefore, while we remain uncircumcised, that is, impure, touch the holy body, but only when we have been made pure by the true circumcision of the Spirit. . . . As, therefore, the Holy Spirit had not yet been sent down to us, for he had not yet ascended to the Father, he repulses Mary as not yet having received the Spirit, saying, "Touch me not, for I am not yet ascended to the Father"; that is to say, I have not yet sent down to you the Holy Spirit. And so, the type is applicable to the churches. . . . Therefore,

[18]1 Thess 4:16. [19]See Heb 6:20. [20]NPNF 2 5:241-42*. [21]See above Origen's comment on this verse. [22]Mt 9:13. [23]See Lk 5:31; 7:37; 8:43-44, 48. [24]Ex 12:48.

also, to those who wish to partake of the blessed Eucharist, the ministers of divine mysteries say, "Holy things to the holy," teaching that participation in holy things is the due reward of those who are sanctified in the Spirit. Commentary on the Gospel of John 12.[25]

Jesus Teaches About His Resurrection and Ascension. Theodore of Mopsuestia: It is the custom of our Lord that, while his providence is preparing something, he seems to do something else according to the sense of his words. For instance, this is how he acted with the woman who suffered from hemorrhages.[26] He asked, "Who touched me?"[27] He certainly knew the answer. However he seemed to ask as if he did not know, so that the woman who had touched him might be afraid and manifest the miracle and show her faith though which, since it was adequate, she had received her healing. . . . And it is the same here as well. He first showed himself to the woman after his resurrection and was about to ascend into heaven, and by now he wanted to teach the disciples that they did not only have to believe in resurrection, because their sight testified to the reality of the facts, but also so that they might know he was not going to remain on earth after his resurrection but would also ascend into heaven to receive greater glory with his Father. Since this is so, it seems he says these things to the woman and forbids her to touch him as if she was not supposed to come into contact with his body in the same way anymore, since he was now provided with a different and much more powerful body. But this is the real meaning: Through what he said he wanted both to teach his disciples about his resurrection and his ascension. And this is evident from the fact that he showed himself again to the disciples who were in doubt, and he ordered them to touch the wounds on his body in the spots of the nails. So this is not the reason he kept the woman from coming into contact with him. And we cannot say that she was prevented because she was a woman; indeed, he allowed her to touch his feet many times. If she could not touch him because she was a woman, he would have forbidden her to do so even before. If he had forbidden the woman because his body had been transformed into a better state, he would have not allowed the disciples to confirm with their touch their faith in his resurrection. And then, if she also, by any chance, had doubted, like them, wouldn't he have allowed her to confirm her faith through the contact with him? If someone says that he did not care about the faith of this woman or her unbelief, this is quite foolish. But since he had allowed her to come to him then, is it possible that the reward that he gave her for her faith was the privation of contact with him? And does this not look hateful, especially to educated people? Therefore, with his words he revealed two things: first, that his body after the resurrection was in a stronger and more excellent condition than before and therefore was not to be exposed to any human contact; second, that he would be assumed into heaven, to be connected forever with the Father in honor. Commentary on John 7.20.17.[28]

20:17c *My Father, Your Father; My God, Your God*

Paving the Way to Heaven. Ambrose: For Christ's purpose in the incarnation was to pave for us the road to heaven. Mark how he says, "I go up to my Father and your Father, to my God and your God." On the Christian Faith 3.7.50.[29]

Jesus Announces Firstfruits of Human Nature. Gregory of Nyssa: He becomes the firstborn of the new creation of men and women in Christ by the twofold regeneration, reborn by holy baptism and by that birth that is the consequence of the resurrection from the dead. In both alike he becomes for us the Prince of life,[30] the firstfruits and the firstborn. This firstborn, then,

[25]LF 48:657-60**. [26]See Lk 8:43. [27]Lk 8:45. [28]CSCO 4 3:348-50. [29]NPNF 2 10:250*. [30]See Acts 3:15.

also has brothers. This is who he is referring to when he says to Mary, "Go and tell my brothers, I go to my Father and your Father, and to my God and your God." In these words he sums up the whole aim of his dispensation as man. For humanity rebelled against God and "served those that by nature were no gods."[31] And even though they were the children of God, they became attached to an evil father falsely so called. Therefore, the mediator between God and man,[32] having assumed the firstfruits of all human nature,[33] sends to his brothers the announcement of himself not in his divine character but in that which he shares with us. He says, "I am departing in order to make that true Father, from whom you were separated, to be your Father; and to make that true God from whom you had rebelled to be your God. And I am doing this in my own person. For by those firstfruits that I have assumed, I am in myself presenting all humanity to its God and Father."

Since, then, the firstfruits made the true God to be its God and the good Father to be its Father, the blessing is secured for human nature as a whole, and by means of the firstfruits the true God and Father becomes Father and God of all men and women. Now "if the firstfruits are holy, the lump also is holy."[34] But where the firstfruits, Christ, is—and the firstfruits is none other than Christ—there also are those who are Christ's, as the apostle says.[35] AGAINST EUNOMIUS 2.8.[36]

CHRIST IS DISTINCT FROM THE FATHER. TERTULLIAN: Now, does this mean I ascend as the Father to the Father, and as God to God? Or does it mean I ascend as the Son to the Father and as the Word to God? This is also why this Gospel, at the very end, intimates that these things were ever written ... "that you might believe that Jesus Christ is the Son of God."[37] Wherever, therefore, you take any of the statements of this Gospel and apply them to demonstrate the identity of the Father and the Son, supposing that they serve your views at that point, you are contending against the definite purpose of the Gospel. For these things certainly are not written that you may believe that Jesus Christ is the Father but the Son. AGAINST PRAXEAS 25.[38]

SONSHIP BY NATURE AND SONSHIP BY GRACE. CYRIL OF JERUSALEM: But in case anyone, from simplicity or perverse ingenuity, should suppose that Christ is but equal in honor to righteous people ... it is well to make this distinction beforehand, that the name of the Father is one, but the power of his operation is many. And Christ himself, knowing this, has spoken unerringly, "I am ascending to my Father and your Father." He does not say, "to our Father,"[39] but distinguishing and saying first what was proper to himself, "to My Father," which was by nature. Then he adds, "and your Father," which was by adoption. For however high the privilege we have received of saying in our prayers, "Our Father," who art in heaven, yet this gift is one of loving-kindness. For we call him Father, not as having been by nature begotten of our Father who is in heaven but having been transferred from servitude to sonship by the grace of the Father, through the Son and Holy Spirit. We are permitted to speak this way because of the ineffable loving-kindness [of our Father]. CATECHETICAL LECTURES 7.7.[40]

CHRIST'S FATHER BY NATURE, OUR FATHER BY ADOPTION. CYRIL OF JERUSALEM: The Father, having begotten the Son, remained the Father and is not changed. He begat Wisdom yet did not lose wisdom himself. He begat power yet did not become weak. He begat God but did not lose his own Godhead. Neither did he lose anything himself by diminution or change. He who

[31]See Gal 4:8. [32]See 1 Tim 2:5. [33]The humanity of Christ being regarded as this "firstfruits": unless this phrase is to be understood of the resurrection, rather than of the incarnation, in which case the firstfruits will be his body, and *analabōn* should be rendered by "having *resumed*." [34]Rom 11:16. The next reference following may be to Jn 12:26 or Jn 14: 3; or to Col 3:3. [35]See 1 Cor 15:23. [36]NPNF 2 5:113*. [37]Jn 20:31. [38]ANF 3:621. See also Novatian *On the Trinity* 26. [39]See also Augustine *Tractates on the Gospel of John* 121.3. [40]NPNF 2 7:45-46*. See also John of Damascus *Orthodox Faith* 4.8 and Ambrose *On the Christian Faith* 1.14.90.

was begotten does not lack anything either. Perfect is he who begat, perfect is that which was begotten: God was he who begat, God is he who was begotten; God of all himself, yet giving the Father the title as his own God. For he is not ashamed to say, "I ascend to my Father and your Father, and to my God and your God." But in case you might think that he is a Father of the Son in the same way that he is Father of creation, Christ drew a distinction in what follows. For he did not say, "I ascend to our Father," lest the creatures should be made fellows of the Only Begotten. Instead, he said, "My Father and your Father." He is in one way mine, by nature. He is, in another way, yours, by adoption. And again, "to my God and your God," in one way mine, as his true and only-begotten Son,[41] and in another way yours, as his workmanship.[42] The Son of God then is very God, ineffably begotten before all ages. Catechetical Lectures 11.18-19.[43]

Christ, in Humility, Ranks Himself with Us. John of Damascus: Of those passages which refer to the period after the resurrection, there are several which pertain to his human nature. . . . Other passages speak of Christ's dual nature, such as, "I ascend unto my Father and your Father, and my God and your God." "My God and your God," is to be understood more in an abstract way, as though he were ranking himself with us. Those passages, in general, that are sublime must be assigned to the divine nature, which is superior to passion and body. And those passages that are humble must be ascribed to the human nature. And those passages that are common must be attributed to the compound being, that is, the one Christ, who is God and man. And it should be understood that both [the human and divine] belong to one and the same Jesus Christ, our Lord. For if we know what is proper to each, and perceive that both are performed by one and the same, we shall have the true faith and shall not go astray. Orthodox Faith 4.18.[44]

Two Natures Must Be Distinguished. Gregory of Nazianzus: To give you the explanation in one sentence: You are to apply the loftier expressions to the Godhead and to that nature in him that is superior to sufferings and bodily experiences. But all that is lowly should be applied to the composite condition[45] of him who for your sakes made himself of no reputation[46] and was incarnate. On the Son, Theological Oration 3(29).18.[47]

20:18 *I Have Seen the Lord*

Mary Not Alone. Augustine: While she was going with the other women, according to Matthew, "Jesus met them and greeted them. And they came and held him by the feet and worshiped him."[48] So we gather that there were two visions of angels. We also understand that our Lord too was seen twice: once when Mary took him for the gardener and again when he met them by the way. In this way, by repeating his presence, he strengthens their faith and calms their fears. . . . And so Mary Magdalene came and told the disciples, not alone but with the other women whom Luke mentions.[49] Harmony of the Gospels 3.24.69.[50]

Sin Buried Where It Began. Gregory the Great: See how the sin of the human race was removed where it began. In paradise a woman was the cause of death for a man;[51] coming from the sepulcher a woman proclaimed life to men. Mary related the words of the one who restored her to life; Eve had related the words of the serpent who brought death. Forty Gospel Homilies 25.[52]

---

[41]Compare *Catechetical Lectures* 7.7. The expression "my God" is understood by the Fathers generally as spoken by Christ in reference to his human nature, but Cyril applies this, as well as the other expression "my Father," to the divine nature. So does Hilary *On the Trinity* 4.53; see also Epiphanius *Panarion* 69.55. [42]Eph 2:10. [43]NPNF 2 7:69*. See also Augustine *Sermon* 265F.2 (*WSA* 3 7:265); Hilary *On the Trinity* 1.33 (NPNF 2 9:49). [44]NPNF 2 9:92**. [45]Gregory often speaks of human nature as *our composite being*. Here he means the sacred humanity exclusively; there is no suspicion of Nestorianism or Eutychianism. [46]Phil 2:7. [47]NPNF 2 7:307-8**. [48]Mt 28:9. [49]Lk 24:10-11. [50]NPNF 1 6:214**. [51]Gen 3:6. [52]CS 123:195.

20:19-20 JESUS APPEARS TO HIS DISCIPLES

[19]On the evening of that day, the first day of the week, the doors being shut where the disciples were, for fear of the Jews, Jesus came and stood among them and said to them, "Peace be with you." [20]When he had said this, he showed them his hands and his side. Then the disciples were glad when they saw the Lord.

Overview: John records that it was evening, which indeed was the case for minds darkened with grief (Peter Chrysologus). But Jesus does not delay in comforting his disciples with his presence (Chrysostom). He appeared through doors that were locked, which shows the extent of the disciples' terror, their fear having caused them to lock not only their house but also their hearts (Peter Chrysologus). And yet, Christ still appears among the disciples through those locked doors, giving us a foretaste of what our resurrected bodies will be like (Augustine). He entered through those closed doors with the same body that entered through the closed door of the Virgin's womb (Gregory the Great). What happened with Christ's body after the resurrection is no more amazing than what happened in the miracles he did before the resurrection, such as walking on the water (Caesarius).

Jesus stands among them as true God (Gregory of Nyssa) with death's power banished from his body (Cyril). In his greeting of peace he breathes into them a tranquility as well as a sharing in the Holy Spirit (Maximus). The peace he gave was himself, since his presence always brings tranquility of soul (Cyril). He shows them his hands and his side, demonstrating that what has occurred is a true, bodily resurrection (Irenaeus). When Jesus showed the disciples the scars from his wounds, he proved to us all that the resurrected body is the same body that had died (Theodoret), although now glorified (Jerome). The wounds that brought us healing also heal unbelieving hearts (Leo). Jesus proved he was both human and divine after the resurrection (Leo). Jesus' earlier prophecy that no one would take their joy away[1] is now fulfilled in his presence among them (Chrysostom).

20:19a *Evening of the First Day and Locked Doors*

An Evening More by Grief Than by Time. Peter Chrysologus: It was evening more by grief than by time. It was evening for minds darkened by the somber cloud of grief and sadness because although the report of the resurrection had given the slight glimmer of twilight, nevertheless the Lord had not yet shone through with his light in all its brilliance. Sermon 84.2.[2]

Jesus Does Not Delay. Chrysostom: It was likely that when the disciples heard these things from Mary they would either not believe the woman—or if they did believe her, they would be sad that he had not considered them worthy of such a vision even though he promised to meet them in Galilee. Since this was so, he did not let a single day pass so that they might not dwell on this and become distracted. Rather, he brought them to a state of longing by their knowledge that he was risen and by what they heard from the woman. And when they were thirsting to see him and were greatly afraid (which especially made their yearning greater), he then, when it was evening, presented himself before them. And he did so in a very marvelous way. And why did he appear in the "evening"? Because that was proba-

[1]See Jn 16:22. [2]FC 110:49.

bly when they would be especially fearful. Homilies on the Gospel of John 86.2.[3]

Doors and Hearts Are Locked. Peter Chrysologus: The extent of their terror and the disquiet caused by such an atrocity had simultaneously locked the house and the hearts of the disciples[4] and had so completely prevented light from having any access that for their senses, overwhelmed more and more by grief, the murkiness of night increased and became more pervasive. No darkness of night can be compared with the gloom of grief and fear because they are incapable of being tempered by any light of either consolation or counsel. Sermon 84.2.[5]

The State of Our Resurrected Bodies. Augustine: But since you have repeatedly asked me what I thought about the resurrection of bodies and the future functions of the members in that incorruptibility and immortality, listen briefly to what could with the Lord's help be further discussed. We must hold most firmly that point on which the statement of the holy Scripture is truthful and clear, namely, that these visible and earthly bodies that are now called natural[6] will be spiritual in the resurrection of the faithful and righteous. But I do not know how the character of a spiritual body, unknown as it is to us, can be either comprehended or taught. Certainly there will be no corruption in them, and for this reason they will not then need this corruptible food that they now need. They will, nonetheless, be able to take and really consume such food, not out of need. Otherwise, the Lord would not have taken food after his resurrection. And he offered us an example of bodily resurrection so that the apostle says of him, "If the dead will not rise, neither has Christ risen."[7] When he appeared with all the members of his body and used their functions, he also displayed the places of his wounds.[8] I have always taken these as scars, not as actual wounds, and saw them as the result of his power, not of some necessity. He revealed the ease of this power, especially when he either showed himself in another form or appeared as his real self to the disciples gathered in the house when the doors were closed. Letter 95.7.[9]

Incorruptible but Touchable. Gregory the Great: The Lord's body that made its entrance to the disciples through closed doors was the same as that which issued before the eyes of people from the Virgin's closed womb at his birth. Is it surprising if he who was now going to live forever made his entrance through closed doors after his resurrection, who on his coming in order to die made his appearance from the unopened womb of a virgin? But because the faith of those who beheld it wavered concerning the body they could see, he showed them at once his hands and his side, offering them the body that he brought in through the closed doors to touch. By this action he revealed two wonderful, and according to human reason quite contradictory, things. He showed them that after his resurrection his body was both incorruptible and yet could be touched. . . . By showing us that it is incorruptible, he would urge us on toward our reward, and by offering it as touchable he would dispose us toward faith. He manifested himself as both incorruptible and touchable to show us that his body after his resurrection was of the same nature as ours but of a different sort of glory. Forty Gospel Homilies 26.[10]

Resurrection Was One More Miracle. Caesarius of Arles: You ask me and say, If he entered through closed doors, where is the bulk of his body? And I reply, If he walked on the sea, where was the weight of his body? But he [walked on the sea] as the Lord. Did he, then, because he arose, cease to be the Lord? What about the fact that he also made Peter walk upon the sea?[11] What divinity could do in the one, faith fulfilled in the other. Christ was able to do it, and Peter

[3]NPNF 1 14:324-25**. [4]See also his *Sermon* 81.2. [5]FC 110:49-50. [6]*Animalia*, cf. 1 Cor 15:44. [7]1 Cor 15:16. [8]See Lk 24:15-43; Mk 16:12-14. [9]*WSA* 2 1:419**. [10]CS 123:201. [11]Mt 14:29.

could because Christ willed it. Therefore, when you begin to examine the reasonableness of miracles by your human senses, fear that you may lose your faith. Do you not know that nothing is impossible for God? So when anyone tells you, If he entered through closed doors there was no body, answer him on the contrary, No, if he was touched there was body, and if he ate there was a body. The one thing he did by a miracle, the other by nature. Sermon 175.2.[12]

Jesus Is Truly God. Gregory of Nyssa: He did not remain in death's power. The wounds that his body had received from the iron of the nails and spear offered no impediment to his rising again. After his resurrection he showed himself whenever he wanted to his disciples. When he wished to be present with them, he was in their midst without being seen, needing no entrance through open doors. . . . All of these occurrences, and whatever other similar facts we know about his life, require no further argument to show that they are signs of deity and of a sublime and supreme power. The Great Catechism 32.[13]

Death's Power Banished from the Body. Cyril of Alexandria: By his unexpected entry through closed doors Christ proved once more that by nature he was God and also that he was none other than the one who had lived among them. By showing his wounded side and the marks of the nails, he convinced us beyond a doubt that he had raised the temple of his body, the very body that had hung on the cross. He restored that body that he had worn, destroying death's power over all flesh, for as God, he was life itself. Why would he need to show them his hands and side if, as some perversely think, he did not rise again bodily? And if the goal was not to have the disciples think about him in this way, why not appear in another form and, disdaining any likeness of the flesh, conjure up other thoughts in their minds? But he obviously thought it was that important to convince them of the resurrection of his body that, even when events would have seemed to call for him to change the mode of his body into some more ineffable and surpassing majesty, he nonetheless resolved in his providence to appear once more as he had been in the past [i.e., in the flesh] so that they might realize he was wearing no other form than the one in which he had suffered crucifixion. Our eyes could not have endured the glory of his holy body, if he had chosen to reveal it to his disciples before he ascended to the Father. Anyone who reflects on the transfiguration will easily infer this is the case. . . . since, it says, they could not endure the sight but fell on their faces.[14] Commentary on the Gospel of John 12.1.[15]

20:19b *Peace Be With You*

The Spirit Breathes Tranquility. Maximus the Confessor: Through his greeting of peace he breathes on them and bestows tranquility as well as a sharing in the Holy Spirit. Chapters on Knowledge 2.46.[16]

The Peace of Christ. Cyril of Alexandria: When Christ greeted his holy disciples with the words "peace be with you," by peace he meant himself, for Christ's presence always brings tranquility of soul. This is the grace Paul desired for believers when he wrote, "The peace of Christ which passes all understanding will guard your hearts and minds."[17] The peace of Christ which passes all understanding is in fact the Spirit of Christ, who fills those who share in him with every blessing. Commentary on the Gospel of John 12.1.[18]

20:20 *Jesus' Hands and Side and the Disciples' Rejoicing*

A True Bodily Resurrection. Irenaeus: As Christ rose in the substance of flesh and

[12]FC 47:434*. See also Jerome *Letter* 108.24 and *Against Jovinianus* 1.36. [13]NPNF 2 5:500. [14]Mt 17:6. [15]LF 48:667-68**. [16]*MCSW* 157. [17]Phil 4:7 [18]LF 48:668-69**.

pointed out to his disciples the mark of the nails and the opening in his side (now these are the tokens of that flesh that rose from the dead), so "shall he also," it is said, "raise us up by his own power."[19] What, then, are mortal bodies? Can they be souls? Not at all, for souls are incorporeal when compared with mortal bodies. . . . We must therefore conclude that it is in reference to the flesh that death is mentioned. This [flesh], after the soul's departure, becomes breathless and inanimate and is decomposed gradually into the earth from which it was taken. This, then, is what is mortal. And it is concerning this that [Paul] says, "He shall also enliven your mortal bodies."[20] Against Heresies 5.7.1.[21]

The Marks of the Nails. Theodoret of Cyr: And so the reason why the Lord stood in the midst of the disciples, even though the doors were closed,[22] after the passion but not before it, was that you might know that your body was sown as a physical body but raised as a spiritual body.[23] But in order that you might not think that what rises is something different, when Thomas did not believe in the resurrection, he shows him the marks of the nails. He shows him the scars of the wounds.[24] He who healed everybody even before the resurrection could have healed himself—especially after the resurrection, could he not? Yes, but through the marks of the nails that he shows he teaches that it is this [body], while through the closed doors by which he enters, he reveals that it is not such a [body as it was]. It was this [body], in order that he might fulfill the goal of the divine plan by raising that which had died, but it was such a body [as it was], in order that it might not lapse into corruption again and not be subject to death again. Dialogue 2.56.[25]

A Glimpse of Glorified Resurrected Bodies. Jerome: The substance of our resurrection bodies will certainly be the same as now, though of higher glory. For the Savior after his descent into hell had the same body in which he was crucified. He showed the disciples the marks of the nails in his hands and the wound in his side. Against Jovinianus 1.36.[26]

Healing Wounds of Unbelieving Hearts. Leo the Great: He offers to the doubters' eyes the marks of the cross that remained in his hands and feet and invites them to handle him with careful scrutiny. He does this because the traces of the nails and spear had been retained to heal the wounds of unbelieving hearts, so that not with wavering faith but with the most certain conviction they might comprehend that the nature that had been lain in the sepulcher was to sit on God the Father's throne. Sermon 73.3.[27]

Jesus Is Human and Divine After the Resurrection. Leo the Great: He showed the wound in his side, the marks of the nails and all the signs of his quite recent suffering, saying, "See my hands and feet, that it is I. Handle me and see that a spirit does not have flesh and bones, as you see me have,"[28] in order that the properties of his divine and human nature might be acknowledged to remain still inseparable. He also did this so that we might know the Word was not different from the flesh so that we can also confess that the one Son of God is both the Word and flesh. Letter 28.5.[29]

Jesus' Prophecy of Joy Comes True. Chrysostom: Do you see the words issuing in deeds? For what he said before the crucifixion, that "I will see you again, and your heart shall rejoice, and your joy no one will take from you,"[30] this he now accomplished in deed. But all these things led them to a most exact faith. For since they had an endless war with the Jews, he continually repeated "Peace be to you," giving them consolation to counterbalance the strife. And so this was the first word that he spoke to them after the resurrection. (Similarly Paul keeps on saying,

[19]1 Cor 6:14. [20]Rom 8:11. [21]ANF 1:532**. [22]See Jn 20:19. [23]See 1 Cor 15:44. [24]See Jn 20:27. [25]FC 106:156-57. [26]NPNF 2 6:374**. [27]NPNF 2 12:187**. [28]Lk 24:39. [29]NPNF 2 12:42**. [30]Jn 16:22.

"Grace be to you and peace."). To the women, however, he gives good news of joy, because they were in sorrow and had received this as the first curse. Therefore he gives good news to each in their own situation: to the men he gave peace because of their war; to the women he gave joy because of their sorrow. Then having put away all painful things, he tells of the victory of the cross, and this was *the* "peace." Homilies on the Gospel of John 86.2-3.[31]

[31]NPNF 1 14:325**; PG 59:470.

20:21-23 The Gift of the Spirit for Forgiveness

[21]Jesus said to them again, "Peace be with you. As the Father has sent me, even so I send you." [22]And when he had said this, he breathed on them, and said to them, "Receive the Holy Spirit. [23]If you forgive the sins of any, they are forgiven; if you retain the sins of any, they are retained."

Overview: Jesus reiterates his comfort for the troubled minds of the disciples (Peter Chrysologus). He commissions the disciples in love (Peter Chrysologus), sending them on a mission to preach his message of repentance and forgiveness. They were in no way to follow their own will but the will of him that sent them (Cyril). As the Father had sent his Son in love, so now he sends his disciples, who may undergo the same persecution Jesus did (Gregory the Great). He gradually prepares them to receive more and more of the Spirit (Gregory of Nazianzus). Christ gives his Spirit to the disciples more than once after the resurrection: He first gave it while he was on earth and later from heaven when the Spirit descended on the disciples at Pentecost, where they manifested the Spirit's power (Augustine). This was the second breath of the Spirit, the first breath in Genesis having been stifled by willful sin (Cyril of Jerusalem), while the second would enliven their faith to be bold in the preaching of the Gospel (Theodore). The Spirit, which is the breath of God (Cyril), is the Son's to give (Athanasius). He prepares the apostles for being sent by breathing his Spirit on them, giving them the spiritual power to remit sins (Chrysostom). The authority that the apostles have is found in Christ, and their unity, and that of the church that grew from them, is traced back to their one Lord, who binds them together through the Spirit (Cyprian).

Forgiveness is given by the Spirit through all of Christ's apostles who receive his authority (Theodore) to both forgive and retain sins. Both binding and loosing sin are allowed to the church; neither is allowed to heresy (Ambrose). Christ gave this authority to all of the apostles (Jerome) and confirms the sentence they pronounce (Chrysostom). They can only forgive what God forgives (Origen). The transformative power of ordination given by the Spirit to the apostles provided them with the strength they needed to fulfill their calling (Cyril). But those who receive such power through the gift of ordination should understand that with great power comes great responsibility (Gregory the Great, Chrysostom).

20:21 *Peace Again, and the Disciples' Commissioning*

Peace Reiterated to Comfort Troubled Minds. Peter Chrysologus: What does this repetition in bestowing peace mean, except that he wants the tranquility that he had announced to their minds individually also to be kept collectively among them by granting peace repeatedly? He knew, at any rate, that they were going to have far from insignificant struggles in the future stemming from his delay, with one boasting that he had persevered in faith[1] and another in grief because he had doubted.[2] . . . Peter denies,[3] John flees,[4] Thomas doubts, all forsake him:[5] unless Christ had granted forgiveness for these transgressions by his peace, even Peter, who was the first in rank of all of them, would have been considered inferior and undeserving of his subsequent elevation to the primacy. Sermon 84.5.[6]

He Sends Them in Love. Peter Chrysologus: The mention of his having been sent does not diminish him as Son but declares that what he wants to be understood here is not the power of the one who sends but the charity of the one who has been sent. This is why he says, "Just as the Father," not the Lord, "has sent me, so I send you." In other words, I send you no longer with the authority of a Master but with all the affection of someone who loves you. I send you to endure hunger, to suffer the burden of chains, to the squalor of prison, to bear all kinds of punishments and to undergo bitter death for all: all of which charity, and not power, enjoins on human minds. Sermon 84.6.[7]

The Apostolic Mission. Cyril of Alexandria: Christ says that he sent the apostles even as the Father had sent him, that they might fully comprehend their mission: to call sinners to repentance and to minister to those who were caught up in evil, whether of body or soul. In all their dealings on this earth, they were not in any way to follow their own will but the will of him who sent them. They were also called to save the world by their teaching, so far as was possible. And in truth we shall find that holy disciples were eager to show the utmost enthusiasm in performing all these things. It is not difficult for people to see this, if they give their attention to the Acts of the Apostles and the words of the holy Paul. Commentary on the Gospel of John 12.1.[8]

The Father Sends the Son, the Son Sends You. Gregory the Great: The Father sent his Son, appointing him to become a human person for the redemption of the human race. He willed him to come into the world to suffer—and yet he loved his Son whom he sent to suffer. The Lord is sending his chosen apostles into the world, not to the world's joys but to suffer as he himself was sent. Therefore as the Son is loved by the Father and yet is sent to suffer, so also the disciples are loved by the Lord, who nevertheless sends them into the world to suffer. Forty Gospel Homilies 26.[9]

20:22 *The Breath of the Spirit Given and Received*

The Gradual Manifestation of the Spirit. Gregory of Nazianzus: [Christ's disciples] were able to receive [the Spirit] on three occasions: before he was glorified by the passion, after he was glorified by the resurrection and after his ascension. . . . Now the first of these manifests him—the healing of the sick and casting out of evil spirits and so does that breathing on them after the resurrection, which was clearly a divine inspiration. And so too the present distribution of the fiery tongues. But the first manifested him indistinctly, the second more expressly, this present one more perfectly, since

[1]Peter, perhaps. [2]Thomas; see Jn 20:28. [3]See Mt 26:69-75. [4]See Mk 14:51-52. See also *Sermon* 78.4, 8 for the identification of the fleeing youth with John, although it was likely John Mark, rather than John the Evangelist. [5]See Mt 26:56. [6]FC 110:51*. [7]FC 110:51-52*. [8]LF 48:671**. [9]CS 123:201-2.

he is no longer present only in energy but . . . substantially, associating with us and dwelling in us. On Pentecost, Oration 41.11.[10]

Twofold Giving of the Spirit. Augustine: But the reason why, after his resurrection, he both gave the Holy Spirit, first on earth, and afterward sent him from heaven,[11] is in my judgment this: that "love is shed abroad in our hearts,"[12] by that gift itself, whereby we love God and our neighbors, according to those two commandments, "on which hang all the law and the prophets."[13] And Jesus Christ signified this by giving them the Holy Spirit once on earth because of the love of our neighbor and a second time from heaven because of the love of God. And if some other reason may perhaps be given for this double gift of the Holy Spirit, at any rate we ought not to doubt that the same Holy Spirit was given when Jesus breathed on them, of whom he says, "Go, baptize all nations in the name of the Father, and of the Son and of the Holy Spirit,"[14] where this Trinity is especially commended to us. It is therefore he who was also given from heaven on the day of Pentecost, that is, ten days after the Lord ascended into heaven. On the Trinity 15.26.46.[15]

Receiving the Spirit Distinguished from Being Clothed in It. Cyril of Jerusalem: This was the second time he breathed on human beings—his first breath[16] having been stifled through willful sins.[17] . . . But though he bestowed his grace then, he was to lavish it yet more bountifully. And he says to them, I am ready to give it even now, but the vessel cannot yet hold it. For awhile therefore receive as much grace as you can bear. And look forward for yet more. "But stay in the city, until you are clothed with power from on high."[18] Receive it in part now. Then, you shall wear it in its fullness. For the one who receives often possesses only a part of the gift. But the one who is clothed is completely enfolded by his robe. Catechetical Lectures 17.12.[19]

The Life-Giving Power of the Spirit. Theodore of Mopsuestia: With these words he teaches them the identity of the giver and the distributor of all these goods. His "breathing" convinces them to have no doubt about this because the body was created in the beginning as immobile and inanimate but then received life, which it did not have in itself when the soul entered into it through "breathing," as the blessed Moses said.[20] After Jesus breathed for the first time, he mentioned the Spirit in order to show that, as then nothing prevented the body from living even though it did not by nature possess [life], which the soul by entering gave it, so now they had to believe that the body of human beings was made imperishable through resurrection, because the Spirit who gives it this strength is powerful. Therefore he said to them, You must truly believe in what has been said to you and must have no doubts about the resurrection. You must not reject the honor of the apostolate because you are scared of being sent as messengers of a new doctrine into the world. You will indeed receive the effect of the Spirit, which, at the right time, will confer on you resurrection and immortality.

Through the Spirit, you will receive in this life an amazing, supernatural strength to perform unheard-of miracles by a mere word. You will be able to face easily any afflictions that may befall you because of those who oppose your preaching. And even though there were many other things to be accomplished in them through the Spirit, without mentioning them, he mentioned the most important argument of all. Here, he says, is what will clearly demonstrate to you the strength of the Spirit. Indeed, as soon as you receive it, you will be able to absolve the sins of whomever you want, as well as to pronounce a sentence of condemnation against anyone. If you, who are

[10]NPNF 2 7:383. [11]Acts 2:4. [12]Rom 5:5. [13]Mt 22:37-40. [14]Mt 28:19. [15]NPNF 1 3:224**; see also Novatian *On the Trinity* 29. [16]See Gen 2:7. [17]Of Adam and Eve. [18]Lk 24:49. [19]NPNF 2 7:127*. [20]Gen 2:7.

human, after receiving the gift of the Spirit, will be able to do all those things that are of God—indeed, only he has the power to judge—I leave to you to consider what the effectiveness of the Spirit is. Once you have received it, you must no longer doubt. Commentary on John 7.20.22.[21]

The Holy Spirit Is the Breath of God. Cyril of Alexandria: The Son, sharing the same nature as God the Father, has the Spirit in the same manner that the Father would be understood to have the Spirit. In other words, the Spirit is not something added or which comes from without, for it would be naïve—even insane—to hold such an opinion. But God the Father has the Spirit, just as each one of us has our own breath within us that pours forth from the innermost parts of the body. This is why Christ physically breathed on his disciples, showing that as the breath proceeds physically from the human mouth, so too does Christ, in a manner befitting God, pour forth the [Spirit] from the divine essence. Commentary on the Gospel of John 9.1.[22]

The Spirit Is the Son's to Give. Athanasius: [He gave the Spirit] to the disciples, demonstrating his Godhead and his majesty and intimating that he was not inferior but equal to the Spirit. And so, he gave the Spirit, saying, "Receive the Holy Spirit," and "I send him," and "he shall glorify me," and "Whatever he hears is what he shall speak."[23] ... Through whom then and from whom is it that the Spirit should be given but through the Son, to whom also the Spirit belongs? And when were we enabled to receive it, except when the Word became man? Discourses against the Arians 1.12.50.[24]

Prepared to Receive the Spirit. Chrysostom: How is it that he says elsewhere, "If I do not go away, he[25] will not come,"[26] and yet he gives them the Spirit here? Some say that by breathing he did not give them the Spirit but prepared them to receive the Spirit by breathing on them. For if Daniel's senses were so overpowered by the sight of the angel,[27] how would they have been overwhelmed in receiving that unutterable gift, if he had not first prepared them for it! ... It would not be wrong, however, to say that they received then the gift of a certain spiritual power, not to raise the dead and do miracles but to remit sins. For the gifts of the Spirit are of different kinds. Homilies on the Gospel of John 86.3.[28]

The Beginning Proceeds from Unity. Cyprian: To all the apostles, after his resurrection, he gives an equal power and says, "As the Father has sent me, even so send I you: Receive the Holy Spirit. Whoever's sins you remit, they shall be remitted to him. And whoever's sins you retain, they shall be retained." And yet, that he might promote unity, he arranged by his authority the origin of that unity, as beginning from one ... so that the beginning proceeds from unity. And this one church, also, the Holy Spirit in the Song of Songs designated in the person of our Lord, saying, "My dove, my spotless one, is but one. She is the only one of her mother, elect of her that bore her."[29] The Unity of the Church 4.[30]

20:23 *The Breath of the Spirit and Forgiveness*

The Apostles Receive Christ's Authority. Theodore of Mopsuestia: What truly wonderful gifts! Indeed, it does not only give the power over the elements and the faculty to make signs and wonders but also concedes that God may name them [judges], and therefore the servants receive from him the authority that is proper to him. The prerogative to absolve and retain sins only belongs to God, and the Jews sometimes raised this objection with the Savior, saying, "Who can forgive sins but God alone?"[31] The Lord generously gave this authority to those

[21]CSCO 4 3:354-55. [22]LF 48:303**. [23]Jn 16:14. [24]NPNF 2 4:336**. [25]The Comforter. [26]Jn 16:7. [27]Dan 10:18-19. [28]NPNF 1 14:325**; PG 59:471. [29]Song 6:9. [30]ANF 5:422*. [31]Mk 2:7.

who honored him. COMMENTARY ON JOHN 7.20.22-25.[32]

THE CHURCH FORGIVES AND RETAINS SIN. AMBROSE: They affirm that they are showing great reverence for God, to whom alone they reserve the power of forgiving sins. But in truth no one does him greater injury than those who choose to prune his commandments and reject the office entrusted to them. For the Lord Jesus himself said in the Gospel, "Receive the Holy Spirit; whoever's sins you forgive they are forgiven to them, and whoever's sins you retain, they are retained." Who is it that honors him most, the one who obeys his bidding or the one who rejects it?

The church holds fast its obedience on either side by both retaining and remitting sin. Heresy is on the one side cruel and on the other disobedient. It wishes to bind what it will not loosen and will not loosen what it has bound, whereby it condemns itself by its own sentence. For the Lord willed that the power of binding and of loosing should be the same, and he sanctioned each by a similar condition. So whoever does not have the power to loose does not have the power to bind. For as, according to the Lord's word, the one who has the power to bind also has the power to loose, their teaching destroys itself, inasmuch as those who deny that they have the power of loosing ought also to deny that of binding. For how can the one be allowed and the other disallowed? It is plain and evident that either each is allowed or each is disallowed in the case of those to whom each has been given. Each is allowed to the church; neither is allowed to heresy. For this power has been entrusted to priests alone. It is only right, therefore, that the church, which has true priests, claims it. Heresy, which does not have the priests of God,[33] cannot claim it. And by not claiming this power heresy pronounces its own sentence, that not possessing priests it cannot claim priestly power. CONCERNING REPENTANCE 1.2.6-7.[34]

THE CHURCH FOUNDED ON ALL OF THE APOSTLES. JEROME: But you say the church was founded on Peter,[35] although elsewhere[36] the same is attributed to all the apostles, and they all receive the keys of the kingdom of heaven, and the strength of the church depends on them all alike, yet one among the twelve is chosen so that when a head has been appointed, there may be no occasion for schism. AGAINST JOVINIANUS 1.26.[37]

THE MASTER CONFIRMS THE SENTENCE OF THE SERVANTS. CHRYSOSTOM: Anyone who considers how much it means to be able, in his humanity still entangled in flesh and blood, to approach that blessed and immaculate Being[38] will see clearly how great the honor is that the grace of the Spirit has bestowed on priests.[39] It is through them that this work is performed, and other work no less than this in its bearing on our dignity and our salvation.

For earth's inhabitants, having their life in this world, have been entrusted with the stewardship of heavenly things, and they have received an authority that God has not given to angels or archangels. Not to them was it said, "Whatever you bind on earth shall be bound in heaven, and whatever you loose, shall be loosed."[40] Those who are lords on earth have indeed the power to bind, but only people's bodies. But this binding touches the very soul and reaches through heaven. What priests do on earth, God ratifies above. The Master confirms the decisions of his servants. Indeed, he has given them nothing less than the whole authority of heaven. For he says, "Whoever's sins you forgive are forgiven, and whoever's sins you retain, they are retained." What authority could be greater than that? "The Father has given all judgment to the Son."[41] But I see that the Son has placed it all in their hands. For they have been

[32]CSCO 4 3:357. [33]This is not a denial of the validity of Novatian ordinations, which were admitted by the Eighth Canon of the Council of Nicaea, but of their lawful jurisdiction. [34]NPNF 2 10:330**. [35]Mt 16:18. [36]Mt 18:18. [37]NPNF 2 6:366**. Origen makes a similar comment in his *Commentary on Matthew* 12.11 (ANF 10:546). [38]That is, God. [39]Or pastors. [40]See Mt 18:18. [41]Jn 5:22.

raised to this prerogative, as though they were already translated to heaven and had transcended human nature and were freed from our passions.

Again, if a king confers on one of his subjects the right to imprison and release again at will, that person is the envy and admiration of all. But although the priest has received from God an authority as much greater than that, as heaven is more precious than earth and souls than bodies, some people think he has received so slight an honor that they can imagine someone entrusted with it actually despising the gift. God save us from such madness! For it is patently mad to despise this great office without which we cannot attain to salvation or God's good promises. For if one "cannot enter into the kingdom of heaven unless he is born again of water and the Spirit,"[42] and anyone who does not eat the flesh of the Lord and drink his blood is excluded from eternal life,[43] and all these things can happen through no other agency except their sacred hands (the priests', I mean), how can anyone, without their help, escape the fire of Gehenna or win his appointed crown? On the Priesthood 3.5.[44]

When to Forgive, When to Retain. Origen: Consider the person inspired by Jesus as the apostles were and who can be known by his fruits[45] as someone who has received the Holy Spirit and become spiritual by being led by the Spirit as a son of God to do everything by reason.[46] This person forgives whatever God forgives and retains sins that cannot be healed, serving God like the prophets by speaking not his own words but those of the divine will. So he, too, serves God, who alone has authority to forgive. On Prayer 28.8.[47]

Transforming Power of Ordination. Cyril of Alexandria: After dignifying the holy apostles with the glorious distinction of the apostleship and appointing them ministers and priests of the divine altar, as I have just said, he at once sanctifies them by promising his Spirit to them through the outward sign of his breath, that we might be firmly convinced that the Holy Spirit is not alien to the Son but consubstantial with him and through him proceeding from the Father. He shows that the gift of the Spirit necessarily attends those who are ordained by him to be apostles of God. And why? Because they could have done nothing pleasing to God and could not have triumphed over the snares of sin if they had not been "clothed with power from on high"[48] and been transformed into something other than they were before. . . . [Jesus] consecrates by actual sanctification, making people partakers in his nature, through participation in the Spirit and in some sort strengthening the nature of humanity into a power and glory that is superhuman. Commentary on the Gospel of John 12.1.[49]

With Great Power Comes Great Responsibility. Gregory the Great: It is pleasant to observe the disciples, lifted up to a height of glory equal to the burden of humility to which they were called. You see how they not only acquire peace of mind concerning themselves but even receive the power of releasing others from their bonds. They share in the right of divine judgment so that as God's vicars they may withhold forgiveness of sins from some and grant it to others. So it was fitting that only those who had consented to be humbled for the sake of God be raised up by him. Those who feared God's strict judgment were made judges of hearts. Those who were themselves fearful of being condemned condemn some and set others free. Their place in the church is now held by the bishops. Those who obtain the position of governing receive authority to loose and to bind. It is a great honor, but the burden is heavy. In truth it is difficult for one who does not know how to exercise control over his own life to become the judge of someone else's life. Forty Gospel Homilies 26.[50]

---

[42]Jn 3:5. [43]See Jn 6:53. [44]COP 71-73*. [45]Mt 7:16, 20; Lk 6:44. [46]See 1 Cor 2:14-15; Rom 8:14; Gal 5:18. [47]*OSW* 150-51*. [48]Lk 24:49. [49]LF 48:671-73**. Leo the Great cites this same passage when urging that ordinations should take place on Sundays, since that is the day Jesus ordained his apostles. See *Letter* 9.2. [50]CS 123:204*.

Importance of Priestly Vigilance. Chrysostom: You should hold your pastor[51] in high honor. You care about your own affairs, and if you care for them well you won't have to give an account to anyone else. But your pastor, even if he orders his own life well, if he does not have an anxious concern for your life as well, yes and of all those around him, he is sent to hell with the evildoers. . . . Therefore, knowing the greatness of their danger, give them a large measure of your goodwill. . . . They should receive your most favorable attention. But if you join with the rest in trampling on them . . . and throw them into despondency, you weaken their hands and render them, as well as yourselves, an easy prey to the waves, no matter how courageous they are. . . . You have respect for secular authorities, but when God appoints do we despise him who is appointed and abuse him and besmirch him with ten thousand reproaches, and though forbidden to judge our brothers, do we sharpen our tongue against our pastors? . . . I am not saying that I approve of those who exercise their pastorate unworthily, but I do greatly pity them and weep for them. . . . And even if there is much to say against the way they have lived their lives, this in no way invalidates what they do by commission from God. . . . But why am I speaking only of pastors? Not even an angel or archangel can do anything on its own. The Father, Son and Holy Spirit do it all while the pastor only furnishes the tongue and the hand. For it would not be right that the salvation of those who come to the sacraments in faith should be endangered by another's wickedness.[52] Homilies on the Gospel of John 86.4.[53]

[51]The Greek speaks of "priests," but both can be rightly understood. [52]Augustine makes the same point in his writings against the Donatists. [53]NPNF 1 14:326**; PG 59:471-72.

20:24-29 JESUS APPEARS TO THOMAS

[24]Now Thomas, one of the twelve, called the Twin, was not with them when Jesus came. [25]So the other disciples told him, "We have seen the Lord." But he said to them, "Unless I see in his hands the print of the nails, and place my finger in the mark of the nails, and place my hand in his side, I will not believe."

[26]Eight days later, his disciples were again in the house, and Thomas was with them. The doors were shut, but Jesus came and stood among them, and said, "Peace be with you." [27]Then he said to Thomas, "Put your finger here, and see my hands; and put out your hand, and place it in my side; do not be faithless, but believing." [28]Thomas answered him, "My Lord and my God!" [29]Jesus said to him, "Have you believed because you have seen me? Blessed are those who have not seen and yet believe."

Overview: Thomas, a twin not only in name but also in how he writes of divine things, is absent when Christ appears (Origen). His absence is not contradicted by Luke's account of the Emmaus disciples' return to the Eleven (Bede). His return was for our benefit since his questioning helped confirm our belief (GREGORY THE GREAT). Even though Thomas was absent, he still received the gift of the Spirit, just as Eldad and Medad did when they were absent from the seventy elders who had received the Spirit under Moses (CYRIL).

Thomas's request to see Jesus' wounds is what the other apostles would have liked to do as well, but he also exhibits precision and carefulness in his request (ORIGEN). He believes the disciples concerning Jesus' death but not his resurrection (AMMONIUS). Jesus shows Thomas his pierced hands and feet, showing Israel its only ever crucified king (JUSTIN). Jesus also proves to the disciples that it is a bodily resurrection he has undergone. The disciples were assembled on the eighth day when Jesus appeared among them, a practice that still continues as the church gathers on the eighth day to receive its risen Lord in the Eucharist (CYRIL). Jesus delays his appearance eight days to allow Thomas to be instructed by the other disciples as well as increasing his desire and future faith (CHRYSOSTOM). Although Jesus' appearance despite the locked doors is difficult to understand, we should also admit the limits of our senses in understanding things beyond our comprehension (HILARY).

Jesus condescends to our senses in order to prove he is truly resurrected (CHRYSOSTOM) with a body that has real flesh and bones (THEODORET) and is witnessed to by those who handled the Word of life (TERTULLIAN). The wounds evidence the fact that it is the same body raised that had died (HIPPOLYTUS), albeit more glorious (JEROME). He chose not to wipe away the traces of the wounds, which also causes one to wonder whether martyrs will retain their wounds (AUGUSTINE). Jesus then tells Thomas to put his hand in his side to further prove the resurrection—but how could Thomas's hand survive such an encounter with the living God unless God's grace enabled him (ROMANUS)? This act, and all the other resurrection evidences, proves beyond a doubt the fact of the resurrection (GREGORY OF NYSSA) so that those of us who were absent, like Thomas, should take to heart Jesus' imperative to stop doubting and believe (GREGORY OF NAZIANZUS). Jesus led Thomas to a confession of his divinity (ATHANASIUS, AMBROSE). When Thomas touched Christ's flesh, he believed he touched God (CASSIAN, AUGUSTINE). In a minority opinion, Theodore expresses his own doubts that Thomas knew that Jesus was God. He rather believes Thomas was only praising God for the accomplished miracle (THEODORE). But the consensus of patristic opinion is that while Thomas did indeed see Christ's flesh, he confessed the divinity, which he could not see (GREGORY THE GREAT). Throughout this account, Christ shows his patience with Thomas's lack of faith, and ours (CYRIL), since he knows that many blessings that lead to resurrection are indeed hidden under the outward veil of suffering (AMBROSE). It is comforting then to know that our faith rests on more than the eyes can see (LEO, JOHN OF CARPATHUS).

20:24 *Thomas, Called Didymus, Is Absent*

A TWIN IN WORD. ORIGEN: "Thomas" is called Didymus, which means "Twin," because he was a kind of twin in word, writing the divine things in two ways and copying Christ, who spoke to those outside of his circle in parables, but to his own disciples he spoke privately about everything. And it is not improper to say that Christ's genuine disciples achieve this double equipment in word that Thomas perhaps had already but even more so afterward. But it may be said that the interpretation of this alone has been recorded because the Evangelist was concerned that Greeks coming into contact with the gospel should notice the peculiarity of the interpretation of the only name specially interpreted, so as to find the cause of his name being set forth also in Greek. FRAGMENT 106 ON THE GOSPEL OF JOHN.[1]

DOES JOHN CONTRADICT LUKE? BEDE: But

[1]AEG 6:140; GCS 10(4):561-62.

why does John say that Thomas was not with them, when Luke writes that two disciples, one of whom was Cleopas, on their return to Jerusalem [from Emmaus] found the Eleven assembled and those who were with them?[2] We must understand that Thomas had gone out and that in the interval of his absence, Jesus came and stood in the midst. Exposition on the Gospel of Luke 6.24.36.[3]

Thomas Absent for Us. Gregory the Great: It was not an accident that that particular disciple was not present. The divine mercy ordained that a doubting disciple should, by feeling in his Master the wounds of the flesh, heal in us the wounds of unbelief. The unbelief of Thomas is more profitable to our faith than the belief of the other disciples. For the touch by which he is brought to believe confirms our minds in belief, beyond all question. Forty Gospel Homilies 26.[4]

Did Absent Thomas Receive the Spirit? Cyril of Alexandria: How, then, someone may not unreasonably inquire, if Thomas was absent, was he in fact made partaker in the Holy Spirit when the Savior appeared to the disciples and breathed on them, saying, "Receive the Holy Spirit"? We reply that the power of the Spirit pervaded every person who received grace and fulfilled the aim of the Lord who gave him to them. And Christ gave the Spirit not to some only but to all the disciples. Therefore, if any were absent, they also received him, the munificence of the giver not being confined to those only who were present but extending to the entire company of the holy apostles. And that this interpretation is not strained, or our idea extravagant, we may convince you from holy Scripture itself, bringing forward as a proof a passage in the books of Moses. The Lord God commanded the all-wise Moses to select seventy elders from the assembly of the Jews and plainly declared, "I will take of the Spirit that is on you and will put it on them."[5] Moses, as he was asked, brought them together and fulfilled the divine decree. Only it happened that two of the men who were included in the number of the seventy elders were left behind and remained in the assembly, that is, Eldad and Medad. Then when God put on them all the divine Spirit, as he had promised, those whom Moses had collected together immediately received grace and prophesied. But none the less also the two who were in the assembly prophesied, and, in fact, the grace from above came on them first. Commentary on the Gospel of John 12.1.[6]

20:25 *Thomas Has to See and Feel for Himself*

Reopening Old Wounds. Peter Chrysologus: Why does the hand of a faithful disciple in this fashion retrace those wounds that an unholy hand inflicted? Why does the hand of a dutiful follower strive to reopen the side that the lance of an unholy soldier pierced? Why does the harsh curiosity of a servant repeat the tortures imposed by the rage of persecutors? Why is a disciple so inquisitive about proving from his torments that he is the Lord, for his pains that he is God, and from his wounds that he is the heavenly Physician? . . .

Why Thomas, do you alone, a little too clever a sleuth for your own good, insist that only the wounds be brought forward in testimony to faith? What if these wounds had been made to disappear with the other things? What a peril to your faith would that curiosity have produced? Do you think that no signs of his devotion and no evidence of the Lord's resurrection could be found unless you probed with your hands his inner organs that had been laid bare with such cruelty? Brothers, his devotion sought these things, his dedication demanded them so that in the future not even godlessness itself would doubt that the Lord had risen. But Thomas was curing not only

[2]See Lk 24:33. [3]CCL 120:417. [4]CS 123:206-7**. [5]Num 11:17. [6]LF 48:678-79**.

the uncertainty of his own heart but also that of all human beings. And since he was going to preach this message to the Gentiles, this conscientious investigator was examining carefully how he might provide a foundation for the faith needed for such a mystery.[7] . . . For the only reason the Lord had kept his wounds was to provide evidence of his resurrection. Sermon 84.8.[8]

Thomas Is a Precise Person. Origen: Thomas seems to have had some precision and carefulness about him, which is shown also by what he said. He most likely did not believe those who said they had seen the Lord. It could have been an apparition, like what had happened in Matthew.[9] I think this was the feeling of the other apostles too, but especially of Thomas. That the other apostles had some such thought on seeing Jesus is clear from there being written, "They supposed it was an apparition,[10] and he answered and said to them, "Handle me and see, for a spirit does not have bones and flesh as you see me having."[11] Fragment 106 on the Gospel of John.[12]

Thomas Believes the Death but Not the Resurrection of Jesus. Ammonius: Thomas was charged with being a real curiosity seeker because he thought the resurrection was impossible. Thus, he not only said "unless I see" but also "unless I touch," lest somehow what he saw turned out to be an illusion. Therefore, when Thomas had heard from the disciples that Christ had been injured by a spear, Thomas believed them, even though he had not seen it. However, he did not believe their report of the resurrection, as if it were beyond reason. He did not say this so much out of unbelief but out of grief, because he himself had not been deemed worthy of seeing the risen Christ. It fit God's purpose that Thomas did not believe, so that we all might know through him that the body that had been crucified had been raised. Since Thomas wanted to see the wounds all around Christ's flesh, as well as his flesh itself, to see if he had risen, Thomas was searching for him. Fragments on John 633.[13]

Jesus Is the Only Crucified King. Justin Martyr: David refers to Jesus' suffering and to the cross in a parable of mystery in Psalm 22[:16-18], "They pierced my hands and my feet." . . . But you still maintain that this very psalm does not refer to Christ because, in your blindness, you fail to realize that no one in [the Jewish] nation who has been called king or Christ has ever had his hands or feet pierced while alive or has died in this mysterious fashion—that is, by the cross—except this Jesus alone. Dialogue with Trypho 97.[14]

The Physical Resurrection. Cyril of Alexandria: We are taught by the slight lack of faith shown by the blessed Thomas that the mystery of the resurrection is effected on our earthly bodies and in Christ as the firstfruits of the human race. He was no phantom or ghost, fashioned in human shape, simulating the features of humanity, nor yet, as others have foolishly surmised, a spiritual body that is compounded of a subtle and ethereal substance different from the flesh. For some attach this meaning to the expression "spiritual body." Since all our expectation and the significance of our irrefutable faith, after the confession of the holy and consubstantial Trinity, centers in the mystery concerning the flesh, the blessed Evangelist has very pertinently put this saying of Thomas side by side with the summary of what preceded. For observe that Thomas does not simply desire to see the Lord but looks for the marks of the nails, that is, the wounds on his body. For he affirmed that then, indeed, he would believe and agree with the rest that Christ had indeed risen again, and risen in the flesh. Commentary on the Gospel of John 12.1.[15]

20:26 *Jesus' Appearance to Thomas on the Eighth Day*

[7]On this point, see also Gaudentius *Sermon* 17 (PL 20:961-62). [8]FC 110:52-54**. [9]Mt 24:5. [10]Gk *phantasma*. [11]lk 24:39. [12]*AEG* 6:139-40; GCS 10(4):561. [13]*JKGK* 354. [14]ANF 1:247-48**. [15]LF 48:682**.

THE EUCHARISTIC ASSEMBLY. CYRIL OF ALEXANDRIA: With good reason, then, are we accustomed to have sacred meetings in churches on the eighth day. And, to adopt the language of allegory, as the idea necessarily demands, we indeed close the doors,[16] but Christ still visits us and appears to us all, both invisibly as God and visibly in the body. He allows us to touch his holy flesh and gives it to us. For through the grace of God we are admitted to partake of the blessed Eucharist, receiving Christ into our hands, to the intent that we may firmly believe that he did in truth raise up the temple of his body. . . . Participation in the divine mysteries, in addition to filling us with divine blessedness, is a true confession and memorial of Christ's dying and rising again for us and for our sake. Let us, therefore, after touching Christ's body, avoid all unbelief in him as utter ruin and rather be found well grounded in the full assurance of faith. COMMENTARY ON THE GOSPEL OF JOHN 12.1.[17]

WHY THE DELAY? CHRYSOSTOM: And why does he not appear to him immediately, instead of "after eight days"? He does so in order that, in the meantime, being continually instructed by the disciples and hearing the same thing repeated, he might be inflamed with more eager desire and be more ready to believe for the future. But where did he learn that his side had been pierced? He heard it from the disciples. How then did he believe that but not believe the other story? Because the latter was very strange and wonderful. But observe the truthfulness of the disciples and how they hide no faults, either their own or others', but record them with great veracity. Jesus again presents himself to them and does not wait to be asked by Thomas or to hear any such thing. Rather, before Thomas could even speak, Jesus prevented him and fulfilled his desire, showing that even when Thomas spoke those words to the disciples, he was present. For he used the same words, though in a reproachful manner, and added instruction for the future. HOMILIES ON THE GOSPEL OF JOHN 87.1.[18]

ADMIT THE LIMITS OF YOUR SENSES TO UNDERSTAND. HILARY OF POITIERS: The Lord stoops to the level even of our feeble understanding. He works a miracle of his invisible power in order to satisfy the doubts of unbelieving minds. Explain, my critic, the ways of heaven—explain his action if you can. The disciples were in a closed room. They had met and held their assembly in secret since the passion of the Lord. The Lord presents himself to strengthen the faith of Thomas by meeting his challenge. He gives him his body to feel, his wounds to handle. He, indeed, who would be recognized as having suffered wounds must necessarily produce the body in which those wounds were received. I ask at what point in the walls of that closed house the Lord bodily entered. The apostle has recorded the circumstances with careful precision: "Jesus came when the doors were shut and stood in the midst." Did he penetrate through bricks and mortar or through stout woodwork—substances whose very nature it is to bar progress? For there he stood in bodily presence; there was no suspicion of deceit. Let the eye of your mind follow his path as he enters. Let your intellectual vision accompany him as he passes into that closed dwelling. There is no breach in the walls; no door has been unbarred. Yet, see how he stands in the midst whose might no barrier can resist. You are a critic of things invisible; I ask you to explain a visible event. Everything remains firm as it was. No body is capable of insinuating itself through the interstices of wood and stone. The body of the Lord does not disperse itself, to come together again after a disappearance. Yet where does the one who is standing in their midst come from? Your senses and your words are powerless to account for it. The fact is certain, but it lies beyond the region of human explanation. If, as you say, our account of the divine birth is a lie, then prove that this account of the Lord's entrance is a fiction. If we assume that an event

[16]Closing the doors occurred in the ancient church service at the time of the eucharist. [17]LF 48:684*. [18]NPNF 1 14:327**.

did not happen, because we cannot discover how it was done, we make the limits of our understanding into the limits of reality. But the certainty of the evidence proves the falsehood of our contradiction. The Lord did stand in a closed house in the midst of the disciples; the Son was born of the Father. Deny not that he stood, because your puny wits cannot ascertain how he came there; renounce instead a disbelief in God the only-begotten and perfect Son of God the unbegotten and perfect Father that is based only on the incapacity of sense and speech to comprehend. ON THE TRINITY 3.20.[19]

20:27 *Put Your Finger Here, and See My Hands*

THE SIGNS OF THE RESURRECTION. CHRYSOSTOM: It is worth inquiring how an incorruptible body showed the prints of the nails and was tangible to a mortal hand. But do not be disturbed. What took place was a matter of condescension. For that which was so subtle and light as to enter in when the doors were shut was entirely lacking all density. But this marvel was shown so that the resurrection might be believed and so that people might know that it was the crucified one himself and not another who rose instead of him. This is why he arose bearing the signs of the cross, and it is also why he eats. At least the apostles repeatedly made this a proof of the resurrection, saying "we, who did eat and drink with him."[20] As, therefore, when we see him walking on the waves before the crucifixion, we do not say that his body is of a different nature but the same as our own. So after the resurrection, when we see him with the prints of the nails, we do not say that he is therefore still mortal. It was for the sake of the disciple that he appeared in this way. HOMILIES ON THE GOSPEL OF JOHN 87.1.[21]

HE HAS REAL FLESH WITH BONES. THEODORET OF CYR: Before the passion he predicted his bodily death each time, saying that he would be handed over to the high priest's followers and proclaiming the trophy of the cross.[22] But after the passion, when he rose from the dead on the third day and, since the disciples doubted that he had been raised, he appeared to them in his actual body. [He] declares that he has real flesh with bones, presents his wounded side to their eyes and shows them the marks of the nails.[23] DIALOGUE 2.18.[24]

WITNESSES WHO HANDLED THE WORD OF LIFE. TERTULLIAN: Marcion chose to believe that Jesus was a phantom, denying to him the reality of a perfect body. Now, not even to his apostles was his nature ever a matter of deception. He was truly both seen and heard on the mount. True and real was the draught of wine at the marriage of [Cana in] Galilee. True and real also was the touch of the then believing Thomas. Read the testimony of John: "That which we have seen, which we have heard, which we have looked on with our eyes and our hands have handled, of the Word of life."[25] False, of course, and deceptive must have been that testimony, if the witness of our eyes and ears and hands by nature is a lie. ON THE SOUL 17.[26]

THE SAME BODY RAISED THAT DIED. HIPPOLYTUS: He calls him, then, "the firstfruits of them that sleep,"[27] as the "first-begotten of the dead."[28] For he, having risen and wanting to show that that same [body] had been raised that had also died, when his disciples were in doubt, called Thomas to him and said, "Reach here. Handle me, and see. For a spirit does not have bone and flesh, as you see me have." In calling him the firstfruits, he testified to that which we have said, that is, that the Savior, taking to himself the flesh out of the same lump, raised this same flesh and made it the firstfruits of the flesh of the righteous, in order that all we who have believed in the

[19]NPNF 2 9:67-68**. [20]Acts 10:41. [21]NPNF 1 14:328*. [22]See Mt 20:18-19. [23]See also Lk 24:39. [24]FC 106:139-40. [25]1 Jn 1:1. [26]ANF 3:197. [27]1 Cor 15:20. [28]Col 1:18.

hope of the risen one may have the resurrection in expectation. FRAGMENT 3.[29]

THE SAME FLESH, BUT MORE GLORIOUS. JEROME: After the resurrection we shall have the same members that we now use, the same flesh and blood and bones, for it is not the nature of these that is condemned in Holy Scripture but their works. . . . The true confession of the resurrection declares that the flesh will be glorious, but without destroying its reality. And so, when the apostle says, "This [flesh] is corruptible and mortal,"[30] his words denote this very body, in other words, the flesh that was then seen. But when he further adds that it "puts on incorruption and immortality," he is not saying that what was put on [i.e., the clothing] does away with the body that it adorns in glory. Rather, it makes that body glorious that previously lacked glory. When the more worthless robe of mortality and weakness is laid aside, then we can be clothed with the gold of immortality and the blessedness of strength as well as virtue. AGAINST JOHN OF JERUSALEM 28-29.[31]

WILL MARTYRS RETAIN THEIR WOUNDS? AUGUSTINE: The love we bear for the blessed martyrs causes us—how, I do not know—to desire to see in the heavenly kingdom the marks that they received for the name of Christ. And possibly we shall see them. For this will not be a deformity but a mark of honor and will add luster to their appearance as well as a spiritual (if not a bodily) beauty. . . . For even though the blemishes of the body will not be found in any resurrected body, the evidences of virtue can hardly be called blemishes. CITY OF GOD 22.19.[32]

WHO PROTECTED THOMAS'S HAND? ROMANUS MELODUS:

Who protected the hand of the disciple which was not melted
At the time when he approached the fiery side of the Lord?[33]
Who gave it daring and strength to probe
The flaming bone? Certainly the side was examined.
If the side had not furnished abundant power,
How could a right hand of clay have touched
Sufferings which had shaken Heaven and earth?
It was grace itself which was given to Thomas
To touch and to cry out,
"Thou art our Lord and God."

Truly the bramble which endured fire was burned but not consumed.[34]
From the hand of Thomas I have faith in the story of Moses.
For, though his hand was perishable and thorny, it was not burned
When it touched the side which was like burning flame.
Formerly fire came to the bramble bush,
But now, the thorny one hastened to the fire;
And God, Himself, was seen to guard both.
Hence I have faith; and hence I shall praise
God, Himself, and man, as I cry,
"Thou art our Lord and God."

For truly the boundary line of faith was subscribed for me
By the hand of Thomas; for when he touched Christ
He became like the pen of a fast-writing scribe[35]
Which writes for the faithful. From it gushes forth faith.
From it, the robber drank and became sober again;
From it the disciples watered their hearts;
From it, Thomas drained the knowledge

[29]ANF 5:240**; GCS 1 2:254. [30]1 Cor 15:53. [31]NPNF 2 6:438-39**. [32]NPNF 1 2:498**. [33]Romanus finds a unique poetic way to communicate the fact that the disciples were in the presence of the now-glorified body of the human-divine Jesus. See also his *Kontakion on the Baptism of Christ* 5.12, where he connects John the Baptist's touching of the human-divine Christ with Uzzah (2 Sam 6:6-8), who died when he touched the ark. [34]Ex 3:3-5. [35]Ps 44:2 (43:3 LXX).

which he sought,
For he drank first and then offered drink
To many who had a little doubt. He
persuaded them to say,
"Thou art our Lord and God."
Kontakion on Doubting Thomas 30.1-3.[36]

No One Now Can Doubt the Resurrection's Power. Gregory of Nyssa: Once he had accustomed people to seeing the miracle of resurrection in other bodies, he confirmed his word in his own humanity. You already received a glimpse of that word working in others—those who were about to die, the child who had just ceased to live, the young man at the edge of the grave, the putrefying corpse, all alike restored by one command to life. . . . Now look at him whose hands were pierced with nails, look at him whose side was transfixed with a spear. Pass your fingers through the print of the nails, thrust your hand into the spear wound. You could surely guess how far within your hand would reach by the breadth of the external scar since the wound that gives admission to the hand shows to what depth the iron entered. If he then has been raised, well may we utter the apostle's exclamation, "How do some say that there is no resurrection of the dead?"[37] Since, then, every prediction of the Lord is shown to be true by the testimony of events—in fact, we not only learned this from his words but also received the proof in his deeds from the very same people who returned to life by resurrection—what other occasion is left for those who do not believe? Let us rather bid farewell to those who pervert our simple faith by "philosophy and vain deceit."[38] Let us instead hold on to our confession [of the resurrection] in its purity, a confession that we have learned through the gracious words of the prophet, "You shall take away their breath, and they shall fail and turn to dust. You shall then send forth your Spirit, and they shall be created, and you shall renew the face of the earth."[39] On the Making of Man 25.12-13.[40]

An Imperative to Believe. Gregory of Nazianzus: If, like a Thomas, you were left out when the disciples were assembled to whom Christ shows himself, when you do see him do not be faithless. And if you do not believe, then believe those who tell you. And if you cannot believe them either, then have confidence in the print of the nails. On Holy Easter, Oration 45.24.[41]

20:28 *My Lord and My God!*

The Crucified Was God. Athanasius: Let them therefore confess, even they who previously denied that the crucified was God, that they have erred. For the divine Scriptures bid them, and especially Thomas, who, after seeing upon him the print of the nails, cried out, "My Lord and my God." Letter 59.10, To Epictetus.[42]

Like Father, Like Son. Ambrose: You have read that the Father is both Lord and God: "O Lord my God, I will call on you, hear me."[43] You find the Son to be both Lord and God, as you have read in the Gospel, that, when Thomas had touched the side of Christ, he said, "My Lord and my God." So just as the Father is God and the Son Lord, so too the Son is God and the Father Lord. The holy designation changes from one to the other. The divine nature does not change, but the dignity remains unchangeable. For they are not [as it were] contributions gathered from bounty but free-will gifts of natural love. For unity has its special property, and the special properties are bound together in unity. On the Holy Spirit 3.15.108.[44]

Thomas Touches God. John Cassian: Thomas, when he touched the flesh, believed that he had touched God, saying, "My Lord and my God." For they all confessed but one Christ, so as not to make him two. Do you therefore believe

[36]*KRBM* 1:329-30. [37]1 Cor 15:12. [38]Col 2:8. [39]Ps 104:29-30 (103:29-30 LXX). [40]NPNF 2 5:417**. [41]NPNF 2 7:432*. [42]NPNF 2 4:574*. [43]Ps 30:2 (29:3 LXX). [44]NPNF 2 10:150*.

him? And do you believe in such a way that Jesus Christ the Lord of all, both Only Begotten and firstborn, is both creator of all things and preserver of humanity and that the same person is first the framer of the whole world and afterward redeemer of humankind? On the Incarnation of the Lord Against Nestorius 6.19.[45]

Touching the Flesh, He Invokes the Word. Augustine: But when Jesus showed Thomas the very places where he had his doubts, Thomas exclaimed, "My Lord and my God." He touched his flesh, he proclaimed his divinity. What did he touch? The body of Christ. Was the body of Christ the divinity of Christ? The divinity of Christ was the Word; the humanity of Christ was soul and flesh. Thomas could not touch the soul, but he could perceive it, because the body that had been dead was moving about alive. But that Word is subject neither to change nor to contact, it neither regresses nor progresses, neither fails nor flourishes, because in the beginning was the Word, and the Word was with God, and the Word was God." That is what Thomas proclaimed. He touched the flesh, he invoked the Word, because "the Word became flesh and dwelt among us."[46] Sermon 145a.[47]

Thomas Praises God for the Miracle. Theodore of Mopsuestia: And [Thomas] touched him carefully, and when he discovered the truth, confessed his fault by saying, "My Lord and my God!" What does this mean? While Thomas did not believe before that the Savior had resurrected from the dead, now he calls him Lord and God? This is not likely. Thomas, the doubtful disciple, does not call Lord and God the one whom he touched—in fact, the knowledge of the resurrection did not teach him that the resurrected one was God. Rather, he praised God for the accomplished miracle, being astonished for the miracles that he saw. Commentary on John 7.20.27-29.[48]

20:29 *Seeing Is Not Believing*

Thomas Sees One Thing, Believes Another. Gregory the Great: When the apostle Paul says that "faith is the ground of things to be hoped for, the proof of things that are not evident,"[49] it is clear that faith is the proof of those things that cannot be made evident. Things that are evident no longer involve faith but recognition. Why then, when Thomas saw and when he touched, was it said to him, "Because you have seen me, you have believed"? Because he saw one thing, and he believed another; divinity could not be seen by a mortal person. He saw a human being, and he confessed him as God. . . . But we also rejoice at what follows, "Blessed are those who have not seen and have believed." Certainly this saying refers to us who keep in our minds one whom we do not see in his body. It refers to us, but only if we follow up our faith with our works. That person truly believes who expresses his faith in his works. Forty Gospel Homilies 26.[50]

Christ's Patience with Thomas and Us. Cyril of Alexandria: Jesus said to him, "Because you have seen me, Thomas, you have believed. Blessed are those who have not seen and yet believe." These words were wonderfully pertinent, and they can be of very great help to us. They demonstrate once again how much he cares for our souls, for he is good, and as Scripture says, "He wants everyone to be saved and to come to a knowledge of the truth."[51] Even so, this saying of his may surprise us. As always, Christ had to be patient with Thomas when he said he would not believe and with the other disciples too when they thought they were seeing a ghost. Because of his desire to convince the whole world, he most willingly showed them the marks of the nails and the wound in his side. Because he wanted those who needed such signs as a support for their faith to have no possible reason for doubt, he even took food, although he had no need for it. . . . But when

[45]NPNF 2 11:601*. [46]Jn 1:1, 14. [47]*WSA* 3 4:443*. [48]CSCO 4 3:358. [49]Heb 11:1. [50]CS 123:207*. [51]1 Tim 2:4.

anyone accepts what he has not seen, believing on the word of his teacher, the faith by which he honors the one his teacher proclaims to him is worthy of great praise. Blessed, therefore, is everyone who believes the message of the holy apostles who, as Luke says, were eyewitnesses of Christ's actions and ministers of the word. If we desire eternal life and long for a dwelling place in heaven, we must listen to them. Commentary on the Gospel of John 12.1.[52]

Blessing Hidden in Suffering. Ambrose: There are some . . . who think a blessed life is impossible in this body, weak and fragile as it is. For we have to suffer pain and grief, weeping, illness—all in this body. . . . It is not a blessing to be in the midst of suffering. But it is a blessing to be victorious over it and not to be bullied by the power of temporal pain. Suppose that things come that are considered terrible because of the grief they cause, such as blindness, exile, hunger, violation of a daughter, loss of children. Who will deny that Isaac was blessed, who did not see in his old age, and yet gave blessings with his benediction?[53] Was not Jacob blessed who, leaving his father's house, endured exile as a shepherd for pay,[54] and mourned for the violated chastity of his daughter[55] and suffered hunger?[56] Were they not blessed on whose good faith God received witness, as it is written: "The God of Abraham, the God of Isaac and the God of Jacob"?[57] A wretched thing is slavery, but Joseph was not wretched. In fact, clearly he was blessed when, while a slave, he checked the lusts of his mistress.[58] What shall I say of holy David, who bewailed the death of three sons,[59] and, what was even worse than this, his daughter's incestuous connection?[60] How could he be unblessed from whom the author of blessedness himself sprung who has made many blessed? For "blessed are they who have not seen yet have believed." All these felt their own weakness, but they bravely prevailed over it. What can we think of as more wretched than holy Job, either in the burning of his house, or the instantaneous death of his ten sons or his bodily pains?[61] Was he less blessed than if he had not endured those things whereby he really showed himself approved?

It is true that in these sufferings there is something bitter and that we cannot use mind over matter to hide this pain. I should not deny that the sea is deep because in shore it is shallow, or that the sky is clear because sometimes it is covered with clouds, or that the earth is fruitful because in some places there is only barren ground or that the crops are rich and full because they sometimes have wild oats mingled with them. So, too, count it as true that the harvest of a happy conscience may be mingled with some bitter feelings of grief. In the sheaves of the whole of a blessed life, if by chance any misfortune or bitterness has crept in, is it not as though the wild oats were hidden or as though the bitterness of the tares was concealed by the sweet scent of the corn? Duties of the Clergy 2.5.19-21.[62]

Salvation Rests on More Than Eyes Can See. Leo the Great: It is the strength of great minds and the light of firmly faithful souls unhesitatingly to believe what is not seen with the bodily sight and to focus your affections where you cannot direct your gaze. And from where should this godliness spring up in our hearts or how should someone be justified by faith, if our salvation rested on those things only that lie beneath our eyes? And so, our Lord said to Thomas, who seemed to doubt Christ's resurrection until he had tested by sight and touched the traces of his passion in his very flesh, "because you have seen me, you have believed; blessed are those who have not seen and yet have believed." Sermon 74.1.[63]

Courageous Endurance. John of Carpathus: Blessed are those who, when grace is

[52]LF 48:691-92**. [53]Gen 27:28. [54]Gen 31:41. [55]Gen 34:5. [56]Gen 42:2. [57]Ex 3:6. [58]Gen 39:7. [59]2 Sam 12:16;13:31; 18:33. [60]2 Sam 13:21. [61]Job 1:14—2:10. [62]NPNF 2 10:46-47**. [63]NPNF 2 12:188**.

withdrawn, find no consolation in themselves but only continuing tribulation and thick darkness, and yet they do not despair. Rather, strengthened by faith, they endure courageously, convinced that they do indeed see him who is invisible. Texts for the Monks in India 71.[64]

[64]*TP* 1:315.

20:30-31 Purpose of the Gospel

[30]Now Jesus did many other signs in the presence of the disciples, which are not written in this book; [31]but these are written that you may believe that Jesus is the Christ, the Son of God, and that believing you may have life in his name.

Overview: When he speaks of the many other signs, John here intimates that he did not include everything the other Evangelists recorded (Theodore). Many signs that he did include, both before and after the resurrection, were needed so that the disciples might truly believe that Jesus was the Son of God (Chrysostom). John wrote this Gospel because he foresaw the blasphemous heresies that would follow (Irenaeus). He intended that his readers would believe that Jesus is the Christ, the Son of God (Tertullian, Hilary). We believe in his name, that is, we believe through him because he is the life (Chrysostom). John inserts this ending here, as a sort of preface to the ensuing narrative, in order to give a special prominence to the last chapter that follows (Augustine).

20:30 *Many Other Signs in the Disciples' Presence*

Other Evangelists' Accounts Sufficient. Theodore of Mopsuestia: With these words the Evangelist shows that there were countless signs that the Savior performed before the disciples. In addition, he testifies that the words of the Gospels are true, namely, those scattered accounts composed accurately by the other [Evangelists] but were omitted by him. With his words here he demonstrates that he did not report those words without any polemical intention, but he shows that the words of the other [Evangelists] are true and are sufficient for the one who comes in faith and considers, reads and understands them. Commentary on John 7.20.30-31.[1]

Many Signs Before and After the Resurrection. Chrysostom: For as before the resurrection it was necessary that many signs should be done, in order that they might believe that he was the Son of God, so it was also necessary after the resurrection, in order that they might admit that he had arisen. Another reason why he added "In the presence of his disciples" is because he conversed with them alone after the resurrection. Therefore he also said, "The world sees me no more."[2] Homilies on the Gospel of John 87.2.[3]

20:31 *Believing in Christ the Son of God*

John Foresaw Heresies. Irenaeus: The Gospel knew no other Son of man but him who

[1]CSCO 4 3:358-59. [2]Jn 14:19. [3]NPNF 1 14:328*.

was of Mary, who also suffered. There was no Christ who flew away from Jesus before the passion. The Gospel knew about him who was born as Jesus Christ the Son of God and that this same person suffered and rose again, as John, the disciple of the Lord verifies, saying, "But these are written so that you may come to believe that Jesus is the Messiah, the Son of God, and that through believing you may have life in his name." [He foresaw] blasphemous systems that divide the Lord, as far as lies in their power, saying that he was formed of two different substances. Against Heresies 3.16.5.[4]

The Reason for the Gospel Account. Tertullian: Why does this Gospel, at its very termination, intimate that these things were ever written unless, to use its own words, it is so "that you might believe that Jesus Christ is the Son of God"? Whenever, therefore, you take any of the statements of this Gospel and apply them to demonstrate the identity of the Father and the Son, supposing that they serve your views there, you are contending against the definite purpose of the Gospel. For these things certainly are not written that you may believe that Jesus Christ is the Father but the Son. Against Praxeas 25.[5]

What Is True Faith? Hilary of Poitiers: The one reason that he alleges for writing his Gospel is that all may believe that Jesus is the Christ, the Son of God. If it is sufficient for salvation to believe that he is the Christ, why does he add "the Son of God"? But if the true faith is nothing less than the belief that Christ is not merely Christ but Christ the Son of God, then assuredly the name of Son is not attached to Christ as a customary appendage due to adoption, seeing that it is essential to salvation. If then, salvation consists in the confession of the name, must not the name express the truth? If the name expresses the truth, by what authority can he be called a creature? It is not the confession of a creature but the confession of the Son that shall give us salvation. To believe, therefore, that Jesus Christ is the Son of God is true salvation, is the acceptable service of an unfeigned faith. For we have no love within us toward God the Father except through faith in the Son. On the Trinity 6.41-42.[6]

Jesus Is Life. Chrysostom: He speaks in general to humankind, showing that it is not the one who we believe in but on ourselves that he bestows a very great favor "in his name," that is, "through him." For he is the Life. Homilies on the Gospel of John 87.2.[7]

An Ending and a Preface. Augustine: This paragraph indicates, as it were, the end of the book. But afterward, there is still the account of how the Lord manifested himself at the sea of Tiberias and in the draught of fishes where special reference is made to the mystery of the church and its future character in the final resurrection of the dead. I think, therefore, it is arranged in this way in order to give special prominence to the fact that the end of the book has, as it were, been interposed, and that this ending was meant to be a kind of preface to the narrative that was to follow, in order in some measure to give it a position of greater eminence. Tractates on the Gospel of John 122.1.[8]

[4]ANF 1:442*. [5]*TTAP* 170**. [6]NPNF 2 9:113*. [7]NPNF 1 14:328*. [8]NPNF 1 7:439**.

21:1-11 Jesus and the Amazing Catch of Fish

[1]After this Jesus revealed himself again to the disciples by the Sea of Tiberias; and he revealed himself in this way. [2]Simon Peter, Thomas called the Twin, Nathanael of Cana in Galilee, the sons of Zebedee, and two others of his disciples were together. [3]Simon Peter said to them, "I am going fishing." They said to him, "We will go with you." They went out and got into the boat; but that night they caught nothing.

[4]Just as day was breaking, Jesus stood on the beach; yet the disciples did not know that it was Jesus. [5]Jesus said to them, "Children, have you any fish?" They answered him, "No." [6]He said to them, "Cast the net on the right side of the boat, and you will find some." So they cast it, and now they were not able to haul it in, for the quantity of fish. [7]That disciple whom Jesus loved said to Peter, "It is the Lord!" When Simon Peter heard that it was the Lord, he put on his clothes, for he was stripped for work, and sprang into the sea. [8]But the other disciples came in the boat, dragging the net full of fish, for they were not far from the land, but about a hundred yards[m] off.

[9]When they got out on land, they saw a charcoal fire there, with fish lying on it, and bread. [10]Jesus said to them, "Bring some of the fish that you have just caught." [11]So Simon Peter went aboard and hauled the net ashore, full of large fish, a hundred and fifty-three of them; and although there were so many, the net was not torn.

m Greek *two hundred cubits*

Overview: The disciples go fishing, no longer afraid (Chrysostom). One might ask, however, why they return to fishing after all that had happened (Gregory the Great). However, there is nothing wrong with the disciples continuing to earn a livelihood after their conversion (Augustine, Gregory the Great). Jesus then reveals himself to them, although not all at once, so that they are not afraid to talk with him (Chrysostom). They have caught no fish, figuratively speaking, under the types and shadows of the old covenant, but then the Sun of righteousness arrives, and their nets are full (Ammonius). He addresses them as children, which is the ideal mindset for discipleship (Clement). At a word from the Lord, they cast their nets, even as they had also done when he first called them, and the fish multiplied even as Christians now are multiplying when the Word is proclaimed (Augustine). As the more contemplative of the two, John is the first to recognize that it is the Lord, while Peter, as the more fervent one, is the first to come to him (Chrysostom). None of them dared to ask who he was because they knew he was God (Jerome). Once they recognize him, Peter, who was stripped to the waist, dives into the water as though he were diving for the pearl of great price (Ephrem). Once they reach the shore, Jesus eats fish with the disciples to once again prove his resurrection, since they may have thought they had seen a spirit instead of a body (Jerome). The fish he serves them is the firstfruits of their catch (Cyril).

John records the number of fish caught as 153, which has any number of symbolic interpretations. It can be seen as a symbol for the fullness of grace of all those who partake of the Spirit (Augustine) as Peter brings the catch of the fullness of the Gentiles (100) and the elect of Israel (50) to Christ for the glory of the Trinity (3)

(Ammonius). Or one might also think of this number as pertaining to the end of the world using an arithmetic triangle that utilizes the prime number 17 (Augustine). The unbroken nets symbolize the unified church unbroken by schism in the face of the stresses of the world (Augustine). Christ came in from the sea, which is the world tossed about, onto the solid shore (Gregory the Great). He committed the church then to Peter, since he is the one who brings the catch of fish safely to the shore (Gregory the Great), where there is true rest (Gregory the Great). In this catch of fishes, contrasted with the earlier catch at the beginning of his ministry, Jesus has the disciples cast their net on the right side. The church also keeps those of the right hand after death in the sleep of peace until it is brought safely to shore in the life to come (Augustine).

21:1-2 *The Disciples Go Fishing*

The Disciples Are Free to Move About and Work. Chrysostom: Do you see that he does not remain with them continually, nor is his presence with them the same as before? He appeared, for instance, in the evening, and then disappeared. Then after eight days he appeared once again, and again he disappeared. Then he appeared later again by the sea, and then another time, causing great awe. But what does John mean when he says Jesus "showed" himself? It is clear from this that he was not seen unless he condescended to be seen because his body was from this time forward incorruptible and of unmixed purity. But why has the writer mentioned the place? To show that he had now taken away the greater part of their fear so that they now ventured out from their home and went about everywhere. For they were no longer shut up at home but had gone into Galilee to avoid danger from the Jews. Simon, therefore, comes to fish. For since neither [Christ] was with them continually, nor was the Spirit yet given, nor were they at that time yet entrusted with anything and so had nothing to do, they returned to their trade. Homilies on the Gospel of John 87.2.[1]

Why Return to Fishing? Gregory the Great: We may ask why Peter, who was a fisherman before his conversion, returned to fishing, when it is said, "No one putting his hand to the plow, and looking back, is fit for the kingdom of God."[2] Forty Gospel Homilies 24.[3]

The Disciples Continue to Earn a Livelihood. Augustine: If the disciples had done this when Jesus was lying in the grave and before he rose from the dead ... we might think they did so out of despair. But now after he has risen from the grave, after seeing the marks of his wounds ... after he breathed the Holy Spirit on them ... all at once they become what they were before, fishers, not of people but of fishes. We must remember then that they were not forbidden by their apostleship from earning their livelihood by a lawful use of their skills, provided they had no other means of living.... For if the blessed Paul did not use that power that he had with the rest of the preachers of the gospel, as they did, but went to warfare using his own resources in case the Gentiles, who were aliens from the name of Christ, might be offended at an apparently minor doctrine; if, educated in another way, he learned a craft he never knew before so that, while the teacher worked with his own hands, the hearer might not be burdened—how much more might Peter, who had been a fisherman, work at what he knew if he had nothing else to live on at the time? But how is it that he had nothing, someone will ask, when our Lord promises, "Seek first the kingdom of God and his righteousness, and all these things shall be added to you"?[4] Our Lord, we answer, fulfilled this promise by bringing them the fishes to catch, for who else brought them? He did not bring on them that poverty that obliged them to go fishing, except in order to

[1]NPNF 1 14:328**; PG 59:475. [2]Lk 9:62. [3]CS 123:180**. [4]Mt 6:33.

exhibit a miracle. TRACTATE ON THE GOSPEL OF JOHN 122.2-4.[5]

RETURNING TO WORK AFTER CONVERSION. GREGORY THE GREAT: We know that Peter was a fisherman, whereas Matthew was a tax collector. Peter returned to fishing after his conversion, but Matthew did not again sit down to his business of tax collecting, because it is one thing to seek to make a living by fishing and another to increase one's gains by money from the tax office.[6] For there are some businesses that cannot—or hardly can—be carried on without sin. And these cannot be returned to after conversion. FORTY GOSPEL HOMILIES 24.[7]

THE DISCIPLES BOUND TO ONE ANOTHER. CHRYSOSTOM: Having then nothing to do, they went fishing, and they did this at night because they were terribly frightened. Luke also mentions this,[8] but this is not the same occasion. And the other disciples followed because from that time on they were bound to one another, and at the same time desired to see the fishing and use their leisure time well. While they were working and tired, Jesus presents himself before them and does not reveal himself all at once so that they enter into conversation with him. HOMILIES ON THE GOSPEL OF JOHN 87.2.[9]

21:3-4 *The Disciples Catch Nothing*

FEW FISH CAUGHT UNDER THE TYPES AND SHADOWS. AMMONIUS: This is the whole import of this passage: Those who had completed their work in the darkness, before the disciples, had not caught anyone in their nets and snatched them from demonic deceit. They may have caught a very few people, which is almost the same thing as nobody. Not even those who served the types and shadows had been caught, since they also despised the divine law and obeyed instead human commandments. Even worse, the multitude of the Gentiles had also not been caught by the nets, since they did not receive the teachings of God. But when "the sun of righteousness" came, that is, the one who hungered after the salvation of the human race, he did not find anything edible among them. He told them to cast forth the word of the gospel, which is the teaching, on the right side of the boat. One can understand that the law and the prophets had been casting forth their words on the left side. By the grace of the one who gave the order, the disciples drew in many. For the marvel on this matter surpasses the fish of the apostles. FRAGMENTS ON JOHN 636.[10]

21:5 *Children, Have You Any Fish?*

THE SIMPLICITY OF CHILDREN IDEAL FOR DISCIPLESHIP. CLEMENT OF ALEXANDRIA: Pedagogy is the training of children, as is clear from the word itself. It remains for us to consider the children whom Scripture points to and then to give the *Paedagogue*[11] charge of them. We are the children. In many ways Scripture celebrates us and describes us in many different figures of speech, giving variety to the simplicity of the faith by diverse names. Accordingly, in the Gospel, "the Lord, standing on the shore, says to the disciples"—they happened to be fishing—"and called aloud, 'Children, have you no fish?' " In this way he addresses those who were already in the position of disciples as children . . . setting before us, for our imitation, the simplicity that is in children. CHRIST THE EDUCATOR 1.5.[12]

21:6 *There Were Many Fish*

THE TWO CATCHES OF FISH. AUGUSTINE: The Lord appeared to his disciples after his resurrection by the sea of Tiberius and found them fishing, although they had caught nothing. While fishing at night, they caught nothing. Day dawned, and they made a catch because they saw

[5]NPNF 1 7:439-40**. [6]At that time, this job was often abused for economic gain. [7]CS 123:180**. [8]Lk 24:37. [9]NPNF 1 14:328**; PG 59:475. [10]*JKGK* 355. [11]Instructor. [12]ANF 2:212.

Christ the day, and at a word from the Lord they cast their nets and made a catch. Now we find two catches of fish made by Christ's disciples at a word from Christ. The first one refers to when he chose them and made them disciples.[13] The second one refers to this current period after he had risen from the dead. Let us compare them, if you agree, and take careful note of the differences between them. It has a lot to do, after all, with the consolidation of our faith.

On the first occasion, then, when the Lord came across the fishermen whom he had not found previously, they had also caught nothing all night, having worked hard without result. He ordered them to throw out the nets. He did not say, on the right, he did not say, on the left, but he simply said, "Throw out the nets." Before the resurrection, the nets were let out all over the place. After the resurrection, the right side is chosen. Next, in the first catch of fish, the boats are overloaded, the nets are breaking. In this last one after the resurrection, there is no overloading of the boat or breaking of the seine. When they fished the first time, the number of fish caught is not mentioned. This time, after the resurrection, a definite number of fish is mentioned. So let us carry on with the first, in order to arrive at the last.... In the first account we have the nets, the nets of the word, the nets of preaching. Here are the nets. Let the psalm tell us, "I proclaimed, and I spoke. They were multiplied beyond counting."[14] It is as plain as a pikestaff that it is happening now. The gospel is being proclaimed, Christians are multiplying beyond counting. If they all lived good lives, they would not be overloading the boat. If they were not divided by heretics and schisms, the net would not be breaking....

The last catch of fish refers to the holy church that exists now in the few, toiling away among the many who are evil. This holy church will be realized in that certain, definite number in which no sinner will be found.... And they will be big fish because they will all be immortal, all destined to live without end. What can be bigger than what has no end? And the Evangelist made it his business to give your memory a flashback to the first catch of fish. Why else did he add, after all, "And though they were such big fish, the nets were not torn"? It was as though he were saying, "Remember that first catch of fish, when the nets were torn." This will be the kingdom of heaven, no heretics will be barking, no schismatics setting themselves apart. All will be inside, all will be at peace. SERMON 229M.1.[15]

21:7 *Peter and John See the Lord*

THE DIFFERENT RESPONSES OF PETER AND JOHN. CHRYSOSTOM: When they recognized him, the disciples Peter and John again exhibited their different temperaments. The one was more fervent, the other more contemplative. The one was ready to go, the other more penetrating. John is the one who first recognized Jesus, but Peter is the first to come to him. HOMILIES ON THE GOSPEL OF JOHN 87.2.[16]

THE DISCIPLES KNEW HE WAS BOTH GOD AND MAN. JEROME: After his resurrection, Jesus was standing on the shore; his disciples were in the ship. When the others did not know him, the disciple whom Jesus loved said to Peter, "It is the Lord." For virginity is the first to recognize a virgin body. Jesus was the same as he was before, yet he was not seen alike by all as the same. And immediately it is added, "And no one dared ask him, 'Who are you?' for they knew that he was the Lord." No one dared because they knew that he was God. They ate with him at dinner because they saw he was a man and had flesh. It was not that he was one person as God, another as man: but, being one and the same Son of God, he was known as man, adored as God. AGAINST JOHN OF JERUSALEM 35.[17]

PETER DIVES FOR THE PEARL OF GREAT PRICE. EPHREM THE SYRIAN. Men stripped their clothes off and dived and drew you out, pearl! It

[13]Lk 5:1-11. [14]Ps 40:5 (39:6 LXX). [15]*WSA* 3 6:315-16*. See also Augustine's comment on Jn 21:11. [16]NPNF 1 14:329*. [17]NPNF 2 6:443**.

was not kings that put you before people, but those naked ones who were a type of the poor and the fishers and the Galileans. For clothed bodies were not able to come to you.[18] They came that were stripped as children. They plunged their bodies and came down to you. And you much desired them, and you helped them who thus loved you. They gave you good news: their tongues before their hearts did the poor [fishermen] open and produced and showed the new riches among the merchants. On the wrists of people they put you as a medicine of life. The naked ones in a type saw your rising again by the seashore. And by the side of the lake, they, the apostles[19] of a truth, saw the rising again of the Son of your Creator. By you and by your Lord the sea and the lake were beautified. The diver came up from the sea and put on his clothing. And from the lake too Simon Peter came up swimming and put on his coat; clothed as with coats, with the love of both of you, were these two. The Pearl, Hymn 5.3-4.[20]

21:9-10 *Jesus Eats Fish*

Jesus Eats to Prove the Resurrection. Jerome: Our Lord ate to prove the resurrection, not to give his palate the pleasure of tasting of honey. He asked for a fish broiled on the coals that he might confirm the doubting apostles who did not dare approach him because they thought they saw not a body but a spirit. Against John of Jerusalem 34.[21]

The Firstfruits of Their Catch. Cyril of Alexandria: They see a fire of coals, for the Savior had kindled a fire miraculously and put a fish on it that he had caught by his ineffable power. This too he had done by design. For it was not the hand of the holy apostles or the preaching of these spiritual fisherman among the human race that started the work. For he first caught one fish as the firstfruits of those who were to come (not that we mean one precisely, for by one is signified a small number). Then afterward the disciples caught the multitude in their nets, being enabled by his divine bidding to catch what they were fishing for. Commentary on the Gospel of John 12.1.[22]

21:11 *Peter Brings the Net to Shore with 153 Fish*

The Catch of the Gentiles and the Elect of Israel. Ammonius: Peter drags the dragnet with the others, bringing the catch to Christ. The hundred can be understood to mean the fullness of the Gentiles. The fifty refers to the elect of Israel who have been saved. And the three set one's mind on the revelation of the holy Trinity, to whose glory the life of the believers who were caught in the dragnet is naturally connected. Fragments on John 637.[23]

The Mystery of the 153 Fish and the Unbroken Nets. Augustine: When to the number of 10, representing the Law,[24] we add the Holy Spirit as represented by 7,[25] we have 17. And when this number is used for the adding together of every serial number it contains, from 1 up to itself, the sum amounts to 153. For if you add 2 to 1, you have 3 of course. If to these you add 3 and 4, the whole makes 10, etc.[26] . . . All therefore who are sharers in such grace are symbolized by this number, that is, are symbolically represented. This number has, besides, three times over, the number of 50, and 3 in addition, with reference to the mystery of the Trinity; while, again, the number of 50 is made up by multiplying 7 by 7, with the addition of 1, for 7 times 7 make 49. And the 1 is added to show that there is one who is expressed by 7 on account of his sevenfold operation. And we

[18]Ephrem perhaps is referring to those clothed in sin who are plunged into the waters of baptism, which he here parallels to Peter's plunge into the water to find the pearl of great price—Christ. [19]The same word in Syriac means "naked" and "apostle." [20]NPNF 2 13:297-98*. [21]NPNF 2 6:442*. [22]LF 48:699**. [23]*JKGK* 355. [24]Symbolized by ten commandments. [25]See Is 11:2-3 and the sevenfold gift of the Spirit. [26]That is, 1+2+3+4+5+6+7+8+9+10+11+12+13+14+15+16+17=153.

know that it was on the fiftieth day after our Lord's ascension that the Holy Spirit was sent, for whom the disciples were commanded to wait according to the promise.[27] It was not, then, without a purpose that these fishes were described as so many in number, and so large in size, that is, as both 153 and large. Tractates on the Gospel of John 122.8-9.[28]

The Sea Signifies the World. Gregory the Great: The question also arises as to why, after his resurrection, the Lord stood on the shore while his disciples were laboring in the sea, when before his resurrection he walked on the waves of the sea[29] in his disciples' sight. . . . What does the sea indicate but this present age, which is tossed about by the uproar of circumstances and the waves of this corruptible life? What does the solidity of the shore signify but the uninterrupted continuity of eternal peace? Therefore since the disciples were still held in the waves of this mortal life, they were laboring on the sea. But since our Redeemer had already passed beyond his perishable body, after his resurrection he stood on the shore. Forty Gospel Homilies 24.[30]

The Church Entrusted to Peter. Gregory the Great: Why was Peter the one who brought the net to land? Our holy church had been entrusted to him.[31] It was to him individually that it was said, "Simon, son of John, do you love me? Feed my sheep."[32] What was afterward disclosed to him in words was now indicated to him by an action. Because the church's preacher was to part us from the waves of this world, it was surely necessary that Peter bring the net full of fish to land. He dragged the fish to the firm ground of the shore because by his preaching he revealed to the faithful the stability of our eternal home. He accomplished this by his words and by his letters, and he accomplishes it daily by his miraculous signs. . . . When the net is said to be full of large fish, we are told how many, namely, 153. Forty Gospel Homilies 24.[33]

A Symbol of Unity. Gregory the Great: Seven and ten multiplied by three make fifty-one. . . . The fiftieth year was a year of rest to the whole people from all their work. In unity is true rest. For where division is, true rest cannot be. Forty Gospel Homilies 24.[34]

The Mystery of the Church at the End. Augustine: The miracle of the catch of fish is a great mystery in the great Gospel of John. And it is recorded in the last chapter to commend it all the more forcefully to our attention. There were seven disciples taking part in that fishing expedition: Peter, Thomas, Nathanael,[35] the two sons of Zebedee and two others whose names are not given. This number refers to the end of time because time is counted by periods of seven days. The statement "When morning arrived, Jesus stood on the shore" also pertains to the end because the shore is the end of the sea and therefore signifies the end of the world. Tractates on the Gospel of John 122.6.[36]

A Type of the Church. Augustine: The Lord indicated here the kind of character the church would have in the end of the world, just as by that other draught of fishes[37] he indicated its present character. The one our Lord did at the beginning of his ministry, the other after his resurrection. The former draught of fishes signified the mixture of bad and good that composes the church at present. The latter signified the good alone that it will contain in eternity when the world is ended and the resurrection of the dead completed. Furthermore, on that previous occasion Jesus did not stand on the shore but went into a ship which was Simon's and asked him to put out a little from the land. . . . In the former

[27]See Acts 1:4. [28]NPNF 1 7:442-43. See also Augustine's *Letter* 55.17.31 (NPNF 1:313-14). [29]Mt 14:25. [30]CS 123:180*. [31]Mt 16:18. [32]Jn 21:17. [33]CS 123:182*. [34]CS 123:183**. [35]In his comments on Jn 1:45-51, Augustine had not included Nathanael among the Twelve. See his *Tractates on the Gospel of John* 7.17 (NPNF 1 7:54). [36]NPNF 1 7:441**. [37]See Lk 5:1-11. Augustine contrasts this earlier catch of fish with John's account here.

account they put the fishes that were caught into the ship and did not, as here, draw the net to the shore. . . . The one account took place before the resurrection, the other after the resurrection of the Lord because in the earlier account it signified our being called by the Lord. The account here signifies our being raised from the dead.

In the earlier account the nets are not thrown to the right or to the left so that we might think he was indicating either the good if it was to the right, or the bad if it was to the left. Instead, he has them throw the nets indifferently: "Let down your nets for a draught" is all that he says, meaning that the good and bad were mixed together. But here in this later account he says, "Cast the net on the right side of the ship," to signify those who should stand on the right hand, the good. . . . But those who belong to the resurrection of life, that is, to the right hand, and are caught within the net of the Christian name, shall only appear on the shore, that is, at the end of the world, after the resurrection. This is why they were not able to draw the net into the ship and unload the fishes, as they were before. . . . The church keeps these of the right hand, after death, in the sleep of peace, as it were, in the deep till the net comes to shore. Tractates on the Gospel of John 122.7.[38]

[38]NPNF 1 7:441-42**.

21:12-14 Jesus Invites the Disciples to Eat with Him

[12]Jesus said to them, "Come and have breakfast." Now none of the disciples dared ask him, "Who are you?" They knew it was the Lord. [13]Jesus came and took the bread and gave it to them, and so with the fish. [14]This was now the third time that Jesus was revealed to the disciples after he was raised from the dead.

Overview: Jesus ate with his disciples on the shore just as the bodies of the just will eat, not because they need to, but because they want to (Augustine). The disciples were in awe of him because he no longer shielded his divine power from them (Chrysostom). Just like the meal they were eating on the shore, Christ is the broiled fish who suffered and is consumed; he is the bread that came down from heaven (Augustine). The seven disciples present for this meal signify the future eschatological banquet when all things will be brought to perfection (Gregory the Great). John speaks of this appearance of Jesus as the "third time," which is a reference to manifestations of Jesus, not to days, since Jesus obviously appeared to his disciples more than three times (Augustine). All these appearances only cause us to look forward even more to our own resurrection (Chrysostom).

21:12 *Come and Eat*

Resurrected Bodies Eat Out of Desire, Not Necessity. Augustine: The bodies of the righteous at the resurrection will need neither any fruit to preserve them from dying of disease or the wasting decay of old age nor any bodily nourishment to prevent hunger and thirst. For they will be endowed with such a sure and inviolable gift of immortality that they will not eat because they have to, but only if they want to. Not the power but the necessity of eating and drinking shall be taken away from them . . . just like our Savior after his resurrection took meat and drink with his disciples, with spiritual but still real flesh, not for the sake of nourishment, but in an exercise of his power. CITY OF GOD 13.22.[1]

THEY WERE IN AWE. CHRYSOSTOM: "They knew that it was the Lord," and therefore they did not ask him, "Who are you?" But seeing that his form was altered and full of awe, they were greatly amazed and wanted to ask something about it. But fear, and their knowledge that he was not someone else but the same person, checked the inquiry, and they only ate what he created for them by exercising greater power than before. For here he no longer looks to heaven, nor does he perform those human acts he did before, thereby showing that those things that he did previously were done by way of condescension. HOMILIES ON THE GOSPEL OF JOHN 87.2.[2]

21:13-14 *Jesus Feeds the Seven Disciples*

BREAD ALLUDES TO THE SACRAMENT. AUGUSTINE: Mystically, the broiled fish is Christ who suffered. And he is the bread that came down from heaven.[3] The church is united to his body in order to participate in everlasting blessedness. This is why he says, "Bring of the fish that you have now caught," in order to signify that all of us who have this hope and are in that number seven of disciples, which represents the universal church here, partake of this great sacrament and are admitted to this bliss. TRACTATE ON THE GOSPEL OF JOHN 123.2.[4]

SEVEN DISCIPLES SIGNIFY THE ESCHATOLOGICAL BANQUET. GREGORY THE GREAT: By holding this last feast with seven disciples . . . he declares that only those who are full of the sevenfold grace of the Holy Spirit shall be with him at his eternal feast. All time here on this earth unrolls in seven days, and the number seven indicates those who now rise above earthly things in their pursuit of perfection. It signifies those who are not bound by love of this world, who when tempted by anything at all do not suppress the [positive] desires that have arisen in them. These are the ones who feast at this final banquet in the presence of Truth. . . . Desire then to be filled with the presence of this Spirit. Weigh carefully what you do now for its impact on your future at that banquet. FORTY GOSPEL HOMILIES 24.[5]

JESUS' POSTRESURRECTION APPEARANCES. AUGUSTINE: We find in the four Evangelists ten distinct appearances of the Lord to different persons after his resurrection: First was to the women near the sepulcher;[6] the second to the women returning from the sepulcher;[7] the third, to Peter;[8] the fourth, to the two going to Emmaus;[9] the fifth, to the large number in Jerusalem when Thomas was not present;[10] the sixth when Thomas saw him;[11] the seventh at the sea of Tiberias;[12] the eighth by all the Eleven on a mountain of Galilee mentioned by Matthew;[13] a ninth when for the last time he sat eating with the disciples;[14] a tenth when he was seen no longer on earth but lifted up in the cloud as he ascended into heaven.[15] HARMONY OF THE GOSPELS 3.25.83.[16]

REFERENCE TO DAYS WHEN HE APPEARED. AUGUSTINE: [The "third time"] is a reference not to appearances but to days. In other words, the first day includes all of his manifestations of himself on the day of his resurrection, then the second day occurs eight days after that when Thomas saw and believed, and now the third day occurs with the draught of fishes. And afterward

[1]NPNF 1 2:256-57**. [2]NPNF 1 14:329*; PG 59:475-76. [3]See Jn 6:41. [4]NPNF 1 7:444*. [5]CS 123:184-85**. [6]Jn 20:14. [7]Mt 28:9. [8]Lk 24:36. [9]Lk 24:15. [10]Jn 20:19-24. [11]Jn 20:26. [12]Jn 21:1. [13]Mt 28:16-17. [14]Mk 16:14. [15]Mk 16:19; Lk 24:50-51. [16]NPNF 1 6:223-24**.

as often as he saw them up to the time of his ascension. Tractate on the Gospel of John 123.3.[17]

Looking Forward to Our Resurrection. Chrysostom: Perhaps when you heard these things, you glowed and called those happy who were then with him along with those who shall be with him at the day of the general resurrection. Let us then make every effort so that we may see that admirable face. For if when now we hear, we are so enflamed, and desire to have been in those days that he spent upon earth, and to have heard his voice and seen his face and to have approached and touched and ministered unto him—consider how great a thing it will be to see him no longer in a mortal body or doing human actions but with a bodyguard of angels, being ourselves also in a form of unmixed purity, and beholding him and enjoying the rest of that bliss which surpasses all language. Therefore I beseech you, let us use every means so as not to miss such glory. For nothing is difficult if we are willing, nothing burdensome if we apply ourselves. "If we endure, we shall also reign with him."[18] Homilies on the Gospel of John 87.3.[19]

[17]NPNF 1 7:444**. [18]2 Tim 2:12. [19]NPNF 1 14:329*; PG 59:476.

21:15-19 Jesus' Reinstatement of Peter

[15]When they had finished breakfast, Jesus said to Simon Peter, "Simon, son of John, do you love me more than these?" He said to him, "Yes, Lord; you know that I love you." He said to him, "Feed my lambs." [16]A second time he said to him, "Simon, son of John, do you love me?" He said to him, "Yes, Lord; you know that I love you." He said to him, "Tend my sheep." [17]He said to him the third time, "Simon, son of John, do you love me?" Peter was grieved because he said to him the third time, "Do you love me?" And he said to him, "Lord, you know everything; you know that I love you." Jesus said to him, "Feed my sheep. [18]Truly, truly, I say to you, when you were young, you girded yourself and walked where you would; but when you are old, you will stretch out your hands, and another will gird you and carry you where you do not wish to go." [19](This he said to show by what death he was to glorify God.) And after this he said to him, "Follow me."

Overview: Jesus deals gently with Peter in not bringing up his denial, nor does he reproach him directly for what had taken place (Chrysostom). Peter's threefold denial is answered by a threefold confession (Jerome) as he effaced his former sin and received a threefold restoration (Ambrose). Peter is restored by the good Shepherd and then called, along with those ministers who follow in his steps, to feed his lambs (Augustine), which are the young Christians who later mature into the sheep Peter is also called to tend (Theodore). This is how we show the love Christ was asking for from Peter, by serving our neighbor (Chrysostom)—what a true shepherd would do—out of love for God and the sheep (Aphrahat). When the prince of pastors commissions Peter to be a pastor, he also cautions him and all pastors to remember that those sheep are his, not theirs (AUGUSTINE), and to remember their own fall so that they are merciful to their flocks (ROMANUS).

Jesus asks a shaken (JEROME) and more cautious Peter (BEDE) a second and a third time if he loves him and then charges him and all the disciples and ministers with a threefold command to feed the sheep (THEODORE). To feed Christ's sheep is to feed the faith of those who believe in him by exercising proper pastoral care (BEDE). Peter's threefold confession in response to his threefold denial mirrors the triple name of the confession of the Trinity in baptism, which is administered by the shepherds to those of their flock who would be sanctified and strengthened (CYRIL). Our Lord's questioning and Peter's confession of love ends in the call for a selfless love that focuses on God and the neighbor rather than oneself (AUGUSTINE). Peter was being called on to love the sheep even to the point of giving up his own life, even as his Lord had done (AUGUSTINE). We who are shepherds cannot but serve in the same way where we are called to do so (GREGORY THE GREAT).

Peter desires to suffer for Jesus, which he did not do when he was younger but will be privileged to do in his older age (CHRYSOSTOM, THEODORE). Peter will arrive at his death, which is the ultimate crown of victory of pastors and their shepherds (EPHREM), having washed away his denial with his tears (AUGUSTINE). Jesus' prophecy concerning Peter is fulfilled when he is fastened to his own cross upside down by Nero in Rome at the same time as Paul (EUSEBIUS). Peter had earlier promised that he would die for the Lord—a promise that he could not keep during our Lord's passion but did ultimately keep when he delivered up himself to martyrdom on behalf of his deliverer (AUGUSTINE). Earlier, Jesus had summoned his disciples to follow him for training; now he summons them to follow him without fear for the real mission (AUGUSTINE). Peter responds to this call, becoming the teacher not only of Jerusalem but of the whole world (CHRYSOSTOM).

21:15 *Do You Love Me? Feed My Sheep.*

JESUS DOES NOT BRING UP THE DENIAL. CHRYSOSTOM: Why, having passed by the others, does he speak with Peter on these matters? He does so because he was the chosen one of the apostles, the mouthpiece of the disciples and the leader of the band. This is why Paul went up, at one time, to inquire of him rather than of the others. And at the same time he does this to show him that he must now be joyful since the denial was put behind him. And so, Jesus entrusts to him primacy over his brothers. He does not bring up the denial, nor does he reproach him for what had taken place. Rather, he says, If you love me, preside over your brothers, and now show them the warmth of love that you have always shown and in which you rejoiced. And the life that you said you would lay down for me, now give for my sheep. HOMILIES ON THE GOSPEL OF JOHN 88.1.[1]

THREEFOLD CONFESSION OF PETER'S LOVE. AMBROSE: It is Peter, chosen by the Lord himself to feed his flock, who merits three times to hear the words "Feed my little lambs; feed my lambs; feed my sheep." And so, by feeding well the flock of Christ with the food of faith, he effaced the sin of his former fall. For this reason he is admonished three times to feed the flock. He is asked three times whether he loves the Lord in order that he may confess him three times whom he had denied three times before his crucifixion.[2] ON THE CHRISTIAN FAITH 5, PROLOGUE 2.[3]

CHRIST'S QUESTION TO PETER. AUGUSTINE: Christ rose again in the flesh, and Peter rose in the spirit because, when Christ died in his passion, Peter died by his denial. Christ the Lord was raised from the dead, and out of his love he raised Peter. He questioned him about the love he was confessing and entrusted him with his sheep. After all, what benefit could Peter confer on

[1]NPNF 1 14:331**. [2]Mt 26:69-75. [3]NPNF 2 10:284**. See also Jerome *Letter* 42.2 (NPNF 2 6:57).

Christ by the mere fact of his loving Christ? If Christ loves you, it is to your advantage, not Christ's. And if you love Christ, it is to your advantage, not Christ's. And yet Christ the Lord wanted to indicate how people ought to show that they love Christ. And he made it plain enough by entrusting him with his sheep. "Do you love me?" "I do." "Feed my sheep." All this once, all this a second time, all this a third time. Peter made no other reply than that he loved him. The Lord asked no other question but whether he loved him. When Peter answered, our Lord did nothing else but entrust his sheep to him. Sermon 229N.1.[4]

Love for Your Neighbor. Chrysostom: There are indeed many other things that are able to give us boldness toward God and to show us bright and approved, but that which most of all brings good will from on high is tender care for our neighbor—which is what Christ requires of Peter here. Homilies on the Gospel of John 88.1.[5]

Feed the Lambs. Theodore of Mopsuestia: Jesus promoted Peter and placed him as the head of the lambs of his herd and said, "Feed my lambs," that is, all those who believe in me and who, because they were instructed only recently, are weaker. And for this reason, it is necessary that you carry their burden, and protect them, and comfort them in their weakness and nourish them with the grace that was given to you. Commentary on John 7.21.15.[6]

Shepherds in the Line of Christ and Peter. Aphrahat: O pastors! Imitate that diligent pastor, the chief of the whole flock, who cared so greatly for his flock. He brought near those who were far away. He brought back the wanderers. He visited the sick. He strengthened the weak. He bound up the broken. He guarded those who were well fed. He gave himself up for the sake of the sheep. He chose and instructed excellent leaders, and committed the sheep into their hands and gave them authority over all his flock. For he said to Simon Cephas, "Feed my sheep and my lambs and my ewes." So Simon fed his sheep and fulfilled his calling and handed over the flock to you and departed. And so you also must feed and guide them well. For the pastor who cares for his sheep engages in no other pursuit along with that. He does not make a vineyard, or plant gardens, or fall into the troubles of this world. Never have we seen a pastor who left his sheep in the wilderness and became a merchant, or one who left his flock to wander and became a husbandman. But if he deserts his flock and does these things, he thereby hands over his flock to the wolves. Demonstration 10.4.[7]

Feed My Sheep, but Remember They Are Mine. Augustine: He is being armed for weightier and greater matters. He is told "Feed my sheep," a task that was certainly going to mean danger for the flesh but glory for the spirit. Just think how much he was going to suffer for the name of Christ by feeding the sheep of Christ! "Feed my sheep, feed my lambs." I mean, if you love me, what present are you going to give me? The prince of pastors made him a pastor so that Peter would feed Christ's sheep, not his own. . . .

"Feed my sheep." Why? Because you love me, because you are devoted to me, I am committing my sheep to you. Feed them, but remember they are mine. Heretical leaders, though, wish to make their own the sheep that are really Christ's. All the same, they are forced . . . to set the stamp of Christ on them. They may make them their own private flock, but they still have to register them in the Lord's name. Sermon 229O.3.[8]

Bearing the Lord's Brand. Augustine: Feed "my" sheep; he did not say "yours," did he? Feed, good servant, the Lord's sheep that bear the

[4]*WSA* 3 6:320*. [5]NPNF 1 14:331*. [6]CSCO 4 3:359-60. [7]NPNF 2 13:384-85**. [8]*WSA* 3 6:324-25. See also Bede *Homily* 2.22 (CS 111:224-25).

Lord's brand. After all, was Paul crucified for you, or were you baptized in the name of Peter and Paul?[9] So feed his sheep, washed in his baptism, sealed in his name, redeemed with his blood. "Feed," he says, "my sheep." Sermon 295.5.[10]

Remember the Mercy You Have Received. Romanus Melodus:

Peter, look to me as to how you educate;
remembering your own fall, sympathize with all;
Mindful of the maiden who caused your fall, do not be harsh;
If conceit attacks you, hear the sound of the cock's crow,
And remember the tears with whose streams I washed you,
I who alone know what is in your heart.

Peter, do you love me? Feed my flock, and love those whom I love, sympathizing with sinners.
Heed my mercy to you, since I received you who had thrice denied me.
You have a thief as gatekeeper of Paradise to give you courage.[11]
Send him those whom you wish. Because of you, Adam turned to me
Saying, "O Creator grant to me the robber as gatekeeper, and Cephas as keeper of keys.
Thou who alone dost know what is in the heart."

Kontakion on the Mission of the Apostles 31.5-6.[12]

21:16 *A Second Time*

A Condemned Peter Prepared for Love. Jerome: If the faith of the apostle Peter is shaken by his Lord's passion, it is so that with bitter weeping he may hear the soothing words "Feed my sheep." Letter 38.1.[13]

Peter Is More Cautious the Second Time. Bede: Peter also restrained himself in this inquiry of our Lord's by answering cautiously, for he remembered earlier on, when Christ's passion was drawing near, he had attributed greater constancy to himself than he possessed. Homilies on the Gospels 2.22.[14]

Simon Supervises the Shepherd. Theodore of Mopsuestia: A second time he said to him, "Tend my Sheep," that is, Simon, tend the men who are mature in faith and possessing proven wisdom, who obey you in the prescribed degrees of the church, in the apostolate, in the priesthood, and in the pastoral office. Commentary on John 7.21.16.[15]

21:17 *The Third Time*

Service to Christ. Theodore of Mopsuestia: The Savior does not say to him, fast, or keep watch for me. But, since the pastoral care of souls is more worthy and more useful to the community, he entrusts him with this. I, he says, need nothing: feed my sheep, and return to me the love with which I loved you, because I will take your care for them as care devoted to me. Commentary on John 7.21.17.[16]

Feed Them Properly. Bede: What [Christ] said to [Peter] at this point, "Feed my sheep," was surely the same thing that he had said to him more clearly before his passion, "But I have asked on your behalf that your faith may not fail you, and once you have recovered, strengthen your brothers."[17] To feed Christ's sheep is to strengthen those who believe in Christ, lest their faith fail them, and to devote oneself ceaselessly [to seeing to it] that they may make greater and greater progress in their faith. However, we must look carefully at the fact that his feeding of the Lord's flock is not to be carried out with one single approach but should rather be multifaceted.

[9]1 Cor 1:13. [10]*WSA* 3 8:199. [11]Lk 23:43; *Acta Pilati*, 26. [12]*KRBM* 1:341. [13]NPNF 2 6:47**. [14]CS 111:222*. [15]CSCO 4 3:360. [16]CSCO 4 3:360-61. [17]Lk 22:32.

A director must diligently see to it that earthly necessities are not lacking to his subjects and also be careful in providing them with examples of virtues along with words of preaching. . . . When those who are under his care may perhaps themselves have fallen into error, he as a righteous person should, according to the word of the psalmist, "accuse them mercifully and rebuke them,"[18] but he should not soothe their hearts with the oil of harmful approval. This too is one of the obligations of a pious shepherd. HOMILIES ON THE GOSPELS 2.22.[19]

THREEFOLD CONFESSION OF BAPTISM. CYRIL OF ALEXANDRIA: Here is a type given to the churches in that they ought to ask for a threefold confession of Christ from those who have chosen to love him by coming to him in holy baptism. And, by dwelling on this passage, instructors in religion may arrive at the knowledge that they cannot please the chief shepherd, that is, Christ, unless they take thought for the health of the sheep of his fold and their continual well-being. . . . Surely it is true to say that they are doing the Lord himself service who take, as it were, by the hand the mind of those who have been admitted to the faith and who are expected to be called to maturity in this faith. They are, in fact, eager to establish them firmly in the faith by every help that they can offer. Therefore, by his thrice-repeated confession the thrice-repeated denial of the blessed Peter was done away with. And, by the saying of our Lord, "Feed my lambs," we must understand a renewal as it were of the apostleship already given to him, washing away the disgrace of his fall that came in the intervening period and obliterating his faintheartedness that arose from human infirmity. COMMENTARY ON THE GOSPEL OF JOHN 12.1.[20]

SELFLESS LOVE. AUGUSTINE: To the threefold denial there is now appended a threefold confession, that his tongue may not yield a feebler service to love than to fear and imminent death may not appear to have elicited more from the lips than present life. Let it be the office of love to feed the Lord's flock, if it was the signal of fear to deny the Shepherd. Those who have this purpose in feeding the flock of Christ, that they may have them as their own and not as Christ's, are convicted of loving themselves, and not Christ, from the desire either of boasting, or wielding power or acquiring gain, and not from the love of obeying, serving and pleasing God. Against such, therefore, there stands as a wakeful sentinel this thrice-inculcated utterance of Christ, of whom the apostle complains that they seek their own, not the things that are Jesus Christ's.[21] For what else do the words "Do you love me? Feed my sheep" mean than if it were said, If you love me, do not think of feeding yourself but feed my sheep as mine and not as your own. Seek my glory in them, and not your own; my dominion, and not yours; my gain, and not yours. Otherwise, you might be found in the fellowship of those who belong to the perilous times, lovers of their own selves, and all else that is joined on to this beginning of evils. . . . With great propriety, therefore, Peter is asked, "Do you love me?" And he is found replying, "I love you." And then the command to "Feed my lambs" is applied to Peter, not only once but also a second and a third time, which also demonstrates here that love and liking are one and the same thing.[22] For the Lord, in the last question, did not say "*Diligis* me," [as he had the first two times] but, "*Amas* me?" Let us, then, love not ourselves, but him. And in feeding his sheep, let us be seeking the things which are his, not the things which are our own. For in some inexplicable way that I cannot understand, everyone who loves himself, and not God, does not love himself. And whoever loves God, and not him-

[18]Ps 141:5 (140:5 LXX). [19]CS 111:224*. [20]LF 48:703. [21]See Phil 2:21. [22]See also Augustine's discussion in *City of God* 14.7. Ancient Christian writers often emphasized the distinction between the four different Greek words for "to love." Augustine, however, was the only one found who dealt with the distinctions on this particular passage, although here as elsewhere he equates *phileō* and *agapaō* rather than distinguishing them.

self, that is the person who loves himself. For whoever cannot live by himself will certainly die by loving himself. The person, therefore, who loves himself while losing his own life does not really love himself. But when [Christ], who preserves life, is loved, a person who does not love himself ends up loving all the more when he does not love himself for this reason, namely, that he may love him [i.e., Christ] by whom he lives. Tractates on the Gospel of John 123.5.[23]

Be Ready to Die for My Sheep? Augustine: In this case, however, the Lord Jesus Christ is entrusting the slave with sheep he bought with his blood, and so he requires of the slave the capacity to suffer to the point of shedding his blood. It is as though he were saying, "Feed my sheep. I am entrusting my sheep to you." What sheep? "The ones I bought with my blood. I died for them. Do you love me? Be ready to die for them." And as a matter of fact, while that human slave of a human master would pay money for sheep destroyed, Peter paid the price of his blood for sheep preserved. Sermon 296.4.[24]

Do Not Neglect Your Calling. Gregory the Great: It appears from these words that, if one who is able refuses to feed the sheep of almighty God, he shows that he does not love the chief Shepherd. For if, in order to accomplish the good of all, the Only Begotten of the Father came forth from the concealment of the Father into our midst, what shall we say if we prefer our privacy over the good of our neighbors? And so, rest is to be desired by us with all our heart. And yet for the advantage of many it should sometimes be laid aside. For, as we ought with full desire to fly from occupation, so, if there should be a lack of anyone available to preach, we need to put a willing shoulder under the burden of occupation. And this we are taught by the conduct of two prophets [Jeremiah and Isaiah], one of whom attempted to shun the office of preaching,[25] while the other desired it.[26] Letter 7.4.[27]

21:18 *Peter's Old Age*

Young and Old Age Contrasted. Chrysostom: But how is it that after having said, "When you were young," he added, "When you are old"? By this he meant that Peter was not young at that time (because he was not), though still not yet an old man, but rather one in the prime of life. So why then did he recall to his memory his former life? He did so to make clear to Peter his standard of values. In the eyes of the world the young man is useful, the old useless. In life with me, Jesus says, this is not the case. Rather, when old age has come on, then nobility shines brighter and courage becomes more illustrious, being unimpeded by youthful passion. This he said not to terrify but to rouse Peter, for he knew about his love and that he long had yearned for this blessing. At the same time he declares the kind of death he will die. For since Peter always wanted to be in danger for his sake, "Be of good cheer," he says, "I will so satisfy your desire that, what you didn't suffer when you were young, you will suffer when you are old." Homilies on the Gospel of John 88.1.[28]

Jesus Predicts Peter's Glorious Martyrdom. Theodore of Mopsuestia: Since the Lord saw that he was tortured by the memory of the past, and that he was heavily burdened and grieved at remembering his denial, he revealed to him what he would suffer for his denial. Peter himself resigned everything to the knowledge of our Lord who taught him about the great change in circumstances he would undergo when he said, Do not be afraid about the future. Indeed I know that your love for me is so firm that you will be crucified for me upside down. And since these words of the Lord were not clear, they were explained by the evangelist: "He said this to indicate the kind of death by which he would glorify God."

[23]NPNF 1 7:445-46**. [24]*WSA* 3 8:205. [25]See Jer 1:6. [26]See Is 6:8. [27]NPNF 2 12:210-11**. [28]NPNF 1 14:332**; PG 59:479.

"Someone else will fasten a belt," because those who die the death of the cross are fastened to the wood. When Nero ordered his execution on the cross, Peter asked his executioners to crucify him upside down, that is, with his head down and his feet up. He did this so that simple people might not worship him like they did Christ because of their, otherwise, identical passion. Therefore, Peter taught people to worship the cross of the Lord [and not his], in order not to give those who like to argue the pretext to object: "In what does the cross of the Lord differ from that of Simon? Both of them were fixed to the cross in the same manner." Therefore he changed how he would die on his cross. . . . The words, "and take you where you do not wish to go," are said because the crucified must necessarily be bound by others where he doesn't want to be. Commentary on John 7.21.18-19.[29]

21:19 *A Death That Glorifies God*

The Reward of Faithful Pastors. Ephrem the Syrian: The Lord did not hand over his little flock to its pastor until he had received genuine pledges. He received the threefold [confession] that [Simon] had professed as trustworthy pledges for the three [denials]. Therefore, when his Master said [to him], "Do you love me?" our Lord was wanting to receive from him his true love so that, after having given the pledge of his love, [Simon] might receive [Jesus'] sheep as a flock. When [the Lord] saw that his mouth was confessing and that his tears were a seal, he gave him the reward reserved for pastors, namely, death, since this is the crown of victory of the pastors and their shepherds. [The Lord] was not able to give Simon the allotted portion of death until he had received from him [the pledge of] his love. For in the same way our Lord would not have given his life for his little flock if it had not been on account of his love for it. Commentary on Tatian's Diatessaron 9.5.[30]

Jesus Prophesied Peter's Martyrdom. Augustine: Peter accomplished later on by the grace of God what he had previously been unable to do by self-reliance. You see, after the Lord had entrusted him with his, not Peter's sheep, to feed them, not for himself but for the Lord, he told him about his future martyrdom, which he had forfeited the first time because he had been in much too much of a hurry. "When you are older," he said, "someone else will gird you and carry you where you do not wish to go. He said this, though, to signify by what death he was going to glorify the Lord." It came about that Peter arrived at his martyrdom, having washed away his denial with his tears. What had been promised him by the Savior could not be taken away from him by the tempter. Sermon 285.3.[31]

The History of Peter Recorded. Eusebius of Caesarea: [Nero] publicly announced himself as the first among God's chief enemies and so was led on to the slaughter of the apostles. It is, therefore, recorded that Paul was beheaded in Rome itself[32] and that Peter likewise was crucified under Nero.[33] This account of Peter and Paul is substantiated by the fact that their names are preserved in the cemeteries of that place even to the present day. It is confirmed likewise by Caius, a member of the church, who arose under Zephyrinus, bishop of Rome. He, in a published disputation with Proclus,[34] the leader of the Phrygian heresy,[35] speaks as follows concerning the places where the sacred corpses of the aforesaid apostles are laid: "But I can show the trophies of the apostles. For if you will go to the Vatican[36] or to the Ostian way, you will

[29]CSCO 4 3:362-63. [30]*ECTD* 156-57**. [31]*WSA* 3 8:97. [32]See Clement of Rome *To the Corinthians* 5. [33]Ibid. [34]This Proclus probably introduced Montanism into Rome at the beginning of the third century. According to Pseudo-Tertullian (*Against All Heresies* 7), he was a leader of one division of the Montanists, the other division being composed of followers of Aeschines. He is probably to be identified with the *Proculus noster*, classed by Tertullian, in *Against Valentinus* 5, with Justin Martyr, Miltiades and Irenaeus as a successful opponent of heresy. [35]The sect of the Montanists. It was called the "Phrygian heresy" from the fact that it took its rise in Phrygia. [36]According to an ancient tradition, Peter was crucified upon the hill of Janiculum, near the Vatican, where the church of San Pietro in Montorio now stands. A more probable tradition makes the scene of execution the Vatican hill itself, where

find the trophies of those who laid the foundations of this church." And that they both suffered martyrdom at the same time is stated by Dionysius, bishop of Corinth, in his epistle to the Romans in the following words: "You have thus by such an admonition bound together the planting of Peter and of Paul at Rome and Corinth. For both of them planted and likewise taught us in our Corinth. And they taught together in the same way in Italy and suffered martyrdom at the same time."[37] I have quoted these things in order that the truth of the history might be still more confirmed. Ecclesiastical History 2.25.5-8.[38]

Christ Dies for Peter First, Not Vice Versa. Augustine: Such was the end reached by that denier and lover—elated by his presumption, prostrated by his denial, cleansed by his weeping, approved by his confession, crowned by his suffering. This was the end he reached, to die with a perfected love for the name of him with whom by a perverted forwardness he had promised to die. After he was strengthened by Christ's resurrection, Peter would do what in his weakness he had promised prematurely. For the necessary order was that Christ should first die for Peter's salvation and then that Peter should die for the preaching of Christ. The boldness thus begun by human temerity was an utter inversion of the order that had been instituted by the Truth. Peter thought he was going to lay down his life for Christ[39]—the one to be delivered on behalf of the deliverer—seeing that Christ had come to lay down his life for all his own, including Peter, which, you see, was now done. From here on out, a true strength of heart (because it was graciously given) may be assumed for incurring death itself for the name of the Lord and not a false one presumptuously usurped through an erroneous estimate of ourselves. Tractates on the Gospel of John 123.4.[40]

Called to Attain the Prize. Augustine: He said, "Follow me," but not in the same way as when he had previously called the disciples. Then too, certainly, he said, "Follow me."[41] But then it was to school he was summoning them; now it is to the prize giving. Sermon 147.3.[42]

Peter Will Glorify God. Chrysostom: Christ told Peter not that he would die, but that he would "glorify God." In this way, we learn that suffering for Christ is both an honor and glory for the sufferer. "And when he had spoken this, he said, "Follow Me." Here again Jesus alludes to his tender carefulness, and to Peter's being very closely attached to himself. If anyone should ask, "How then did James assume the see at Jerusalem?" I reply that Christ appointed Peter, not as Bishop of this see, but as Doctor of the whole world. Homilies on the Gospel of John 88.1.[43]

Nero's circus was and where the persecution took place. In the fourth century the remains of Peter were transferred from the Catacombs of San Sebastiano (where they are said to have been interred in 258) to the Basilica of St. Peter, which occupied the sight of the present basilica on the Vatican. [37]Gk *kata ton auton kairon.* The *kata* allows some margin in time and does not necessarily imply the same day. Dionysius is the first one to connect the deaths of Peter and Paul chronologically, but later it became quite the custom. One tradition put their deaths on the same day, one year apart (Augustine and Prudentius, e.g., are said to support this tradition). Jerome (*On the Lives of Illustrious Men* 1) is the first to state explicitly that they suffered on the same day. Eusebius puts their martyrdom in 67, Jerome in 68. The Roman Catholic Church celebrates the death of Peter on June 29 and that of Paul on June 30 but has no fixed tradition as to the year of the death of either of them. See notes in NPNF 2 1:129-30 for this and the previous notes. [38]NPNF 2 1:129-30**. See also Tertullian *Scorpiace* 15 (ANF 3:648). [39]See Jn 13:37. [40]NPNF 1 7:445*. [41]Mk 1:17. [42]*WSA* 3 4:449. [43]NPNF 1 14:332**.

21:20-23 THE BELOVED DISCIPLE

[20]Peter turned and saw following them the disciple whom Jesus loved, who had lain close to his breast at the supper and had said, "Lord, who is it that is going to betray you?" [21]When Peter saw him, he said to Jesus, "Lord, what about this man?" [22]Jesus said to him, "If it is my will that he remain until I come, what is that to you? Follow me!" [23]The saying spread abroad among the brethren that this disciple was not to die; yet Jesus did not say to him that he was not to die, but, "If it is my will that he remain until I come, what is that to you?"

Overview: The disciple whom Jesus loves is the priest, martyr and teacher who now sleeps at Ephesus (Eusebius). Peter asks about John's future as one with whom he would be closely bound in the subsequent history of the apostles (Chrysostom). Our text ensures our understanding of Peter's love for our Lord even as it also ensures we know of our Lord's love for John. But the love he has for us now is only a shadow of that love that is yet to be realized in the life to come, when there will be nothing that would hinder his love for us (Augustine). Jesus again invites the disciples to follow him, but this time they can expect to suffer and die for the name, except John, whom Jesus did not want to suffer martyrdom (Augustine). Because of this, there was an unfounded expectation that John would remain alive until the Lord's return (Tertullian). John's writings, however, attest that he never believed there was such a promise, nor would he yield to such an empty hope (Ambrose). Peter, as John's close friend, is concerned about what would happen to John, but history tells us that John lived seventy-three more years after Jesus' ascension, dying in peace and serenity during the time of Trajan (Theodore).

21:20 *The Disciple Whom Jesus Loved*

The Disciple Leaned on the Lord's Breast. Eusebius of Caesarea: For in Asia also great luminaries have fallen asleep who will rise again on the last day of the advent of the Lord, when he shall come with glory from heaven and shall search out all the saints. . . . And this is also where John is, who leaned on the bosom of the Lord, who was a priest wearing the miter, a martyr and a teacher, and he sleeps at Ephesus. Ecclesiastical History 3.31.3.[1]

21:21 *Lord, What About This Man?*

Peter Speaks Up for John. Chrysostom: Why has Peter reminded us of [John's] reclining? Not without cause or by chance but to show us what boldness Peter had after the denial. For he who then did not dare to question Jesus but turned this task over to another was now entrusted with the chief authority over the brothers. And not only does he not commit to another what relates to himself, but he himself now puts a question to his Master concerning another. John is silent, but Peter speaks. He also shows here the love that he had toward him. For Peter greatly loved John, as is clear from what followed, and their close union is shown both throughout the Gospel and also in the Acts.[2] When therefore Christ had foretold great things of Peter and committed the world to his care and had foretold his martyrdom and testified that his love was greater than that of the others, desiring to have John also to share in this with him, he said, "And

[1]FC 19:189. [2]See Acts 3-4.

what shall this man do? Shall he not travel the same road with us?" On that other occasion, because he is not able himself to ask the question, he put John forward. Similarly, now desiring to return the favor and supposing that John would want to ask about matters pertaining to himself but lacked the courage, he himself undertook the questioning. HOMILIES ON THE GOSPEL OF JOHN 88.2.[3]

21:22 *What Is That to You? Follow Me!*

CONTEMPLATION AND ACTION. AUGUSTINE: There are two states of life, therefore, preached and commended as revealed to the church from heaven: the one being in faith, the other in sight; one remaining in time in a foreign land, the other residing in the eternal heavenly dwelling. . . . The first was signified by the apostle Peter, the other by John. . . . And so, it is said to Peter, "Follow me" by imitating me in the endurance of temporal evils. [But of John it is said], "Let him remain" till I come to restore everlasting bliss. And this may be expressed more clearly in this way: Let action that is perfected, informed by the example of my passion, follow me; but let contemplation that has only just begun remain until I come, to be perfected when I come. For the godly fullness of patience, reaching forward even unto death, follows Christ; but the fullness of knowledge remains until Christ comes, to be manifested then. For here the evils of this world are endured in the land of the dying, while the good things of the Lord shall be seen in the land of the living. For in saying, "I want him to remain till I come," we are not to understand that John was supposed to remain on earth, or to abide permanently, but he was, rather, to wait. Therefore, what is signified by John shall certainly not be fulfilled now, but when Christ comes.

But what is signified by Peter to whom it was said, "Follow me," except that his [and our] following must be done now, or it will never reach the expected outcome. In such an active life, the more we love Christ the more easily we are delivered from evil. But he loves us less as we now are, and therefore delivers us from this state of being so that we may not always be such as we are. There [in heaven], however, he loves us more; for we shall not have anything about us to displease him, or anything that would cause Christ to separate us from him. He loves us here for the purpose of healing and delivering us from everything he doesn't love. Here, therefore, he loves us less because it is a place where he does not want us to remain. There [in heaven] he will love us in an even larger measure as the place toward which he would have us to be passing as we leave behind the place where he knows we would otherwise perish. Let Peter therefore love him, that we may obtain deliverance from our present mortality; let John be loved by him, that we may be preserved in the immortality to come. TRACTATES ON THE GOSPEL OF JOHN 124.5.[4]

PETER FOLLOWS, JOHN REMAINS. AUGUSTINE: The Lord either said what he said to Peter about his martyrdom, or he said it about the gospel of John. As regards the martyrdom and this "Follow me," [he means] suffer for me, suffer what I did. Because Christ was crucified, Peter too was crucified . . . while John experienced none of this. That is what is meant by, "It is thus that I wish him to remain." Let him fall asleep without wounds, without torment, and wait for me. You, Peter, "Follow me," suffer what I did. That's one way these words can be explained. . . .

As regards the Gospel of John, though, this is what I think is meant: that Peter wrote about the Lord, others too wrote; but their writing was more concerned with the Lord's humanity. . . . But while there is something about the divinity of Christ in Peter's letters, in John's gospel it is very much to the fore. . . . He soared above the clouds and soared above the stars, soared above the angels, soared above every creature and arrived at the Word through which all things were made. SERMON 253.5.[5]

[3]NPNF 1 14:332*; PG 59:480. [4]NPNF 1 7:450-51**. [5]*WSA* 3 7:150*.

21:23 *The Rumor About John Not Dying*

An Unfounded Rumor. Tertullian: John underwent death, although concerning him there had prevailed an unfounded expectation that he would remain alive until the coming of the Lord. On the Soul 50.[6]

A Tradition of John's Burial. Augustine: But still, as I began to say, if some deny the death of Moses, whom Scripture itself, in the very passage where we read that his sepulcher could nowhere be found,[7] explicitly declares to have died. How much more may occasion be taken from these words where the Lord says, "Thus do I wish him to stay till I come," to believe that John is sleeping but still alive beneath the ground? In fact, we have a tradition about him (which is found in certain apocryphal scriptures) that he was present, in good health, when he ordered a sepulcher to be made for himself. And that, when it was dug and prepared with all possible care, he laid himself down there as in a bed and became immediately dead. And yet, as those think who so understand these words of the Lord, [he was] not really dead but only lying like one in such a condition. And while he was considered "dead" he was actually buried [according to this tradition] when asleep and that he will so remain until the coming of Christ, making known meanwhile the fact of his life by the bubbling up of the dust, which is believed to be forced by the breath of the sleeper to ascend from the depths to the surface of the grave. I think it quite superfluous to contend with such an opinion. For those may see for themselves who know the locality whether the ground there does or has done to it what is said regarding it, because, in truth, we too have heard of it from those who are not altogether unreliable witnesses.[8] Tractates on the Gospel of John 124.2.[9]

Nothing to Fear in Death. Ambrose: There is, then, nothing for us to fear in death, nothing for us to mourn, whether life, which was received from nature be rendered up to it again, or whether it is sacrificed to some duty that claims it, and this will be either an act of religion or the exercise of some virtue. And no one ever wished to remain as at present. This has been supposed to have been promised to John, but it is not the truth. We hold fast to the words and deduce the meaning from them. He himself in his own writing denies that there was a promise that he should not die, that no one from that instance might yield to an empty hope. But if to wish for this would be an extravagant hope, how much more extravagant would it be to grieve without rule for what has happened according to rule! On His Brother Satyrus 2.49.[10]

Peter Wants to Know What Will Happen to John. Theodore of Mopsuestia: Peter turned to the secret decision of providence and saw from a distance the disciple John, son of thunder, who followed slowly, admiring the great and sublime promise made by our Lord to Peter. . . . Since John lived long, that is, seventy-three years after the ascension of the Lord to the time of Trajan, and died after all the other apostles in peace and serenity by natural death, the Lord alludes to this by saying, If I want him to live long enough so that he may remain until my return, you do not need to investigate this. Only pay attention to what is yours, that is, take care of your work and follow me. Commentary on John 7.21.20-23.[11]

---

[6]ANF 3:228 [7]Deut 34:6. [8]Augustine reports an almost supernatural phenomenon that was supposedly taking place at the ground where John was buried, as having an almost living and breathing appearance of the soil. [9]NPNF 1 7:448**. [10]NPNF 2 10:181**. [11]CSCO 4 3:363.

21:24-25 COMMENDATION OF THE GOSPEL

[24]This is the disciple who is bearing witness to these things, and who has written these things; and we know that his testimony is true.

[25]But there are also many other things which Jesus did; were every one of them to be written, I suppose that the world itself could not contain the books that would be written.

Overview: John wrote only one Gospel, although he had enough material for many (Eusebius). In this Gospel, he often appeals to the love Christ had for him and he for Christ as a motivation for why he wrote the Gospel (Chrysostom), although it would seem these last sentences were possibly written by another (Theodore). Either way, John was obviously not writing this Gospel in order to curry favor, since he left out many of the miracles and includes other less flattering occasions (Chrysostom), nor could he record everything Jesus did, since Christ's glory and the many miracles he did were too immense to be contained in a single book (Gregory of Nyssa). And so we wait for that day, along with the Evangelist John, when we shall understand everything fully and meet one another at the gates of the city above (Cyril). But as we wait, let us continue to carefully study and apply what we have learned from this Gospel so that we may attain to all the good things Christ has in store for us (Chrysostom). And now we bring to a close this commentary on the harp of the Spirit, the heavenly theologian and apostle John.

21:24 *The Disciple Who Wrote This Gospel*

The Writings of John. Eusebius of Caesarea: John, who reclined on the bosom of Jesus,[1] has left us one Gospel, although he confessed that he might have written so many that the world could not contain them. And he wrote also the Apocalypse, but he was commanded to keep silence and not to write the words of the seven thunders. He has left also an epistle of very few lines; perhaps also a second and third. But not all consider them genuine, and together they do not contain one hundred lines. Ecclesiastical History 6.25.9-10.[2]

John Wrote the Gospel out of Love. Chrysostom: Why is it then, that, when none of the others do so, he alone uses these words and that for the second time witnessed to himself? For it seems to be offensive to the hearers. Why then does he do it? He is said to have been the last one who embarked on writing [a Gospel]. Christ[3] had moved and roused him to the work, which is why he continually sets forth his love, alluding to the cause by which he was impelled to write. Therefore he also continually makes mention of it, to make his record trustworthy and to

[1]See Jn 13:23. [2]NPNF 2 1:273*. [3]Alternatively, *God*.

show that he came to this work motivated by that love. "And I know,"[4] he says, "that the things are true that he says." Homilies on the Gospel of John 88.2.[5]

The End of the Gospel Is by Another. Theodore of Mopsuestia: The interpreter [that is, Theodore himself] says that the words, "But there are also, etc." are not by John but by someone else.[6] Commentary on John 7.21.24-25.[7]

21:25 *The World Itself Not Big Enough*

John Did Not Write to Curry Favor. Chrysostom: And so it is clear, [John is saying], that I was not writing to curry favor. For I certainly could not have been acting to gain favor when I have not even related as many miracles (of which there were many) as the others have. I have omitted most of them, instead bringing forward the plots of the Jews, the stoning, the hatred, the insults, the reviling and showing how they called him a demoniac and a deceiver. And so I certainly could not have been acting to gain favor. For anyone who wanted to court favor would have done the opposite, namely, rejecting what was worthy of reproach in favor of the more glorious details. Since then he wrote what he did from full assurance, he does not decline to produce his own testimony, challenging people separately to inquire into and scrutinize the circumstances. Homilies on the Gospel of John 88.2.[8]

The Immensity of Christ's Work of Creation. Gregory of Nyssa: Holy Scripture omits all idle inquiry into substance as superfluous and unnecessary. And I think it was for this reason that John, the son of thunder, who with the loud voice of the doctrines contained in his Gospel rose above that of the preaching that heralded them, said at the close of his Gospel, "There are also many other things that Jesus did, so many that, in fact, if all of them were written, I suppose that even the world itself could not contain the books that should be written." He certainly does not mean by these the miracles of healing, for of these the narrative [in general terms] leaves none unrecorded, even though it does not mention the names of all who were healed. For when he tells us that the dead were raised, that the blind received their sight, that the deaf heard, that the lame walked and that he healed all kinds of sickness and disease, he does not in this leave any miracle unrecorded but embraces each and all in these general terms. But it may be that the Evangelist means this in his profound wisdom: that we are to learn the majesty of the Son of God not by the miracles alone that he did in the flesh. For these are little compared with the greatness of his other work. . . . For since God has made all things in wisdom and to his wisdom there is no limit,[9] . . . the world that is bounded by limits of its own cannot contain within itself the account of infinite wisdom. If, then, the whole world is too little to contain the teaching of the works of God, how many worlds could contain an account of the Lord of them all? For perhaps it will not be denied even by the tongue of the blasphemer that the maker of all things that have been created by the mere fiat of his will is infinitely greater than all. If, then, the whole creation cannot contain what might be said respecting itself—for this is, according to our explanation, what the great Evangelist is testifying to—how should human shallowness contain all that might be said of the Lord of creation? Answer to Eunomius's Second Book.[10]

[4]Chrysostom replaces the first person plural "we know" with "I know" without further explanation. [5]NPNF 1 14:333**; PG 59:480-81. [6]The Greek version of Theodore's commentary expands on the Syriac text of this "someone else," saying, "This is probably an addition that was placed at the margin by one of the scholars [Gk *philoponoi*] to show that the miracles that were performed by the Lord were more than those written, and partly by mistake, in ignorance it was placed by others inside and became part of the text of the gospel. Later, time and habit caused it to appear in the gospels, and so all believers are certain that it is a true part of the text and the true ending of what was written in the gospel" (EC 7:146). [7]CSCO 4 3:364. [8]NPNF 1 14:333**; PG 59:481. [9]Ps 147:5 (146:5 LXX). [10]NPNF 2 5:262**.

Evangelists Meeting Above with the Faithful. Cyril of Alexandria: Very great, then, says the apostle, will be the number of the miracles that God has done, and altogether without number will the list of his deeds be seen to be. And out of many thousands have these that are recorded been taken, as not being inadequate to profit to the uttermost those who read them. And let no one who is of a teachable spirit and loves instruction, John implies, blame the one who wrote this book because he has not recorded the rest. For if "the things" that he did "had been written"—every one, without any omission—then such an immeasurable number of the books would have filled the world. We maintain that, even as it is, the power of the Word has been displayed more than abundantly. For it is open to everyone to observe that a thousand miracles were performed by the power of our Savior. The preachers of the Gospels, however, have recorded the more remarkable of them, in all probability. They recorded what could best be confirmed by their hearers in incorruptible faith and those that would provide instruction in morality and doctrine. They did this so that, conspicuous for the orthodoxy of their faith and glorified by many works that result in righteousness, they might meet at the very gates of the city above. And, being joined to the church of the firstborn in the faith, they might at length attain to the kingdom of heaven in Christ. Commentary on the Gospel of John 12.1.[11]

Continually Study and Apply What You Have Learned. Chrysostom: Let us, therefore, pay careful attention to the words, and let us not stop reading and searching them through, for it is from their continual application that we ultimately benefit. We can then cleanse our life so as to cut up the thorns of sin and the cares of the world, which are fruitless and painful. And just as the thorn, however it is held, pricks the holder, so the things of this life, on whatever side they are grasped, give pain to the one who clings and cherishes them. Spiritual things are not like this. They resemble a pearl in that whichever way you turn it, it delights the eyes. . . . Let us then lighten ourselves and expand our horizons as we grow in maturity by getting rid of the evil things of this life and practicing the good. Let us obtain everlasting goods, then, through the grace and mercy of our Lord Jesus Christ with whom to the Father and the Holy Spirit be glory, dominion and honor, now and forever, world without end. Amen. Homilies on the Gospel of John 88.3.[12]

Commentary Concluded. Theodore of Mopsuestia: And here we conclude . . . this commentary on the harp of the Spirit, on the heavenly theologian and Apostle who is the friend of the glory of the Lord, the holy John the younger. Commentary on John 7.21.25.[13]

[11]LF 48:707-8**. [12]NPNF 1 14:333-34**. [13]CSCO 4 3:364.

Appendix
Early Christian Writers and the Documents Cited

The following table lists all the early Christian documents cited in this volume by author, if known, or by the title of the work. The English title used in this commentary is followed in parentheses with the Latin designation and, where available, the Thesaurus Linguae Graecae (=TLG) digital references or Cetedoc Clavis numbers. Printed sources of original language versions may be found in the bibliography of works in original languages.

Adamantius (Origen)

Concerning Right Faith in God *(De recta in Deum fide)* TLG 2950.001

Ambrose

Concerning Repentance *(De paenitentia)* Cetedoc 0156
Concerning Virgins *(De virginibus)* Cetedoc 0145
Death as a Good *(De bono mortis)* Cetedoc 0129
Duties of the Clergy *(De officiis ministrorum)* Cetedoc 0144
Expositions on the Gospel of Luke *(Expositio evangelii secundum Lucam)* Cetedoc 0143
Isaac, or the Soul *(De Isaac vel anima)* Cetedoc 0128
Jacob and the Happy Life *(De Jacob et vita beata)* Cetedoc 0130
Letters *(Epistulae)* Cetedoc 0160
Liturgy of Hours *(Nunc Sancte nobis Spiritus)*
On His Brother Satyrus *(De excessu fratris Satyri)* Cetedoc 0157
On Paradise *(De paradiso)* Cetedoc 0124
On the Christian Faith *(De fide)* Cetedoc 0150
On the Holy Spirit *(De Spiritu Sancto)* Cetedoc 0151
On the Mysteries *(De mysteriis)* Cetedoc 0155
On the Patriarchs *(De patriarchis)* Cetedoc 0132
Sermon Against Auxentius *(Sermo contra Auxentium de basilicas tradendis)* Cetedoc 0160
Six Days of Creation *(Exameron)* Cetedoc 0123
The Sacraments *(De sacramentis [Dub.])* Cetedoc 0154

Ambrosian Hymn Writer

Easter Hymn, At the Lamb's High Feast *(Ad regias Agni dapes)*

Ambrosiaster

Commentary on 1 and 2 Corinthians *(In epistulas ad Corinthios)*
Questions on the Old and New Testaments *(Quaestiones Veteris et Novi testimenti)* Cetedoc 0185

Ammonius
Fragments on John *(Fragmenta in Joannem [in catenis])* TLG 2724.003

Andrew of Crete
Homily 8 on Lazarus *(Homiliae 8, in Lazarum quatriduanum)*

Aphrahat
Demonstrations *(Demonstrationes)*
Apollinaris of Laodicea
Fragments on John *(Fragmenta in Joannem [in catenis])* TLG 2074.038

Athanasius
Discourses Against the Arians *(Orationes tres contra Arianos)* TLG 2035.042
Homily on the Resurrection of Lazarus *(Catechesis in festum pentecostes)*
Letter to Epictetus *(Epistula ad Epictetum)* TLG 2035.110
Letter to Serapion *(Epistulae quattuor ad Serapionem)* TLG 2035.043
On the Incarnation *(De incarnatione verbi)* TLG 2035.002

Augustine
Against Two Letters of the Pelagians *(Contra duas epistulas Pelagianorum)* Cetedoc 0346
Answer to Maximus *(Contra Maximinum)* Cetedoc 0700
Christian Instruction *(De doctrina Christiana)* Cetedoc 0263
City of God *(De civitate Dei)* Cetedoc 0313
Confessions *(Confessionum libri tredecim)* Cetedoc 0251
Discourse Against the Arians *(Contra sermonem Arianorum)* Cetedoc 0702
Explanations of the Psalms *(Enarrationes in Psalmos)* Cetedoc 0283
Harmony of the Gospels *(De consensu evangelistarum libri iv)* Cetedoc 0273
Letters *(Epistulae)* Cetedoc 0262
On Baptism *(De baptismo)* Cetedoc 0332
On Eighty-three Varied Questions *(De diversis quaestionibus octoginta tribus)* Cetedoc 0289
On Rebuke and Grace *(De correptione et gratia)* Cetedoc 0353
On the Gift of Perseverance *(De dono perseverantiae)* Cetedoc 0355
On the Spirit and the Letter *(De spiritu et littera)* Cetedoc 0343
On the Trinity *(De trinitate)* Cetedoc 0329
Reply to Faustus the Manichaean *(Contra Faustum)* Cetedoc 0321
Sermons *(Sermones)* Cetedoc 0284
Tractates on the Gospel of John *(In Johannis evangelium tractatus)* Cetedoc 0278

Basil of Seleucia
Homily on Lazarus *(Homilia in Lazarum)* TLG 2800.019

Basil the Great
Against Eunomius *(Adversus Eunomium)* TLG 2040.019
Concerning Baptism *(De baptismo libri duo)* TLG 2040.052
Letters *(Epistulae)* TLG 2040.004

On the Holy Spirit *(De spiritu sancto)* TLG 2040.003
Sermons *(Sermones de moribus a Symeone Metaphrasta collecti)* TLG 2040.075

Bede
Commentary on the Acts of the Apostles *(Expositio actuum apostolorum)* Cetedoc 1357
Exposition on the Gospel of Luke *(In Lucae evangelium exposition)* Cetedoc 1356
Exposition on the Gospel of Mark *(In Marci evangelium exposition)* Cetedoc 1355
Homilies on the Gospels *(Homiliarum evangelii libri ii)* Cetedoc 1367

Caesarius of Arles
Sermons *(Sermones)* Cetedoc 1008

Cassian, John
Conferences *(Collationes)* Cetedoc 0512
On the Incarnation of the Lord Against Nestorius *(De incarnatione Domini contra Nestorium)* Cetedoc 0514

Chromatius of Aquileia
Sermons *(Sermones)* Cetedoc 0217+(M)

Clement of Alexandria
Christ the Educator *(Paedagogus)* TLG 0555.002
Fragments *(Fragmenta)* TLG 0555.008
Stromateis *(Stromata)* TLG 0555.004

***Constitutions of the Holy Apostles* (*Constitutiones apostolorum*)** TLG 2894.001

Cosmas of Maiuma
Kanon for the Fifth Day *(Hymni 6, Pro Magna Quinta Feria)*

Council of Constantinople 381
Nicene-Constantinopolitan Creed, Third Article (Greek Text)

Cyprian
Letters *(Epistulae)* Cetedoc 0050
On Mortality *(De mortalitate)* Cetedoc 0044
The Lord's Prayer *(De dominica oratione)* Cetedoc 0043
The Unity of the Church *(De ecclesiae catholicae unitate)* Cetedoc 0041

Cyril of Alexandria
Commentary on the Gospel of John *(Commentarii in Joannem)* TLG 4090.002
Glaphyra on Genesis, Numbers etc. *(Glaphyra in Pentateuchum)* TLG 4090.097

Cyril of Jerusalem
Catechetical Lectures *(Catecheses ad illuminandos)* TLG 2110.003
Sermon on the Paralytic *(Homilia in paralyticum juxta piscinam jacentem)* TLG 2110.006

Diadochus of Photice

On Spiritual Perfection *(Capita centum de perfectione spirituali)*	
Didache *(Didache xii apostolorum)*	TLG 1311.001

Didymus the Blind

Fragments on John *(Fragmenta in Joannem [in catenis])*	TLG 2102.025
On the Holy Spirit *(Liber de Spiritu Sancto)*	Cetedoc 0615

Dionysius of Alexandria

Fragments *(Fragmenta)*

Ephrem the Syrian

Commentary on Tatian's Diatessaron *(In Tatiani Diatessaron)*
Hymn Against Julian: On the Church *(Carmina adversus Julianum Imperatorem Apostatam, adversus doctrinas falsas et Judaeos)*
Hymns on Virginity *(Hymni de virginitate)*
Memra for the Fifth Day of Great Week *(Sermones in Hebdomadam Sanctam)*
The Pearl *(Hymnen de fide)*

Eusebius of Caesarea

Commentary on the Psalms *(Commentaria in Psalmos)*	TLG 2018.034
Ecclesiastical History *(Historia ecclesiastica)*	TLG 2018.002
Minor Supplements to Questions to Marinus *(Supplementa minora ad quaestiones ad Marinum)*	TLG 2018.032
Proof of the Gospel *(Demonstratio evangelica)*	TLG 2018.005
To Marinus, Supplement xx *(Supplementa ad quaestiones ad Marinum)*	TLG 2018.031
To Stephanus *(Quaestiones evangelicae ad Stephanum)*	TLG 2018.028

Flavian of Chalon-sur-Saône

A Hymn for Holy Thursday: "Heaven and Earth Rejoice" *(Tellus ac aethra jubilent)*

Gaudentius of Brescia

Sermons *(Tractatus vel sermons)*
Two Tractates on Exodus *(Tractatus paschales)*

Gregory of Nazianzus

Against the Arians and on Himself, Oration 33 *(Contra Arianos et de seipso)*	TLG 2022.041
Against the Eunomians, Theological Oration 1(27) *(Adversus Eunomianos)*	TLG 2022.007
In Defense of His Flight to Pontus, Oration 2 *(Apologetica)*	TLG 2022.016
Letters *(Epistulae)*	TLG 2022.001
On Holy Baptism, Oration 40 *(In sanctum baptisma)*	TLG 2022.048
On Holy Easter, Oration 45 *(In sanctum pascha)*	TLG 2022.052
On Pentecost, Oration 41 *(In pentecosten)*	TLG 2022.049
On the Great Athanasius, Oration 21 *(In laudem Athanasii)*	TLG 2022.034
On the Holy Lights, Oration 39 *(In sancta lumina)*	TLG 2022.047
On the Holy Spirit, Theological Oration 5(31) *(De spiritu sancto)*	TLG 2022.011

On Theology, Theological Oration 2(28) *(De theologia)*	TLG 2022.008
On the Son, Theological Oration 3(29) *(De filio)*	TLG 2022.009
On the Son, Theological Oration 4(30) *(De filio)*	TLG 2022.010

Gregory of Nyssa

Against Eunomius *(Contra Eunomium)*	TLG 2017.030
Answer to Eunomius's Second Book *(Contra Eunomium)*	TLG 2017.030
Homilies on the Song of Songs *(In Canticum canticorum)*	TLG 2017.032
Letters *(Epistulae)*	TLG 2017.033
On the Holy Trinity *(Ad Eustathium de sancta trinitate)*	TLG 2017.001
On the Making of Man *(De opificio hominis)*	TLG 2017.079
On Virginity *(De virginitate)*	TLG 2017.043
The Great Catechism *(Oratio catechetica magna)*	TLG 2017.046

Gregory Thaumaturgus

Twelve Topics on the Faith *(De fide capitula duodecim)*	TLG 2063.028

Gregory the Great

Forty Gospel Homilies *(Homiliarum xl in evangelica)*	Cetedoc 1711
Homilies on Ezekiel *(Homiliae in Hiezechihelem prophetam)*	Cetedoc 1710
Letters *(Registrum epistularum)*	Cetedoc 1714
Morals on the Book of Job *(Moralia in Job)*	Cetedoc 1708

Hesychius of Jerusalem

Easter Homily *(Homilia i in sanctum pascha)*	TLG 2797.030
Homily on St. Lazarus *(Homilia i in sanctum Lazarum)*	TLG 2797.038

Hilary of Poitiers

On the Trinity *(De trinitate)*	Cetedoc 0433

Hippolytus

Fragments on Genesis *(Fragmenta in Genesim)*	TLG 2115.004
Fragments on Proverbs *(Fragmenta in Proverbia)*	TLG 2115.013
Fragments on Two Robbers *(De duobus latronibus)*	TLG 2115.022
On the Gospel of John and the Resurrection of Lazarus *(In evangelium Joannis et de resurrectione Lazari [Dub.])*	TLG 2115.023

Ignatius of Antioch

Epistle to the Trallians (longer version) *(Epistulae interpolatrae et epistulae suppositiciae [recensio longior])*	TLG 1443.002

Irenaeus

Against Heresies *(Adversus haereses)*	Cetedoc 1154

Isidore of Seville
Etymologies (Etymologiarum sive Originum libri xx) Cetedoc 1186

Jacob of Sarug
Homily on Three Baptisms

Jerome
Against John of Jerusalem *(Contra Johannem Hierosolymitanum)* Cetedoc 0612
Against Jovinianus *(Adversus Jovinianum)* Cetedoc 0610
Commentary on Matthew *(Commentarii in evangelium Matthaei)* Cetedoc 0590
Homily 87, On John 1:1-14 *(Homilia in Johannem evangelistam [1:1-14])* Cetedoc 0597
Letters *(Epistulae)* Cetedoc 0620
The Perpetual Virginity of Mary *(Adversus Helvidium de Mariae virginitate perpetua)* Cetedoc 0609

John Chrysostom
Commentary on Galatians *(In epistulam ad Galatas commentarius)* TLG 2062.158
Homilies on Colossians *(In epistulam ad Colossenses)* TLG 2062.161
Homily on Holy Saturday *(Homilia in sabbatum sanctum in Gregory of Antioch De Baptismo Christi sermons duo)*
Homilies on the Acts of the Apostles *(In Acta apostolorum)* TLG 2062.154
Homilies on the Gospel of John *(In Joannem [homiliae 1-88])* TLG 2062.153
Homilies on the Gospel of Matthew *(In Matthaeum [homiliae 1-90])* TLG 2062.152
Letters to Olympias *(Epistulae ad Olympiadem)* TLG 2062.088
On the Priesthood *(De sacerdotio)* TLG 2062.085
Poem on Prayer *(In Ecloga i-xlviii ex diversis homiliis [Sp.])* TLG 2062.338
Sermon on St. Peter and Elijah *(In sanctos Petrum et Heliam [Sp.])* TLG 2062.127
Sermon on the Betrayal by Judas *(De proditione Judae [Sp.])* TLG 2062.030

John of Carpathus
Texts for the Monks in India (in *Philocalia*)

John of Damascus
Orthodox Faith *(Expositio fidei)* TLG 2934.004

John the Elder (John of Dalyatha)
Letters *(Epistulae)*

Justin Martyr
Dialogue with Trypho *(Dialogus cum Tryphone)* TLG 0645.003

Leo the Great
Letters *(Epistulae)* Cetedoc 1657
Sermons *(Tractatus septem et nonaginta)* Cetedoc 1657

***Letter to Diognetus* (*Epistula ad Diognetum*)** TLG 1350.001

Mark the Hermit
No Righteousness by Works *(De his, qui putant se ex operibus justificari)*
On the Spiritual Law *(De lege spirituali)*

***Matins for Holy Thursday* (*Τριωδιον Κατανυκτικον*)**

Maximinus
Sermons *(Collectio Veronensis: De lectionibus sanctorum evangeliorum [Dub.])* Cetedoc 0694
Maximus the Confessor
Chapters on Knowledge *(Capita gnostica)* TLG 2892.009
The Four Hundred Chapters on Love *(Capita de caritate)* TLG 2892.008
Various Texts on Theology *(Diversa capita ad theologiam et oeconomiam spectantia [Sp.])* TLG 2892.011

Melito of Sardis
A Discourse with Antoninus Caesar *(Apologia [Sp.])*

Methodius
On the Resurrection *(De resurrectione)* TLG 2959.003

Novatian
On the Trinity *(De Trinitate)* Ceteodc 0071

Origen
Against Celsus *(Contra Celsum)* TLG 2042.001
Commentary on Matthew
(Commentarium in evangelium Matthaei [lib.12-17]) TLG 2042.030
(Commentaria in evangelium Matthaeum [Mt 22:34-27:63]) TLG 2042.028
Commentary on the Epistle to the Romans *(Commentariorum in Epistolam B. Pauli ad Romanos)*
Commentary on the Gospel of John
(Commentarii in evangelium Joannis [lib. 1, 2, 4, 5, 6, 10, 13]) TLG 2042.005
(Commentarii in evangelium Joannis [lib. 19, 20, 28, 32]) TLG 2042.079
Fragments on the Gospel of John *(Fragmenta in evangelium Joannis [in catenis])* TLG 2042.006
Homilies on Exodus *(Homiliae in Exodum)* TLG 2042.023
Homilies on Leviticus *(Homiliae in Leviticum)* TLG 2042.024
On First Principles *(De principiis)* TLG 2042.002
On Prayer *(De oratione)* TLG 2042.008

***The Passing of Mary* (*Transitus Mariae*)**

Peter Chrysologus
Sermons *(Collectio sermonum)* Cetedoc 0227+

Peter of Alexandria
Canonical Epistles *(Epistula canonica)* TLG 2962.004

Fragment *(Fragmenta de eo, quod Hebraei decimam quartam primi mensis lunae usque ad Hierosolymorum excidium recte statuerint)*

Potamius of Lisbon
On Lazarus *(De Lazaro)*

Proclus of Constantinople
Homily on the Palm Branches *(Homilia 9: In ramos palmarum)*

Prosper of Aquitaine
On the Ungrateful People *(De ingratis Carmen)*

[Pseudo]-Athanasius
Fourth Discourse Against the Arians *(Oratio quarta contra Arianos)* TLG 2035.117

Quodvultdeus
Third Homily on the Creed *(Sermo 3: De symbolo III)* Cetedoc 0403

Romanus Melodus
Kontakia *(Cantica)* TLG 2881.001

Rufinus of Aquileia
Commentary on the Apostles' Creed *(Expositio symboli)* Cetedoc 0196

Severian of Gabala
Homily on the Washing of the Feet *(Homilia de lotione pedum)*

Severus of Antioch
Cathedral Homilies *(Homiliae cathedrales)*

***Shepherd* of Hermas (Hermas, *Pastor*)** TLG 1419.001

***Stichera for the Third Hour of Holy Friday* (*Τριωδιον Κατανυκτικον*)**

Tertullian
Against Marcion *(Adversus Marcionem)* Cetedoc 0014
Against Praxeas *(Adversus Praxean)* Cetedoc 0026
An Answer to the Jews *(Adversus Judaeos)* Cetedoc 0033
Apology *(Apologeticum)* Cetedoc 0003
On Idolatry *(De idololatria)* Cetedoc 0023
On Monogamy *(De monogamia)* Cetedoc 0028
On Patience *(De patientia)* Cetedoc 0009
On Prayer *(De oratione)* Cetedoc 0007
On the Resurrection of the Flesh *(De resurrectione mortuorum)* Cetedoc 0019
On the Soul *(De anima)* Cetedoc 0017

On the Veiling of Virgins *(De virginibus velandis)*	Cetedoc 0027
Scorpiace *(Scorpiace)*	Cetedoc 0022
The Chaplet *(De corona)*	Cetedoc 0021

Theodore of Heraclea

Fragments on John *(Fragmenta in Joannem [in catenis[)*	TLG 4126.004

Theodore of Mopsuestia

Commentary on John *(Commentarius in evangelium Johannis Apostoli)*
Commentary on John, Fragments *(Fragmenta graeca)*

Theodoret of Cyr

Dialogues *(Eranistes)*	TLG 4089.002
Letters *(Epistulae: Collectio Sirmondiana [1-95])*	TLG 4089.006
(Epistulae: Collectio Sirmondiana [96-147])	TLG 4089.007

Theophilus of Alexandria

Sermon on the Mystical Supper *(In mysticam coenum)*

The Tree of the Cross (De ligno crucis)

Bibliography of Works in Original Languages

This bibliography refers readers to original language sources and supplies Thesaurus Linguae Graecae (=TLG) or Cetedoc Clavis (=Cl.) numbers where available. The edition listed in this bibliography may in some cases differ from the edition found in TLG or Cetedoc databases.

Adamantius (Origen). "De recta in Deum fide." In *Origenes Opera omnia*. Edited by J.-P. Migne. PG 11, cols. 1713-884. Paris: Migne, 1857. TLG 2950.001.

Ambrose. "De bono mortis." In *Sancti Ambrosii opera*. Edited by Karl Schenkl. CSEL 32, pt. 1, pp. 701-53. Vienna, Austria: F. Tempsky; Leipzig, Germany: G. Freytag, 1897. Cl. 0129.

———. "De excessu fratris Satyri." In *Sancti Ambrosii opera*. Edited by Otto Faller. CSEL 73, pp. 207-325. Vienna, Austria: Hoelder-Pichler-Tempsky, 1895. Cl. 0157.

———. "De fide libri v." In *Sancti Ambrosii opera*. Edited by Otto Faller. CSEL 78. Vienna, Austria: Hoelder-Pichler-Tempsky, 1962. Cl. 0150.

———. "De Isaac vel anima." In *Sancti Ambrosii opera*. Edited by Karl Schenkl. CSEL 32, pt. 1, pp. 639-700. Vienna, Austria: F. Tempsky; Leipzig, Germany: G. Freytag, 1897. Cl. 0128.

———. "De Jacob et vita beata." In *Sancti Ambrosii opera*. Edited by Karl Schenkl. CSEL 32, pt. 2, pp. 1-70. Vienna, Austria: F. Tempsky; Leipzig, Germany: G. Freytag, 1897. Cl. 0130.

———. "De mysteriis." In *Sancti Ambrosii opera*. Edited by Otto Faller. CSEL 73, pp. 87-116. Vienna, Austria: Hoelder-Pichler-Tempsky, 1955. Cl. 0155.

———. *De officiis ministrorum*. Edited by Maurice Testard. CCL 15. Turnhout, Belgium: Brepols, 2000. Cl. 0144.

———. *De paenitentia*. Edited by Roger Gryson. SC 179. Paris: Éditions du Cerf, 1971. Cl. 0156.

———. "De paradiso." In *Sancti Ambrosii opera*. Edited by Karl Schenkl. CSEL 32, pt. 1, pp. 263-336. Vienna, Austria: F. Tempsky; Leipzig, Germany: G. Freytag, 1897. Cl. 0124.

———. "De patriarchis." In *Sancti Ambrosii opera*. Edited by Karl Schenkl. CSEL 32, pt. 2, pp. 123-60. Vienna, Austria: F. Tempsky; Leipzig, Germany: G. Freytag, 1897. Cl. 0132.

———. "De sacramentis (Dub.)." In *Sancti Ambrosii opera*. Edited by Otto Faller. CSEL 73, pp. 13-85. Vienna, Austria: Hoelder-Pichler-Tempsky, 1955. Cl. 0154.

———. "De spiritu sancto." In *Sancti Ambrosii opera*. Edited by Otto Faller. CSEL 79, pp. 5-222. Vienna, Austria: Hoelder-Pichler-Tempsky, 1964. Cl. 0151.

———. *De virginibus*. Italian and Latin. Translated with introduction, notes and appendixes by Franco Gori. Milan: Biblioteca Ambrosiana; Rome: Città nuova, 1989. Cl. 0145.

———.. "Epistulae; Epistulae extra collectionem traditae." In *Sancti Ambrosii opera*. Edited by Otto Faller and Michaela Zelzer. CSEL 82. 4 vols. Vienna, Austria: F. Tempsky; Leipzig, Germany: G. Freytag, 1968-1990. Cl. 0160.

———. "Exameron." In *Sancti Ambrosii opera*. Edited by Karl Schenkl. CSEL 32, pt. 1, pp. 1-261. Vienna, Austria: F. Tempsky; Leipzig, Germany: G. Freytag, 1897. Cl. 0123.

———. *Expositio evangelii secundum Lucam*. Edited by Marcus Adriaen. CCL 14. Turnhout, Belgium:

Brepols, 1957. Cl. 0143.
———. "Nunc Sancte nobis Spiritus." In *HBM*, p. 35. Edited by Matthew Britt. Rev. ed. New York: Benziger Brothers, 1924.
———. "Sermo contra Auxentium de Basilicas tradendis." In *Sancti Ambrosii opera*. Edited by Michaela Zelzer. CSEL 82, pt. 3, pp. 82-107. Vienna, Austria: Hoelder-Pichler-Tempsky, 1982. Cl. 0160.
Ambrosian Hymn Writer. "Ad regias Agni dapes." In *HBM*, p. 144-45. Edited by Matthew Britt. Rev. ed. New York: Benziger Brothers, 1924.
Ambrosiaster. *In epistulas ad Corinthios*. Edited by Heinrich Joseph Vogels. CSEL 81 2. Vienna, Austria: Hoelder-Pichler-Tempsky, 1968.
———. *Quaestiones Veteris et Novi testamenti*. Edited by Alexander Souter. CSEL 50. Vienna, Austria: F. Tempsky; Leipzig, Germany: G. Freytag, 1908. Cl. 0185.
Ammonius. "Fragmenta in Joannem (in catenis)." In *JKGK*, pp. 196-358. Edited by Joseph Reuss. Texte und Untersuchungen 89. Berlin: Akademie-Verlag, 1966. TLG 2724.003.
Andrew of Crete. "Oratio VIII: In Lazarum quatriduanum." In *Opera omnia*. Edited by J.-P. Migne. PG 97, cols. 959-80. Paris: Migne, 1860.
Aphrahat. "Demonstrationes (IV)" In *Opera omnia*. Edited by R. Graffin. Patrologia Syriaca 1, cols. 137-82. Paris: Firmin-Didor, 1910.
Apollinaris of Laodicea. "Fragmenta in Joannem (in catenis)." In *JKGK*, pp. 3-64. Edited by Joseph Reuss. Texte und Untersuchungen 89. Berlin: Akademie-Verlag, 1966. TLG 2074.038.
Athanasius. "Catechesis in festum pentecostes." Translated by Joseph Buchanan Bernardin. *AJSL* 57, no. 3 (1940), 262-90.
———. "De incarnatione verbi." In *Sur l'incarnation du verbe*. Edited by C. Kannengiesser. SC 199, pp. 258-468. Paris: Éditions du Cerf, 1973. TLG 2035.002.
———. "Epistula ad Epictetum." In *Opera omnia*. Edited by J.-P. Migne. PG 26, cols. 1049-70. Paris: Migne, 1887. TLG 2035.110.
———. "Epistulae quattuor ad Serapionem." In *Opera omnia*. Edited by J.-P. Migne. PG 26, cols. 525-676. Paris: Migne, 1887. TLG 2035.043.
———. "Orationes tres contra Arianos." In *Opera omnia*. Edited by J.-P. Migne. PG 26, cols. 813-920. Paris: Migne, 1887. TLG 2035.042.
Augustine. *Confessionum libri tredecim*. Edited by L. Verheijen. CCL 27. Turnhout, Belgium: Brepols, 1981. Cl. 0251.
———. "Contra duas epistulas pelagianorum." In *Sacti Aurelli* Augustini. Edited by Karl Franz Urba and Joseph Zycha. CSEL 60, pp. 423-570. Vienna, Austria: F. Tempsky; Leipzig, Germany: G. Freytag, 1913. Cl. 0346.
———. "Contra Faustum." In *Sancti Aurelii Augustini*. Edited by Joseph Zycha. CSEL 25, pp. 249-797. Vienna, Austria: F. Tempsky; Leipzig, Germany: G. Freytag, 1891. Cl. 0321.
———. "Contra Maximinum." In *Opera omnia*. Edited by J.-P. Migne. PL 42, cols. 743-814. Paris: Migne, 1861. Cl. 0700.
———. "Contra sermonem Arianorum." In *Opera omnia*. Edited by J.-P. Migne. PL 42, cols. 683-708. Paris: Migne, 1861. Cl. 0702.
———. "De baptismo." In *Sancti Aurelii Augustini*. Edited by Michael Petschenig. CSEL 51, pp. 143-375. Vienna, Austria: F. Tempsky; Leipzig, Germany: G. Freytag, 1948. Cl. 0332.
———. *De civitate Dei*. In *Aurelii Augustini opera*. Edited by Bernhard Dombart and Alphons Kalb. CCL 47, 48. Turnhout, Belgium: Brepols, 1955. Cl. 0313.
———. *De consensu evangelistarum libri iv*. In *Sancti Aurelii Augustini*. Edited by Francis Weihrich. CSEL 43. Vienna, Austria: F. Tempsky; Leipzig, Germany: G. Freytag, 1904. Cl. 0273.

———. "De corruptione et gratia." In *Opera omnia*. Edited by J.-P. Migne. PL 44, cols. 915-46. Paris: Migne, 1845. Cl. 0353.

———. "De diversis quaestionibus octoginta tribus." In *Aurelii Augustini opera*. Edited by A. Mutzenbecher. CCL 44A, pp. 11-249. Turnhout, Belgium: Brepols, 1975. Cl. 0289.

———. "De doctrina christiana." In *Aurelii Augustini opera*. Edited by Joseph Martin. CCL 32, pp. 1-167. Turnhout, Belgium: Brepols, 1962. Cl. 0263.

———. "De dono perseverantiae." In *Opera omnia*. Edited by J.-P. Migne. PL 45, cols. 993-1034. Paris: Migne, 1861. Cl. 0355.

———. "De spiritu et littera." In *Sancti Aurelii Augustini*. Edited by Karl Franz Urba and Joseph Zycha. CSEL 60, pp. 155-229. Vienna, Austria: F. Tempsky; Leipzig, Germany: G. Freytag, 1913. Cl. 0343.

———. "De Trinitate." In *Aurelii Augustini opera*. Edited by William John Mountain. CCL 50-50A. Turnhout, Belgium: Brepols, 1968. Cl. 0329.

———. "Enarrationes in Psalmos." In *Aurelii Augustini opera*. Edited by Eligius Dekkers and John Fraipont. CCL 38, 39, 40. Turnhout, Belgium: Brepols, 1956. Cl. 0283.

———. *Epistulae 185-270*. In *Sancti Aurelii Augustini*. Edited by A. Goldbacher. CSEL 57. Vienna, Austria: F. Tempsky; Leipzig, Germany: G. Freytag, 1911. Cl. 0262.

———. "In Johannis evangelium tractatus." In *Aurelii Augustini opera*. Edited by R. Willems. CCL 36. Turnhout, Belgium: Brepols, 1954. Cl. 0278.

———. "Sermones." In *Augustini opera omnia*. Edited by J.-P. Migne. PL 38 and 39. Paris: Migne, 1844-1865. Cl. 0284.

———. *Sermones*. In *Aurelii Augustini opera*. Edited by Cyrille Lambot. CCL 41. Turnhout, Belgium: Brepols, 1961. Cl. 0284.

———. "Sermones." In *MiAg* 1. Edited by Germain Morin. Rome: Tipografia poliglotta vaticana, 1930. Cl. 0284.

———. *Sermons pour la pâque*. Edited by Suzanne Poque. SC 116. Paris: Éditions du Cerf, 1961. Cl. 0284.

Basil of Seleucia. *Homilia in Lazarum*. Edited by Mary B. Cunningham. AnBoll 104, pp. 170-77. Brussels: Société des Bollandistes, 1996.

Basil the Great. "Adversus Eunomium." In *Opera omnia*. Edited by J.-P. Migne. PG 29, cols. 497-774. Paris: Migne, 1857. TLG 2040.019.

———. "De baptismo libri duo." In *Opera omnia*. Edited by J.-P. Migne. PG 31, cols. 1513-1628. Paris: Migne, 1885. TLG 2040.052.

———. *De spiritu sancto*. In *Basile de Césarée: Sur le Saint-Esprit*. Edited by Benoit Pruche. SC 17. Paris: Éditions du Cerf, 2002. TLG 2040.003.

———. "Epistulae." In *Saint Basil: Lettres*. Edited by Yves Courtonne. Vol. 2, pp. 101-218; vol. 3, pp. 1-229. Paris: Les Belles Lettres, 1961-1966. TLG 2040.004.

———. "Sermones de moribus a Symeone Metaphrasta collecti." In *Opera omnia*. Edited by J.-P. Migne. PG 32, 1115-382. Paris: Migne, 1857. TLG 2040.075.

Bede. ìExpositio actuum apostolorum.î In *Bedae opera*. Edited M. L. W. Laistner. CCL 121, pp. 3-99. Turnhout, Belgium: Brepols, 1983. Cl. 1357.

———. "Homiliarum evangelii." In *Bedae opera*. Edited by David Hurst. CCL 122, pp. 1-378. Turnhout, Belgium: Brepols, 1956. Cl. 1367.

———. "In Lucae evangelium exposition." In *Bedae opera*. Edited by David Hurst. CCL 120, pp. 1-425. Turnhout, Belgium: Brepols, 1960. Cl. 1356.

———. "In Marci evangelium expositio.î In *Bedae opera*. Edited by David Hurst. CCL 120, pp. 431-648. Turnhout, Belgium: Brepols, 1960. Cl. 1355.

Caesarius of Arles. *Sermones Caesarii Arelatensis*. Edited by Germain Morin. CCL 103, 104. Turnhout, Belgium: Brepols, 1953. Cl. 1008.
Cassian, John. *Collationes xxiv*. Edited by Michael Petschenig. CSEL 13. Vienna, Austria: F. Tempsky; Leipzig, Germany: G. Freytag, 1886. Cl. 0512.
———. "De incarnatione Domini contra Nestorium." In *Johannis Cassiani*. Edited by Michael Petschenig. CSEL 17, pp. 233-391. Vienna, Austria: F. Tempsky; Leipzig, Germany: G. Freytag, 1888. Cl. 0514.
Chromatius of Aquileia. "Sermones." In *Opera*. Edited by Jospeh Lemarié. CCL 9A, pp. 3-182. Turnhout, Belgium: Brepols, 1974. Cl. 0217.
Clement of Alexandria. "Fragmenta." In *Clemens Alexandrinus*. Vol. 3, 2nd ed. Edited by Otto Stählin, Ludwig Früchtel and Ursula Treu. GCS 17, pp. 193-230. Berlin: Akademie-Verlag, 1970. TLG 0555.008.
———. "Paedagogus." In *Le pédagogue [par] Clement d'Alexandrie*. 3 vols. Translated by Marguerite Harl, Chantel Matray and Claude Mondésert. Introduction and notes by Henri-Irénée Marrou. SC 70, 108, 158. Paris: Éditions du Cerf, 1960-1970. TLG 0555.002.
———. "Stromata." In *Clemens Alexandrinus*. Vol. 2, 3rd ed., and vol. 3, 2nd ed. Edited by Otto Stählin, Ludwig Früchtel and Ursula Treu. GCS 15, pp. 3-518 and GCS 17, pp. 1-102. Berlin: Akademie-Verlag, 1960-1970. TLG 0555.004.
Constitutiones apostolorum. In *Les constitutions apostoliques*, 3 vols. Edited by Marcel Metzger. SC 320, 329, 336. Paris: Éditions du Cerf, 1985-1987. TLG 2894.001.
Cosmas of Maiuma. "Hymni." In *S. P. N. Germani Opera omnia*. Edited by J.-P. Migne. PG 98, cols. 475-83. Paris: Migne, 1860.
Cyprian. "De dominica oratione." In *Sancti Cypriani episcopi opera*. Edited by Claudio Moreschini. CCL 3A, pp. 87-113. Turnhout, Belgium: Brepols, 1976. Cl. 0043.
———. "De ecclesiae catholicae unitate." In *Sancti Cypriani episcopi opera*. Edited by Maurice Bévenot. CCL 3, pp. 249-68. Turnhout, Belgium: Brepols, 1972. Cl. 0041.
———. "De mortalitate." In *Sancti Cypriani episcopi opera*. Edited by Manlio Simonetti. CCL 3A, pp. 15-32. Turnhout, Belgium: Brepols, 1976. Cl. 0044.
———. *Epistulae*. Edited by Gerardus Frederik Diercks. CCL 3B, 3C. Turnhout, Belgium: Brepols, 1994-1996. Cl. 0050.
Cyril of Alexandria. "Commentarii in Joannem." In *Sancti patris nostri Cyrilli archiepiscopi Alexandrini in D. Joannis evangelium*. Edited by P. E. Pusey. Culture et Civilisation. Oxford: Clarendon Press, 1872. Reprint, Brussels, 1965. TLG 4090.002.
———. "Glaphyra in Pentateuchum" In *Opera omnia*. Edited by J.-P. Migne. PG 69, cols. 9-678. Paris: Migne, 1859. TLG 4090.097.
Cyril of Jeruslaem. "Catecheses ad illuminandos 1-18." In *Cyrilli Hierosolymorum archiepiscopi opera quae supersunt omnia*." Vol. 1, pp. 28-320; vol. 2, pp. 2-342. Edited by Wilhelm Karl Reischl and Joseph Rupp. Munich: Lentner, 1860. Reprint, Hildesheim: Olms, 1967. TLG 2110.003.
———. "Homilia in paralyticum juxta piscinam jacentem." In *Cyrilli Hierosolymorum archiepiscopi opera quae supersunt omnia*." Vol. 2, pp. 405-26. Edited by Wilhelm Karl Reischl and Joseph Rupp. Munich: Lentner, 1860. Reprint, Hildesheim: Olms, 1967). TLG 2110.006.
"De ligno crucis." See "De Pascha." In *S. Thasci Caecili Cypriani opera omnia*. Edited by Wilhelm A. Hartel. CSEL 3, pt. 3, pp, 305-8. Vienna, Austria: F. Tempsky; Leipzig, Germany: G. Freytag, 1868.
Diadochus of Photice. *Capita centum de perfectione spirituali*. In *Oeuvres spirituelles*. Edited by Eduard des Places. SC 5. 3rd ed. Paris: Éditions du Cerf, 1966.
Didache xii apostolorum. In *Instructions des Apôtres*, pp. 226-42. Edited by Jean Paul Audet. Paris: Lecoffre,

1958. TLG 1311.001.
Didymus the Blind. "Fragmenta in Joannem (in catenis)." In *JKGK*, pp. 177-186. Edited by Joseph Reuss. Texte und Untersuchungen 89. Berlin: Akademie-Verlag, 1966. TLG 2102.025.
———. "Liber de Spiritu Sancto." In *Opera*. Edited by J.-P. Migne. PL 23, cols. 109-62. Paris: Migne, 1865. Cl. 0615.
Dionysius of Alexandria. "Fragmenta." See *The Letters and Other Remains of Dionysius of Alexandria*. Edited by Charles Lett Feltoe. Cambridge Patristic Texts. Cambridge: Cambridge University Press, 1904.
Ephrem the Syrian. "Carmina adversus Julianum Imperatorem Apostatam, adversus doctrinas falsas et Judaeos." In *S. Ephraemi Syri, Rabulae Episcopi Edesseni, Balaci Aliorumque Opera selecta*, pp. 3-20. Edited by Julian Joseph Overbeck. Oxford: Clarendon, 1865.
———. *Hymnen de fide*. Edited by Edmund Beck. 2 vols. CSCO 154, 155. (Scriptores Syri 73, 74). Louvain: Secrétariat du Corpus, 1955.
———. *Hymni de virginitate*. Edited by Edmund Beck. 2 vols. CSCO 223, 224 (Scriptores Syri 94, 95). Louvain: Secrétariat du Corpus, 1962.
———. *In Tatiani Diatessaron*. In *Saint Éphrem: Commentaire de l'Évangile Concordant–Text Syriaque* (Ms Chester-Beatty 709), vol. 2. Edited by Louis Leloir. Leuven and Paris: Peeters Press, 1990.
———. *Sermones in Hebdomadam Sanctam*. Edited by Edmund Beck. CSCO 412 (Scriptores Syri 181). Louvain: Secrétariat du Corpus, 1979.
Epistula ad Diognetum. In *A Diognète*. 2nd ed. Edited by Henri Irénée Marrou. SC 33. Paris: Éditions du Cerf, 1965. TLG 1350.001.
Eusebius of Caesarea. *Commentaria in Psalmos*. In *Opera omnia*. Edited by J.-P. Migne. PG 23. Paris: Migne, 1857. TLG 2018.034.
———. "Demonstratio evangelica." In *Eusebius Werke, Band 6: Die Demonstratio evangelica*. Edited by Ivar A. Heikel. GCS 23. Leipzig: Hinrichs, 1913. TLG 2018.005.
———. "Historia ecclesiastica." In *Eusèbe de Césarée. Histoire ecclésiastique*, 3 vols. Edited by Gustave Bardy. SC 31, pp. 3-215; 41, pp. 4-231; 55, pp. 3-120. Paris: Éditions du Cerf, 1952, 1955, 1958. TLG 2018.002.
———. "Quaestiones evangelicae ad Stephanum." In *Opera omnia*. Edited by J.-P. Migne. PG 22, cols. 879-936. Paris: Migne, 1857. TLG 2018.028.
———. "Supplementa ad quaestiones ad Marinum." In *Opera omnia*. Edited by J.-P. Migne. PG 22, cols. 983-1006. Paris: Migne, 1857. TLG 2018.031.
———. "Supplementa minora ad quaestiones ad Marinum." In *Opera omnia*. Edited by J.-P. Migne. PG 22, cols. 1007-16. Paris: Migne, 1857. TLG 2018.032.
Flavian of Chalon-sur-Saône. "Tellus ac aethra jubilent." In *Thesauri hymnologici hymnarium*. Edited by Clemens Blume. Analecta Hymnica Medii Aevi 51, pp. 77-78. Leipzig: O.R. Reisland, 1908.
Gaudentius of Brescia. "Tractatus paschales." In *S. Gaudentii episcopi brixiensis tractatus*. Edited by Ambrosius Glück. CSEL 68. Vienna, Austria: Hoelder-Pichler-Tempsky, 1936.
———. "Tractatus vel sermons." In *Opera omnia*. Edited by J.-P. Migne. PL 20, cols. 843-1002. Paris: Migne, 1845.
Gregory of Nazianzus. "Adversus Eunomianos (orat. 27)." In *Gregor von Nazianz: Die fünf theologischen Reden*, pp. 38-60. Edited by Joseph Barbel. Düsseldorf: Patmos-Verlag, 1963. TLG 2022.007.
———. "Apologetica (orat. 2)." In *Opera omnia*. Edited by J.-P. Migne. PG 35, cols. 408-513. Paris: Migne, 1857. TLG 2022.016.
———. "Contra Arianos et de seipso [orat. 33]." In *Opera omnia*. Edited by J.-P. Migne. PG 36, cols. 213-37. Paris: Migne, 1886. TLG 2022.041.
———. "De filio (orat. 29)." In *Gregor von Nazianz. Die fünf theologischen Reden*, pp. 128-68. Edited by Jo-

seph Barbel. Düsseldorf, Germany: Patmos-Verlag, 1963. TLG 2022.009.
———. "De filio (orat. 30)." In *Gregor von Nazianz. Die fünf theologischen Reden*, pp. 170-216. Edited by Joseph Barbel. Düsseldorf, Germany: Patmos-Verlag, 1963. TLG 2022.010.
———. "De spiritu sancto (orat. 31)." In *Gregor von Nazianz. Die fünf theologischen Reden*, pp. 218-76. Edited by Joseph Barbel. Düsseldorf, Germany: Patmos-Verlag, 1963. TLG 2022.011.
———. "De theologia (orat. 28)." In *Gregor von Nazianz: Die fünf theologischen Reden*, pp. 62-126. Edited by Joseph Barbel. Düsseldorf: Patmos-Verlag, 1963. TLG 2022.008.
———. *Epistulae*. See *Saint Grégoire de Nazianze Lettres*. 2 vols. Edited by Paul Gallag. Paris: Société d'edition "Les Belles Lettres," 1964-1967. TLG 2022.001.
———. "In laudem Athanasii (orat 21)." In *Opera omnia*. Edited by J.-P. Migne. PG 35, cols. 1081-128. Paris: Migne, 1857. TLG 2022.034.
———. "In pentecosten (orat 41)." In *Opera omnia*. Edited by J.-P. Migne. PG 36, cols. 427-52. Paris: Migne, 1858. TLG 2022.049.
———. "In sanctum baptisma (orat. 40)." In *Opera omnia*. Edited by J.-P. Migne. PG 36, cols. 360-425. Paris: Migne, 1858. TLG 2022.048.
———. "In sancta lumina [orat. 39]." In *Opera omnia*. Edited by J.-P. Migne. PG 36, cols. 336-60. Paris: Migne, 1858. TLG 2022.047.
———. "In sanctum pascha [orat. 45]." In *Opera omnia*. Edited by J.-P. Migne. PG 36, cols. 624-64. Paris: Migne, 1858. TLG 2022.052.
Gregory of Nyssa. "Ad Eustathium de sancta trinitate." In *Gregorii Nysseni opera*. Vol. 3.1, pp. 1-16. Edited by Werner William Jaeger. Leiden: Brill, 1958. TLG 2017.001.
———. "Contra Eunomium." In *Gregorii Nysseni opera*, 2 vols. Vol. 1.1, pp. 3-409; vol. 2.2, pp. 3-311. Edited by Werner William Jaeger. Leiden: Brill, 1960. TLG 2017.030.
———. "De opificio hominis." In *Opera S. Gregorii*. Edited by J.-P. Migne. PG 44, cols. 124-256. Paris: Migne, 1863. TLG 2017.079.
———. "De virginitate." In *Grégoire de Nysse. Traité de la virginité*. Edited by Michel Aubineau. SC 119, pp. 246-560. Paris: Éditions du Cerf, 1966. TLG 2017.043.
———. "Epistulae." In *Gregorii Nysseni opera*. Vol. 8.2, pp. 1-95. Edited by George Pasquali. Leiden: Brill, 1959. TLG 2017.033.
———. "In Canticum canticorum (homiliae 15)." In *Gregorii Nysseni opera*. Vol. 6, pp. 3-469. Edited by Herman Langerbeck. Leiden: Brill, 1960. TLG 2017.032.
———. "Oratio catechetica magna." In *Gregorii Nysseni opera*. Vol. 3.4, pp. 1-106. Edited by Ekkehard Mühlenberg. Leiden: Brill, 1996. TLG 2017.046.
Gregory Thaumaturgus. "De fide capitula duodecim." In *Excavations at Nessana, vol. 2: Literary Papyri*, pp. 155-58. Edited by L. Casson and E. L. Hettich. Princeton, N.J.: Princeton University Press, 1950. TLG 2063.028.
Gregory the Great. "Homiliae in Hiezechihelem prophetam." In *Opera*. Edited by Mark Adriaen. CCL 142, 3-398. Turnhout, Belgium: Brepols, 1971. Cl. 1710.
———. "Homiliarum xl in evangelica." In *Opera omnia*. Edited by J.-P. Migne. PL 76, cols 1075-1312. Paris: Migne, 1857. Cl. 1711.
———. *Moralia in Job*. Edited by Mark Adriaen. CCL 143, 143A, 143B. Turnhout, Belgium: Brepols, 1979-1985. Cl. 1708.
———. *Registrum epistularum*. 2 vols. Edited by Dag Norberg. CCL 140, 140A. Turnhout, Belgium: Brepols, 1982. Cl. 0714.
———. *San Gregorio Magno Commento Morale a Giobbe*, vol 1. ODGM 1 1. Edited by Paolo Siniscalco. Rome: Città Nuova Editrice, 1992.

Hermas. "Pastor." In *Die apostolischen Väter 1: Der Hirt des Hermas*. Edited by Molly Whittaker. GCS 48, 2nd ed., pp. 1-98. Berlin: Akademie-Verlag, 1967. TLG 1419.001.

———. "Homilia i in sanctum pascha." In *Homélies pascales*. Edited by Michel Aubineau. SC 187, pp. 105-66. Paris: Éditions du Cerf, 1972. TLG 2797.030.Hesychius of Jerusalem. "Homilia i in sanctum Lazarum." In *Les homélies festales d'Hésychius de Jérusalem*. Vol. 1. Edited by Michel Aubineau. *SubHag* 59, pp. 402-27. Brussels, Belgium: Société des bollandistes, 1978. TLG 2797.038.

Hilary of Poitiers. *De trinitate*. Edited by Pieter F. Smulders. CCL 62 and 62A. Turnhout, Belgium: Brepols, 1979-1980. Cl. 0433.

———. "De trinitate." In *Opera omnia*. Edited by J.-P. Migne. PL 10, cols. 1-472. Paris: Migne, 1845. Cl. 0433.

Hippolytus. "De duobus latronibus." In *Hippolyt's kleinere exegetische und homiletische Schriften*. Edited by Hans Achelis. GCS 1 2, p. 211. Leipzig: Hinrichs, 1897. TLG 2115.022.

———. "Fragmenta in Genesim." In *Hippolyt's kleinere exegetische und homiletische Schriften*. Edited by Hans Achelis. GCS 1 2, pp. 51-53, 55-71. Leipzig: Hinrichs, 1897. TLG 2115.004.

———. "Fragmenta in Proverbia." In *Hippolyt's kleinere exegetische und homiletische Schriften*. Edited by Hans Achelis. GCS 1 2, pp. 157-67, 176-78. Leipzig: Hinrichs, 1897. TLG 2115.013.

———. "In evangelium Joannis et de resurrectione Lazari (Dub.)." In *Hippolyt's kleinere exegetische und homiletische Schriften*. Edited by Hans Achelis. GCS 1 2, pp. 215-20, 224-27. Leipzig: Hinrichs, 1897. TLG 2115.023.

Ignatius of Antioch. *Epistulae interpolatae et epistulae suppositiciae (recensio longior)* (Sp.). In *Patres apostolici*, vol. 2, 3rd ed., pp. 94-112. Edited by Franz X. Funk and F. Deikamp. Tübingen: H. Laupp, 1913.

Irenaeus. "Adversus haereses, livres 1-5." In *Contre les hérésies*. Edited by Adelin Rousseau, Louis Doutreleau and Charles A. Mercier. SC 34, 100, 152, 153, 210, 211, 263, 264, 293, 294. Paris: Éditions du Cerf, 1952-82. Cl. 1154 f.

Isidore of Seville. *Etymologiarum sive originum libri xx: Recognovit brevique adnotatione critica instruxit*. Edited by W. M. Lindsay. Oxford, 1911. Repr. Oxford: Oxford University Press, 1989. Cl. 1186.

Jerome. *Adversus Helvidium de Mariae virginitate perpetua*. Edited by J.-P. Migne. PL 23, cols. 193-216. Paris: Migne, 1845. Cl. 0609.

———. "Adversus Jovinianum." In *Opera omnia*. Edited by J.-P. Migne. PL 23, cols. 211-338. Paris: Migne, 1865. Cl. 0610.

———. *Commentarii in evangelium Matthaei*. Edited by David Hurst and Marcus Adriaen. CCL 77. Turnhout, Belgium: Brepols, 1969. Cl. 0590.

———. "Contra Johannem Hierosolymitanum." Edited by J.-P. Migne. PL 23, cols. 371-412. Paris: Migne, 1845. Cl. 0612.

———. *Epistulae*. Edited by I. Hilberg. CSEL 54, 55, 56. Vienna, Austria: F. Tempsky; Leipzig, Germany: G.F. Freytag, 1910-1918. Cl. 0620.

———. "Homilia in Johannem evangelistam (1:1-14)." In *Opera, Part 2*. Edited by Germain Morin. CCL 78, pp. 517-23. Turnhout, Belgium: Typographi Brepols Editores Pontificii, 1958. Cl. 0597.

John Chrysostom. "De proditione Judae (Sp)." In *Opera omnia*. Edited by J.-P. Migne. PG 49, cols. 373-92. Paris: Migne, 1862. TLG 2062.030.

———. "De sacerdotio." In *Jean Chrysostome. Sur le sacerdoce*. Edited by Anne Marie. Malingrey. SC 272, pp. 60-372. Paris: Éditions du Cerf, 1980. TLG 2062.085.

———. "Ecloga i-xlviii ex diversis homiliis (Sp)." In *Opera omnia*. Edited by J.-P. Migne. PG 63, cols. 567-902. Paris: Migne, 1862. TLG 2062.338.

———. "In Acta apostolorum (homiliae 1-55)." In *Opera omnia*. Edited by J.-P. Migne. PG 60, cols. 13-384. Paris: Migne, 1862. TLG 2062.154.

———. "In epistulam ad Colossenses." In *Opera omnia*. Edited by J.-P. Migne. PG 62, cols. 299-392. Paris: Migne, 1862. TLG 2062.161.

———. "In epistulam ad Galatas commentarius." In *Opera omnia*. Edited by J.-P. Migne. PG 61, cols. 611-82. Paris: Migne, 1859. TLG 2062.158.

———. "In Joannem (homiliae 1-88)." In *Opera* omnia. Edited by J.-P. Migne. PG 59, cols. 23-482. Paris: Migne, 1862. TLG 2062.153.

———. *In Matthaeum (homiliae 1-90)*. In *Opera omnia*. Edited by J.-P. Migne. PG 57-58. Paris: Migne, 1862. TLG 2062.152.

———. "In sanctos Petrum et Heliam [Sp.]." In *Opera omnia*. Edited by J.-P. Migne. PG 50, cols. 725-36. Paris: Migne, 1862. TLG 2062.127.

———. "Homilia in sabbatum sanctum." See "De baptismo Christi sermons duo." In Gregory of Antioch, *Opera omnia*. Edited by J.-P. Migne. PG 88, cols. 1866-84. Paris: Migne, 1860.

———. *Lettres á Olympias*. 2nd ed. Edited by Anne Marie Malingrey. SC 13. Paris: Éditions du Cerf, 1968. TLG 2062.088.

John of Carpathus. In *Philokalia*. 5 vols. Edited by Gergios Antnios Galits. Thessalonik: "To perivoli ts Panagias," 1987-1989.

John of Dalyatha. *La collection des letters de Jean de Dalyatha*. Edited by R. Beulay. PO 39, fasc. 3. Turnhout, Belgium: Brepols, 1978.

John of Damascus. "Expositio fidei." In *Die Schriften des Johannes von Damaskos*, vol. 2, pp. 3-239. Edited by Bonifatius Kotter. PTS 12. Berlin: De Gruyter, 1973. TLG 2934.004.

Justin Martyr. "Dialogus cum Tryphone" In *Die ältesten Apologeten*, pp. 90-265. Edited by Edgar J. Goodspeed. Göttingen, Germany: Vandenhoeck & Ruprecht, 1915. TLG 0645.003.

Lenten Triodion. ΤΡΙΩΔΙΟΝ ΚΑΤΑΝΥΚΤΙΚΟΝ ΠΕΡΙΕΧΟΝ ΑΠΑΣΑΝ ΤΗΝ ΑΝΗΚΟΥΣΑΝ ΑΥΤΩ ΑΚΟΛΟΥΘΙΑΝ ΤΗΣ ΑΓΙΑΣ ΚΑΙ ΜΕΓΑΛΗΣ ΤΕΣΣΑΡΑΚΟΣΤΗΣ. ΑΘΗΝΑΙ: ΕΚΔΟΣΕΙΣ ΦΩΣ, 1958.

Leo the Great. "Epistulae." In *Opera omnia*. Edited by J.-P. Migne. PL 54, pp. 593-1218. Paris: Migne, 1846. Cl. 1657.

———. *Tractatus septem et nonaginta*. Edited by Antonio Chavasse. CCL 138 and 138A. Turnhout, Belgium: Brepols, 1973. Cl. 1657.

———. "Tractatus septem et nonaginta." In *Opera omnia*. Edited by J.-P. Migne. PL 54, pp. 111-552. Paris: Migne, 1846. Cl. 1657.

Mark the Hermit. "De his, qui putant se ex operibus justificari." In *Marc le moine: Traités*. Edited by Georges-Matthieu de Durand. SC 445, pp. 130-201. Paris: Éditions du Cerf, 1999.

———. "De lege spirituali." In *Marc le moine: Traités*. Edited by Georges-Matthieu de Durand. SC 445, pp. 74-129. Paris: Éditions du Cerf, 1999.

Maximinus. "Collectio Veronensis: De lectionibus sanctorum evangeliorum (Sp.)." In *Scripta Arriana Latina I*. CCL 87, pp. 1-145. Edited by Roger Gryson. Turnhout, Belgium: Brepols, 1982. Cl. 0694.

Maximus the Confessor. "Capita de caritate." In *Opera omnia*. Edited by J.- P. Migne. PG 90, cols. 959-1080. Paris: Migne, 1860. TLG 2892.008.

———. "Capita gnostica." In *Opera omnia*. Edited by J.- P. Migne. PG 90, cols. 1084-173. Paris: Migne, 1860. TLG 2892.009.

———. "Diversa capita ad theologiam et oeconomiam spectantia (Sp.)." In *Opera omnia*. Edited by J.- P. Migne. PG 90, cols. 1185-462. Paris: Migne, 1860. TLG 2892.011.

Melito of Sardis. See "Pseudo-Melito: Apologies." In *Spicilegium syriacum*, pp. 41-51. Edited by William Cureton. London: Rivingtons, 1855.

Methodius. "De Resurrectione." In *Methodius*. Edited by G. Nathanael Bonwetsch. GCS 27, pp. 226-420 *passim*. Leipzig: Hinrichs, 1917. TLG 2959.003.

Nicene-Constantinopolitan Creed, Third Article (Greek Text). In *Acta conciliorum oecumenicorum*. Vol. 1.1.7. Edited by Eduard Schwartz. Berlin: de Gruyter, 1929.

Novatian. "De Trinitate." In *Opera*. Edited by Gerardus Frederik Diercks. CCL 4, pp. 11-78. Turnhout, Belgium: Brepols, 1972. Cl. 0071.

Origen. "Commentaria in evangelium Matthaeum (lib. 12-17)." In *Origenes Werke*, vol. 10.1-2. Edited by E. Klostermann. GCS 40.1-2. Leipzig: Hinrichs, 1935. TLG 2042.030.

———. "Commentaria in evangelium Matthaeum (Mt 22:34-27:63)". In *Origenes Werke*, vol. 11. Edited by E. Klostermann. GCS 38 2. Leipzig: Hinrichs, 1933. TLG 2042.028.

———. "Commentarii in evangelium Joannis (lib. 1, 2, 4, 5, 6, 10, 13)." In *Origene. Commentaire sur saint Jean*. 3 vols. Edited by Cécil Blanc. SC 120, 157, 222. Paris: Éditions du Cerf, 1966-1975. TLG 2042.005.

———. "Commentarii in evangelium Joannis (lib. 19, 20, 28, 32)." In *Origenes Werke*, vol. 4. Edited by Erwin Preuschen. GCS 10, pp. 298-480. Leipzig: Hinrichs, 1903. TLG 2042.079.

———. "Commentariorum in Epistolam B. Pauli ad Romanos." In *Der Römerbriefkommentar des Origenes: Kritische Ausgabe der bersetzung Rufins, Buch 4-6*. Edited by C. P. Hammond Bammel. AGBL 33. Freiburg: Herder, 1997.

———. "Contra Celsum." In *Origène Contre Celse*. Edited by Marcel Borret. SC 132, 136, 147 and 150. Paris: Éditions du Cerf, 1967-1969. TLG 2042.001.

———. "De oratione." In *Origenes Werke*, vol. 2. Edited by Paul Koestchau. GCS 3, pp. 297-403. Leipzig: Hinrichs, 1899. TLG 2042.008.

———. *De principiis*. In *Origenes Werke*, vol. 5. Edited by Paul Koetschau. GCS 22. Leipzig: Hinrichs, 1913. TLG 2042.002.

———. "Fragmenta in evangelium Joannis (in catenis)." In *Origenes Werke*. Vol. 4. Edited by Erwin Preuschen. GCS 10, pp. 483-574. Leipzig: Hinrichs, 1903. TLG 2042.006.

———. "Homiliae in Exodum." In *Origenes Werke*, vol. 6. Edited by Willem A. Baehrens. GCS 29, pp. 217-30. Leipzig: Hinrichs, 1920. Cl. 0198/TLG 2042.023.

———. "Homiliae in Leviticum." In *Origenes Werke*, vol. 6. Edited by Willem A. Baehrens. GCS 29, pp. 332-34, 395, 402-7, 409-16 Leipzig: Teubner, 1920. TLG 2042.024.

Peter Chrysologus. "Collectio sermonum." In *Opera omnia*. Edited by J.-P. Migne. PL 52, cols. 183-680. Paris: Migne, 1859. Cl. 0227+.

———. *Collectio sermonum a Felice episcopo parata sermonibus extravagantibus adjectis*. 3 vols. In *Sancti Petri Chrysologi*. Edited by Alexander Olivar. CCL 24, 24A and 24B. Turnhout: Brepols, 1975-1982. Cl. 0227+.

Peter of Alexandria. "Epistula canonica 12." In *Discipline générale antique*. Vol. 2. Les canons des Pères grecs. Fonti. Fascicolo IX, pp. 33-57. Edited by Périclès Pierre Joannou. Rome: Tipografia Italo-Orientale "S. Nilo," 1963. TLG 2962.004.

———. "Fragmenta de eo, quod Hebraei decimam quartam primi mensis lunae usque ad Hierosolymorum excidium recte statuerint." In *Opera omnia*. Edited by J.-P. Migne. PG 18, cols. 511-12. Paris: Migne, 1857.

Potamius of Lisbon. "De Lazaro." In *Opera omnia*. CCL 69A, pp. 165-95. Turnhout, Belgium: Brepols, 1999.

Proclus of Constantinople. "Homilia 9: In ramos palmarum." In *Opera omnia*. Edited by J.-P. Migne. PG 65, cols. 772-22. Paris: Migne, 1858.

Prosper of Aquitaine. *De ingratis Carmen*. Edited by Charles T. Huegelmeyer. Patristic Studies 95. Washington, D.C.: Catholic University of America Press, 1962.

[Pseudo-]Athanasius. "Oratio quarta contra Arianos." In *Die pseudoathanasianische "IVte Rede gegen die*

Arianer" als 'κατὰ 'Αρειανῶν λόγος' ein Apollinarisgut, pp. 43-87. Edited by Anton Stegmann. Rottenburg: Bader, 1917. TLG 2035.117.
Quodvultdeus. "Sermo 3: De symbolo III." In *Opera*. CCL 60, pp. 303-63. Edited by René Braun. Turnhout, Belgium: Brepols, 1976. Cl. 0403.
Romanus Melodus. "Cantica." In *Romanos le Mélode: Hymnes*. Edited by J. Grosdidier de Matons. SC 99, 110, 114, 128, 283. Paris: Éditions du Cerf, 1964-1981. TLG 2881.001.
Rufinus of Aquileia. "Expositio symboli." In *Opera*. Edited by Manlio Simonetti. CCL 20, pp. 125-82. Turnhout, Belgium: Brepols, 1961. Cl. 0196.
Severian of Gabala. "Homilia de lotione pedum." Translated by A. Wenger. *REBy* 25, pp. 225-29. Paris: Institut français d'études byzantines, 1967.
Severus of Antioch. *Les Homiliae cathedrales de Sévère d'Antioche: Traduction syriaque de Jacques d'Édesse, Homélies 40-55*. Edited by M. Brière, F. Graffin and C. J. A. Lash. PO 36, fasc. 1, no. 167. Turnhout, Belgium: Brepols, 1971.
Tertullian. "Adversus Judaeos." In *Tertulliani opera*. Edited by E. Kroymann. CCL 2, pp. 1339-96. Turnhout, Belgium: Brepols, 1954. Cl. 0033.
———. "Adversus Marcionem." In *Tertulliani opera*. Edited by E. Kroymann. CCL 1, pp. 437-726. Turnhout, Belgium: Brepols, 1954. Cl. 0014.
———. "Adversus Praxean." In *Tertulliani opera*. Edited by E. Kroymann and E. Evans. CCL 2, pp. 1159-205. Turnhout, Belgium: Brepols, 1954. Cl. 0026.
———. *Apologeticum*. In *Tertulliani opera*. Edited by Eligius Dekkers. CCL 1, pp. 77-171. Turnhout, Belgium: Brepols, 1954. Cl. 0003.
———. "De anima." In *Tertulliani opera*. Edited by J. H. Waszink. CCL 2, pp. 781-869. Turnhout, Belgium: Brepols, 1954. Cl. 0017.
———. "De corona." In *Tertulliani opera*. Edited by E. Kroymann. CCL 2, pp. 1037-65. Turnhout, Belgium: Brepols, 1954. Cl. 0021.
———. "De idololatria" In *Tertulliani opera*. Edited by August Reifferscheid and George Wissowa. CCL 2, pp. 1101-24. Turnhout, Belgium: Brepols, 1954. Cl. 0023.
———. "De monogamia." In *Tertulliani opera*. Edited by Eligius Dekkers. CCL 2, pp. 1229-53. Turnhout, Belgium: Brepols, 1954. Cl. 0028.
———. "De oratione." In *Tertulliani opera*. Edited by Gerardus Frederik Diercks. CCL 1, pp. 255-74. Turnhout, Belgium: Brepols, 1954. Cl. 0007.
———. "De patientia." In *Tertulliani opera*. Edited by J. G. Ph. Borleffs. CCL 1, pp. 299-317. Turnhout, Belgium: Brepols, 1954. Cl. 0009.
———. "De resurrectione mortuorum." In *Tertulliani opera*. Edited by J. G. Ph. Borleffs. CCL 2, pp. 919-1012. Turnhout, Belgium: Brepols, 1954. Cl. 0019.
———. "De virginibus velandis." In *Tertulliani opera*. Edited by Eligius Dekkers. CCL 2, pp. 1207-26. Turnhout, Belgium: Brepols, 1954. Cl. 0027.
———. Scorpiace.î In *Tertulliani opera*. Edited by August Reifferscheid and George Wissowa. CSEL 20, pp. 144-79. Vienna, Austria: F. Tempsky; Leipzig, Germany: G. F. Freytag, 1890. Cl. 0022.
Theodore of Heraclea. "Fragmeta in Johannem." In *JKGK*, pp. 65-176. Texte und Untersuchungen 89. Edited by Joseph Reuss. Berlin: Akademie-Verlag, 1966.
Theodore of Mopsuestia. *Commentarius in evangelium Iohannis Apostoli*. 2 vols. Edited by Jacques Marie Vosté. CSCO 115, 116 (Scriptores Syri ser. 4, vol. 3). Paris: Typographeo Reipublicae, 1940.
———. "Fragmenta graeca." In *Essai sur Théodore de Mopsueste*. Edited by Robert Devreesse. Studi e testi 141, pp. 305-419. Città del Vaticano: Biblioteca apostolica Vaticana, 1948.
Theodoret of Cyr. "Epistulae: Collectio Sirmondiana (epistulae 1-95)." In *Théodoret de Cyr: Correspon-*

dance II. Edited by Yvan Azéma. SC 98, pp. 20-248. Paris: Éditions du Cerf, 1964. TLG 4089.006.
———. "Epistulae: Collectio Sirmondiana (epistulae 96-147)." In *Théodoret de Cyr: Correspondance III*. Edited by Y. Azéma. SC 111, pp. 10-232. Paris: Éditions du Cerf, 1965. TLG 4089.007.
———. "Eranistes." In *Theodoret of Cyrus: Eranistes*, pp. 61-266. Edited by Gérard H. Ettlinger. Oxford: Clarendon Press, 1975. TLG 4089.002.
Theophilus (of Alexandria). "In mysticam coenum." In *Opera omnia*. Edited by J.-P. Migne. PG 77, cols. 1016-29. Paris: Migne, 1864.
Transitus Mariae. In *Apocalypses Apocryphae: Mosis, Esdrae, Pauli, Johanni, item Mariae dormitio, additis Evangeliorum et actuum Apocryphorum supplementis*, pp. 113-36. Edited by Konstantin von Tischendorf. Hidesheim, Germany: Georg Olms, 1866.

Bibliography of Works in English Translation

Ambrose. *Hexameron, Paradise, and Cain and Abel.* Translated by John J. Savage. FC 42. Washington, D.C.: The Catholic University of America Press, 1961.

———. *Letters.* Translated by Mary Melchior Beyenka. FC 26. Washington, D.C.: The Catholic University of America Press, 1954.

———. "Liturgy of Hours, Terce." In *HBM,* p. 35. Translated by Cardinal Newman. Edited by Matthew Britt. Rev. ed. New York: Benziger Brothers, 1924.

———. *Select Works and Letters.* Translated by H. De Romestin. NPNF 10. Series 2. Edited by Philip Schaff and Henry Wace. 14 vols. 1886-1900. Reprint, Peabody, Mass.: Hendrickson, 1994.

———. *Seven Exegetical Works.* Translated by Michael P. McHugh. FC 65. Washington, D.C.: The Catholic University of America Press, 1972.

———. *Theological and Dogmatic Works.* Translated by Roy J. Deferrari. FC 44. Washington, D.C.: The Catholic University of America Press, 1963.

Ambrosian Hymn Writer. "Easter Hymn, At the Lamb's High Feast." Translated by Robert Campbell. In *HBM,* p. 35. Edited by Matthew Britt. Rev. ed. New York: Benziger Brothers, 1924.

Andrew of Crete. "Homily 8, on Lazarus." In "Andreas of Crete's Homilies on Lazarus and Palm Sunday: The Preacher and His Audience." Translated by Mary B. Cunningham. In *Preaching, Second Century, Tertullian to Arnobius, Egypt before Nicaea,* pp. 22-41. Edited by Elizabeth A. Livingstone. StPatr 31. Leuven: Peeters, 1997.

Aphrahat. "Demonstration IV, On Prayer." In *The Syriac Fathers on Prayer and the Spiritual Life,* pp. 5-25. Translated by Sebastian Brock. CS 101. Kalamazoo, Mich.: Cistercian Publications, 1987.

———. "Select Demonstrations." In *Gregory the Great, Ephraim Syrus, Aphrahat,* pp. 345-412. Translated by James Barmby. NPNF 13. Series 2. Edited by Philip Schaff and Henry Wace. 14 vols. 1886-1900. Reprint, Peabody, Mass.: Hendrickson, 1994.

Athanasius. "Homily on the Resurrection of Lazarus." In Joseph Buchanan Bernardin, "The Resurrection of Lazarus." *AJSL* 57 (1940): 262-90.

———. "Letter to Serapion." In C. R. B. Shapland, *The Letters of Saint Athanasius Concerning the Holy Spirit.* NewYork: Philosophical Library, 1951.

———. "Letter to Serapion." In *The Holy Spirit,* pp. 98-108. Translated by J. Patout Burns and Gerald M. Fagin. MFC 3. Wilmington, Del.: Michael Glazier, 1984.

———. *Selected Works and Letters.* Translated by Archibald Robertson. NPNF 4. Series 2. Edited by Philip Schaff and Henry Wace. 14 vols. 1886-1900. Reprint, Peabody, Mass.: Hendrickson, 1994.

Augustine. *Anti-Pelagian Writings.* Translated by Peter Holmes and Robert Ernest Wallis. NPNF 5. Series 1. Edited by Philip Schaff. 14 vols. 1886-1889. Reprint, Peabody, Mass.: Hendrickson, 1994.

———. *City of God, Christian Doctrine.* Translated by Marcus Dods. NPNF 2. Series 1. Edited by Philip Schaff. 14 vols. 1886-1889. Reprint, Peabody, Mass.: Hendrickson, 1994.

———. *The City of God Books VIII-XVI.* Translated by Gerald Walsh and Grace Monahan. FC 14. Washington, D.C.: The Catholic University of America Press, 1952.

———. *Eighty-three Different Questions.* Translated by David L. Mosher. FC 70. Washington, D.C.: The

Catholic University of America Press, 1982.
———. *Expositions on the Book of Psalms.* Edited from the Oxford translation by A. Cleveland Coxe. NPNF 8. Series 1. Edited by Philip Schaff. 14 vols. 1886-1889. Reprint, Peabody, Mass.: Hendrickson, 1994.
———. *Expositions of the Psalms, 51-98.* Translated by Maria Boulding. *WSA* 17-18. Part 3. Edited by John E. Rotelle. New York: New City Press, 2001-2002.
———. "Harmony of the Gospels." In *Sermon on the Mount, Harmony of the Gospels, Homilies on the Gospels,* pp. 65-236. Translated by William Findlay, S. D. F. Salmond and R. G. MacMullen. NPNF 6. Series 1. Edited by Philip Schaff. 14 vols. 1886-1889. Reprint, Peabody, Mass.: Hendrickson, 1994.
———. "Homilies on the Gospel of John." In *JFB,* pp. 56-57, 102-3, 136-37. Edited by Edith Barnecut. New York: New City Press, 1993.
———. *Homilies on the Gospel of John, Homilies on the First Epistle of John, Soliloquies.* Translated by John Gibb et. al. NPNF 7. Series 1. Edited by Philip Schaff. 14 vols. 1886-1889. Reprint, Peabody, Mass.: Hendrickson, 1994.
———. *Letter 1-99.* Translated by Roland Teske. *WSA* 1. Part 2. Edited by John E. Rotelle. New York: New City Press, 2001.
———. "The Letters of St. Augustine." In *Prolegomena, Confessions, Letters,* pp. 219-593. Translated by J. G. Cunningham. NPNF 1. Series 1. Edited by Philip Schaff. 14 vols. 1886-1889. Reprint, Peabody, Mass.: Hendrickson, 1994.
———. "On the Holy Trinity." In *Augtustine: On the Holy Trinity, Doctrinal Treatises, Moral Treatises,* pp. 1-128. Translated by Author West Haddan. NPNF 3. Series 1. Edited by Philip Schaff. 14 vols. 1886-1889. Reprint, Peabody, Mass.: Hendrickson, 1994.
———. *Sermon on the Mount, Harmony of the Gospels, Homilies on the Gospels.* Translated by William Findlay, S. D. F. Salmond and R. G. MacMullen. NPNF 6. Series 1. Edited by Philip Schaff. 14 vols. 1886-1889. Reprint, Peabody, Mass.: Hendrickson, 1994.
———. *Sermons.* Translated by Edmund Hill. *WSA* 1-11. Part 3. Edited by John E. Rotelle. New York: New City Press, 1990-1997.
———. *The Trinity.* Translated by Stephen McKenna. FC 45. Washington, D.C.: The Catholic University of America Press, 1963.
———. *The Writings Against the Manichaeans and Against the Donatists.* Translated by J. R. King. NPNF 4. Series 1. Edited by Philip Schaff. 14 vols. 1886-1889. Reprint, Peabody, Mass.: Hendrickson, 1994.
Basil the Great. "Concerning Baptism." In *Ascetical Works,* pp. 339-430. Translated by M. Monica Wagner. FC 9. New York: Fathers of the Church, Inc., 1950.
———. *Letters and Select Works.* Translated by Blomfield Jackson. NPNF 8. Series 2. Edited by Philip Schaff. 14 vols. 1886-1889. Reprint, Peabody, Mass.: Hendrickson, 1994.
———. *On the Holy Spirit.* Translated by D. Anderson. Crestwood, N.Y.: St. Vladimir's Press, 1980.
Basil of Seleucia. "Homily on Lazarus." Translated by Mary B. Cunningham. *AnBoll* 104 (1986):178-84.
Bede. *Commentary on the Acts of the Apostles.* Translated by Lawrence T. Martin. CS 117. Kalamazoo, Mich.: Cistercian Publications, 1989.
———. *Homilies on the Gospels.* Translated by Lawrence T. Martin and David Hurst. 2 vols. CS 110 and 111. Kalamazoo, Mich.: Cistercian Publications, 1991.
Caesarius of Arles. "Sermons." In *The Church,* pp. 37, 43 and 185-86. Translated by Thomas Halton. MFC 4. Wilmington, Del.: Michael Glazier, 1985.
———. *Sermons 81-186.* Translated by Mary Magdeleine Mueller. FC 47. Washington, D.C.: The Catholic University of America Press, 1964.
Cassian, John. *The Conferences.* Translated and annotated by Boniface Ramsey. ACW 57. New York:

Paulist Press, 1997.
———. *Sulpicius Severus, Vincent of Lerins, John Cassian*. Translated by Edgar C. S. Gibson. NPNF 11. Series 2. Edited by Philip Schaff and Henry Wace. 14 vols. 1886-1900. Reprint, Peabody, Mass.: Hendrickson, 1994.
Clement of Alexandria. *Fathers of the Second Century: Hermas, Tatian, Athenagoras, Theophilus, and Clement of Alexandria*. Translated by F. Crombie et al. ANF 2.
Edited by Alexander Roberts and James Donaldson. 10 vols. 1885-1887. Reprint, Peabody, Mass.: Hendrickson, 1994.
"Constitutions of the Holy Apostles." In *Lactantius, Venantius, Asterius, Victorinus, Dionysius, Apostolic Teaching and Constitutions, 2 Clement, Early Liturgies*, pp. 385-508. Edited by James Donaldson. ANF 7. Edited by Alexander Roberts and James Donaldson. 10 vols. 1885-1887. Reprint, Peabody, Mass.: Hendrickson, 1994.
Cosmas of Maiuma. "Kanon for the Fifth Day of Great Week." In *The Eucharist*, pp. 385-92. Translated by Daniel J. Sheerin. MFC 7. Edited by Thomas Halton. Wilmington, Del.: Michael Glazier, 1986.
Cyprian. In *Hippolytus, Cyprian, Caius, Novatian*, pp. 267-596. Translated by Ernest Wallis. ANF 5. Edited by Alexander Roberts and James Donaldson. 10 vols. 1885-1887. Reprint, Peabody, Mass.: Hendrickson, 1994.
———. "On Mortality." In *Born to New Life: Cyprian of Carthage*, pp. 105-27. Edited by Oliver Davies. Translations by Tim Witherow with an introduction by Cyprian Smith. London: New City, 1991.
Cyril of Alexandria. "Commentary on John." In *Cyril of Alexandria*, pp. 96-129. Translated by Norman Russell. The Early Church Fathers. London: Routledge, 2000.
———. *Commentary on the Gospel of John*. Vols. 1-2. Translated by Philip Edward Pusey and Thomas Randell. LF 48. Edited by Henry Parry Liddon. London: Rivingtons; Oxford: James Parker, 1885.
———. "Glaphyra on Numbers." In *JFB*, pp. 38-39. Edited by Edith Barnecut. New York: New City Press, 1993.
Cyril of Jerusalem. "Catechetical Lectures." In *S. Cyril of Jerusalem, S. Gregory Nazianzen*, pp. 1-202. Translated by Edward Hamilton Gifford et al. NPNF 7. Series 2. Edited by Philip Schaff and Henry Wace. 14 vols. 1886-1900. Reprint, Peabody, Mass.: Hendrickson, 1994.
———. "Sermon on the Paralytic." In *The Works of Saint Cyril of Jerusalem*, pp. 207-22. Translated by Leo P. McCauley and Anthony A. Stephenson. FC 64. Washington, D.C.: The Catholic University of America Press, 1970.
Diadochus of Photice. "On Spiritual Perfection." See "On Spiritual Knowledge and Discrimination." In *TP* 1, pp. 254-96. Translated and edited by G. E. H. Palmer, Philip Sherrard and Kallistos Ware. London: Farber and Farber, 1979.
Didache. In *AF*, pp. 251-69. Translated by J. B. Lightfoot and J. R. Harmer. Edited by M. W. Holmes. 2nd ed. Grand Rapids, Mich.: Baker, 1989.
Dionysius of Alexandria. "Fragments." In *Gregory Thaumaturgus, Dionysius the Great, Julius Africanus, Anatolius and Minor Writers, Methodius, Arnobius*, pp. 81-120. Translated by S. D. F. Salmond. ANF 6. Edited by Alexander Roberts and James Donaldson. 10 vols. 1885-1887. Reprint, Peabody, Mass.: Hendrickson, 1994.
Ephrem the Syrian. *Commentary on Tatian's Distessaron*. See *ECTD*. Translated and edited by C. McCarthy. Journal of Semitic Studies Supplement 2. Oxford: Oxford University Press for the University of Manchester, 1993.
———. *Hymns*. Translated and introduced by Kathleen E. McVey. Preface by John Meyendorff. Classics in Western Spirituality. New York: Paulist Press, 1989.
———. "Memra for the Fifth Day of Great Week (Holy Thursday)." In *The Eucharist*, 137-43. Trans-

lated by Daniel J. Sheerin. MFC 7. Edited by Thomas Halton. Wilmington, Del.: Michael Glazier, 1986.

———. "The Pearl." In *Gregory the Great, Ephraim Syrus, Aphrahat*, pp. 293-301. Translated by J. B. Morris. NPNF 13. Series 2. Edited by Philip Schaff and Henry Wace. 14 vols. 1886-1900. Reprint, Peabody, Mass.: Hendrickson, 1994.

Eusebius of Caesarea. "Church History." In *Eusebius: Church History, Life of Constantine the Great, and Oration in Praise of Constantine*, pp. 73-403. Translated by Arthur Cushman McGiffert. NPNF 1. Series 2. Edited by Philip Schaff and Henry Wace. 14 vols. 1886-1900. Reprint, Peabody, Mass.: Hendrickson, 1994.

———. *Ecclesiastical History: Books 1-5*. Translated by Roy J. Deferrari. FC 19. Washington D.C.: The Catholic University of America Press, 1953.

———. *Proof of the Gospel*. 2 vols. Translated by W. J. Ferrar. London: SPCK, 1920. Reprint, Grand Rapids, Mich.: Baker, 1981.

———. "To Marinus." In *AEG* 6, pp. 119-23. Translated by Harold Smith. London: Society for Promoting Christian Knowledge, 1929.

Flavian of Chalon-sur-Saône. "A Hymn for Holy Thursday: 'Heaven and Earth Rejoice.'" In *The Eucharist*, pp. 384-85. Translated by Daniel J. Sheerin. MFC 7. Edited by Thomas Halton. Wilmington, Del.: Michael Glazier, 1986.

Gaudentius of Brescia. "Two Tractates on Exodus." In *The Eucharist*, pp. 85-93. Translated by Daniel J. Sheerin. MFC 7. Edited by Thomas Halton. Wilmington, Del.: Michael Glazier, 1986.

Gregory of Nazianzus. "Orations." In *Cyril of Jerusalem, Gregory of Nazianzen*, pp. 203-434. Translated by Charles Gordon Browne and James Edward Swallow. NPNF 7. Series 2. Edited by Philip Schaff and Henry Wace. 14 vols. 1886-1900. Reprint, Peabody, Mass.: Hendrickson, 1994.

Gregory of Nyssa. "Homilies on the Song of Songs." In *FGTG*, 158-59. Translated and edited by Jean Daniélou and Herbert Musurillo. New York: Charles Scribner's Sons, 1961. Reprint, Crestwood, N.Y.: St. Vladimir's Seminary Press, 1979.

———. "On Virginity." In *Ascetical Works*, pp. 6-75. Translated by Virginia Woods Callahan. FC 58. Washington D.C.: The Catholic University of America Press, 1967.

———. *Select Writings and Letters of Gregory, Bishop of Nyssa*, pp. 33-248. Translated by William Moore and Henry Austin Wilson. NPNF 5. Series 2. Edited by Philip Schaff and Henry Wace. 14 vols. 1886-1900. Reprint, Peabody, Mass.: Hendrickson, 1994.

Gregory Thaumaturgus. "Twelve Topics on the Faith." In *Gregory Thaumaturgus, Dionysius the Great, Julius Africanus, Anatolius and Minor Writers, Methodius, Arnobius*, pp. 50-53. Arranged by A. Cleveland Coxe. ANF 6. Edited by Alexander Roberts and James Donaldson. 10 vols. 1885-1887. Reprint, Peabody, Mass.: Hendrickson, 1994.

Gregory the Great. *Forty Gospel Homilies*. Translated by David Hurst. CS 123. Kalamazoo, Mich.: Cistercian Publications, 1990.

———. "Letters." In *Leo the Great, Gregory the Great*, pp. 73-243, and *Part II: Gregory the Great, Ephraim Syrus, Aphrahat*, pp. 1-116. Translated by James Barmby. 2 vols. NPNF 12 snf 13. Series 2. Edited by Philip Schaff and Henry Wace. 14 vols. 1886-1900. Reprint, Peabody, Mass.: Hendrickson, 1994.

———. *Morals on the Book of Job*. Translated by Members of the English Church. 4 vols. LF 18, 21, 23 and 31. Oxford: John Henry Parker, 1844-1850.

Hesychius of Jerusalem. "Easter Homily." In *JFA*, pp. 56-57. Edited by Edith Barnecut. New York: New City Press, 1992.

———. "Homily on St. Lazarus." In *Les homélies festales d'Hésychius de Jérusalem*. 2 vols. Edited by Michel Aubineau. *SubHag* 59. Brussels: Société des Bollandistes, 1978-1980.

Hilary of Poitiers. "On the Trinity." In *Hilary of Poitiers, John of Damascus*, pp. 40-233. Translated by E. W. Wastson et al. NPNF 9. Series 2. Edited by Philip Schaff and Henry Wace. 14 vols. 1886-1900. Reprint, Peabody, Mass.: Hendrickson, 1994.

———. "On the Trinity." In *JFC*, pp. 66-67. Edited by Edith Barnecut. New York: New City Press, 1994.

Hippolytus. "Fragments on the Two Robbers." In *AEG* 6, p. 96. Translated by Harold Smith. London: Society for Promoting Christian Knowledge, 1929.

———. *Hippolytus, Cyprian, Caius, Novatian, Appendix*. Arranged by A. Cleveland Coxe. ANF 5. Edited by Alexander Roberts and James Donaldson. 10 vols. 1885-1887. Reprint, Peabody, Mass.: Hendrickson, 1994.

———. "On the Gospel of John and the Resurrection of Lazarus." In *AEG* 4, pp. 164-84 passim. Translated by Harold Smith. London: Society for Promoting Christian Knowledge, 1928.

Ignatius of Antioch. "Epistle to the Trallians (longer version)." In *The Apostolic Fathers with Justin Martyr and Irenaeus*, pp. 66-72. Translated by A. Cleveland Coxe. ANF 1. Edited by Alexander Roberts and James Donaldson. 10 vols. 1885-1887. Reprint, Peabody, Mass.: Hendrickson, 1994.

Irenaeus. "Against Heresies." In *The Apostolic Fathers with Justin Martyr and Irenaeus*, pp. 309-567. Translated by A. Cleveland Coxe. ANF 1. Edited by Alexander Roberts and James Donaldson. 10 vols. 1885-1887. Reprint, Peabody, Mass.: Hendrickson, 1994.

Jacob of Sarug. "The Epiklesis in the Antiochene Baptismal Ordines." In *Symposium Syriacum 1972*, pp. 183-218. Translated by Sebastian Brock. OrChrAn 197. Rome: Pontifical Oriental Institute, 1974.

Jerome. "Homily 87, on John 1:1-14." In *Homilies 60-96*, pp. 212-20. Translated by Sister Marie Liguori Ewald. FC 57. Washington, D.C.: The Catholic University of America Press, 1966.

———. *Letters and Select Works*. Translated by W. H. Fremantle. NPNF 6. Series 2. Edited by Philip Schaff and Henry Wace. 14 vols. 1886-1900. Reprint, Peabody, Mass.: Hendrickson, 1994.

John Chrysostom. *Homilies on Galatians, Ephesians, Philippians, Colossians, Thessalonians, Timothy, Titus, and Philemon*. Translated by Gross Alexander et al. NPNF 13. Series 1. Edited by Philip Schaff. 14 vols. 1886-1889. Reprint, Peabody, Mass.: Hendrickson, 1994.

———. *Homilies on the Acts of the Apostles and the Epistle to the Romans*. Translated by J. Walker et al. NPNF 11. Series 1. Edited by Philip Schaff. 14 vols. 1886-1889. Reprint, Peabody, Mass.: Hendrickson, 1994.

———. "Homilies on the Gospel of John." In *Homilies on the Gospel of Saint John and the Epistle to the Hebrews*, pp. 1-334. Translated by Philip Schaff. NPNF 14. Series 1. Edited by Philip Schaff. 14 vols. 1886-1889. Reprint, Peabody, Mass.: Hendrickson, 1994.

———. *Homilies on the Gospel of Saint Matthew*. The Oxford translation. NPNF 10. Series 1. Edited by Philip Schaff. 14 vols. 1886-1889. Reprint, Peabody, Mass.: Hendrickson, 1994.

———. "Homily on Holy Saturday." In *JFA*, pp. 54-55. Edited by Edith Barnecut. New York: New City Press, 1992.

———. "Letters to Olympias." In *On the Priesthood, Ascetic Treatises, Select Homilies and Letters, Homilies on the Statues*, pp. 289-304. Translated by W. R. W. Stephens et al. NPNF 9. Series 1. Edited by Philip Schaff. 14 vols. 1886-1889. Reprint, Peabody, Mass.: Hendrickson, 1994.

———. "Sermon on the Betrayal by Judas." In *The Eucharist*, pp. 143-47. Translated by Daniel J. Sheerin. MFC 7. Edited by Thomas Halton. Wilmington, Del.: Michael Glazier, 1986.

———. *Six Books on the Priesthood*. Translated by Graham Neville. Crestwood, N.Y.: St. Vladimir's Seminary Press, 1977.

John of Carpathus. "Texts for the Monks in India." In *TP* 1, pp. 298-321. Translated and edited by G. E. H. Palmer, Philip Sherrard and Kallistos Ware. London: Faber and Faber, 1979.

John of Damascus. "Orthodox Faith." In *Hilary of Poitiers, John of Damascus*, pp. 1-101 (part 2). Translated

by S. D. F. Salmond. NPNF 9. Series 2. Edited by Philip Schaff and Henry Wace. 14 vols. 1886-1900. Reprint, Peabody, Mass.: Hendrickson, 1994.
John the Elder [John of Dalyatha]. "Letters." In *The Syriac Fathers on Prayer and the Spiritual Life*, pp. 330-37. Translated by Sebastian Brock. CS 101. Kalamazoo, Mich.: Cistercian Publications, 1987.
Justin Martyr. "Dialogue with Trypho, a Jew." In *Apostolic Fathers, Justin Martyr, Irenaeus*, pp. 194-270. Translated by A. Cleveland Coxe. ANF 1. Edited by Alexander Roberts and James Donaldson. 10 vols. 1885-1887. Reprint, Peabody, Mass.: Hendrickson, 1994.
The Lenten Triodion. Translated by Mother Mary and Archimandrite Kallistos Ware. London: Faber and Faber Limited, 1977. Reprint, South Canaan, Penn.: St. Tikhon's Seminary Press, 2002.
Leo the Great. "Sermons." In *JFB*, pp. 26-27, 44-45, 60-61. Edited by Edith Barnecut. New York: New City Press, 1993.
———. "The Letters and Sermons of Leo the Great, Bishop of Rome." In *Leo the Great, Gregory the Great*. Translated by Charles Lett Feltoe. NPNF 12. Series 2. Edited by Philip Schaff and Henry Wace. 14 vols. 1886-1900. Reprint, Peabody, Mass.: Hendrickson, 1994.
Letter to Diognetus. In *AF*, pp. 251-59. Translated by J. B. Lightfoot and J. R. Harmer. Edited by M. W. Holmes. 2nd ed. Grand Rapids, Mich.: Baker, 1989.
Mark the Hermit. See "St. Mark the Ascetic." In *TP* 1, pp. 110-46. Translated and edited by G. E. H. Palmer, Philip Sherrard and Kallistos Ware. London: Farber and Farber, 1979.
Maximus the Confessor. *Maximus the Confessor: Selected Writings*. Translated by George C. Berthold with Jaroslav Pelikan and Irénée-Henri Dalmais. Classics of Western Spirituality. New York: Paulist Press, 1985.
———. "Various Texts on Theology." In *TP* 2, pp.164-284. Translated and edited by G. E. H. Palmer, Philip Sherrard and Kallistos Ware. London: Farber and Farber, 1981.
Melito of Sardis. "A Discourse with Antoninus Caesar." In *Twelve Patriarchs, Excerpts and Epistles, The Clementia, Apocryphal Gospels and Acts, Syriac Documents*, pp. 751-56. Translated by B. P. Pratten. ANF 8. Edited by Alexander Roberts and James Donaldson. 10 vols. 1885-1887. Reprint, Peabody, Mass.: Hendrickson, 1994.
Methodius. "On the Resurrection." In *AEG* 4, passim. Translated by Harold Smith. London: Society for Promoting Christian Knowledge, 1928.
Novatian. "Treatise Concerning the Trinity." In *Fathers of the Third Century: Hippolytus, Cyprian, Caius, Novatian, Appendix*, pp. 611-44. Translated by Robert Ernest Wallis. ANF 5. Edited by Alexander Roberts and James Donaldson. 10 vols. 1885-1887. Reprint, Peabody, Mass.: Hendrickson, 1994.
Origen. "Commentary on Matthew." In *AEG* 4, passim; *AEG* 6, passim. Translated by Harold Smith. London: Society for Promoting Christian Knowledge, 1928-1929.
———. *Commentary on the Epistle to the Romans, Books 1-5*. Translated by Thomas P. Scheck. FC 103. Washington D.C.: The Catholic University of America Press, 2001.
———. *Commentary on the Gospel According to John, Books 1-10 and 13-32*. Translated by Ronald E. Heine. FC 80 and 89. Washington, D.C.: The Catholic University of America Press, 1989-1993.
———. "Commentary on the Gospel of Matthew." In *Gospel of Peter, Diatessaron, Testament of Abraham, Epistles of Clement, Origen, Miscellaneous Works*, pp. 411-512. Translated by John Patrick. ANF 9. Edited by Allan Menzies. 10 vols. 1885-1887. Reprint, Peabody, Mass.: Hendrickson, 1994.
———. "Fragments on the Gospel of John." In *AEG* 4, pp. 1-19, 164-98 passim. *AEG* 5, pp. 101-12, 205-32, 275-319, passim; *AEG* 6, passim. Translated by Harold Smith. London: Society for Promoting Christian Knowledge, 1928-1929.
———. *Homilies on Genesis and Exodus*. Translated by Ronald E. Heine. FC 71. Washington, D.C.: The Catholic University of America Press, 1982.

———. *Homilies on Leviticus: 1-16*. Translated by Gary Wayne Barkley. FC 83. Washington, D.C.: The Catholic University of America Press, 1990.

———. "On Prayer." In *OSW*, pp. 81-170. Translated by Rowan A. Greer. Classics of Western Spirituality. New York: Paulist, 1979.

———. "On Prayer." In *Prayer; Exhortation to Martyrdom*, pp. 15-140. Translated by John J. O'Meara. ACW 19. Westminster, Md.: Newman Press, 1954.

———. *Tertullian (IV); Minucius Felix; Commodian; Origen (I and III)*. Translated by Frederick Combie. ANF 4. Edited by Alexander Roberts and James Donaldson. 10 vols. 1885-1887. Reprint, Peabody, Mass.: Hendrickson, 1994.

The Passing of Mary. In *Twelve Patriarchs, Excerpts and Epistles, The Clementia, Apocryphal Gospels and Acts, Syriac Documents*, pp. 592-98. Translated by Alexander Walker. ANF 8. Edited by Alexander Roberts and James Donaldson. 10 vols. 1885-1887. Reprint, Peabody, Mass.: Hendrickson, 1994.

Peter Chrysologus. *Selected Sermons, Vols 2-3*. Translated by William B. Palardy. FC 109 and 110. Washington, D.C.: The Catholic University of America Press, 2004-2005.

———. "Sermons." In *JFA*, pp. 44-45. Edited by Edith Barnecut. New York: New City Press, 1992.

———. "Sermons." In *JFC*, pp. 44-45, 116-17. Edited by Edith Barnecut. New York: New City Press, 1992.

Peter of Alexandria. "The Canonical Epistle." In *The Writings of Methodius, Alexander of Lycopolis, Peter of Alexandria, and Several Fragments*, pp. 292-322. Edited by Alexander Roberts and James Donaldson. ANCL 14. Edinburgh: T & T Clark, 1869.

———. "Fragments." In *Gregory Thaumaturgus, Dionysius the Great, Julius Africanus, Anatolius and Minor Writers, Methodius, Arnobius*, pp. 280-83. Translated by James B. H. Hawkins. ANF 6. Edited by Alexander Roberts and James Donaldson. 10 vols. 1885-1887. Reprint, Peabody, Mass.: Hendrickson, 1994.

Proclus of Constantinople. "Homily 9: On the Palm Branches." In *Proclus Bishop of Constantinople: Homilies on the Life of Christ*, pp. 150-53. Translated by Jan Harm Barkhuizen. ECS 1. Brisbane, Australia: Centre for Early Christian Studies, Australian Catholic University, 2001.

Prosper of Aquitaine. "On the Ungrateful People." In *ECLP*, pp. 115-17. Translated by Carolinne White. The Early Church Fathers. London: Routledge, 2000.

[Pseudo-]Athanasius. "Fourth Discourse Against the Arians." In *Selected Works and Letters*, pp. 433-47. Translated by Archibald Robertson. NPNF 4. Series 2. Edited by Philip Schaff and Henry Wace. 14 vols. 1886-1900. Reprint, Peabody, Mass.: Hendrickson, 1994.

Quodvultdeus. *Quodvultdeus of Carthage: The Creedal Homilies*. Translated by Thomas Macy Finn. ACW 60. New York: Newman Press, 2004.

Romanus Melodus. *Kontakia of Romanos, Byzantine Melodist*. 2 vols. Translated and edited by Marjorie Carpenter. Columbia, Mo.: University of Missouri Press, 1970-1973.

Rufinus of Aquileia. "Commentary on the Apostles' Creed." In *Theodoret, Jerome, Gennadius, Rufinus: Historical Writings, etc.*, pp. 541-63. Translated by William Henry Fremantle. NPNF 3. Series 2. Edited by Philip Schaff and Henry Wace. 14 vols. 1886-1900. Reprint, Peabody, Mass.: Hendrickson, 1994.

Severian of Gabala. "Homily on the Washing of the Feet." In *JFA*, pp. 50-51. Edited by Edith Barnecut. New York: New City Press, 1992.

Shepherd of Hermas. In *Fathers of the Second Century: Hermas, Tatian, Athenagoras, Theophilus, and Clement of Alexandria*, pp. 9-55. Translated by F. Crombie. ANF 2. Edited by Alexander Roberts and James Donaldson. 10 vols. 1885-1887. Reprint, Peabody, Mass.: Hendrickson, 1994.

Tertullian. *Latin Christianity: Its Founder, Tertullian*. Arranged by A. Cleveland Coxe. ANF 3. Edited by

Alexander Roberts and James Donaldson. 10 vols. 1885-1887. Reprint, Peabody, Mass.: Hendrickson, 1994.

———. "Tertullian." In *Tertullian (IV); Minucius Felix; Commodian; Origen (I and III)*, pp. 5-166. Translated by S. Thelwall. ANF 4. Edited by Alexander Roberts and James Donaldson. 10 vols. 1885-1887. Reprint, Peabody, Mass.: Hendrickson, 1994.

———. *Tertullian's Treatise Against Praxeas*. Edited by Ernest Evans. London: SPCK, 1948.

Theodore of Mopsuestia. *Commentary on the Gospel of John*. Translated George Kalantzis. ECS 7. Strathfield, Australia: St. Pauls Publications, 2004.

Theodoret of Cyr. *Eranistes*. Translated by Gerard H. Ettlinger. FC 106. Washington, D.C.: The Catholic University of America Press, 2003.

———. "Theodoret." In *Theodoret, Jerome, Gennadius, Rufinus: Historical Writings, etc.*, pp. 1-348. Translated by Blomfield Jackson. NPNF 3. Series 2. Edited by Philip Schaff and Henry Wace. 14 vols. 1886-1900. Reprint, Peabody, Mass.: Hendrickson, 1994.

Theophilus (of Alexandria). "Sermon on the Mystical Supper." In *The Eucharist*, pp. 148-57. Translated by Daniel J. Sheerin. MFC 7. Edited by Thomas Halton. Wilmington, Del.: Michael Glazier, 1986.

"The Tree of the Cross." In *ECLP*, pp. 137-39. Translated by Carolinne White. The Early Church Fathers. London: Routledge, 2000.

See the volume *Commentary Index and Resources* for a collection of supplemental ACCS material, including a comprehensive Scripture index and authors/writings index.

Subject Index